Latin American Radicalism

Latin American Radicalism

A Documentary Report on
Left and Nationalist Movements

EDITED BY

IRVING LOUIS HOROWITZ

JOSUÉ DE CASTRO

JOHN GERASSI

RANDOM HOUSE

NEW YORK

Library of Congress Catalog Card Number: 68–14515

*Manufactured in the United States of America
by American Book–Stratford Press*

*Book design by Victoria Dudley
Binding design by Mary M. Ahern*

ACKNOWLEDGMENTS

"U.S. Hegemony and the Future of Latin America," by Celso Furtado, appeared originally in the September, 1966, issue of *The World Today,* the monthly journal published by the Royal Institute of International Affairs, London. "Seven Erroneous Theses About Latin America," by Rodolfo Stavenhagen, first appeared in *New University Thought.* "Electoral Politics, Urbanization, and Social Development in Latin America," by Irving Louis Horowitz, was first published in *Urban Affairs Quarterly,* Volume II, Number 3 (March, 1967), pages 3–35, by permission of the publisher, Sage Publications, Inc. "The United States and the Latin American Left Wings," by John J. Johnson, is reprinted by permission of the *Yale Review*. "Violence and Politics in Latin America," by Merle Kling, first appeared in *Sociological Review Monograph*, #2, 1967. "Control and Cooptation in Mexican Politics," by Bo Anderson and James D. Cockcroft, originally appeared in *International Journal of Comparative Sociology*, Volume 7, Number 1, March, 1966. "The Alliance That Lost Its Way," by Eduardo Frei Montalva, is reprinted by special permission from *Foreign Affairs*, April, 1967. Copyright © 1967 by the Council on Foreign Relations, Inc., New York. "Internal Colonialism and National Development," by Pablo Gonzalez-Casanova; "Mass Immigration and Modernization in Argentina," by Gino Germani, and "Political Strategies of National Development in Brazil," by Hélio Jaguaribe, are reprinted by permission of *Studies in Comparative International Development*.

Preface

The preparation of a documentary reader differs considerably from the task of writing a book. In a documentary the need is for broad coverage rather than a unified, systematic approach. There is the further assumption that the purpose of a documentary is to acquaint the reader with a range of materials no one person can do justice to or encompass. In this case the goals of a documentary have been eminently fulfilled. While there have been many readers on the subject of Latin America, this is, to the best of our knowledge, the first documentary which singles out for special attention the role of the left in Latin America.

Often enough documentaries on Latin America have a left-wing emphasis elliptically, almost inadvertently, since in some sense the left is where the action is. Nonetheless the task of making explicit the role of the Latin American left remained undone. It is our shared feeling that a need exists to make plain what the ferment on the left represents. For if one can speak of the *polarization* of left and right in America, one must also take note of the *pluralization* within the left that has taken place in fact as a consequence of this larger polarization.

The division of labor in the book—representing as it does the cooperation of a sociologist, a geographer, and a journalist—is made possible by the common realization that there is a need for reappraisal no less than a necessity for a recognition of the radical tradition within Latin America. But in addition to being linked together by an acceptance of broad radical premises for the hemisphere, the division of labor in the book reflects the backgrounds of each of us. It seemed natural to divide the book into three sections: the first, with hemispheric nationalism as its binding theme; the second, with the overall theme of social and economic structure; and the third, with the overriding concerns directed at the political and military aspects of the current situation. Obviously all divisions represent an arbitrary cutoff point taken for the convenience of the editors and does not necessarily reflect a sharp difference in the role performance or in goal orientation. Yet certainly in Latin America, the themes of nationalism, social development, and political revolution can hardly be said to exist in a vacuum oɪ in isolation from one another. And it is to be hoped that the reader will bear in mind this truth; and the fact that we are aware of these linkages.

Whether it likes to admit it or not, Latin America is underdeveloped. Though, obviously, some of the countries are far better off than the rest, all of them are ultimately completely dependent on one or more of the world's major powers (inevitably the United States), and that alone makes the continent underdeveloped. It also explains why the left is meaningful to the continent's young—and why the solutions offered by traditional American scholars (not to mention the State Department) are irrelevant. Those solutions, as the essays in this book make abundantly clear, are based either on bad faith or a series of illusions which must be destroyed. Among such illusions are the convictions that there are modernizing militarists in backward societies, that a middle-class sector will somehow rise above its self-serving properties to become a democratic bulwark between wealth and poverty, and that agricultural technology is somehow sufficient to encourage economic development without requiring transformation in the social bases of agricultural relations.

The direct consequence of discarding these illusions is the understanding that the nations of Latin America have the right not only to make revolutions, but also to make re-revolutions. Considering that the United States has had one singularly successful revolution, it has tended to forget the possibility that other revolutions may become atrophied or simply fail entirely. Therefore, the right of remaking a revolution, in nations such as Mexico and Bolivia, or even in those that had their revolutions much earlier, must be accepted. This right of re-revolution is perhaps hardest for the United States, as well as the Soviet Union, to accept. Revolutions are not sacred events. They become sacred only when regimes harden and calcify.

In sum, the standpoint of the Latin American left as it emerges in this documentary account is that the scenes and the scenarios of problems in the hemisphere exist from the Rio Grande to Tierra del Fuego, but that the sources of many of the problems are external to the hemisphere; and at this point in historical time are located in the United States.

It might be concluded that the defining characteristic of Latin American radicalism internally is the need for social development; and that would mean the elimination of internal colonialism. But the basic international need is for political revolution; and that would entail the expulsion of foreign imperialism. Whether in fact this two-pronged attack by the left on what they perceive to be the sources of continental misery will succeed, or whether the analysis they offer is too simplistic to provide a satisfactory program or prognosis, remains to be seen. But this documentary account attempts to record the present state of the great struggle to bring Latin America into the twentieth century before the advanced part of the world gets out of this century.

Irving Louis Horowitz
Josué de Castro
John Gerassi

Contents

xi

Part I

THE SOCIOECONOMIC PIVOT

The Norm of Illegitimacy:

The Political Sociology

of Latin America

IRVING LOUIS HOROWITZ

THE PAPERS selected for inclusion in this section meet several interlocking criteria: (1) They share an attempt to develop a general understanding of Latin America as a whole, rather than any one community, city, or nation. (2) They each take a critical social problem—labor-management relations, internal colonialism, the role of the intelligentsia—and see how that problem reveals area-wide commonalities. (3) In the main, they have a strong tendency to emphasize problems of stability and instability in the area, and where their crucial sources derive from. (4) They are mainly generalist papers written by major social scientists. That they also have strong biases and positions does not alter the factual content of their work. (5) Finally, each paper, in its own way, illustrates a concern with the norm of illegitimacy, the nonfunctional, nonequilibrated basis of political rules, economic policies, and social systems that for the most part currently define the area as an authentic entity over and apart from any of its national or regional parts.

For my part, I wish to attempt my own synthetic overview of the social structure, institutions, and ideologies of Latin America. It will be clear that I owe a great deal to some of the people represented in this section—particularly scholars such as Stavenhagen, Casanova, Kling, and Furtado. But the best way of indicating such indebtedness, aside from their actual repre-

3

sentation in the volume, is to avoid banal blurbs on their efforts, and instead attempt a genuine utilization of their intellectual inputs in my own output. So let me turn to the question of legitimate and illegitimate authority in Latin American social structures.

Contrary to academic mythology and sociological folklore, we are faced not with inadequate data in the area of Latin American studies, but rather conflicts between severely circumscribed and limited theories that work well enough for national units, and a collection of data about Latin American societies having little correlational significance at the hemispheric level. Macroanalysis has been especially weak in the area of Latin America for various reasons, and primary among these is that almost every kind of theory about a developing nation has a contradictory outcome when applied to different nations within the hemisphere.

The dilemma of forging an adequate theory is not restricted to the practical side. There is also the broader confusion surrounding the concept of legitimacy. As in so many other areas, Weber turned Marx upside down. For Marx, the state represents a monopoly of illegitimate power because politics is merely the organized machinery of one class for oppressing the others. For Weber, on the other hand, the state is organized primarily as a service agency, not a power dispenser. The state is thus an administrative staff having a monopoly on the legitimate use of force in order to enforce order in society.[1] It is evident then that for Marx the essence of the state is power; while for Weber the core of the state is authority.

Without wishing to resolve such a pervasive dualism in the sociological literature by fiat, for the purpose of this study I accept that certain societies do operate in Weberian terms, while others operate in terms of the Marxian conception. More specifically, those societies which over a long period of time display norms sanctioned in law and made viable through mass participation can be considered legitimate; those societies that rest visibly and demonstrably on unaccepted or barely tolerated power structures and relations can be considered illegitimate. One might declare that nations as different as Great Britain and

[1] Compare and contrast Karl Marx and Friedrich Engels, *Manifesto of the Communist Party.* New York: International Publishers, 1932, pp. 31–32; and Max Weber, *The Theory of Social and Economic Organization.* New York: Oxford University Press, 1947, p. 154.

the Soviet Union illustrate forms of legitimated authority; most nations of Latin America illustrate forms of illegitimacy.

It is important to distinguish between illegitimacy and violence. Latin American societies operating in terms of the norm of illegitimacy, while often prone to greater outbursts of mass violence, just as often display an institutionalization of illegitimacy which drastically reduces the amount (and certainly the quality) of violence manifest in them. Illegitimacy may function as a Paretan device to circulate elites in the absence of either laws sanctioned at the top or recognized as valid guidelines at the bottom end of society. The definition used herein is that legitimacy is the perception of the state as a service agency rather than an oppressive mechanism, and that this perception is cemented by a common adhesion to either legality or mass mobilization. The norm of illegitimacy, to the contrary, is the perception of the state as primarily a power agency which is cemented by a common reliance on illegal means to rotate either the holders of power or the rules under which power is exercised.

THE INTERNAL DYNAMICS OF ILLEGITIMACY

Consider the relationship of the middle classes and militarism. During the fifties the most popular theory advanced by scholars and policy-makers alike held that to the extent to which the size of the middle class is increased, there is a decrease in the extent of military involvement in political and social life. United States policy between 1957 and 1962 was largely based on the premise of this middle-class salvation theory of Latin America.

The data do show (as far as Uruguay and Costa Rica are concerned) that with an increase in the size of the middle class there has been a parallel decrease in the size of the military. Yet even this is dubious, given the election of a military leader as President of Uruguay and the increased participation of Costa Rica in Central American regional defense schemes. But in turning to countries like Argentina and Brazil, which also have large and growing middle classes—as a matter of fact the Argentine middle class is the largest in all Latin America—we find the reverse situation. Instead of showing an inverse correlation between middle-class growth and militarism, there are parallel growth lines of militarism and the middle class. The same is true for Brazil. And the steady promotion of "civic action" programs, with their direct appeals to middle-class military cooperation, only serves to stimulate such outcomes. In fact, a coalition between the urban bourgeoisie in Rio de Janeiro and São Paulo, and the military, served to oust the João Goulart regime in 1964. The middle sectors, far from weakening military dominion, had the reverse effect. The situation in Peru and Argentina, while showing national idiosyncrasies, is analogous in that there too, military interaction with the middle classes provides stability with legitimacy. Clearly, prima facie theorizing is inadequate as a guide to the understanding of Latin American social structure. Unfortunately, when the myth of middle-class salvation broke down, it was replaced by an even less tenable myth, that of military salvation.

Old myths about the military die hard. There is a school of thought which attributes to the military a unique developmental orientation. We are told: if this generation wants to attain a rapid rate of development, social science must stop treating the military as pariahs. It is claimed that given the unique organizational efficiency of the military, the degree of their mobilization, the degree to which they have constant labor available for social purposes, and the degree to which they are a national force and symbol, they are not only a force for development, but may well turn out to be a unique force.[2] An empirical look at the data does not drive us to any such optimistic prospects for military rule. They fail to show that the military are especially good at promoting a developmental pattern, at least in Latin America.[3]

The military have simply failed to act as an autonomous or unified group. Oftentimes they act as agents of other social

[2] The best example of this kind of approach is in the United States Department of Defense, "Civic Action: The Military Role in Nation-Building," *Armed Forces Information and Education*, Vol. III, No. 14 (January 15, 1964). For a more recent example along similar lines, see Willard F. Barber, "The American Concept of Counterinsurgency: Some Latin American Applications." Presented at the American Association for the Advancement of Science, Washington, D.C., December 26, 1966 (mimeographed).

[3] I have attempted to summarize the position of Latin American military in my study of "The Military Elites," in *Elites in Latin America*, Seymour Martin Lipset and Aldo Solari, eds. New York: Oxford University Press, 1967, pp. 146–189.

classes or powerful government alignments. The view of the military as leaders in civic action, with respect to Latin America, ignores one of the gravest difficulties of all, namely, the exorbitant cost factor in their maintenance. The military establishment is expensive and wasteful. When a country like Chile buys twenty subsonic jet fighters, that portion of the federal budget intended for agrarian reform or industrial modernization is seriously impaired. The developmental *ideology* of the military, even when present, is thus undermined by their feudalistic *organization*. The so-called modernizing military phenomenon does not stem from a sober appraisal of the complex social stratification system so much as from a profound search for the key to hemispheric stability.

It is not exclusively the contradictory aspects of Latin American development that make a general theory an elusive goal, but the degrees of variation found in the social structure of the hemisphere. Recently, for example, one writer has distinguished eight different types of working-class organizations that can be found and correlated with different nations. They are the following: (1) countries with little urban or industrial concentration and with a small middle class; (2) countries with isolated mass situations, without a large urban industrial concentration, and with a small middle class; (3) countries with isolated mass situations, without large urban concentrations, and with a large middle class in their urban sector; (4) countries with little urban and industrial concentration, but with a large middle class; (5) countries with large urban-industrial concentrations, and a large middle class in their urban sectors; (6) countries with isolated mass situations, but without large urban-industrial concentrations and a large middle class.[4] While, formally speaking, such tabular compilations are useful—and can be transformed into elements of an operational appraisal—listing of differences is no more a theory of Latin America than noting the existence of different regions can be said to comprise a theory of United States development. Nor will simplified attempts at correlational analysis take us very far, since the Boliv-

---

[4] Torcuato Di Tella has pointed out key differences related to the above and provided a useful typology for examining working-class organization. See, *El sistema político argentino y la clase obrera*. Buenos Aires: Editorial Universitaria de Buenos Aires, 1964; also see his paper on "Populism and the Working Class in Latin America," in *Government and Politics in Latin America*. New York: Frederick A. Praeger, 1968.

ian working class exhibits political influence well beyond its
economic level of existence, and likewise, the organizational
strength of the Chilean working class exhibits a marked superiority with respect to that of Argentinian workers who, in turn,
have a higher economic life style.

For many years, between 1945 and 1965, the nation-by-
nation accounting system has served to overcome traditionalist
obstructions placed in the path of intelligent theory construction
by the *pensadores* and *historiadores*. But compensation has led
to overcompensation—to the idealization of the nation as a
unique unit of analysis. The limits of the nation-building model
of analysis have not been accounted for. The needs of constructing a usable theory for the continental complex have not been
explored. Although a significant start in overcoming a reliance
on linear models has been made by Rodolfo Stavenhagen, the
debris of nonsensical, but widely held notions of Latin America,
persists.[5] It is now imperative to elaborate upon generalizations
that help us to comprehend the level at which Latin America
does exist as a unit.

We should first consider certain assumptions about the nature
of Latin American politics that may appear outrageous at first
glance. Above all, we must take a critical look at the doctrine
that demands for survival require the stable maintenance of a
democratic, libertarian, or parliamentarian order. The likelihood is that the reverse is more nearly the case. In order for a
political system to "survive" in Latin America, it must peren-
nially change its policies and generate instability as a survival
pattern. This is not to say that instability must be attributed to a
deliberate plan. Rather, the political-military complex can respond to latent structural sources of instability, such as population explosion, crop failures, transportation and communication
breakdowns, etc., in such a way as to manipulate these structural deformities for the purpose of maintaining political illegitimacy.

The maintenance of political illegitimacy has deep roots in
the colonial history of Latin America. Under the Spanish legal
and political organization the king held a position above the
law. But this formula also involved acceptance rather than an
imposition upon the masses. The basic juridical formula of the

5 Rodolfo Stavenhagen, "Seven Erroneous Theses About Latin America,"
New University Thought, Vol. 4, No. 4 (Winter, 1966–67), 25–37.

crown being above the law had as its corresponding political formula the idea of acceptance rather than violence. The non-violent character of illegitimacy makes possible its continuance even at present. As one scholar recently noted:

> The rule of the Spanish king was authoritarian in the sense that it was not bound by legal enactments and regulations. Under the Spanish conception of law, the king was acting within the system of *derecho* but without being subject, in practice, to the *ley*. The term *derecho* refers to the system of law in general, including its philosophical and idealistic aspects. The word *ley* applies to enacted legislation. Although it might sound redundant, the Spanish monarch was in possession of an "authoritarian" authority.[6]

This translegal status of rulers, combined as it was with incredibly detailed laws binding the ruled to the state, is therefore a longstanding condition.

Let us then start with what might be termed the norm of illegitimacy, or the norm of conflict, and consider those norms based on a consensualist apparatus to be largely inoperative. This kind of approach provides something valid and valuable in the study of Latin American society, namely, the comprehension of illegitimacy as a style of "doing business." Such an approach allows us to ask an entirely different set of questions than is generally asked by nation-building approaches to Latin America: In effect, how has the area engendered an "institutionalization of crisis" as a *normative* pattern of politics?

The methodological component in this dilemma is that we have sound treatises on each nation *in* Latin America, but correspondingly unsound doctrines *on* Latin America. The sociology of international stratification is roughly at the stage the formal study of social stratification was a quarter of a century ago. The units of measure are different, but the problems are roughly analogous. The work of the thirties convinced many that crude measures of social class needed refinement. This led to a series of doctrines that treated every subclass as a unique entity that was qualitatively distinct from other subclasses. Now, in the study of Latin America, and as a reaction

[6] Frank Jay Moreno, "The Spanish Colonial System: A Functional Approach," *The Western Political Quarterly,* Vol. XX, No. 2, Part 1 (June, 1967), 308–320.

to the totalistic approaches of the "big thinkers" of the classical tradition, the nation or even parts of nations have come to be defined as unique entities that are qualitatively distinct from other nations in the hemisphere. Mexico, Brazil, and Argentina have produced their "exceptionalist" theorists in good number. At a time when some researchers have given up the quest for a unified theory of the hemisphere, they have pointedly produced a sophisticated body of literature that is qualitatively superior to what previously existed. Yet, even in the results achieved, a certain parallelism with social stratification doctrines of yesteryear can be detected. While sophisticated studies of every nation in Latin America are available—Casanova of Mexico,[7] Germani of Argentina,[8] Furtado on Brazil,[9] Fals-Borda on Colombia,[10] to name but a few—there is no significant study of Latin America as a whole which can serve as an explanatory theory about the continent. The position can now be taken that available nation-by-nation accounts have a fragmentizing effect on theoretical generalizations of a hemispheric dimension, and hence result in the general acceptance of static models of Latin American social structure.

To accept the idea of nation-building as fundamental is no less unsatisfactory than to accept the idea that class uniqueness defines all aspects of stratification. To begin with, it is hard to prove that the idea of nationality is any more powerful than that of religion, ethnicity, urbanism, industrialism, or any other organizing principle of social life. Indeed, in many nations, the idea of nationhood is a referent only for the urban middle classes. But beyond the formalistic objections that might be

[7] Pablo González-Casanova, *La democracia en México*. Mexico City: Ediciones Era, 1965.

[8] Gino Germani, *Estructura social de la Argentina*. Buenos Aires: Editorial Raigal, 1955; and *Política y sociedad en una época de transición: de la sociedad tradicional a la sociedad de masas*. Buenos Aires: Editorial Paidós, 1962.

[9] Celso Furtado, *The Economic Growth of Brazil*. Berkeley and Los Angeles: University of California Press, 1963; and *Diagnosis of the Brazilian Crisis*. Berkeley and Los Angeles: University of California Press, 1965.

[10] Orlando Fals-Borda, *La violencia en Colombia: Estudio de un proceso social* (with Hernán Guzmán Campos and Eduardo Umaña Luna). Bogotá: Ediciones Tercer Mundo, 1963 (second edition); *La subversión en Colombia: el cambio social en la historia*. Bogotá: Ediciones Tercer Mundo, 1967.

raised by a pluralistic framework is the empirical objection to nation-building approaches that would deny the reality of Latin America.[11] There *are* commonalities: in social history, in class composition, in political organization, in language cluster, and above all, in the common subordinate positions the nations of Latin America occupy with respect to the United States.

In dealing with Latin America as a real entity we are no longer confined to nation-building concepts. It is the line, perhaps the chain, between the United States center and the Latin American peripheries that becomes the organizing link for understanding what constitutes Latin America. The relations between nearly every nation of Latin America and the United States are more direct (at the technological, political, and military levels) than the relations between any two nations within Latin America. This is particularly plain in the military sphere, where the United States is the organizing element which fuses the various hemispheric defense pacts, and which unabashedly provides an ideological cement to such operations.[12] This is not to deny the relevance of civil or military arrangements among Latin American nations, but only to indicate that such relations are derivative rather than originative, secondary rather than primary.[13] Therefore, in explaining the absence of legitimation in both its political and military aspects we are compelled to introduce the external factor—the role of imperialism.

Latin American elites, while neither impotent or unified, are not legitimized by a pluralist ideology, nor are they formed primarily through social demands from the masses. Therefore, such elites often lack valued skills of public administration or civic expertise on one side, and the sure knowledge of popular support on the other. These states often acquire power by unstructured methods. They breed counterelites that similarly dismiss technical standards of competence and have a like

---

[11] One scholar who has come to appreciate the reality of Latin America and use it as an organizing principle in his work is Donald Marquand Dozer, *Latin America: An Interpretive History.* New York: McGraw-Hill Book Company, 1962.

[12] See in particular the statement by General Robert W. Porter, Jr., USA Commander in Chief, United States Southern Command (Panama), before the House Foreign Affairs Committee on the FY 1968 Military Assistance Program. (April 25, 1967.)

[13] See Juan Saxe-Fernández, "El consejo de defensa Centroamericano y la *pax americana,*" *Cuadernos Americanos,* Vol. CLII, No. 3 (May–June, 1967), 39–57.

contempt for the popular classes. What evolves are neo-Falangist systems. There is no elite in Latin America which legitimizes itself simply by legal succession of its power. Rather, there are class columns of particularistic power, each a pillar supporting a weak public government, and each cancelling the other classes' or sectors' potential for total power. Falangism is basically a system in which multiple elites have a mutual cancellation effect in order to support a public-government structure. But each also has the power to prevent any other class or group from ruling for any extensive length of time. What each lacks is the power to maintain, establish, and legitimize that rule for a long period of time. In this way Falangism promotes the personalist style, the *caudillo* system. But since Falangism is a model for maintaining delicate balances between groups of equal weight by a strong central leader, any displacement of weight creates a crisis in the system as a whole. That is why the area has been run more by Machiavellian foxes than by Platonic lions.

Revolution, or the coup d'état, is often greeted with a sigh of relief by participating social sectors, no matter what the political coloration of the regime or the class involved in the *golpe*. The constancy of such revolutions provides a means to alleviate the tension of groups pulling with equal strength in all directions at once. The *golpe* is a *politically* distributive mechanism without being a *socially* disruptive mechanism. It is a means of changing established policy. No government is thereby ever able to fully legitimize itself by electoral procedures alone, thus producing what I call the "norm of illegitimacy." Long-range periods of constitutional, or at any rate, tranquil government rule become a heavy price to pay for many elite groups whose bases of power remain insecure—or never were secure. They must act quickly, decisively, since candidates who fill office for a legally prescribed period become a threat. If national office were legitimized in electoral procedures, many traditionalistic pillars of society would collapse. It is precisely to prevent their own collapse that such elite groupings of Latin America institute a norm of illegitimacy. This situation has been appreciated by Charles Anderson, when he noted that "with the possible exception of Perón, political intervention by the military in Latin America does not seem to have the effect of overhauling the power system of the society. Rather, under military governments in Latin America, holders of important power capabilities in the society are assured that their position in the society will not be endangered, and are permitted some participation in the political process."[14]

Why are elite groupings of Latin America unable to develop legitimizing models, and why are working classes unable to develop revolutionary models? In part it is because the management of their affairs is oftentimes not in their own hands. For example, although the working class of Brazil may be well organized into unions, and even constitute a "labor aristocracy," the fact is that the unions themselves are often dependent on the whims of the political organization of the state apparatus. This was particularly true during the period from Vargas to Goulart. The state apparatus, for its part, is contingent for its support upon coffee growers and the profits that they bring in from Parana. In turn the coffee growers in the south are dependent on the international monetary system which regulates the price of coffee, and even regulates the supply of, and demand for, coffee. In other words, elite formations lack a leadership base to press their members' claims and are not free to bargain, to negotiate a public policy. These elites have status without corresponding power. They have enough status to counteract the pressure of other groups, but not enough power to rule. Only the military can act freely to establish new balances and relieve the strain of equal pull in all directions. This it may do by permitting new elite groups to penetrate the political processes, but this mediating role only makes the army the backbone of illegitimacy. The military are themselves too tied into foreign interests and too involved with commercial activities to do anything more than underwrite the norm of illegitimacy throughout the hemisphere.

The most sophisticated stage of the internal dynamic of illegitimacy is reached when military structures are overturned by other portions of the military elite. This serves to circulate elites without running even the small risks inherent in civilianization of the nation. This sort of military rule is clearly indicated by the fact that not long after the Ecuadorian National Congress was dissolved by the military junta it allowed a constituent assembly to be elected on October 16, 1966, to write a new constitution. More realistically, the three-man army

[14] Charles W. Anderson, "Toward a Theory of Latin American Politics," in *Occasional Paper No. 2* in *The Graduate Center for Latin American Studies,* Nashville: Vanderbilt University, February, 1964.

junta was overthrown by an air force group, who in turn underwrote the Conservative Party rule and appointed Otto Arosemena Gómez as interim President.[15] This indicates how extensive the norm of illegitimacy is in Latin American politics—a form of politics that the military are largely responsible for, and yet a form of rule clearly unsuited to long-range mass political mobilization. For this reason, among others, civilian parties continue to prevail in the formal political infrastructure. Thus, the most advanced form of the norm of illegitimacy is observed when a ruling military junta merely threatens to civilianize itself—i.e., liberalize its conditions of rule—and other portions of the military rapidly move into the political arena to sustain the norm of illegitimacy.

Now are nation-building and revolution-making related to one another? How do such interconnections fit into any known facts about Latin America?

To establish such a connection we have to appreciate the role of the Latin American Samurai—the free-floating nineteenth-century *caudillo* turned professional twentieth-century officer—in a situation that demanded nationalism but disallowed populism.

Since the armed forces of Latin America are interest armies, the analysis of military phenomena cannot be based on one structural type of armed force, such as the federal army sponsored by the national state, but must take into account those military groupings representing other elite (or would-be elite) interests: regional armies and gendarmeries sponsored by local subgovernmental units; feudal and private armies sponsored by the superordinate class, race, or ethnic groups. This classification illustrates not only the divisions within the military, but also how the norm of illegitimacy finds organizational representation and ideological expression in the military sector no less than in the political sector.

Militarism is not simply a professional activity in Latin America. Because of its internal-control character it seeps into the life styles of Latin American society in a way which is uncharacteristic of other regions of the world. The military ethic is far more extensive and more potent than the simple numerical count of the size of the armed forces and general staff would

---

[15] Cf. *Political Handbook and Atlas of the World: 1967*, Walter H. Mallory, ed. New York and Evanston: Harper & Row, 1967.

reveal. Precisely because the military underwrites the militarization of civil administration, it reinforces illegitimacy and becomes the key source of right-wing nationalism. Since the military is dominated by international powers, its nationalism is more rhetorical than real.

It might be objected that this view tends to consider the military a foreign body in the structure of social classes. In point of fact, the military are clearly integrated into most Latin American societies. However, it is important to recognize that the military are not a social class in themselves, but function as extensions of certain classes; i.e., they are attached to the landed aristocracy or to the urban middle classes. They only rarely act as a class for themselves, even if they sometimes seem to act as a group in themselves. This marginal role in the social structure accentuates the instability of overt military rule. They are compelled to solicit support from one or another sector of the class network; this then creates the basis for further *golpes* and illicit politics.

This satellitic role of the military is particularly apparent in Latin America (it is particularly well hidden in the Middle East) because of the well-defined and longstanding class network existing in Latin America. The "Nasserist option" does not really obtain. Nasserism depends for its strength on an ill-formed, misshapen "classlessness" which exists primarily in many parts of the Middle East. The role of the military as a force for national development, such as the monumental achievement made by Ataturk and the Kemalist forces in Turkey, simply cannot be replicated in Latin America because of the well-established sophistication of class organization in Latin America. Therefore, if the military is not a "foreign body" in Latin America, neither is it a unique force chosen by history to determine the destiny of Latin America.

THE IMPERIAL DYNAMICS OF ILLEGITIMACY

Take three terms like "modernization," "industrialization," and "development," which in the social science literature are used with such remarkable interchangeability that one begins to wonder why three words are required at all. From my perspective, however, these words not only mean entirely different things, but are often at odds with one another.[16] Consequently, we have a linguistic barrier to a unified theory of Latin America. The indicators which we have of the Latin continent, used in connection with modernization, and when employed with any degree of precision, seem to refer to things extending from electrification, creature comforts, the construction of supermarkets and highways to the unfolding of innovative cultural forms.

Many indicators of modernization—life expectancy, literacy of the masses, sophisticated communication and transportation networks—seem to link up with the urban process. Indeed, modernization is oftentimes used as a surrogate for the urban process. On the other hand, the concept of development is often spoken of as a surrogate for industrialization. The measures used in defining economic development—per capita national production, the consumption of energy, the population employed in business, commerce, and service industries—are intimately linked to industry. This distinction between modernization and industrialization is not simply academic. Even if we confine ourselves to the measures above, it is plain that the degree of modernization can diverge radically from that of industrialization. Argentina is as "modern" a society as West Germany, while both Brazil and Mexico are much closer to the big three of the United States, England, and Germany than they are to the Afro-Asian new nations. However, if we substitute measures of industrial potency, developmental levels reveal themselves to be radically different from modernization scales. At the industrial level, Argentina and Brazil appear more akin to the Congo and Haiti, rather than to the big three Western powers.[17] Seen in this light, the ideology behind the "revolution in rising expectations" is anchored to the modernization process, while the ideology of "revolution from below" is clearly anchored to the industrialization process. Thus, development might be said to encompass a double interchange—the inter-

[16] I have tried to express the nature of such terminological differences in *Three Worlds of Development: The Theory and Practice of International Stratification*. New York and London: Oxford University Press, 1966.

[17] See Gino Germani, *Política y sociedad en una época de transición: de la sociedad tradicional a la sociedad de masas*. Buenos Aires: Editorial Paidós, 1962.

action of modernization and industrialization forming the core problems of developmental processes and strategies alike.

Economic theory has been adapted to clarify these differences between modernization and industrialization. However, it cannot go beyond its own limits as a science; it can ably *translate* into a more precise language the dilemmas of development, but it is no more in a position to *resolve* these dilemmas than phrenology was able to settle problems of mental disorder. Monetarism has been used, especially in present-day Brazil and Argentina, as a device for moving beyond the import-substitution bottleneck into the modern economic sector without revolution. Structuralism has been used, especially in Mexico in the thirties, Cuba in the sixties, and now to a lesser extent in Chile, to overcome import-substitution bottlenecks by creating a more potent national heavy industrial and mining pattern. The link of structuralism is to industrialization what the link of monetarism is to modernization.[18]

Each strategy of economic growth has its own strains, and each creates political spinoffs. The monetaristic solutions create internal colonial stress by sharpening the conflict between have and have-not sectors, between the largely urban sectors and the largely rural sectors. Thus modernization creates the seeds of social disequilibrium by sharpening the strain between sectors. The structuralistic solutions, in an effort to escape the control by foreign imperial economies of their national economy, face a different set of problems, but a set no less harsh in its implications. In order to lay the basis of an industrial society, a considerable amount of sacrifice is required of the lower classes, the rural classes, and even the middle classes. But what is sacrificed is precisely what monetarism can buy: creature comforts and a high standard of personal living, nothing short of the most visible results of "modernization." Thus, structuralism too creates a strain toward disequilibrium within the underdeveloped societies of Latin America.

In short, monetarism and structuralism, which both start out with great expectations to alleviate the material conditions which create revolutions, seem to end up as economic ideologies, inadvertently inducing that which is most dreaded in the

[18] See David Felix, "Monetarists, Structuralists, and Import-Substituting Industrialization," *Studies in Comparative International Development,* Vol. I, No. 10 (1965), 137–153.

other—further dependence on the external economic sector.[19]

Modernization and developmental orientations do not exclude revolutionary alternatives and may parallel an increase rather than a decrease in revolutionary sentiment. The problem of this paradoxical convergence is this: Latin Americans perceive the most modern results of technology in other countries, but rarely do they acquire the industrial means for creating such results on an autonomous basis. Attempts to emulate and replicate specific national models oftentimes end in frustration and puzzlement. Frustration of mass goals, which is produced as much by awareness of cases of advancement as by failure, makes for revolutionary types of people and for revolutionary types of situations. Revolutionary sentiments are not simply a consequence of underdevelopment, but more properly a result of polarization between developed and underdeveloped sectors. And these polarities confront each other in Latin America not exclusively as a class question, but as a question in international stratification. The large-scale foreign corporation, along with the large-scale penetration of foreign military-bureaucratic forces, produces the same effect in the "periphery" as it does at the "cosmopolitan center": it serves to absorb foreign wealth and soak up foreign labor power.

The factor of illegitimacy is enhanced by the simple device of removing basic strategy decisions from the Latin American orbit and centering them in the imperial concentration points. To successfully execute such control, however, a portion of the Latin American decision-making elites, whether military or civilian in background or occupation, becomes intimately involved in the satisfactory conduct of the local groupings. Thus, instead of being linked to the developmental process, a portion of the local elites becomes tied to the security of foreign investments. Since this imperial dynamic has the deeper effect of placing the legitimating agencies in foreign control, the actions of the nation-state system in Latin America tend heavily to become repressive. The norm of illegitimacy is therefore guaranteed by an imperial system that sees the constant circulation of local elites as beneficial to its own interests.

The power of the imperial center to determine the form of

[19] This dovetailing of outcomes between monetarism and structuralism is made painfully, if inadvertently, clear in the set of papers on *Inflation and Growth in Latin America,* Werner Baer and Isaac Kerstenetzky, eds. (A Publication of the Economic Growth Center, Yale University). Homewood, Illinois: Richard D. Irwin, Inc., 1964.

Latin American societies is perhaps best illustrated by the case of Bolivia. This country exhibited many tendencies present in Mexico and Cuba: an authentic popular revolution (the MNR [*Movimiento Nacional Revolucionario*] in 1952); a powerful trade union organization; and widespread political mobilization—conditions which are clearly necessary ingredients in any model based on legitimation from below. However, the economic fortunes of the nation, while emancipated from "internal colonialists," remained linked (more firmly than ever) to the foreign purchasers of Bolivian natural resources. The radical labor movement, which had the power to cancel the national bourgeoisie, found itself overmatched in competition with the international bourgeoisie. Bolivia became the most heavily subsidized nation per man in the entire world (including all the Near Eastern nations). The United States became the effective underwriter of what was supposedly the most radical political structure in South America. But if the Bolivian miner found his wages improved over prerevolutionary times, the Bolivian political structure found itself even more dependent on foreign capital than in the prerevolutionary era. Thus, far from guaranteeing legitimacy from below, such foreign imperial dominion only returned the situation to a status quo ante, in which the military sector performed its classic function of guaranteeing survival through illegitimacy.

Although it is readily admitted that United States policy, at both the diplomatic and defense levels, is a contributory factor in Latin American militarism, such an admission still perceives of such intervention as a response to, or a product of, local circumstances. I would advance the proposition that what has increasingly taken place is the foreign management of internal conflicts in Latin America. This raises the possibility of a new United States imperialism based on political rather than economic considerations, and therefore tactically dedicated to indirect management of Latin American military establishments rather than direct interventionism. With the rise of overall strategies on a grand scale, with the assertion that the basic purpose of United States national policy is to promote and secure a structure of hemispheric relationships compatible with the values of the United States, local control, idiosyncratic regimes, and classical Latin American strongmen must themselves be bridled—so that the local military no less than the local political administration are plugged into the norm of illegitimacy as a way of maintaining stability by virtue of the requirements of Pax Americana.

The new imperialism is conducted largely through political policy whose principal instrument is military assistance, with increasing emphasis on the preparation of the armed forces for counterinsurgency operations. As General Porter made perfectly plain in Congressional testimony, the aims of security must take priority over national development.

> The Military has frequently proven to be the most cohesive force available to assure public order and support of resolute governments attempting to maintain internal security. Latin American armed forces, acting in conjunction with the police and other security forces, have helped to control disorders and riots, contained or eliminated terrorists and guerrillas, and discouraged those elements which are tempted to resort to violence to overthrow the government.[20]

It will be observed that illegitimacy of rule is markedly different from the use of violence as an agency of mass political mobilization. For what the imperial center requires is a continuation of illegitimacy, but not a continuation of violence. Hence, the classic function of the coup d'état is aborted. It becomes an instrument to prevent, rather than stimulate, rapid, unchallenged social change.

The norm of illegitimacy is underwritten by military assistance programs that transform disparate, peripheral, and regional military caciques representing indigenous factors into a highly coordinated and unified grouping representing an international commitment against Communist penetration of the hemisphere. Joint military operations between the nations of Latin and North America, standardization of equipment, arranging central command structures, increasing the number of conferences, and meetings at regional as well as continental levels all serve to transform random types of illegitimate rule into a normative pattern of illegitimacy, or, at the least, a search for order in transnational terms, i.e., in terms of the interests of the cosmopolitan center.

[20] Porter, *op. cit.* For confirmation that Porter represents the dominant U.S. policy and not simply an idiosyncratic viewpoint, see the testimony of Lincoln Gordon on the "Foreign Assistance Act of 1966," *Hearings Before the House Committee on Foreign Affairs,* Washington: USGPO, 1966, p. 372; and Richard R. Clark, "U.S. Military Assistance in Latin America," *Army Digest* (September, 1966), 18–19.

Such programs, however, circumscribe the level and form of the political activity of Latin American military establishments. They are faced with the choice of supporting United States policy in order to develop counterinsurgency capabilities (and hence undermine any sort of legitimation that would be derived from mass participatory revolution), or supporting nationalistic factions and jeopardizing their foreign assistance pacts (hence negating the military elite as a factor in policy-making in Latin America). Whatever the particular decisions taken now, United States policies of military globalism tend to make obsolete earlier efforts at a standard typology of Latin American military styles and forms based exclusively on internal political affairs.

There are severe limits placed upon any autonomous developmental pattern in Latin America. To be sure, these are old nations which have long histories. They are also far more developed than most Asian countries and most African countries in terms of the size of their respective modernized sectors. But the most important point is that Latin America shows the face of the future to other sectors of the Third World. It reveals plainly that liberation from colonialism is radically different from liberation from imperialism. Indeed, the positive termination of the colonial phase may, as a matter of fact, stimulate imperial investment—both in terms of money and manpower. Furtado has expressed the special characteristics of economic instability which made possible the current imperial stage of illegitimacy:

> In Latin America, development induced by the industrial revolution in Europe and the United States was enough to transform part of the economic systems inherited from the colonial epoch, but not enough to create autonomous systems able to generate further growth. Hence, Latin America remained on the "periphery" of advanced industrial economies at a time when markets for primary products were far from able to generate the dynamism required.[21]

The norm of illegitimacy can arise only in a context where structural requisites for legitimate authority are absent. Legitimate authority can be institutionalized through either mechanisms of law or mechanisms of class. But if mechanisms of law

[21] Celso Furtado, "U.S. Hegemony and the Future of Latin America," *The World Today: The Royal Institute of International Affairs.* Vol. 22, No. 9 (September, 1966), 375–85.

are inadequate to meet the demands of the society, and mechanisms of class are too underdeveloped to come to the fore, and if both the legal machinery of the state and the class potency of the state are blocked by imperial factors, then the whole discussion of the nature of legitimation involves an examination of imperialism.[22] Modernization and industrialization express the contradiction in developmental terms, just as imperialism and nationalism express the contradiction in geopolitical terms. For this reason it is necessary to understand the connections between these dual processes if a theory of legitimation is to be forged.

It might be asked: Why doesn't a similar imperialism lead to similar results the world over? If there is an imperialist factor, should it not show up as roughly equivalent in its inputs and consequences the world over? One response that presents itself is that the United States has differential commitments the world over; hence, radically different consequences flow from its involvement. When one speaks of the "overextension of United States commitment," it is hard to imagine that Africa can be viewed in the same way as Latin America. Although a similar set of "interests" may obtain, there are widely varying "obligations." The basic problem for the United States in the second half of the twentieth century is its "security." In determining this security, the place of Latin America is far more central than that of Africa. In Latin America, development induced by the industrial revolution was enough to transform part of the economic system inherited from the colonial epoch, but not enough to create an autonomous system capable of generating autonomous growth. In this, Latin America, precisely because of its profound *modernization*, is more directly linked to the cosmopolitan centers of industrialism than are the nations of Africa and Asia. The latter remain traditional, but also politically far more mobile and freewheeling. Thus, the special relationship of Latin America for North America, and vice versa, creates a special set of results.

In the nineteenth century imperialism was a less weighty phenomenon than now. However, if we take the relationship of the British Empire to the growth of Brazil, or if we examine the

---

22 Whatever the evidential shortcomings, this response to the logic of the situation is well appreciated by Andrew Gunder Frank in his work on *Capitalism and Underdevelopment in Latin America: Historical Studies of Chile and Brazil*. New York and London: Monthly Review Press, 1967.

history of British colonial overseas relationships in Argentina in the nineteenth century, we will see that everything from the organization of the cattle industry to the organization of the railroads is directly related to the impact of the overseas factor. Whether we consider Spanish colonial rule in the eighteenth century, British colonial rule in the nineteenth century, or United States colonial rule in the twentieth century, one of the essential constants in Latin America—however shifting in form —has been the presence of an imperial factor. And it is the integration of traditionalistic classes with highly sophisticated international monetary elites that provides the material bases for the norm of illegitimacy.

What becomes clear is that the norm of illegitimacy is serviceable both to the internal needs of the political-military order which gives visible direction to Latin American policies and to the international needs of the economic order which limits the directions that the indigenous elements may chance upon. Thus nationalism from within and imperialism from without, far from being at loggerheads over the management of Latin America, serve more often than not to complement each other. The touching faith in nationalist solutions as a means for transcending imperial domination simply ignores the character of the nationalisms in Latin America. The nationalism of the right, which has prevailed in nearly every country of the Southern Hemisphere, offers scant optimism for avoiding imperial control. Indeed, such "nationalist" leaders of the "whole people" as Juan Perón, Getulio Vargas, and Rojas Pinilla were compelled to abandon their optimal plans for a countervailing imperialism of the Southern Hemisphere and settle for a "partnership" with foreign corporate wealth. They were trapped in the supreme contradiction of satisfying the requirements of the neo-Falangist elite arrangement, and hence having to finance their nationalistic ambitions through outside sources—the much maligned foreign capital.

Given this set of circumstances, a theory of Latin America cannot avoid being incorporated into a larger framework of the interplay of nationalism and colonialism. The definition of Latin America is itself a consequence of this interplay. If this formulation strikes the observer as crude, lacking in sophistication, so be it! The objective situation is itself crude and lacking in sophistication. The norm of illegitimacy is informally sanctioned from the lowest petty official living off bribes in some remote customs house in Asunción or São Paulo to the highest official living off the mineral produce of Latin America in some highly visible counting house in New York or London. To break the cycle of crisis and collapse, to eliminate the norm of illegitimacy as an operational code for Latin America means to break the organizational impasse created by both local bureaucrats and imported businessmen.

Appendix: Some Qualifying Aspects to the Norm of Illegitimacy

As I indicated at the outset, we do not have any adequate general social theory of Latin America. And although I would maintain that the kinds of approaches outlined herein, focusing on the interpenetration of national elites and imperial investors, is the main pivot in a system of survival through illegitimacy, this by no means explains the actual behavior of *all* Latin American nations. While it might be quite serviceable for sixteen of them, there are at least four cases—Chile, Cuba, Mexico, and Uruguay (and perhaps Costa Rica)—where the norm of illegitimacy does not obtain, certainly not in "ideal-typical" form. But rather than resort to a mobilization-integration model[23] which indeed was a first serviceable attempt at a general theory, I should rather like to explain why, at least in two cases—Mexico and Uruguay—the norm of illegitimacy does not presently obtain.[24]

The first fact to take into consideration about Uruguay is that from its inception there existed a relatively strong parallel dualism: A rural political party representing landholding economic interests; and an urban party representing middle-class and organized working-class interests. The stability of its politi-

[23] Gino Germani, "Social Change and Intergroup Conflicts," in *The New Sociology,* Irving Louis Horowitz, ed. New York and London: Oxford University Press, 1964, pp. 391–408.

[24] My reasons for omitting Cuba and Chile from consideration here are that in the case of Cuba, I have attempted to provide some sort of accounting elsewhere. See "The Stalinization of Castro," *New Politics,* Vol. IV, No. 4 (1966); and "Cuban Communism," *Trans-Action,* Vol. 4, No. 10 (October, 1966). In the case of Chile, my knowledge is far too limited to even make an attempt at an educated guess.

cal system was therefore more a result of the neatness in the
division of power, in the stability of the equilibrium, than in any
perfectly meshed network of mass mobilization and integration.[25]

The neatness of class and elite divisions is itself a consequence of the second major fact about Uruguay. It evolved as a
buffer state separating the two titans of the Southern Hemisphere: Brazil and Argentina. Thus, it comes into existence
without the myriad of subclass pressure groups and shadow
elites which pervade nearly every other nation in the hemisphere. Uruguay has no need to call upon the military to expand
or contract civil power, since the balancing act was achieved by
administrative fiat at the start of its national independence
period. At the same time, Uruguay is in a position to function in
terms of legitimate authority, since such small-nation legitimacy
itself provides essential security to the large nations which it
borders. Whatever the nature of Brazilian and Argentine politics, they nonetheless retain a shared interest in seeing to it that
Uruguay is ran on at least semidemocratic principles.

At the same time, the satellitic aspects of Uruguay are also
reinforced by the fact that, like Denmark and Finland, Uruguay
is a modernized nation and not a developmental nation. It has
been moved to evolve satellitic economic relations without
sacrificing its political autonomy. Indeed, Uruguay has engaged
in an historic trade-off characteristic of a number of more
advanced small nations: it performs a willing (or at least a
knowing) satellitic economic role in exchange for a guarantee
of political sovereignty.

The exceptional circumstances in Uruguay's historical evolution—its parity of class cleavage and absence of parasitic
sectors, and its trade-off of economic independence for political
sovereignty—serves to explain why this small "Switzerland of the
Western Hemisphere" is able to escape the hard fate of its more
powerful neighbors. Yet it would not be quite accurate to say
that Uruguay is a legitimate polity in the classical sense, since
what one finds is a peculiar withering away of state power. The
political system in Uruguay serves to allocate bureaucratic

[25] See my study, "La política urbana en Latinoamérica," *Revista Mexicana de Sociología,* Vol. XXVIII, No. 1 (January, 1967). I might add
in this connection that the discussion on Uruguay was omitted from the
English-language version of this paper.

functions and to adjudicate the claims of various social factions; however it does not have real autonomous power to act. This situation could thus be described as semilegitimacy.

In a country like Mexico one might inquire: Does not legitimate authority obtain? Is there not an orderly transfer of power? Have there been any revolutionary upheavals since the revolution of 1920? Is there any evidence of a military coup d'état coming? Surely, if the question of legitimacy is linked to the satisfactory management of succession crises, Mexico would be the direct opposite of Argentina or Peru. But is such a criterion of formalistic succession on much better footing than personal charisma? Several kinds of answers can be fashioned.

Mexico did have a twentieth-century national revolution, which, at the very least, gives to it a degree of autonomy absent in most other countries in the hemisphere. But Mexico is now undergoing a crisis of a very profound sort. Mexico is a single-party state. It has one major party which regularly receives between 85 and 90 percent of the vote; two minor parties, one left and one right, share the remaining ballots. The choice of officialdom is increasingly becoming an internal matter, through the party mechanism. The PRI (Partido Revolucionario Institucional) party mechanism is becoming a political IBM system: balancing out the needs, requests, and demands of different sectors. The Mexican polity has been properly characterized as "a complicated system of exchanges between interest groups and an oligarchy that provides decisive and sometimes rather ruthless leadership."[26] The pillars of power are becoming increasingly uneven, and the possibility of tumultuous change is pressing.

The crisis has not been made manifest in Mexico precisely because the public sector of the economy has become so powerful, bureaucratic, and entrenched that it is even hard for a class such as the private industrial class to exercise any autonomous power. The Mexican military budget has been considerably enlarged in the last three years. The widely reported growth of sporadic guerrilla insurgency and the recent student riots at the National University of Mexico have each indicated the growth of illegitimate forms of political behavior. The steady investment in domestic rather than foreign industry taking place in

26 Bo Anderson and James D. Cockcroft, "Coöptation in Mexican Politics," *International Journal of Comparative Sociology*, Vol. 7, No. 1 (March, 1966), 11–28.

Mexico has exacted a high toll from the nation's working classes. The high growth rate of Mexico's economy has prevented any outbreak of mass violence. But what would happen if there were a growth-rate decline or a weakening of Mexico's economy as a result of a concerted boycott by the Central American Trade Association is difficult to ascertain.

In a country like Mexico the abortive character of the 1910–20 revolution is beginning to have its effects. Nonetheless it should be kept in mind that Mexico is still one of the most *stable* regimes in the hemisphere. Yet even a background in revolution does not exempt Mexico from the legitimacy crisis. For although Mexico achieved its legitimacy through mass revolution, it was able to guarantee its polity only in the thirties, when it successfully carried through an oil nationalization plan that met with the hearty disapprobation of the United States. Mexico's problem is to maintain this network of legitimacy in a period when its economic resources are now large enough to compete with the United States, at least on a regional basis, but not powerful enough to cancel United States interests as a whole. How Mexico can manage the dynamics of imperialism will thus become a critical factor in evaluating its long-run chances for perpetuating legitimate rule.

Therefore, as in the case of Uruguay, Mexico too reveals a peculiar deterioration of state power, or at least its inability to define its power in any context other than that provided by the ruling political party. The Mexican state does not have powers to act; the PRI does have such powers. This type of situation, where the party rather than the polity is endowed with legitimacy, could be described as *quasi-legitimacy*.

In the two negative cases introduced—Uruguay and Mexico —one finds not simply a generalized confrontation of legitimate versus illegitimate forms of polity, but rather some sophisticated shadings that reveal elements of both, and virtues (or vices) of neither.

Three inescapable and interrelated conclusions appear to follow from this analysis. First, military or quasi-military rule in most parts of Latin America, whatever achievements it may register, is a surrogate for legitimate authority, utilizing force to prevent legitimacy from evolving. Further, there is scant evidence that the cycle of illegitimacy encouraged by military *golpes* encourages either modernizing attitudes or basic industrial growth. Second, the norm of illegitimacy is fostered and promoted from the "cosmopolitan center." Imperialism directly affects political socialization in Latin America, and inhibits the maturation of independent pluralistic forms of government. Third, it can be ascertained that those nations least subject to the norm of illegitimacy are also among the most rapidly developing nations in the hemisphere and among the most democratically ruled. Without wishing to assign arbitrary causal sequences for which there is scant evidence, it is nonetheless possible to see that the cycle of illegitimacy must be broken at some point if Latin America is to fulfill its noblest ambitions.

The System and the Social Structure of Latin America

RAÚL PREBISCH

DISTRIBUTIONAL PRIVILEGE AND THE EFFICACY OF THE SYSTEM

Social Mobility and the Dynamic Elements

THE CHANGES in the production pattern and structure of the economy that are called for by the spread of modern technology entail, in their turn, a transformation of the social structure in order to impart dynamic force to the economic system and promote income redistribution. Under the prevailing social structure a large proportion of the savings potential of the upper-income groups is left untapped, together with much of the potential embodied in human, land, and capital resources.

During the period of externally geared development, technology made little headway. It gained most ground in export activities and in the activities allied to them in one way or another. The techniques introduced were usually simple, and compatible with a social structure based on land monopolization and extensive farming methods. Complex techniques were also introduced from time to time, but in those cases the activities involved were far from being an integral part of Latin American life, since they generally constituted foreign enclaves, particularly in so far as the exploitation of natural resources was concerned.

The industrialization movement had no radical effect upon

29

this state of affairs. Another upper stratum was added to the existing structure and the middle class was gradually drawn into it, becoming numerically stronger in the process, but failing to establish a definite personality of its own.

During the first stage of industrialization there was actually no need for changes to be made in the social structure. The kind of industrialization that took place was mainly extensive, characterized by fairly easy techniques and the lack of any imperative need to make intensive use of the scanty capital and of the human resources available; in this it resembled the extensive type of farming indulged in on large estates.

The possibilities of this type of development are nearly exhausted. In order to quicken its tempo, modern techniques must be introduced into agriculture and yield substantially raised. Industry will have to advance toward increasingly complex patterns, explore the possibilities of finding the markets it needs abroad, and rapidly conquer the vast area within the region where underconsumption is rife.

Why is it necessary to transform the social structure if this new stage of accelerated development is to supervene? There are cogent reasons. The social structure has an adverse effect on development in two respects that are of supreme importance: (a) the emergence of the dynamic elements in a given society; and (b) the way in which these elements play their part in the production process.

Modern production techniques have an ever-increasing need of these dynamic elements—men of initiative, drive, and resolution who are capable of taking risks and shouldering responsibility. They are needed at a vast number of levels, ranging from skilled workers to top-level technical experts and the organizers and administrators of all the phases of the economic process. They are also required in other branches of human activity. The need for these dynamic elements increases at a rate far more rapid than that of development itself. In other words, if development is speeded up, the task of singling out and training such men will have to be pursued much more vigorously. In industry alone, it has been calculated that for every 1 percent by which production increases, there will have to be 4 percent[1] more technicians in every category to ensure production effi-

[1] See F. H. Harbison, *The Process of Educational Planning,* Information document No. 5, Conference on Education and Economic and Social Development in Latin America, March, 1962.

ciency. The same is true of other branches of economic activity.

What is being done in this connection in Latin America is little enough if the magnitude of the problem and the marked differences between the Latin American countries are taken into account. A considerable human potential is left untapped, since very few dynamic elements succeed in forcing their way up from the lower and middle strata of society. Naturally, a larger proportion comes from the middle strata, although there are often serious obstacles in the way of their absorption. The lack of proper social mobility is clear evidence of social stratification.

The starting point for social mobility is education. By now it is fully recognized that education in Latin America has fundamental shortcomings, that there is a high illiteracy rate, and that the educational system bears no relation to the requirements of economic development, quite apart from the serious deficiencies that exist in other basic cultural respects.

But this is not all. Strictly speaking, the extremely low income level of half the population and the straitened circumstances of much of the remainder prevent the dynamic elements from emerging and taking advantage of the whole range of opportunities for education and technical training, even when these exist. The first concrete expression of an income redistribution policy should be in this field, through social investment in the development and training of human resources and in the provision of effective means of access to education at all levels. This would bring about a new order of things in which the dynamic elements that reach the upper strata would be proportionate to the numerical size of the social strata from which they come. Perhaps one of the most decisive factors in the remarkable development first of the United States and then of the Soviet Union—despite the fundamental divergencies in their systems—has been the common denominator of a highly active process of social mobility which had not been observable previously under the aegis of industrialization.

These dynamic elements are not confined exclusively to the economic field, but pertain to society as a whole. They are the men who set their stamp on each generation. Although their opportunities for education and for rising in the social scale are severely limited, this does not diminish their *élan vital* or the strength of their aspirations. And if the sluggish pace of development prevents their being turned to account in the economic and social process and hampers their ascent to the different levels of activity within this process, there is a natural feeling of resentment, and their pent-up energy will inevitably brim over into other channels. What course these dynamic elements will eventually follow if the slow rate of development persists is another of the unknown quantities in Latin America, and herein lies one more great opportunity for exercising rational control over the forces of economic and social development.

Privilege and Its Effects on
Incentives to Economic Activity

Nevertheless, the mere fact of bringing these dynamic elements to the fore and giving them training does not necessarily mean that they will effectually fulfill their function in the economic and social development process. At this point we are confronted with the other outstanding problem linked to the social structure. In the Latin American countries certain forms of privilege considerably weaken the incentive to technical progress in all its manifestations. And consequently, the chances of getting the best out of the men of initiative and ability that modern technology requires is seriously lessened.

It is common knowledge that the extreme disparities in the size of landed properties militate against the application of up-to-date intensive farming techniques—in the case of the latifundia, because they yield a lucrative income without the introduction of such practices, and in that of the minifundia, on account of their very poverty and ineffectiveness.

But this state of affairs is not confined to the land. In industry too the edge of the incentives to technical progress has been blunted by excessive protection and the positions of privilege it creates. Private enterprise needs constant application of the spur of competition to keep it on the alert. And in Latin American industry as a whole, competition is seldom very keen. Here we are treading on delicate ground, where—to forestall misinterpretations—a clear line of demarcation must be drawn between criticism of the operation of the system and fair acknowledgment of what industrialization has achieved.

The role of private enterprise is not only to establish new industries and expand those already in existence, but also to turn the limited capital available to the best possible account.

This is essentially a matter of having the right men to call on. Protection carried to excess affords no encouragement to train efficient workers and make good use of their services. Production equipment is often misguidedly used, with the result that its performance is inferior to that registered even in countries with medium industrial yields, not to mention those where productivity is high. Several factors combine to determine this situation: the organization of the factory and the system of distribution of labor, defective raw materials, inadequate supervision, careless treatment of machinery and plant. All these problems can be solved. That is, they can be solved provided private enterprise does not confine its efforts to the initial functions of promotion. It must also be indefatigable in its endeavors to increase yields and reduce costs. And this is where nothing can replace the spur of competition.

In the shelter of high tariff barriers and other import restrictions or prohibitions, anticompetitive practices, if not virtually monopolistic combines, have become widespread. Well-equipped establishments operate alongside others whose costs are high, in a sort of tacit mutual benefit society, the latter safeguarding their marginal existence and the former reaping the big profits that accrue from the cost differential.

Of the need for income redistribution measures to redress the existing grave social disparities, no further evidence is required than has already been submitted. But such measures do not represent a complete and basic solution, since the disparities in question, and the forms they assume, are largely the outcome of the defective operation of the economic system; there is no close relation between personal income and the real contribution made by its recipients to the economic and social development process.

This defective pattern of distribution does not, of course, enhance the prestige of the system of private enterprise in the Latin American countries, despite the fact that in each of them many cases are observable in which a high income level is clearly the result of technical progress and of ability to innovate, to introduce new methods, to give better service to the community. It is men with just such capabilities that are needed for the acceleration of development. By virtue of social mobility and competition, increasing numbers of them must be given the opportunity to rise from the ranks and receive the necessary training.

In discussion of such topics, the relation between these two decisive factors in economic progress is often forgotten. Free enterprise and competition are inseverably linked, since in default of the latter the former is doomed to wilt in the atmosphere of privilege. Given a combination of the two, there will be abundant scope for private enterprise and its energetic participation in the planning of development.

Reflection will show that the ability of a small number of people to concentrate in their hands a high proportion of collective income has its roots deep in history. Our ancestors failed to do what other equally new or even newer societies did to clear the way for economic development and stabilize the foundations of democracy—namely, abolish privilege in respect of land ownership. In these latitudes, the great fortunes of the past derived largely from appropriation of the land and its subsequent rise in value. To this was later added the further privilege created by excessive protection. And at all stages, there has been inflation as a powerful instrument for the arbitrary acquisition of wealth.

No attempt is made here to analyze all the factors that have conduced to the concentration of wealth and income, since in that case attention would have to be devoted to the consequences of the misuse of political power or of certain types of artificial state intervention in economic activity, as well as to the effects of restrictive business combines and certain harmful practices fostered by defective organization or supervision of the banking system. Only the principal determinants are indicated, the most widespread, whose significant influence on income distribution and the efficacy of the economic system is giving rise to serious manifestations of social strife.

All these forms of privilege in the distribution of wealth and income are sapping the energies of the dynamic elements in process of emergence, undermining their capacity for struggle and achievement. Of those who are prevented from becoming an active part of the economic system, by its lack of dynamism, some are driven by their very sense of frustration, and the contrast between their own situation and that of the more fortunate, into the resentful attitude of which something has already been said; while others, especially those from the middle strata of society, seek refuge in public administration, a field of activity that is as apt to demoralize the dynamic elements as to attract those that are not dynamic, those that have been unable to find a niche in private economic activity, either because of the latter's own shortcomings, or because the aforesaid divorce between education and development has disqualified them to do so.

In such circumstances, functions and functionaries spread and multiply in the civil and military spheres. And the state, whether or not prompted by essential considerations, takes on entrepreneurial activities and indulges in different forms of intervention or control which—dictated as they are by the wish to remedy deficiencies in the system—seldom deal with development phenomena, much less promote development, since they are frequently of a negative or interdictory character.

Thus, alongside men who discharge their functions with efficiency and public spirit, there are many who take shelter behind these other forms of privilege incorporated in the social structure. The latter tend to assimilate the living patterns of the ruling groups and to rely on their patronage, thus wasting the reforming power they might have wielded at their own social level.[2]

These social phenomena emanate essentially from the lack of dynamism of the development process and at the same time tend to aggravate it, not only because state action is diverted into the channels indicated above, but also because the dynamic elements are devitalized, and net capital formation is thus deprived of substantial resources.

INFLATION AND THE SOCIAL STRUCTURE

The Social Background of Inflation

The power of certain social groups to exercise an arbitrary influence over the distribution of income is what lies behind inflation in Latin America. It gives rise to factors that have a direct or indirect inflationary impact. This impact is direct, if recourse is had to credit expansion as a means of meeting investment requirements, instead of to the restriction of con-

[2] See José Medina Echavarría, *Economic Development in Latin America. Sociological Considerations* (E/CN.12/646).

sumption, or if the necessary effort to meet the government deficit by taxation or budgetary means is shirked, either in boom periods, when this effort is relatively easy, or in slump periods, when it becomes difficult. The effect of the factors in question is indirect, when it is the broad masses of the population that have to bear the consequences of the existence of structural stumbling blocks to development and of the regressive methods chosen to deal with these obstacles. This is particularly true of import substitution activities, whose costs, plus the excessive profit margins permitted by tariff protection, are transferred to prices; and it also applies to the higher cost of certain agricultural products, often important items of mass consumption, mainly because of the obstacles to increased production arising from the prevailing form of land tenure. These and other elements constitute nonmonetary inflationary factors.

The lower strata of the Latin American population are beginning to use their growing political and trade union power to defend themselves against the rise in prices resulting from these monetary and nonmonetary inflationary factors. They are doing so by means of wage increases, in the first place, and secondly, by obtaining social security benefits and other state services intended to improve their situation. But when increases in wages, social security contributions, and indirect taxes are not or cannot be absorbed by entrepreneurs' profits, as is generally the case, they force up costs and are transferred to prices, thus promoting credit expansion, and leading to new increases in wages, security benefits, and taxes, in the all-too-familiar spiral. This does not mean that some of the workers and employees do not generally succeed in recouping themselves for the effects of price increases, and even in more than offsetting them; but they do so only at the expense of other social groups. The chief victims are the rural workers, who have no trade union power, generally receive little or nothing in the way of social security benefits, and do not enjoy the same state services as people in the towns. Other groups affected are those workers and employers, either active or retired, who because they are less well-equipped to defend themselves are left behind when it comes to wage increases, or those who share with the entrepreneurs the ill-effects of currency overvaluation on the income of export or substitution activities, which also aggravate the

tendency for the external sector to become a development
bottleneck. Lastly, the understandable reluctance to increase
taxes or public utility rates in proportion to the wage increases
of those employed by the state or by the enterprises concerned
enables the rest of the community to defend their real income to
a corresponding extent, but not on any lasting basis, since the
deficit resulting from such attitudes inevitably leads to a blanket
rise in prices.

These delays in raising the wages of the groups left in the
rear, and in adjusting exchange rates, taxes, and public utility
tariffs, cannot continue indefinitely, and as the underprivileged
groups succeed in gaining ground and the state changes its
attitude, the spiral is given increasing impetus, and is even
further intensified if the pace of economic activity is reduced.

Reluctance to Adopt Drastic Solutions

Thus the spiral gradually exhausts its corrective effects and
becomes an increasingly disruptive influence. Unquestionably,
this is fully known and understood. But what other recourse
remains if basic solutions are shirked? Letting the spiral take its
course is generally the easiest way out in the short run. It is
usual to resort to what is feasible from a political point of view
even if it is not advisable from a rational standpoint.

Suffice to note the obvious contrast between the formidable
opposition usually aroused by any attempt to even up distributional disparities through tax reform, and the very liberal nature
of certain social security benefits and state services whose costs
fall, in the last analysis (although very unevenly), on the broad
masses of the population who are supposed to benefit. Much the
same is true of mass wage and salary increases.

But what is the point of these solutions? They are certainly
not simple. The problem is greatly complicated by the fact that
to the elements of traditional inflation have been added those
others whose elimination will be a lengthy business, since they
derive from structural weaknesses.

In the traditional type of inflation, of a monetary character,
real wages can recoup their losses at the expense of inflationary
entrepreneurial profits. But the situation is different when price
increases have a nonmonetary basis. This is a question of
inflationary elements which, because they cannot be absorbed

by increases in productivity, have long and steadily been moving up the spiral.

In such cases the basic solution can only be more rapid development, accompanied by a policy of income redistribution. However, this takes time, and during the interval an anti-inflationary policy means a sacrifice by the lower strata of the population such as could only be tolerated from the psychological and political standpoints if an expansionist policy were simultaneously introduced to stimulate the use of the economy's idle capacity, with the ensuing rapid rise in income, and a policy of austerity regarding the higher groups, to reduce their consumption sharply and promote an increase in investment. All this should be combined with the timely contribution of international resources. The resulting improvement in the rate of development would be the only means of compensating real wages for what they had lost through the nonmonetary forms of inflation.

As can be seen, this is a strictly political aspect of the problem, since a solution of this nature requires, in addition to the firm decisions involved, the full support and understanding of the masses, although this support must not be undermined by premature or excessive pressure or demands that would wreck the whole program of rehabilitation and expansion.

Stabilization Policy

Thus monetary stabilization is not conceivable except in relation to a policy of economic development and social justice. In fact, regarding stabilization as a solution in itself has often led to failure in the laudable attempt to end inflation.

The principal instrument of this type of stabilization is credit machinery. Undeniably, an external imbalance can be temporarily eliminated through a reduction of total income brought about by restrictive use of this instrument. It can be eliminated, but not remedied, since however long the depressive effects of the policy involved may be endured, sooner or later rational measures aimed at recovery will have to be taken, and the consequent rise in income will resurrect the external disequilibrium.

With respect to internal imbalances, an attempt to remedy the government deficit by economic contraction generally has exactly the opposite effect, because of its depressive repercussions on the country's tax capacity, and also—to the detriment of investment—on the capacity to save.

From another standpoint, the social strife implicit in inflation is generally intensified by the dynamic weakness that is the inability of the system as it functions at present to absorb the population displaced from rural areas and those already living in the towns who have been unable to find employment in productive activities. In the meantime, these people take refuge in unskilled personal services, and redundant or unnecessary work in private and state activities, and the brunt of all this is borne by the lower social strata. Thus, lack of dynamism becomes another of the potent causes of nonmonetary inflation.

In the final analysis the superfluous staff taken on in private administration, who do not produce a corresponding amount of goods and services, create pressure on the goods and services produced by others, and thus provide a powerful stimulus to the inflationary spiral.

Here too the simplistic approach has its own formula, which is merely to send these superfluous workers packing. One of the implicit advantages of credit restriction is in fact to break public or trade union resistance to these so-called economic rehabilitation measures. Here again, all that is done is to side-step a problem which must be faced, namely, that of increasing the pace of development to correct the lack of dynamism.

Our frank stand against such simplistic views is usually interpreted as defense of inflation and opposition to anti-inflationary measures. This is far from being the case, since inflation, in the final analysis, is the result of a structure that is curbing development, both by preventing full use of the savings potential and by putting obstacles in the path of technical progress. Thus the problem of inflation is inseparable from the development problem, and monetary policy must be an integral part of the policy of economic and social development. Otherwise anti-inflationary measures are sooner or later doomed to failure.

But continuing inflation is not a valid alternative either. As we wrote some time ago in another paper: "If the system under which we live cannot develop without it, inflation will be an alternative that leads nowhere. For it corrodes the economy and dangerously disrupts society. Impossible, then, to deny the rationality of inflation as an instrument, not to infuse the system with dynamic vigour, but to sweep it inexorably onward to disintegration."[3]

Two Types of Foreign Capital

The Persistence of Enclaves

The social structure handed down from the times of externally geared development was associated with the characteristic type of foreign investment aimed mainly at serving, in one way or another, the interests of the major centers of which the undertakings concerned were an offshoot. They continue essentially, now as then, to lean toward the development of mineral resources, export and allied activities, and public utility concessions.

These are the enclaves to which reference has already been made. In those days, any inflow of advanced techniques was confined to them. They made no attempt to disseminate such techniques within the country, nor was there any reason for them to do so, since extensive farming of the land by the country's own rural population usually required no more than a rudimentary technology. Moreover, such private enterprise as emerged from time to time in our countries to engage in activities similar to those of the enclaves often ended in the domestic efforts being engulfed by them or disappearing under their economic pressure.

However, this did not affect the compatibility of the foreign enterprises with the prevailing social structure. On the contrary, the latter is gaining strength and substance as time goes by; the ruling groups—relying on their privileged position as landowners—are enjoying the benefits of the steady increase in the value of the land deriving from population growth and from the externally geared development fostered by the foreign enterprises. At the same time they participate, albeit tangentially, in the activities of these enterprises, chiefly by being of service to them in their relations with the public authorities. They are thus

3 See "Economic Development or Monetary Stability: the False Dilemma," *Economic Bulletin for Latin America*, Vol. VI, No. 1, March, 1961, p. 25.

able to lead that typical life of ease which is conducive to the
enjoyment of European culture—cultural development within
underdevelopment—and to participation in political campaigning (often confined to these same ruling groups), the broad
masses being called upon regularly or occasionally to accommodate their internal differences.

These enclaves of the past, which are still with us, must either
change of themselves or give way to domestic enterprise. The
days when foreign enterprise came in to do what Latin America
could not are definitely over. We need the outside world to help
us to cultivate our own ability, so that the population as a whole
can be brought to share in the process of development. Thus,
the foreign enterprise must be a nucleus for the dissemination of
technology, as it already is in some cases.

While there are a few encouraging signs of such a change,
much still remains to be done. Of course, the proportion of net
income left in a given country by these enterprises is usually
larger than before, when they were relatively small. But the
nationals concerned generally have little—if any—access to
technology, and decisions are taken abroad, without the country's influencing them to any great extent, however important
they may be to its interests. There are even cases where the
actual pattern of exports is beyond the control of Latin American trade policy.

There is a pressing need for new formulas to solve these
problems, not only in connection with this form of business
activity per se but also because the new formulas in question
will help to create an atmosphere conducive to the cooperation
of foreign capital in the new stage of industrialization which
must be embarked upon without delay.

Strictly speaking, a clear distinction must be made between
two types of foreign capital: the outdated type, with the enclaves which still subsist, and the new type, which takes a
determined share in the intensive process of industrialization.

Other Problems of Foreign Capital

Of course, this latter mode of procedure also raises some
problems, but they can be solved without too much difficulty.
Among the more important are those deriving from the policy
of the country itself.

In the first place, the huge profits made by some firms. The profit incentive is clearly essential if foreign private enterprise is to be attracted. However, it should be the consequence of the advanced techniques such firms bring into the country, the new patterns of production, organization, and marketing they introduce into the local milieu. No impartial view can call this in question. But here too the effects of undue protection and inflation are felt, to which must be added some cases of spurious incorporation of foreign capital under the protection of official action itself. As regards this whole state of affairs, the Latin American governments are in a position to apply corrective measures not so much to suppress its effects as to attack its very causes with respect to both foreign and domestic firms.

The other problem, which demands a much greater and more sustained effort, is the technical and economic inferiority of Latin American enterprise as compared with its foreign counterpart. We have many times commented on this. While it is a quite natural phenomenon, measures leading to the progressive establishment of a reasonable balance should be adopted. Elsewhere in the present document reference is made to these measures, which need not be confined to the Central American Common Market, although it is there that the need for them is most pressing.

Rightly considered, undue protection also influences the technical inferiority of the domestic enterprise because it weakens the initiative of the executives and thus does not encourage them to improve their techniques. On more than one occasion we have seen domestic firms either absorbed or dislodged by foreign enterprises when engaged in activities in which it would not have been difficult—with greater initiative and more funds —to assimilate new production techniques.

Even more complicated is the problem created by some firms which are part of international trusts and which, by dividing the markets among themselves, usually hamper the domestic production effort. Here state intervention, either to do what has to be done or to let others do it, is unavoidable.

Moreover, in a development plan it is quite right that each country should clearly define those priority areas in which it would like to have the cooperation of foreign private enterprise. While no attempt can be made to suggest these areas here and now, it would seem obvious that, in a program designed to encourage exports, foreign enterprise has a very important part to play, both because of its knowledge of export practices and external markets, and on account of its level of technical and economic know-how, which domestic firms cannot usually attain in a short time. Here, as in any other industrial activity, a partnership between foreign and Latin American enterprise might be a very suitable solution, from the standpoint both of dissemination of techniques and of improved relations with domestic interests. Such a partnership should be a clearly defined objective in the granting of tax exemptions by capital-importing countries. Otherwise, foreign investment might carry undue weight in some branches of economic activity, which would be undesirable from various points of view.

By thus acting as an agent for the propagation of advanced techniques within the country concerned, the foreign enterprise would play a part in the development of Latin America very different from the role it had in the past, notwithstanding the significance of its contribution to externally geared development. In those days, however, the existing type of foreign enterprise fitted easily into the social structure, and as this structure changes to meet the exigencies of development, the foreign enterprise must inevitably change as well.

PLANNING AND THE OPERATION OF
THE ECONOMIC SYSTEM

Public Administration As It Reflects the Social Structure

If Latin American private enterprise is lagging behind the requirements of development, it is not surprising that the same is true of public administration. Its organization is a survival from times past, with additions and adjustments, but without basic changes.

It is not that there is any unawareness of the defects of the public administration, or any lack of urgent calls for reform; but for reasons similar to those that have led to the maintenance of the existing social structure, and others as well, the public administration in our countries has not undergone any change.

Actually, the prevailing type of public administration is in line with the social structure. The fact that nearly half the active population makes out a living in agriculture has had no more effect than to procure the allocation of a tiny fraction of budget resources for technological research and the dissemination of its findings, since the prevailing system of land tenure does not demand such measures. Taxation, properly used, is a powerful instrument for economic development and distributional justice, and our countries' experience would suffice, in combination with some external assistance, to enable us to organize the tax machinery efficiently, prevent evasion, and modify the fiscal system in general. If this has not been achieved in the way and to the extent necessary, the resistance of the ruling groups is largely to blame. Many other examples could be mentioned. Broadly speaking, these groups do not demand efficiency; and what is more serious, the political movements of the lower groups have seldom made much endeavor to improve public administration.

In fact, all the old ways survive, and one clientele gives way to another in the administration, since there are few Latin American countries that have an effective civil service. Quantity rather than quality is the basis of staffing, and the poor salaries —in some cases reduced by inflation to unbelievably low levels, until the spiral makes it possible to recover what has been lost, or a part of it—drive away the most able and disorganize the whole system.

Given this state of affairs, the plan—essentially popular in its origin—of transferring certain foreign-owned enclaves to national ownership has often had disastrous results. This does not mean that it is impossible to find or train men who can run such activities efficiently, but the impetus of strong feeling is not enough; judicious selection, discipline, and steadfastness are a *sine qua non.*

Nevertheless, it would be a mistake to see in all this merely the play of economic interests, political pressures, or perhaps the warping of certain state machinery from its true purpose. There is a background of inertia, of perpetuation of inefficiency, which is preventing the public administration in Latin America from adapting itself to the requirements of economic development, except in a few special cases. This applies to simple as well as to complicated functions, and the result is apparent in the needless trammeling of economic activity—in fact, of all activities that bear any relation to the state—and in every imaginable kind to inefficient and time-consuming procedure. Naturally, ours has the weaknesses inherent in all bureauc-

racies, but it displays marked symptoms of underdevelopment
as well. In short, the public sector betrays itself as behind the
times, not only in its administrative functions, but also in the
inadequacy of the existing machinery when it comes to bringing
new ideas to the fore, and formulating and carrying out a
rational development policy.

Plans and Planning

In our countries the state is not organized for the last-named
functions. This must be frankly admitted, now that we are
beginning to open our minds to the idea of planning. Plans are
beginning to be put forward, but the actual work of planning, in
the broadest and most responsible sense, is either nonexistent or
exists only in embryo.[4]

Planning has three separate aspects, although they are all
closely linked: (a) the conception of the plan, (b) the translation of the plan into a series of practical measures and specific
projects, and (c) the administrative organization required for
the two previous tasks and for the execution and supervision of
the plan, as well as its constant adjustment to changed circumstances. In other words, an economic and social development
plan entails the planning of a public administration capable of
furthering its objectives.

The most significant advance has been achieved mainly in the
first phase, that of conception. Much less progress has been
made in planning proper, although there are signs that the
governments are beginning to recognize the significance of this
fact.

Once the overall development targets have been quantified,
together with individual goals for the various economic and
social sectors, and the funds necessary to achieve them have
been determined, the next step should be to embark on the
actual measures and specific projects at once. Many of these can
even be prepared and carried out as the plan takes shape. However, this does not generally happen with the necessary dispatch, even in cases where there are sufficient internal or
external funds for the preparation of projects. It is not unusual
to find measures that clash with the aims of the plan, for when

---

[4] The Secretariat has carried out a study on the existing situation in this
field. See *Progress in the Planning Field in Latin America* (E/CN.12/
677).

there is no proper planning organization, there is generally a characteristic dichotomy between current problems and development problems, between immediate action and planning, as if these were not merely two sides of the same coin.

Thus, a plan without planning activity is pointless. At best it is the rational formulation of a body of ideas, valuable enough as an ordered presentation of problems and possible ways of solving them, but not as a complex of elements that can serve as the basis for practical action.

Furthermore, as a result of the pressure of circumstances, plans have often tended to be drawn up by a small group of people who have been unable to make use of the piecemeal experience of a host of government departments—the experience of the vast number of people who will have to execute the plan without having had the opportunity of cooperating in the determination of its aims. In other words, the body responsible for formulating the plan is often superimposed on the existing administrative organization without in any way becoming a part of it. There must be an effort to achieve integration, following one basic principle: the plan must not be created only from above; it must come from below, traveling up through all the responsible levels of the administration.

All these weaknesses are easy to understand, and in no way detract from the admirable achievement of those governments who have undertaken the formulation of plans; if they had not done so, the weaknesses in question would not have appeared. The next step is to carry out the far from easy task of making the administrative machinery capable of responding to the needs of planning. The unremitting labor it involves can only be successfully undertaken if a firm decision at the top has the backing of the senior officials in the administration, since they must all take an active part in the work of planning.

The Power of the State and Ways of Exercising It

From another standpoint, this planning task, the effort to act consciously upon the forces of development, means giving the state considerable power. We cannot deny this or escape the anxious misgivings that often trouble even those who are convinced of the need to carry out the structural changes referred to and clear the way for state planning, to say nothing of those who are strongly opposed to such a course. How far will the endeavor to regulate the forces of development subordinate individuals to the power of the state? Shall we have to sound a retreat in the historic struggle to prevent the dominion of a few men, of a minority, over the rest of the community? Is there a basic conflict between the acceleration of development and a steady advance toward democracy? Or can we succeed in synthesizing these two aims by giving Latin American democracy an economic and social content?

An understandable confusion exists regarding all this. If we are to achieve a synthesis we must, in influencing the forces of development, combine economic and social aims with political objectives. And to reconcile the two we must effect a harmonious combination of state action with individual initiative. The state will not prescribe the conduct of individuals—that is, say what they must do or leave undone in their economic activity. It acquires an impersonal power, not over them, but over the forces that actuate them. This power must be exercised basically by means of incentives to economic action rather than by coercion once the structural problems that stifle development have been overcome, because coercive elements in the operation of the system open the way to arbitrary dominion of the state over the individual.

This is a fundamental and crucial point which it is essential to clarify. We must consider whether the ways in which the state carries out its plan to regulate the forces of development do or do not interfere with the behavior of the individual, or endanger the independence of his personal decisions.

In this context, what is the significance of state action to ensure that better use is made of the savings potential? What consequences will flow from the way in which the state tries to influence individual enterprise in order to induce it to fulfill the aims of the plan? How far is the technical action of the state likely to affect the independence of personal decisions?

Let us look first at the problem of capital formation. A distinction must be drawn between the initial steps to make full use of the savings potential and the subsequent operation of the system. As to the former, this problem cannot be envisaged solely in the light of the distributional privileges that characterize the present social structure, since these must be gradually reduced and eliminated by structural reforms.

Thus, the problem of capital formation must also be considered from the standpoint of the ultimate operation of the system. Once the structural changes have taken place, the state will have to continue intervening by means of incentives to encourage saving, or by taking part of personal income in the form of taxes.

Only experience can show how far this aim can be attained by means of incentives, and how far coercion will have to be used. Nevertheless, there are limits beyond which coercion cannot be pushed within the existing institutional systems, since to do so would dangerously weaken incentives to economic activity. This is a most important point, since once these limits have been exceeded the way will be open to direct economic action by the state and to the concentration of economic power in its hands, thus increasing its capacity to interfere in the personal freedom of action of the individual.

But as long as this extreme is not reached, the power of the state, great as it may be, can be exercised at an absolutely impersonal level, without implying in any way the subordination of the individual. Consumption can be restricted in relation to income levels, not to persons. Every man will be free to consume and to use his savings as he wishes. The same can be said of measures for redistributing income: this should be done in relation not to the individual, but to his social level, so that it can be raised without distinction of persons.

But even if the validity of these arguments were admitted, the discovery of the unknown quantity would not be complete. In order to regulate the forces of development, the state must influence individual enterprise in economic activity. And another question immediately arises: will this not give the state the opportunity of interfering with personal freedom of action, of compelling the individual to do what he does not want to do? Furthermore, why must the state intervene? Is not the play of market forces sufficient to guide individual decisions?

The response to these questions covers two main points: (a) the state must intervene because the pointers afforded by the market do not always lead to action that will promote the most economic use of the available resources, and (b) it must do so because the indications provided by market forces have a bearing only on some of the decisions of the individual, not on all of them, and in particular, not on those that are of considerable importance in development. State intervention is essential to guide private activity, and to induce it, without coercion of any kind, to fulfill certain development aims.

We will not concern ourselves with the first point. I have elsewhere explained how the labor-cost/capital-cost ratio has been distorted, at the expense of the most economic use of resources. This situation can also be remedied on an impersonal basis, by the creation of certain conditions that will induce private enterprise to take one path or another, without compulsory measures of any kind.

Now let us consider the second point. As we know, the indications that determine individual economic behavior in the market are given by price movements. Price is an effective pointer to the road that new investment should follow. This applies to most goods and services, and the state usually has no reason to intervene, except when the operation of competition is distorted.[5] However, it can enable individuals to make their own forecasts on the basis of better information on market movements and the probable course of future demand.

But there are a small number of goods and services, of strategic importance in economic development, in the case of which investments take a relatively long time to bring in a return and price is no guide. A deficit in the supply of these goods and services usually has a serious effect on the development of the whole economy. This is where the state must supply other pointers to make up for the lack of spontaneous indicators, and provide inducements to private enterprise to follow the pointers in question. In Latin America critical situations have arisen most frequently in connection with energy, transport, and public utilities in general, with agricultural production, and with import substitution. In none of these fields does the market provide any sound indicators, and consequently private enterprise cannot act effectively without state guidance. Future demand must be estimated in accordance with the desired rate of income growth, production conditions must be studied, and investment promoted a number of years in advance—by means of incentives offered by the state. All this is beyond the capacity of private persons operating in the market.

With respect to import substitution—which holds and must continue to hold such an important place in our national and regional development planning—this special feature of course exists. In a number of cases demand estimates must relate to

[5] Naturally, there are also noneconomic reasons—ethical, health, or cultural factors—which may make state action advisable, but this has nothing to do with planning.

goods imported not directly, but as the component parts of the finished article. Consequently the price system plays no part. When the goods in question are replaced by domestically produced articles, these components have to be imported—whether in the form of raw materials or intermediate goods—and so do the capital goods needed to manufacture the articles concerned. All this can be foreseen, and such prevision is essential if investment is to be correctly channeled and the external bottleneck avoided. The development of industrial exports that must take place in order to solve this problem will introduce new factors into the work of anticipating future demand, as regards exports both to the Central American Common Market and to the rest of the world.

As can be seen, although this task of guiding private enterprise by state intervention is of considerable importance, it can be carried out without coercion, by the mere deployment of incentives and disincentives. Thus there is no encroachment of any kind on the independence of individual decisions, nor is the behavior of individuals governed by what the state determines in each case.

The same can be said of technical action by the state to stimulate the assimilation of modern technology. This is a question not only of guiding individual enterprise, but of direct state action, both in research and the spread of technology, and in respect of the education needed to apply this technology. The price system can play no part in solving these problems. It is the state, for the most part, that must determine what is best to be done and how to do it, and must make large-scale investment. But this does not impose any kind of compulsion on individuals to use this technology, or to train themselves to apply it. This too is a matter of incentives and disincentives.

However, there is one very important exception, relating to the conservation and use of natural resources. Here coercive measures are required in order to prevent the destruction of a country's natural wealth by private enterprise, but this action too is impersonal in character.

Direct Economic Action by the State

The state does not need to have all the power in its hands in order to regulate the forces of development and social progress. But it is easy to see why there is still a great deal of confusion as to the meaning of planning action by the state to achieve this aim, since until a few years ago planning took place only as part of a socialist conception of the economy.

Under the influence of the socialist experience, it is often thought that direct economic action by the state is essential to planning action. Thus the discussion frequently wanders off on to the hackneyed topic of the merits or demerits of private enterprise as opposed to state enterprise. This abstract plane is certainly not the appropriate one for the discussion, since it has to be made clear what kind of private enterprise is thus being extolled.

Is it simply and solely the form that prevails in the present social structure, or is it the type that would rise vigorously to the surface if that structure were changed?

If the second question were answered in the affirmative, and not the first, the discussion could be confined to indicating those typical cases in which, even if the system were to acquire its full dynamic impetus, there would be weighty reasons for state action in our countries. Some of these reasons have to do with economic development. There are cases in which the state has had to undertake activities in the strategic areas of the economic system, or make investments which have not proved attractive to private enterprise. In other instances, state action has had the virtue of building up a technical capacity that would have been difficult to achieve otherwise.

Apart from these development considerations, there are other motives that in Latin America's experience are generally important: avoidance of an excessive concentration of economic power, and consequently of political influence, in private hands; and the taking-over by the state of enterprises that by their nature are monopolistic, or of activities which might otherwise be carried out by international combines that limit competition, and are unfavorable to certain national development aims.

But all these weighty reasons, and others that are perhaps less so, are extraneous to the actual requirements of planning, since the state, as already indicated, can effectively achieve its development objectives by incentives and disincentives to private enterprise. And from this point of view, direct state action would be justified if such instruments did not give the desired results.

These considerations relating to the tools to be used are of great pragmatic importance, and the following aspect of the problem should be approached on a pragmatic basis too. Needless to say, planning requires the state to undertake highly complex functions. One of the reasons for the lack of ability to tackle certain development problems demonstrated thus far by the public administration in our countries has been the proliferation of tasks and responsibilities, great and small, which generally overburden officials at the higher levels. It is true that this is above all a question of good organization and delegation of responsibilities within the administrative hierarchy; but it is equally undeniable that the farther state action is extended, the more difficult it will be for the higher levels of the administration to devote attention to decisions on development planning.

The essential aim must be to make the state more capable of regulating the forces of development by means of the machinery of the system, without interfering with the personal behavior of the individual. There is nothing inherent in planning or in the dissemination of modern technology that must lead to the subordination of the individual at the expense of his fundamental rights.

The Alliance for Progress

and Peaceful Revolution

xxxx
xxxxxxxxx
xxxxxxxx

PAUL N. ROSENSTEIN-RODAN

OF ALL the underdeveloped areas of the world, Latin America is the least poor. In 1965 her 230 million inhabitants had an income (gross domestic product) of over $90 billion, or $400 per head. This is almost three times the per capita income of the other underdeveloped areas and six times the per capita income of India and Pakistan. True, the difference is probably smaller in terms of real purchasing power, but when all adjustments have been made for inflation, per capita incomes in Latin American nations are still around twice that of other underdeveloped countries and four times that of India and Pakistan.

Indeed, judged in terms of annual income alone, Venezuela ($950 per capita) and Argentina ($680 per capita) should not even be considered underdeveloped, while Mexico, Chile, Uruguay, and Panama have incomes per head of over $450, which is just above what is normally considered underdeveloped income. The fact is that these six countries, with 37.6 percent of Latin America's population and 55 percent of her gross domestic product, today have incomes similar to those of Italy or Holland during the early 1950s.

That leaves four countries—Bolivia, Ecuador, Honduras and Paraguay—accounting for around 6 percent of Latin American population, to form the least developed group. At the bottom of the income scale there is Haiti, a special case of extreme poverty by any standard, with an income per head of $65.

Even when we move to those countries accounting for the bulk (54.4 percent) of Latin America's population, where per capita incomes average between $260 and $410, we find that Brazil is usually ranked among the more developed countries in

Latin America because of her high degree of industrialization and development potential. To a large extent this is also true of Colombia, followed at some distance by Peru.

It is precisely because Latin America has a much higher income than the other underdeveloped areas that her economic performance seems so disappointing. After all, it is the poor countries who encounter the greatest obstacles in their thrust toward self-sustained economic growth. It is more difficult for them to increase the savings needed for better education and more investment. With a higher income there is more scope to maneuver and to save; there *could* be more lubricating oil in the growth mechanism.

Latin America should be nearer to her growth goal than other underdeveloped areas. Ninety percent of her population should be able to realize, within a decade, not just a room and a chicken in every pot, but self-sustained economic growth. Certainly, the Alliance for Progress goal of increasing income per head by 2.5 percent a year does not seem unrealistic.

Unfortunately, the economic history of the last fifteen years does not come up to these expectations. Between 1950 and 1965 the average growth in per capita income was 2 percent per annum, which was not markedly higher than that in Asia and Africa. Moreover, the rate of increase was actually falling during this period: it was 2.3 percent in 1950–55, 2 percent in 1955–60, and 1.7 percent in 1960–65! Of course, part of the slowdown was due to accelerated population increase, but that is also true in other underdeveloped regions. It is also true that in 1964–65 income per head did increase 2.5 percent, but this was largely due to such special factors as very good crops in Argentina and improved terms of trade. Moreover, the improvement was not sustained in 1966.

How do we account for this relatively disappointing performance? And why was the Alliance for Progress unable to overcome the obstacles? Here are some of the most immediate reasons:

First, the level of real capital formation, the basis of economic growth, has not increased sufficiently. Gross investment as a percentage of GNP remained disappointingly stable in most countries during the whole period, and in the last five years only El Salvador, Guatemala, Nicaragua, and Panama succeeded in raising it. Between 1951 and 1964 savings in Latin America rose from 16.3 to 16.9 percent of GNP, while income increased over

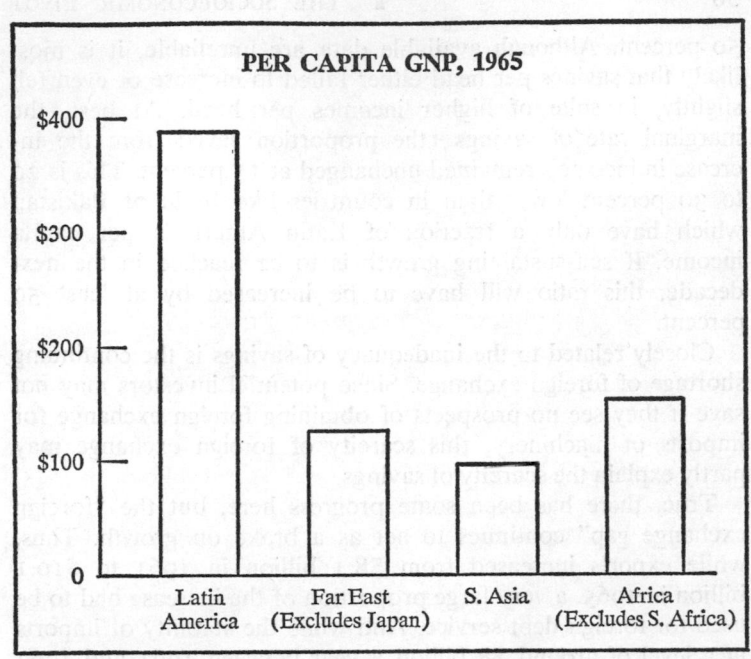

PER CAPITA GNP, 1965

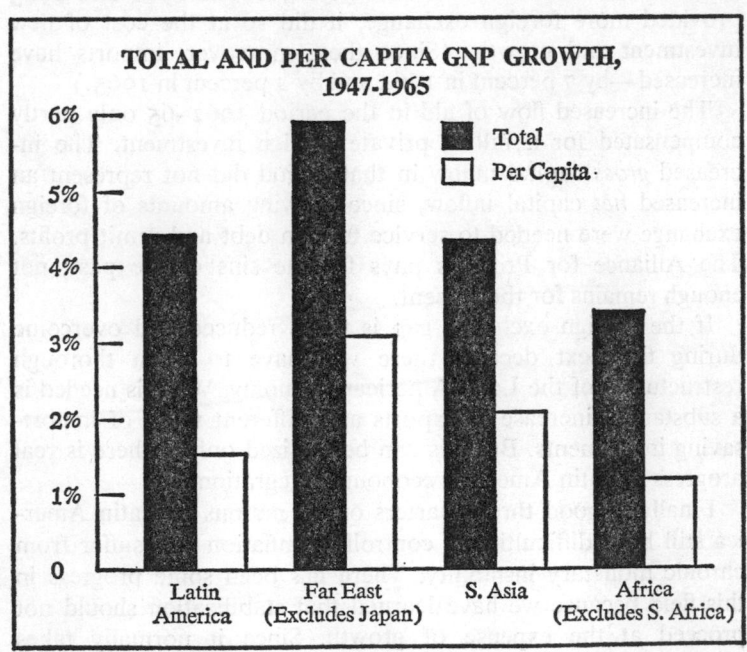

TOTAL AND PER CAPITA GNP GROWTH, 1947-1965

Total
Per Capita

50 percent. Although available data are unreliable, it is most likely that savings per head either failed to increase or even fell slightly, in spite of higher incomes per head. At best, the marginal rate of savings (the proportion saved from the increase in income) remained unchanged at 15 percent. This is 20 to 30 percent lower than in countries like India or Pakistan which have only a fraction of Latin America's per capita income. If self-sustaining growth is to be reached in the next decade, this ratio will have to be increased by at least 50 percent.

Closely related to the inadequacy of savings is the continuing shortage of foreign exchange. Since potential investors may not save if they see no prospects of obtaining foreign exchange for imports of machinery, this scarcity of foreign exchange may partly explain the scarcity of savings.

True, there has been some progress here, but the "foreign exchange gap" continues to act as a brake on growth. Thus, while exports increased from $8.1 billion in 1961 to $10.1 billion in 1965, a very large proportion of the increase had to be used for foreign debt service. And while the stability of imports at a level of around $8 billion a year between 1961 and 1963 provided more foreign exchange, it did so at the cost of new investment and growth. (Since then, moreover, imports have increased—by 7 percent in 1964 and by 4 percent in 1965.)

The increased flow of aid in the period 1962–65 only partly compensated for a fall in private foreign investment. The increased *gross* capital inflow in that period did not represent an increased *net* capital inflow, since growing amounts of foreign exchange were needed to service foreign debt and remit profits. The Alliance for Progress pays for the sins of the past; not enough remains for the present.

If the foreign exchange gap is to be reduced and overcome during the next decade, there will have to be a thorough restructuring of the Latin American economy. What is needed is a substantial increase in exports and different types of import-saving investments. But this can be realized only if there is real progress in Latin American economic integration.

Finally, a good three-quarters of the nations of Latin America still have difficulties in controlling inflation and suffer from chronic monetary instability. There has been some progress in this field because we have learned that stabilization should not proceed at the expense of growth. Since it normally takes several years to increase the production and supply of domestic foodstuffs, only a gradual stabilization is attempted. Even so, in terms of growth, the price of stabilization policies in some countries (Argentina, Brazil, and Colombia, for example) seems to be high, while the reduction in inflation has not been as much as was planned. The lack of monetary stability may increase the deficiency of savings and also impede progress in Latin American integration.

Growth is not the only objective of the Alliance. Improved income distribution is another goal. The basic objective of the modern development creed and of the Alliance for Progress is not equality of income, but equality of opportunity. Such equality cannot be established overnight; still, it is most important to create a justified hope that the children will have a better fate than their parents. When a high rate of growth is achieved, social, and not only economic, progress is possible; when economic growth is below a critical (high) level, *any* progress is bound to be small.

In Latin America there are three basic inequalities:

(1) *Inequality between the employed and the unemployed.* The right to work is the very minimum equality of opportunity that modern society must provide; there is no substitute for full employment. Yet we are nowhere near realizing this goal in Latin America, and it will take a real effort over the development decade of the Alliance to reach it.

The Alliance for Progress target growth rate of 5.5 percent a year was not just an arithmetical exercise of providing a 2.5 percent increase in income per head for a population growing at 3 percent per annum. It was based on the assumption that only such a high rate of growth would provide a sufficient industrial drive to create new jobs. Indeed it may well be an underestimation; a 6 percent rate of growth may be needed, since modern industry is in general capital-intensive.

Remember that to fulfill 80 or 85 percent of this target growth rate—as many Latin American countries have done during the recent years of the Alliance—does not mean that four-fifths of the employment target has been fulfilled. Substantial *additional* job opportunities only begin to be created at a minimum threshold level of growth of somewhere between 5 to 6 percent a year. Thus, fulfilling four-fifths of the target growth rate may well mean fulfilling only one-fifth of the employment target.

There does not seem to be a choice here between doing a little less or a little more. This is an *either/or* situation: no middle way exists. We can sacrifice the *prospect* of a better standard of living by giving priority to an *immediate* increase in employment through public works, subsidized handicrafts, etc. This would increase employment in the short run, but lead to a very much lower rate of growth, less savings, and therefore, to lower capital formation. Thus, in the long run, more employment tomorrow means less employment the day after tomorrow than would otherwise be possible. Or we can aim at absorbing unemployment at a high level of productivity through large-scale, capital-intensive but highly productive industrialization. This implies high savings and investment, and a high rate of economic growth—5.5 to 6.5 percent for the economy as a whole, and around 9 to 10 percent per annum in the industrial sector. It will take at least five to ten years to reach full employment that way—but it is *the* way of defeating poverty and of reaching sustained growth. There are no halfways of solving the employment problem—and solved it will have to be if the Alliance for Progress is to mean anything.

(2) *Inequality between the rural and the urban regions.* At present, income per head of agricultural workers is between one-third and one-half lower than the (low) income of workers outside agriculture. Reducing this inequality will involve far more than agrarian reform. Excessive protectionism has kept the level of industrial prices too high, with the result that the domestic terms of trade between agricultural and industrial products are even worse than those existing in the world market. A thorough reform of tariff policy, which, incidentally, is also needed for effective industrial growth, must be implemented. Imperfections in the marketing and distribution of agricultural products must be reduced. Incentives must be provided for modernization of agricultural production. This means subsidies for such things as fertilizer, land reclamation, etc. It also means the establishment of minimum prices for two- or three-year periods in order to reduce the risks and uncertainties of selling. Unfortunately, we are only at the beginning of such a policy, and only in a few countries.

Once implemented, such policies may reduce somewhat the emigration of the agricultural population into towns. But industrialization will also have to provide better employment opportunities for the inflow of workers into the towns, as well as incentives and markets for increased agricultural output.

(3) *Inequality between the poor and the rich.* This is the least important, although the most publicized, inequality. Effective growth normally brings about effective redistribution of income. The share of labor in national income is around 50 percent in Latin America (or up to 60 percent in some of the more advanced countries). It will rise, as it has risen in high income development countries, toward 70 percent. A built-in redistribution of income has to be introduced, not at the expense of productivity and incentives, but through fiscal savings and income policies.

How successful has the Alliance for Progress been in moving Latin American economies toward self-sustaining economic growth? We have to be careful here to distinguish between progress achieved by the Alliance for Progress and progress realized by the Latin American economy. It is true, for instance, that the rate of growth in 1964 and 1965 reached a level of 2.5 percent per head, which would be satisfactory if it could be sustained. Unfortunately, a large part of this growth was due to good crops and improved terms of trade, not to specific achievements of the Alliance.

But while there have been disappointments and failures, there have also been partial successes. The Alliance has been responsible for a gradual improvement in the coordination of economic policy. Today a minister of agriculture or of industry will be more in touch with the minister of finance than used to be the case. Stabilization policies are also better planned—and in some cases better executed. Economic policies are less inconsistent than previously, although, of course, still very far from ideal. Most governments at least make an effort not to get drowned in day-to-day problems. Of course, emergencies still come first: to reach the long run you have to survive the short run. Planning begins when one can keep one's head above water. But the need to think of the day after tomorrow is at least recognized.

There has also been real progress in the fiscal area. Higher government revenues, for instance in Brazil and Chile, are due to more efficient collection, and in some cases, to fiscal reforms. Higher revenues are not always reflected in a higher budget surplus, since current expenditures often rise. Still, the inflationary impact of budget deficits has been reduced during the years of the Alliance beyond anything known in the past. At the same time, there has been a more clearly articulated emphasis on social progress in government spending. Most important here—more important even than housing—has been the increase in spending for education, a basic condition of equality of opportunity.

The flow of aid has increased far above the shockingly insufficient levels of the past. Today a growing, if insufficient, proportion of aid consists of program loans, although most aid still goes for monetary stabilization rather than for development. Clearly, if there are to be more program loans, there will have to be better and more numerous development programs. Thus we have a vicious circle: no program loans without programs, no programs without program loans. This circle must be broken.

Finally, the life of the Alliance for Progress has been prolonged for another decade to make up for time lost. And a great deal of time *has* been lost. The fact is that, in spite of the achievements mentioned above, the basic restructuring of the Latin American economy and society has not been proceeding as we hoped. At the rate Latin America has been going in the last five years, even another decade would not achieve the peaceful revolution which is the ultimate objective of the Alliance for Progress.

So far we have examined the proximate causes for this disappointing performance. The ultimate cause, however, is the lack of drive, mystique, and elan which alone could overcome the normal inertia and resistance to change. A peaceful revolution is much more difficult to achieve than a violent one. People are prepared to die on the barricades for common sense, for a gradually better living—but not for the middle way.

To create a heroic spirit of mission, an enthusiasm for a peaceful revolution is the main task confronting Latin American leadership. It is a difficult task, but it is not impossible. The New Deal, the Anglo-Scandinavian Socialism and Full Employment Welfare State, the Marshall Plan, the development mystique of Nehru's India, the euphoria of the Kennedy days in the United States—all show that it can be achieved. Except for Chile, it is conspicuously missing in Latin America today. Yet it is the *sine qua non* of success. It cannot be achieved cheaply, for there are no bargains in history. But it is not too late. We have lost many battles, but we have not lost the war.

U.S. Hegemony and
the Future of Latin America

CELSO FURTADO

WITHIN the group of nations termed the Third World—nations for whom the problems of development come before all others —Latin America occupies a special position, in view of the peculiarity of its relations with the United States. Almost all the underdeveloped African and Asian countries have achieved political independence within the last two decades and are at present led by a generation that emerged during the revolutionary struggle. The consciousness of victories achieved lends optimism to their behavior and even leads them to overestimate their strength and capabilities in the effort to overcome underdevelopment. In Latin America, on the contrary, there is a general consciousness of living through a period of decline. On the one hand, the phase of "easy" development, through increasing exports of primary products or through import substitution, has everywhere been exhausted. On the other, the region is becoming aware that the margin of self-determination, in its search for ways of coping with the tendency toward economic stagnation, is being daily reduced as the imperative of U.S. "security" calls for a growing alienation of sovereignty on the part of national governments. This difference in the historical situation explains, to some extent, the disparity between the psychological attitudes currently observable among the Latin American peoples and the other peoples of the Third World. To the optimism of the latter is opposed the feeling of revolt that prevails among Latin Americans, particularly in the younger generation. Latin American society is currently going through a revolutionary phase, as a consequence of the penetration of modern technology and the emergence of new collective aspirations within the framework of institutions ill-equipped to absorb this new technology or to interpret and satisfy these aspirations.

It is a notorious fact that the revelant political problems of Latin American countries are of direct interest to the authorities responsible for U.S. security, who are in a position to interfere decisively in the working out of a solution for these problems. It is only natural, therefore, that Latin Americans should become increasingly preoccupied with the following questions: (*a*) what exactly is understood by U.S. security? and (*b*) to what degree are the interests of this security compatible with the Latin American revolution?

U.S. SPHERE OF INFLUENCE

A new international order is now inevitably evolving as the methods of the cold war become obsolete, though what form it will take is not yet clear. It is perfectly obvious, however, that without some basic understanding between the principal centers of power the diplomatic processes envisaged in the United Nations Charter are of little value. The fundamental problem is, therefore, to discover the likely trends of this basic understanding. The Russians, having redefined their security problems in the light of their technological advance, are apparently no longer concerned with maintaining a strictly regimented sphere of influence. On the contrary, they now seem inclined to think that a return to a pluralist international system, necessarily implying the break-up of the Western bloc led by the United States, would increase their relative influence; this pluralism would probably lead to an aggravation of the "contradictions" between the principal capitalist nations, and this could only operate to the Russian advantage. By progressively "liberalizing" their sphere of influence, the Russians seem to be working toward the creation of a new international order in which the principle of self-determination will have a not altogether secondary role to play. Behind this lies the idea that, in the long run, capitalism, at least in the form propounded by the United States, is not viable for most of the countries of the Third World. The latter, in changing their social order, are much more likely to move away from American influence. In this way, a "community of socialist nations" would tend to grow quite naturally and the Soviet Union would assume legitimate leadership as *primus inter pares* in such a community. The United States, on the other hand, conscious that a "conclusive and world-wide victory over Communism" is no longer possible, seems to be inclined to define the supreme aim of her foreign policy as the defense of the integrity of the "free world."[1] This is a difficult aim to achieve since it requires, on the one hand, strict delimitation of the perimeter of a sphere of influence extending over a number of continents, and on the other, the development and successful application within that sphere of influence of social techniques capable of preventing significant changes in the social structures of numerous countries at different stages of development.

The attempt by the United States to define her area of influence vis-à-vis the Soviet Union passed its conclusive test at the time of the so-called Cuban rocket crisis in October, 1962. This confrontation established that the Soviet Union cannot give unlimited guarantees of defense to a country in the North American sphere of influence which attempts to break away from U.S. hegemony by means of effecting changes in its social structure. American victory in this decisive case consisted in conducting the crisis in such a way that the Soviet Union was faced with the alternatives of having to unleash a thermonuclear war or of recognizing the "right" of the United States to limit the sovereignty of any country within her orbit, even after such a country had succeeded in changing its social structure. In the final analysis, therefore, this means that a country which changes its social structure, and in this way moves out of the U.S. orbit of influence, can be "tolerated" but will not be recognized by the dominant power. The doctrine was estab-

---

[1] In cold-war jargon, the term "free world" refers more or less vaguely to all the countries outside the Soviet and Chinese orbits of influence. By historical tradition, the Americans have a marked aversion for the concepts of "empire" and "imperialism" when used to explain their own policy. Recently an English political analyst attempted to demonstrate that this was an unfounded prejudice, since the Americans "in the last 20 years, have been carrying out with unparalleled maturity and generosity, their imperial obligations." (See Henry Fairlie, "A Cheer for American Imperialism," in the *New York Times Magazine,* July 11, 1965.) I prefer, however, to stick to the concept of a "sphere of influence" which has been used by someone as well integrated in the North American political establishments as Walter Lippmann.

64 THE SOCIOECONOMIC PIVOT

lished that defense of such a "tolerated" country must always fall within the sphere of so-called limited warfare, the possibility of a thermonuclear confrontation being excluded. To establish this doctrine, the United States paid the price of risking a nuclear holocaust; and it is by the price paid that the importance of the victory should be measured. All the indications are that the United States is pursuing a similar aim in the case of Vietnam: namely, to create a situation that, by the very nature of its dynamic, will force the principal contender—in this case China—to acknowledge the limits of its own strength.

PROBLEM OF SOCIAL INSTABILITY

Once the perimeter of the U.S. sphere of influence has been established and any outside military interference has been neutralized, the problem arises as to whether U.S. hegemony is able to maintain a high degree of social stability within its area of influence. In this respect, we must draw attention to two points: first, that the basic variable which determines the contemporary historic process is provided by technological development; secondly, that the speed with which modern technology must penetrate the underdeveloped world in order to overcome initial resistance and ensure continuity of development inevitably provokes a series of social reactions incompatible with the preservation of most of the preexisting structures.

In the United States, the nature of this problem is slowly coming to be understood. For a long time the problem was simply considered an aspect of the cold war: the social instability of the Third World was attributed to the "Machiavellian" actions of the Soviet Union, and it was held that the only solution to the problem lay in "containing" the "aggressive" Power. Referring to the Eisenhower Administration, Professor Morgenthau writes: ". . . both the thought and actions of our government tend toward the assumption that the Soviet Union is not only the exploiter of world revolution—which is correct—but also its creator—which is a convenient absurdity."[2] Later

[2] Hans Morgenthau, *The Political and Military Strategy of the United States* (1954), reproduced in *Politics in the Twentieth Century* (University of Chicago Press, 1962), Vol. II, p. 21.

the doctrine emerged, formulated by MIT technicians led by W. W. Rostow, according to which the aims of U.S. foreign policy could more easily be fostered by properly organized "foreign aid" programs for underdeveloped countries.[3] It was accepted that the development process could be oriented from outside, the U.S. aim being to "create independent, modern and developing States."[4] The whole problem was to help underdeveloped countries to overcome their initial difficulties and attain a point of "self-supporting development." Implicit in this theory is the idea that once the pains preceding "takeoff" have been assuaged, any serious risk of social instability would cease to exist.

This theory, which enjoyed a great vogue at one stage and produced its most brilliant efflorescence in the Alliance for Progress, came in for serious criticism in the period that followed. It has been argued that one should not forget that development itself, even when oriented from outside, creates social instability since it "undermines the cultural structure and religious order."[5] This line of thought emphasizes the fact that the aim of U.S. policy, namely, to keep intact its sphere of influence, must never be lost sight of, and that any particular country's development should be considered as a means of attaining this end. "As a rule," writes Professor Wolfers, "the most effective type of aid will be the aid that promises to give the greatest satisfaction to those élite groups who are eager to keep the country out of Communist or Soviet control." In a recent book, political scientist John S. Pustay, a major in the U.S. Air Force, reminds us that "the very programs designed to promote socioeconomic development (for example, the Alliance for Progress) will in themselves create tensions and dislocations as the old and indigenous way of life is replaced by a new and alien mode of living. Therefore, the military will be called upon to back the civil police in providing stability during this period

[3] The ideas of this group are expressed in a study presented to a special Senate Committee in July 1957, *The Objectives of United States Economic Assistance Programs.*

[4] W. W. Rostow, *The Stages of Economic Growth* (1959), reproduced in W. F. Hahn and J. C. Ness, eds., *American Strategy for the Nuclear Age* (New York, Doubleday, 1960).

[5] Arnold Wolfers, *Military or Economic Aid: Questions of Priority.* A report to the Presidential Committee for the Study of Military Aid, July 1959, reproduced in *American Strategy for the Nuclear Age,* p. 386.

of social turmoil."[6] As the leading power, the United States must concern herself with the creation of supranational structures to ensure this stability if she does not want to run the risk of growing defections inside her sphere of influence. Until such supranational structures are created, the United States herself will have to bear the responsibility for providing internal social stability in all countries falling within her orbit. In one of his last speeches in the United Nations, Adlai Stevenson made it clear that "as long as the international community is not prepared to rescue the victims of clandestine aggression, national force will have to fill the gap."

"Security" Versus "Development"

For the United States, therefore, the basic problem in the second half of the twentieth century is the problem of her "security," that is to say, the question of the type of world-wide organization that will prevail as a consequence of the current technological revolution, and that must be compatible with the preservation of the American way of life inside U.S. territory and the defense of American economic interests outside. From the Latin American point of view, on the other hand, the great problem is that of "development," that is to say, the problem of gaining access to the fruits of this technological revolution.

It must be borne in mind that Latin America's political and social institutions were essentially transplanted from Europe and that from the very beginning the Latin American national economies existed as a frontier of the European, or at a more recent stage, of the European and North American economies. The characteristics of capitalist industrial development, which proceeded within the framework of powerful national states, provoked from the outset a heavy concentration of the fruits of technical progress; this inevitably created poles of technological advance, giving rise to geographical concentration of income and wealth. Such a process can be observed in the European continent itself, where, up to the Second World War, the central, eastern, and southern European countries, despite their

[6] John S. Pustay, *Counter-insurgency Warfare* (New York, Free Press of Glencoe, 1965).

integration in the regional economy, had practically no access to the fruits of technological progress at the end of a century of industrial revolution. In Latin America, development induced by the industrial revolution in Europe and the United States was enough to transform part of the economic systems inherited from the colonial epoch, but not enough to create autonomous systems able to generate further growth. Hence, Latin America remained on the periphery of advanced industrial economies at a time when markets for primary products were far from able to generate the dynamism required.

Attempts at industrialization of an "import-substitution" type for a time provided an alternative and allowed further changes to be made in the economic structures of some countries. However, the type of industrial organization practicable in certain historical conditions cannot be independent of the type of technology to be adopted. The technology which Latin America has to assimilate in the second half of the twentieth century effects a considerable saving in manpower and is extremely exacting with regard to the size of the market. In the conditions at present prevailing in the region, the rule tends to be monopoly or oligopoly and progressive concentration of income; and this in turn, by conditioning the pattern of demand, directs investment toward certain industries, which are precisely those requiring a high capital coefficient and those most exacting with regard to the size of the market. In Latin America, experience has proved that this substitutive form of industrialization tends to lose its impulse once the phase of "easy" substitutions has been exhausted, and leads eventually to stagnation.[7]

At present, Latin America is faced with the ineluctable necessity of introducing profound changes into its institutional framework in order to lay the foundations for development. These changes will have to be oriented in three directions: (*a*) in such a way that technological change is prevented from provoking concentration of income and distorting the allocation

[7] Of the Latin American countries that have made substantial advances in the "substitution" type of industrialization, Mexico is the only case which has not yet shown a clear tendency toward stagnation. It must, however, be taken into account that this is the only country in the group which has promoted far-reaching agrarian reform and eliminated the political influence of the feudally based oligarchy. On the other hand, Mexico is notable for the great development of her export of services (tourism), an activity that absorbs considerable manpower.

of productive resources, thus reducing the efficiency of the economic system; (*b*) in the sense of widening the present and potential size of markets through schemes for regional economic integration; and (*c*) by influencing the actual orientation of technological development in terms of the specific requirements of the present phase of Latin America's modernization process. Obviously, therefore, development in Latin America cannot simply result from spontaneous market forces. Only the conscious and deliberate action of central decision-making organs can ensure that it is properly worked out. What is currently called the Latin American Revolution is really the recognition of this problem and the attempt—intermittent and desultory as yet—to create a system of political institutions that can guide the social changes needed to make development viable. Since the present ruling classes fail to understand the nature of the problem and are determined to maintain the status quo, those in Latin America who are actually struggling for development are, whether or not consciously, playing a revolutionary role.

Let us now see how the problems of U.S. "security" tie in with those of Latin American development. Since the Latin American area is the innermost circle of the U.S. zone of influence, it is only natural that the latter country's policy of hegemony should be conducted there in exemplary fashion. From the Latin American point of view, the Cuban rocket crisis must be interpreted as bringing the Monroe Doctrine up to date. According to the new rules, two options are open to the countries of Latin America: political and economic integration under U.S. hegemony, each particular situation being defined within the sphere of influence of the superpower, or dislocation from this sphere of influence. In the latter event, however, the country in question can only hope to have its sovereignty "tolerated" according to rules laid down for each individual case by the dominant power. These rules can be rigid enough to render internal pressures uncontrollable, and they can make survival of the regime (as in the present case of Cuba) a heavy onus on any powers outside the sphere of influence who become politically involved in the issue. The recent Dominican experience made it clear that the United States is not prepared to tolerate any further defections within the inner circle of her zone of influence. Until the external perimeter of the sphere of influence is more solidly established—and this could be a consequence of solving the Vietnam issue—it can be expected that a rigid line of intolerance will prevail in the Latin American area.

If we admit that the military aspects of the "security" problem in the region have been solved by implicit Soviet acceptance of a new definition of the Monroe Doctrine, we can infer that the economic aspects will now come to the fore. It is likely, therefore, that the domestic problems of each individual Latin American country, particularly in the economic sphere, will become of increasing interest to the organs responsible for U.S. external security. As the most probable path (other than open subversion, which would be dealt with on the military level) that a Latin American country can follow in order to move out of the U.S. sphere of influence is to effect changes in its economic policy, the latter will have to be strictly controlled from outside if stability is to be maintained. At the same time, since one of the prerequisites for averting major changes in economic policy is the preservation of existing power structures, strict vigilance will have to be maintained over the political processes, and in addition, a control mechanism for preventive action must be introduced into individual countries if the enormous cost of international police action is to be avoided.

As soon as U.S. "security" is defined as implying the maintenance of the social status quo in Latin America, it becomes perfectly clear that the autonomy of the countries in the region (assuming that Latin American nations and states are something more than the temporary power structures) to supervise their own development is reduced to very little. This doctrine implies that fundamental decisions must be taken at a higher level, probably in the political center of the sphere of influence or in some "supranational" organ to which effective power may have been delegated by that political center. We must therefore ask what type of "development" the United States envisages for Latin America. This question has never been the subject of open discussion in government circles, since Congress has regarded economic aid as a mere complement of military aid, which was defined strictly within the orbit of security policy. Recently the problem has been attracting some attention, but chiefly on the technical-administrative level. As Professor Edward Mason observes: "Recently AID has given increased attention to this problem and has attempted to formulate for some of the principal aid-receiving countries a so-called Long-Range Assistance Strategy which spells out U.S. economic,

political, and security interests in the countries in question, the
conditions necessary to their attainment, and the relevant instrument of foreign policy."[8]

U.S. BUSINESS CORPORATIONS

Although no unanimous conclusion has been reached on all
aspects of this complex problem, there is already an accepted
doctrine in the United States in so far as at least one point is
concerned: namely, that a decisive role in Latin American
development is being undertaken by private American companies and that U.S. "aid" policy should be conducted principally through them. The report of the Clay Committee was
emphatic on this point, and in recent years both Congress and
the Administration have shown considerable concern to create
conditions for the effective operation of political guarantees and
economic incentives to enable private U.S. firms to carry out
this important function. "Guarantee" agreements have been
signed with Latin American governments permitting private
U.S. companies operating in their territories to enjoy a privileged position in comparison with identical companies operating
at home. At the same time, measures such as the Hickenlooper
amendment create political "super-guarantees" for U.S. companies by subjecting local governments to a permanent threat.
In the words of Professor Mason: "It would seem that the
government has gone about as far as it can go to promote U.S.
private foreign investment in Latin America without outright
subsidization."[9] In this context, private investment means,
whether explicitly or implicitly, investment by the large corporations, since the small American business firm possesses neither
the capacity nor the means to operate abroad.

The first problem that arises from the Latin American point
of view is to establish what type of political organization is
likely to be compatible with a regional economic system controlled chiefly by powerful American corporations. It is easy to
infer that the most attractive sectors for these corporations are
those producing goods or services in which technological devel-

[8] Edward S. Mason, *Foreign Aid and Foreign Policy* (New York,
Harper & Row for Council on Foreign Relations, 1964), p. 48.
[9] *Ibid.*, p. 90.

opment plays an important role. Without going into other aspects of the problem, we must remember that the large American corporation is a powerful private bureaucracy, exercising public or semipublic functions, whose integration into U.S. political society has up to now remained undefined. Professor Andrew Hacker reminds us that "Unlike the religious and guild structures of earlier centuries, the large firm of today has no theoretical rationale linking power, purpose, and responsibility."[10] Hence no way has yet been found of integrating these large corporations, whose functions are becoming increasingly public, into the structure of a pluralistic political society. At the same time, government is becoming increasingly powerless against these great corporations, since even in the United States "government is weaker than the corporate institutions purportedly subordinate to it. . . ."[11] Even Adolf Berle, the leading authority on this subject, who cannot be suspected of animosity toward the large company, draws attention to the fact that the board of directors of a large corporation derives power from no one but itself, "it is an automatic self-perpetuating oligarchy."[12] The enormous power at present possessed by these large corporations has not the slightest claim to legitimacy. Professor Berle tells us in the U.S. the doctrine is taking shape that "where a corporation has the power to affect a great many lives (differing from the little enterprise which can be balanced out by the market) it should be subject to the same restraints under the Constitution that apply to an agency of the federal or state government."[13] Called upon to operate in Latin America with a number of privileges, outside the control of U.S. antitrust legislation, and with U.S. political and military protection, the great American corporation must of necessity become a superpower in any Latin American country. Since a large proportion of the basic decisions on orientation of investment, location of economic activity, orientation of technology, and the degree of integration of the national economies rests in the hands of these large corporations, it is quite clear that the exist-

[10] Andrew Hacker, "Corporate America," Introduction to *The Corporation Take-Over* (New York, Harper & Row, 1964), p. 2.
[11] *Ibid.*, p. 11.
[12] A. A. Berle, "Economic Power and the Free Society," included in *The Corporation Take-Over*, p. 91.
[13] *Ibid.*, p. 99.

ing national states will come to play an increasingly secondary role.

Such a regional "development project," which tends to render obsolete the idea of nationality as the principal political force in Latin America, offers many attractions to important sectors of the local ruling classes, who see in it an ingenious formula for deflating the "nationalism" which they hold responsible for most of the current social unrest. If most of the state's substantive functions in controlling the economic and social development process were taken away, then the current political ferment characterizing many Latin American countries would in all probability tend to diminish and government could then function principally on the "technical" level. We would have attained, by the opposite path, the Saint Simonian ideal of replacing the government of men by the administration of things.

Leaving aside the question of whether such a situation could be reconciled with the traditions of Latin American culture and merely considering some of the technical aspects of the problem, there is ample reason to believe that such a "development project" is not viable in current Latin American conditions. The great U.S. corporation seems to be as inadequate an instrument for dealing with Latin American problems as is a powerful mechanized army faced with guerrilla warfare. The large corporation with its advanced technology and high capitalization, particularly when backed by numerous privileges, produces the same effect in an underdeveloped economy as large exotic trees introduced into an unfamiliar region: they drain all the water, dry up the land, and disturb the balance of flora and fauna. In effect, indiscriminate penetration into a fragile economic structure by large corporations, characterized by their high degree of administrative inflexibility and enormous financial power, tends to provoke a structural imbalance difficult to correct—for instance, a greater differentiation in living standards between groups of the population and a rapid increase of open or disguised unemployment. If control by the national governments is further reduced, allowing the large U.S. corporations to operate with even greater freedom than they now enjoy, the tendency to concentration of economic activity is likely to be accentuated, aggravating the existing differences in living standards between social groups and geographical areas, and the final result will be a real or potential increase of social tensions. Since economic decisions of a strategic nature would fall outside the scope of Latin American governments, these tensions would tend to be regarded, on the local political plane, solely from their negative viewpoint; state action would therefore have to be essentially repressive in character.

Economic development in the problematical conditions Latin America is called upon to face at the moment requires, however, the cooperation of large masses of the population and active participation by important sectors of this population. This is why the most difficult tasks are of a political rather than a technical nature. Hard political decisions must be taken and this can be done only if such action is supported by the existing national centers of political power. The principle of nationality is therefore vital for the present phase of Latin American development. Today, more than ever, this concept is extraordinarily functional and any measure taken to weaken the Latin American states as political centers, able to interpret national aspirations and to rally the people around common ideals, will limit the region's development possibilities. Thus, Latin America's economic integration can be justified only if it is conceived in terms of defining common policy between national states and not as a coordinating link between the great foreign enterprises operating in the region.

CONCLUSIONS

In conclusion, one can enumerate certain points:

(1) Under the conditions of nuclear equilibrium obtaining at present between the superpowers, the exercise of supranational hegemony can be justified only in the light of the interest of the power wishing to exercise such hegemony.

(2) Spheres of influence no longer have any significance for the superpowers from the point of view of their military security.

(3) From the standpoint of the countries of the Third World, spheres of influence are nothing but systems of economic domination, which lessen their freedom of maneuver as they seek to adapt their political and social structures to development requirements.

(4) U.S. hegemony in Latin America, by underpinning the anachronistic power structure, constitutes a serious obstacle to development for the majority of countries in the region.

(5) The U.S. Government's program for development in Latin America, based as it is on the activities of the great American business corporations and on preventive control of "subversion," is not viable, except as a means of freezing the social status quo.

(6) The success of development policy in Latin America will depend first of all on the capacity of its promoters to mobilize the great mass of the population in the region. This can be done only from each national political center and in conformity with national values and ideals.

(7) Economic integration will serve the development needs of the region only if it stems from a common policy formulated by really independent national governments and not from the coordination of the interests of the great foreign business enterprises operating in Latin America.

The Central American Defense
Council and Pax Americana

JOHN SAXE-FERNÁNDEZ

THE FUNDAMENTAL characteristic of Central American history
in the sixties is the presence of a series of powers conducive to
the economic, and eventually political, coordination of that
area.

The military aspect of such an "integration" is analyzed in
this article. In this field, as in the economic one, the development and leadership, the source and the drive for action originate essentially from the efforts toward "regionalization," actually encouraged by American industry and foreign policy.
Whereas the expanding multinational corporations of the
United States primarily benefit from the Central American
Common Market,[1] on the military side the main objective is to

[1] One of the main objectives in forming the Central American Common
Market was to attract foreign investment. The level of foreign control
over the principal Central American industries is higher than in any
other Latin American region. This problem was highlighted by investments of W. R. Grace in Central America and by United Fruit Company's purchase of strategic industrial plants. The familiar pattern of
conflict between the local nationalists who fear further economic dominance and foreign corporations who wish to invest funds or establish
branch manufacturing operations has been resolved by guarantees by the
Central American governments on investments and "expected" profits of
foreign companies. For an analysis of the internal structural conditions of
the Central American economy see: "La integración económica Centro-
americana," by Joseph Moscarella; "La industrialización y sus problemas
en la América Central," by Joseph Mills; and "Sistema de pagos y
comercio Intercentroamericano," by Jorge González del Valle, in *Integración de América Latina*, Miguel S. Wionczek, ed., Fondo de Cultura

75

coordinate the Central American armed forces by means of an international organization based on the two pillars of American military strategy in the underdeveloped countries: (a) counter-insurgency, and (b) programs of civic military action.

The ideological and organizational model generated in the Isthmus, which tends to extend itself to the inter-American level by means of the recent and sporadic inter-American Peace Force, is part of the American military metaphysics, whose role is to perpetuate the existing system of international stratification.[2]

BRIEF HISTORICAL SUMMARY

The Central American Defense Council (CONDECA) was formally established in 1964 as a defensive instrument incorporated to the Central American States Organization (ODECA). This military block gathers the respective defense ministers in a council whose function is to coordinate joint military actions in order to improve "collective safety . . . in case of an eventual communist aggression in Central American

---

Económica, México D.F., 1964, pp. 273–328; Oscar Zamora Salgado, *El sector externo del mercado común Centroamericano*, Universidad Autónoma de México, Master's thesis, 1964. For a historical perspective see Thomas Karnes, *The Failure of the Union: Central America, 1828–1960*, Chapel Hill, University of North Carolina Press, 1961. For recent United Fruit Company's investments see "UFCO Buys 40% Interest in Central America of Polymer International," *Wall Street Journal (WSJ)*, April 6, 1966, p. 32; "UFCO Bought Numar S. A." *WSJ*, July 23, 1965; "Central Americans Lift Trade by Tariff Cuts. Arrow Shirt, Other Companies Rush In," *WSJ*, March 10, 1965, p. 1; "Export-Import Bank Loaned Industria Firestone de Costa Rica $3.2 Million to Build Tire Plant Near San José," *WSJ*, May 25, 1966, p. 25; "Inter-American Development Bank Approved Loan of $15 Million to Central America," *WSJ*, January 31, 1967, p. 23. (The loan is to develop highways, industrial centers, telecommunications facilities, and interconnection of electric power systems, all of which are American enterprises. The Central American governments will pay the interest charges.
[2] An analysis of the difficult dilemmas and alternatives of the present international system of stratification is presented in a clear and systematic way by Irving L. Horowitz, *Three Worlds of Development: The Theory and Practice of International Stratification.* Oxford University Press, 1966.

territory".[3] Costa Rica, which officially has no army, and
Panama, which has a national police, would be given a chance to
participate actively in CONDECA in the future. A recent
meeting of the council, which took place in San Salvador in mid-
1966, modifies the constitutional act to include not only the
"armies" but also "the Ministries of National Security." This
measure favors the effective integration of the two countries
mentioned above.

Internal Causes

(a) The idea of a Central American army has been especially cherished by Guatemala and Nicaragua. Both the national
guard of Nicaragua, led by Anastasio Somoza, Jr., and the
Guatemalan army have enough manpower, equipment, and
funds to secure them a predominant position in the formulation,
direction, and operation of strategies and programs of military
action carried on by CONDECA.

With American military encouragement, the heads of the
armed forces of these two countries succeeded in organizing a
consulting conference between the representatives of the high
Central American military hierarchy in July, 1961. The outcome of this meeting was a joint petition to their respective
governments urging the creation of a defense council and an
intelligence service attached to it with the purpose of controlling
what they called "subversive communist agents who infiltrate
the area."[4] To quote the New York Times, in those days the
military feared a possible Cuban expansionism ". . . and each
country, due to a series of changes in the political alliances and
economic pressures, suspected the other as possible sources of
invasion to their respective territories."[5] Mutual suspicion and
mistrust reached their highest point. The Southern Command of
the United States,[6] based at the Canal Zone, intervened in order

[3] Latin American Times, New York, July 9, 1965, and Le Monde, Paris,
July 4–5, 1965.

[4] New York Times, October 29, 1961.

[5] Ibid.

[6] For a historical analysis of the creation of the Southern Command and
other bilateral treaties between Panama and the United States see: House
of Representatives Committee on Foreign Affairs: The Story of Panama,
Washington, 1915; Panama Canal Zone Governor's Annual Report,
1914–1935, Washington, D.C., U.S. Government Printing Office, 1915–
1936.

to restore good relations and mutual cooperation. As a result, "Operation Brotherhood" was carefully planned; it consisted of a series of maneuvers which took place in Honduras, in August and September, 1962. The basis for this military exercise was a hypothetical guerrilla attack on Tegucigalpa's Tocontín Airport. "Army units totaling 1,500 from Honduras, Guatemala, El Salvador, Nicaragua, Colombia and the Canal Zone took part in the hypothetical defense . . . The maneuvers were the first to be held outside the Canal Zone since 1959. They emphasized U.S. determination to defend the strategic isthmian area, considered a primary Communist target."[7]

In December of the same year (1962), a new constituent charter of the ODECA was signed, creating, among other organizations, a council of defense ministers to watch over the safety of the Central American collectivity. A few years later, the presidents of El Salvador, Nicaragua, Costa Rica, and Honduras expressed their wish to create an "effective defense system." Cautiously, they expressed their will that such a "defense system" be compatible with the principle of nonintervention.

(b) With CONDECA working since 1964, the ministers, advised by the United States, started a program of military operations with the purpose of preparing "defensive" actions against Cuba. In 1965, for example, "Operation Falconview" took place, a military exercise to defend the Isthmus against invasion and subversive infiltration from "the Caribbean."[8]

The Cuban Revolution generated in Central American oligarchic-military circles a panic comparable only to the one created in Washington. Because of this, the strengthening of military power in that area was considered an unavoidable necessity. It must be pointed out, however, that the strategy in relation to Cuba has not only been defensive but also offensive. Guatemala, Nicaragua, as well as other countries—including Costa Rica—have allowed (and still allow) their territories to be used by groups of Cuban exiles, who are financed, trained, and directed by the Central Intelligence Agency, in order to eventually overthrow the present Cuban regime.[9] As was described by

[7] *Hispanic American Report,* California, University of California, November, 1962, p. 797.

[8] *Latin American Times,* New York, August 25, 1965.

[9] A detailed description of the activities of CIA, the Cuban exiles, and the bases and training camps in Central America is provided by Haynes

Manuel Artime to Haynes Johnson: "Since March 17, 1960, President Eisenhower authorized the CIA to organize, train, and equip Cuban refugees as a guerrilla force in order to overthrow Castro."[10] With a tenacity which is normal in those who receive a strong economic stimulus, Artime, Emilio Núñez Portuondo, and Aureliano Sánchez continue to get ready in Central America for an operation which, they hope, will be more successful than the Bay of Pigs.

(c) With the exception of Costa Rica, the Central American military establishments behave as the supreme arbiters in the political life of their respective countries. In general, army actions are basically measures of internal repression. In this sense, the influence they can have on CONDECA is perceived as an additional guarantee to maintain—and even increase—their hegemony over the population, and above all to ensure the already gigantic influence that they have on political life. (A detailed description of the equipment and personnel of the Central American armed forces is included in Appendix 1 of this essay.)

External Causes

The external pressures to create CONDECA clearly originate from the general directives underlying present North American foreign policy. As U.S. Assistant Secretary for inter-American Affairs Jack Hood Vaughn said:

> The United States hope to develop close relations with the Central American Defense Council organization, which will strengthen the defenses against the forces of International Communism which threaten our society.[11]

Hood Vaughn's enthusiasm toward CONDECA can be justified in terms of the general American strategy: CONDECA is the first regional military organization "officially" created in the American hemisphere and it is hoped that it will be a small-

Johnson, with Manuel Artime *et al.*, *The Bay of Pigs*, New York, Dell Publishing Co. Inc., 1964.

[10] *Ibid.*, p. 30. Artime continues: "Six years earlier, the President made a similar decision involving CIA guerrillas in a Latin American country: Guatemala . . . a similar success was expected in Cuba."

[11] *Latin American Times*, New York, August 25, 1965; *New York Times*, August 23, 1965, p. 12.

scale experience leading to a similar inter-American organization.

In 1965, President Johnson urged the nations of the hemisphere to develop some kind of collective military force that would be authorized to intervene in the internal affairs of Latin American nations threatened by "wars of national liberation." As he expressed it:

> Out of the Dominican crucible the twenty American Nations must now forge a stronger shield against disaster . . . In today's world . . . the old distinction between the civil war and international war has already lost much of its meaning.[12]

After the President, Secretary of State Dean Rusk maintained that "the hemisphere needs to take up again the question of constituting some stand-by force on a continuing basis, on prompt call, and the organization of a political machinery for taking hemispheric tensions promptly in the face of fast-moving events."[13]

NORTH AMERICAN MILITARY POLICY IN LATIN AMERICA

North American military policy has undergone a noticeable change in the sixties. It is divided into two periods: one from 1942 to 1960, in which a series of measures to guarantee the defense of the continent against any external aggression are established, and another since 1960, which emphasizes programs of internal repression and civic military action.

1. During the Second World War, the United States Congress granted a help of $400 million worth of equipment to the Latin American military establishments. In 1942 all the Latin American nations agreed to cooperate with the United States when, in a declaration issued in Rio de Janeiro, they stated that any act of aggression from a non-American state to any American nation would be considered as an aggression to all the countries under the agreement. At the end of the war, this structure was perpetuated in the Chapultepec Act (1945), which was later incorporated in the 1947 Rio de Janeiro Treaty. From 1952 on,

12 *New York Times*, May 29, 1965, pp. 1–2.
13 *New York Times*, May 30, 1965, IV, p. 4.

UNITED STATES MILITARY AID
TO LATIN AMERICA, 1952–1961

Fiscal Year	Amount (In dollars)
1952	200,000
1953	11,200,000
1954	34,500,000
1955	31,800,000
1956	30,400,000
1957	43,900,000
1958	47,900,000
1959	54,000,000
1960	53,700,000
1961	91,600,000

Source: Remarks by Senator Gruening in
Senate Debate, August 21, 1962. Reported
in Congressional Record, p. 14414.

military assistance to Latin America was considerably increased
under the Mutual Security Act of 1951.

Under the Mutual Security Act, a variety of terms and conditions had to be met before the Latin American nations could
"benefit" from military assistance. Two of the basic requirements to obtain funds were: (a) subscription to bilateral treaties, and (b) authorization to establish American military missions.[14]

2. In the early sixties, North American civil and military
strategists realized that the Soviet Union was not threatening the
Latin American continent with a massive attack. As Hovey
comments:

The policy of getting ready for the external defense of the
hemisphere, typified by the Pact of Rio de Janeiro and indicated
by the nature of North American military assistance, seemed to
imply preparations for a non-existent threat.[15]

On the other hand, the Soviet Union's development of intercontinental missiles and nuclear weapons made obvious the

[14] See J. Lloyd Mecham, The United States and Inter-American Security
1889–1960, Texas, University of Texas Press, 1961, p. 335 ff.
[15] Harold Hovey, United States Military Assistance, New York,
Frederick A. Praeger, 1965, p. 57.

uselessness of Latin American armies in the eventuality of a
Third World War.

The attention of the strategists was concentrated on the
"wars of national liberation," which stirred the so-called underdeveloped world. The Cuban Revolution finally shattered the
nervous system of Imperial United States. As an answer, the
previous policy of "external defense" was abandoned in favor
of policies of "internal security," which include the immediate
military preparation to fight against any type of subversion. The
era of "counterinsurgency" began, a prophylactic military term
equivalent to "counter-revolution." As a part of such a strategy
the Alliance for Progress program was initiated. This program,
together with those of civic military action, tends to create anti-
subversive "prophylactic belts."[16] Brigadier General Enemark
expressed this idea before the American Senate Foreign Relations Committee:

> The role of Latin American security forces (not only the police
> but also the Army) is of a basic importance. In order for the
> Alliance for Progress to have any chance of success, the govern-
> ments must have enough power to control subversion, prevent
> terrorism and eliminate flows of violence which may reach un-
> manageable proportions.[17]

In the beginning of the Alliance for Progress era, Latin
American armed forces began to receive the explicit approval of
the American Congress. In 1961, a study mission sent by the
American Senate, after a tour of Latin America, advised the
American Government to "take a more favorable attitude
toward the military groups in most Latin American countries.
. . . We are convinced that the military are not only the sole
forces of stabilization, but they also promote democratic insti-
tutions and progressive changes of a socio-economic nature."[18]
After Kennedy's assassination, Assistant Secretary of State

16 Edmundo Flores, "La Alianza para la Reacción," *Cuadernos Americanos* XXV, Vol. CXLV, March–April, 1966 (Mexico City).
17 *House Foreign Affairs Committee* CY 62, "Testimony of Brigadier
General Enemark," Washington, D.C., U.S. Government Printing Office,
1962, p. 268.
18 "Study Mission to South America (November–December, 1961),"
Senate 87th Congress, 2nd Session, Doc. N 91, Washington, D.C., U.S.
Government Printing Office, 1962.

Thomas Mann saw to it that such opinions reached the American executive power.

With the exception of naval defense programs, military assistance to Latin America is concentrated on internal security and civic military action projects. To implement these programs, higher budgets were promoted, adequate training and equipment provided, and military bureaucracies reorganized:

(a) *Budget*. When counterinsurgency and civic action programs were established early in 1960, United States military assistance to Latin America doubled. It is estimated that in the decade of the fifties the yearly average of United States military assistance to Latin America was $35 million, while for the years 1960 to 1965, the annual average was over $70 million.[19]

(b) *Equipment and training* are being provided according to the new strategic requirements.[20] The so-called School of the Americas in the Canal Zone has trained over 16,000 Latin American students in counterinsurgency and civic action. According to the annual report of the United States Defense Department, "the emphasis of the training has been given to counterinsurgency. . . . The courses and operations of counterinsurgency . . . were started in July, 1961, and they take place four times a year."[21] As of 1964, from a total of 16,343 Latin American students trained, 8,154 were Central Americans. By countries the distribution was as follows:

Country	Number
Costa Rica	1,639
El Salvador	358
Guatemala	958
Honduras	810
Nicaragua	2,969
Panama	1,420
TOTAL for Central America	8,154
TOTAL for Latin America	16,343[21a]

[19] W. Barber and C. N. Ronning, *Internal Security and Military Power,* Ohio State University Press, 1966, p. 145.
[20] *Department of Defense Annual Report, 1962,* Washington, D.C., U.S. Government Printing Office, Vol. LV, September 19, 1966.
[21] *Ibid.,* p. N 1421.
[21a] Barber and Ronning, *op. cit.,* p. 149.

(c) *Bureaucracy.* The Latin American armed forces leadership is trained at the Army Special Warfare Center at Fort Bragg, North Carolina. This training center is under the United States Continental Army Command (CONARC) supervision. Its purpose is to conduct the training of the "special forces," psychological warfare, and counterinsurgency units. The courses and training received by the Latin American personnel were described by Assistant Secretary of State Edwin M. Martin. The training program includes subjects such as "riot control, counter-guerrilla operations and tactics, intelligence and counter-intelligence, and other subjects which will contribute to the maintenance of public order, and the support of Constitutional Governments."[22]

The counterinsurgency and civic action blueprint has been extended to every aspect of the program of military aid to Latin America. William S. Gaud, Administrator for the International Development Agency (AID) said recently at a press conference: "That program—of military aid—is directed towards training for internal security and Civic Action."[23] Lincoln Gordon, former Assistant Secretary for Inter-American Affairs, maintains that the "Latin American Armed Forces are developing an increasing capacity to face any threat to their internal security."[24]

(d) *The Heirs of Camelot.* After the "Camelot debacle" (a U.S. government project in Latin America in which many U.S. social scientists became involved) a series of projects covering the same grounds was initiated:

1. *Project Role* "is studying the changing roles of indigenous military establishments."
2. *Project Resettle* "is probing the problems of agrarian colonization in cooperation with the Peruvian Government."
3. *Project Simpático* "is an effort in Colombia to analyze military civic action programs and their effect on the attitudes of people."

22 "Communist Subversion in the Western Hemisphere." A statement by Assistant Secretary of State E. M. Martin. Latin American Subcommittee of House Committee on Foreign Affairs. February 19, 1963. *Department of State Bulletin,* March 18, 1963, pp. 406–407.
23 *Department of State Bulletin,* September 19, 1966, Vol. LV, N 1421, p. 420.
24 "Foreign Assistance Program for Latin America," *Department of State Bulletin,* Vol. LIV, N 1408, June 20, 1966, p. 985.

COUNTERINSURGENCY AND CIVIC ACTION
ORGANIZATIONAL MODEL FOR TRAINING*

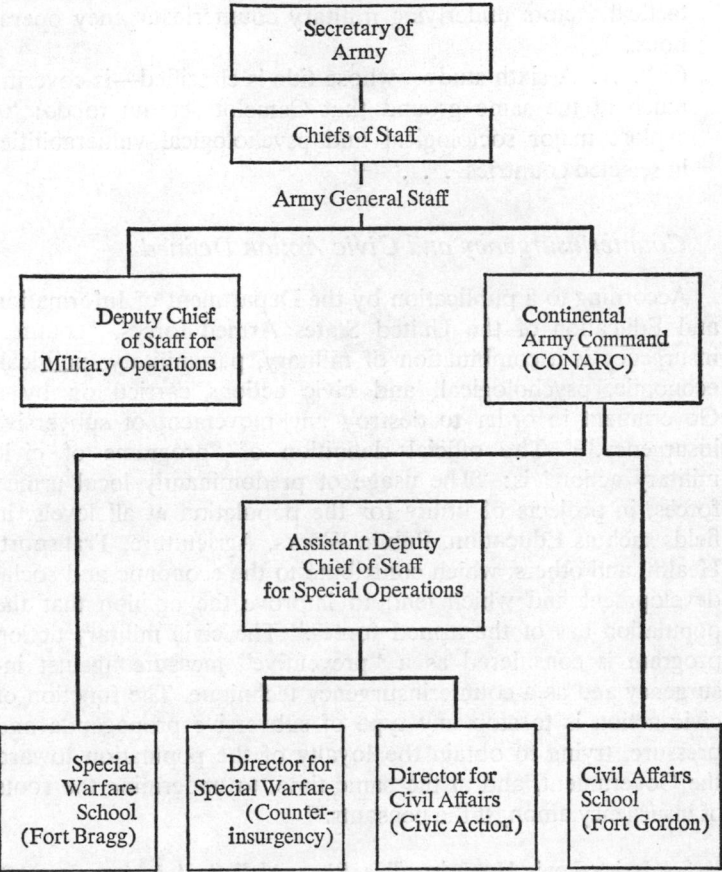

Secretary of Army

Chiefs of Staff

Army General Staff

Deputy Chief of Staff for Military Operations

Continental Army Command (CONARC)

Assistant Deputy Chief of Staff for Special Operations

Special Warfare School (Fort Bragg)

Director for Special Warfare (Counter-insurgency)

Director for Civil Affairs (Civic Action)

Civil Affairs School (Fort Gordon)

*United States Department of the Army, Organizations for counterinsurgency and Civic Action. (Civil Affairs School, Fort Gordon, Ga., 1964).

4. *Project Secure* "is a study of internal security problems such as riot control."

5. *Project Numismatics* "is an analysis of the strategic and tactical factors underlying military counterinsurgency operations."

6. ". . . A sixth study—whose title is classified—is covering much of the same ground that Camelot set out to do: 'to explore major sociological and psychological vulnerabilities in selected countries . . .' "[25]

Counterinsurgency and Civic Action Defined

According to a publication by the Department of Information and Education of the United States Armed forces, "counterinsurgency is a combination of military, paramilitary, political, economic, psychological, and civic actions carried on by a Government in order to destroy any movement of subversive insurgency."[26] The official definition of "programs of civic military action" is: "The usage of predominantly local armed forces, in projects of utility for the population at all levels, in fields such as Education, Public Works, Agriculture, Transport, Health, and others, which contribute to the economic and social development and which tend to improve the opinion that the population has of the armed forces." The civic military action program is considered as a "preventive" measure against insurgency and as a counterinsurgency technique. The function of civic action is to stop any type of subversive propaganda and pressure, trying to obtain the loyalty of the population toward the Government, and at the same time, to undermine the roots of insurgency amongst the peasants.[27]

[25] See Irving Louis Horowitz, *The Rise and Fall of Project Camelot: Studies in the Relationship Between Social Science and Practical Politics.* Cambridge, Mass., M.I.T. Press, 1967; also useful in this connection is John S. Tompkins, *The Weapons of World War III:* The Long Road Back from the Bomb. New York, Doubleday Company Inc., 1966, p. 11.

[26] *Annual Forces Information and Education for Commanders,* Vol. 3, N 14, January 15, 1964.

[27] *Ibid.* A series of preventive activities are going on in Latin America today: "More than 250 teams of Army, Navy, and Air Force men are working on a variety of special projects ranging from engineering and medical help in the training of local military and police units in counterguerrilla tactics. Venezuela, for example, has been able to improve substantially its control of guerrilla and terrorist elements with U.S.-trained

To the counterinsurgency and civic action blueprint we must add the services of the local intelligence organizations, trained and directed by the Central Intelligence Agency. In general, the role of these "intelligence" services is to infiltrate and sabotage revolutionary movements at the level of leadership. The effectiveness of this combination is obvious from the results obtained in Venezuela, Guatemala, Colombia, and Peru, where guerrilla activities have been controlled and the guerrilla leaders systematically eliminated.

The consequences of this kind of military assistance on the political structure of Latin America have no precedents. The traditionally weak civil political structures, as opposed to the military, are reduced to virtual impotence. The impact of those kinds of programs on the poor and underdeveloped countries of Central America is still greater. John D. Powell shows how military aid has given to every member of the national guard of Nicaragua, under the leadership of "Tachito" Somoza, an average of $930 worth of equipment and training in order to impose their power and to lead violent actions over a population whose annual income per capita is $205. In the case of Guatemala, the "military aid" has provided the average soldier with a power worth $538 (in equipment and training) to exert violence over the average Guatemalan, whose annual income is $185.[28]

A parallel between the rationalizations under which *caudillismo* was nurtured and the slogans behind counterinsurgency and civic action programs is not difficult to visualize. The ideology for *caudillismo* was provided by nineteenth-century European Positivism under the motto *Orden y Progreso* (Order

---

military and police units. In Peru, the Government has made good progress against guerrilla concentrations with its U.S.-trained and -supported Army and Air Force. In Colombia, training and a few helicopters have aided the Army to re-establish Government control in the rural insurgent areas. The Bolivian Army is being trained and equipped to counter intermittent violence in the mines. A Guatemalan counterinsurgency force is being supported with weapons, vehicles, radios, and training. And our military assistance to Uruguay is oriented toward improving the small arms, ammunition, communications, and transportation equipment of its security forces. . . . On another front, the Army maintains operations research in Rio de Janeiro . . ." John Tompkins, *op. cit.,* pp. 11–12.

[28] John Duncan Powell, "Military Assistance and Militarism in Latin America," *The Western Political Quarterly,* V. 18, June, 1965, pp. 382–392.

U.S. Military Assistance to Central America

Country	Cumulative U.S. military aid, 1950–1962 (Thousand dollars)	Cumulative U.S. military aid per member of Armed Forces (In dollars, July, 1962)
Nicaragua	3,813	930
El Salvador	1,136	169
Honduras	2,324	529
Guatemala	4,311	538
Panama	929	n.a.
Costa Rica	832	n.a.

Sources: Agency for International Development. U.S. Foreign Assistance, July 1, 1945 to June 30, 1962. Statistics and Reports Division, AID, Washington, D.C., 1961. See also John Duncan Powell, *op. cit.*

and Progress). The rationalization for today's version of *caudillismo* is provided by North American militarism. Instead of *orden* we have counterinsurgency, and *progreso* is translated as civic military action.

The basic deficiency of *caudillismo* and its incorporation into counterinsurgency and civic action programs is that it fails to provide the necessary democratic institutional mechanisms through which socioeconomic conflicts could be released. If a political catastrophe is to be avoided in the face of intensified economic stress and despairing demographic pressure, different interest groups (including labor unions, the intelligentsia, and peasant organizations) must be given proper institutional channels to express their tensions and demands. Gino Germani and Kalman Silvert maintain that "the military will be reduced to their barracks and their professional functions alone only when Latin American countries develop sufficiently complicated power structures and a society sufficiently flexible and integrated . . . when socioeconomic conflicts have found institutionalized expression within a common framework of shared norms."[29] While agreeing with these authors, we must also add that current emphasis on militaristic solutions and increased military intervention in civilian affairs tends to inhibit the growth of efficient political systems. This tendency is observed not only in the banana republics but also in Latin America's

[29] Gino Germani and Kalman Silvert, "Politics and Military Intervention in Latin America," in *Political Development and Social Change*, ed. by Jason L. Finkle and Richard W. Gable. New York, John Wiley, 1966, pp. 397–401.

biggest nations. A typical case is the recent militarization of Brazil, where the armed forces took over the executive, legislative, and judiciary powers at the municipal, state, and federal levels; militarized the labor unions; wiped out political parties and made a mockery of all democratic institutions. In Argentina (and, with few exceptions, in the rest of Latin America) a similar situation prevails. A good share of responsibility for this condition has to be assigned to North American military policies. They inflate military power. While the counterinsurgency program trains and arms the Latin American armies, increasing their superiority over the average citizen in any situation of physical conflict, civic action provides an ideological frame which justifies and encourages military intervention in situations which would normally be under civilian control:

> If "civic action" would mean tractors *instead of* tanks, encouragement of civic action could be justified even if there are doubts as to whether the military is the best and most economical agency to conduct such operations. But if we insist that civic action must not detract from military capabilities—and the U.S. Congress has made this stipulation with the U.S. military's concurrence—then civic action is likely to mean tractors *in addition* to tanks.[30]

To their image as the champions of anti-Communism, the Latin American military have added that of economic messiahs. In fact, contemporary Latin American militarism is ideologically directed against both "Communist infiltration" *and* "civilian inefficiency." All military takeovers occurring between 1960 and 1965 were rationalized thusly.

Civilians are incapable of: (a) controlling Communist infiltration, and (b) solving economic problems. This attitude is exemplified by the remarks two Chilean military officers made after attending a joint inter-American military maneuver: "(our) foreign colleagues seemed more convinced that it was their mission to save the hemisphere not only from the Communists but also from the Civilians."[31]

The exuberant power gained by Latin American armed forces in the last five years seems to be placing them as a determining factor in political-economic and even social events. It seems as

[30] Barber and Ronning, *op. cit.,* p. 236.
[31] *New York Times,* December 24, 1964, p. 5.

if the increase in their power is reaching the takeoff stage, at which they generate their own power with a high degree of autonomy from their respective political systems and an equally high degree of dependence on their foreign benefactors.

The growing militarism generated not only by the programs previously described but also by the explicitly favorable attitude of the United States toward military regimes is insulting to all Latin American countries. Senator Wayne Morse, alarmed by these tendencies, declared the following, when the 1967 program for military aid was being discussed:

> The mild attitude of the United States towards the military establishments in Latin America has contributed to deny Argentina a Constitutional government. The example set by the United States by extending the economic and military aid to the staffs of the Dominican Republic, Guatemala, Honduras, Ecuador, and El Salvador, contributed to the gestation of Castelo Branco's coup d'etat in Brazil. Moreover, when we decided almost automatically to approve of such a regime and to offer it great amounts of money as aid, we encouraged the Argentinian military to overthrow their government. . . . All our reasonings that our military aid tends to teach the civilian groups to control the military, have been completely contradicted by such events. The situation was deplorable enough when these coups used to happen in the small Central American republics. Now they have spread to Brazil and Argentina.[32]

The Washington decision makers should be reminded that the periods of unprecedented *orden* and notable *progreso* provided by the caudillos were followed by national political cataclysms: "Thirty years of Díaz's 'prosperity' were followed by nearly twenty years of civil war. Thirty years of Gómez's 'prosperity' were followed successively by a period that came seriously close to civil war . . . and an extended period of violence. . . . The demise of Trujillo after twenty years of uninterrupted 'peace' and 'economic development' has left the Dominican Republic ripe for civil war. . . . No North American needs to be told what followed the prosperity of the Batista regime in Cuba."[33]

[32] "What Should Be the Foreign Aid Policy of the United States?" Senate 89th Congress, 2nd Session, Doc. 89. Washington, D.C., U.S. Printing Office, 1966.
[33] Barber and Ronning, *op. cit.*, pp. 40–41.

What ought to concern us is what will follow Central American *Orden y Progreso* as well as Castelo Branco's and Costa e Silva's prosperity in Brazil, and General Onganía's peace and tranquillity in Argentina. We are acutely aware of the Vietnamese nightmare, with its napalm conflagrations and human tragedy. After the Dominican affair we know that if something goes wrong in Brazil or Argentina—or for that matter in any Latin American republic—we can no longer assume immunity from American infantrymen and the latest Phantom jets. The Vietnamese experience is therefore more than an irritating irrelevancy for inter-American affairs.

CONDECA AND PAX AMERICANA

America's modest military aid in Latin America is decidedly more effective than its mercenary forces in Europe and Asia, not, however, in holding back Communists, but in holding up military oligarchies . . . Viewed in the physical and economic context of a poor country in Central America, U.S. military assistance no longer appears small and innocent.

J. W. FULBRIGHT

A careful reading of the military aid program for 1967 presented by the Defense Department before the American Senate shows that the main objectives of counterinsurgency could be attained more efficiently by coordinating and unifying the human and technical resources of the Latin American armed forces. With this purpose in mind, an attempt has been made to reduce as much as possible any military rivalries which could endanger such an objective.[34] For example, it has been planned to increase meetings and conferences of military leaders to encourage an exchange of ideas and "to reinforce friendship ties and mutual understanding."[35] A meeting of this kind took place in Argentina at the end of 1966. Joint military operations are being planned for the near future.

CONDECA's organization and activities fit this pattern perfectly. CONDECA has a staff composed of higher hierarchy

[34] *Department of Defense Annual Report, 1962, op. cit.*, pp. 112–113.
[35] *Ibid.*

representatives of the armies and the security offices of Central
America. This organization is advised by the Central Intelli-
gence Agency (CIA), which provides information, and by the
Central American representatives of the three branches of the
American military system: the Army, the Navy, and the Air
Force.

In order to obtain the coordination of both human and technical capabilities, CONDECA has done the following:

(a) It has standardized and unified the organizing system of
the six armies. This measure implies the immediate improvement of the systems of mobilization of troops and light equipment. Special attention is given to air transport and to the joint
operations carried on by the infantry and the air force. This is
so because in antiguerrilla strategy, air logistics is closely
related to the ground movement of counterinsurgency troops.

It is generally accepted that in case of insurgency the respective national army will operate in the first place. If such an army
is unable to carry on a fast "prophylaxis," then, at its demand,
it will receive the necessary reinforcements if, and only if, the
control potential in other supposedly critical areas is not
thereby considerably weakened. This coordination is facilitated
by the existence of

(b) A standardized type of training. As we already pointed
out, this is carried out not only by the military missions in the
respective countries but also in the common training centers,
especially at the school situated in the Canal Zone;

(c) A standardized type of equipment. This fortunate convergence of factors is superimposed by an organizing system
with branches of command and organization graphically represented in the following way:

This diagram of relationships provides two levels of coordination: one between the Central American military establishments and the other between the American military system and
CONDECA. In this structure, United States entities control all
levels.

If this model were generalized to an inter-American level, the
American military system would absorb the human resources of
all the military establishments in Latin America. As long as this
organization exists, the Pentagon can direct its attention to
other areas of the world, since the Latin American armies,
coordinated by an organization whose decision-making body is

CONDECA AND THE AMERICAN MILITARY ESTABLISHMENT:
An Organizational Model[36]

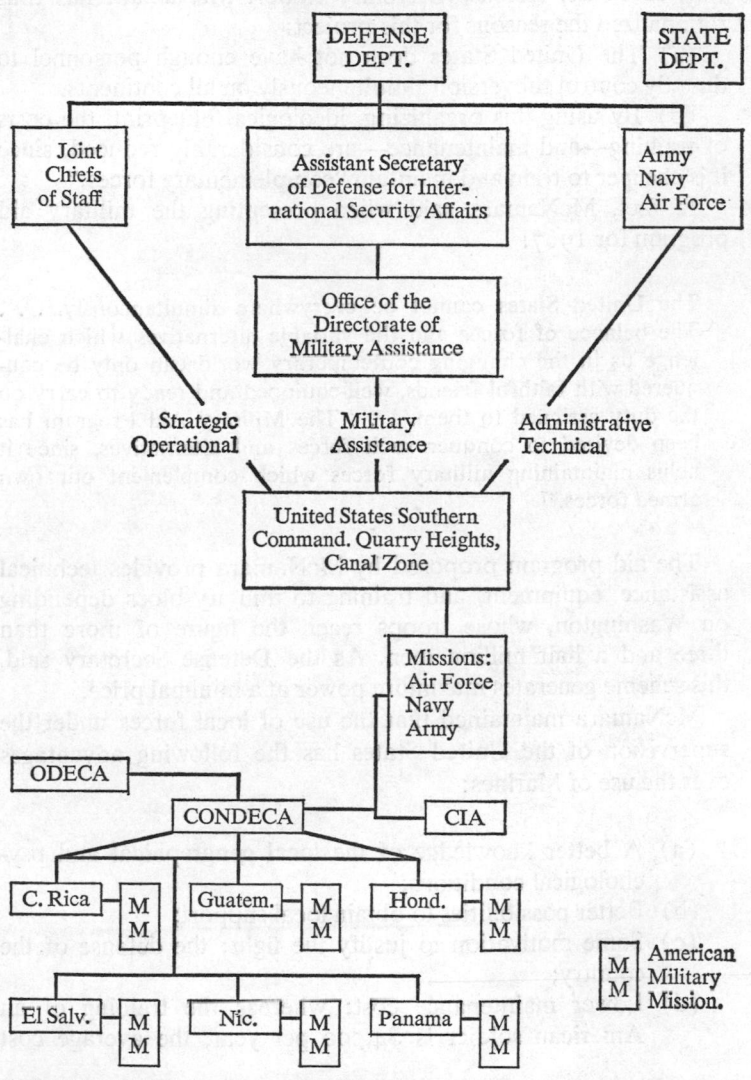

[36]In this diagram CONDECA's organizational chart is integrated to the composition and organization of the Office of the Secretary of Defense. Civil Affairs School, Fort Gordon, Ga., 1964. (See Barber and Ronning, *op. cit*. p. 102).

in Washington (with a minimum of American personnel), would collectively control any subversive movement in their own countries. Defense Secretary Robert McNamara has thus rationalized the reasons for this project:

(a) The United States does not have enough personnel to directly control subversion simultaneously on all continents.

(b) By using this organizing, ideological blueprint, the costs of training—and maintenance—are considerably reduced, since it is cheaper to train and maintain "complementary forces."

In fact, McNamara said when presenting the military aid program for 1967:

> The United States cannot be everywhere simultaneously. . . . The balance of forces and the variable alternatives which challenge us in the changing contemporary world can only be conquered with faithful friends, well-equipped and ready to carry on the duty assigned to them. . . . The Military Aid Program has been devised to conquer such forces and alternatives, since it helps maintaining military forces which complement our own armed forces.[37]

The aid program proposed by McNamara provides technical assistance, equipment, and training to military blocs depending on Washington, whose troops reach the figure of more than three and a half million men. As the Defense Secretary said, this scheme generates maximum power at a minimal price.

McNamara maintained that the use of local forces under the supervision of the United States has the following advantages over the use of Marines:

(a) A better knowledge of the local geographical and psychological conditions;
(b) Better possibilities to obtain local support;
(c) Some motivation to justify the fight: the defense of the country;
(d) Lower maintenance cost: whereas the training of an American soldier is $4,500 per year, the average cost

[37] "Statement of R. McNamara, Secretary of Defense, before the Senate Foreign Relations Committee in Support of the Fiscal Year 1967 Military Assistance Program," April 20, 1966, in *What Should Be the Foreign Policy of the United States?*, p. 79. See also Defense appropriations for 1967, 89th Congress, 2nd Session, Part 1.

per capita of the "complementary" armed forces is $540 per year.[38]

As is traditionally done, the program proposed by the Department of Defense was unanimously approved by the Senate. It seems that the reasons given by McNamara and the experiences of the so-called Inter-American Peace Force in the Dominican Republic convinced the senators of the advantages, economic no less than political, which could be derived by encouraging the creation of a CONDECA at an inter-American level.

CONCLUSION

Together with the pessimism created by the increasing militarization of Latin America[39] there exists the necessity and the responsibility to understand the dilemmas with which the present military situation confronts us, in all their theoretical and practical implications:

(a) The organizing ideological pattern of CONDECA tends to spread throughout the continent, involving all the countries of Latin America without exception.

(b) There is clear evidence that, with the expansion of this military pattern, the armed forces tend to increase their area of action and control to the political, economic, and social fields. Everything seems to indicate that the greater the dependence on external forces to increase this control, the greater the alienation—and autonomy—of the armed forces in relation to the corresponding political system. Such a tendency will continue to increase as long as military establishments are nurtured in a technical environment divorced from the larger implications of politics and economy.

(c) The Pax Americana tends to become universal, not inside the frame of a humanitarian idealism (as demonstrated by the genocidal war in Vietnam and the illegal intervention in

---

[38] *Ibid.*
[39] The present militarization of Latin America has not respected the old civilian tradition that Uruguay and Costa Rica have always represented in Latin American history. (For Uruguay, see footnote 27.) The Costa Rican case is described in detail in Appendix 2.

the Dominican Republic), but inside the amoral but technically efficient premises of a military logistic.

(d) Such premises need to be known in detail in their social and economic aspects (civic military action) and in the military ones (counterinsurgency), since they defy, in a very effective way, all orthodox revolutionary premises.

With Henri Edmé,[40] we must realize that revolution is no longer an imminent, unavoidable, and victorious reality, but only a possibility. In order for this possibility to become reality, it is necessary to build a theory which will interpret and respond to the technological-ideological models of the type we examine in this essay. Without such a theory, all revolutionary action is doomed to failure:

> The coincidence of the modification of circumstances and of human activity can only be conceived and understood as revolutionary practice.
>
> Karl Marx, *Thesis on Feuerbach*

APPENDIX I: DESCRIPTION OF THE
CENTRAL AMERICAN MILITARY ESTABLISHMENTS

In Guatemala military service is obligatory for two years for male citizens between eighteen and fifty years of age. The army is composed of approximately 8,500 men. The air force, composed of 500 well-trained officers, is equipped with a F-51D Mustang squadron; a squadron of B-26 Invaders (light bombers); a squadron of C-47 transports and T-33 jet trainers. There is a national police of 3,000 men, which can be coordinated with the army in case of emergency. Part of the officer's training takes place in the polytechnic school, and, as in the rest of Central America, in different institutions for military training in the United States and in the Canal Zone.

Nicaragua has a national guard composed of 220 officers and from 4,000 to 6,000 soldiers, with a well-trained reserve of over 4,000 men. Such numbers, however, are quite conservative estimates of the actual force of the national guard. The air force

---

[40] Henri Edmé, "Révolution en Amérique Latine?" *Les Temps Modernes*, year 21, May, 1966, Paris, 2013–2038.

had jets, P-51 Mustang squadrons, Thunderbolt F-47 fighter-bombers and C-47 and C-45 transport squadrons, as well as a considerable number of training planes.

The army of El Salvador is organized into four territorial divisions with ten infantry regiments, an artillery regiment, a cavalry regiment. There also exists a flying arm and a small naval arm. The air force has a 0-47 transport and several combat and training units which include some F-4U5 fighter-bombers.

In accordance with the Central American Convention in Washington, the army of Honduras is limited to 2,500 soldiers, including a national guard organized into 23 infantry companies and an artillery battery. The air force includes two squadrons of Corsair fighter-bombers and some P-5Y Privateers, and a small number of C-47 and C-46 transports.

In Costa Rica the army was abolished as a permanent institution in 1948. A civil guard of 1,200 men took the place of the previous army. However, a private paramilitary organization of the fascist type, called "Free Costa Rican Movement," has recently been created. This group trains its members in the military art and has been tacitly approved not only by the previous government (Orlich: 1962–1966), but also by the present one (Trejos: 1966–1970), which has even included some of its members in the government and in the civil guard.

Panama has no army. The national police has an authorized number of soldiers fixed at 3,900.

Main Characteristics: In all these military establishments, emphasis has been given to the use of light weapons such as machine guns, flamethrowers, and rifles. The main combat unit is the infantry.

APPENDIX 2

CONDECA HAS been up to now a dynamic, expensive organization and it promises to be very useful in maintaining the existing order in the banana republics. Among its most immediate programs are: (a) the carrying out of joint military operations; and (b) succeeding in actively incorporating Costa Rica and Panama.

The next military exercise that CONDECA will carry out is

called "Operation Nicarao," and it will certainly make history in the Republic of Costa Rica, since it is the first "war game" for the otherwise pacific and demilitarized "Central American Switzerland." The lesson that Costa Rica has to learn—and to pay for—has been a difficult one. Everything seems to indicate that Cost Rica will learn it and pay for it.

With the innocence of a newborn, a high officer of the civil guard headquarters of Costa Rica described Operation Nicarao to me in the following way: "Of course, we will have two sides. We will assume the presence of 'subversive guerrillas' coming from Cuba and from continental China." To my question of why they included China, the high officer told me in a confidential manner that the "intelligence services" which advise CONDECA maintain that China will invade Central America in 1970.

In any case, what we must basically understand is that Operation Nicarao is essentially a diving board by means of which Costa Rica jumps (and is thrown) into the "Central American swimming pool." The brand-new administration of Professor José Joaquín Trejos is doing the diving right now. The style and the technique are strictly creole.

When a Costa Rican government wants to make drastic changes in policies and public administration, it generally announces such decisions during a period when the national congress is in recess. This tactic tends to diminish the opposition and the political impact generated by the legislative assembly, which, in this country, is the ideal political forum. During the congressional recess of August, 1966, the dismissal of some important officers who held positions generally considered "sacred" in Costa Rica was announced. Among other highly polemical activities in the national milieu, the participation of Costa Rica in Operation Nicarao became public knowledge thanks to an infiltration of the security systems. According to the details given by the press, in order to avoid any conflicts of a formal (constitutional) type, the American Air Force will be in charge of the transportation of the Costa Rican troops (which are now being trained in Panama) directly to Nicaragua where the operation will take place. This news was immediately confirmed by the president. Costa Rica was an active member of the club.

On August 20, 1966, the following step tending to the militarization of the country was taken: The newspaper *La*

Nación announced in its first page the imminent inauguration of
a program of civic military action, promoted, planned, and
financed by the Southern Command. According to the security
minister, the Costa Rican civil guard will be directly financed by
the Southern Command in order to carry out educational and
public health activities at an "ultra-rural level."

A month later the Costa Rican university students started a
campaign against the participation of Costa Rica in CON-
DECA. In a document published in *La Prensa Libre* (September 14, pp. 1–2), the Federation of University Students said:

Considering:

1. That article 12 of the Political Constitution of the Republic
of Costa Rica, in which the Army as a regular institution is outlawed, must be interpreted in a restrictive way with reference to
the state of national defense, that is, as a state of emergency,
meaning by this danger against the State and the Supreme
Powers;
2. That, in consequence, the Council for Central American
Defense pretends to institutionalize, at an international level, a
military force which, by itself, is unnecessary for our country;
3. That CONDECA, the same as the Interamerican Peace Force,
may become the instrument of imperialistic interests and, in fact,
it is already the instrument of the interests of militaristic groups
which dominate several of the Central American countries;
4. That the principle of autodetermination of the peoples is
threatened by a military force at an international level, as proved
by the unjustified creation and intervention of the so-called Inter-
american Peace Force;
5. That the Government Council has been willing at all moments
to follow the game of the Central American militarists endangering the institutional regime of our country, helping to create at a
Central American level an institution which is forbidden by constitutional law in our juridical ordinances;

We agree:

1. In energetically repudiating any participation of our government in the creation of CONDECA, and in claiming vehemently
a correct interpretation, by the Government, of Article 12 of the
Constitution which reflects faithfully the will of the legislator and
the popular feeling according to the juridical experience of our
people;
2. In condemning the attempt by Central American militaristic

groups to institutionalize a force which justifies violence and anti-democratic action which:

(a) Endangers the sovereignty of the Central American peoples affecting fundamentally the principle of self-determination;

(b) threatens with the destruction of democratic institutions in the Central American countries which have a civilian regime;

(c) increases the power of the Military in Nicaragua, Honduras, El Salvador, and Guatemala, countries which live in a constant struggle towards their liberation from the military castes.

JOSÉ A. ALFARO (President)
MARCOS V. TRISTAN ORLICH
(Secretary of Judicial Review)

The day this document was published, according to the editorial in *La República* on September 15, 1966, "All of a sudden the city of San José was cut in two, its commercial activities and the traffic in Avenida Central and nearby streets was almost paralyzed. . . . Three bombs exploded in different places in the city. . . . They had succeeded in creating an artificial climate of protest, terrorism, and public unrest." The morning daily then asks: "Who is trying to create this artificial climate? Who is interested in breaking our traditional national harmony? . . . Who are those who have received the training for these actions?"

In the following weeks, terrorism continued to spread fear and indignation among the usually peaceful neighbors of San José. The mass media concluded immediately that everything was a Communist plot. According to *La República* (September 22, 1966), the explosions "correspond to the line of 'sabotage and terrorism,' typical of red activities." Such a condemnation seems to be premature. However, immediately, some right-wing pressure groups started to demand the creation of an army in order to stop Communism, which overnight had become a threat for the public security of the country. The conservative and wealthy Berta de Gerli shouted from her *La Nación* column "Bitter Drops" (September 22, 1966):

The defenses that Costa Rica must have cannot be inconsistent or weak any longer. It is very beautiful to keep repeating that we have "more teachers than soldiers" but the reality of a period full of evils requires a constant vigilance if we do not want to continue facing serious, very serious, surprises.

On September 25, *La Juventud* of the National Liberation Party denounced from *La República* (p. 15) that "anonymously, the anticommunists of fascist and nazi tendencies have put into circulation a sheet in which, shamelessly, they support Central American militarism and they justify the despotic policies of the Argentinian dictator, under pretense that they respond to his will to 'repress the communist groups of the Argentinian universities.' "

The activities and the training of the paramilitary organization Free Costa Rica Movement have come into the discussion of this serious matter. Some months before the terrorist events, a bomb arsenal was found in the metropolitan district of Tibas. The individuals arrested, according to declarations made by the minister of public security, were members of that organization. The news was suppressed and officially "rectified."

Although it is difficult to clarify objectively the origin of these terrorist activities, the fact is that they essentially benefit those groups which favor the militarization of Costa Rica and its incorporation in CONDECA. The "state of emergency" has been effectively used to counteract the opinions and the antimilitary activities of the university students and of *La Juventud* of the National Liberation Party.

Seven Erroneous Theses

About Latin America

RODOLFO STAVENHAGEN

IN THE massive literature dealing with social and economic development and underdevelopment produced in recent years, many doubtful, mistaken, and ambiguous theses have appeared. Many of these are accepted as the working truth, and form a major part of the conceptual framework of Latin American intellectuals, politicians, students, researchers, and professors. Neither facts nor recent research, which contradict these theses, have been able to weaken them. Constant repetition in innumerable books and articles, particularly foreign ones, have given these concepts a growing life of their own, turning some of them, despite growing evidence to the contrary, into dogmas.

In this article I will deal with the sociological theses, since the debate about similar mistaken economic theses has been quite widespread.

The first thesis:
The Latin American countries are dual societies.

In essence this thesis affirms that two different, and to a certain extent independent—though necessarily connected—societies exist in the Latin American countries: one is an archaic, traditional, agrarian, and stagnant or retrogressive society; the other is a modern, urban, industrialized, dynamic, progressive, developing society. The "archaic society" is characterized by personal and family (kinship) relations; by traditional institutions (ritual co-parenthood, certain types of collective labor, certain forms of personalistic political domination, and patron-client relationships); by rigid stratification of ascribed social statuses (i.e., where the individual's status in the social structure is determined by birth, with little likelihood of change during his lifetime); and by norms and values which exalt—or at least accept—the status quo and the inherited traditional forms of social life, which are said to constitute an obstacle to economically "rational" thought. The "modern society," on the other hand, supposedly consists of the type of social relations which sociologists call secondary, determined by interpersonal actions which are motivated by rational and utilitarian ends; by functionally oriented institutions; and by comparatively flexible social stratifications, in which status is attained through personal effort, and is expressed by quantitative indices (like income or level of education) and social function (like occupation). In the so-called "modern society," the norms and values of the people tend to be oriented toward change, progress, innovation, and economic rationality (e.g., maximum benefits at minimum costs).

According to this thesis, each of the two societies facing each other in the Latin American countries has its own characteristic dynamics. The first, the "archaic society," has its origins in the colonial epoch (or perhaps earlier), and preserves many ancient cultural and social elements. It changes little, or does so very slowly. At any rate, changes are not internally generated, but are imposed upon it by the modern society. The other society, the "modern" one, is oriented toward change; it generates within itself its own transformations and is the focal point of economic development, whereas the "archaic" society constitutes an obstacle to such development.

The dual society thesis is expressed on a more sophisticated level by positing an alleged duality between feudalism and capitalism in the Latin American countries. In fact, it is claimed that in a large part of Latin America a feudal type of society and economic structure exists, which constitutes the base for retrogressive and conservative social and economic groups (i.e., the landowning aristocracy, the oligarchy, local political strongmen, etc.). On the other hand, the theory affirms, there exist nuclei of a capitalist economy, in which we find the entrepreneurial, progressive, urbanized middle classes. Implicit in this description is the idea that "feudalism" is an obstacle to development in Latin American countries and must be eliminated to give way for a progressive capitalism, which will be developed by the entrepreneurial capitalists for the benefit of the country as a whole.

There is no doubt that in all the Latin American countries great social and economic differences exist—between rural and urban areas, between the Indian and non-Indian populations, between the mass of peasants and the urban and rural elites, and between the very backward and the relatively developed regions.

Nevertheless, these differences do not justify the use of the concept of dual society for two principal reasons. First, the relations between the "archaic" or "feudal" regions and groups and the "modern" or "capitalistic" ones represent the functioning of a single unified society of which the two poles are integral parts; and second, these two poles originate in the course of a single historical process.

Let us take the first point. What is important is not the mere existence of two "societies" or a "dual society"—two contrasting poles at the ends of a socioeconomic continuum—but rather the relationships which exist between these two "worlds" and which bind them into a functional whole. To the extent that the localized development of certain areas in Latin America is based on the use of cheap labor (is this not what principally attracts foreign capital to our countries?), the backward regions —those that provide the cheap labor—fulfill a specific function in the national society and are not merely zones in which, for one reason or another, development has not taken place. Moreover, the archaic zones are generally exporters of raw materials to the urban centers of the country and abroad. As we shall see later, the developed areas of the underdeveloped countries operate like a pumping mechanism, drawing from their backward, underdeveloped *hinterland* the very elements that make for their own development. This situation is not new to the underdeveloped countries. It is the result of a long historical process that began with the expansion of mercantilist and colonialist Europe.

Let us turn now to the second point, the single historical process which gave rise to the two poles of Latin American society. The conquest of Latin America was accomplished principally in the context of commercial goals. Essentially, it was accomplished by a series of joint (private and state) mercantile enterprises. In some regions veritable feudal areas were created by means of *encomiendas* and *mercedes* (respectively, grants of Indian labor and land, by which the Spanish Crown rewarded the conquerors). The conquered indigenous populations were subjected to the most brutal oppression and exploitation on the part of the Spaniards. In the same way that the slavery of the African Negroes on the Caribbean and Brazilian sugar plantations satisfied the needs of a mercantilist economy oriented toward the consumer markets, Europe too was not a closed, self-sufficient economy (as was the case in classical European feudalism), but in turn satisfied the needs of the export mining industry and of agriculture which supplied these mining centers or the European markets.

During the whole colonial epoch, the driving force of the Latin American economy was the mercantilist-capitalist system. The Spanish and Portuguese colonies were large producers of raw materials which supplied various European markets, directly or indirectly, and thus contributed to the later industrial development of Western Europe. The "feudal" economy, if it ever really existed, was subsidiary to the dynamic centers—the mines and export agriculture—which, in turn, responded to the needs of the colonial metropolis.

The one constant factor of the colonial economy was the search for and control of cheap labor for the colonial enterprises. First the colonists tried enslaving the indigenous populations; then the slavery of Africans was introduced. Later they assured themselves of servile Indian labor through a series of arrangements which varied from the *encomienda* to the forced distribution of Indian workers. The "feudal" living and working conditions of the majority of the Indian peasant population reduced to a minimum the costs of production in mining and in colonial agriculture. Thus, the "feudalism" in labor relations may be considered a function of the development of the colonial economy in its entirety, which, in turn, formed an integral part of the world mercantilist system.

The colonial economy was subjected to strong cyclical variations. In Brazil, one after another of the major industries grew and then declined. This was true for the primitive extraction of wood, sugar production in the great slave plantations of the Northeast, mining in the central part of the country, the extraction of rubber in the Amazon, and finally, during this century, coffee production in the South and Southeast of Brazil. Each one of these cycles brought an epoch of growth and prosperity to the area in which it occurred. Each corresponded at that moment to a foreign demand. And each one left, in the end, a stagnant, underdeveloped, backward economy and an archaic social structure. In a large part of Brazil, then, *underdevelopment followed upon and did not precede development.* The underdevelopment of these areas is largely the result of a previous period of development that was of short duration, followed by the development of new activities in other parts of the country.

This pattern also can be observed in the rest of Latin America, principally in the mining zones which flourished in one epoch and whose economies decayed thereafter. The economic cycles of colonial Latin America were determined, in large part, by the economic cycles of the Western world. In Middle America, Indian communities that are now closed, isolated, and self-sufficient were not always like that. On the one hand, the colonists displaced the Indian populations, which were removed to inhospitable and isolated zones in which their living standards were reduced to a miserable subsistence level; on the other hand, during the periods of economic depression, those communities which had previously been relatively integrated into the global economy cut themselves off from the world and were depressed through necessity to a subsistence level. We see, then, that in historical terms development and underdevelopment are connected in Latin America, and that frequently the development of one zone implies the underdevelopment of others. We also see that the "feudal" conditions largely respond to the needs of the colonial metropolis and the colonial elite, whom it is hardly possible to define as feudal.

The kind of relationships that were established between a colonial metropolis and its colonies were repeated within the colonial countries themselves, in the relationships that developed between a few "poles of growth" and the rest of the country. As Spain was to her colonies, so the centers of colonial power in New Spain (and in the rest of Latin America) stood to the outlying, backward areas that surrounded them.

Indeed, the backward, underdeveloped regions of our countries have always played the role of *internal colonies* in relation to the developing urban centers or the productive agricultural areas. And in order to avoid the mistaken idea that there are two (or more) independent social and economic systems at work in the Latin American countries, we propose to describe the situation in terms of *internal colonialism* rather than in terms of "dual societies." This will become clearer as we discuss the next thesis.

The second thesis:

Progress in Latin America will come about by the spread of industrial products into the backward, archaic, and traditional areas.

This diffusionist thesis is found at many levels. Some speak of an urban—or Western—culture which will spread gradually over the world, and which will little by little absorb all the backward and primitive peoples. Others speak of the effects of modernization as if it was a spot of oil which spreads slowly outward from a central focus. Others affirm that all stimuli for change in the rural areas come of necessity from the urban zones. The fact that transistor radios, bicycles, toothpaste, and Coca-Cola can be found in the most remote parts of the world is cited to support these arguments.

This thesis implies three others, which are not always stated as clearly: (1) the development of the modern sector, which is essentially expansionist, brings with it *ipso facto* the development of the traditional and archaic sector; (2) the "transition" from traditionalism to modernism is a current, permanent, and inescapable process which will eventually involve all traditional societies; and (3) the centers of modernism themselves are nothing but the result of the diffusion of "modernist" traits (technology, know-how, the spirit of capitalism, and, of course, capital) which come from the already developed countries. The thesis can be considered mistaken for the following reasons:

A. While it is certain that a large number of consumer goods have been distributed to the underdeveloped areas in recent years, this does not automatically imply the development of these areas, if by development we mean an increase in per capita output of goods and services, and in the general social welfare. Often this diffusion of products is nothing but the diffusion of the culture of poverty into the backward, rural areas, for it involves no basic institutional changes.

B. The spread of manufactured industrial goods into the backward zones often displaces flourishing local industries or manufactures, and therefore destroys the productive base for a significant part of the population, provoking what is known as rural proletarianization, rural exodus, and economic stagnation in these areas.

C. The same process of diffusion has contributed to the development of a class of merchants, usurers, middlemen, monopolists, and moneylenders in the backward rural areas, in whose hands is concentrated a growing part of the regional income; and who, far from constituting an element of progress, represent an obstacle to the productive use of capital and to development in general.

D. The "diffusion" is often nothing more than the extension into the rural areas of monopolies and monopsonies, with negative consequences for a balanced and a harmonious development.

E. The process of diffusion of *capital* has taken place *from* the backward to the modern areas. Constant decapitalization of the underdeveloped areas in Latin America accompanies the migration of the best trained part of the population out of the backward zones: young people with a bit of education who are looking for better opportunities in other areas. It is not the presence or absence of factory-made goods, but this unfavorable outward flow from the backward zones which determines the level of development or underdevelopment of these areas.

F. This process of "diffusion," to which are attributed so many beneficial results, has been going on in Latin America for more than 400 years—and aside from certain dynamic focal points of growth, the continent is still as underdeveloped as ever.

*   *   *   *

In reality, the correct thesis would be: the progress of the modern, urban, and industrial areas of Latin America has taken place at the expense of backward, archaic, and traditional zones. In other words, the channeling of capital, raw materials, abundant foods, and manual labor coming from the backward zones permits the rapid development of these poles or focal points of growth, and condemns the supplying zones to an increasing stagnation and underdevelopment. The trade relations between the urban and the backward areas is unfavorable to the latter in the same way that the trade relations between underdeveloped and developed countries on a world scale are unfavorable to the underdeveloped countries.

The third thesis:
The existence of backward, traditional, and archaic rural areas is an obstacle to the formation of an internal market and to the development of a progressive and national capitalism.

It is claimed that progressive national capitalism—located in the modern industrial and urban centers—is interested in agrarian reform, the development of the Indian communities, the raising of minimum wages paid to agricultural workers, and other programs of a similar sort. This thesis is mistaken for the following reasons:

A. With rare exceptions, no progressive or national capitalism exists in Latin America, nor do the international conditions exist which would allow its development. By a "progressive" and "national" capitalism, we mean one which is committed in word and in deed to the independent economic development of the country—i.e., of the masses of the population. This would mean the formulation and acceptance by the capitalist class of economic policies furthering: (a) diversified agriculture for the internal market; (b) transformation of the country's principal raw materials for use in the country itself; (c) increasing industrialization; (d) a high rate of reinvestment in the country's agriculture; (e) increasing state participation in large economic enterprises; (f) strict control of foreign investments and their subordination to national needs; (g) strict control over exports of capital and profits; (h) preference for nationally owned enterprises over foreign-owned companies; (i) strict limitation of unnecessary imports; (j) strict limitation of the manufacture of nonessential consumer goods; and other such objectives.

These policies are not being pursued in most Latin American countries, and the countries that have tried at one time or another to implement them have suffered tremendous external political and economic pressures. The recent history of Brazil is a case in point. After the U.S.-supported military coup in that country in 1964, the previous economic policies which had furthered a progressive and national capitalism were thrown overboard in favor of the increasing control of the economy by U.S. corporations. The same thing has happened in Argentina,

Chile, Bolivia, and other countries. With the exception of Mexico (and at one time, of Brazil), the "national bourgeoisie" in Latin American countries does not have enough power or influence anywhere to make its interests really felt.

B. Up to this time—and for the foreseeable future—a significant internal market exists among the urban population, a market which is growing continuously and which is not yet fully supplied. On the other hand, in these same urban areas there is an industrial sector that works at less than full capacity for reasons that have little to do with the internal market, but rather with profits; and for a long time there will be no need for these industries to do more than supply the growing urban zones. That is to say, metropolitan areas like Lima, Callao, São Paulo, Santiago, and Mexico City can grow economically for the indefinite future without necessarily effecting any basic changes in the structure of the backward rural areas, the internal colonies.

The fourth thesis:
The national bourgeoisie has an interest in breaking the power and the dominion of the landed oligarchy.

It has often been said that there is a profound conflict of interests between the new elites (or the new upper class), represented by modern commercial and industrial entrepreneurs, and the old elite (or the traditional upper class), which derives its prominence from the ownership of the land. Although the latifundist aristocracy was eliminated by revolutionary means in some Latin American countries (however, always by the people, never by the bourgeoisie), there does not seem to be a conflict of interests between the bourgeoisie and the oligarchy in the other countries. On the contrary, the agricultural, financial, and industrial interests are often found in the same economic groups, in the same companies, and even in the same families.

For example, much of the capital coming from the archaic latifundias of Northeast Brazil is invested by their owners in lucrative enterprises in São Paulo. And in Peru, the grand families of Lima, associated with progressive foreign capital, are also the owners of the major "feudal" latifundias in the Andes. There is no structural reason why the national bourgeoisie and the latifundist oligarchy should not understand one another; on the contrary, they complement each other very well. And in those cases where there is a possibility of a conflict of interests (as with some legislation which would benefit one group and be prejudicial to the other, for example), there is no lack of bourgeois or military government which will give ample compensation to the group whose interest is prejudiced. The disappearance of the latifundist oligarchy has been exclusively the result of popular movements, not of the bourgeoisie. The bourgeoisie finds a very good ally in the landowning oligarchy in maintaining internal colonialism, which in the last analysis benefits both of these social classes equally.

The fifth thesis:
Latin American development is the work and creation of a nationalist, progressive, enterprising, and dynamic middle class, and the social and economic policy objectives of the Latin American governments should be to stimulate "social mobility" and the development of that class.

There is probably no other thesis about Latin America more widespread than this one. It is supported by researchers, journalists, and politicians; it is the theme of seminars and conferences, the subject of voluminous books, and one of the implicit but basic assumptions of the Alliance for Progress; it has been transformed into a virtual dogma. But this thesis is false, for the following reasons:

A. In the first place, the concept "middle class" itself contains ambiguities and equivocations. If it deals, as is often the case, with middle-income groups situated between the two extremes of a given economic scale, then it is not a social class but a statistical aggregate. Generally, however, this concept refers to people who have a certain type of occupation, particularly in the tertiary sector of the economy—in commerce or services—and mostly in the urban areas. In this case, it refers to white-collar workers, the bureaucracy, businessmen, and certain professions. At times this concept also refers to certain social groups which have no place in the traditional structural model of Latin America, in which there supposedly exists only a landed aristocracy and peons without land. All other groups, from the small landowners to the urban population as a whole, are then lumped together under the catchall term "middle class." As long as there is no clear definition of this term, information concerning the virtues and potentialities of this "middle class" is only a subjective opinion of those who state it.

B. Very often the term "middle class" is a euphemism for "ruling class." When one speaks of the entrepreneurs, the financiers, and the industrialists in relation to the development of the Latin American countries, reference is made to a class which has the power in the society, which occupies the apex of the social, economic, and political pyramid, and which makes, as such, the overall decisions which affect these countries. In other words, the class in question is in no sense "middle."

C. This thesis of the middle class usually suggests the idea of a potentially majoritarian mass of the population, primarily recruited from the lower strata of society, which will sooner or later totally occupy the social universe. At that time, it is implied, the upper classes will no longer have any economic importance, nor the lower classes any numerical importance. There could be nothing more utopian or mistaken. The growth of the tertiary economic sector is no guarantee of development, nor will the growth of the middle social sectors (a statistical fiction) guarantee the disappearance of the economic and social inequalities of society. No matter how accelerated the growth of these middle strata may be in Latin America as a whole, the growth of the lower income groups in both the countryside and the city on the one hand, and that of the miniscule upper income strata on the other, is still greater.

D. The sectors which compose the middle class in its restricted sense—small and medium-sized farm owners, small businessmen, public employees, small entrepreneurs, artisans, different types of professionals, etc. (i.e., those who work on their own or who receive a salary for nonmanual labor)—usually do not have the characteristics which are attributed to them. Instead, they are economically and socially dependent upon the upper strata; they are tied politically to the ruling class; they are conservative in their tastes and opinions, defenders of the status quo; and they search only for individual privileges. Far from being nationalists, they like everything foreign—from imported clothing to the *Reader's Digest*. They constitute a true reflection of the ruling class, deriving sizable benefits from the internal colonial situation. This group constitutes the most important support for military dictatorships in Latin America.

E. The concept "middle class" is also understood at times in terms of the consumption habits of a certain part of the population. In this way, for example, the fact that the peasants buy bottled beer instead of chicha or pulque, or that the urban population buys furniture or electrical appliances on credit, is considered by some as an indisputable sign that we have taken great steps in the march toward a "middle class" civilization. Everyone in Latin America, these authors tell us, has "the aspirations of the middle class." It is only a question of time as to when these aspirations will be realized. This assertion is incorrect for the following reasons:

A social class is not defined by the articles it consumes, nor does the level of aspirations reveal the structure of social institutions and the quality of intergroup relations. The diffusion of manufactured articles is directly related to the overall level of technology as well as to effective demand. The majority of the population—particularly in the urban areas—can enjoy this type of consumption, to some extent, but it requires no basic change in the class structure or in the inequalities of income, social status, political power, or labor relations.

The creation of "aspirations" or "necessities" of a certain type is increasingly the result of an all-powerful advertising industry which has infiltrated all social milieus. Levels of aspiration are rising everywhere, but so is the level of unfulfilled aspirations; and this, as any psychologist would confirm, leads to rising levels of frustration and feelings of deprivation. Thus, the aspirations of the middle class could well be transformed into revolutionary consciousness.

Furthermore, economic studies have demonstrated that in Latin America the proportion of wages in the national income —on which most of the population is dependent—tends to diminish, while the profits and capital returns of a minority tend to increase. This tendency, which has been accelerated in recent years by the process of inflation (especially in countries like Argentina, Brazil, Chile, Bolivia, and Colombia), does not fit with the idea of the slow, harmonious growth of the middle class.

F. The strengthening of the middle class, as a goal of social policy, is not essentially intended to further economic development in a country, but rather to create a political force capable of supporting the existing ruling class, and of serving as a buffer in the class struggles which endanger the stability of the existing social and economic structure. The ideologues of the middle class have lamented that this class was not sufficiently strong in Cuba to oppose the socialist revolution. On the other hand, they give credit to the "middle class" for the fact that the Mexican and Bolivian revolutions have become "stabilized" and "institutionalized."

The so-called middle classes are closely tied to the existing economic and political structure, and lack an internal dynamic which could transform them into promoters of an independent economic development. Their relative numerical importance is one thing, and their condition and capacity as a class to make decisions which could affect economic structures and processes is altogether another thing. It is noteworthy that the authors who are most attached to the idea of the growth of the middle class give little or no importance to the fact that the lower strata still constitutes the largest part of the Latin American population.

G. Finally, the thesis of the middle class tends to obscure the fact that there are tensions, oppositions, and conflicts between ethnic groups as well as between classes in Latin America; that the social and economic development of the Latin American countries depend, in the last analysis, upon an adequate solution to these conflicts; and that the growth of the "middle sectors" (as one North American author calls them), though very impressive in certain regions, does not contribute to the solution of these problems. At times, such growth may even postpone a solution and sharpen the conflicts.

The sixth thesis:
National integration in Latin America is the product of miscegenation.

This thesis is frequent in the countries which have major ethnic problems—those that have a large proportion of Indians in the population, and Brazil, with its Negro population. It is argued that the Spanish and Portuguese colonization of America brought two main racial groups, two civilizations, into confrontation, and that the process of national integration represents both a biological and a cultural mixture. In the Indo-American countries, it is thought that ladinoization (acculturation of Indians) constitutes a universalizing process in which the major differences between the dominant white minority and the Indian peasant masses will disappear. It is said that out of the traditional bipolar social structure a new, intermediate biological and cultural element is appearing—the Ladino, or Cholo, or mestizo, or mulatto, as the case may be—who bears the "essence of nationality" and who possesses all the virtues necessary for progress in Latin American countries.

The fallacy in this thesis is that biological and cultural mixing (a common process in many parts of Latin America) does not constitute, in itself, a change in the existing social structure.

National integration, as an objective process, and the birth of a national consciousness, as a subjective process, depend on structural factors (i.e., on the nature of the relations between men and between social groups) and not on the biological or cultural attributes of certain individuals. National integration (in the sense of full participation of all citizens in the same cultural values, and the relative equality of social and economic opportunities) will be achieved in the Indian areas not with the development of a new bio-cultural category, but with the disappearance of internal colonialism. In the internal colonies of our countries, the mestizos (or racially mixed population) are, in fact, representatives of the local and regional ruling class who help to maintain the Indian population in a state of oppression. They have not the slightest interest in true national integration. On the other hand, in the increasingly important urban centers, the immigrant rural population, often of Indian stock, is rapidly "integrated" from the national point of view; but this is due more to the positions which it occupies in the class structure than to the process of miscegenation.

Furthermore, the thesis of miscegenation very often hides a racist prejudice (which may be unconscious); in the countries where a majority of the population has Indian traits, biological miscegenation signifies "whitening," and in that sense citing the virtues of miscegenation really hides anti-Indian biases. The same prejudice is found in the cultural version of this theory— indeed, it means the disappearance of Indian culture. Thus, making miscegenation the prerequisite for national integration condemns the Indians of America, a group which numbers in the tens of millions, to a slow cultural agony.

The seventh thesis:
Progress in Latin America will only take place by means
of an alliance between the workers and the peasants, as a
result of the identity of interests of these two classes.

We cannot leave this discussion of Latin America without referring to a thesis which is quite prevalent among the orthodox left. Indeed, on the basis of theories developed by Lenin and Mao Tse-tung, it is said that the success of the democratic revolution in Latin America depends on the ability of the working and peasant classes to forge a common front against the reactionary bourgeoisie and against imperialism. In this regard, it would be well to consider the following facts:

A. One of the indisputable steps in all democratic revolutions is agrarian reform. But the acquisition of land by the peasantry through a noncollectivist agrarian reform transforms them into proprietors whose class interests are those of other landed proprietors.

B. The objective interests of the peasants and the workers are not identical in the matter of agrarian reform. An agrarian reform usually implies an initial diminution of food deliveries to the cities, the effects of which are first felt by the working class. It also means the channeling of public investments into the rural sectors, with a consequent disfavoring of the urban sector—which, as we have seen, is about the only sector that really benefits from economic development in a situation of internal colonialism.

C. The struggle of the urban working class (which is politically more powerful than the peasantry) for higher wages, more and better public social services, price controls, etc., finds no seconding in the peasant sector because benefits obtained by the working class in this way are usually obtained at the cost of agriculture—i.e., the peasants. In other words, the urban working class of our countries is also a beneficiary of internal colonialism. That is one of the reasons why a truly revolutionary labor movement does not exist in Latin America.

D. In nineteenth-century England the expulsion of peasants from the land and their migration to the industrial sweatshops signified a diminution of their standard of living; in Czarist Russia rural-urban mobility was strictly limited and the worker-peasant alliance was made in the field of battle; and in People's

China the same alliance was forged in the fight against the Japanese invaders. In sharp contrast to all of these examples, rural emigration is not only possible for the discontented of the countryside in Latin America, but in most cases it represents an improvement in economic and social conditions (even in the *favelas,* the *barriadas,* the *ranchos,* or the *colonias proletarias*— the shantytowns—of the Latin American cities), as compared with conditions in the countryside. One can theorize that the revolutionary consciousness of the peasants increases in *inverse* proportion to the possibility of their individual upward social mobility, and that this relationship would hold even more strongly if the latter also implies geographic mobility.

E. We may also suppose that the more severe the internal colonialism in Latin America (i.e., the greater the difference between the metropolis and its internal colonies), the further the possibilities of a true political alliance between workers and peasants will be reduced. The example of recent events in Brazil and Bolivia should illustrate this point.

* * * *

These seven theses do not include all the erroneous theories and concepts about the social structure of Latin America; but most of the others are related in one way or another to these, and are derived from them, and the reader will be able to recognize them when he next encounters them.

Internal Colonialism and
National Development

PABLO GONZÁLEZ-CASANOVA

POLITICAL FRONTIERS have directly or indirectly influenced the formulation and use of sociological categories. Certain categories have appeared and have been treated in relation to the internal problems of a nation or territory, and others in relation to international problems, without systematically fixing points of interconnection; that is, without sufficiently investigating up to what point the categories generally used to explain internal problems also serve to explain international problems and vice versa.

The idea of civilization has corresponded generally to an international or universal analysis of history, while the notion of dual or plural society has corresponded to internal analyses of underdeveloped nations or territories. The concept of classes and social strata has been applied to the internal study of societies without being related to the conflicts between nations. The concept of colonialism has been used, above all, as an international phenomenon which explains relations between different peoples and nations. Occasionally, extrapolations of categories have been made, as in speaking of "proletarian nations" or the "stratification of nations." The principal exception to the statement above is the notion of culture, which has been systematically applied to nations, regions, communities, and classes. These general circumstances have obscured or placed on a lesser level a certain type of phenomenon, which does not adjust its limits to "traditional" categories.[1]

1 Rupert Emerson, *From Empire to Nation: The Rise of Self-Assertion of Asian and African Peoples* (Cambridge, Mass.: Harvard University Press, 1960), p. 342.

The purpose of the present article is to focus upon the relatively interchangeable character of the notion of colonialism and of colonial structure, emphasizing colonialism as an internal phenomenon. Along with this, the purpose is to point out how colonialism functions as a phenomenon which is not only international but intranational. Its exegetical value for the problems of development might result in a growing appreciation of the common points between the new nations of Africa and Asia and the old "new nations" of America, where a dual society still exists and where there has been a process of development and of mobilization which has not yet been completed.

The notion of "internal colonialism" has its roots in the great independence movement of the old colonies. The experience of independence has customarily stimulated new notions about independence and development. With *political* independence the notion of an integral independence and of a neocolonialism slowly arises. With the creation of the nation-state as a motor of development and the disappearance of the "imperialistic ogre," there appears a need for technicians and professionals, for contractors and capital. With the disappearance of the direct domination of foreigners over natives, the notion of domination and exploitation of natives by natives emerges. In the political and historical literature of the nineteenth and twentieth centuries it can be observed how the Latin American countries absorbed these new experiences. The "pro-Indian" and liberal literature of the nineteenth century points to the substitution of the domination of Spaniards by that of the creoles. Interestingly, the exploitation of the Indians continues, having *the same characteristics* it had before independence.

This syndrome has been registered again with the present proliferation of new nations. Emerson notes that "the end of colonialism" by itself only eliminates problems that arise directly from foreign control. But the "oppression" of some sectors over others continues—an "oppression" felt by some sectors as more intolerable than the continuation of the colonial Government. Coleman points out that in the new nations "for special reasons bound to the rationalization of colonialism, this class—the military, the clergy, and the bureaucracy—supports the idea of the 'divine right' of the educated to govern; and its members have been affected by the bureaucratic-authoritative predispositions derived from the traditional society or the co-

120   ▓ THE SOCIOECONOMIC PIVOT

lonial experience."[2] Hoselitz observes that ". . . the upper
classes, including many government intellectuals, are prepared
to manipulate the unprotected masses in a way similar to that
used by the foreign masters whose rule they have broken."[3]
Dumont gathers the complaints of the Congo peasants ("Independence is not for us . . .") and of Cameroon peasants ("We
are headed for a worse colonialism of class . . ."), and he
himself says: "the rich behave like white colonials . . ."[4]
Fanon, in his renowed book *Les Damnés de la Terre* analyzes
the substitution of the foreign exploiters by native exploiters—
stressing above all the "struggle of classes."[5] C. Wright Mills, in
a seminar organized by the Latin American Center for Research
in the Social Sciences, observed with precision a few years ago:
"Given the uneven type of development that Professor Lambert
has so clearly outlined, the developed sections in the interior of
the underdeveloped world—in the capital and in the coast—are
a curious species of imperialistic power, which has, in its own
way, internal colonies."[6] It would be useless to continue quoting more authors. All serious students of the economic and
political problems of the new nations have registered these
facts.

Understanding the facts of internal colonialism remains sporadic. A deeper study of the problem invites a series of delimita-
tions searching for a structural definition which may serve as a
sociological explanation of development. The delimitation of
the phenomenon involves three problems. First, whether this
category is really different from others which the social sciences
presently use, and which analyze behavior in a similar way
through distinctions between town and country, "master" and

2 James S. Coleman, "The Political Systems of the Developing Areas,"
The Politics of the Developing Areas, ed. Gabriel A. Almond and James
S. Coleman (Princeton, N.J.: Princeton University Press, 1960), p. 548.
3 Bert F. Hoselitz, *Sociological Aspects of Economic Growth* (Glencoe,
Ill.: The Free Press, 1962), p. 148.
4 René Dumont, *L'Afrique Noire est mal partie* (Paris: Editions du
Seuil, 1962), pp. 7, 8, 221 ff.
5 Frantz Fanon, *Les Damnés da la Terre* (Paris: Maspero, 1961),
p. 111 ff.
6 C. Wright Mills, "The Problem of Industrial Development," *Power,
Politics and People,* ed. Irving L. Horowitz (New York: Oxford University Press, 1963), p. 154.

"servant," worker and manager in the first stage of capitalism; social classes and the establishment and solution of social conflicts; dual society or the social strata. Second, avoiding the use of this category in the processes of rationalization, justification, refutation, and irrational and emotional manipulation as occurs with all categories that refer to *conflicts* in the world and *tension* within the scientific literature. Third, locating the exegetical and practical value confronting other categories such as that of Weber's Protestant Ethic; Parsons' and Hoselitz' "ascription," "fulfillment," or "success"; McClelland's "achieving society"; Lerner's empathy"; and Lipset's "value orientation" as exhibited in his book on the United States as a new nation.

The question facing the acceptance of a new category for the study of development, such as internal colonialism, is clear: How does this category serve to explain the phenomenon of development from a sociological point of view, in its behavioral context? What kind of analytical value does it have? To what point will this category explain the same phenomenon already explained by other categories as the city and country, the social classes, the dual society, or the social strata? How can we prevent the use of this category in a vague, emotional, irrational, or aggressive way? Finally, what practical "operational significance,"[7] from the point of view of the politics of development, does this category have? To these questions should be added others about the behavior of the phenomenon and its explanatory value, throughout the "stages of development," and at different levels of social mobilization.

The fact that dominant groups and classes in new nations play similar roles to those played by the old colonials may be deplorable, but it is not of primary interest. What we seek is its potential as a sociological explanation of problems of underdeveloped societies. We will aproach the problem in two ways: one which allows the typification of colonialism as an integral phenomenon, changeable from an international to an internal category; and another which permits us to see how the phenomenon has occurred in a new nation which has reached the "takeoff stage," and which has already been through an era of

[7] John H. Adler, "Some Policy Problems in Economic Development," *Economic Development and Cultural Change,* IX, No. 2 (January, 1961).

agrarian reform, industrialization, construction of the infrastructure. Thus, we will treat the problem of internal colonialism in a nation as a stage of industrial process, whose experience may be politically typical and relevant to the "newcomers."

Originally the term *colony* was used to designate a territory
occupied by emigrants from a mother country. Thus Greek
colonies were settled by immigrants from Greece who went to
live in Roman territories such as North Africa. This classic
meaning of the term *colony* remained in use until the modern
era. By the nineteenth century a recurrent characteristic of
colonies attracted attention: the dominance exercised by immigrants over indigenous populations. By the middle of the last
century, Herman Merivale observed this change of meaning in
the term. Then *colony* was understood to mean, both in official
circles and in common language, possession of a territory in
which European emigrants dominated indigenous peoples.

Presently, in speaking about colonies or colonialism, allusion
is made above all to the domination of some people by others.
The term has come to have a violent connotation. It has become
a kind of accusation, and in certain circles even its use is taboo.
In the United Nations, "non-self-governing territories" are
spoken about, a term which contains a built-in self-definition.
According to Article 23 of the United Nations Charter, these
are "territories whose inhabitants have not yet attained total self-
government." In the United Nations different delegations have
tried to sharpen this definition. The delegation from the United
States made a contribution that may have a certain empirical
value. According to its observations, the term as used in the
Charter "seems applicable to any territory, administered by a
member of the United Nations, that does not enjoy self-government in the same measure as the metropolis."[8] The French
delegation pointed out three facts that should be considered in
defining a colony: "dependence in relation to a member state;
responsibility exercised by this state in the administration of the
territory; and the existence of a population that has not completely attained self-government." The Soviet delegation suggested that "territories without their own government are possessions, protectorates, or territories that do not participate in
the election of higher administrative bodies." India declared
that "territories that do not govern themselves can be defined

[8] *United Nations Document A/74,* October 21, 1946, pp. 5–6.

and included with all those territories in which the rights of inhabitants, their economic status and their social privileges are regulated by another State." Egypt pointed out that the determining factor "is the state of dependence of a nation with respect to another with which it has no natural bonds. In this respect all extrametropolitan territories, whose population, language, race, and culture are different from those of the people they are dominated by, should be considered as territories lacking self-government."[9]

If we take these observations about the colonial phenomenon in elaborating a concrete political definition, we observe that a colony is: (1) A territory without self-government. (2) It is in an unequal position with respect to the metropolis where inhabitants do govern themselves. (3) The administration and responsibility for administration is a concern of the state which dominates it. (4) Its inhabitants do not participate in elections of higher administrative bodies, i.e., rulers are assigned by the dominating country. (5) The rights of its inhabitants, their economic situation, and their social privileges are regulated by another state. (6) This position does not correspond to natural bonds—but rather to artificial models which are the product of conquest or of international concession. (7) Colonial inhabitants belong to a race and culture different from that of the dominating people. Customarily they also speak a different language.

These characteristics, with the exception of the last, are in effect *produced* in any colony. The last one is *found* to be so, not always, but in the majority of instances. As exceptions, we could note the colonies which formed the United States, Argentina, Canada, or Australia. Yet even in these cases the colonists lived near native populations who had racial and cultural differences from their own. These natives were, in the main, not employed in the work of the colony, and they were often exterminated or dislodged from their territories. And if American colonialists did not use the natives in the colony's work, the importation of Negroes and of the Negro culture produced effects similar to the relations characteristic of colonial life elsewhere.

However, these illustrations are not sufficient to explain the nature of a colony. On one hand, we are dealing with a

[9] Emil J. Sady, *The United Nations and Dependent Peoples* (Washington, D.C.: The Brookings Institution, 1957), pp. 78–79.

formalistic juridical-political definition, whose attributes may be absent even without the colonial situation disappearing; and without permitting the statistical treatment of a true variable which moves from a *colonial structure* to an *independent structure.* On the other hand, a formal definition omits mention of the immediate and more general function which the domination of some peoples over others fulfills, and the form in which this domination takes place. "The object of colonies," Montesquieu wrote more than two hundred years ago, "is to carry on commerce in better conditions than can be found with the neighboring peoples with whom the advantages are reciprocal. It has been affirmed," he added, "that only the metropolis can negotiate with the colony and this for a good reason, because the object of the colonial establishment has been the extension of commerce and not the foundation of a city or a new empire."[10]

To this immediate and more general function of the colonial phenomenon are added others of a cultural, political, and military type, which have a longer-lasting effect and functions that deviate from the general one. International development occurs within the colonial structure: the expansion of "civilization," social and technical progress, the westernization of the world, evangelization and proselytization, the diffusion of liberal and socialist ideas. It occurs in a framework of uneven relations between developed and underdeveloped countries. The motives of colonization are not only economic, but military, political, and spiritual. But the economic and commercial functions of colonies are immediate and general. They mark a recurrent pattern in the colonial process.

Montesquieu spoke of these functions when he sided with those who affirmed that "only the metropolis can negotiate with the colony." From his viewpoint it was natural that the metropolis should monopolize the colony's commerce, and prevent any commercial competition unfavorable to the urban center. Merivale said it with even greater clarity: "To adjust our economic notions about the profits of a particular country, the profits in question must be something exclusive and monopolized."[11] This important concept is not only useful in analyzing

[10] Montesquieu, *L'Esprit des lois,* Chapter XXI, 1748.
[11] Herman Merivale, *Lectures on Colonization and Colonies: Delivered Before the University of Oxford in 1840 and 1841* (London, 1861), p. 188.

typical colonies (those territories that are completely colonial and dependent on an empire), but also in studying the degree of dependence and independence from colonial status.

Every time there is a colony, there exists, in effect, a condition of monopoly in exploiting natural resources, work, the import-export trade, and fiscal revenues. This is not a tautological affirmation. The dominant country monopolizes the colony, and prevents other countries from exploiting its natural and human resources. This monopolization is extended to mass culture and to the sources of information. The colony thus becomes isolated from other nations. All contact with the outside and with other cultures is funneled through the colonial power. When colonial dominion grows stronger, it is because it extends its economic and cultural monopoly. The colonialist policy consists precisely in reinforcing the economic and cultural monopoly through military, political, and administrative domination. In these conditions one can approach the study of colonialism and dependence through the monopoly exercised by one country over another. As this monopoly becomes accentuated, colonization is accentuated. This monopoly permits the extensive exploitation of the resources of the colony: buying and selling through institutionalized conditions of inequality. At the same time, this deprives other empires from gaining access to the benefits of this type of unequal relationship, while depriving the native population of the tools of negotiation, of their natural riches, and in great measure, of the fruits of their labor.

The monopoly isolates the colony from other empires and other countries, and in particular from other colonies. This is characteristic of various phenomena in present-day colonial society, some of which have been pointed out by Myrdal.[12]

(1) The colony acquires characteristics of a complementary economy to the empire. It accommodates itself to the economy of the metropolis. The exploitation of natural resources is a function of the demand by the metropolis which seeks to integrate colonies into the empire's economy. This gives rise to a distorted development of colonial sectors and regions, a development which is reflected in the means of communication, in the irregular birth and growth of cities, etc. Colonialism

---

[12] Cf. Gunnar Myrdal, *Teoría económica y regiones subdesarrolladas* (México: Fondo de Cultura Económica, 1959), pp. 69 ff.

foments a process of *change* other than of development.[13] The
lack of economic integration in the interior of the colony, the
lack of communication between zones of the colony and neighboring colonies corresponds to a lack of general cultural integration.

(2) The colony acquires other characteristics of dependency
which facilitate colonial treatment. In international commerce
the colony not only depends upon a single metropolitan market
but also on a predominant sector—mineral or agricultural—and
on a predominant product—gold or silver, cotton, sugar, copper, or tin. Thus the colony arises in a handicapped context
which in turn is a consequence of dependence on a single
market, a single sector, or a predominant or single product.
This increases the power of the metropolis and its possibilities
to negotiate from a position of strength with the colony, preventing competition from other empires, and preventing the
colony from competing with the mother country. The capacity
of the colony for negotiation is thus minimal. Monopoly adapts
itself to different types of colonies and colonial systems; in
some, fiscal monopoly predominates, in others the monopoly of
natural resource exploitations, still in others, the monopoly of
foreign trade.

(3) The colony is also used as a monopoly for the exploitation of cheap labor. The concessions of land, water, mines, and
commercial licenses for establishing new enterprises are granted
only to the inhabitants of the metropolis, to their descendants,
or to a few natives whose alliance is eventually solicited.

(4) The standards of life in the colonies are different from
those in the metropolis. The workers—slaves, serfs, peons,
laborers—receive the minimum necessary for subsistence and
often less.

(5) Repressive systems predominate in the solution of class
conflicts; these are longer lasting and more violent than in the
metropolis.

(6) The entire system tends to increase the international
inequality, and the economic, political, and cultural inequalities
between metropolis and colony.[14] It also increases internal

[13] François Perroux, *L'Economie du XXe siècle* (Paris: Presses Uni-
versitaires de France, 1961), pp. 195, 408, 557.
[14] This is the direct or immediate effect. Indirectly and in the longer
run, the colonial growth, as Marx recognized, "dissolved the semi-bar-
baric communities, the semi-civilized communities, breaking their eco-

racial inequalities of caste, of exemptions; religious, rural, urban, and class inequalities. This inequality is particularly important for the comprehension of the colonial society and is closely tied to the dynamics of dual or plural societies.

The existence of dual societies coincides and is interwoven with the existence of colonialism—even though we should distinguish between "immigrant colonies" and "agrarian colonies" on one hand, and "exploitation colonies" on the other. The former have tended to be homogeneous societies, which "have moved in the direction of equality with respect to the Mother Country, in finances as well as in industrial equipment, and towards a political independence, formal or potential."[15] But at the same time, the position of dependence, typically colonial, is accentuated in the "exploitation" colonies and in the plantations revealing heterogeneous cultures. "The colonial society as a general rule consists of a series of groups more or less conscious of themselves, often separated amongst themselves for reasons of colour, and who try to live their separate lives within a single political frame. *In sum, colonial societies tend to be plural societies.*"[16]

In reality it is difficult to ascertain whether inequality in technical development has more influence over the formation of the colonial system than the colonial system itself has on uneven development. It is true that dual or plural societies occur through the contact of two civilizations, one technically more advanced than the other.[17] It is also true that the dual or plural society occurs through colonial development. It characterizes the colonial growth. The ideology of the "highly endowed European" versus the "semilogical Indian" disguises the way in which the latter is exploited by the former, and the way in which their economic relations are reinforced through discriminatory procedures. The colonial structure is tightly bound

---

nomic basis . . . provoking a great social revolution." See Karl Marx, "British Rule in India," *On Colonialism* (Moscow: Foreign Languages Publishing House), p. 36. I would add that this process of international acculturation leads to opposition to colonialism itself.

[15] Celso Furtado, *The Economic Growth of Brazil* (Berkeley and Los Angeles: University of California Press, 1963).

[16] E. C. Walter, *Colonies* (Cambridge and London: Cambridge University Press, 1944), p. 72.

[17] Cf. Jacques Lambert, *Os dois Brasils* (Rio de Janeiro: Ministerio da Educação e Cultura, 1959).

# #

47474747### ### al### ch# ## ####

to the plural society, to uneven development, and to combined forms of exploitation, simultaneous rather than successive as in the classic European models of development. In effect, in the colonies the slave and feudal relations are combined and coexist with capitalist and state-owned enterprises. Heterogeneity—technical, institutional, and cultural—coincides with a structure in which the relations of domination and exploitation are relations between heterogeneous and culturally different groups.

This characteristic of internal colonial life has psychological and political implications which can be determined only within their natural framework. Racism and racial discrimination are the historical legacy of the conquest of some peoples by others —from antiquity to the expansion of the great empires and colonial systems of the modern era. Hobson, thinking in terms of superior and inferior races, noted that "always when superior races establish themselves in territories where inferior races can be profitably used for manual work and agriculture, for mining and domestic work, the latter do not tend to die off but rather come to constitute a servile class."[18] Racism appears in all the colonies where two cultures are found, in Hispanic America, in the Near and Far East, in Africa. It is the official dogma of English colonization. It corresponds to the color barrier that the Japanese set in the Asian countries they dominated during World War II, despite their famous slogan of "Asia for the Asians." Racism and racial segregation are essential in the colonial exploitation of some peoples by others. They influence all configurations of development in colonial cultures. They are a brake in the processes of acculturation. In the interchange and transmission of advanced techniques to the dominated population, in the occupational mobility of native workers who tend to remain in unskilled jobs, in the political and administrative mobility of the native people, racism and discrimination correlate with the political psychology of colonialism.

Colonial psychology and colonial behavior have been little studied. We do not have a rigorous and empirical study on the "colonial personality," as necessary and useful as this would be. The authors who have dealt with this problem have often done so in an accusative form. Readers participate emotionally, accepting or rejecting the accusations. Something similar occurs in studies of the colonized, their psychology and personality.

[18] John A. Hobson, *Imperialism: A Study* (London: George Allen and Unwin Ltd., 1948), p. 253.

The small book by Memni,[19] with its very acute observations, and the clinical cases that Fanon registered in his work as a psychiatrist[20] are among the best of a large quantity of political denunciations made by travelers, historians, and ideologists. Clearly, within this situation two of the most characteristic problems of the colonialist personality consist in a complicated welter of attitudes ascribing the treatment of individuals according to the place they occupy in the social scale. A complicated etiquette exists in colonial society which fixes the terms in which one should and must address oneself to different social groups, "the degree of courtesy or rudeness acceptable," the types of "humiliations that are natural."[21] Memni adds that "a group of conducts, of learned reflexes, exercised from very early infancy, underlies colonial racism. This has so spontaneously been incorporated into the gestures, even to the most banal words, that it constitutes one of the most solid structures of the colonialist personality."[22] To these complicated forms of humiliation and courtesy typical of *ascription* in the traditional society is added the *dehumanization* of the colonized. His being perceived as a thing finds an appropriate parallel in the studies of Nazi psychology.

This phenomenon gives place to processes of manipulation, sadism, and aggression so often found in the accusations against colonial treatment. "What serious sense of duty is felt when facing an animal or a thing? This is what the colonized is made increasingly to resemble. Because of this the colonizer can adopt a double standard for judging himself as a superior being to the colonized. For him, the colonized driving an automobile is a spectacle to which he cannot become accustomed. The colonialist denies the colonized all normal character. He sees him as a monkey-like pantomime. An accident, even a grave one, which affects the colonized almost makes him laugh. The machine-gunning of a colonized multitude may bring an indifferent shrug. For the rest, the weeping of a native mother who cries over the loss of her son or husband only vaguely

[19] Cf. Albert Memni, *Portrait du colonisé précédé du portrait du colonisateur* (Paris: Correa, 1957).

[20] Fanon, *op. cit.*, appendix.

[21] K. N. Panikkar, *L'Asie et la domination occidentale du XVᵉ siècle à nos jours* (Paris: Eds. du Seuil, 1956), p. 145.

[22] Memni, *op. cit.*, p. 114.

reminds the colonialist of the sorrow of a mother or a wife."[23]

This psychology, with complicated rules of treatment, with prejudices, and perceptions of the colonized man as a thing, is linked to the internal policy of the colonial society, to a policy of manipulation and discrimination which appears in the juridical, educational, linguistic, and administrative order which tends to sanction and increase the social dichotomies and the relation of domination and exploitation characteristic of colonies. On this point, the historical juridical literature is sufficient, and requires neither restatement nor summarization.

But if these are the typical characteristics of colonialism, the problem now lies in knowing to what degree they are found in what we have called "internal colonialism" and to what degree the phenomenon of internal colonialism does actually exist.

It is well known that upon reaching independence, the old colonies' international and internal structure does not suddenly change. The international social structure continues in great part along the same path and continues a policy of "decolonization." This has been observed both by the rulers of the new nations and by the European investigators. In the internal domain, approximately the same thing happens, although the problem has not received emphasis other than occasional observations.

The new nations preserve, above all, the dichotomous character and contradictory types of relations similar to those found in colonial society. The problem consists in investigating up to what point the characteristics, attributes, and variables typical of colonialism and colonial society are found in the new nations and their social structure, their position at a given moment, and their dynamics and their behavior throughout the different stages of development. What value might this investigation have? Here we must attempt to answer some of the questions formulated earlier. Up to what point is this category of internal colonialism different from others used by the social sciences? To what extent can it be studied in a systematic and precise way? And what exegenic value can it have in a sociological analysis of development?

Internal colonialism corresponds to a structure of social relations based on domination and exploitation among culturally heterogeneous, distinct groups. If it has a specific differ-

[23] *Ibid.*

ence with respect to other relations based on superordination, it inheres in the culture heterogeneity which the conquest of some peoples by others historically produces. It is such conquests which permit us to talk not only about cultural differences (which exist between urban and rural populations and between social classes) but also about differences between civilizations.

The colonial structure resembles relations of domination and exploitation typical of the rural-urban structure of traditional society and of underdeveloped countries,[24] insofar as a population integrated by several social classes (urban or colonial) dominates and exploits a population integrated by different classes (rural or colonized). This process resembles foreign colonialism because cultural differences between the city and country are acute. However, internal colonialism stands apart because cultural heterogeneity is historically different. It is the result of an encounter between two races, cultures, or civilizations, whose genesis and evolution occurred without any mutual contact up to one specific moment. The conquest or the concession is a fact which makes possible intensive racial and cultural discriminations, thus accentuating the *ascriptive* character of colonial society.

On the other hand, the colonial structure resembles the relations of domination and exploitation typical of the English factory proprietors and the foremen at the beginning of the nineteenth century, who did not hesitate in using the whip on the shoulders of children when they did not work or fell asleep. As Hoselitz points out, they operated in conditions similar to those of the foreign colonists and natives of the underdeveloped countries: "abundance of labor, masses of people who had to adjust to the discipline and regularity of the industrial society, in which the manipulation, without brakes and often inhuman, offered ample profits in production, money, and social power."[25] The colonial structure and internal colonialism are distinguished from the class structure since colonialism is not only a relation of exploitation of the workers by the owners of raw materials or of production and their collaborators, but also a relation of domination and exploitation of a total population (with its distinct classes, proprietors, workers)

[24] John H. Kautsky, *Political Change in Underdeveloped Countries* (New York: John Wiley & Sons, 1962), pp. 15, 17; Hoselitz, *op. cit.*, pp. 162 and 195–96.
[25] Hoselitz, *op. cit.*, pp. 194–98.

by another population which also has distinct classes (proprietors and workers). Internal colonialism reveals many differences with the structure of classes, and sufficient differences
with the city-country structure to be used as an analytical
instrument. Its exegetic function will help make these differences clear.

Being a category which takes up phenomena of *conflict* and
exploitation, internal colonialism, as other similar categories,
merits an analytical and objective study if we want to increase
our understanding of essential problems in underdeveloped
societies and derive from its precise knowledge an operational
and exegenic wealth. To that aim we can undertake studies
similar to Shannon's[26] (when measuring with different instruments, the capacity of nations to be independent) or, like
Deutsch[27] (when he measures the mobilization of the marginal population in the processes of development) making an
inventory of the basic tendencies and patterns of internal colonialism.[28]

The appendix to this study includes a table with the different
attributes and variables we have registered of anthropological
findings on the Indians' position in Mexico. Many of these
variables do not present analytical problems. Some of them
correspond to indicators which are objectives of the national
and international statistical register. The measurement of monopoly and dependence, of agrarian and fiscal discrimination,
official credits, public investment or salaries in terms of the low
living standards of the Indian population—or the "para-colo-
nized" population—might present minor problems.[29]

[26] L. W. Shannon, "Is Level of Development Related to Capacity for
Self Government?", *The American Journal of Economics and Sociology,*
July 17, 1958, No. 4, pp. 367–82.
[27] Karl W. Deutsch, "Social Mobilization and Political Development,"
The American Political Science Review, September, 1961, LV, No. 3,
pp. 493 ff.
[28] Karl W. Deutsch, "Toward an Inventory of Basic Trends and Patterns," *Comparative and International Politics,* March, 1960, XIV, No. 1,
pp. 39–57.
[29] In some cases, official statistics are available. We tried to find in the
case of Mexico correlations by Indian–non-Indian regions, without
finding significant coefficients, probably because the population which
does not speak only Indian tongues, in the proximities of the Indian
communities, has conditions of life similar to these. We are now trying to
obtain census cards for a stricter analysis of the relation between the
prevalence of Indian dialect and life styles.

This is not the case with many other characteristics. Direct work is necessary in any investigation based on categories which cover phenomena of conflict and exploitation. Perhaps Myrdal's classic work, *An American Dilemma,* and the abundant use he makes of the techniques of historical and documentary evidence combined with field-work techniques might be suitable in this type of study. The obstacles are not insurmountable, although they are formidable.

The practical and political value of internal colonialism throughout the different stages of social development and social mobilization is clearly perceived when this phenomenon's characteristics are placed within a concrete setting. Mexican social structure might be usefully examined in this context.

Mexico is a country which obtained its political independence 150 years ago. It has distributed 48 million hectares of arable land to 2½ million peasants, ending the old latifundist system. Its rural population was less than 50 percent in 1960 (the rural-urban limit being 2,500 inhabitants). In this same year, only 53 percent of the labor force was in agriculture, and the rest in secondary or tertiary industrial activities. The rate of integrating the population into the national development process is very high.[30] With the triumph of the great liberal and progressive movements, from independence to the social revolution of 1910, the *official* and *national* symbols of this "mestizo" country are the Indians: Cuahtemoc, who fought against the Spanish conquerors, and Juárez, who as a child spoke only Mixtec, an Indian dialect, and who was a full-blooded Indian. In schools and in secular society generally Indians are objects of veneration. The cementing, symbolic value they have corresponds to a mestizo society, without racial prejudices in the national orbit or in the national ideology. The Indian problem of Mexico is seen—in governmental and intellectual circles—as a cultural rather than a racial problem. It is linked to the ideology of the Revolution. Politicians attribute to the Indian innumerable positive values, pride of a progressive nativist policy.

However, the Indian problem subsists: the number of inhabitants five years of age or over who do not speak Spanish, but only an Indian dialect or language, was more than one million

[30] Pablo González-Casanova, "Sociedad plural y desarrollo: el caso de México," *América Latina,* V, No. 4 (October-December, 1962), pp. 31–61.

in 1960—that is, 3.8 percent of the national population over five years of age. The number of inhabitants who speak an Indian language or dialect and garble some Spanish was almost two million in 1960. This constitutes 6.4 percent of the population. From a linguistic point of view, the Indian problem covers more than 10 percent of the population. If indicators other than language are used in defining the Indian—work techniques, institutions—the number of Indians "grows to about 20 or 25 percent," that is, they comprise more or less seven million inhabitants.

The condition of these inhabitants, particularly the least acculturated among them, exhibits many characteristics typical of internal colonialism. These occur despite the period of national independence, the revolution period, the agrarian reform, sustained development and industrialization, civic pride, or even the cultivation of a folk ideology.

The forms internal colonialism takes are the following, as registered by anthropologists in repetitive though unsystematic ways:

(a) The "dominant center" or "metropolis" (in Mexico, the cities of San Cristóbal, Tlaxiaco, Huauchinango, Sochiapan, Mitla, Ojitian, Zacapoaxtla, etc.). It exercises a monopoly over Indian commerce and credit. The interchange is plainly unfavorable to the Indian communities. It takes the shape of a permanent decapitalization of these communities to the lowest levels. Isolation of the Indian communities with respect to any other center or market is visible. Monoculture, deformation, and dependence of the Indian economy, each coincides with commercial monopoly.

(b) An exploitation of the Indian population by the different social classes of the Ladino population exists. "Tlaxiaco," says an anthropologist, referring to an urban center, "presents heterogeneous forms of social stratification. Its social composition has a pronounced effect on the division of classes. But the characteristic of these social classes is the fact that they rest on the exploitation of the Indian as a worker or producer."[31] The exploitation is combined—a mixture of feudalism, slavery, capitalism, forced and salaried work, partnerships, peonage, and gratuitous "free" domestic services.

The plundering of the Indian communities fulfills two func-

31 Alejandro D. Marroquín, "Economía de las zonas indígenas," pp. 37–38.

tions as during the colonial era: it deprives Indians of their land, and it converts them into peons or paid workers. The exploitation of one population by another corresponds to differential salaries for equal work. Such is the case with the exploitation of Indian artisans by the Ladino population (wool, textile, palm, wicker, ceramics). It extends from linguistic discrimination ("I was a worm until I learned Spanish") to discrimination in modes of dress, until higher juridical, political, and trade union discrimination is realized. This coincides with colonial attitudes of local and federal functionaries, and of Ladino political leaders. Finally, this situation corresponds to differences of culture and life style which can be registered according to the type of population: Indian or Ladino.

The following are observed facts: amongst Indian communities a subsistence economy is predominant. Monetary and capitalization levels are minimum. Land is in advanced stages of decay and of low quality (when it can be used at all) for agriculture. Agriculture and cattle-raising processes are deficient; seeds are of poor quality; animals are often diseased and smaller than others of their kind. Techniques of cultivation are backward—pre-Hispanic or colonial—(hoe, ax, windlass). Levels of productivity are low. Life standards are lower than in non-Indian regions (more insalubrity, mortality, infant mortality, and illiteracy). There is an aggravated lack of essential services (schools, hospitals, water, electricity). Prostitution and alcoholism are fomented by procurers and Ladinos. There is aggression of rich communities against poor ones (real and symbolic). The culture is magico-religious. Economic manipulation is based on a prestige economy, while political manipulation (oppression, collective vote) is widely practiced. These characteristics correspond to typical colonial stereotypes in which Indians are considered as "unreasonable people," "lazy, good for nothing," and in which the violation of rules of courtesy, language, dress, tone of voice on the part of the Indians often provokes violent verbal and physical abuse from the Ladinos.

National development and mobilization, the increase of communications, and the size of the market have provided an outlet for the more aggressive members of these Indians communities. As soon as they dress like mestizos, speak Spanish, participate in the national culture, the situation of the Indian corresponds to the different strata they occupy in the society. At the national level the problem is certainly not a racial one. There are two problems that do have national importance. First, the federal government itself maintains a discriminatory policy, consciously or unconsciously. Agrarian reform has much less importance in the Indian regions. The fiscal charge is proportionally higher for these regions, while credits and investments are proportionally lower.[32] Second, if the above characteristics, typical of internal colonialism, are found integrally in a population that comprises only 10 percent of the total—at the crossroads of Ladino and Indian Mexico—this fact has a natural interaction with the national society as a whole, in which there is a continuum of colonialism—from the society which integrally exhibits all colonial characteristics to those regions and groups in which only residues of paracolonialist manipulatory forms remain.

Restricting ourselves to the case of Mexico, we see that internal colonialism has various operational functions whose tendencies and deviation deserve analysis as a viable hypothesis in like situations.

(1) In dual-economy societies, internal forms of colonialism remain after political independence and social changes occur.

(2) Internal colonialism as a *continuum* of the social structure of the new nations limits social mobilization and maximum participation in the development process. This can constitute an obstacle to the negotiated solution of conflicts in the institutional and rational forms of what Dahrendorf calls "post-capitalist" society. Colonialist stereotypes, the perception of the native as a thing and his manipulation, can be found in the colonialist continuum and might explain some of the resistance to the democratic evolution of these societies.[33]

(3) In part, colonialism explains the uneven development of underdeveloped countries. The laws of the market and the scarce political participation and organization in subdeveloped zones simultaneously serve to maintain a "dynamic of inequality" and prevent the processes of egalitarianism characteristic of development from emerging.[34]

[32] Pablo González-Casanova, "México: El ciclo de una revolución agraria," *Cuadernos Americanos* (January-February, 1962), pp. 7–29.

[33] Pablo González-Casanova, *La democracia en México: estructura política y desarrollo económico* (Mexico, Editorial Era, 1965).

[34] Pablo González-Casanova, "México; desarrollo, subdesarrollo," *Desarrollo Económico*, III, Nos. 1–2, April-September, Buenos Aires, Argentina.

(4) The practical and political value of "internal colonialism" is perhaps distinguished from like categories in that these others provide a psychologistic and value-oriented analysis, useful for the design of policies of communication, propaganda, and education. It must be noted that *internal colonialism* is above all structural. It is bound to the policy of the national government (of national integration, internal communication, and expansion of the national market). It has a political and economic value in accelerating these processes and in conceiving specific instruments—economic, political, and educational —which will deliberately accelerate the processes of decolonization, not only externally but internally. Then, the processes of development may be enhanced by this increased understanding of the mechanisms of colonialism.

APPENDIX

The Forms of Internal Colonialism

(A) Monopoly and Dependence

1. The "dominant center" or metropolis and the isolation of the native community (areas of difficult access, lack of means of communication, cultural isolation).

2. Monopoly of commerce and trade by the "dominant center" (relations of unfavorable interchange for the native community, speculation, acquisition of premature harvests, hoarding of merchandise).

3. Monopoly of credit (usury, control of native production).

4. Monoculture, population economically active, dedicated to agriculture and secondary production.

5. Deformation and dependence of the native economy.

6. Decapitalization.

7. Migration, exodus, and mobility of the natives.

8. Reinforcement of the dependence (juridical, political, military, and economic measures).

(B) Relations of Production and Social Control

1. Joint exploitation of the Indian population by the different social classes of the Ladino population.

2. Combined exploitation (slavery, feudal, capitalist, partnerships, peonage, free services).

3. Plunder of communal and private lands, creation of wage earners.

4. Salaried work (differential salaries: mines, mills, coffee plantations).

5. Exploitation of the artisan (wool, textile, palm, wicker, ceramics).

6. Social discrimination (humiliation and oppression).

7. Linguistic discrimination.

8. Juridical discrimination (utilization of the law against the Indian; abuse of his ignorance of the law).

9. Political discrimination (colonialist attitudes of local and federal functionaries, lack of political control by the natives in own municipalities).

10. Discrimination in union-hiring policies.

11. Agrarian discrimination.

12. Fiscal discrimination (taxes and excises).

13. Discrimination in public trade.

14. Discrimination in official credit.

15. Other forms of discrimination (barter, measurements, weights).

16. Process of displacement of the Indian by the Ladino (as governor, proprietor, merchant).

17. Policy reinforcing the combined systems of exploitation.

(C) *Culture and Living Standards*

1. Subsistence economy, minimum monetary level, minimum capitalization.

2. Land of accentuated poverty or low quality (when available), improper for agriculture (in sierras) or of good quality (isolated).

3. Deficient agriculture and cattle-raising.

4. Backward techniques of exploitation (pre-Hispanic or colonial).

5. Low level of productivity.

6. Standards of living lower than the Ladinos' (health, mortality, infant mortality, illiteracy).

7. Lack of services (schools, hospitals, water, electricity).

8. Magico-religious culture and economic manipulation (prestige economy) and political manipulation (collective vote).

9. High incidence of alcoholism and prostitution.
10. Aggressiveness of some communities against others (real and symbolic).
11. Routine, traditionalism, conformity.
12. Political reinforcement of traditionalism (technical and ideological) of conformity, and of aggression of some communities against others.

General Sources:

Julio de la Fuente: "Indian population" (unpublished); Alejandro Marroquín: "Problemas económicos de las zonas indígenas" (unpublished); Alejandro Marroquín: "Problemas económicos de las comunidades indígenas de México" (course program, mimeographed), México, 1960; M. O. de Mendizábal: "Los problemas indígenas y su más urgente tratamiento," *Obras Completas, IV,* México, 1946; M. T. de la Pena: "Panorama de la economía indígena de México" (Primer Congreso Indigenista Interamericano, Pátzcuaro, 1946); Jorge A. Vivo: "Aspectos económicos fundamentales del problema indígena" (*Rev. América Indígena,* III, No. 1, January, 1947); Manuel Gamio: "Consideraciones sobre el problema indígena"; L. Loyo: "Estudio sobre la distribución de los grupos indígenas de México" (Primer Congreso Indigenista Interamericano, Pátzcuaro, 1946); L. Aguirre Beltrán: "Instituciones indígenas en el México actual . . ."; Alfonso Caso: 'Definición del indio y de lo indio," *Indigenismo* (Instituto Nacional Indigenista, Mexico), 1958.

Electoral Politics, Urbanization,

and Social Development

in Latin America

IRVING LOUIS HOROWITZ

ELECTORAL politics is the implementation of major decisions by noncoercive means. The two most important facts to recognize about the enormous land mass stretching from the Río Bravo to Tierra del Fuego are the degree to which such political power is concentrated in the big cities of the coastal regions or high plains, and the concentration of this power among economic classes integral to the upper social stratum. Electoral politics is restricted to specific types of positions and professions linked to the money economy. The polarization of political life into electoral and pressure groups is central to an understanding of Latin American political culture. The faith in electoral politics, in its turn, is fused to the universalistic and achievement values found in urban life.[1]

The following remarks are acknowledged to be tentative. Indeed, given the state of data reliability on Latin America, it is hard for anyone to speak in any but a cautious way.[2] There are,

[1] See Seymour M. Lipset, "Some Social Requisites of Democracy, Economic Development and Political Legitimacy," in *American Political Science Review*, LIII, No. I (March, 1959), pp. 69–105.

[2] Any such exploration as this comes up against problems of data reliability, data comparability, and the simple fact that the measures we now have are often of a crude sort, and hence unsuitable for specialized cross-cultural or comparative international purposes. For an excellent

nonetheless, enough pieces of information—of an ethnographic as well as an economic nature—to posit a set of hypotheses which at least warrant further investigation.

The division between urban and rural dwellers is more pointedly a rift between "classes" who inhabit the cities and "masses" of disenfranchised peasants and rural laborers who live in the countryside.

The power structures of Latin American countries are typically oligarchical. In his work on Brazilian careers and social structure, Anthony Leeds,[3] elaborating upon the model developed by A. S. Teixeira,[4] has pointed out that the Brazilian power structure (with reference to political pressure groups) shapes up as a cupola in which classes alone engage in politics. The masses are simply not included by these classes in basic calculations concerning the distribution of power and wealth. Hence the advanced cities rise on a precarious and asynchronous social structure. Enveloping this is a combination of fixed bureaucracy and the Church.[5] The power structure itself is divided in relatively even proportions: coffee interests, military and civil servants, social security personnel, railway and port workers, maritime personnel, highway and road builders, heavy and light industrial interests, and bank workers. Even though such an equilibrium model does not account for the circulation of elites, it does help to illustrate the continued gap between class and mass; and of equal weight, the instability of elite sectors.

Without too much effort a parallel design can be worked out

summary of present needs and dilemmas, see Roger Messy and Hans Pederson, "Statistics for Economic Development with Special Reference to National Accounts and Related Tables," in Werner Baer and Isaac Kerstenetzky (eds.), *Inflation and Growth in Latin America* (Homewood, Ill.: Richard D. Irwin Co., 1964), pp. 112–42.

[3] Anthony Leeds, "Brazilian Careers and Social Structure: A Case History and Model," in Dwight B. Heath and Richard N. Adams (eds.), *Contemporary Cultures and Societies of Latin America* (New York: Random House, 1965).

[4] Anisio S. Teixeira, *Educação não e privilegio* (Rio de Janeiro: Jose Olympio, 1952).

[5] That this model with respect to the Church at least requires serious modification in the light of recent events is made clear by David Mutchler, "Roman Catholicism in Brazil," in *Studies in Comparative International Development*, I, No. 8 (1965), pp. 103–117.

for Mexico, which shares with Brazil the distinction of rapid urbanization combined with an enormous agricultural sector. In many instances, they both exhibit a higher rate of urbanization, which may be considered the *style* of modernization, than of industrialization, which may be considered the *substance* of modernization. Of particular importance in the Mexican case is the politicalization of the bureaucracy, which is not set up to accommodate the majority of mass groups. Despite differences in formal parliamentary arrangements, Mexico and Brazil are both politically inelastic systems. Undue growth of any one interest sector causes profound and immediate disequilibrium in the precariously built edifice. In both countries there is incessant political maneuvering to modify and even stifle regional development at the expense of prescribed nuclear centers.

Given the nature of competing and conflicting elements within a modern class system, added to continuing traditional factionalisms, democratic falangism, in which the national state becomes the exclusive lever of growth, itself beomes a source of instability. This is the case even for the more highly developed Latin American societies. In Mexico not simply the state but the Central Executive Committee of the ruling party (PRI) harnesses nearly all forms of national authority,[6] while in Brazil the creation of a ruling party (ARENA) has had the same effect—*sans* the benevolence of the Mexican system.

Summarizing a mass of data, Pablo González-Casanova has recently shown that even in a nation such as Mexico, where economic growth rates and political stability indices are quite high, the urban-rural dichotomy with respect to electoral politics remains fully intact. Because of their significance, his findings are worth quoting at length:

(a) The agricultural population, and particularly the rural working class that is far poorer than the economically active population as a whole, is that which has a lesser proportion of members who belong to worker organizations. (b) The political parties, which in all parts of the world are predominantly urban organizations, in Mexico, as far as can be determined, do not have either the characteristics or the dimensions of citizen orga-

6 See Robert E. Scott, *The Mexican Government in Transition* (Urbana: University of Illinois Press, 1959). For a verification of single-party domination, see William V. D'Antonio and Richard Suter, *Primary Elections in a Mexican Municipio; New Trends in Mexico's Struggle Toward Democracy* (mimeographed, 1965).

nizations in highly developed countries. The citizens, and particularly those who live in the countryside, are marginal to the parties—passive instruments of its leadership. (c) The rural population, that is to say, the poorest, are those who vote least; it is the general tendency of this sector to be most marginal to the voting process. (d) The illiterate population is connected with the lowest voting percentages. (e) The rural population that does not vote displays the least opposition (to the official party in power) of any group. (f) The poorest States are those where the least electoral opposition is registered.[7]

The prima facie situation is clear: the gap between the political and the apolitical at the same time represents and symbolizes the rupture between urban and rural life.

The actual degree of the urban class versus rural mass schism would seem mitigated by the fact that the landed aristocracy forms an essential *class* ingredient in the power structure of Brazil. In fact, however, the landed aristocracy has changed its function—from a feudal aristocracy tied to local interests to a supplier of primary goods for national and international markets. It has also exchanged its characteristic, traditionalist *Gemeinschaft* orientation for a highly refined, modernist *Gesellschaft* outlook.[8] Directly put, the source of traditional *wealth* may still be the land, but the sources of *power* are clearly in the urban centers. And no class in Latin America knows this better than the often besieged but rarely beaten landed aristocracy. The "struggle" between city and country from the perspectives of the landed aristocracy has therefore become largely mythic and nostalgic. This newly retooled sector is, properly speaking, a landed capitalist class neatly absorbed in and defined by the larger urban political apparatus.

What mediates intensive class competition is the safety-valve aspect of internal migration. The movement of the peasantry from the rural areas to urban centers in countries such as Brazil, Mexico, and Peru has clearly served to reduce revolutionary discontent in these nations. However, this is by no means a universal highroad to lessening class antagonism in Latin America. In Argentina, for example, the movement from rural regions to urban centers provided a revolutionary base to

---

[7] Pablo González-Casanova, *La democracia en México* (Mexico City: Ediciones Era, 1965), p. 107 *et passim*.

[8] See Aldo E. Solari, *Sociología rural latinoamericana* (Buenos Aires: Editorial Universitaria de Buenos Aires, 1963).

the Peronist movement. Only when cities do in fact relieve social and economic sources of discontent by enlarging upon industrial opportunities do the mass agencies of revolution become shriveled. And this withering away of the revolutionary impulse is not so much a function of ecological motility as it is of industrial mobility.[9]

In Latin America local versus national distinction in types of political participation is less important than in the United States. The felicitous phrase of Scott Greer, "metropolitics," implies the sort of local vis-à-vis national politics found in the United States, where there is a high division of political labor based on a constant strain between local and national politics. Local and national elites compete for control of the "metro-polity," i.e., metropolitan activities.[10] But in Latin America the division is rather between urbanism as the style and locale of electoral politics in contrast to ruralism as the style and locale of pressure politics. This is one reason why in the industrially backward nations of Latin America (such as Paraguay and Haiti) there seems to be no noticeable upward movement of politicians from a local to national level. The more backward the national economy, the more strictly a national politician is beholden to a class sector. Class interest, being national, cuts across regional interests and local issues. But for this very reason the "cosmopolitan" political style is a source of weakness, since a politician cannot rely on a local or regional voting base to protect him in times of major crisis and upheaval.

Throughout Latin America the population of the cities is growing faster than that of the countryside. The disproportionate rate of growth signifies a deep transformation in power

[9] Urgently needed to test the effects of both internal migration and foreign immigration on the urban-industrial complex are studies of specific cities. Some efforts in this connection are contained in Hector Ferreire Loria, *Evolução industrial de São Paulo* (São Paulo: Livraria Martins Editora, 1954); Fernando Henrique Cardoso, "The Structure and Evolution of Industry in São Paulo: 1930–1960," *Studies in Comparative International Development,* Vol. 1, No. 5 (1965); Irving L. Horowitz, "The Jewish Community of Buenos Aires," *International Review of Community Development,* Whole No. 9 (Summer, 1962), 187–213; Tulio Halperín Donghi, "La expansión Granadera en la Campaña de Buenos Aires," *Desarrollo Económico,* III, No. 1–2, 57–110.

[10] Scott Greer, *Metropolitics: A Study of Political Culture* (New York: John Wiley & Sons, 1963).

relations and power balances, as urbanization and politicaliza-
tion are intimately associated.

Even very developed nations are captives to, no less than
makers of, their history. Latin America is certainly no exception. First, history bequeathed Spanish and Portuguese conquerors who were more concerned with extracting wealth than
with establishing permanent settlements. Cities were built in
coastal areas, the better to ship goods and grain. Needless to
add, such cities were often built without much concern for the
Indian inheritance, or for regional social characteristics. These
neo-European centers were often more in touch with the needs
of Old Spain than with those of New Spain. As such, the urban
process raised *social* aspiration levels without relieving *economic* pressures.

Second, nature bequeathed a series of fine, easy-to-settle
coastal regions. In marked contrast, the interior of Latin America is characterized by climatic extremes and severe topological
obstacles. Thick jungles rise up to meet steep and youthful
mountains. Nature combined with society in contributing to
uneven regional development. Thus, the rural sectors, where
agricultural production is dominant, is seriously limited by
factors of topology and general geography. The economic
differences between rural and urban politics should not prevent
an appreciation of the geographic proximities between these two
main sectors.

Third, there is a Latin life style which values immediate
gratification more highly than postponed or future reward. This
cultural style stifled internal national development—first, because of the pot-of-gold orientation and second, because of the
constant emphasis on spending rather than investing. The drive
toward internal migration and exploration characteristic of the
westward expansion in North America gave way to the drift
toward coastal comfort in Latin America. Cultural factors
conspired with nature and with history to create in Latin
America an asymmetry of rural and urban development which
remains intact to this day.[11]

This series of imbalances is reflected in current statistics
showing the ratio of city dwellings to national population

[11] For an acute examination of this imbalance, see Kingsley Davis, "The
Urbanization of the Human Population," *Cities* (New York: Alfred A.
Knopf [A Scientific American Book], 1965), pp. 3–24.

146   ⚏ THE SOCIOECONOMIC PIVOT

figures. As Table I illustrates, Latin American nations tend to
suffer from "the problem of Goliath's head"—a situation in
which a giant urban head rests on a demographically minute
rural body. Blanksten has noted that "there is no Latin American country in which there has been a trend away from urbanization; everywhere the impressive fact has been the movement

TABLE I

CENTRALIZATION OF LATIN AMERICAN POPULATION

Country	Population of largest metropolitan area	Metro-politan area as percent of nation	National population*	Census year
Uruguay	1,204	46.5	2,592	1963
Argentina	9,334(a)	44.5	20,959	1960
Brazil	29,685(b)	41.8	70,967	1960
Costa Rica	499	36.4	1,370	1963
Bolivia	1,170	33.2	3,520	1964
Chile	2,430	32.9	7,374	1960
Cuba	1,998	28.0	7,134	1963
Panama	273	25.4	1,076	1960
Venezuela	1,757(b)	23.4	7,524	1961
Nicaragua	275	17.3	1,593	1964
Peru	1,875	17.3	10,857	1961
Paraguay	305	16.8	1,817	1962
Dominican Republic	529(a)	15.3	3,452	1964
Colombia	2,221(a)	14.7	15,908	1963
Mexico	5,520	14.4	38,400	1963
Guatemala	573	13.4	4,278	1964
Ecuador	506	11.0	4,585	1962
El Salvador	256	10.2	2,511	1961
Honduras	154	7.7	2,008	1963
Haiti	250	6.3	4,000	1961

* In thousands.
(a) Includes suburban and non-nuclear regions in the totals, i.e., they
are "megalopolis" figures rather than central-city figures.
(b) Includes population of the two largest metropolitan areas.
Source: *The Statesman's Yearbook Statistical and Historical Annual for
the Year 1965–1966* (New York: St. Martin's Press, 1965); and ECLA,
"Geographic Distribution of the Population of Latin America and Regional Development Priorities," *Economic Bulletin for Latin America*,
Volume 8, No. 1 (March, 1963).

TABLE II
URBANIZATION OF THE LATIN AMERICAN POPULATION

Country	(Estimated) Total urban population (1965)	Urban regions as percent of nation	(Estimated) Total urban population (1970)	Urban regions as percent of national population	Percent increase in urban population
Argentina	16,100	74.1	17,600	74.3	0.2
Bolivia	1,300	35.0	1,400	35.0	—
Brazil	40,590	49.3	52,850	55.1	5.8
Chile	5,962	68.7	7,115	72.6	3.9
Colombia	9,611	53.1	12,274	57.9	4.8
Costa Rica	509	34.8	628	34.9	0.1
Dominican Republic	1,185	33.3	1,530	36.1	2.8
Ecuador	1,834	38.2	2,264	38.7	0.5
El Salvador	1,102	39.3	1,304	40.4	1.1
Guatemala	1,521	34.3	1,946	37.6	3.3
Haiti	730	15.9	810	16.2	0.3
Honduras	518	23.2	645	25.0	1.8
Mexico	22,300	54.7	27,900	62.6	7.9
Nicaragua	683	41.7	836	44.3	2.6
Panama	504	40.9	577	40.1	−0.8
Paraguay	694	35.6	797	35.6	—
Peru	5,250	46.6	6,520	50.1	3.5
Uruguay	1,971	72.5	2,095	72.5	—
Venezuela	6,005	67.4	7,913	72.9	5.5

Source: Inter-American Development Bank, *Social Progress Trust Fund* (Fifth Annual Report; Washington, D.C., 1965).

toward the city, the swelling of urban populations."[12] This fact, firmly established in the available data, indicates that the base of political power has shifted to the urban regions.

A further indication that this tendency toward urban concentration is expanding emerges from a consideration of Table II. It provides a conservative estimate of population expansion in the urban sectors in relation to the nation as a whole. Here one can immediately see that the countryside, far from enveloping the

[12] George I. Blanksten, "The Politics of Latin America," Gabriel A. Almond and James S. Coleman (eds.), in *The Politics of the Developing Areas* (Princeton, New Jersey: Princeton University Press, 1960), p. 470.

urban regions, is rapidly being abandoned in favor of the cities. While this table offers no information on the numbers of people, or percentage increase, for the capital city in relation to the smaller urban centers, present trends indicate a greater concentration in the large cities than presently exists. The rate of urbanization is especially higher in such rapidly industrializing societies as Brazil, Chile, Colombia, Mexico, and Venezuela. Indeed, on an average, these countries exhibit a rate of urbanization more in keeping with geometric population bursts than with currently modest rates of industrialization.

Whether this drive toward the city is due to "push" factors (difficulties in rural life) or "pull" factors (attractions of urban life) is difficult to ascertain. The tendency in Latin American studies is to emphasize push factors: the lack of opportunity for change in status; the displacement of functions by rapid farm mechanization; the high degree of soil exhaustion in many areas; the ineffective administration, marketing, and serving facilities in rural areas.[13] On the other hand, the fact that the flow to large cities is significantly greater than actual opportunities for stable employment or adequate housing indicates the existence of large-scale pull factors. The attraction of the city cannot be attributed to industrial growth alone, since the rate of urbanization is much higher (often twice as high) than the rate of industrialization. This "lure" is undoubtedly linked to achievement drives, to the desire to give children the advantages of education, health welfare, general culture, etc., associated with city life throughout the world.[14]

The essential sociological undertaking begins with this chicken-and-egg problem. First, what is the nature of the mix between push and pull factors? Second, why do some families or family heads migrate to the cities, while others of like background and training do not? Third, why do those who migrate often appear more stable and more rational than their offspring —as one notes in the case of Oscar Lewis' ethnographic studies.[15] Fourth, why do some of those who make a relatively

[13] See for example Gino Germani, *Política y sociedad en una época de transición: de la sociedad tradicional a la sociedad de masas* (Buenos Aires: Editorial Paidós, 1962).

[14] See Philip M. Hauser (ed.), *La urbanización en América Latina* (Paris: UNESCO, 1962). This work emphasizes the pull factors in the urbanization process.

[15] Oscar Lewis, *The Children of Sánchez* (New York: Random House,

satisfactory adjustment to urban patterns leave their positions and return to the agricultural settlement from whence they came? These unresolved questions indicate the extent to which social-psychological factors in migration to the cities have yet to be correlated to basic economic and political data.[16]

The political officials of Latin America, by virtue of their urban focus—their attentiveness to the needs of union officials, petty bureaucrats, urban-centered militarists, export-import middlemen, and businessmen—are compelled to give short shrift and second place to rural reform. Insistence of political leaders on agrarian reform, whether through expropriation or through some more cautious device like high taxation, has often been a primary cause for the toppling of regimes. The political demise of João Goulart was in large part due to his insistence on reform, both economic and electoral, in rural Brazil. Similar experiences have been frequent in Central America. In Mexico, even after the revolution had been consolidated in 1917, politicians showed a profound reticence to engage in the politics of agrarian reform. Partial land reform finally took place in the mid-1930s under the rule of Lázaro Cárdenas. As one commentator recently observed: "Widespread distribution did not begin until twenty-five years after the first blood was spilled and almost twenty years after the Mexican Constitution was amended."[17] Where thoroughgoing agrarian reform was enacted in the wake of revolutionary ferment, as in Cuba in 1960, this very simultaneity almost brought down the government. Castro's strategy of total land redistribution led to many economic and political complications with the middle sectors who at first encouraged the Revolutionary regime, and he continued his program only at the cost of losing their support. Thus,

1961); and *La Vida: A Puerto Rican Family in the Culture of Poverty* (New York: Random House, 1966).

16 Significant work in this direction has recently been undertaken by Joseph A. Kahl, *A Study of Career Values in Brazil and Mexico* (mimeographed, 1965); and from a psychological perspective, see John F. Santos, "A Psychologist Reflects on Brazil and Brazilians," E. N. Baklanoff (ed.), in *New Perspectives of Brazil* (Nashville: Vanderbilt University Press, 1966), pp. 233–263; and Rogelio Díaz-Guerrero, "Neurosis and the Mexican Structure," *American Journal of Psychiatry*, No. 112 (1955), pp. 411–417.

17 See John P. Powelson and Anatole A. Solow, "Urban and Rural Development in Latin America," *The Annals of the American Academy of Political and Social Science*, Vol. 360 (July, 1965), pp. 48–62.

because of the political risks involved, a serious alteration of the land tenure system seems to entail revolution rather than reform. The Latin American record thus far would indicate that a solution to this land problem in "reform-mongering" terms has been largely unsuccessful.

But our main concern is how the tremendous shift of the population from rural-agricultural to urban-industrial pursuits has restructured basic power loci. First, political machinery can serve to displace direct revolutionary action by absorbing the goals without the methods of revolutionary movements. To the extent urbanization takes place in such a way as to further the growth of an electoral party apparatus, direct revolutionary solutions become difficult to initiate. At the same time, and despite its ideological propensities, urban politicalization often makes exceedingly difficult the landholding classes' traditional recourse to illegality, terror, and intimidation.[18]

Second, the traditional classes are faced with the need to engage in coalition politics for the first time. Isolated, they are no longer capable of exercising effective or exclusive political power, either directly or through appointed *"gorila"* military personnel. The more closely these rural landholding interests are linked to the international economy, the more they become enmeshed in big-city life and its bureaucratic-industrial norms. The rural mass versus urban class dichotomy is therefore actually sharpened by the emergence of the latifundists as an additional oppressive urban class factor.

Third, control of the leading city (or cities) in nearly every nation of Latin America now signifies effective political control of the nation. The rural-based, nineteenth-century *caudillo* can rarely frighten a city into obedience. Sarmiento's great fear of the rural "barbarians" overrunning urban "civilization" has become historically interesting rather than socially relevant.[19]

[18] See Glaucio Ary Dillon Soares, "The Political Sociology of Uneven Development in Brazil," in Irving L. Horowitz (ed.), *Revolution in Brazil: Politics and Society in a Developing Nation* (New York: E. P. Dutton & Co., 1964), pp. 164–195.

[19] D. F. Sarmiento's account reflected the traditional liberal fear of *caudillos* like Rosas and Quiroga, rather than any dislike of rural values as such. See his classic statement in *Facundo: Civilización y barbarie* (1845) (New York: Doubleday & Co., Colección Hispánica, 1961); also see his more visionary statement, *Argirópolis: capital de los estados confederados.* Vol. XIII of the *Obras de D. F. Sarmiento.* (Buenos Aires: Publicado bajo los auspicios del gobierno Argentino, 1896).

Indeed, the more likely situation is for the urban-based, political-military cadre to stamp out significant military threats in the countryside. Sometimes, when rural strength is unbroken, as in the case of Colombia, the urban political regime arranges a compromise solution between contending factions. This solution is made possible not only by the strength of the urban region, but by the non-ideological, patrimonial character of many rural struggles in Latin America.

Fourth, the city provides a great deal of personal stability in contrast to the rural regions. The legal bases of city life are far less problematic than those of rural life. This assertion may seem to be contradicted by the large numbers of *golpes* and *manifestaciones* in the cities, but in fact such events only redistribute power among the holders of power, and do not shatter the structure of power as such. These *golpes* and *manifestaciones,* however dramatic, are momentary in their effect.

Fifth, the violent characteristics of life in the backlands, the very absence of any regulative machinery, makes politics a more openly violent encounter between forces and hence tends to eliminate the role of the political mediator. The fact that agrarian disputes are often jurisdictional, concerning who has the rights to what lands at what time and in what proportion, further weakens the possibilities of leadership emerging from the agricultural sector by dividing the potential holders of rural power among themselves. However, relative to the urban sector, these agrarian upper-class interests are increasingly losing ground as they become (*a*) merged with commercial activities in the cities; (*b*) engaged in combat with radical or revolutionary forces; and (*c*) lose their indispensability to the structure of the national economy.

Above all, urbanization—whether or not linked to industrialization—enfranchises large numbers of people by bringing them into contact with political organizations. Whether political eligibility is a consequence or a cause of the urban division of labor is less important than its having taken place in the cities. This drastically affects the structure and distribution of state power. The redistribution of power is not necessarily more democratic because it is based in cities, but it must be more facile and opportunistic (i.e., responsive to the will of the people) to survive.[20]

[20] See Francisco C. Weffort, "State and Mass in Brazil," *Studies in Comparative International Development,* Vol. II (1966), No. 12; and for

As the urban process matures, and as the rural sector shrinks in importance, political rights tend to be uniformly diffused throughout the nation. The mobilization and integration of the masses in Latin America thus tends to be funneled through the urbanization process.

In Latin America the extent of the division of labor, or at least the degree to which differentiated social classes can be identified, varies from city to city and region to region. In Buenos Aires and Montevideo one can tell the difference between a middle-class white-collar worker and a blue-collar factory worker by the color and cut of their clothes. These class divisions can be noticed only in circumstances of relatively advanced industrialization, and in large-sized cities. The middle-sized cities of Latin America tend to have a relatively low degree of industrial rationalization and a correspondingly undifferentiated class system.[21] They remain suppliers of raw materials, where perhaps the first stages of processing may take place. One study notes that for one middle-sized Mexican city, the rule of thumb for lower-class membership is simply "any person who earned his living by working with his hands."[22] In other words, the main distinction is still between "hand" work and "head" work, rather than more sophisticated indicators of urbanization.

Inevitably, because political decisions in Latin America are desperate pragmatic choices to stave off chaos and the choices are made by the classes to the exclusion of the masses, the fusion politics of urban Latin America has been from its inception highly unstable. Of the thirteen multiparty systems listed as unstable in a recent factor analytic survey, nine are in Latin America: Argentina, Brazil, Dominican Republic, Ecuador, El

an empirical account of this process, see Orlando M. Carvalho, *Política do município* (Rio de Janeiro: Agir Editores, 1946).

[21] What is meant here by low degree of industrial rationalization is simply the absence of diversification, not necessarily the quality of goods manufactured.

[22] Andrew H. Whiteford, *Two Cities of Latin America: A Comparative Description of Social Classes* (Garden City, N.Y.: Doubleday & Co., 1964), pp. 136–138. The same situation seems to be the case for Brazil. See Charles Wagley, *Amazon Town: A Study of Man in the Tropics* (New York: The Macmillan Co., 1953).

Salvador, Guatemala, Panama, Peru, and Venezuela.[23] These nine countries are also those in Latin America (with two exceptions, Argentina and Venezuela) with the largest agricultural sectors. In each case, the rural sector exceeds half the total population, which is another way of saying that the majority of their citizens are non-participants in the electoral political process. It is instructive to note that in a nation such as Mexico, with high urban concentration, there is a correspondingly high political participation even in the rural regions.[24]

The relationship between population and politics must now be placed in focus. In another connection, but quite relevant in our investigation, Kornhauser has pointed out that

> Non-participation results in lack of exposure to information and indoctrination concerning democratic values, and in the lack of habits of discussion, debate, negotiation, and compromise— modes of conduct indispensable to democratic politics.

He goes on to indicate that in critical times mass movements and revolutionary parties recruit precisely from such non-participants.

> Within all strata, people divorced from community, occupation, and association are first and foremost among the supporters of extremism. The decisive social process in mass society is the *atomization* of social relations; even though this process is accentuated in the lower strata, it operates throughout the society.[25]

Tables III and IV, taken together, provide solid evidence that the structure of political parties is most advanced where indicators of high urban development are clear-cut. Urbanism does not necessarily yield democratic politics; rather, it makes possible the kind of mass participation which is a necessary if not a sufficient cause for democratic politics. The degree of class stratification, the literacy of a population, the number of uni-

---

[23] See Arthur S. Banks and Robert B. Textor, *A Cross-Polity Survey* (Cambridge, Mass.: The M.I.T. Press, 1963), sections 152–155.

[24] González-Casanova, *op. cit.*, pp. 239–245.

[25] William Kornhauser, *The Politics of Mass Society* (Glencoe, Ill.: The Free Press, 1959), p. 73; for a more recent study directed toward developing regions, see David E. Apter, *The Politics of Modernization* (Chicago: The University of Chicago Press, 1965), esp. pp. 453–458.

versity students, the number of voters in the society, and the degree of unionization are sound indicators of urban growth. The decisive issue now (one we shall later deal with in a separate point) is whether this urbanization process is far enough developed to make possible further social change through the reform-mongering impulses of the cities, or whether social change will come through the revolutionary impulses of the countryside.

TABLE III
TYPES OF SOCIAL STRATIFICATION IN LATIN AMERICA
(CIRCA 1950)

Country	Percent in middle and upper brackets of population	Percent engaged in secondary and tertiary activity	Percent of population literate	Number of university students per 1,000 population	Annual rate of urbanization
(a) Middle strata: 20 percent or more, (b) cultural existence, psychology of a middle class, (c) ethnic homogeneity and cultural homogeneity, national identification and considerable level of participation in various sectors, (d) urban-rural differentiation and geographical discontinuity exists but to a lesser degree than in other countries in Latin America:					
Argentina	36	75	87	7.7	17
Uruguay	—	82	95	5.2	14
Chile	22	65	80	3.9	16
Costa Rica	22	43(−)	80	3.9	16
(a) Middle strata: 15 to 20 percent approximately, (b) emerging middle class (but degree of self-identification questionable), (c) ethnic and cultural heterogeneity, sharp unbalance in degree of participation in national society and other aspects, (d) marked discontinuity between rural and urban areas, and considerable regional differences:					
Cuba	22	56	78	3.9	9(−)
Venezuela	18	56	52(−)	1.3(−)	29(+)
Colombia	22	42	63	1.0(−)	17

Symbols (−) too low and (+) too high for quartile ranking.

Source: Gino Germani, "Estrategia para estimular la movilidad social," in J. A. Kahl (ed.), La industrialización en América Latina (Mexico-Buenos Aires: Fondo de Cultura Economica, 1965), pp. 294–95.

(a) *Middle strata: between 15 and 20 percent approximately,* (b) *cultural, psychological, and political existence of middle class* (but see [d]),(c) *ethnic and cultural heterogeneity, marked differences in degree of urbanization and industrialization in certain areas and predominance of rural life in the major part of the country:*

Mexico	20	44	59	0.9(−)	17
Brazil	15	38	49	1.2(−)	13

Country	Percent in middle and upper brackets of population	Percent engaged in secondary and tertiary activity	Percent of population literate	Number of university students per 1,000 population	Annual rate of urbanization

(a) *Middle strata: less than 15 percent, emerging middle strata in some countries, but clear persistence in varying degrees of traditional patterns,* (b) *ethnic and cultural heterogeneity in almost all,* (c) *vast sectors of population still marginal,* (d) *rural pattern predominant, but with regional differences:*

Country	Percent in middle and upper brackets of population	Percent engaged in secondary and tertiary activity	Percent of population literate	Number of university students per 1,000 population	Annual rate of urbanization
Panama	15	45(+)	70(+)	2.6	15(+)
Paraguay	14	46(+)	66(+)	1.3	12
Peru	—	40(+)	42	1.8	11
Ecuador	10	49(+)	56(+)	1.4	12(+)
El Salvador	10	36	40	0.3	9
Bolivia	8	37	12	2.0(+)	8
Guatemala	8	25	29	0.1	10(+)
Nicaragua	—	29	38	0.7	8
Dominican Republic	—	30	43(+)	1.2	10(+)
Honduras	4	24	35	0.7	10(+)
Haiti	3	23	11	—	5

The countries which are consistent for the stated measures of social stratification and mobilization fall at the poles of development. Consistency (herein defined as parallel rankings on four out of five measures given) is shown for Argentina, Uruguay, Chile, Mexico, and Brazil at the highly urbanized pole; and for Honduras, Haiti, Nicaragua, El Salvador among the least urbanized nations.[26]

It is noteworthy that the level expended for education is the only radically asymmetrical feature of Mexico and Brazil. It is also the case that the urbanization rate is disproportionately higher than other developmental measures for at least half the nations of Latin America. Only Cuba reveals a lower rate of urbanization than its norm on the other indicators. This gives quantitative substance to the primacy of "pull" factors in urbanization. Thus it can be hypothesized that rapid development tends to be symmetrical, whereas uneven development tends to be asymmetrical.

The symmetry in economic development does not carry over into political development. The uneven characteristics of political mobilization can be gathered from Table IV. Taking proportions of voters and union membership as central, one finds that only eight nations (Uruguay, Chile, Mexico, Peru, Brazil, Paraguay, Bolivia, and Honduras), when ranked in quartiles, reveal themselves to be either in the same quartile for the two items or apart by only one quartile. It may be significant that high stability in the political culture (whether of a democratic variety as in Chile or an undemocratic variety as in Paraguay) does tend to reveal a correlation between these two variables. The greatest discrepancies appear in Central America, where a high degree of formal legal-parliamentary rules obtain, but a low degree of mass mobilization and integration. As in so many other instances, the Argentine case seems exceptional. Its mobilization, as evidenced by the degree of unionization and voting measures, is extremely high, yet the sort of national integration found in other nations where such measures are consistently high simply does not obtain.

The data appear to indicate that totalitarianism is consonant with both ends of the rank order. Where there is a very high electoral participation there seems to be a strong correlation with stable and totalitarian systems; where there is a very low

---

[26] Irregularities tend to maximize where the level and rate of economic development, as evidenced by the industrialization process, occupies some middle ground. For example, the proportion of the population engaged in secondary and tertiary activities in Panama, Paraguay, Peru, and Ecuador are too high for the kind of stratification and mobility systems exhibited in these countries—all of medium development. On the other hand, the number of university-trained personnel is disproportionately low for such nations as Colombia and Venezuela.

electoral participation there appear to be unstable and authoritarian systems. Venezuela is the exception to this rule. At the other end, where there is a clustering at the median (40 to 60 percent) range, there is a tendency toward stability of either a democratic or authoritarian sort. Again, Chile is an exception, with its relatively low level of electoral participation and high democratic political system.

High unionism is generally correlated with this middle range electoral participation. It serves as a useful, if crude, measure of democratic tendencies. But here too the data inspire caution. Paraguay has an extremely totalitarian system, but through government intervention has organized a large number in union participation. On the other hand, Costa Rica has an exceptionally low level of unionization, which is atypical for a democratic polity.

Finally, such items as voting patterns for Socialist and Communist parties, religious parties, and secular parties present such a mixed mosaic that the search for meaning is at the level of biological explanations of Brownian movement. Ethnographic and qualitative information is vital for making sense of the quantitative data. For example, although the Christian Democrats in Chile have a nominal "clerical" ideology, it is far to the left of many secular political parties in Chile, and even more so than "secular" parties in nations such as Argentina, El Salvador, Panama, or Paraguay.[27]

The "moral" of the data presented in Table IV is to avoid any equation of electoral analysis with political analysis.

In a matrix of correlations in which the items in Table IV were considered (nature of the political system, percent of voters, and percent unionized) and select items from Table III (percent literacy and urbanization rate), it becomes clear that the strongest measure is an inverse relationship between totalitarianism and literacy (−0.661734). No other measure tested shows anywhere near the same relational strength, either positive or negative. However, several qualifying aspects should be listed. First, the scale of democratic, authoritarian, and totalitarian systems is itself unstable. Guatemala had a revolution in the control year (1950), while the growth of repressive mechanisms in Venezuela and Paraguay was becoming evident in this

[27] See Bruce M. Russett and associates, *World Handbook of Political and Social Indicators* (New Haven and London: Yale University Press, 1964), pp. 82–96.

TABLE IV

TYPES OF POLITICAL MOBILIZATION IN LATIN AMERICA
(circa 1950)

Country	Basic nature* of the political system	Percent of voters in adult popu- lation	Political Mobilization		
			Sequence and quartile rank	Percent of workers affiliated with unions	Sequence and quartile rank
Argentina	U mp A	61.8	6	48.4	2
Uruguay	S mp D	58.3	7	24.5	10
Costa Rica	S mp D	57.6	8	4.4	15
Chile	S mp D	37.4	12	31.7	5
Venezuela	S mp A	83.8	2	30.8	6
Cuba	U sp T	69.1	4	80.4	1
Colombia	S mp A	40.2	11	18.4	11
Mexico	S sp D	34.6	14	44.6	3
Brazil	U mp A	34.4	15	26.0	8
Panama	S mp D	56.2	9	1.3	19
Paraguay	S sp T	29.1	17	26.5	7
Peru	U mp A	39.2	12	7.4	14
Ecuador	U mp A	28.4	18	10.4	12
El Salvador	U mp A	29.3	16	3.0	18
Bolivia	U sp A	51.4	10	34.1	4
Guatemala	U mp A	27.5	19	1.1	20
Nicaragua	S sp T	92.7	1	4.1	16
Dominican Republic	U mp T	63.6	5	25.5	9
Honduras	S sp T	36.5	13	9.7	13
Haiti	S sp T	74.2	3	3.6	17

* Code: U (unstable), S (stable)
mp (multiparty), sp (single party)
D (democratic), A (authoritarian), T (totalitarian)

period. Second, any general characterization of political systems into three categories is itself subject to considerable debate. Thus, whether in the long run literacy is related to high democratic values remains difficult to ascertain. One fact that does emerge from the data analysis in the extent to which high educational norms are connected to urban processes.

Rather direct evidence that education in general is connected to urbanization is provided by Harbison and Myers. The information in Table V indicates the extent to which a high agricultural population is inversely related to high-level technical manpower such as teachers and professionals. While expenditures on education seem inconclusively related to levels of development, such expenditures may be indicative of rates of development.

One significant feature not represented in the data is the phenomenon of miseducation.[28] Nations such as Argentina, Uruguay, and Brazil have a relatively decent supply of high-level manpower. However, such proficient manpower is poorly distributed throughout the nation. In fact, cities such as Buenos Aires, Rio de Janeiro, and Caracas have an overabundance of high-level personnel with respect to the short supply available for the nation as a whole. This may help to explain why, even when a nation in Latin America has a large number of technically competent personnel, economic development tends to be dramatically inconsistent in output and equally irregular in ecology.

The interconnection of social stratification and political mobilization is further enhanced by the fact that even small and predominantly agricultural nations, such as the Central American republics, boast of potent urban centers, in which both social and political development is largely concentrated. The technically competent personnel often find themselves involved in one form of government machinery or another. The size of the urban bureaucracy further contributes to the structural imbalances mentioned, by fusing the trained and highly skilled work force not just to the urban center but to the national political apparatus concentrated in that center.

In this fashion the one social sector which, in theory, would be capable of breaking through the yin and yang of a proletarianized bourgeoisie and a bourgeoisified proletariat is itself linked to the stratification system that creates a large politically aware bureaucracy, but one decisively removed from the national interest as a whole.

[28] For two interesting essays on miseducation, see William S. Stokes, "The *Pensadores* of Latin America," in George B. deHuszar (ed.), *The Intellectuals* (Glencoe, Ill.: The Free Press, 1960); and David Nasatir, "Student Action in Latin America," *Trans-Action*, Vol. 2, No. 3, March–April, 1965.

TABLE V

URBANIZATION AND EDUCATION IN LATIN AMERICA
High-level Manpower (10,000)

Country	Percent of population in agriculture	Rank*	Teachers in primary and secondary levels	Physicians and dentists	Expenditures on education as percent of national income
Argentina	25	(01)	88.1	17.5	2.5
Chile	30	(02)	na	7.5	2.4
Uruguay	37	(03)	na	13.0	na
Venezuela	41	(04)	59.4	6.5	4.1
Cuba	42	(05)	36.6	13.0	3.4
Ecuador	53	(06)	40.8	3.0	1.7
Colombia	54	(07.5)	41.1	5.0	2.1
Paraguay	54	(07.5)	78.3	6.0	1.7
Costa Rica	55	(09)	77.5	4.5	4.0
Dominican Republic	56	(10)	24.2	2.5	1.6
Mexico	58	(11.5)	36.0	4.5	1.4
Brazil	58	(11.5)	48.9	5.0	2.6
Peru	62	(13)	44.4	3.0	2.9
Guatemala	71	(14)	34.9	1.2	2.4
Bolivia	72	(15)	28.3	3.5	na
Haiti	83	(16)	20.3	1.0	na

* Nations are ranked in terms of percent population in agriculture. It will be noted that the percentages for the size of the agricultural population vary from the previous tables. This variation is not statistically or qualitatively significant. The difference simply reflects the use of various census reports and population estimates.

Source: Frederick Harbison and Charles A. Myers, *Education, Manpower and Economic Growth* (New York: McGraw-Hill Book Co., 1964), pp. 45–48.

In examining Table VI, describing the economically active population of Latin American nations in terms of occupations, several important, albeit tentative, conclusions can be reached. Where the combined rural working classes and landholding classes are less than 30 percent, as is the case for Argentina,

TABLE VI

URBAN-RURAL DICHOTOMY AND OCCUPATIONAL DISTRIBUTION
(circa 1950) (Percent per 100 Active Population)
   (*Urban Sector*)   (*Rural Sector*)

Country	Urban middle strata	Urban workers	Combined urban	Landowners and medium-sized farming entrepreneurs	Peons and other rural workers	Combined rural
Argentina	28	45	73	8	19	27
Chile	21	50	71	1	28	29
Venezuela	16	45	61	2	37	39
Cuba	21	38	59	—	41	41
Ecuador	10	38	48	1	51	52
Panama	15	31	46	1	53	54
Costa Rica	14	31	45	8	47	55
Paraguay	12	33	45	2	53	55
Colombia	12	32	44	10	46	56
Brazil	13	24	37	2	61	63
Guatemala	6	31	37	2	61	63
Bolivia	7	20	27	1	72	73
El Salvador	9	27	36	2	62	64
Honduras	4	12	16	—	84	84
Haiti	2	12	14	1	85	86

N.B. Included in the urban middle strata are: (a) entrepreneurs in business, industry, and service occupations, that is, persons performing these activities with the aid of dependent personnel, (b) the professions, (c) technicians and managerial personnel, (d) white-collar workers, both public and private. The urban workers include all persons working in the secondary- and tertiary-activity branches and not covered by the preceding categories (mainly persons who are in dependent situations, but also included are persons doing manual work for their own account, without dependents). The category of agricultural landowners and entrepreneurs includes only those persons using wage labor. The category of peons and other rural workers includes farm wage labor and all those working the land as lessees, owners, or on a similar basis, but without having employees working for them.

Source: Gino Germani, "Estrategia para estimular la movilidad social," supra Table III.

Venezuela, and Chile, the political system tends to be multi-party and under urban "liberal" domination. In addition to this, socialist politics in Latin America tends to be city-based, coalitional, and reformist in outlook. Where the rural classes are 40 percent or higher, as is the case in most of Latin America, including Cuba and Brazil, the political system tends to be more exclusively concerned with the class interests of the urban sectors. But these are furthermore the regions where peasant-based revolutionary movements tend to be more violent and more successful, as was the case in Cuba, Bolivia, Guatemala, and Brazil, at one time or other during the postwar era. That such regimes have often been unstable and/or overthrown only accentuates the correlation of urbanism generating political reform and ruralism generating political reaction and revolution.

The statistical evidence unquestionably points to the decisive role which urbanization has played in the political culture of Latin America. Approximately 90 percent of the variance is accounted for when urbanization measures are combined with industrialization measures.[29] Perhaps the most interesting finding, if for no other reason than it is unexpected, is the significance of educational-literacy measures in the determination of the types of political culture found throughout Latin America. It is important to find out that the only other strong correlation also involves education—as a factor in unionization. Whether this is an indirect consequence of the work habitat in the industrial plant, or a direct relationship, is less important than the recognition of the intimate connection of education with vertical social mobility, no less than with political mobilization.[30]

The Latin American urban complex is a center of reform because it contains the bulk of reform-minded social sectors. The Latin American rural complex is the center of both reaction and revolution because class polarization and class disenfranchisement is relatively complete, and because the class variable is not moderated by other factors.

[29] See Neuma Aguiar Walker, "A Quantitative Study of Mobilization in Brazil" (unpublished paper, mimeographed).
[30] See Robert J. Havighurst, "Education and Social Mobility in Four Societies," in A. H. Halsey, J. Floud, and C. A. Anderson (eds.), *Education, Economy and Society* (New York: The Free Press of Glencoe, 1961), pp. 105–120.

Before examining the urban political structure, some commentary on traditional decision-making procedures is in order. A predominantly ascriptive and caste system of relationships has tended to reduplicate itself throughout the social system. The primary context of social relationships has not been that of rights and privileges of equal citizens interacting with one another, but that of superordination and subordination based upon lineage, race, and inherited status. Within this hierarchy, the rural sectors comprised of Indians, mestizos, Negroes, and mulatto elements have tended to occupy the bottom rung. These same elements have relied more on personalism than upon politics to get their way.

The appeals of the *caudillo* to personalist impulses of the rural mass are not unlike a Latin variation upon a Tammany Hall politician. While heaping great contempt upon these rural masses, the *caudillo* at the same time undoubtedly knows their problems and is willing to act on their needs—for a price. What this indicates is a process of co-optation of the lower classes of society by the elite elements for use in military forays, organized civil wars, and even stuffing the ballot boxes in elections. Such co-optation was accomplished through a traditional chain of command involving the authority figures of the various ruling castes. The polarization of political interests provoking such co-optation in the last century was a function of the internecine conflicts of the elite and required no particular understanding of the true nature of these class interests on the part of the co-opted elements. Political conflict could be characterized as vertical polarizations of a society in which competing groups symbolically acted out the demands of various descendant or ascendant elites. Rural politics in Latin America is thus another way of describing the tightly knit elites which have been largely drawn from the agricultural sector. This includes not only landowners but also a heavy percentage of the military leadership. The rural populace as a mass has been marginal to the political process except as its incidental victims and willing or unwilling instruments.

One indication of how this rural *caudillo* style insinuates itself into urban life is provided by Carlos Medina's description of political campaigning among the *favelados* of Rio de Janeiro.

> While the great topics are being discussed, each voter looks for a personal benefaction and each *politico* strives to guarantee his constituency. This is where the most important figure in Brazilian

elections appears: the *cabo eleitoral* . . . He fills the gap between what the candidates proclaim and what they will perform.
Politics is thus imbued with a highly demagogic content. The
candidate presents the voter with a program of action, but to the
individual he promises his personal intervention. It is this which
counts.[31]

Just as it might be said that urban politics is simply politics,
there is another sense in which the personal approach acts to
prevent any meaningful urban reform, by rigorously avoiding
specific issues related to urban life such as slum dwelling,
sanitation and sewage systems, fire-alarm units, garbage disposal trucks, protection against false weights and measures, etc.
Indeed, the only exception to civic disinterest is the police
corps—and that because the police of many large Latin American cities function more as military reserves than as local law
enforcement agents.

Industrialization, bureaucratization, and modernization place
very great strains on this traditional style of unpolitics. It
created the need for symbolic representation of stratified, developed, and highly ambitious class forces, all of which crystallized
in the urban sector. The rise of a multiparty system was in effect
a response to the impossibility of any further continuance of the
anti-politique of violence. It was not a national decision or an
intellectual commitment to make democratic the political order,
but an exhaustion of the rural classes, and an exhibition of
urban preeminence.

Table VII indicates that with the notable exceptions of Argentina and Cuba, there is a significant correlation between deaths
from mass violence and numbers of people engaged in farming
activities. Such highly urbanized nations as Uruguay, Brazil,
and Mexico show little "unsponsored" violence. At the same
time there is an inverse correlation between the urbanization
process and these causes of death. The emergent parliamentary
style in urban politics successfully ordered and centralized its
machinery as a first task, but did little to ameliorate or control
rural politics. For the first time in the twentieth century this
choice in politics pervades Latin America. Constitutional re-

[31] Carlos Alberto de Medina, *A favela e o demagogo*, as quoted in
Richard Morse, "Urbanization in Latin America," *Latin American Research Review*, Vol. I, No. 1 (Fall, 1965), p. 57; on this topic, also see
Andrew Gunder Frank, "Urban Poverty in Latin America," in *Studies
in Comparative International Development*, Vol. 2, No. 5, 1966.

form occurs in the cities and at those junctures in each of the Latin American countries when the choice between centralized state law and rural terror had to be made.

As Table VII shows, while there is evidence for correlating high violence and low urbanization, there is also evidence of high violence coinciding with high urbanization. Perhaps what is involved is violence of different types at different levels of economic development. Before we dismiss the relationship of violence to urbanization, several points should be noted. In each

TABLE VII

THE RURAL-URBAN DICHOTOMY AND GROUP VIOLENCE

Country*	Death from group violence 1950– 1962	Rank†	Percent of popu- lation in farming	Rank†	Percent of popu- lation in cities over 20,000	Rank†
Cuba	2900	1	42	65.5	36.5	26
Bolivia	663	4	72	16.5	19.4	57
Colombia	316	6	55	49.0	22.4	52
Argentina	217	8	25	80.5	48.5	14
Honduras	111	10.5	66	32.0	11.5	80
Venezuela	111	10.5	42	65.5	47.2	15
Paraguay	60	12	55	49.0	15.2	70
Guatemala	57	13	68	28.0	11.2	82
Dominican Republic	31	19	56	47.0	12.2	78
Peru	26	20	60	40.0	13.9	72.5
Panama	25	21	54	51.0	33.1	30
Costa Rica	24	22	55	49.0	15.4	67.5
Ecuador	18	25	53	52.5	17.8	64
Haiti	16	27	83	7.0	5.1	101.5
Nicaragua	16	27	68	28.0	20.1	55

* The nations listed in the above chart cover only the first four deciles, or those nations for which there is a significant number of deaths due to group violence.

† The rankings have not been recomputed for Latin America alone, since in its present form an indication of where this region ranks with respect to the rest of the world can better be ascertained.

Source: Bruce M. Russett et al., *World Handbook of Political and Social Indicators* (New Haven and London: Yale University Press, 1964).

of the three nations which exhibit a correspondence of high violence and high urbanization, there have been major revolutions during the periods covered. Castro in Cuba (a left-wing revolution), Perón in Argentina (a right-wing revolution), and Betancourt in Venezuela (a centrist revolution). Where there have been coups d'état, or revolutions from above, violence continues to be high, despite the relative backwardness of the societies involved. The Mexican Revolution was undoubtedly costly and violent, but the relatively high stability which has obtained since 1920 indicates that once a revolution consolidates and institutionalizes itself, violence sharply declines.[32]

It should be noted that Table VII covers the period between 1950 and 1962. This means that it does not cover the present "guerrilla phase" of violence. It may well be that rural violence may expand, despite the institutionalization of the political system in the urban zones. If my main hypothesis is correct, we can expect to find an increase in violence even in relatively advanced nations of Latin America, but such violence will increasingly be ecologically confined to the rural areas of the advanced nations. Thus, guerrilla violence has already been widely reported in Peru, Brazil, Argentina, and to a lesser degree, even in Mexico. Such violence does not take place in Lima, Rio de Janeiro, Buenos Aires, or Mexico City, but in the rural zones. Leadership for such violent groups may be drawn from the political marginals or "modernizing intellectuals" of the big cities, but the popular masses must be willing and able to engage in combat.

The landed aristocracy is still in a position to command the loyalties of the tradition-bound peasant masses. Instead of having politics as a symbolic recognition of different class interests, the landed interests, through their feudal paternalism, compel the development of politics by other means, that is, by force of arms.[33] This brings the situation to a full circle. The urban-rural dichotomy in Latin America is one in which the old aristocratic ruling classes have at their disposal a mass base of relatively loyal peasants while the new middle classes have at

[32] See Harry Eckstein, *Internal War: Problems and Approaches* (New York: The Free Press of Glencoe, 1964), pp. 1–32.

[33] Cf. Glaucio Soares, "The Political Sociology of Uneven Development in Brazil," *Revolution in Brazil: Politics and Society in a Developing Nation,* Irving L. Horowitz (ed.) (New York: E. P. Dutton & Co., 1964), pp. 164–195.

their disposal the urban working classes who feel they have a vested interest in the going social system. The dichotomization between urban and rural regions begins to develop an autonomous character, and instead of the classical Marxist or European pattern of a struggle between classes, there takes place a struggle between class and mass, with the landed aristocracy becoming increasingly marginal in the political struggle.

What this means in political terms is that the city becomes the reforming area and the countryside becomes the revolutionary area. The Latin American city is now the center of reform. It is the clear representation of middle-class needs and ambitions. But such liberalism is not to be confused with revolutionary sentiments.

When an agrarian revolution succeeds, the likelihood is that the urban reform elements will pay a premium price. The Cuban Revolution is a classic example. First, the trade union movement became politicized under a unified leadership. Second, the urban working class was taxed 4 percent (in some cases 5 percent) of their salary. Third, the urban workers were required to take a "voluntary" cut in wages to stabilize the economy. Fourth, and finally, the essential tasks of the urban proletariat were redefined away from class interests and toward firm cooperation with government planning agencies. Those who protested this natural history of the revolution were severely castigated. Castro, in 1960, made a violent attack on the electricity workers and other urban unions, saying that they "had sold the right of primogeniture of the working class, its right to rule and direct the country, for the miserable pottage of special economic privileges."[34] Clearly then, one function of agrarian revolutions is to treat the urban proletariat as one more special interest group, and not just as the vanguard of the revolution. This mass versus class phenomenon is characteristic of most revolutionary movements in the Latin American sphere. The urban working classes are part of the liberal center, and their voting patterns reveal precisely such tendencies.

The countryside remains the polarized expression of reaction and revolution—of total solutions to total problems. In the absence of an adequate growth of middle-sized cities, or of mass colonization of the hinterlands by the "developed" sectors, this

[34] For this and other statements by revolutionary leaders in Cuba, see Boris Goldenberg, *The Cuban Revolution and Latin America* (New York: Frederick A. Praeger, 1965), esp. pp. 193–213.

condition is likely to remain unchanged. A few ethnographic
illustrations of this should suffice.

In his study of *caudillismo,* Raymond E. Crist long ago
pointed out that

> The destiny of the revolutionary cause in Venezuela was decided
> on the Llanos, for there the patriots enjoyed natural advantages.
> Climate was, for example, a major ally for Paez [José Antonio
> Paez, guerrilla leader of Venezuela who was born near the village
> of Acarigua in 1790]; the rainy season was as disastrous for
> Spanish troops as winter was for Napoleon's Grand Army in
> Russia. As a guerrilla leader, a caudillo, Paez was himself a
> product of the grasslands . . . The common people will con-
> tinue to see in him a reflection of themselves because he was one
> of them and they will, therefore, assign to him the virtues which
> they themselves would like to possess. He was flesh of their flesh
> and blood of their blood; he did not look down on them from
> Olympian heights as did Bolívar, the intellectual. Paez was cer-
> tainly among the greatest caudillos, although he was nothing but
> a guerrilla leader. He had learned nothing about military tactics
> from books, but he knew his country and he knew his people.[35]

The appeal made by Juan Perón to the memory of Manuel
Rosas was an attempt to rekindle mass against class sentiments:
Argentinian nationalism against the cosmopolitanism of Buenos
Aires. Rosas' rule of the whip, his pose as a "white gaucho" and
bearing the holy crusade against enlightenment, against unitar-
ians, against positivists, against freemasons meant nothing or
next to nothing to the rural masses. The lesson of Rosas was
not lost on Perón, for no matter how politically authoritarian
Perón was, and despite the certain disaster his economic policies were leading toward, he could claim with pride and justification that a *social* revolution had been carried out. And even
though this urban *caudillo* (Perón) distinguished himself from
the rural *caudillo* (Rosas) in many ways, the rhetoric of
nostalgic nationalism, of the rural regions against the urban
sectors, received an enormous response. Perón too was anti-
officialist; he was a populist. The contents of this populism,
however, remain as cloudy today, over a decade after the
collapse of Peronism, as ever. If anything is needed to show that

[35] Raymond E. Crist, "Geography and Caudillismo: A Case Study"
[1937], in H. M. Hamill, Jr. (ed.), *Dictatorship in Spanish America*
(New York: Alfred A. Knopf, 1965), pp. 84–85.

reaction and revolution are closer to each other than either are
to reform, the history of Argentina should readily demonstrate
the case.[36]

This concept of the city as essentially a liberalizing rather
than radicalizing environment is reinforced by the interesting
observations of Oscar Lewis.

> The population of Mexico City has very close ties with the rural
> hinterlands. Mexico City is essentially conservative in tradition.
> In Mexico most of the revolutions have begun in the country.
> The city has been the refuge for the well-to-do rural families
> whose local positions were threatened. Mexico City is not as
> highly industrialized as many American cities and does not
> present the same conditions of life. Mexican farmers live in well-
> organized villages that are more like cities and towns than like the
> open-country settlement pattern of American farmers. Finally,
> Tepoztlán is close to Mexico City, not only geographically but
> also culturally. The similarities between the value systems of
> working-class and lower-middle-class families in Mexico City and
> those of Tepoztecans are probably much greater than those
> between, let us say, families from the hill country of Arkansas
> and working- and middle-class families from St. Louis or De-
> troit.[37]

At a different level, and as a result of the migration of the
masses to the cities, there has been a reinforcement of the
reform impulses of city life. The concerns of the city are absorption of the peasantry, making them an industrious group, and
providing them with an effective political franchise which would
help in transforming the urban center from a colonial possession into an industrial base with minimal friction. Germani
indicates that this is the case in Argentina.

> Urbanization gained an unusual impetus with the massive migra-
> tion to the cities from the interior of the country. During the

[36] On the history of Buenos Aires, see Julio Rinaldini, "Buenos Aires,"
in Germán Arciniegas (ed.), *The Green Continent* (New York: Alfred
A. Knopf, 1954), pp. 382–400; and for some marvelous vignettes, see
Roberto Arlt, *Nuevas aquafuertes porteñas* (Buenos Aires: Librería
Hachette, 1960).
[37] Oscar Lewis, "Urbanization Without Breakdown: A Case Study,"
Contemporary Culture and Societies of Latin America, Dwight B. Heath
and Richard N. Adams (eds.) (New York: Random House, 1965), esp.
p. 435.

decade 1936–47 the proportion of *argentinos* born in the provinces who moved to the metropolitan zone of Buenos Aires was
equal to almost 40 per cent of the natural increase of these same
provinces. It was an exodus en masse, by which vast layers of
people from the underdeveloped zones—masses until this moment completely outside the bounds of the political life of the
country—were established in the large cities and particularly in
Buenos Aires.[38]

There are three great differences in migration patterns from the
early twentieth century to now, according to Germani. First, the
rhythm of the earlier patterns was much slower, since the urban
population growth lasted over at least three decades; second,
the masses that exerted political pressure and led toward effective universal suffrage were not immigrants themselves (who,
being foreigners, were participating only indirectly and with
difficulty in political processes), but their offspring; and lastly,
above all, it was a matter of a rise of the newly formed middle
class, leaving a nascent urban proletariat in a subordinate situation. These large masses, transplanted in short order to the
cities, transformed suddenly from rural *peones,* artisans, or
persons with hardships into industrial workers, acquired a
political significance without at the same time finding the institutional channels necessary for integrating themselves into the
normal functioning of the democracy.
    Strong evidence is provided by Johnson that this combination
of working-class mobilization *without* any corresponding class
integration, far from adding to social unrest, gave great support
to the middle classes. The working classes not only changed the
social morphology of city life, but provided precisely that sort
of battering rod for the bourgeois parties which in Europe were
channelized into socialist parties. "When the middle sectors
struck out on their own and began to provide the urban laborers
with direction, their intractability was converted into a political
asset. Everywhere the industrial workers contributed significantly to the initial victories of the middle sector leadership."[39]
The bourgeoisification of the workers thus proceeded through
the general urbanization process.

[38] Gino Germani, "The Transition to a Mass Democracy in Argentina,"
loc. cit., pp. 468–469.
[39] John J. Johnson, *Political Change in Latin America: The Emergence
of the Middle Sectors* (Stanford: Stanford University Press, 1958),
pp. 41–42.

The rurally based *caudillo* gives the masses their reflection in a charismatic personalistic leader able to register their frustrations through his will. Thus, the *caudillo* is everywhere celebrated among those masses who were often most exploited by the military clique. This is because while the *caudillo* saw his role as redeemer of national unity by converting the city into an arm of the state—in other words a right-wing image of national restoration—the peasantry saw in him the means of their liberation from oppressiveness of politics as such.

The residue of strength which the new-style *caudillo* retains among marginal groups—especially transitional groups in the process of moving from rural to urban centers—cannot be ignored in weighing this "populist-officialist" dichotomy. The *caudillo,* in his personalist appeals and in his public display of gifts and goods to the very poor, is an exemplar of the "doer" (military man) over and against the "talker" (political man). The strength of General Manuel Odría in the *barriadas* of Lima and of Juan Perón in the *villas miseria* of Buenos Aires indicates the continued identification with authority figures of a large portion of the unabsorbed spillover into semi-urban life.[40]

Hirschman's analysis of reform and revolution in terms of gaming analogies offers some cogent arguments as to why traditional classes *should,* if they were rational and in control of the political system, adopt "reform-mongering" tactics. Yet, as Hirschman himself indicates, there is "only a remote chance that the maneuver will work." But he urges this chance be taken, or face the specter of revolution, "the last of our possible outcomes."[41] However, this is not the last outcome. Revolutions are neither ultimate nor irrevocable. They may even

---

[40] François Bourricaud, "Structure and Function of the Peruvian Oligarchy," *Studies in Comparative International Development,* Vol. II (1966), No. 2; and Irving L. Horowitz, "Modern Argentina: The Politics of Power," *The Political Quarterly,* Vol. 30, No. 4 (October-December, 1959), 400–410.

[41] Albert O. Hirschman, *Journeys Toward Progress: Studies of Economic Policy-Making in Latin America* (New York: The Twentieth Century Fund, 1963), pp. 251–297. It is interesting to note that although Hirschman dedicates his book (in part) to Celso Furtado—calling him an "arch-reformmonger"—Furtado never so designates himself. Indeed, his own analysis of the revolutionary process in the Northeast stands in sharp contradiction to the Hirschman strategic approach. See Celso Furtado, *Dialética do desenvolvimento* (Rio de Janeiro: Editora Fundo de Cultura, 1964), pp. 137–155.

happen more than once. Reaction, or in economic terms, stagnation, is the ultimate outcome.

Hirschman's analysis would probably be more appropriate for factory owners in urban regions than for landholders in rural regions. Indeed, they have often, although with some reluctance, accepted unionization on precisely the grounds that the alternatives would be mass proletarian uprisings. The same approach seems to fall on deaf ears among the traditional classes. Several reasons, structural rather than strategic, suggest themselves for this capacity of the urban regions to accept and absorb reform-mongering, and the incapacity of the rural regions to do likewise. First, the notion of traditionalism implies a fixed relationship of superordination and subordination—which when threatened, threatens the entire social system based on the patron-laborer relationship. Second, it is far easier to divide money than land into equal shares. Land tenure and land ownership lead to total change. It is not something which landlords and peons are able to divide into equal shares. Third, the function of the factory owner is to provide investment capital, incentive, organizational skills, etc., all of which make him relatively understandable to the factory worker. But when the landholder loses his authority he can rarely, if ever, replace it with real offerings. Fourth, the rise of universalistic criteria tends to depersonalize relations, hence it "impersonalizes" solutions. These, at any rate, provide some explanation for why industrialization tends to yield reform rather than revolution, and why the opposite is the case in the rural areas of Latin America. The question persists, nonetheless, as to why reform-mongering has not dominated political styles to a greater extent.

Scott indicates that for Mexico at least there is a direct correlation between social class and political socialization. "The 10 or so percent who share participant political culture norms are found primarily in the upper and in the stable middle-middle class; of these no more than 1 or 2 percent could be characterized as viewing politics from the prospective of the more nearly democratic 'civic culture' of Almond and Verba."[42] Scott goes on to cite factors, primarily of a psychological type, that may account for this lag in mass politicalization. He cites the

[42] See Robert E. Scott, "Mexico: The Established Revolution," in Lucien W. Pye and Sidney Verba (eds.), *Political Culture and Political Development* (Princeton, New Jersey: Princeton University Press, 1965), pp. 330–395.

authoritarian values inculcated by the Church, the traditionalist *machismo* inculcated by the primary socializing agents of family and friends, the mistrust of collective action bred by poor work relationships, the stubbornness of rural values that tend to carry over perhaps more in Mexico than elsewhere—given the traditionalistic aspects of Mexico City. Whatever the causes of this lag in politicalization, the consequences are clear enough: the homogenization of the power structure and its tendency to become a bureaucratic elite. This process tends to confirm the stereotyped visions of politics in Latin America among Latin Americans. Thus, if the politics of reform are well-nigh impossible in the rural regions, they become difficult even in urban areas because the interest parties have never been able to succeed, and ideological parties have never been required to meet the pragmatic test of success.

The strategy of urban development is just as necessary to determine the future course of politics in Latin America as the strategy of industrial development. Urbanism can be viewed as coincidental and parallel with the growth of industrialization, rather than as a stage on the road to industrialization.

According to figures compiled by the United Nations, in those Latin American nations considered most developed (Argentina, Chile, Venezuela, and Brazil), the level of urbanization is approximately twice that of the level of industrialization. Whereas, in those nations often thought to be the less developed (Bolivia, Ecuador, Paraguay, and Peru) the percentage of urbanization and industrialization is in an almost exact one-to-one ratio. Thus, we either thoroughly redefine what development means, or what is more rational and simple, appreciate the fact that while urbanization is a necessary condition for industrial growth, it is also true that urbanization is consonant with a relatively low degree of industrialization. Such cities as Recife in Brazil and Puebla in Mexico attest to this. Thus, it would be short-sighted and intellectually risky to assume that urbanism is but a stage on the road to industrialism. Blumer has indicated that

> Early industrialization is neutral with regard to each of the four basic conditions which set the character of the classes of early industrial workers. Industrialization does not account for the

differences in the composition of these classes; it does not
account for the differences in the industrial milieux; it does not
account for the differences in outside conditions of life; and it
does not account for the definitions used to interpret experience
and to organize action. We have to look elsewhere for explanations of the make-up, the experiences, and the conduct of the
working classes that come into existence.[43]

Single causation theories of industrialism as the leading
factor in revolutionary discontent may be useful, but it must be
recognized that to the extent a society is rapidly industrialized
with a minimum of transitional fissures, to that extent, the city,
the cradle of such industrial enterprises, tends to promote
reform movements in contrast to revolutionary movements.
Industrial classes develop organizational solidarity, a sense of
upward mobility within the larger moneyed portions of the
society, and a firm conviction that their specific class needs can
be met by a "fair share" and fair distribution theory rather than
by revolutionary activities as such. This seems to be indicated
by the ideologies of Mexican, Argentinian, and Brazilian labor
movements.[44] This would further be reinforced by the close,
almost paternalistic ties of the trade unions with the dominant
political forces in each country.

The supreme importance of the question of urban politics in
Latin America is its direct political implications for the current
situation. For the difference between urban and rural attitudes
may be seen not just in contrasting attitudes toward change, but
in a mode of life where change is institutionalized (the city
complexes), in contrast to a mode of life where change is
apocalyptic and sporadic (the rural regions).[45]

There are three essential strategies of change now current:
the United States strategy of concentrating on developing a

[43] Herbert Blumer, "Early Industrialization and the Laboring Class,"
The Sociological Quarterly, I, No. 1 (January, 1960), 13.
[44] Michael Everett, "The Political Role of Trade Unions in Mexico"
(mimeographed); Neuma Aguiar Walker, "The Organization and Ideology of Brazilian Labor," in Irving L. Horowitz (ed.), *Revolution in
Brazil* (New York: E. P. Dutton & Co., 1964), pp. 242–256; Torcuato S.
Di Tella, *El sistema político argentino y la clase obrera* (Buenos Aires:
Editorial Universitaria de Buenos Aires, 1964).
[45] See Nels Anderson, "The Urban Way of Life," *International Journal
of Comparative Sociology*, III, No. 2 (December, 1962), 186–187.

national politics of a multiclass variety, the Soviet model of developing a politics of an industrial class variety, and a Chinese model of developing politics on the basis of mass peasant movements. What is involved is nothing short of the choice between reform and revolution on one side and between two strategies for making revolution on the other. While it may well be, indeed is even likely, that Latin America will create its own political mixtures (as it has until now), it is worth at least listing the choices as they are seen from the main political and ideological centers of the world.

If the United States model is to become successfully integrated in Latin America, it will be necessary for the class-mass dichotomy to be eliminated, and for a genuine national politics to emerge. The difficulty thus far has been the remarkable ineptitude and even corruption of the middle sectors. For the Soviet model to emerge as successful, the industrial class within the cities would have to see itself as linked to the peasant mass in the countryside, and see its own role in politicalization as the essential agent of revolution. For this orthodox Soviet view, the group which controls the cities controls the nation. However, the aspirations of the working class have moved closer to the middle sectors than to the peasant masses in most instances. The third model, the Chinese strategy, is the reverse. In the Maoist view the peasant mass surrounds the urban centers and overwhelms all the minority classes. In this doctrine, in the initial phase of revolution at least, he who controls the countryside controls the nation. The supreme difficulty with this approach for Latin America is the heavy concentration of the population in the coastal regions—and the increased reliance upon migration rather than recourse to revolution to secure mass goals.

It has been said that "the cities of Latin America are laboratories for the examination and analysis of emerging social classes, for the exploration into the social effects of industrialization, and for studies of social change."[46] This is certainly the case for North American social scientists. But it must equally, if indeed not more emphatically, be kept in mind that the cities of Latin America, for its inhabitants, are labyrinths

[46] Andrew H. Whiteford, *Two Cities of Latin America: A Comparative Description of Social Classes* (Garden City, New York: Doubleday & Co., 1964), p. 255.

of sharp class differentiation, examples of industrial distortions produced by centuries of both external and internal colonialism. These cities are essential proving grounds for social change based on social reform, and when that fails, for change based on social revolution.

The United States and
the Latin American Left Wings

JOHN J. JOHNSON

BETWEEN early 1964 and April, 1965, Latin American–United States relations experienced a surface calm unequalled since the Second World War. The specter of Castroism appeared less threatening to official circles in the United States and Latin America than it had earlier. In March, 1964, the overthrow of President João Goulart swung Brazil safely back into the hemisphere camp. Then, in a presidential election held in September, 1964, Chilean voters showed an overwhelming preference for the Christian Democrat candidate, Eduardo Frei, over his Socialist-Marxist opponent, Salvador Allende, who had stated that if elected he would work to strengthen Chilean economic and diplomatic ties with the Communist-bloc countries and to nationalize those parts of Chile's industrial economy most directly under foreign control. In March, 1965, the Chilean Christian Democrats won a sweeping congressional victory. The climate produced by these developments seemed to promise warmer relations between the United States and Latin America. There was, indeed, a strong tendency in the United States to forget that there had been no abatement of the basic social, economic and political inequalities that had led to the erosion of relations in the first place.

Then came the unilateral intervention in the Dominican Republic. Acting as if from instinct, outraged political and intellectual leaders in a number of the republics promptly charged that the United States was reverting to its policies of the 1920's.

Meanwhile, Washington warned that the inability or un-

willingness of Latin American governments to react decisively
to real or imagined threats to the security of the hemisphere
would not deter the United States from responding to those
threats in a manner it considered appropriate. On October 12,
1966, Thomas Mann, Undersecretary of State for Economic
Affairs, in addressing the annual meeting of the Inter-American
Press Association convened at San Diego, affirmed the right-
eousness of the United States' position. Before Secretary
Mann's address it had already become clear that whatever else
the intervention meant in terms of United States–Latin American policy, it had shattered any delusion that cooperative
ventures, such as the Alliance for Progress, were narrowing the
gap of misunderstanding between Washington and the responsible civilian leaders of Latin America. The deep implication of
the intervention can be understood only if we appreciate that
since 1945 the pace of change in Latin America has accelerated
so fast that international relations have been unable to keep in
step.

Even the most cursory examination of the state of Latin
America reveals that everywhere the traditional structure of the
republics is crumbling as millions abandon established values
for new ones that are often transitory and rooted in the moment. Political and economic power are shifting with increasing
speed from the traditionally structured hacienda to the as yet
unorganized cities. Historically privileged minorities no longer
enjoy unchallenged power. New groups are forcing traditional
ones to accept political and social subordination. The last
remnants of mutual interest between the "haves" and the "have
nots" are under attack. This development is most apparent in
the cities, but it is evident even on the haciendas, and especially
on the holdings devoted to large-scale commercial agriculture.

Like other members of his society, Juan Pueblo, the symbol
of the great working mass in Latin America, is becoming restless and self-willed in his personal search for social justice,
money, and status. Whether at any given moment Juan Pueblo
leans toward traditional democratic practices or seeks simple
solutions to his complex problems, the record shows that he
increasingly responds to the appeals and programs of the non-
Communist leftists.

The leftist groups to whom the new and insecure urban
dwellers are tempted to look—and whom the United States

tends to overlook—hold the key to the future of Latin America, and to United States–Latin American relations. They are, as a rule, well to the left of the current Latin American regimes that the United States supports (with varying degrees of enthusiasm but which it nonetheless supports). At least until they achieve power, the leftist elements will keep Latin America agitated socially, economically, and politically. Just as surely, they will keep alive the apprehension their countries hold toward the United States.

Currently the non-Communist left wings are important power factors in all but four of the republics. They do not figure significantly in Cuba, which appears to have been moved body and soul into the Communist camp, leaving for the moment no opportunity for overt opposition of a serious nature. For two quite different reasons, the non-Communist leftists in Mexico, Costa Rica, and Uruguay are effectively removed from the sources of power. First, those societies have developed viable political systems, which up to now have absorbed interest groups as they have emerged. Second, Mexico and Costa Rica and to a lesser extent Uruguay have thus far maintained a sufficient degree of economic momentum to satisfy the minimum demands of nearly their entire population.

In the other republics, the non-Communist leftists break down into essentially three main groupings. The first two groupings are primarily political in nature. One is represented by the left in Brazil prior to April 1, 1964. Similar elements are to be found in Ecuador, Venezuela, and Argentina. The second group is illustrated by the current Chilean regime of Christian Democrat Eduardo Frei. Its most representative example is probably found in Peru, where it is currently supporting the reform measures of the Belaúnde Terry administration. The third grouping, the "angry left," is both the most characteristic of the Latin American left wing movements and the hardest to identify.

The United States government hailed with thinly veiled pleasure the overthrow of Brazil's leftist president, João Goulart, and within hours recognized the military-dominated regime that had forced Goulart into exile in Uruguay. From the beginning the United States has worked closely with the Castelo Branco regime, as witness the cooperation of the two republics in the Dominican peace force. Five months after Goulart's ouster the

United States, with equal public enthusiasm, greeted leftist Eduardo Frei's electoral landslide over Salvador Allende in the Chilean presidential elections.

In view of the United States' response to these two developments in the leftist camp, it is worthwhile to compare the kinds of leftism that they—Goulart at the moment of his overthrow from office and Frei as he campaigned for the presidency—represent.

There was a striking similarity in the programs of the two men. Both were secular in their outlook: Goulart was frankly anticlerical and openly defied Catholic lay groups; Frei, though convinced that religion has an important place in modern society, stood for rigid separation of Church and State, and strongly supported public education. In mid-1965, Frei had an audience with Pope Paul VI, a meeting that would have been unlikely between Allende, had he won, and the Prelate.

Both Frei and Goulart regarded urban industrial development as the major political problem, and regarded agrarian reform as a major social obligation. It is generally granted that Frei was sincere and perhaps even realistic when he called for land reform designed to give title to 100,000 rural but landless families, approximately 15 percent of Chile's total population. Goulart's commitment to agrarian reform is not so clear. His opponents insist that during his brief tenure as president he acquired over a million acres of land to add to his already large holdings in the south of Brazil. Many responsible individuals have found it extremely difficult, if not impossible, to reconcile his seeming mania for land and his fervent public statements favoring drastic agrarian reform.

Both Goulart and Frei demanded a new deal in international trade that would make their countries more dependent upon exchange of goods and less dependent upon aid. Frei insisted that he would trade anywhere so long as it benefited Chile and that he would do this without reference to the Cold War. Neither Goulart nor Frei felt that his nation's economic problems could be solved simply by signing inter-American agreements. Both hoped instead to resolve them in a world rather than a hemispheric context, although the Chilean was not as insistent upon this as was his Brazilian counterpart.

Frei and Goulart were both, at heart, state planners. They were committed to the proposition that, in developing countries, growth is more important than who is responsible for it. Each man, as a consequence of his views on state planning, strongly supported heavy public involvement in economic growth and social welfare. Each held that capitalism degrades human dignity. Both were highly nationalistic and insisted on tight regulation of foreign investment. Frei promised to "Chileanize" copper, which for half a century has provided Chile with some 60 percent of its foreign exchange. To Frei, Chileanization meant state control of the copper industry without totally eliminating foreign investors, whose holdings in Chile approximate one billion dollars. Frei has since carried out his copper policy over the objections of the extreme left, which called for full nationalization.

Despite these similarities, Goulart and Frei were far apart in a number of vital areas. Goulart was a political pragmatist, with a "come as you are" philosophy. He was interested first of all in power; he asked for votes, not commitment, and was prepared to bypass constitutional procedures, even to resort to violence, in order to gain his ends. Frei, on the other hand, offered a social Christian doctrine which he urged his supporters to accept along with his social and economic reform program. He convinced the Chilean voters and the United States that he stood foursquare for peaceful revolution within Chile's legal and constitutional framework.

Goulart, although not a Communist himself, in his last frantic days in office turned increasingly to the Communists in his political household. Frei, while acknowledging that Chilean Communists were battling for many legitimate causes, made it clear that he believed that he could win those causes as readily with democratic and Christian allies as with Communist ones. In publicly attributing constructive roles to the Communists, Frei reflected the attitude of many Chilean non-Communists leftists. They are not alarmed by Marxist Communism because they have grown up with it, and have in fact borrowed heavily from it in developing their own political, social, and economic doctrines.

Two salient points about the non-Communist leftists in Latin America emerge: first, they range over a broad social-economic spectrum; second, they do not have the same distrust of Communism that the population of the United States as a whole has. The apparently contradictory attitude of the United States in greeting the downfall of Goulart and election of Frei with equal enthusiasm suggests that the United States, however reluctantly, has come to accept those leftists who can control their clienteles. Frei was able to do this; Goulart was not.

Political leaders such as Goulart and Frei receive much support for their programs from what I have called the angry left. It could as well be called the intellectual left, since it is comprised almost solely of men of letters, professionals, and university students. The angry leftists are those who refuse to be satisfied with the state of their fellow men or who simply hate unanimity, and there are many of the latter persuasion in the Spanish–Portuguese-speaking world. Those who are angry constitute a very small proportion of the total population, but what they lack in numbers they make up for in tenacity.

Unlike the Goularts and Freis, who live on votes, the angry leftists thrive on ideas. They seem to prefer to be leaders without responsibility. This may be just as well, for when they do assume high office they are often dreadful administrators.

The angry left suffers from exaggerated concern with what its historical image will be. Its members fear that they may be looked upon as someone's tool. This often prevents them from giving full cooperation to politicians of their own countries or to international organizations.

The angry leftists distinguish themselves from other political leftists in a number of ways. Unlike many politicians, the angry leftists refuse to rest upon their laurels. Should their present goals somehow be miraculously achieved they would immediately come forward with new and more demanding ones. They can be impossibly unreasonable when they argue ideas from their hearts instead of their heads. They can keep the social scientists reeling as they variously place the blame for the wretchedness of their land on priests, the military, the Indian, the foreigner, on democracy, dictatorship, bookishness, ignorance, or even divine intervention. They may be totally irrational in drawing distinctions between their own cultures and those of the remainder of the Western world.

Those of the angry left who draw the sharpest distinctions between their own societies and those of other Western nations do so out of a conviction that the remainder of the West refuses to accept them and their nations as equals. They are torn on the one hand by the cultural and spiritual estrangement they feel, and on the other, by a desire to resemble the prestige cultures of the West without appearing to depend on them. Their bewilderment as to where they fit into the cultural pattern of the West often drives them to seek security behind a wall of xenophobic nationalism.

Regardless of how they are accepted by their own people or are viewed from abroad, the angry leftists perform an indispensable service. They have a long and proud tradition of breaking lances in the name of causes that seemed hopeless but were eventually won. They are men of conscience where the privileged are too often socially unconscious. Since 1918 university students have carried a heavy share of responsibility for keeping new ideas boiling, new objectives alive. In that year in Córdoba, Argentina, students began a university reform movement which soon found a warm reception throughout most of the republics. The universities ceased to be sanctuaries for privileged elites and classical students but became essentially centers for political action. Since then the ideal student has been a political combatant, or as the Peruvian literary critic Luis Alberto Sánchez has preferred to say, "a belligerent soldier in the social struggle."

During periods of dictatorship the students have been the shock troops of the opposition. They are the civilians who have been killed, martyred, and exiled. When democratic regimes have control, the students are expected to continue as agitators and apostles of the as yet unfulfilled revolution. Few would deny the students the right to their felt need to fight the status quo. They have seen too many politicians mount their horses from the left and descend from the right, and they have witnessed so much opportunism, favor-trading, and corruption that they are entitled to a substantial amount of sustained indignation.

However, their behavior and tactics often leave much to be desired. They are prone to feel that only they can make a revolution and that they must do it before they graduate. Their conviction drives them to become agitators before they have become students of political science; they are inclined to depend too heavily upon borrowed slogans and not heavily enough upon reason. Therefore they can easily come under the influence of student leaders who have had the benefit of training by experts in the ideological struggle. This occurred at the National University of Venezuela in Caracas a few years ago. There, seventeen- and eighteen-year-olds were taught to believe that their supreme responsibility was to protect Communists and *fidelistas* who hid behind the autonomy of the University. Students who had no thought of becoming Communists themselves, in effect, took it upon themselves to protect the Communists from Venezuelan courts.

The extreme leftist infiltration of university student movements has by no means been limited to Venezuela. In Peru, for example, there have been times when key student organizations in the four-hundred-year-old University of San Marcos in Lima and the University in Trujillo have been under the control of *fidelistas*. The strong extreme-leftist influence in the University of Concepción, Chile, was brought to the attention of the hemisphere in late 1965 when Senator Robert Kennedy visited its campus and was submitted to various abuses.

What is as much or more to the point—in the struggle for student attention, politics very often is given precedence over the classroom. Agitational politics often take students away from their studies for prolonged periods of time. If they push too hard they may see their institutions closed down. The result is that if students do graduate they do so as professionals without vocations, and when their turn has come to participate in government they ordinarily lack adequate technical administrative skills to initiate and sustain original reform programs.

But again, it matters little whether or not one approves the students' political activities. Such activities will continue and students will have a disproportionate degree of influence so long as competing power centers remain divided. There is a probability that dogmatic ideological ballast may prove more important than political sophistication when it comes to changing the social and economic structure of the republics.

The nations of Latin America will have to meet new situations for which the past furnishes little precedent, and, therefore, predictions are dangerous. Nevertheless, it seems likely that the power of the non-Communist leftists, of both the political and angry types, will increase before it subsides. The range of developments favoring them is nearly limitless, and the range of circumstances threatening them is narrow indeed. Leftism as an ideology appeals particularly to young people, who are willing to challenge the convictions of their elders and are less committed that their elders to traditional institutions. Latin America's population, taken as a whole, is one of the youngest in the world. Figures compiled by the Inter-American Development Bank show that in mid-1965 over 42 percent of the area's total population were under fifteen years of age and over 51 percent under twenty years of age. Comparable figures for the United States were approximately 31 percent and 39 percent respectively. Brazil and Mexico together had over 54 percent of Latin America's total population, and 54.5 percent of their combined population were under twenty years of age. Among the Latin American republics, Costa Rica had the highest percentage (58.7) of citizens under twenty years of age.

Implicit in these demographic figures are three good reasons why the left will prosper: (1) Latin America's population is to an unusual degree in age groups requiring expensive services such as schools and medical care. The record of the past indicates that the governments will find it difficult to provide those services in sufficient amounts to satisfy the working groups. At the moment, for example, the area, taken in its entirety, is putting approximately 2 percent of its gross product into education as compared to 5.75 percent for the United States with its markedly older population. (2) Persons of working age will have to provide for so many dependents that the prospect of their achieving satisfactory levels of living for themselves and their families appears slight unless new and aggressive institutions are established. (3) Industry and commerce are unlikely to develop fast enough to absorb today's children into well-paying jobs. The enormity of that responsibility can be appreciated when it is realized that by 1975 Latin America must somehow provide approximately 29 million new jobs, of which only about 4 million can be expected to come from the agricultural sector.

The situations that large Brazil and small El Salvador face call attention to the dilemmas confronting their sister republics. Brazil, with one-half the population, must provide as many new jobs each year as does the United States. Demographic projections strongly support the view that Brazil not only cannot expect any letup in the demand for new jobs but must, in fact, anticipate an acceleration of those demands. Brazil's population picture substantiates this view. Its population in 1960 was about 71 million. By 1970 its population will be in the neighborhood of 97 million, by 1980 around 132 million, by 1990 an estimated 180 million, and by the year 2000 a potentially dangerous 245 million. If the margin of error in these figures is not unduly excessive, during the last decade of this century Brazil's population will surge upward at the rate of 6.5 million, or more than the present total annual increment for all of Latin America. And population growth must be translated into job opportunities if anything resembling stability is to be attained.

In some respects El Salvador's potential problems are even more overwhelming than Brazil's. The little Central American republic does not have an industrial-commercial base such as Brazil's from which to launch a broad-gauged and continuing economic revolution of the nature needed to meet the job requirements of its burgeoning population. El Salvador's current population of approximately 3 million will rise an estimated 66 percent, to 5 million by 1981. At that point in time El Salvador will have one person for every acre of its land mass, including volcanoes. And unless economic growth is somehow maintained at an unprecedented level, El Salvador could two decades hence be on its way to becoming another Haiti.

Another situation favoring the leftists is that in Latin America leftism is first of all an urban phenomenon. And the cities of Latin America are growing at a fantastic rate. Buenos Aires, which during the 1940's was overrun by rural people who rushed to attach themselves to the dictator Perón, is the only exception. Between 1950 and 1960 São Paulo increased its population 78 percent, to 4,357,000; Mexico City, 60 percent, to 4,800,000; Caracas, 62 percent, to 1,356,000; and Lima, 95 percent, to 1,262,000. The major urban centers have grown rapidly because, despite their grossly inadequate provision for the welfare of the working man, they have provided more variety and a better life than the countryside.

A vast majority of those freshly funneled into the major cities have given the non-Communist left the first opportunity to satisfy their minimum demands. In general, only after the newcomers felt that the reformist elements had betrayed them have they turned to the extreme left.

Organized labor represents still another development favoring the non-Communist lefts. Urban labor forces are only beginning to come into their own and clearly there is, at the present time, little correlation between labor's numerical strength and its voice in the process of change. Still, it would seem that organized labor has the potential to become the core around which major reform movements might develop. Labor's weakness to date may be ascribed to four developments. First, only a small minority of urban workers have been unionized. Even in a modern society such as Chile's, fewer than three in

ten urban workers belong to a union. Second, constant inflation
has forced the unions to concentrate their efforts on periodically
obtaining very large wage increases. Third, only in Uruguay,
Chile, and Costa Rica are there genuine free trade union movements. Elsewhere the unions generally are controlled by the
State. Not unusually, labor organizations are financed by the
State because the workers cannot afford to pay union dues.
Under such circumstances it is not surprising that in bargaining
sessions between labor and capital the State is the arbiter.
Fourth, labor suffers in terms of power because the strike is
relatively ineffective (for the reasons suggested above), and
because specialization has not reached the point where strikes
can bring activity to a standstill.

Despite government intervention in the labor movement, the
unions in recent years seem more often to have won victories
than to have suffered defeat. Organized labor's major setback
since Castro came to power occurred in Brazil. There, following
the overthrow of President Goulart in April, 1964, a military
regime named labor leaders who could be trusted to reflect the
views of the nation's military-dominated government.

There will be no shortage of angry university students. Despite the general neglect of education noted above, enrollment is
growing in the universities where leftist agitation tends to
spawn; the total university enrollment is now in the neighborhood of 680,000. By 1970 the republics hope to enroll a total
of 985,000—still less than a fourth of the number who already
attend colleges in the United States, but large for societies
whose rate of development is slow. Discontent within the university communities can be expected to increase if the public
bureaucracies and industry do not expand rapidly enough to
absorb the graduates who will enter the job market over the
next few years. The prospects of such a development actually
occurring are not bright. Already the supply of university
graduates seeking employment in appointive public offices
greatly exceeds the demand, and there is little to suggest that
managerial positions in private enterprise will be able to take up
the slack.

The employment opportunities for those trained in the hu-
manities, particularly in education and law, appear especially
unfavorable. The unpromising future of students in those fields
is significant because they have been the ones who, at both
undergraduate and graduate levels, have been most inclined to

engage in agitational politics. Their political radicalism can be explained in part by long exposure to reform-minded professors. In the case of the prospective teacher, there is the added consideration that he cannot look forward either to an adequate salary or social prestige. The lawyer, who historically has sought security in public and private bureaucracies rather than in private law practice, is faced with growing competition for the positions in public and private enterprises to which he feels entitled by virtue of his academic training.

The non-Communist left wing will prosper because Latin America is growing up politically and socially. The various social-economic groups will settle their differences increasingly in political combat rather than in street scuffles and guerrilla skirmishes. This is the kind of political climate that the non-Communist leftists welcome because they feel sure, and with good reason, that they have numbers and time on their side. In this regard one should note that, despite *fidelista* violence in Venezuela and rather widespread political violence in Ecuador and Santo Domingo during 1965, political violence directly involving civilians is dropping rapidly in most republics. In fact, although Latin America as a whole has had an extraordinary amount of disorder and instability, violence is not generalized there. Since the late 1920's no United States citizen has lost his life in a change of government in Latin America. The area has had only three major wars in a century and a quarter. For three decades before the military took over in 1964, Brazil had maintained a quite respectable record of political nonviolence at the national level. Force has not figured in Uruguayan politics for a half-century now. Chile in particular has a deep-seated tradition of nonviolence in politics, symbolized by the fact that no Chilean president has ever been assassinated. In marked contrast with the past, violence arising from military coups is more and more directed against opposing elements within the armed forces themselves and less and less often against civilians.

A further factor which may be expected to favor the non-Communist leftists is that radical reformism has become fashionable, and for the political opportunists not only fashionable but profitable. Just about everywhere that honest elections for national offices are held, reformists are growing stronger at the expense of the traditionalists. In 1960 in Brazil, Jânio Quadros, running as an independent, and promising all things to all men, won an overwhelming presidential victory. In the 1964 Chilean presidential contest 95 percent of the vote went to parties that are so far left in their social and economic thinking that they make Johnson Democrats indistinguishable from McKinley Republicans. Meanwhile, as the nations of Latin America develop closer contacts with one another, the policies of a reformist regime in one country will tend to have healthy repercussions in neighboring republics.

Several conclusions may be drawn. First of all, Latin Americans have a long way to go to translate their notions of dignity and the good life into the reality for which they yearn. A vast majority of us can find some comfort in the fact that, except in Cuba, they are seeking the solutions to their frustrating problems through relatively democratic institutions. Democratic practices do permeate political life in Latin America under all but the harshest of dictatorships. One of the remarkable recent developments favoring democracy in the area has been a shift away from violence and personal authoritarianism to greater reliance upon manipulation, persuasion, and group consensus.

Second, we should not forget that the interplay between new hopes and old ways almost inevitably produces conflicts susceptible to exploitation by extremists of both the right and the left and by external powers as well. Development is disruptive. The records show that too often friends of democracy do not appreciate this. Most particularly, the records show that friends of democracy have not been perceptive in distinguishing between those who feel a sincere and urgent need for reform but prefer to work within democratic frameworks, and those who demand reform at all costs. The democrat who refuses to distinguish between the leftist elements, and excuses himself with the explanation that the non-Communist leftists are Communists in democratic garb, is like a man sitting on a keg of TNT—sure in the knowledge that it will eventually lose its potency and oblivious to the possibility that someone in the meantime may light the fuse to it.

Third, democratic institutions in Latin America are on trial as never before to show their capacity to meet demands imposed upon them for social and economic progress. They need support wherever they can find it.

Fourth, it is easy but dangerous to stick with a loser, but that is just what we are doing at this moment in each of the Latin

American countries. The proof is that Washington is supporting the most socially conservative elements that could possibly win an honest election, and doing that grudgingly.

Can we out of loyalty afford to go down to defeat with a leadership that has lost touch or is losing touch with the popular masses? Or do we have a moral responsibility to stay in touch with the human substructure? We would seem to have that moral obligation, both to ourselves and to the non-Communist reform elements of Latin America. There the popular masses can no longer go unheeded. The elite members of society, who when torn between the fear of failure and the fear of the masses have preferred failure, are on their way out. The non-Communist leftists seek to absorb the masses rather than to crush them. The absorption process will take place and it will do so amidst great social turbulence. The United States must know when to show sympathy rather than suspicion, and when the choices are not clear opt for the future rather than the past. To do otherwise is to invite alienation from the great and growing masses of the Latin American republics.

Violence and Politics

in Latin America

MERLE KLING

*At times it seems to me that the absence of bloodshed and
death drives us desperate, as if we feel ourselves alive only
when surrounded by firing squads and destruction . . .*
    DON GAMIEL BERNAL, a character in a novel by Carlos
Fuentes, *The Death of Artemio Cruz.*

FORCE or violence, as Marx observed, may be "the midwife of
every old society which is pregnant with the new,"[1] but neither
Marx nor less paternal students of the ontogeny of revolutions
recognize the capacity of political midwives to affect the hered-
ity of the political offspring that they deliver. Modal studies of
revolution, drawing upon the French and Russian revolutions
for illustrative data, specify the causes of major revolutions,
describe patterns in the rhythms of revolutionary movements,
assess the durable consequences of revolutionary upheavals.
But possible links between varieties of violence and revolutionary outcomes are left unexplored. For well-known studies of
revolution, written by authors who wear the conceptual spectacles provided by the political cultures of the United States and
Great Britain, treat violence with literary and analytical economy. After all, their political cultures evaluate violence as
aberrant, exceptional behavior.

[1] Cited in Frederick Engels, *Herr Eugen Dühring's Revolution in
Science (Anti-Dühring)* (New York: International Publishers, 1939),
p. 203.

191

Yet, just as elections may be regarded as manifest aspects of political systems in Western Europe and the United States, revolutions, with their accompanying violence, may be regarded as an aspect of the political culture of many Latin American political systems. Thus elections (in some political systems) and revolutions (in other political systems) become related to distinctive political expectations, demands, and norms; to distinctive standards of recruitment of political elites; to alternative definitions of political skill within political systems; and to divergent strategies for the pursuit of power.

ELECTIONS AND NONVIOLENT POLITICAL SYSTEMS

Elections constitute integral elements of nonviolent political systems in contemporary British and North American societies. Socialized into acceptance of nonviolent methods of political competition, virtually all relevant parties to political conflict in these societies expect elections to take place and consider it right that they should take place. The political culture—the prevailing, widely distributed beliefs, values, cognitions, and affective responses—sanctions the resolution of contests for public office by election, by vote, and condemns the intrusion of violence within the arena of internal political conflict. The advocate of violence in these societies, consequently, not only defies the formal juridical rules of the political system; he attacks the psychological supports of the juridical system, since he threatens highly salient norms.

Violent behavior is not absent from British and North American societies, but it is *predominantly* oriented toward nonpolitical objects. Violence does not significantly affect the choice of governmental leaders, the articulation and aggregation of group interests, the patterns of authority for the entire society, the content of domestic and foreign policies, or the allocation of large, tangible resources. Experts in the employment of organized violence, military personnel, compete for rewards but do not fire their weapons, or threaten to fire their weapons, in order to assist one group of political competitors as against another, to force the adoption of one public policy as opposed to another.

Means become linked with ends. Acceptance of the discipline

and restraint of means (elections) is accompanied by contraction of the scope of change envisioned as ends (goals). Advocacy of violence in a political system that has assimilated the norms of elections can be justified only on behalf of drastic changes, on behalf of millennial goals. Since violence represents a deviant means by the standards of such a political culture, it can be embraced only on behalf of deviant ends. A group that acquiesces in the election norms of a nonviolent political culture, accordingly, exposes its goals to subtle forces of attrition. For it proves difficult to maintain, simultaneously, loyalty to apocalyptic visions and prosaic rules of electoral competition. In a culture of political nonviolence, revolutions, rather than elections, mark rapid and profound transitions in public policies and the massive restructuring of a political system.

The United States and Great Britain, therefore, exemplify political systems in which (1) elections take place regularly and frequently; (2) violence is oriented predominantly toward nonpolitical objects; (3) experts in the manipulation of violence do not utilize their expertise in order to determine public policies and to designate leading governmental personnel; (4) the process of political socialization discourages the selection of violence as an appropriate method for political participation; (5) advocacy of, or resort to, violence is widely perceived as a deviant means associated with the pursuit of deviant ends relative to prevailing norms; and (6) elections are compatible with divergent, but circumscribed, policy outcomes.

REVOLUTIONS AND A CULTURE OF POLITICAL VIOLENCE

In contrast with the United States and Great Britain, many Latin American political systems are characterized by manifestly violent political behavior and acceptance of violence as a "legitimate" means for the pursuit of power.

1. *Frequency of revolution.* The popular image of Latin America as an area of endemic revolution is warranted. The resolution of succession problems by methods not authorized by constitutional prescription is a recurring phenomenon, and the replacement of leading personnel, notably presidents, by acts of violence is common. "Between independence and World War I," Edwin Lieuwen notes, "the Spanish-American republics

experienced 115 successful revolutions and many times that number of abortive revolts."[2] In the two decades 1931–1950, there were 58 successful revolutions.[3] During the period between 1940 and 1955, the office of president in Latin American countries was occupied by 121 men, forty-two of whom remained in office less than one year, and there were 136 successions to the presidency.[4] Between January 1, 1950 and January 1, 1965, as the following list indicates, at least 40 successful revolutions occurred. If all the changes in the office of president or the leadership of juntas or the composition of executive councils in Haiti (May 1957) and the Dominican Republic (January 1962 and December 1963) were included, the number would be even larger.

May 1950	Haiti	May 1957	Colombia
May 1951	Bolivia	June 1957	Haiti
May 1951	Panama	July 1957	Guatemala
March 1952	Cuba	October 1957	Guatemala
April 1952	Bolivia	January 1958	Venezuela
December 1952	Venezuela	January 1959	Cuba
June 1953	Colombia	October 1960	El Salvador
May 1954	Paraguay	May 1961–	Dominican
June 1954	Guatemala	January 1962	Republic
August 1954	Brazil	August 1961	Brazil
December 1954	Honduras	November 1961	Ecuador
January 1955	Panama	March 1962	Argentina
September 1955	Argentina	July 1962	Peru
November 1955	Argentina	March 1963	Peru
November 1955	Brazil	March 1963	Guatemala
September 1956	Nicaragua	July 1963	Ecuador
October 1956	Honduras	September 1963	Dominican
December 1956	Haiti		Republic
February 1957	Haiti	October 1963	Honduras
April 1957	Haiti	April 1964	Brazil
May 1957	Haiti	November 1964	Bolivia

[2] *Arms and Politics in Latin America*, revised edition (New York: Frederick A. Praeger, 1961), p. 21.

[3] Lee Benson Valentine, *A Comparative Study of Successful Revolutions in Latin America, 1941–1950* (Stanford University: Ph.D. dissertation, 1952), pp. 246–247.

[4] Huey Carl Camp, *Presidential Politics in Latin America: The Dynamics of Power* (Washington University, St. Louis: Ph.D. dissertation, 1965), Table XXXVI, pp. 442–443.

During the period 1950–1965, consequently, revolutions took place in sixteen of the twenty Latin American republics. Only in Mexico, Uruguay, Chile, and Costa Rica was the period marked by the absence of revolution.

2. *Pervasive political violence.* Every election campaign does not culminate in victory. Every outburst of political violence does not culminate in revolution. While displays of politically oriented violence are not confined to successful campaigns for control of the presidency in Latin America, the political systems are permeated by acts of violence. If each violent action does not result in revolution—and it does not—the frequency of acts of political violence, nevertheless, encourages the perception of violence as a highly visible means for pursuing political ends.

Although fragmentary reporting and dissimilar criteria for the inclusion and exclusion of evidence prevent the compilation of uniform and complete inventories of violence in Latin America, data on the pervasiveness of political violence in the area are impressive and relatively abundant. One study noted "some 3,500 Latin American insurgency and insurgency-related events" for the period 1946–1963.[5] The same study comments upon the historical continuity of violence in the area:

> Historians have grown haggard in the task of counting up all the insurgencies and civil wars to which the "Age of the Caudillos" gave rise. Venezuela, for example, had suffered 52 important revolts by 1912. Bolivia had more than 60 "revolutions" by 1898 and had assassinated six presidents. Colombia had experienced 27 civil wars, one of which claimed 80,000 and another 100,000 lives. These are among the more extreme examples but many of the other republics did not lag far behind.[6]

And a statistical summary of the incidence of internal wars, 1946–1959, compiled by Harry Eckstein from the *New York Times Index,* illustrates the ubiquity of political violence in Latin America. In his summary, unequivocal cases include warfare, turmoil, rioting, terrorism, mutiny and coups, and equivocal cases include plots, administrative action, and two quasi-private cases that may not be politically oriented.[7]

5 Atlantic Research Corporation, Georgetown Research Project, *A Historical Survey of Patterns and Techniques of Insurgency Conflicts in Post-1900 Latin America* (Arpa Project 4860) (1964), pp. ii–iii.

6 *Ibid.,* p. 51.

7 *Internal War: The Problem of Anticipation* (January 15, 1962, mimeographed), Appendix I, p. 3.

INCIDENCE OF INTERNAL WARS, 1946–1959

	Unequivocal	Unequivocal and Equivocal
Argentina	35	57
Bolivia	34	53
Brazil	36	49
Chile	9	21
Colombia	42	47
Costa Rica	16	19
Cuba	80	100
Dominican Republic	2	6
Ecuador	26	41
El Salvador	4	9
Guatemala	32	45
Haiti	32	40
Honduras	10	11
Mexico	27	28
Nicaragua	13	16
Panama	23	29
Paraguay	19	29
Peru	20	23
Uruguay		1
Venezuela	26	36

In the light of the evidence, political violence cannot be regarded as aberrant behavior in Latin America. It is recurring, chronic, and rule-conforming rather than heteroclite. If participants in a political culture of nonviolence expect periodic elections, then politically orientated members of Latin American societies should expect unscheduled but regular manifestations of political violence. For violence, as Harry Eckstein strikingly points out in a series of generalized propositions, is capable of becoming a self-perpetuating style of political behavior:

> In some societies, the most manifest cause of internal war seems to be internal war itself, one instance following another, often without a recurrence of the conditions that led to the original event. This means that political disorientations may be followed by the formation of a new set of orientations, establishing a predisposition toward violence that is inculcated by the experience of violence itself. In such cases, internal wars result not from specifiable objective conditions, and not even from the loss of legitimacy by a particular regime, but from a general lack of

receptivity to legitimacy of any kind. Violence becomes a political style that is self-perpetuating. . . .[8]

3. *The roles of experts in violence.* Although military personnel in the United States and Great Britain are not political eunuchs, their roles are relatively restricted. They are likely to articulate interests of limited scope, particularly the competing interests of armed services for budgetary allocations, but they are not likely to perform functions of interest aggregation, general political socialization and recruitment, authoritative rule-making and rule-interpretation. Typically, they do not announce their support for, or opposition to, programs of medical care for the aged, plans for the nationalization of railroads, or alternative schemes for financing education. Since their doctrinal training tends to identify the symbolism of "politics" with prohibited activity, military personnel in the United States, in the process of acquiring professional standards of behavior, are encouraged to develop little preoccupation with a large variety of policy outcomes.

One element in Latin American systems of political violence is the *diffuseness,* rather than the specialization, of the roles of experts in violence. They do not merely promote interests of various segments of the armed forces and administer, actively or latently, severe sanctions in order to enforce policies formulated by authoritative decision-makers. They conspicuously engage in the selection of governing personnel, the promulgation of public policies, the resolution of succession crises, the competition for office, and the allocation of budgetary resources. Among Latin American military personnel, technical competence in the employment of violence merges with a concern for the diverse policy outputs of the political system.

The low demands for combat duty by Latin American military units against foreign enemies, moreover, mean that military personnel and material can be mobilized for participation in revolutionary maneuvers and interservice rivalries, and that a trained military bureaucracy is available, and possibly eager, to discharge administrative duties that are carried on ineptly (at least in the eyes of some) by civilian officials. Obviously, military personnel are equipped and trained to participate effectively in Latin American revolutions. Thus a study of twenty-

8 "On the Etiology of Internal Wars," *History and Theory,* Volume IV, Number 2 (1965), pp. 150–151.

198   ▮ THE SOCIOECONOMIC PIVOT

nine successful revolutions during the period 1941–1950 concludes: "The military played a significant role in the 29 revolutions."[9] Another study of Latin American presidents between 1940 and 1955 notes that "national military contingents account for thirty-nine of fifty-seven forcefully attained shifts of presidential personnel."[10]

The ability of military personnel to occupy the office of president in Latin American societies provides an additional measure of their political influence and power, and the evidence of the recruitment of Latin American presidents from the ranks of military officers is revealing. "To take a single year," according to Edwin Lieuwen, "in 1954 thirteen of the twenty republics were ruled by military presidents." Moreover, between 1930 and 1957, "fifty-six military men . . . held the presidential office in the twenty Latin American republics for as long as a year."[11]

Examination of the professional backgrounds of the 121 men who held the office of president in a Latin American country at some time during the period 1940–1955 yields particularly striking results. Relevant data on occupational background were secured for 116 presidents. They were classified into professional categories, and since many presidents (25 percent of the military group and more than 75 percent of the civilian group) qualified for more than one category, the total number is greater than the number of men who held office. The number of presidents, classified according to professional background, follows:

Military	51
Legal profession	33
Educators	31
Communications media—writers, journalists, owners of newspapers, etc.	18
Medical doctors	10
Bankers and financiers	9
Landowners, agriculturalists	8
Other (businessmen, managers, engineers, architects, etc.)	19

[9] Lee Benson Valentine, *op. cit.*, p. 261.
[10] Huey Carl Camp, *op. cit.*, p. 164.
[11] *Op. cit.*, pp. 122, 129.

As the study that collected these data points out:

> . . . the military grouping is larger by far than any single . . .
> grouping in the civilian segment of the sample. Furthermore,
> the members of the military are one of the most homogeneous
> occupational groups . . . Multiple occupational classifications
> appear much more frequently among the civilian presidents than
> they do in the military category.

In fact, every state in Latin America had at least one president
with a background of professional military service between
1940 and 1955.[12]

Not only do military personnel often secure presidential office
in Latin America, but they tend to maintain themselves in office
for prolonged periods. *Continuismo,* extension of the term of
office of an incumbent by a variety of legalistic and manipula-
tive devices, not uncommonly is associated with the tenure of a
military president. Hence, men of military background, while
constituting only 42.1 percent of the total number of presidents
during the period 1940–1955, held office for almost two-thirds
of the time; "nonmilitary" presidents, accounting for 57.9 percent of the presidents, held the position for only 36.6 percent of
the time.[13]

In the culture of political violence that prevails in Latin
American societies, skill in the provocation and organization of
violence is not concentrated exclusively in the hands of professional soldiers. Other competitors for power and influence, too,
learn to rely upon techniques of violence—however arcane and
private the motivations for violence—to pursue their public
goals. Thus students engage in frequent riots, sometimes store
and fire weapons from inside the legal sanctuary of the universities, and manifest considerable militancy and belligerency in
advocating public policies. The "professional student" of the
Latin American university may not qualify as a "professional
revolutionary," since he lacks the stable party commitment and
ideological sophistication (or rigidity) that Lenin set down as
requisites for the role; but his preoccupation with public affairs
and experience in combatting organized police and military
forces often make him approximate the role of "professional

[12] Huey Carl Camp, *Caudillismo: An Empirical Approach* (Washington
University, St. Louis: M.A. dissertation, 1960), *passim.*
[13] *Ibid.,* p. 431.

revolutionary" in the sense of one who maintains a sustained interest in the pursuit of governmental authority by means of violence. The culture of political violence, consequently, accommodates both the expert and counter-expert, or amateur, in violence. And when some of the "amateurs" secure training in guerrilla tactics and terrorism, the line dividing the expert from the amateur becomes fluid. In any case, where expectations of peaceful governmental transitions are low, individuals and groups not integrated into regular military formations also seek to acquire expertise in the techniques of violence. The revolutionary, whether the appellation professional is attached to him or not, like the military man of diffuse political functions, serves to differentiate a culture of political violence and to emphasize the role of experts in violence in such a culture.

4. *Legal and formal concomitants of violence.* Not surprisingly, there are legal and formal corollaries of the patterns of violence in Latin America: (1) frequent replacement and revision of written constitutional documents; (2) conspicuous departures from prescribed constitutional norms in political behavior; (3) recurrent suspensions of constitutional guarantees, declarations of states of siege, and the conduct of government by decree; and (4) the institutionalization of procedures for exile, including the right of asylum.

In many Latin American countries, constitutions are rather casually discarded when a revolution takes place, the convening of a constituent assembly for the drafting of a fresh document is not a rare event, and the proclamation of a new constitution does not presage an era of documentary continuity. Constitutions, in brief, come and go. During a period of a hundred years, Bolivia had ten constitutions, Ecuador thirteen, and Venezuela fifteen. Under these conditions, the transiency of constitutional documents makes it difficult to elevate them to the level of symbols of legitimacy.

Glaring discrepancies between relatively unambiguous written legal prescriptions and political practice are common in Latin America. Despite constitutional requirements, legislatures may not be convened, elections may be indefinitely postponed, the independence of the judiciary may remain unrecognized, principles of federalism or decentralization may be circumvented, the power of the executive may be exercised without constraint, and elaborate statements of civil liberties and social welfare allowed to stand as rhetorical ideals uncontaminated by observance. In the Latin American political culture of violence, only the politically naïve search constitutional documents for significant clues to the operation of political systems, and only scholars with vested interests in legalistic studies can rationalize meticulous explications of constitutional texts.

Since constitutions are not sacrosanct, the suspension of constitutional guarantees, the promulgation of a state of siege, and the conduct of government by means of presidential decrees are recurrent phenomena. Nomenclature varies, but every constitution in Latin America authorizes these practices. Governing personnel, especially presidents, therefore, can invoke a formal clause to curb speech, press, petition, and assembly; to threaten property rights at least temporarily; and to restrict the activities of opposition groups. And the subsequent ritualistic approval of residential decrees by a legislative body may prove perfunctory.

In an environment of constitutional uncertainty and violent competition for governmental office, the treatment of political opponents, obviously, presents a special problem to an incumbent regime. Some measures at the disposal of Latin American governments are relatively conventional: surveillance, confinement, imprisonment. But exile and rights of asylum have become uniquely stylized aspects of the political systems of Latin America. Like the sequence of movements in a bullfight, the ritual of asylum and exile of political leaders in Latin America is enacted in conformity with relatively inflexible precedents. The political figure who threatens a regime but is vulnerable to punitive action by coercive organs of the government escapes to a foreign embassy; the incumbent regime expresses doubt that the "escaped" politician qualifies for asylum, since he has committed "common crimes" (including, if a deposed president, the theft of public funds); after the lapse of a suitable period, the government quietly permits the refugee in a foreign embassy to depart from the country. Persistent efforts at extradition or the denial of safe conduct into exile are rare.

The legal and formal aspects of Latin American political systems thus serve to maintain and perpetuate violence. For overt acts of violence yield an output of constitutional instability, disregard for prescribed legal norms, conducting government through executive orders, and the institutionalization of procedures for exile and asylum. In turn, these legal and formal concomitants feed back into the system and contribute to the perpetuation of violence, since constitutions do not inspire respect, prescribed legal rules do not impose effective restraints, decision-making by the executive is customary, and the rule of asylum, by protecting the loser in a violent political struggle, does not discourage revolutionary conspiracies.

5. *Convergence of proximate and early socialization.* Contemporary social scientists seek the sources of political attitudes and modes of political behavior in the nonpolitical, as well as political, experiences of members of a political system. Politically relevant responses, it now is explicitly acknowledged, are learned in families, religious organizations, and schools, as well as in political parties and governmental bureaucracies. Harry Eckstein, accordingly, has pointed out that congruent socializing experiences may serve as a support for stable, democratic political systems. On the other hand, the cues emanating from the various institutions of a society may undermine the stability of a system: authoritarian family structures and officially promulgated democratic norms during the period of the Weimar Republic in Germany often are cited as illustrations of incongruence in a political system. Moreover, as Almond and Verba point out, the effects of nonpolitical patterns of authority may be "culminative." In their words: "If one finds oneself consistently in social situations where one has a voice over decisions, this is more likely to result in a general sense of competence than if the experience with participation in one area is not matched by similar experiences in other areas."[14]

There is a consensus among observers, both participant and disengaged, regarding the models of behavior and attitudes encouraged by nonpolitical agencies of socialization (the family, the Church, and less formally organized institutions) in Latin America. These sensitive reporters of impressions, who lean toward the interpretive essay as a congenial form of expression, emphasize the compatibility between the values and styles imparted by nonpolitical institutions and the perpetuation of patterns of political violence and revolution in Latin American political behavior.

The theme of *machismo* dominates the literature of psychological insight devoted to Latin America. The political world preponderantly is a man's world, and the male learns to value

14 Gabriel A. Almond and Sidney Verba, *The Civic Culture* (Princeton, New Jersey: Princeton University Press, 1963), pp. 369–370.

qualities of masculinity: "Men especially are expected to be men. One takes pride in being *'muy hombre.'* "[15] By means of vocabulary, dress, grooming, posture, and promiscuity, the man seeks to demonstrate his virility. He acquires a sensitive shell to protect personal dignity and is expected to respond aggressively to threats of *dignidad:* "Response [to an affront] must be immediate, direct and normally violent."[16] And *machismo,* a consequence of socializing experiences within the family, is linked to an adult predisposition for acts of violence. In the words of Octavio Paz: ". . . the essential attribute of the *macho*—power—almost always reveals itself as a capacity for wounding, humiliating, annihilating."[17] To put it in psychological jargon: aggression and violence often are externalized, rather than internalized, by members of Latin American societies.

While acts of violence may be motivated by feelings of inferiority and resentment and encouraged by the cult of *machismo,* orientations toward death in Latin America facilitate the acceptance of the fatal consequences of acts of violence. Whereas death is banished from daily, familiar, and "normal" activities (and thus fears of it relegated to the unconscious) in Anglo-Saxon cultures, awareness of death is maintained at a high level of consciousness in Latin American societies. Religious rituals, often representing a blend of Roman Catholicism and autochthonous beliefs, accord frequent and visible recognition to the reality of death. The death motif is incorporated into toys and pastries. Death masks and representations of skeletons figure prominently in religious processions. Funeral rites are elaborate, and in Mexico, the Day of the Dead is enthusiastically celebrated. The language employed by Octavio Paz suggests virtually a *mystique* of death: "To die and to kill are ideas that rarely leave us. We are seduced by death."[18]

Much of the psychological capability for violence may be drained off by nonpolitical activities. A good deal of the energy

---

[15] Norman Raymond Humphrey, "Ethnic Images and Stereotypes of Mexicans and Americans," *The American Journal of Economics and Sociology,* Vol. 14, No. 3 (April 1955), p. 309.

[16] *Ibid.,* p. 310.

[17] *The Labyrinth of Solitude* (New York: Grove Press, Inc., 1961), p. 82.

[18] *Ibid.,* pp. 57–58.

available for violent behavior may be siphoned off directly into acts of homicide and fights between individuals; or indirectly, by exhibitions of verbal aggression; or vicariously, by attendance at bullfights. But for a minority, politics, especially revolutionary politics, can provide a significant outlet. Early socialization produces tensions that seek resolution in violence, approved social styles for males encourage belligerent behavior, participation in political violence may provide reassurance for those who boast of a masculinity that is suspect, and prevailing values condone acts of violence, including political violence. Hence an active minority engaged in acts of political violence is inhibited neither by a political system that brands such acts as illegitimate nor by internalized values that censure resorting to violent methods. Since neither the standards of society or conscience are wrenched by outbreaks of political violence, individuals may mobilize their psychic resources of aggression to take part in student riots, demonstrations, political terrorism— and revolution. Their induction into politics, in the phrase of Verba and Almond, takes place "through experience with violent revolution."[19] And thus there is a congruence between early socialization and later modes of political action: nonpolitical agencies of socialization have laid the foundations for a culture of political violence.

6. *Compatibility of revolutionary means with diverse ends.* The sequel to elections in a culture of political nonviolence may include limited changes in public policies, but is not likely to be marked by a radical rearrangement of the political system or drastic changes in a wide variety of public policies. In contrast, the range of possible outcomes accompanying a revolution, in a culture of political violence, is extremely broad: the greater the degree of compatibility between violence and the prevailing norms of a political system, the greater the range of policy outputs that may accompany the employment of violence. In such a culture, since millennial aspirations need not be invoked to justify violence, a revolution, like an election in other cultures, may merely rotate personnel. Also like an election, it may serve as a prelude to the introduction of relatively limited changes in public policies. But unlike an election, a revolution

[19] Sidney Verba and Gabriel A. Almond, "National Revolutions and Political Commitment," in Harry Eckstein, editor, *Internal War: Problems and Approaches* (New York: The Free Press of Glencoe, 1964), p. 206.

may shift personnel, eliminate certain social classes, radically modify the capabilities of various interests to exert influence and power, and transform the system for absorbing and resolving public conflicts. The spectrum of changes engendered by elections in a culture of political nonviolence form a rather small arc. A much larger arc, however, is required to accommodate the range of changes generated by revolution in a culture of political violence. Revolutionary means are compatible with highly diverse ends.

Thus some revolutions in Latin America substitute one military officer for another as president, and leave the political system intact and public policies unaffected. The goal of such revolutions appears as a variant of the familiar slogan of an election campaign: "Throw the rascals out!" Other revolutions tamper little with the political system, but modify the proportion of royalties on mineral exploitation claimed by the local government. Yet other revolutions (the Cuban and the Mexican are conspicuous examples) reorder the political structure, change the symbolic environment and drastically transform public policies. Significantly, the introduction of these far-reaching changes is preceded by relatively prolonged periods of violence. And the politically socializing effects of participation in a particular form of violence are suggested by Fidel Castro himself: "Had I understood the imperialist phenomenon, I would then [at an early stage in the conflict with Batista] have truly become a Marxist-Leninist. But to reach that point I had to have two years of armed conflict . . ."[20]

Despite certain functional similarities between elections and revolutions, consequently, the potential scope of the changes stimulated by elections and revolutions differs. In a culture of political nonviolence, a revolution signals drastic changes; in a culture of political violence, a revolution *per se* may or may not be a harbinger of drastic change. For a culture of political violence authorizes means that may yield widely divergent ends, whereas a culture of political nonviolence imposes rather severe restrictions on the scope of change that may be pursued by means sanctioned by that culture. Since politically relevant violence neither occurs rarely nor produces uniform outcomes in Latin America, social scientists with good cause have become preoccupied with the study of violence—under such rubrics as

[20] Quoted in interview with C. L. Sulzberger, *New York Times,* November 7, 1964.

internal war, revolution, and instability—in its varied manifestations in Latin America.[21]

21 For a critical analysis of recent approaches to the study of political
violence, see Lawrence Stone, "Theories of Revolution," *World Politics*,
Vol. XVIII, No. 2 (January, 1966), pp. 159–176.

Trade Unionism as an Instrument

of the Latin American Revolution

EMILIO MASPERO

INTRODUCTION

LATIN AMERICA is today in the throes of a revolutionary process. Forces of all kinds are being mobilized either to impede or to advance the revolution. Against this background of social ferment, organized labor is playing an increasingly important role, both among urban and rural workers. It will be my purpose to describe Latin America's democratic trade-union movement of Christian inspiration, which, with its own unique ideology, program, and spirit, is attempting to introduce a positive and perhaps decisive factor into Latin America's social revolution.

There is no one democratic force in Latin America today that can by itself provide a complete and definite solution to the enormous problems confronting the area. Christians by themselves cannot hope to provide the solution. It seems, however, that their voice will be increasingly heard during the coming struggle. The new presence of democratic and Christian trade-union forces, dynamic and powerful, is a fact that can no longer be disregarded; it must be more and more taken into account by anyone attempting to understand Latin America, and especially its social ferment.

In our Christian approach to trade unionism, we naturally want to organize all the workers, so as to promote the integral and collective interests. We hope through organization to provide for social, economic, moral, and cultural development of workers, and to contribute thereby to the overall development of nations. The type of trade unionism that we specifically advocate is characterized by the adjective "Christian." The term Christian, as we use it, has no sectarian, religious, ecclesiastical, theological, or dogmatic implications. We use the term simply to refer to the social philosophy and the ethic of Christianity as they apply to trade unionism—as they inspire its orientation, its direction, and its methods. Our unionism is based on some very fundamental ideas, attitudes, and moral concepts that are common to all men of good will. Christian trade unionism is not dependent upon any ecclesiastical authority, nor is it guided by the specified apostolic goals of official Catholic action groups. In the Christian trade-union organizations of Latin America, one finds neither religious nor ecclesiastical discrimination. All workers can enter our organizations simply by accepting our principles and programs. Our leaders and members include men of different faiths, and their status within our organizations is in no way affected by their religious beliefs.

In Latin America, trade unionism constantly comes face to face with the greed for power of Communism, with the utilitarian ambitions of capitalism, and with the programs of various dictators and political parties. The forces with which Latin American trade unions must contend or cooperate are almost always based upon a particular ideology. In such a situation, ideological neutrality is untenable, and trade unionism is itself forced to choose an ideology. We have chosen the social philosophy of Christianity.

This explanation has seemed to me necessary as an introduction, since certain Americans who choose to oppose us refer to "secular" trade unionism as if Christian trade unionism, by contrast, were clerical and denominational. We *also* constitute a secular trade unionism, but not *neutral* trade unionism. We take our inspiration from that which, we are convinced, is the most sure and best solution for the present drama of Latin American workers and peasants, oppressed by injustice and hunger and misery, but desirous of finally seeing the light of their social redemption.

THE SOCIAL REVOLUTION IN LATIN AMERICA

The social revolution is on the march in Latin America, and it may be well to define certain terms, as we use them there:

Cuartelazo: an armed coup promoted by a military faction against legally constituted authority.

Golpe de estado: an armed uprising which can be led by the military or by civilians and political parties and caudillos (popular leaders).

Insurrección: also an armed and violent uprising, but with the participation of vast sectors of the population.

Subversión: activity carried out in a cunning, underhanded manner to create opposition to legally constituted authority.

Sedición: agitation aimed at provoking disturbance and disorder in order to undermine constituted authority.

Revuelta: armed and violent uprising against legal authority, generally an isolated, momentary, and disorganized action.

Until now Latin America has experienced an interminable succession of *cuartelazos, golpes de estado, insurrecciones, subversiones, sediciones,* and *revueltas* of every kind, shape, and form. Since independence from Spain (around 1810) to the present, there have been more than 300 such operations. In Guatemala alone no fewer than 60 *golpes* and *cuartelazos* have taken place since 1948.

There are many people who still live with an artificial image of Latin America which is the product of tourist agencies and the great international news agencies. Latin America is still regarded as a little-known continent of people of quick temperament who make all kinds of promises and fulfill none, who are more inclined to talk than to work, and who often prefer appearances to profound and fundamental values. They emerge as emotional and unstable lovers of sun, siesta, the guitar, political polemics, and the easy life. Within this picturesque framework great publicity is given in the United States and Europe alike to the unending chain of so-called Latin American revolutions. This is about the only time we are accorded front-page honors in the newspapers.

But these are not revolutions in the true sense of the word. With the exception of Mexico, Bolivia, and Cuba, our misnamed revolutions have not passed beyond the point of movements provoked by caudillos, classes, or parties for the purpose of taking political power, but without intending to change the established order. A caudillo or military leader—to give one example—at a given moment manages to glue together forces in opposition to another caudillo or military leader. The victor takes over the government as booty and administers the public

210   ■ THE SOCIOECONOMIC PIVOT

power for the satisfaction of his own personal interests. Thus, in
cadence with the more or less bloody revolts, one chief executive follows another, with no substantial change of regime. The
political, juridical, social, and economic structures continue
unchanged. It is the same boat, the same route, but with another
captain wearing a different uniform.

The true revolution is deliberately produced in accordance
with a given ideology; it calls for rapid and fundamental change,
embracing all basic structures (political, juridical, economic,
and social). In this sense Latin America is living its most profoundly revolutionary moment ever. Never before have the
foundations of the existing order been so shaken as now, and at
all levels.

There are those who claim that the revolution is being
provoked by international Communism, or by the political
maneuvering of demagogues hoping for a rapid rise to power.
Others claim that revolution in Latin America is not imminent,
that it is merely a fashionable word being bandied about at the
moment because the Cuban Revolution has aroused the passions of the youth.

We must emphasize that neither international Communism,
nor the demagoguery of politicians, nor the aroused emotions of
our youth are the source of the revolutionary process in Latin
America. Even if Communism had never existed in Cuba or
elsewhere in the world, even if the demagoguery of politicians
and the spirited enthusiasm of our youth were absent, we would
still face today in Latin America all of the exigencies and
consequences of a sweeping and thorough revolutionary process.

The social revolution is provoked by the very reality of Latin
America itself. The causes of the revolution lie in the current
political, legal, economic, and social structures; they originate
also in the basic needs of human beings who, even in the space
age, have not been able to procure the most fundamental
material requirements for living with dignity.

Latin America occupies 16 percent of the face of the earth
and contains 6 percent of world population. It is the most
sparsely populated continent on earth. Yet in this rich and
thinly populated area, 130 million Latin Americans will go to
bed hungry tonight, living in a permanent state of malnutrition,
according to statistics of the UN Food and Agriculture Organization (FAO).

Just a couple of years ago, Dr. Mardones Restat, Director of Children's Hospital in Santiago, Chile, announced that of the 30,000 Chilean babies who died before the age of one, 20,000 died of hunger. And it must be remembered that Chile is by no means the poorest country of Latin America. Neither is it the most disorganized, since it has had the good fortune of 130 years of constitutional life and only three years of dictatorship.

In August of 1960, my trade-union travels took me to El Salvador, the smallest and most densely populated country of Latin America. In the streets of San Salvador, I witnessed a tragic parade. More than 50,000 peasants staged a demonstration march in the streets, demanding a new law establishing, not a minimum wage, but a *minimum diet*. In mid-twentieth century! In a so-called Christian continent.

In Haiti, the poorest country of the world and the most forgotten of Latin America, thousands of families eat just one meal a day, other thousands between two and five a week, and countless masses live on fruit, plunder, or beggary. To make matters worse, more than seven million tons of cultivable Haitian land are lost to the sea each year through erosion. It is a nation threatened by total erosion.

Even in Mexico, fifty years after the realization of the first peasant revolution in Latin America, 80 percent of the people are poorly fed. Forty-six percent live on a diet based completely on corn. The average consumption of proteins per day is less than one-third of that in the United States.

In Northeast Brazil, a region larger in land area than the United States, chronic hunger suffered by millions of human beings inspired the famous book, *The Geography of Hunger,* by Josué de Castro, who located this region in the black cordon of world hunger and misery.

In other days, hunger was a disgrace which demanded resignation to the will and providence of God. Today, hunger is immoral and unjust.

In 1959, I saw in the piers at Houston Bay a line of Liberty ships tied up side by side for ten miles. They were filled with United States surplus food. In that year, the surplus American agricultural production was valued at $7 billion in milk, eggs, meat, and cotton. It is a similar story in the case of some European countries, such as France, for example. Science, technology, mechanics, government planning, and the ordering

212 ■ The Socioeconomic Pivot

of work are causing the land to produce more and more. Humanity has at its disposal all the necessary means to feed all human beings who inhabit the earth.

But the majority of Latin Americans are not only deprived of bread for the body, but also of opportunities to nourish their minds and spirits. At this time there are more than 70 million illiterates in Latin America. Adding the semi-illiterates, it can be said that two-thirds of all Latin Americans have not been included into essential, literate civilization and culture. And the population increases at a more rapid rate than in the United States, Russia, Europe, or Africa. The rate of population growth (2.5 percent) produces 2.5 million new Latin Americans a year. Between 1960 and 1975, the Latin American population increase will be 100 million—from 200 million souls to 300 million. At the present rate of economic growth it will take Latin America forty-five years to reach the level of gross income now enjoyed by Western Europe. But by that time the population of our continent will exceed 500 million.

Elemental necessities cannot be satisfied, and population grows at an ever-increasing rate, generally outstripping economic development and growth. More mouths to feed and less food. More workers and fewer jobs. More minds to cultivate and fewer resources for basic education. More families to be housed and fewer houses. More sick and fewer doctors.

The imbalance between the prices of products which we export and those of the imports caused Latin America to lose $10 billion during the decade 1950–60, according to CEPAL, the UN economic organization for Latin America. According to data revealed in the U.S. Senate, the flight of capital from Latin America during the same period was $15 billion.

At the same time the United States represents 6 percent of world population and monopolizes 40 percent of world wealth, Latin America, Asia, and Africa, with 60 percent of world population, enjoy only 17 percent of the riches.

A new factor injected into this tragic socioeconomic climate has finally triggered the revolutionary process. Until very recently, a political, cultural, economic, and social oligarchy controlled the destinies of our republics, virtually unchallenged by the passive, inarticulate masses—the victims of the oligarchy's exploitation. Today one witnesses a growing awareness among the Latin American masses not only of the fact that they are being exploited, but of the possibility of breaking out of the vicious circle of misery, injustice, and immorality. This awareness is emerging not only among the urban laboring classes, but also among farm and mining laborers, and even among the forgotten Indian communities of our countries.

In 1962 a group of Ecuadorian Indians descended from the mountains that surround the capital city of Quito, asked to see the president of the republic, and eventually were allowed to address these words to him: "We are tired of living as animals in the mountains. We want to have the same homes, the same cars, the same job opportunities which you people have here in the cities. And if these opportunities are not given to us peacefully, we will all descend from the mountains and claim them by force."

The best men of the continent are on the side of the revolution. Shortly before the late President Kennedy traveled for an historic meeting with Premier Khrushchev, he made the following statement to his people: "Our knees do not tremble before the word revolution. On the contrary, we believe in the revolution in Africa, in Latin America, in Asia and in the Middle East. And this," he added, "is the greatest revolution in human history."

True, there are those in Latin America and elsewhere who would explain the facts and alternatives in simplistic terms. For some, it is a matter of selecting models for economic development, of choosing between capitalism and Communism. Others place the problem on a religious plane, as if it represented the great encounter between Christ and anti-Christ. The choice, they say, is between Communism and Christianity. Still others say the destiny of Latin America lies in the alternative democracy-or-dictatorship, simplifying all in mere political terms.

Granted that a new economic system is needed. Models must be chosen for economic development. Spiritual values must be defended, as well as political, social, and juridical systems. But these are only part of the alternative. A choice must be made for or against the revolution. In this sense, Latin America is becoming increasingly more divided into two clearly defined groups: those of us who seek the revolution because we wish to save man and his dignity, and those who oppose the revolution because their knees shake for fear of losing privileges, riches, comforts, and powers. This is the true alternative: revolution or counterrevolution. On both sides of this question there are many dictators, many democrats, many capitalists, many Communists, and many Christians.

THE PRESENT TRADE-UNION SITUATION IN LATIN AMERICA

Trade Unionism and Underdevelopment in Latin America

The phenomenon of underdevelopment creates a special situation which determines many of the characteristics of trade unionism in its world. Special situations created by the phenomenon of underdevelopment gravitate strongly in the determination of characteristics of trade unionism in the underdeveloped world.

In Latin America, most national and foreign capital has been invested in speculative activities, where profits are larger. Thus, we have suffered from a form of colonialist capitalism. More than 65 percent of Latin America's income derives from agricultural production, and close to 85 percent of our exports are raw materials. Industrial capitalism is not strongly established, and this is one of the reasons for the historical weakness of trade unionism in Latin America where, as in the rest of the world, syndicalism has emerged primarily as an organized reaction to industrial capitalism.

Trade unionism has made its most notable gains in organizing Latin American workers employed in the production of raw materials such as sugar, bananas, oil, copper, and coal. These workers, however, represent only a small minority of the active labor force, and enjoy a privileged position in comparison to the great majority of the laboring masses. In Venezuela, for example, the oil workers' organization includes only 2 percent of the country's working population.

There are some 25 million aborigines in Latin America, sometimes classified as sub-Americans because of the hopelessness of their situation and the misery that has for so long characterized their lives. This Indian element has always been hostile toward trade-union organizations. Consequently, the labor movement has been able to make little progress among a significant portion of the population.

Latin America is agriculturally structured, and the determining factor in this structure is the landed oligarchy, which not only controls the land but determines the methods of agricultural production. More than 80 million agricultural workers in Latin America are almost completely without effective union organization. The system of agrarian feudalism presided over by autocratic rulers in alliance with the military inevitably works against the union movement. Unaware, moreover, of the possibilities for aiding themselves through organization, the peasants have almost always sought temporary amelioration through the paternalism of political bosses or caudillos. They have not understood the potentialities of a class-based trade-union organization. To make the situation worse, the urban trade unionism of the industrial workers has generally been jealous and professionally exclusive and has restrained rural organization, on some occasions opposing it altogether.

Illiteracy also stands in the way of the organized labor movement. The two-thirds of the Latin American population that is either illiterate or semiliterate is comprised of the working classes. Their very illiteracy renders them less accessible to the labor organizer.

Every year structural and technological unemployment mounts in Latin America. Every year there are more workers and fewer jobs. Argentina, one of the countries that had managed for a fairly long period to maintain a satisfactory situation of full employment, has now entered a crisis situation, with unemployment soaring. In more and more of our countries there are hunger demonstrations. They are one additional bitter manifestation of the desperation of millions of people who cannot find work. Trade-union leaders know very well that the masses of the unemployed cannot easily be organized. Only with relatively full employment can trade unions thrive, and especially in a climate that is hostile to them in so many ways.

Despite the background of increasing general unemployment, a continual rise in employment in the public-service sector has been taking place. In many Latin American countries, however, there are no laws that encourage the organization of public-service employees into unions. What is more, governments often try to block such attempts.

In addition, the peculiar conditions of Latin America lead to continual political instability. Until a short time ago, this instability was provoked by struggles among oligarchical or caudillo factions which came to power and were deposed by a *golpe de estado*. Today the causes of political instability go deeper. We have entered a revolutionary period whose effects are not merely political, but social as well.

Because of the lack of political stability and especially the absence of effective democratic processes, serious problems beset union organization and action. There is a close and indispensable relationship between unionism on the one hand, and democracy and liberty on the other. Without democracy there can be no effective unionism, and without authentic unionism—and only free unionism is authentic—there is no possibility of building stable and popular democracies in our countries.

Latin American workers and their unions have always been the victims of dictatorial governments. Even self-styled liberal and republican governments have tolerated and encouraged the most serious social and economic injustices. To make matters worse, when labor is favored by a particular administration, it is likely to be persecuted by the next, for it has never been allowed to develop autonomous strength. The governments of Latin America have continually set up all kinds of controls over union organizations. Usually these controls are intended to assure a labor monopoly for those union organizations attached to the party or caudillo currently in power. When political power changes hands, the labor movement is thoroughly disrupted.

Political parties constantly exercise their paternalism over almost all of the organizations within our countries, and thus diminish the strength and vitality of worker movements. By means of partisan paternalism, conservative forces as much as the Communists infiltrate labor movements. Neither conservative nor Communist forces view the unions as anything but tools to be employed for gaining political power.

Militarism in Latin America runs the gamut from the most reactionary elements to those favoring Nasserism. Almost always, though, the armed forces are linked to the interests of the landowning oligarchy and the industrial bourgeoisie. In attempting to act as the supreme arbiter of the political destinies of our countries, military men have been hostile to organized labor, and thus have only added to the already numerous obstacles before the union movement.

Religious and spiritual influences have sometimes been used to misinterpret and distort the true objective of trade unionism, discrediting and impeding the movement. With a view toward easy proselytizing, religious forces have tried to use existing trade unions or create new ones to emphasize exclusively spiritual and pious considerations. Lacking a true temporal program, religious forces many times have simply used trade unions to advance a particular faith, thus mixing and confusing the temporal and spiritual realms.

The weaknesses of the Latin American trade-union movement can by no means be explained solely in terms of spiritual, social, or religious forces external to it. Internal lack of efficiency and numerous errors of leadership must be acknowledged.

The history of our labor movement abounds in examples of sacrifice, generosity, heroism, and above all, loyalty to the workers and their interests. Nevertheless, a great part of the responsibility for the present union situation falls upon the trade-union leaders. There have been unscrupulous leaders who have misused union funds; leaders who have failed to defend the workers' interests; leaders who have sold out to the employers, the political parties, the governments, and even police; leaders without community spirit who have used their unions as instruments of personal self-aggrandizement. Many labor leaders have become millionaires through trade unionism. They live in a way that insults the misery and hunger of the majority of the workers, whom they supposedly represent.

Today, a great majority of the Latin American workers distrust the trade-union leaders who have not been capable of rising to the moral challenge. They have come to fear the exploitation of labor leaders as much as the economic system in which they are trapped. This situation destroys the faith and hope of the laboring masses as well as the effectiveness and dynamism of trade unionism. It is very difficult to find in the present labor movement militant and active members who feel that the trade union represents an ideal of personal and collective liberation, and who are willing to dedicate the better part of their lives to working toward this liberation. Corruption and a bureaucratic approach to leadership have exhausted the sources of idealism—both of leaders and workers.

In order for trade unionism to become a movement for the integral promotion of the workers' interests, it is necessary that each member feel himself a part of a collective whole. In many unions, the affiliated working masses are passive elements whose passivity is deliberately fostered by the union leaders to maintain themselves in power. Many trade unions have not called assemblies, have not held elections of officers, and have not consulted the workers about strikes, conflicts, or the negotiation and signing of contracts for very long periods of time. Often, all the unions seem to do is to withhold union dues every month and refuse to allow the rank and file any voice in controlling the investment and use of these funds.

In addition to these external and internal forces that operate against them, Latin American labor unions have had to contend with adverse influences from abroad. The University of Chicago Research Center on Economic Development and Cultural Changes published a study in 1960 for the U.S. Senate Subcommittee on American Republics Affairs of the Committee on Foreign Relations entitled *United States Business and Labor in Latin America*. In the chapter dealing with the labor movements, the following observation is made:

> The labor unions in the United States and the labor unions of Latin America must both sincerely recognize and accept the differences of the labor organizations in the two areas of the Western hemisphere. They must accept that this diversity corresponds to the basic differences in historical and cultural background as well as to the differing existing situations, tasks, and experiences. Every attempt to pattern Latin American organizations after North American models or vice-versa would not only fail but would have disastrous results for true democratic cooperation. The democratic labor organization should be fundamentally differentiated from communist-dominated ones by the recognition of the diversity of similar international organizations and by an absolute repudiation of the idea that only one philosophy and method of efficient operation can exist for all labor organizations.

This analysis is profoundly true and touches on one of the factors that has contributed most to the creation of the unsatisfactory condition of trade unionism in Latin America. Influences exerted by countries with different cultural and historical backgrounds and at different stages of economic, social, and political development have done great harm to Latin America's union organizations. Two principal currents of influence have

affected our unions—one from the United States, the other from
the Soviet Union.

In 1918, with the establishment of the Pan American Labor
Confederation (COPA), the United States began officially a
policy of encouraging a coordinated labor movement for the
entire Western Hemisphere patterned after the North American
model. At present this objective is being waged more vigorously
than ever before. Even the Alliance for Progress, created in
response to the challenges of the cold war and the tragic situation in Cuba, is being used as an instrument to foster the growth
of United States–style trade unionism in Latin America. Although North American trade unions are primarily responsible
for the campaign now under way in Latin America, largely
controlling and financing it, they are aided by various official
agencies of their government. Labor attachés of United States
embassies in South America are among the many officials connected with the State Department who do all in their power to
take an active part in directing the internal processes of the
Latin American trade-union movement, usually with detrimental consequences.

This has created confusion among Latin American workers.
They see that various United States labor leaders who come to
Latin America to encourage the use of U.S. organization
methods are often guided by the best intentions. Yet, these men
appear to have some direct connections with the United States
Government, whose representatives are active in promoting
United States–style trade unionism. These Government representatives seem officially committed to the support of political
administrations, often dictatorships, that symbolize the exploitation of the working classes. Moreover, the United States Government is traditionally associated with an overriding interest in
protecting the profit-making opportunities of its citizens in Latin
America, rather than in aiding native workers.

The influence exercised by United States labor has often
distorted trade unionism in Latin America, bringing to it an
orientation not suitable to the local reality. This has been true in
regard to the struggle against Communism. In the United States,
Communism is viewed as a physical menace to the established
way of life and to the institutions that have brought a considerable degree of well-being to the vast majority of citizens
that are, therefore, widely cherished. In Latin America, Communism is seen as a means of change, as a possible solution to

an unsatisfactory way of life. In the Latin American countries, the temptation to try something new grows from day to day. Negative anti-Communism, often associated simply with blind opposition to change, is habitually fostered by American foreign policy. The result is that many organizations which are under the influence of North American trade unionism become confused and their perspectives distorted in their struggle for democracy and social justice. The policies of American diplomats and labor leaders have often worked to the advantage of Communism, which sometimes appears as the only source of hope for the workers and peasants in the absence of alternatives to the present, unacceptable situation.

A distinguished North American labor leader has written: "For free unionism, capitalism is as necessary as water for fish." This statement appears to be applicable within the North American context, even though I might not subscribe totally to it were I a North American. It certainly reveals the orientation of North American unions. In the United States capitalism is not opposed. Instead, the people have become docile members and beneficiaries of a system which, as it has evolved, has shown itself capable of improving the lives of the laboring masses.

Latin American laborers are disconcerted when the voice of United States trade unionism preaches the advantages of free enterprise and popular capitalism. Among the majority of urban laborers and peasants, free-enterprise capitalism is regarded as one of the most formidable forces opposing their betterment. After 150 years of private initiative, free enterprise, and free competition, in Latin America there are more than 130 million undernourished, more than 70 million illiterates, and the lowest economic growth rate in the Western world.

Democracy has many times been confused with capitalism, as if the capitalist system were essential to democracy. The fact is that the majority of the governments on our continent, wrongly called democratic, have always been in the hands of financial oligarchies that have practiced exploitation through capitalism. For us in the Christian trade-union movement, democracy is the political form that the social revolution we hope to wage will introduce. This democracy has nothing to do with capitalism as it now exists in Latin America. To function and to perfect itself in our environment, democracy must transcend the present capitalist system and introduce for the first time democratic principles, not only into the political but also into the social and economic orders. Given the value judgments that tend to attach to these words in Latin America, the penchant to picture capitalism and democracy as bedfellows has caused many to lose hope in political freedom, to reject democracy, and to incline toward totalitarianism.

North American unionism has always professed to be a pragmatic and nonpartisan movement. Thus, it has avoided assuming an ideological, philosophical, or doctrinaire character. Its only concern has been the struggle for bread and butter and the continuing material progress of the workers.

Pragmatism and nonpartisanship—although we might disagree that such nonpartisanship really exists even in the United States —may be suited to North America. In Latin America, where ideological struggles caused by Communism, by opposing political tendencies, and by the revolutionary climate become more intensive every day, pragmatism and nonpartisanship can do positive harm. Our ideological struggles can be compromised neither by pragmatism, nor avoided by nonpartisanship. A strictly pragmatic or nonpartisan trade union in Latin America is vulnerable to Communist infiltration, to exploitation by political opportunism. A union of this type has as much chance to exercise effective leadership within Latin America's revolutionary process as a blind man has to cross a busy city intersection against the stoplight safely.

It is undeniable that in Latin America, with its hungry millions, trade unionism cannot disengage itself from the struggle for "bread and butter." But a major factor at stake is to gain for the organized forces of labor a decisive and preponderant participation in the social revolution. And this will never be done within a collective-bargaining framework which, even in the United States, some of the better labor leaders are beginning to question.

Besides, there is nothing more dangerous than to attempt to impose a single method or philosophy in the workers' movement as if there were just one road to reach a synthesis between liberty and justice.

Institutional pluralism is one of the most essential aspects of progressive and humanistic democracy. However, many North American union leaders who travel continuously throughout our countries, and many Latin American union leaders who are influenced and supported economically by North American labor organizations, insist more and more emphatically that they alone have the right to speak for democratic trade unionism. They further contend that two differently oriented democratic labor union movements cannot coexist in the Western Hemisphere. One must be either with them or against them. By this stand, they introduce an almost fanatical sectarianism into the hemisphere's union movement.

The Communist influence has been even more inimical to the autonomy of Latin American labor organizations. Cuba presents a very clear case. True, the Cuban phenomenon can be considered from one point of view as an accelerator of the revolutionary process on our continent. But the present Cuban experience is more a counterrevolutionary phenomenon that has hindered the Latin American social revolution, which must always seek its own and original channels. Owing to the presence of international Communism the Cuban labor movement has lost its autonomy and become, in effect, counterrevolutionary in nature.

Communists have contributed very little to the cause of trade unionism in Latin America. However misdirected, the initiative of North American trade unions has, at least, aided in the organization of numerous groups and has rendered some positive service. Communists, on the other hand, have always preferred to penetrate, infiltrate, and dominate the existing trade unions so that they can bring them into line with imperialistic Communist strategy.

The forces of genuine Latin American trade unionism claim for themselves not only a dignified independence from foreign influences but also the right to follow the methods, philosophy, and objectives appropriate to their unique environment. It is the conviction of Latin American Christian trade unionism that the social revolution and the fate of the continent must be in the hands of the Latin Americans themselves. Nobody will be able to save them if they themselves do not want to be saved, and if they do not develop their own and effective means to accomplish the social revolution.

Until very recently, instead of having a revolutionary trade unionism, we have had a servile imitation of alien models, sometimes tamed and limited by the governments that happened to be in power, often corrupted and demoralized by the moral weakness of our leaders, and at times conservative and conformist in its programs and its goals. We need revolutionary

leaders and tactics, a revolutionary doctrine, and a revolutionary mystique.

CLASS AND THE SOCIAL REVOLUTION

To participate in the Latin American revolutionary process it
is necessary to have a clear revolutionary conscience and will.
But desire is not enough. The revolution must be carried out
with organized forces, a revolutionary doctrine, revolutionary
tactics and strategies, and a revolutionary mystique.

The social revolution in Latin America must be a moral
revolution, embodying a set of values and a concept of man and
society that will result in human liberation and lead to continuity and stability. We must reject all movements that might
militate against the dignity of man. Taking this into account,
and accepting the fact that existing trade unionism in Latin
America has often denied to city laborers and rural peasants the
chance to become effective instruments of the revolutionary
process, there seemed no alternative to introducing a new type
of labor organization. Accordingly, the Latin American Confederation of Christian Trade Unionism (CLASC) was founded
in 1954. Today it boasts a formidable membership of young
workers in every country and territory of Latin America, including the three Guianas and most of the English-speaking Caribbean.

CLASC is the first sizable trade-union movement of Christian
and democratic inspiration in Latin America. Why, in a Christian continent, was there not prior to 1954 an organized
Christian trade-union movement? Why did fifty years of anarchist, socialist, Communist, and United States influence have
to transpire before a firm, powerful, and enduring Christian
orientation could be introduced into the labor movement?

It is true that at the beginning of the twentieth century
Christian Democratic trade unions did arise, however ephem-
erally, in several Latin American countries. At this time similarly oriented unions were being founded in Europe. In 1910,
the basis of a Christian trade-union movement already existed
in Argentina and a similar movement was under way in Chile.
Before long, though, the leaders of this movement were banished from both Argentina and Chile. In Uruguay and Brazil,

the initial endeavors to form Christian trade unions represented little more than an attempt to provide social insurance as well as religious and spiritual protection for the members. The National Catholic Center of Labor (CCNT) existed in Mexico until 1927, and at times provided serious competition for the powerful regional Confederation of Mexican Laborers (CROM), which was dominated by anarchist, socialist, and Marxist ideas. But the religious persecution unleashed in the late 1920s destroyed the CCNT.

Aside from local political assaults, what crushed the Christian trade-union movement in the first third or half of the twentieth century was the lack of concern of organized Christian thought with questions of social justice. The Catholic Church has historically achieved magnificent success in Latin America by extending charity and by paternalistically administering doles. While it was providing schools for the few and erecting magnificent and costly temples, the Church failed to realize—until it was almost too late—that the Latin American masses would some day come to desire not charity and alms, but social justice.

Moreover, many Church leaders—bishops, priests, and laymen—seemed (and some of them continue to seem so) completely committed to the existing social order. At best, they have been passive and indifferent in their attitudes toward it. Often, they acted directly to favor the economic, social, political, and cultural structures that benefited only the oligarchy. Given this background, the workers, when they began to become aware of and to rebel against the injustices of the established order, inevitably turned against the Church. In their quest for justice the masses were alienated from the Church and subsequently they have often been attracted to Communism, or else reduced to anarchistic desperation.

Until very recently, Latin American Catholicism concerned itself almost exclusively with the external happiness of its members rather than with substantially bettering the unjust and miserable social conditions from which workers and peasants suffered. Temporal factors were not considered, and resorting to political expedients and labor organizations to improve material conditions was frowned upon and equated with Communist and criminal agitation.

In this atmosphere no authentic Christian trade-union movement could make headway. Thus, at least until the end of World

War II, Marxian viewpoints were bound to influence, if not dominate, Latin American union activities. Since the end of the war, however, new phenomena have appeared. Christians and many Church leaders have begun to commit themselves to the cause of social revolution. One need only read the September 18, 1962, pastoral letter of the Chilean bishops on social justice, or reflect on the impact that the Chilean Jesuits have had in courageously urging basic social change through their organ *Mensaje,* to understand the magnitude of the transformation that has occurred.

In trying to comprehend the new approach of the Church, it is also most enlightening to read some of the pastoral letters issued in recent years by bishops of other Latin American countries. These letters recommend social action by Christians, and urge agrarian reform and general restructuring of the socioeconomic order in the name of Christian conscience. They also condemn capitalism and its exploitation of workers and peasants. In the new Christian generation of Latin America, the young clergyman, a specialist in temporal as well as theological matters, thoroughly familiar with the economic, social, and political problems of our day, is at the very least a catalyst in the revolutionary process. Throughout Latin America, young clergymen and lay leaders have come to realize the need to break with the present order and destroy the privileges of a small minority so as to bring hope to the masses and make possible their full participation in the national existence.

Throughout Latin America, young Christian democrats are winning the enthusiasm and stirring the hopes of the great majority of the independent-thinking sectors. Christian trade unionism is the expression among the workers and peasants of the reform and revolutionary aspirations that have seized hold of the transformed Christian thought in Latin America. Christian trade unionism accepts the need for the social revolution, and does not shy away from the attendant risks. It is prepared to use all effective means to make this revolution serve the needs of an integrated democracy in Latin America—democracy in the political, social, and economic structures, always animated by Christian respect for the dignity of man. Christian trade unionism is ideological, because it is not possible to remain neutral when confronting the revolutionary process. One must make a choice from among the various models of social and economic development. We have chosen as our basis of operation the social philosophy of Christianity, and the social and economic goals associated with an integral concept of man and society.

Christian trade unionism is free trade unionism, because it believes that the revolution ought to be made within the framework of freedom and all of its attendant requirements. To the masses there must be given the economic and social basis that freedom implies and without which freedom exists only as a luxury of the minority and an insult to the majority that is enslaved by hunger, misery, and ignorance. Christian trade unionism also avers that freedom is the inspiring force of all authentic trade unionism. Without freedom for the workers to organize and work toward their self-realization and that of the nation as a whole, there can be no authentic trade-union movement.

Christian trade unionism is democratic, not only because it professes the need for an integrated democracy encompassing the political, social, and economic orders, but also because it believes in the workers and because it has faith in the potential and capacity for intelligent sacrifice by the masses. Our movement proclaims that the trade union is the living community of workers who have decided to assert mastery over their own destinies.

Christian trade unionism is unitarian. Its theme is unity in liberty. It aspires to unify all the workers and peasants of Latin America in freedom, without seeking monopolistic privileges, around one doctrine and one program that will epitomize the hopes and the needs of all workers without discrimination.

Christian trade unionism is technical, because it proclaims that the revolution should not be the result of improvisations or emotion, but of planning and method. The revolution that we proclaim is the revolution of responsibilities in which one must, if he desires to take a leading role, prove his capabilities, seriousness, and preparation. To succeed, our revolution must be effective, and in order to be so, it must have technique and a plan. To endeavor to change the economic, legal, political, and social structures without having people technically and morally capable of effecting the transformation is, in effect, to favor the counterrevolution and to doom the countries—the countries that trust in the revolution—to disillusionment and blackest despondency. For this reason, Christian trade unionism attaches primary importance to the training of labor in every kind of skill and technological proficiency. Yearly, thousands of activists and militant members of Christian trade unionism pass through CLASC's international and national institutes, seeking the knowledge that is necessary if they are to be effective labor leaders and to contribute positively to the process of social change within their countries.

Christian trade unionism is autonomous and independent trade unionism. It works energetically toward the creation of autonomous and independent trade-union forces at the loyal service of the workers and their interests. Trade-union autonomy and independence are indispensable prerequisites for the establishment of pluralistic democracies in which organized labor forces have the necessary power to participate in the social and economic life of the country.

Christian trade unionism is revolutionary, because its every effort is directed at changing the situation in Latin America. Its entire policy of collective bargaining, of union education and training, of social services and worker assistance is aimed at gaining the support of the majority of the workers and peasants in order to have the necessary force to provoke or demand substantial changes.

Finally, Christian trade unionism is Latin American trade unionism. One of the most profoundly significant goals of the revolution on our continent is the unification of our countries. This unification must be achieved in such manner as to guarantee our freedom from colonial or imperial influences of any kind. In the future of our continent, there are only two alternatives: solidarity or disintegration. If Latin America is to opt for solidarity, it must employ original instruments that are products of its own culture and experience.

CLASC AND THE UNITED STATES

Relations between the two Americas have been largely dominated by noxious extremes on both sides. Latin Americans oscillate between a spirit of rupture and one of submission. As for the North Americans, they have largely practiced a policy tending to virtual annexation of their southern neighbors, or one of oblivion to their existence.

In Latin America there are those who have made the anti-imperialist struggle a demagogic tactic for obtaining votes or a calculated cold-war maneuver to place our continent under the domination of Soviet imperialism. On the other hand, just as many or more would copy all that comes from the United States because they have decided that it is always better than all that exists in Latin America. They assume the comfortable position of expecting that everything be solved from above, from the North—a servile position without personality.

Logically, these positions obstruct sincere dialogue and the possibility of dignified people-to-people solidarity governed by the canons of mutual respect and the demands of international social justice.

The denunciations of imperialism by Christian trade unionism have not differed substantially with honest and sincere critiques of U.S.-Latin American relations by such North American statesmen as Senator J. William Fulbright and the late President John F. Kennedy. For Christian trade unionism, imperialism is economic, political, or military preponderance, a violation of the principles of mutual respect and solidarity. Our position, however, has never been governed by a spirit of rupture or a calculated maneuver to play into the hands of any other imperialism. We seek to follow our own methods, our own philosophy, our own genuinely Latin American tactics, programs, and strategies in a revolutionary move toward formation of the United States of Latin America.

There are those in both Latin America and the United States who would disfigure this position. Some accuse us of being Communists, crypto-Communists, or fellow travelers, especially when they speak with North Americans of Christian religious convictions. On the other hand, progressive agnostics are told we are "holy-holy types, pious people easily managed by priests and bishops and without any trade-union authenticity." In this manner are deceived many North Americans of good will who sincerely wish to know Latin America better without sectarian intermediaries.

Again, I wish to cite a passage from the study *Business and Labor in Latin America,* conducted by the University of Chicago for a subcommittee of the U.S. Senate:

> The policy to follow with respect to workers organizations should be based in frank recognition of the *diversity* of the labor movements. Although the interests of the United States require the

strengthening of organizations which aspire to development of democratic institutions, there is no reason why these organizations should be guided according to the model of the American trade unions. The spirit of relations between the North American and the Latin American workers organizations should consist in a cooperation of the first with the democratic trade unions of the latter, without attempting to teach them and even less with the intention of imposing on them characteristics of the respective North American organizations. It is obvious that, to make effective the cooperation between the U.S. and Latin American workers organizations, both sides must recognize and accept sincerely the diversity of the workers movements in the different countries of the Western Hemisphere. They must bear in mind that the differences correspond to basic differences of historical antecedents and to the current labor situations, tasks and experiences. Any attempt, conscious or otherwise, to configure the workers movements within the arrangement of a pre-established model would be not only fruitless but disastrous for true democratic cooperation. Democratic workers movements should distinguish themselves from those dominated by the Communists by a recognition of *international plurality* and by an absolute repudiation of any idea that there is only one uniform efficacious way for the entire workers movement.

These objective observations have great value for the Latin American reality. Unfortunately, they have not been borne in mind. North American trade-union organizations have systematically discriminated against the Christian trade-union organizations and made them the object of humiliating scorn. With respect to relations, we have always been granted just one alternative: that we disappear as an organization and a reality so that we might be annexed and absorbed by the trade-union organizations inspired, promoted, and financed in Latin America by North American trade-union organizations and the U.S. Government. There is not the slightest respect for international pluralism. The idea is to monopolize all in order to place it at the service of a formula, and of interests and partial viewpoints of one single sector of the democratic trade unionism of the two Americas—disavowing all the other democratic trade-union organizations which are making their own original efforts in Latin America.

The Alliance for Progress itself, at the trade-union level, is governed by a dangerous discrimination. The original concept of the Alliance contemplates the mobilization of the popular forces to act as the subjects and direct beneficiaries of change and progress in Latin America. Nevertheless, a series of intermediate Washington functionaries entrenched as directors and administrators of the Alliance channel all assistance and aid to trade-union organizations that are controlled by American unions. This policy is in contradiction to the revolutionary orientation given the Alliance by Kennedy and his young team.

We share with the North American workers the Judeo-Christian ethic. Yet, despite this spiritual communion and ethic, there is no systematic dialogue, nor any system of relations based on dignified and fraternal solidarity. Instead, a gigantic wall of silence and of slanted information has been built—the product of sectarianism, opportunism, and a covetous spirit of those who would make democratic trade unionism in Latin America an odious and unjust monopoly.

CHRISTIAN WORKERS WITH THE REVOLUTION

Those of us who believe in Christian values and in democracy as the political form for the Latin American revolution are faced with a tremendous challenge in this most critical moment of Latin American history. The historical objective of the revolution is to establish systems capable of satisfying elemental human necessities. Access to power, riches, and culture must be opened to the popular masses of the continent so that they will become the preponderant factor in their own destinies and those of our countries. We have decided to participate fully in the process of the social revolution precisely because we are Christians and democrats and workers.

As a maneuver for maintaining the status quo, the specter of the *paredón* of Fidel Castro is evoked by reactionary elements in Latin America. But in our continent, we know there exists another *paredón:* the *paredón* of hunger and of misery, of the unemployment and the permanent humiliation of the poor. Between these two *paredones* lies the road of the social revolution in Latin America. One must have the courage to follow this route—the way of hope for the poor. Because in Latin America all is at stake within the hope of the poor. The time is very short for the solution of problems accumulated over many years and festering at once. The instrument for changing the history of our continent lies with those who are capable of capturing the hope of the poor and oppressed. And democratic Christians, both in the political and trade-union spheres, have pledged their lives to the revolution, because hope is a Christian virtue and the Christian message is especially addressed to the poor. We have preferred to break with the existing order and exercise the right to create a future order which will be democratic and Christian. If we fail, more than 200 million human beings will suffer a long black night because hope, and the revolution of Christians, will not have arrived in time.

Part II

THE NATIONALIST PIVOT

Introduction: Not One

Latin America

JOSUÉ DE CASTRO

DRAINED OF ITS LIFEBLOOD and bursting with energy, Latin America, a continent in the throes of development, is a source of concern and a basis of hope. It has to accomplish a revolution and a synthesis. First, it must cast off the feudal yoke, destructive monopolies, acquire economic independence, and allay the hunger of stomachs and hearts. Then, it must reconcile the requirements of revolution with human respect and refrain from sullying the present in the name of a bright future.

Since the Cuban revolution, Latin America is a focus of world attention. Some are lying in wait for the conflagration, predict the great Jacquerie of desperate peoples, and recommend increased exploitation since the good old days are beyond recall. Others, for sometimes identical reasons, seek a means for channeling and impeding the flood they say will be devastating.

Latin America will however resist change in a world that makes change its reason for existence. It has acquired stature, it has expanded, but basically it has remained unchanged. It has not developed because true development does not merely consist in expansion, increased production and higher per capita income, but in social transformation that benefits the community. Forces of resistance, that are the outcome of the conquest and that still prevail, have opposed it. This is the legacy of the feudal origins that hold Latin America together and differentiate it from Anglo-Saxon North America.

A product of agrarian feudalism, Latin America remains the unique twentieth-century feudal continent. All the social forces, all the values, all the new economic systems are embedded in this feudal groundwork. Reference is often made to "relics of a feudal past," whereas, in fact, feudalism still exists, barely concealed behind new façades.

When America was discovered, Europe, from the North to the Pyrenees, was already involved in the Renaissance; feudalism persisted south of the Pyrenees. Spain and Portugal, fully occupied with the wars against Islam, had fallen two centuries behind. Portugal was a landed monarchy, Spain a medieval Catholic kingdom.

In Latin America the conquerors re-created their prosperous feudalism. They had their Renaissance too, but it was a feudal one, and feudalism thereby found new strength in the large landed estates. The discovery of America did not promote a historic evolution but was rather a regression. A social structure that was dying out in Europe found new lease on life.

The *repartimientos* and *encomiendas* are typically feudal. The large capitalists, to whom the Portuguese Crown alloted lands in Brazil, organized their estates in the old style. The monarchy did not possess the necessary means for colonization, lacking money and men. It alloted vast areas to feudal lords, who entered into partnerships with wealthy men of the emerging bourgeoisie. The latter committed part of their fortunes and made use of the credit enjoyed by the aristocracy.

There are four obvious characteristics of Latin American society:

(1) an exploitative economy devoted to the extraction of natural wealth (silver, gold), and the production of one or two foodstuffs (coffee, sugar cane);

(2) an export economy that supplies other countries with raw materials and buys manufactured products from them without any desire or possibility of independent economic development;

(3) a persistent landed feudalism which results in vast areas only slightly or poorly cultivated by owners without liquid assets; and

(4) a society onto which European institutions have been grafted.

Changes have occurred. The population explosion that started in 1940 has reversed the social, economic, and cultural situation on the continent. Men have abandoned the land for the cities, which are inadequate to absorb them. Agricultural employment has fallen and the services sector has swelled. New social categories have emerged without as yet any real class consciousness. The growth in population makes impossible the ownership system, unchanged since the colonial era. The need for agrarian reform is severe, but the results in Mexico and even more so, Bolivia, have not come up to expectation.

Medical progress allows millions to survive, but without any means of making a living they are thrown into a cramped labor market which was already unable to meet the requirements of the population. In 1650 the population of the continent was 12 million. Three centuries later, in 1950, it stood at 163 million. It is now over 220 million and by 1980, Latin America will probably have a population of 297 million; by 2000, it will rise to 500 million.

G. W. Schmeltz has established that to obtain economic domination through a fixed trend in trade exchanges, the percentage of sales and purchases to or from a given trading partner has to, and need only be, equal to at least 40 percent of the total foreign trade and that the latter represents a large fraction of the national product, whereas the foreign exchanges of the dependent state play only a modest role in the general economy. Such is the situation in Latin America. The United States imports and consumes 75 percent of all the raw materials and primary products exported by Latin America. Most Latin American countries maintain a precarious balance by exporting one or two raw materials. If there is a slump in one or another of the raw products, the entire nation is affected by the crisis. It involves a succession of downward trends:

(1)   there is a deficit in the balance of payments and foreign-exchange reserves dwindle and then run dry: short-term capital imports are unfeasible since a discount-rate policy proves to be impossible;

(2)   imports are cut and purchases of capital equipment necessary for varying and diversifying the economy suffer;

(3)   the reduction in imports and exports leads to unemployment; and

(4)   the state finances become unbalanced since

tax revenue is obtained largely from the yield of exports and a drop in sales reduces taxation receipts at a time when the badly affected sectors are calling for help. In order to avoid halting the development plan and to pay out the subsidies required, the State will be tempted to finance itself through inflation. It will also have recourse to fixing import quotas and manipulating foreign exchange rates to the detriment of world exchanges and industrial equipment exports. Inflation and foreign exchange instability discourage the flow of foreign capital and promote expatriation of domestic capital. The expansion of international trade in raw materials is therefore a deciding factor in the growth of underdeveloped countries which, for many years to come, will depend on this for financing agricultural development, industrialization and diversification of their economies. (Pierre Goetschin)

Of course, raw materials are sold at cut rates and manufactured products are expensive: from 1950 to 1960 the ratio between the prices of raw materials and those of manufactured goods decreased by 26 percent, due for the most part to the increase in manufactured products. Thus the rich countries, by buying raw materials cheaply from poor countries and selling them manufactured goods at a high cost, contribute directly to their impoverishment and make them pay for what they get twice over. The price increase for finished products compels poor countries to supply more raw materials so as to acquire the capital equipment they need. The drop in the purchasing power for all exports from developing countries as a result of the deterioration in the terms of exchange (i.e., the ratio between export price and import price) represents nearly $13.1 billion for the years 1950–1961.

Moreover, the raw-materials market proves to be particularly unstable: fluctuations in demand are considerable. A United Nations survey shows the full extent of variations from 1901 to 1950.

The annual price fluctuation reaches 14 percent, which means that from one year to the next, on an average, if the volume of exports remains constant, revenue may increase or decrease by 14 percent. Now a reduction of this extent cancels out all the effects of outside aid:

(1) fluctuations in the market price during the year reach an average of 27 percent over this period and amount to 32 percent of cocoa and 37 percent for rubber;
(2) fluctuations in the export volume amount to 19 percent; and

(3) total fluctuations in export revenue dependent on volumes and prices average about 23 percent from one year to the next, but they can reach 37 percent from a falling cycle to a rising cycle, the average cycle being about four years. This instability in foreign currency revenue therefore adds considerably to the difficulties of developing countries and renders impossible the medium-term forecasting necessary for implementing development programs. For the same quantities, the export revenue for Brazilian coffee, which amounted to $1 billion in 1954, only represented $700 million in 1961.

According to the United Nations the loss for Latin America resulting from the drop in prices for raw materials in a single year was ten times greater than the credits received from the United States and international agencies.

The repatriation of profits constitutes another source of imbalance. Between 1950 and 1961, Latin America received $47.4 billion in the form of loans, gifts, and investments. Of this amount, $20.9 billion, representing profits and interests, was repatriated. The share of foreign capital mounted to $9.6 billion, but at the same time the sums repatriated from Latin American countries to lender countries amounted to $13.4 billion. Finally, therefore, it was Latin America that was lending to the rich countries. If we add the losses caused by the drop in prices of raw materials and the rise in prices of manufactured goods—amounting to $10.1 billion during this same period—we see that in the end $13.9 billion left Latin America for the rich countries during these years.

These circumstances explain the mistrust with which the Latin American countries view the aid programs. They are aware that such programs sustain their state of misery and serve as a security for the favored nations.

Latin Americans shy away when they learn the exact amount of investments and repatriations. From 1950 to 1955 the United States invested $2 billion, chiefly in the raw materials and agricultural plantations sectors, and made a profit of $3.5 billion. Nearly half of this profit, $1.5 billion, was repatriated.

In 1959, from a profit of $775 million, $200 million was reinvested and $575 million repatriated. During the last ten years Latin America has been defrauded of $2.679 billion. Capital investments are directed toward sectors from which they can obtain immediate profits, chiefly in the oil and mining sectors

(51 percent in 1959). Foreign companies insist on drastic guarantees from the governments against risks of devaluation, expropriation, and even war.

A comparison of profits will show that those obtained in Latin America are, depending on the case, 50 to 200 percent higher than those made in the United States. A United Nations survey reveals that the averge profit made in the processing industry in the United States during the postwar years was 15 percent, while the profit obtained by the branch firms in the same industrial sector in Latin America amounted to 23 percent. Even sharper disproportions may be noted in individual cases.

Again during the postwar years, official reports show, for Standard Oil of New Jersey, a profit of 11% in the U.S.A. and 33% in Latin America. In 1948, General Motors made a profit of 25% in the United States and nearly 80% in its Latin American subsidiary companies. The Anaconda Copper Co. obtains a profit in Chile that is 200% higher than in the U.S.A. and, during the same period, Firestone Tires made profits that were four times higher in Latin America.[1]

The Chilean economist Alberto Baltra has estimated that the American trusts that control copper production in his country have, during the last thirty years, derived a net profit of $2 billion, which represents about 40 percent of the total value of copper exports during this period and three times the amount of investments made in Chile.

In 1961 alone, private firms in the United States earned $1.6 billion in interest and profits from their investments in Latin America. If one is to believe these firms' tax returns, they claim to have made a profit of $774 million in 1959 with investments amounting to $8.218 billion. But the Department of Commerce review, *Survey of Current Business,* estimates that the earnings of the major American private firms rose between 1950 and 1959 by 90 percent in Chile, nearly 90 percent in Venezuela, and 30 percent in Argentina.

Since 1960, 90 percent of the long-term credits granted to Latin America by the Export-Import Bank of Washington are 52 percent to the benefit of trusts and cartels.

As a general rule, loan agreements lead to the following results: American goods are supplied at a price higher than the

[1] Johann Lorenz Schmidt, *Deutsche Aussenpolitik,* November, 1961.

current United States price; the loans are made for the benefit of the trusts established in the assisted countries; the goods arrive on American ships, are insured by American firms, and banking transactions are carried out by American banks. In this way they recover 20 to 25 percent of the amounts loaned out.

After the 1929 depression several Latin American countries endeavored to set up a national industry around which they erected protectionist barriers. After many attempts to breach this defensive system, the trusts decided that it would be more profitable to install their factories in these countries. Since they run the mining industries and most of the plantations, they control the major part of the processing industries to which they give new native names. Buyers, unaware that they are dealing with an American trust, order their electrical equipment from the Industria Electrica Mexicana, the little sister, in disguise, of the Westinghouse Electric Corporation.

American capital is concentrated geographically and economically. In terms of geography, of the $7 billion invested in 1956:

> Venezuela received $1.817 billion; Brazil, $1.209 billion; Cuba, $774 million; Chile, $677 million; Mexico, $675 million; Central America, $610 million; Argentina, $470 million; Peru, $354 million; Colombia, $289 million; and others, $133 million.

We have already pointed out that this money is invested in industries that earn profits almost immediately and is of little benefit to local economies. Two billion is devoted to oil extraction, $1.1 billion for ores, $632 million in plantations producing exportable agricultural commodities, $4.95 million in businesses and $1.5 billion in the processing industries.

The economic concentration is demonstrated by these figures from Brazil. Foreign capital, mainly American, controls:

> 50 percent of the iron and rolled-metal industry
> 50 percent of the meat industry
> 56 percent of the textile industry
> 72 percent of electric power production
> 80 percent of cigarette manufacture
> 80 percent of pharmaceutical production

        98 percent of the automobile industry
        100 percent of oil and gasoline distribution

In Peru, Anderson Clayton dominates the wool and cotton production and market. The Grace Company, the Chase Manhattan Bank, the First National City Bank of New York, the Northern Peru Mines, the Marcona Mines and Goodyear establish the prices for agricultural products and control 80 percent of the raw materials. The International Petroleum Company, a subsidiary of the Standard Oil Company of New Jersey, owns the oil that represents 80 percent of national production. The American Smelting and Refining Company and the Cerro de Pasco Corporation, which also owns over 1.200 million acres, reign over copper and other mining products. The Bell Telephone Company has taken over the telephone services.

Venezuela is overflowing with oil. It is the second-largest oil producer in the world and the richest Caribbean state. It has the highest national revenue but it is so badly distributed that the peasant masses are plunged in misery. Standard Oil produces half the black gold, Shell one quarter, Gulf, one-seventh; and Socony, Sinclair, and Phillips, the rest. The second item of wealth, the iron, belongs to Iron Mining, an affiliate of U.S. Steel, to Orinoco Mining, an affiliate of U.S. Steel, and to the Western Ore Company. These companies own half the reserves, estimated at 700 million tons. The Cooper group runs the iron and steel industry; Hawkins the petrochemicals; and Reynold has taken over the bauxite reserves.

Paul Johnson of the *New Statesman* offers this definition of Latin America: "It could have been the kingdoms of the world that the devil showed Christ from the mountain." It possesses more cultivable and extremely productive tropical land than any other continent and three times more agricultural land, per inhabitant, than Asia.

It lies dying on a bed of wealth. It has huge estates, poorly operated or working only for the export market, alongside a dispossessed peasant multitude that toils with ridiculous tools for paltry wages and with only one certitude—misery at birth, misery at death, and from start to finish, daily suffering.

In Chile and Brazil, 2 percent of the population is comfortably settled on 50 percent of the cultivable land. In Venezuela, 3 percent monopolizes 90 percent of the land. In the rest of Latin

America, except in Mexico and Cuba, 5 percent of the population owns half the land. The national agricultural census figures provide an eloquent picture of these contrasts. The predominance of large agrarian estates is one of the causes of Latin America's underdevelopment. The characteristic feature of the latifundium is that it is partially exploited by antiquated means.

The latifundium cumulates all the disadvantages of the large estate and the small enterprise, without enjoying the advantages of one or the other. The direct outcome of the slave system or, more generally, that form of serfdom constituted by the Indian *encomienda,* the latifundian structure, in which the labourer remains personally dependent on the owner and the master has the customary obligation of protecting his subjects, is a complete system of social organization related to the feudal system. The economic function of the latifundium is to produce for the market only on an accessory basis. In the main, it has to meet all the social as well as economic requirements of its inhabitants who, because of their isolated condition and ignorance, have so far known only the most rudimentary needs; for the master, the prestige of a feudal lord and the influence that obedient subjects afford in national politics have often been more important than the income from very limited agricultural productivity. (Jacques Lambert)

The outstanding feature of this rural economy is the absence of any real monetary economy or even a market within these agricultural areas. The consumer and barter economy dominates the countryside and results in limited productivity and a very low standard of living. The peasants are undernourished, they suffer from chronic diseases, and they can neither read nor write. They live outside the national community. They are mere objects of the historical process.

Another form of the large landed estate is the big plantation which combines agrarian capitalism and colonial exploitation and devotes itself to cultivating an export product—coffee, sugar, cotton, or fruit. The estate is run in an industrial manner. Agricultural workers receive a wage and, in many cases, medical treatment. Overseers run the estate for the master, who lives in town. These big plantations have helped to create an agricultural proletariat conscious of its rights and capable of getting them respected. Because they use modern methods, they are also a factor in development.

Jacques Lambert has stressed the evolutive role played by these agricultural units. Effectively, it is these big modern plantations whose intensive production provides the large majority of Latin American countries, which do not have vast mining resources, with the major part of the foreign currency required for their development. Brazil, Colombia, Ecuador, Uruguay, Argentina owe more than half their exports to plantation monocultures. The capitalist plantation has also been useful in integrating rural populations into the developed national society. These plantations have become the centers for modernizing a very antiquated form of agriculture. By providing their personnel with a certain amount of available funds, by facilitating their education, and by granting them social benefits similar to those available in towns, the capitalist plantation, contrary to the latifundium, has contributed to reducing social dualism.

Plantation owners enjoy considerable political power, which they use for their special interests. They invest very little. If they devote 25 percent of their agrarian income to improving their crops, they testify to an awareness of their responsibilities, as pointed as it is rare. The major part of their earnings is wasted on sumptuous building or concealed in American or Swiss bank accounts. In the tropical areas most of the plantations belong to American firms. The famous United Fruit Company, which dominates Guatemala, Honduras, and Costa Rica, owns more than 1,200,000 acres. Before the revolution, the American Sugar Company owned about 30,000 acres in Cuba and controlled 62 percent of the sugar production.

In Latin America, agricultural reform projects spread like mushrooms in the springtime and last about as long. All these governments loudly declare their intention of giving land to the peasants and of reallocating estates, but the results are ridiculous when compared to the stated ambitions. So far Latin America has witnessed only three important land reforms—in Mexico, Bolivia, and Cuba. All three have different features and in the case of Mexico, and more particularly Bolivia, they can easily be subjected to major criticism. But it is not our intention here to analyze these three solutions in detail.

True land reform implies a strictly implemented government plan and also includes sufficiently varied industrialization that will make the nation economically independent, provide work to those who will leave the countryside and offer thousands of new consumers purchasing power. Such an ambition, in practical terms, entails revolution.

All efforts to modernize and stimulate agriculture crash against an antiquated agrarian basic structure. This brief analysis of economic and social conditions reveals bluntly the absolute necessity of radical transformation of agricultural production methods, but this saving effort would only be possible with a complete reshaping of the present rural structures.

This type of reform does not consist in the expropriation or reallocation of land merely to meet the immediate needs of the poor. We consider agrarian reform to be a means of revising the legal and economic relationship between those who own property and those who work it. There must be the will to limit the working of the land, *by written law,* in such a way as to obtain higher, and above all, better distributed output for the benefit of the entire rural community. To accomplish this, one must overthrow inertia, and the barriers set up by acquired or inherited rights and privileges. This radical modification of the economic structure demands a political choice and a policy.

What remains to be seen is whether the supporters of landed feudalism and capitalism will resign themselves to accepting an inevitable evolution or whether they will oppose it with all their strength.

The future of Latin America will be read in the opposition between forces within this system. On the one side are the revolutionary forces led by advance-guard minorities, enlightened and experienced, sometimes unobtrusive or idealist, who are relying on the support of the overwhelming masses of the continent—the outcasts, the defenseless, and the hungry. On the other side are the forces of reaction, also led by a minority— the privileged groups of capitalist bourgeoisie and landed oligarchy—who are an insignificant number but very powerful since they hold all the instruments and means of production, the land, and the political power. These counterrevolutionary forces are able to reinforce their position on the political chessboard because they can count on the alliance and firm support of international capital—the capitalist trusts and international police who protect their interests, the governments and armed forces of capitalist powers, in particular, the United States.

Moreover, this struggle between oppressor groups and the

oppressed masses is a universal phenomenon. It can be seen everywhere in various disguises of racial strife, religious quarrels, conflicts between divergent nationalisms and ideologies. What marks the struggle in Latin America, and distinguishes it, is first of all the enormous disproportion of forces between partisans of the status quo, who are extremely powerful, and the masses who impatiently yearn for revolution but who lack the means for that struggle, from financial resources to cultural preparation. In a world of accelerated transformation one can see dominant groups everywhere making concessions, yielding some of their privileges. Except in Latin America, where the forces of oppression adamantly yield nothing and try to impede the trend of history and progress by systematic violence.

Today Latin America breathes only the stifling air of violence: the radical opposition between the chronic, institutionally organized violence imposed by a false social order which is undisguisedly inhuman, and the acute violence supported by insurgent intellectuals, mass leaders, true representatives of the classes, guerrillas, parties of the left and even certain more advanced Church representatives who rebel against the violence of the Establishment and advocate revolutionary violence to pull apart the machine of continent-wide oppression.

This overall picture of Latin America takes note of the extreme complexity of the human problem on this continent: its immense diversity, its economic, social, and political polymorphism. Really, "Latin America" does not exist. The Latin America of today is a creation of a synthesizing idea just as it was in the sixteenth century an invention of Spanish thinking. The historian Jean Babellon wrote that "Latin America is a Spanish invention" to explain that the discovery of the New World by the crazy visionary Christopher Columbus had been prepared at length in the half-light of medieval Spain, with its Messianic and adventurist thinking, and which was then in the twilight of a decadent feudalism, and impatiently lusting after the delights of fabulous riches hidden in the far-off lands.

The conquistadores who arrived later branded on the hide of the New World all the marks of a Spanish utopia which would be for the personal use of Spaniards or, rather, Europeans. It is this world of baroque splendors and the feudal Renaissance that we have endeavored to paint in this introduction.

But what else has been added through the centuries to these primitive Spanish drawings? Latin America is the Western

Sphinx, frequently enigmatic to less baroque peoples like most Americans and Europeans.

After the Cuban revolution in 1959 and the discovery, by the United States, in 1960, of the powder keg in Northeast Brazil with its peasant leagues, the number of books on Latin America published in the United States rose considerably. Unfortunately, most of these books do not provide North Americans with a true or living image of South America. Generally they are either scholarly works which concentrate on particular aspects, such as anthropology or economics essays, or they are reports by journalists or political commentators who see Latin America through the ethnocentric perspectives of those who live in an industrialized, affluent world. Some are traumatized when they find themselves face to face with the spectacle of misery in this Latin part of the hemisphere. To this list one must add the official and unofficial reports which often fail to give a clear image of this area of the world.

North American government circles, embarrassed by their restless and disquieting neighbors, have not troubled to discover why Latin Americans are so dissatisfied with their northern neighbors. North Americans find that the image in Latin America of relations between the two Americas lends itself to caricature. The truth is that these relations *are* a living caricature of "relations between free nations."

How is one to overcome these difficulties, and many others, to obtain a glimpse of Latin America which shows its people in movement and in action—a portrait that is not set or motionless?

We have tried to overcome these difficulties by arranging this book in symposium form, with analyses by Latin Americans as well as North Americans and Europeans. We selected as collaborators men who are interested in studying the dynamics, the machinery of change in Latin America, and who want to contribute to this change. We have tried to meet the challenge of the Latin American enigma. In an attempt to read on the face of the Latin American Sphinx the most significant features of its historic past and the revelatory signs of the future, we are trying to present a book that can supply an objective idea of the social dynamics of Latin America, of the movements and transfers of the power centers in these developing countries, or, to be more specific, "in these countries where underdevelopment is constantly worsening," as Claude Julien put it. And, as well, a book that might show us a little of the future. Our project was there-

fore designed to analyze present-day reality within a historical
framework. There is no question of predicting the future or making prophecies. *Prospection* is not *forecasting*. Forecasting tries
to give us an idea of probable events to which we shall have to
adapt ourselves, while prospection is aimed at determining the
possible objectives that can be attained. This is what chiefly interests the advance-guard elements throughout the world—to
learn how the future world order will appear so that options may
be taken.

What will be the place of Latin America in the world order of
tomorrow? Any facts that may reveal that future must be understood. The authors of these essays attempt to analyze some of
these facts.

In this introduction I do not want to determine the final positions, the necessary options, the specific actions. This should
come out of the dialogues between readers and authors. After
that, the reader may perhaps be able to discern the sociological
outline of Latin America and then attempt to understand the
Sphinx. Not before. I do not pretend to guide the reader this far.
My aim in this introduction is to take the reader to the threshold
of this discovery and to bring him into contact with authors who,
each in his own way, have put down their experiences and
thoughts. And, more particularly, on those problems that relate
to nationalism and the will for revolution that hold sway from
one end of the continent to the other.

The Violence of Domination: U.S. Power and the Dominican Republic*

FRED GOFF
and MICHAEL LOCKER

INTRODUCTION

THE MASSIVE U.S. military intervention in the Dominican Republic during 1965 greatly clarified the political situation throughout Latin America. Just as Viet Nam focused U.S. interests in Asia, so the Dominican intervention objectified North American intentions throughout the hemisphere. In both places Washington made it painfully clear how far it is willing to go to maintain control over the Third World. The more subtle guises by which the U.S. tried to manipulate events since the days of gunboat diplomacy were stripped away when 20,000 soldiers stormed ashore to crush a nationalist rebellion in Santo Domingo. For most Latin Americans the official reasons offered to justify this action were patently false. To all but most North Americans it was obvious the Dominicans had their independence stolen in order to benefit U.S. economic, political, and military interests. The violence that flared to the surface in this confrontation is buried inside every other covert and overt mechanism the United States utilizes to control the Third World. Domination breeds violence and the potential for organized revolution.

In many respects the Dominican Republic is a small carbon

* Mimeographed. New York: North American Congress on Latin America, 1967.

copy of Cuba. An island republic close to our shores, it lives on a sugar-export economy, has a large Negro and Spanish population, and suffers from a history marked by violent, cruel dictatorship and U.S. intervention. American efforts to dominate the country stretch back to the early 1800's, culminating in the Spanish-American War and the gunboat diplomacy days of Theodore Roosevelt, Taft, and Wilson.[1]

Plagued by long-term economic stagnation, extensive debts to European bankers, and by political chaos, the country was invaded in 1898 by a U.S.-supported secret military expedition led by a wealthy exiled Dominican merchant. The venture failed, but in 1903 and again in 1904 revolts broke out and political leaders, vying for control, sought U.S. protectorate status. Troops landed temporarily to "protect" a sugar estate and lend support to a pro-United States faction; Kuhn, Loeb and Co., a large New York banking house, took over the foreign debts and floated a $20 million bond issue.

In a dozen years from 1904 to 1916, the United States moved from the Roosevelt Corollary to full-scale Marine occupation of the Dominican Republic. First we collected customs, then we forbade insurrection in order to maintain stability, then we held elections with warships in the harbor and sailors or Marines at the polls, then we demanded full control over internal revenues and expenditures as well as over customs, then we demanded the disbanding of the Army and establishment of a Guardia Nacional (Constabulary); then we sent the Marines.[2]

DOMINATION THROUGH OCCUPATION: 1916–1930

U.S. military occupation forces literally ran the country for eight years, ignoring even the fiction of a "Dominican government." In strikingly contemporary language the commanding U.S. admiral announced the occupation:

[1] Histories of the Dominican Republic in English are few and far between. The most thorough account is by the famous State Department diplomat and one-time American Commissioner to the Dominican Republic (1922–25), Sumner Welles, *Naboth's Vineyard: The Dominican Republic, 1844–1924,* 2 vols. (New York, 1928).

[2] John Bartlow Martin, *Overtaken by Events: The Dominican Crisis from the Fall of Trujillo to Civil War* (New York, 1966), p. 28.

. . . for the purpose of supporting the constituted authorities and to put a stop to revolutions and consequential disorders . . . It is not the intention of the United States Government to acquire by conquest any territory in the Dominican Republic nor to attack its sovereignty, but our troops will remain until all revolutionary movements have been stamped out and until such reforms as are deemed necessary to insure the future welfare of the country have been initiated and are in effective operation.[3]

In order to stabilize the financial situation, the military government repressed nationalist forces through a program of "disarmament and pacification." In two eastern provinces, Seibo and San Pedro de Macoris, where large American sugar estates were established, Dominicans took to the hills, harassed the plantations, and conducted guerrilla warfare. The Marines, terming them bandits, hunted the insurgents down mercilessly, terrorizing the local population and committing atrocities. By 1920 the repression, combined with the award of disputed land to United States and Dominican *latifundistas,* raised nationalistic passions almost to the point of full-scale rebellion. Alarmed, the plantation operators banded together under the leadership of an American, Edwin Kilbourne, to pacify the area. With a new Marine Commander they organized local squads of native Dominicans familiar with the terrain. A program of peaceful inducements was initiated after limiting the guerrilla forays and the more important leaders were persuaded to surrender. "The Marines unquestionably sowed the seed of anti-Americanism throughout the Repulbic," especially in the eastern provinces. To this day "in some towns the anniversary of their departure is celebrated as a holiday."[4]

Most of the social and economic programs established during the occupation collapsed when the troops formally withdrew in 1924. But even before withdrawing, the United States insisted on maintaining control over customs until all foreign debts were paid, forced the adoption of a U.S.-drafted electoral code, and

[3] Welles, Vol. 2, p. 777.
[4] Martin, p. 29. On the operations and effects of U.S. occupation see Arthur J. Burks, *Land of a Checkerboard Family* (New York, 1932); Melvin M. Knight, *The Americans in Santo Domingo* (New York, 1928); Dana G. Munro, *Intervention and Dollar Diplomacy in the Caribbean, 1900–1921* (Princeton, 1964); and Marvin Goldwart, "The Constabulary in the Dominican Republic and Nicaragua" in *Latin American Monographs,* No. 17 (Gainesville, 1962).

further strengthened the National Police as a substitute for the old politicized army. Trained and officered by American Marines, the police quickly became the most organized and powerful force throughout the island. It was through this structure that Rafael Leonidas Trujillo made his way, assiduously cultivating friendships with the American officers, conspicuously demonstrating cooperation and cordiality. As he climbed the promotional ladder, with the aid of favorable American recommendations, he mastered the one essential rule for gaining and sustaining political power in the Republic—an understanding that the base of domestic power is rooted primarily in the United States.

DOMINATION THROUGH DICTATORSHIP:
THE ERA OF TRUJILLO

When the National Police was transformed back into the army in 1928, Trujillo assumed the role of chief. Maneuvering carefully behind the scenes he engineered a fake uprising followed by the seizure of cities and the confiscation of weapons on the pretext of preserving order and preventing bloodshed. "One of Trujillo's greatest concerns in this plot was to insure that the government he established would be recognized by the United States."[5] Close contact with the American legation and his influential old Marine Commander, Colonel Cutts, guaranteed Trujillo U.S. support and ultimate success.

Once in power Trujillo proceeded to erect a pervasive and repressive totalitarian regime. The army was his private instru-

[5] Robert D. Crassweller, *Trujillo: The Life and Times of a Caribbean Dictator* (New York, 1966), p. 62. Crassweller's book is a highly authoritative account of the Trujillo period. During World War II the author was an officer in the State Department's Economic Warfare Section. Later he was a partner in a Dominican-Puerto Rican iron mining venture, then became a member of the legal staff of Pan American World Airways. In 1967 he joined the staff of the Council on Foreign Relations to do a two-year study on U.S. policy in the Caribbean.
A discussion of the Dominican armed forces can be found in Howard J. Wiarda, "The Politics of Civil-Military Relations in the Dominican Republic," *Journal of Inter-American Studies,* Vol. II, No. 4 (October, 1965), pp. 465–84.

ment of coercion and terror; the oversize officer corps benefited materially and enjoyed privileged status.[6] At home and abroad he developed a huge espionage apparatus providing the kind of intelligence needed to predict events and manipulate people. By recruiting their sons Trujillo cleverly forced most of the oligarchy into collaboration; blackmail, threats, and economic pressure compelled virtually every man of ability to serve him. Torture and assassination awaited those who resisted. Political opposition was erased or manipulated by co-option, imprisonment, exile, or murder. The Generalissimo personally selected all the national and local appointments, and his own party, manned by an endless string of relatives and cronies, administered a sizable social-welfare program. Every official, high or low, was subjected to constant rotation, public humiliation, or sudden elevation on short notice by orders from "El Jefe."

Beyond this traditional *caudillo* system, Trujillo constructed a fantastic personal economic empire. "At the most, . . . other [*caudillos*] had wanted money for its own sake, or for luxury, display, bribery, or a political purpose. Trujillo, far more than any of them, saw in the entire economic process a source of dominion as potent as the army, as strong as the most rigid political structure."[7] Funds collected from the public and from illicit operations were invested in every conceivable agricultural and industrial enterprise; monopolies usually followed. Import-export taxes and license fees facilitated the harassment and eventual takeover of corporations dealing in foreign trade, the lifeblood of the economy. Moreover, U.S. commodity shortages at the end of World War II raised prices on agricultural exports and propelled the island's elite into relative prosperity. After centralizing banking operations, Trujillo could sell any of his unprofitable businesses to the state for a large profit and make timely reacquisitions. It has been estimated that between 65 and

[6] "During his long rule, the dictator showered continuous favors upon his uniformed backers, the result being that the Dominican Republic built up the most powerful war machine in the Caribbean, a military establishment far out of proportion to the actual security needs of the tiny nation. It included 17,000 troops; 12,000 policemen; light-, medium-, and heavy-tank battalions; and squadrons of fighters, bombers, destroyers, and frigates. The armed forces simply occupied their own nation." Edwin Lieuwen, *Generals vs. Presidents: Neomilitarism in Latin America* (New York, 1964), p. 55.

[7] Crassweller, p. 123.

85 percent of the entire economy eventually ended up in his hands.[8] The monetary fortune accumulated from this empire was not trivial, and the variety of devices it afforded for exercising power was crucial to maintaining the regime.

In the late forties and during the fifties, Trujillo made his move for the most coveted prize in the Dominican economy— the cane sugar industry. A sharp rise in postwar sugar prices attracted Trujillo's attention, but with the exception of relatively small properties held by the Vicini family the entire industry was owned by foreign capital—mainly United States. Fully aware of the financial and political complications involved in entering this economic sector, he proceeded cautiously. After acquiring a small independent mill in 1948, he pushed forward with the construction of an enormous milling installation, Rio Haina, that was put into production in 1953. In order to supply enough cane, he acquired large tracts of land from Dominicans, Canadians, Puerto Ricans, and finally Americans with small holdings. The largest single sugar complex on the island, La Romana, a subsidiary of the American-owned South Puerto Rico Sugar Co., was then handed the technical task of building a railroad for the efficient transportation of cane and managing the entire operation on a profit-sharing basis.

These accomplishments pushed Trujillo into the largest economic deal of his reign—acquisition of the prized U.S. West Indies Sugar Company. A product of the Marine occupation and the efforts of antiguerrilla expert Edwin Kilbourne (president and director of the company), West Indies was the largest geographically dispersed sugar complex on the island: four high-volume mills, along with 30,000 head of cattle, considerable pasture land, coconut plantations on Samana Bay, some coffee

[8] *The Hispanic American Report,* Vol. XV (Events of December, 1962) reported: "Official sources revealed that Trujillo's share of the national wealth had amounted to the following: bank deposits, 22%; money in circulation, 25%; sugar production, 63%; cement, 63%; paper, 73%; paint, 86%; cigarettes, 71%; milk, 85%; wheat and flour, 68%; plus the nation's only airline, its leading newspapers, and the three principal radio and television stations. According to the Swiss daily (Basel) *National Zeitung,* the Trujillo family had deposited no less than $200 million in Swiss banks in the name of fictitious companies."
In the same journal, Vol. XVI (Events of May, 1963), 463: ". . . the dictator owned 10% of the productive land and 10% of the cattle industry; 45% of the nation's active manpower was employed directly in Trujillo enterprises; a further 35% was engaged in the Armed Forces and the government-operated banking, hotel, and electricity systems."

fincas, and a great deal of underdeveloped land. Unlike La
Romana with its powerful South Puerto Rico Corp. connections
to Kuhn, Loeb & Co. and Rockefeller interests, West Indies
could not elicit enough political influence to bring about U.S.
intervention.[9] After some pressure was applied and the word of
Trujillo's desire to buy got out, the stockholders negotiated a
favorable figure ($35,830,000) in three cash installments. As
for South Puerto Rico, Trujillo realized its technical skills were
not replaceable and its powerful connections could be mutually
advantageous in raising the island's U.S. sugar quota.

The sugar acquisitions demonstrated that Trujillo still retained his keen understanding of power relationships within the
United States as well as the limitations they imposed on his
actions. Geographic proximity and the economic strength of the
United States forced any Dominican government to depend on
close and cordial relations with powerful U.S. citizens. To this
end, Trujillo devoted boundless energy and resources in the
form of business deals, sex, flattery, campaign contributions,
bribes, blackmail, even murder. Joseph E. Davies, the archetype
of Trujillo's influential American, was a multimillionaire corporate lawyer (with a major interest in General Foods) turned
New Deal diplomat. In 1931, Davies visited the Republic for
President Roosevelt and brought back a highly favorable assess-
ment of the new regime, which led, in turn, to a lifesaving
moratorium on debt payments and opened up new lines of
credit. A long friendship ensued; Davies visited often to serve as
financial counsel on business ventures and fiscal policy. Along
with Davies, industrialist Herbert May, construction tycoon
Felix Benítez Rexach, diplomat-businessman William Pawley,
and the molasses dealers A. I. and J. M. Kaplan served as

[9] Originally West Indies Sugar was part of a company controlled by the
National City Bank. But in 1931 the company was taken over by less
influential stockholders who counted on the considerable skill and influ-
ence of the management—which included Kilbourne—within the Republic.
On the other hand, South Puerto Rico's connections to Kuhn, Loeb &
Co. (the powerful New York banking house that held the Dominican
government's debt until 1940) existed through stock ownership, loans,
and interlocking directors. Ties to Rockefeller interests (including the
Chase Manhattan Bank and its predecessors, and Standard Oil Co. of
New Jersey) were manifest through interlocking directors and the chief
Rockefeller law firm, Dewey, Ballantine, Bushby, Palmer & Wood, which
was the company's general counsel.

Trujillo's economic liaison with the U.S. financial and business community.[10]

Trujillo never found an equivalent to Davies in the political sphere of the U.S. Establishment, though he managed to significantly influence governmental decisions and public opinion through a chain of well-paid politicians, lawyers, journalists, and lobbyists. Nobody knows how many millions of dollars were passed directly or indirectly to Senators, Representatives, Executive Department employees and other powerful Americans in public life who might protect and promote Trujillo.[11] Such dignitaries, critics as well as supporters, were often invited to his private fiefdom, wined and dined, provided with women and then secretly photographed. The "blackmail photographic library was extensive."[12]

In conjunction with these unsavory tactics, Trujillo produced a continual barrage of propaganda geared to project a favorable image of the Dominican Republic and its benevolent leader. Elections were staged, figureheads occupied the president's office, the capital was "beautified" and anti-Communism took on the trappings of a holy crusade. In order to inflate the

[10] Herbert May was a link to the Pittsburgh Mellon interests which developed a sizable investment in the 1950's for mining bauxite at Cabo Rojo through the Aluminum Company of America.

Benítez, a Puerto Rican who fought Muñoz Marín over the issue of independence, raised capital and equipment for public improvement projects undertaken by his company, the Rexach Construction Co. He was selected by Trujillo to be his political agent in Puerto Rico.

William Pawley was ambassador to Peru (1945–46) and Brazil (1946–48), influential in Washington, and a businessman with diverse holdings in Florida and Cuba. He drafted the Dominican legislation on foreign investments for Trujillo, obtained mineral concessions for U.S. investors and advised the Generalissimo on numerous occasions (e.g., The Galindez Affair).

The Kaplan brothers bought molasses for export to the U.S. and had extensive political power within the liberal wing of the Democratic Party.

[11] The head of Trujillo's military intelligence (SIM) wrote:

"Trujillo had, for instance, price lists for the purchase of some U.S. Congressmen. An ordinary, run-of-the-mill Representative would cost about $5,000 or less. A few House committee chairmen could be had for about three times that much, depending on the committee. Senators came higher, of course. A chairman of a key committee could run from $50,000 to $75,000."

Arturo R. Espaillat, *Trujillo: The Last Caesar* (Chicago, 1963), p. 81.

[12] Martin, p. 35.

country's importance, extravagant foreign embassies were maintained, glamorous trips undertaken, and a world's fair hosted in the capital. In a most clever move to obtain the influential good will of American and European Jewish leaders, an offer was made in 1940 to admit 100,000 Jewish refugees on very liberal terms. Most of these programs and many others were of course meaningless, but in public relations terms they would have to be judged a success. A countless number of public officials and newsmen praised the nation's "progress built on stability" and cooperated with its operations out of innocence, stupidity, or greed.[13]

After 1955, Trujillo built a Congressional power base in the United States centered around his periodic attempts to enlarge the island's share of the extremely lucrative U.S. sugar quota. Since 1934, the United States Government has subsidized the price of raw sugar to regulate supply and stabilize prices for domestic refiners and industrial consumers. A tonnage quota is assigned by Congress (primarily the House Agriculture Committee) to exporting nations and domestic growers guaranteeing the producer a high price and thus assuring delivery. Cuba had always been a preferred nation in the system, receiving the largest quota (providing approximately one-third of all sugar consumed in the United States) by reason of its position as the world's greatest producer. Since the dollar stakes were high and most of the Cuban ventures constituted very substantial *American* investments, the Cuban lobby exercised considerably more leverage than Trujillo and South Puerto Rico Sugar.[14]

[13] The prominent faithfuls who could be counted on to defend the dictator from adverse criticism included Senators Smathers, Thurmond, Ellender, Eastland, Russell, and Jenner; Representatives McCormack, Fulton, Jackson, and Cooley; ex-ambassador (to Peru and Brazil) and special assistant to State and Defense William Pawley; General George Olmstead; and Hearst society columnist Igor Cassini.

[14] This was reflected in the prestige of their lobbyist George W. Ball, a partner in the law firm of Cleary, Gottlieb, Steen and Ball, who represented two Cuban sugar associations before Congress during the 1956 consideration of the Sugar Act. Ball went on to become Under-Secretary of State in the Kennedy and Johnson administrations. Neither Trujillo nor South Puerto Rico ever retained a political figure with as much influence as the Cuban lobby.

The role of prestigious political figures in the sugar-quota lobbying is discussed in Daniel M. Berman and Robert A. Heineman's article "Lobbying by Foreign Government on the Sugar Act Amendments of 1962," *Law and Contemporary Problems* (September, 1963), pp. 416–27.

Thus, it was not until the Cuban Revolution fundamentally altered power relations inside the United States that the Dominican Republic had a chance to sell its greatly expanded sugar exports at preferential quota prices.[15] As United States–Cuban relations deteriorated and Castro cut back sugar production during 1959–60, Trujillo's lobbying in Congress began to bear fruit. By July, 1960, the Cuban quota was cancelled and the Dominican Republic received the largest portion of its subsequent redistribution.[16] Cane production soared and the value of sugar exports doubled.

Yet Castro's revolution was obviously a mixed blessing. On June 14, 1959, Dominican exiles launched an invasion from Cuba which, though unsuccessful, shook Trujillo's regime to its roots. Torture, arrests, and assassinations of prominent Dominicans followed, and for the first time in thirty years, opposition on a large scale developed. By January, 1960, in an unprecedented event, the Roman Catholic Church finally denounced the Trujillo regime. During this same period huge arms expenditures began to sap the economy's strength. In a fit of desperation, Trujillo lashed out in an assassination attempt on an archenemy, Venezuela's social democratic President Rómulo Betancourt. The Organization of American States (OAS) was called into session, Trujillo was denounced, and economic sanctions were imposed.

U.S. support for OAS condemnation and sanctions demonstrated how far Trujillo's U.S. power base had diminished. U.S. investments failed to increase after the early fifties because of the dictator's drive for total monopoly over the economy and

The whole quota system really benefits American-owned producers at home or abroad far more than underdeveloped nations, as has been asserted by its backers. Most of the subsidies, eventually paid for by the American public through higher prices, are collected by U.S. corporations, who then determine their use in terms of profit maximization rather than social needs. Those subsidies which end up with foreign nationals only make the oligarchy richer and more powerful.

[15] Before 1960, most Dominican cane was sold to the British dealers Tate & Lyle. Though the raw sugar was sold at low world market prices, Trujillo's control over labor kept wages so depressed that Dominican sugar producers could still turn a handsome profit.

[16] This was largely due to the efforts of Representative Harold Cooley (D.-N.C.), Chairman of the House Agriculture Committee and virtual sugar czar when it came to setting quotas. Cooley, along with his staff, made several expense-paid trips to the island to "visit" El Jefe and was very favorably disposed to the dictator.

massive corruption. Washington's preoccupation with revolutionary Cuba provided the impetus for a change in policy; in order to alter the traditional nonintervention policy of the OAS and legitimize the destruction of Castro's "dictatorship," a precedent for hemispheric intervention would first be established vis-à-vis Trujillo's regime.[17] Soon after Castro's rise to power, Trujillo and his advisers recognized this dilemma. Survival was possible only by eliminating Castro (to restore the status quo in the Caribbean and U.S. support through "nonintervention") or, barring this, creating a completely new power base resting on an alliance with Cuba and the Eastern bloc. Obviously the latter course placed Trujillo's interests above those of the United States and was therefore fraught with danger. But after thirty years of unscrupulous rule the Generalissimo was hardly prepared to step down without a struggle.

A plot to overthrow Castro in August, 1959, financed by Trujillo, attempted to foster an internal uprising backed by a foreign invasion (from Florida and the Dominican Republic). But the Eisenhower Administration was not yet prepared to back such drastic moves and the CIA hampered the invasion operations. When the Cuban-based conspirators double-crossed Trujillo's agents the plot failed miserably.[18] Without Castro's removal relations continued to deteriorate: "The Department of State increasingly viewed the Dominican tyrant as an embarrassment, an awkward inheritance from an earlier time, now lingering too long and imperiling the future and unwittingly preparing the way for Castroism."[19] Increased U.S. reliance on Domini-

---

[17] Jerome Slater, "The United States, the Organization of American States, and the Dominican Republic, 1961–1963," *International Organization*, Vol. 18, No. 2 (Spring, 1964), 268–91.

[18] This whole episode to overthrow Castro in 1960 is still shrouded in mystery, especially the role of the CIA and the American soldier of fortune William Morgan. A substantial number of Cuban exiles and foreign mercenaries were actually enlisted while Morgan was assigned the task of reactivating the Second Front of Escambray and capturing the city of Trinidad for the invasion landing. After Morgan double-crossed his backers and the invasion fell through many of the Cuban exiles were recruited by the CIA for the Bay of Pigs landing (April, 1961). The United States never supported the plot with much zeal, probably because Washington's policy at this time centered around opposing Castro through isolation rather than direct intervention. For some details see Crassweller, pp. 349–52, and Robert Emmett Johnson, "For a Million Bucks I'll Knock Off Castro," *True* (August, 1967), pp. 12–18.

[19] Crassweller, p. 421.

can sugar imports strengthened the push to stabilize the situation by removing Trujillo. Diplomat-businessman William Pawley, along with his close friend Senator George Smathers (D.-Fla.), visited El Jefe to plead for his abdication in order to facilitate a smooth transition toward democracy. Trujillo refused to comply, military assistance and arm shipments were terminated, and Ambassador Joseph S. Farland contacted the growing internal underground before the United States vacated his diplomatic post in May, 1960.

By this time Trujillo had already moved to offset his increasing isolation through an informal alliance with Cuba and the Eastern bloc. "The two Caribbean outcasts agreed to stop fighting each other and to concentrate on their other problems."[20]

The Communist Party was legalized and only Russian disinterest prevented the establishment of close political relations with the socialist countries. The disestablishment of the Catholic Church and the expropriation of all U.S.-owned property were urged in public. But in contrast to these anti-U.S. moves, Trujillo desperately tried to protect the country's much-valued sugar quota from OAS-inspired sanctions. His lobbyists and diplomatic representatives went to work in and outside the government on the close-knit sugar community. Lawrence Myers, head of the Agriculture Department's sugar office, Thomas Murphy, deputy to Myers, and William Case, an official in the sugar office, were secretly contacted. The lobbyists convinced Representative Harold Cooley (D.-N.C.), powerful Chairman of the House Agriculture Committee, to block legislative moves by the Eisenhower Administration to suspend the quota.[21] When Congress adjourned without final action, executive power prevailed through an order imposing a special tax on Dominican sugar, thereby abolishing windfall quota profits.

Kennedy's rise to power gave Trujillo's lobbyists a new chance to alter U.S. policy. State Department consultant and sugar company executive Adolf A. Berle, Jr., and Under Secre-

[20] *Ibid.*, p. 424.

[21] These facts were uncovered by *New York Times* reporter Tad Szulc, who was shown some of Trujillo's secret files after the dictator's assassination, *New York Times* (July 30, 1962). In another example of the close-knit U.S. business-government sugar community, Lawrence Myers later became President of the National Molasses Company, a subsidiary of the Kaplan brothers' South Western Sugar and Molasses Company which was bought by C. Brewer and Company in 1963.

tary of State Chester Bowles were reached in an effort to have the special sugar tax lifted. Moreover, a special lobbyist (Igor Cassini) convinced Joseph Kennedy that a revolutionary situation was developing and that it would be helpful to send a special envoy to Ciudad Trujillo to assess matters. The State Department's top troubleshooter, Robert Murphy, paid an informal visit and again sought a liberalization of the regime. It was clear to the Kennedy Administration that support among Latin Americans for anti-Castro activities (including the Bay of Pigs) rested in part on anti-Trujillo moves. Without a power base in the executive branch of the United States Government the Dominican dictator was helpless to determine his own fate.

The failure of the Murphy mission set in motion the final stages of a CIA-supported plot to assassinate Trujillo. Chiefly organized by some of his own military officers, the assassination was successfully carried out on May 31, 1961.[22] As an obstacle to, rather than an instrument for, domination, the Great Benefactor had to be removed.

DOMINATION THROUGH STABILIZATION: 1961–1963

With Trujillo's disposal the Kennedy Administration had to choose between maintaining order through support for the remaining repressive apparatus and hated Trujillo cronics or gambling on democracy and social change by favoring the anti-Trujillo forces. U.S. priorities were clearly spelled out by the President in a Cabinet session soon after Trujillo's death.

> There are three possibilities in descending order of preference: decent democratic order, a continuation of the Trujillo regime or a Castro regime. We ought to aim for the first, but we really can't renounce the second until we are sure that one can avoid the third.[23]

In effect, Washington simultaneously attempted to maintain stability and order while encouraging democratization and minor social change. In classical fashion the New Frontiersmen

[22] Norman Gall, "How Trujillo Died," *The New Republic* (April 13, 1963), pp. 19–20.
[23] Arthur M. Schlesinger, Jr., *A Thousand Days: John F. Kennedy in the White House* (Boston, 1965), p. 769.

submerged Dominican interests under North American needs. For six months the United States hesitated to dismantle the old structures now administered by Trujillo's last figurehead president, Joaquin Balaguer, but really in the hands of Trujillo's remaining relatives, military officers, business associates, and gangsters. The island was wracked by bloody repressions and severe unemployment, while the United States encouraged Balaguer to "liberalize" and "democratize" his regime. Conservative and left opposition against Trujilloism without Trujillo sought continued suspension of the U.S. sugar quota to restrain the regime's excesses. Kennedy, realizing this was his most powerful weapon, had to postpone moving against the Trujillistas until the U.S. military, the CIA and its cooperating organizations could penetrate the country's shattered infrastructure, create a conservative alternative regime, and thereby control events. By the end of 1961 a conspiracy of Dominican generals was combined with a show of U.S. naval power offshore near Santo Domingo to force the last of the Trujillo family to leave the island.[24]

The first real political organization after Trujillo's assassination sprang up within the oligarchy, petty bourgeois and professional classes who formed an anti-Trujillo civic-minded association which later became the Union Civica Nacional (UCN) political party. In order to gain a base among the youth and intellectuals, the UCN entered into an unholy alliance with the strongly nationalist 14th of June Movement (IJ4). This alliance, however, was quickly sacrificed in January, 1962, for control of the U.S.-backed interim Consejo de Estado (Council of State) government which was charged with maintaining stability and holding elections the following December. The United States demonstrated its strong backing of the council by lifting economic sanctions, resuming diplomatic relations, restoring military assistance, extending $25 million in emergency credit, and authorizing the purchase of additional sugar under the premium quota price.[25]

The ending of sanctions and the reestablishment of a Dominican sugar quota was undoubtedly crucial. The cane sugar

[24] De Lesseps S. Morrison, *Latin American Mission: An Adventure in Hemisphere Diplomacy* (New York, 1965), Chapters 7–10.
[25] For a description of political maneuvering after November, 1961, see Julio César Martínez, "Revolution and Counter Revolution: The Chessboard," *New Politics*, Vol. IV, No. 2 (Spring, 1965), pp. 47–55.

industry is the largest industrial operation on the island and the
leading contributor to government income in the form of taxes,
foreign exchange, and employment. Privately South Puerto Rico
Sugar's La Romana produces one-third of the cane output,
while the former Trujillo holdings, taken over by the Consejo,
produce a little less than the remaining two-thirds. In 1962 over
90 percent of Dominican cane went to American ports, and
under a newly enacted sugar quota act, both South Puerto Rico
Sugar and the interim government retained influential lobbyists
to jack up quotas even further.

A fundamental question confronting the Consejo and subsequent governments revolved around the fate of the confiscated
Trujillo properties. These represented approximately 65 percent
of Dominican industry in fifty-seven different product sectors,
35 percent of the arable land, and 30 percent of the animal
husbandry.[26] It was an open secret that the UCN hoped to
distribute the holdings to favored private interests if they won
the upcoming elections.

During the 1962 electoral campaign the Partido Revolucionario Dominicano (PRD), headed by twenty-five-year exile
Juan Bosch, presented a platform advocating distribution of
Trujillo land to landless *campesinos,* formation of cooperatives,
an increase in agricultural wages, construction of small town
communal eating halls, public works, and development of new
industry around untapped mineral resources to reduce unemployment. The general object was to diversify agriculture and to
create a consumer economy.

Despite repeated setbacks and unforeseen complications the
holding of elections was guaranteed by the frantic but thorough
manipulations of U.S. ambassador John Bartlow Martin, a man
with strong ties to the ADA (Americans for Democratic Action) liberals in the United States. For example, at one crucial
juncture, Martin wrote:

> Then I called the senior Embassy staff and Williams together, told
> them what I was doing, and told them we must slow down the
> Dominican reaction before it got completely out of control. We
> must immediately talk to all important Dominicans—explain the
> situation, urge everyone to await developments, and reaffirm our
> determination not to abandon the Republic. We divided up the

[26] Dr. Emilio Cordero Michel, "The Dominican Revolution," *Progressive Labor* (December, 1965), p. 68.

people we could see—Consejeros, political party leaders, government men, sugar men.[27]

DOMINATION THROUGH INFILTRATION: THE BOSCH GOVERNMENT

The defeat at the hands of Bosch's social democratic PRD, which received 60 percent of the December, 1962, vote, caught the UCN and its conservative backers by surprise. But Bosch, a self-educated intellectual from humble origins, knew his government would not last long; thirty hours before the polls opened he told a television audience:

> I do not wish to be a candidate because I know the PRD will win the elections and if it does, the government . . . will be overthrown in a short time on the pretext that it is Communist.[28]

As a skeptical business community looked on, Bosch negotiated a $150 million line of credit with a Zurich-based consortium to finance his larger development projects, a departure from the usual U.S. sources. Next he cancelled an oil refinery contract, which Esso, Texaco, and Shell had negotiated with Trujillo and the Consejo, because of the large profits which would leave the country.[29]

[27] Martin, p. 164. Martin was a free-lance journalist and a key speech writer in the 1952 and 1956 presidential campaigns of Adlai Stevenson. He worked on John F. Kennedy's 1960 campaign staff and was subsequently appointed ambassador to the Dominican Republic, arriving in March, 1962.

[28] Juan Bosch, *The Unfinished Experiment: Democracy in the Dominican Republic* (New York, 1965), p. 123.

This book was originally published in Spanish in 1964 by the Centro de Estudios y Documentación Sociales (CEDS) under the title *Crisis de la Democracia de América en la República Dominicana* (Mexico, 1964). CEDS was run in Mexico by social democrat Victor Alba and was financed by the CIA through the J. M. Kaplan Fund. The English edition does not give the translator's name and was published by Frederick A. Praeger, Inc., which was recently exposed as having contracted with the CIA for numerous printing jobs.

[29] Drew Pearson on May 21, 1965 elaborates:

". . . Third factor operating against Bosch, when he was kicked out in September, 1963, was the Texas Oil Co. Sen. Wayne Morse (D-Ore.), in hearings before the Senate Foreign Relations Committee, devel-

Despite these initiatives toward financial independence, Bosch found it necessary to seek United States aid. The Kennedy Administration hoped to make the Dominican Republic a "showcase of democracy" as a counterweight to Cuba.[30] Nevertheless, Bosch found U.S. financial backing hard to obtain. Former businessman Newell Williams, AID director for the Republic, commented: "Ever since Bosch has been in, we've been turned down."[31] Later, toward the end of Bosch's first one hundred days in office, Ambassador Martin noted, "We had committed something over $50 million to last year's Consejo but not a cent for Bosch."[32]

Several aspects of his administration alarmed native and United States investors. An effort was made to rescind several sugar contracts negotiated by the Consejo. While advantageous for U.S. sugar purchasers, these contracts meant a loss of several million dollars in foreign exchange for the Dominican Republic. Former Ambassador Martin wrote:

> The Department [State Department] instructed me to inform the Dominican Government that its failure to honor legitimate contracts with U.S. sugar firms would certainly have most serious repercussions for the Bosch government and might even lead to an invocation of the Hickenlooper amendment which would end AID to the Republic.[33]

Within a week of Bosch's inauguration, *Business Week* attacked him for proposing a "revolutionary constitution" and land reform "which would prohibit operations of U.S.-owned

oped the fact that Duane D. Luther of Texaco, a former member of the cloak-and-dagger OSS, had contributed $2,500 to Bosch's opponent, Viriato Fiallo, and was reported to have plotted the anti-Bosch revolt . . . When I telephoned Luther to get his side of the story, the overseas operator reported that he would not take the call."

Drew Pearson, "The Washington Merry-go-Round" (May 21, 1965) as reported in Gary J. Mounce and Anne H. Sutherland, editors, *After Santo Domingo, What? U.S. Intervention in Latin America*, pp. 11–18, an inquiry sponsored by the University Colloquy on Public Relations, University of Texas, May, 1966, Austin, Texas.

30 See Schlesinger, pp. 769–773, the section entitled "The Showcase That Failed."
31 Martin, p. 389.
32 *Ibid.*, p. 451. AID money was slow in coming. Bosch eventually received authorization for about $50 million in grants and loans.
33 *Ibid.*, p. 355.

sugar companies."[34] An official of La Romana expressed the
fear that Bosch's government might make the Puerto Rican
"mistake" of subdividing the cane lands. "To break up the
Company's lands would wreck Romana."[35] Concern over constitutional provisions about business operations was a constant
theme in discussions between U.S. representatives and all Dominican governments. Much later during the U.S. invasion and
occupation of the Republic in 1965, U.S. negotiators demanded
that the "rebels," who were fighting for a reinstatement of the
1963 Constitution, modify several of its articles. They were
especially troubled by Article 19, giving workers the right to
profit sharing in both agricultural and industrial enterprises;
Article 23, prohibiting large landholdings; Article 25, restricting
the right of foreigners to acquire Dominican land; Article 28,
requiring landholders to sell that portion of their lands above a
maximum fixed by law, excess holdings to be distributed to the
landless peasantry; and Article 66, prohibiting expulsion of
Dominicans from their own country. American negotiators in
1965 proposed an amendment to exempt owners of sugar
plantations and cattle ranches, the largest of these being South
Puerto Rico Sugar's La Romana.[36]

The Constitution also upset the Roman Catholic Church,
especially for its articles legitimizing divorce, secularizing education, declaring juridical equality of legitimate and natural-
born citizens, and for failing to mention the 1954 Concordat
with the Vatican. Papal Nuncio Emanuele Clarizio and Msgr.
Thomas Reilly (a U.S. citizen working in the country under the
authority of the Vatican) both visited Bosch, seeking constitutional changes. When the Constitution was promulgated without
changes, the Church declined to send a representative to the
official ceremony.[37]

---

[34] *Business Week* (March 2, 1963), as quoted by Victor Perlo, *The
Marines in Santo Domingo* (New York, 1965), p. 10. (A pamphlet
published by New Outlook publishers.)

[35] *Latin America Report,* Vol. V, No. 4 (1963), 13.

For a discussion of another controversial piece of Bosch legislation
directly affecting La Romana see Franklin J. Franco, *República Dominicana, Clase, Crisis Y Comandos* (Cuba, 1967), p. 141, on the "Precio
Tope de Azucar" Act. Basically it provided for any profits from sales of
sugar above a ceiling price to be given to the state.

[36] Dan Kurzman, *The Washington Post* (May 25, 1965), as reported by
I. F. Stone's Weekly (May 31, 1965).

[37] Bosch, *Unfinished Experiment,* pp. 128–9.

In short time, inflated anti-Communism flourished and began to undermine Bosch's legitimacy. Even civil-libertarian Ambassador Martin kept constant pressure on Bosch with advice like the following:

> I recommended Bosch couple any changes with other measures—repeal of the old de-Trujilloization law and enactment of a law providing for the trial of military personnel by military tribunals . . . I recommended that Congress adopt a resolution declaring it the sense of the Congress that communism was incompatible with the Inter-American system . . . and that it enact a Dominican version of the Smith act . . . I recommended he hold back on agrarian reform if it entailed confiscation laws.[38]

In practical terms, Martin's anti-Communism reinforced the irrational charges of Dominican rightists which further undermined Bosch's government. A favorite target of right-wing generals was the Inter-American Center for Social Studies (CIDES). Run by a Rumanian-born naturalized American, Sacha Volman, CIDES received its funds and direction from the American-based Institute of International Labor Research (IILR). The IILR in turn was headed by U.S. social democratic leader Norman Thomas and its secretary-treasurer was Volman. All but a fraction of IILR's budget came from the J. M. Kaplan Fund, which was exposed in 1964 by Congressman Wright Patman as a conduit for Central Intelligence Agency funds. Immediately after the armed forces overthrew Bosch, CIDES was sacked and closed while Volman fled the country. Ironically, the military was, in effect, charging a CIA operation was riddled with Communists and Communist sympathizers, though it is now clear CIDES' covert purpose was to assure strong U.S. influence in the PRD and Bosch's government.

Earlier this same Institute of International Labor Research played a crucial role in Dominican politics. At the time of Trujillo's assassination (May, 1961), Juan Bosch was teaching at the Costa Rican Institute of Political Education which Sacha Volman set up in 1959 with CIA funds channeled through the J. M. Kaplan Fund and the IILR. Immediately after Trujillo's assassination Volman was the first man Bosch sent to the Republic to survey the political situation and recommend strategy for the PRD. During 1962 he proceeded to organize a

[38] Martin, p. 487.

300,000-member peasant league (FENHERCA), which played a key role in providing Bosch's PRD with the critical countryside vote in the election (approximately 70 percent of the Dominicans live in rural areas). But once the votes were in Volman abandoned FENHERCA and one of the PRD's strongest bases of organized support deteriorated.

With Bosch in office, Volman reoriented his energies and resources into organizing CIDES, a planning-research center for the government and a training institute for young political organizers and administrators. CIDES was to provide most of the state planning as well as the crucial technical and professional talent for running the government and the infrastructure of the PRD. The Kaplan Fund contributed $35,000 which was supplemented by grants from several other U.S. foundations and government agencies. A $250,000 grant from the Ford Foundation (administered by Brandeis University and ADA leader John P. Roche) paralleled CIDES' work within the government civil service administration. Along with other similar programs, the U.S. Government was thus able to penetrate and manipulate the social democrats (PRD) in the Dominican Republic as well as the government they formed.

As it turned out, the involvement of J. M. Kaplan in the IILR and its Dominican offshoots (FENHERCA and CIDES) was not a fortuitous occurrence. This Caribbean sugar and molasses speculator had arranged a monopoly of Dominican molasses sales during the latter years of the Trujillo era. Introduced to Bosch by Norman Thomas, Kaplan became the Dominican president's personal emissary to business and political circles in New York and Washington. In reality, Kaplan's interest in Bosch's government, both in terms of channeling CIA funds to Volman's operations and maintaining a favorable image for Bosch among his powerful U.S. friends, was directly related to his sugar and molasses operations and associations. One month before Bosch was overthrown Kaplan suddenly decided that his administration was infiltrated with Communists and he withdrew his influential support. This vital break signaled the collapse of Bosch's power base in the United States.[39]

[39] For the background on this subject see: Ruth Shereff, "How the CIA Makes Friends and Influences Countries," *Viet Report* (January–February, 1967); Bosch, pp. 97 and 169–78; Dan Kurzman, "Labor Group Got $1 Million From CIA," *The Washington Post* (February 21, 1967); and Sacha Volman, *Latin American Experiments in Political and Economic Training,* Brookings Institution (Washington, 1964).

But the Kennedy Administration never placed all its bets on infiltrating and controlling the social democratic PRD in order to guarantee U.S. domination. In what amounted to a schizophrenic policy, the Kennedy Administration, while supporting Bosch, simultaneously trained and equipped the antireformist forces that eventually brought down his regime—the armed forces and the police.

> . . . the United States-trained police joined the Army in ousting President Bosch, following which both the police and the anti-guerrilla units, trained during 1963 by a forty-four-man United States Army Mission, were used to hunt down Bosch's non-Communist partisans in the name of anti-Communism.[40]

Bosch never directly confronted the graft-ridden and top-heavy military with its large officer corps and oversize portion of the national budget: "Had I ever made even a single change in the military command, my government would have lasted only weeks, perhaps only days."[41] Nevertheless, the military chafed under several aspects of his administration, especially the abrogation of a special military privilege—the right of trial solely by military tribunals. And, in his last days in office, Bosch fought the purchase of six British warplanes which included a 20 percent kickback for top air force officers.

Although Bosch did curtail military graft, the primary reason the armed forces turned against him was more complex, and behind it lies the specter of Cuba. Batista and his officers' first stop after fleeing Castro's revolutionary militia was San Isidro Air Force base on the outskirts of Ciudad Trujillo.

> The issue that united all those military officers who opposed Bosch for various reasons was the alleged growing Communist influences in his government. For the officers, Communism was neither an ideological, economic, or imperialistic system but only meant as they recalled the case of the Cuban revolution, destruction of the armed forces and death to the officers; and rumors that Bosch's Party was arming a militia seemed to give credence to their fears.[42]

[40] Lieuwen, p. 127.
[41] Bosch, *Unfinished Experiment*, p. 216. A full discussion of the military can be found in Howard J. Wiarda, *Journal of Inter-American Studies*.
[42] Wiarda, *Journal of Inter-American Studies*, p. 480.

The Dominican officers were not used to acting alone, however. Judging from accounts like the following, they were given the go-ahead to overthrow Bosch by their U.S. advisers:

> Cass [Bevan Cass] was having problems of conscience about Bosch. As our naval attaché, he was obliged to urge Dominican officers to support Bosch, but he himself had misgivings about Bosch's attitude toward the Castro Communists . . . and didn't know "how much longer I can go on supporting him like this" . . . he was probably our most influential attaché.[43]

Led by the air force tank commander, Elias Wessin y Wessin, and Trujillo assassin Antonio Imbert Barrera, the armed forces deposed Bosch on September 25, 1963.

The cross-purpose policy of backing both the right and the left went even deeper. The AFL-CIO Latin American trade union federation, ORIT, split the PRD-oriented labor movement with the formation of CONATRAL, a pro-U.S., parallel confederation of Dominican unions organized along the anti-political Sam Gompers line. Aiding in the training of anti-Bosch unionists was the American Institute for Free Labor Development (AIFLD), a bizarre hybrid of AFL-CIO, big business, and U.S. Government interests.[44] Not surprisingly, CONATRAL exhorted the Dominicans one week before the coup, through a one-page newspaper advertisement, to put their faith in the armed forces to defend them against Communism.

[43] Martin, pp. 504–5. According to *Time* staffer Sam Halper, the Dominican armed forces ousted Bosch "as soon as they got a wink from the U.S. Pentagon." See Sam Halper, "The Dominican Upheaval," *The New Leader* (May 10, 1965).

[44] Nine young labor leaders attended the AIFLD school in Washington, D.C.; two were sent to Europe and Israel for special training; and twenty additional leaders attended regional AIFLD schools in Latin America.

The working-class spirit of these training sessions is most difficult to comprehend, given the fact that ALFLD's chairman was J. Peter Grace, President of W. R. Grace and Company and a Director of the First National City Bank. Also on the board are several other leaders of U.S. corporations with heavy investments in Latin America.

For further discussion of the ALFLD see: Sidney Lens, "American Labor Abroad: Lovestone Diplomacy," *The Nation* (July 5, 1965) and George Morris, *CIA and American Labor: Subversion of the AFL-CIO's Foreign Policy* (New York, 1967), Chapter 6.

Shortly after the coup most other labor leaders were in jail, hiding, or had sought asylum.[45]

Ambassador Martin, never overwhelmingly enthusiastic about Bosch, nevertheless sought the State Department's view on the utilization of American warships for reinstating Bosch. The Department refused to intervene unless a "Communist takeover" was imminent. Bosch's downfall was the final blow to the Kennedy hope for peaceful social reform in Latin America. The extremely weak power base in the United States advocating such a program—certain intellectuals, social democrats, some of Kennedy's advisers and a section of the CIA—was no match for threatened business interests, generals, and liberals who put anti-Communism ahead of social change. It should be remembered that Caribbean policy in the early sixties was dominated by a preoccupation with Cuba and the incipient spread of Fidel Castro's revolution. For businessmen, journalists, and State Department officials, the legitimacy of Bosch's administration rested on its ability to contain, through whatever means necessary, the small Castroite left (primarily the nationalistic 14th of June Movement). As mentioned above, Martin went so far as to strongly recommend the enactment of a Dominican Smith Act. Bosch refused. And for the influential power base in the United States concerned with Cuba, this ruled out large-scale support, and therefore survival.

La Romana, already in economic difficulty, was worried about extended strikes, land confiscation, and the disappearance of their cheap labor supply. Exporters, shipping lines, and dock workers feared a loss of business. East Coast sugar refiners and their industrial customers realized an occlusion of their precious commodity from the one large remaining Caribbean source would trigger wild gyrations in sensitive sugar prices. For an industry still shaky from an earlier Caribbean storm, the mere prospect of "another Cuba"—with the attendant loss of an ample supply of cane at stable prices—was too much to bear. Moreover, a crucial development within the sugar industry strengthened the hand of anti-Bosch *golpista* forces. A shortage

[45] Dominican labor, including the numerous splits within the movement, is reviewed in T. D. Roberts *et al., Area Handbook for the Dominican Republic,* U.S. Government Printing Office (Washington, 1966), Chapter 21; and Susan Bodenheimer, "The AFL-CIO in Latin America. The Dominican Republic: A Case Study," *Viet Report* (September–October, 1967), pp. 17–19 and 27–28.

created by Cuban developments temporarily drove the price of world sugar far above the subsidized U.S. quota rate. This guaranteed the Dominican sugar interests a profitable outlet for their commodity in the event of reprisals by the Kennedy Administration. In effect, the Dominican right was gambling on the traditional U.S. willingness to recognize any reactionary government after a decent period of mourning for a departed constitutional order. Bosch was never prepared to deal effectively with a right-wing coup. The early deterioration of Bosch's peasant support organized by CIA-backed Sacha Volman through FENHERCA cut him off from the countryside. Mishandling of his labor support, combined with splitting of the labor confederations by U.S.-trained organizers, deprived Bosch of his most effective weapon against a right-wing coup—a mass-based movement which at any time could be armed to counteract the military. With the cooperation of some reform-minded disgruntled young officers this might have been possible, but Bosch refused to condone the use of violence. What could have been his strongest base of support, an organized labor and peasantry, had been infiltrated and manipulated by the United States.

DOMINATION THROUGH MANIPULATION: THE TRIUMVIRATE

Kennedy, seeing the *golpe* as a heavy blow to the *Alianza*, refused to recognize the new regime and suspended aid; but Kennedy was assassinated. In an effort to gain U.S. diplomatic recognition and economic aid a new government, the so-called Triumvirate, dramatically announced it was threatened by an incipient guerrilla movement aided by Fidel Castro. Actually, some June 14th Movement leaders took to the hills shortly after Bosch's downfall, but the arms they acquired were apparently obtained through a CIA agent (Camilo Todemann) and proved useless. When the guerrillas surrendered, they were mercilessly tortured and executed.[46] The plot produced the desired effect, for one of President Johnson's first foreign policy shifts was to recognize the regimes in the Dominican Republic and Hon-

[46] José Francisco Peña Gómez, "U.S. White Paper on the Dominican Republic," *New America* (December 18, 1965), 5, and Martin, pp. 631–2.

duras. On the same day (December 14, 1963), Thomas Mann was appointed Assistant Secretary of State for Inter-American Affairs. The subsequent Dominican government was headed by Donald Reid Cabral, former auto dealer, close friend of U.S. business and member of the oligarchy. Realizing his power rested with the military, Reid turned his back on the officers' contraband and smuggling operations, thereby winning their tacit support.[47]

The Reid government put an end to economic and social development. With the shelving of the 1963 Constitution, the Bosch reform legislation, and the Zurich consortium credit, large numbers of United States businessmen turned again to the Dominican Republic. George Walker (of the Mellons' Koppers Company), a close Reid friend, had made a visit to the Dominican Republic during the Consejo period (Reid was one of the seven Consejo members) on behalf of the Businessmen's Council on International Understanding. Walker "had brought in high-level U.S. industrialists to study the former Trujillo properties and advise the Consejo what to do with them."[48] It was from these operations that Bosch had hoped to partially finance his social reforms. But Walker recommended gradually selling or leasing the properties to private investors.

The Midland Cooperatives of Minneapolis, Minnesota, landed an oil refinery contract. Falconbridge Nickel Mines, a Canadian-American concern, announced plans to build a $78-million refinery. The Inter-American Development Bank and the AFL-CIO launched a joint housing project. The World Bank gave $1.7 million for a hydroelectric study, replacing the one Bosch intended to finance with European capital.[49]

And there was more. At the same time, plagued by plunging world sugar prices, Reid continued Bosch's austerity program and received International Monetary Fund (IMF) and AID credit and loans as well as a $30-million loan from six U.S. commercial banks.

During the Bosch regime the 18,000 workers at South Puerto Rico's La Romana had won a 30 percent increase in their meager wages. Under Reid, that contract was broken and in February, 1965, one much more favorable to the company was

[47] For a discussion of the Reid Cabral period, see Martin, pp. 47–55.
[48] Martin, p. 116.
[49] *Hispanic American Report*, Vol. XVII (Events of July, 1964), p. 621.

negotiated with a parallel or "ghost" union set up by La Romana. Since low wages are crucial for profits in this marginal industry requiring surplus labor, the company greatly benefited from Reid's antilabor policy. Reid had previously declared a state of siege in Santo Domingo to offset a general strike called by the Sindicato Independiente de Choferes. By spring of 1965 the country was $200 million in debt; there were rumors of a Reid campaign to sell the former Trujillo properties, now in the hands of the state, to private investors; the armed forces were carrying on increasingly flagrant and publicly known contraband operations; and Santo Domingo itself was facing a serious water shortage—Reid had discontinued the renovation and expansion of the city's water system initiated by Bosch. One other persistent rumor was that Reid was planning to rig the promised elections to insure his victory. More than one commentator was led to observe that only U.S. support kept Reid in power.[50]

Meanwhile, in exile, Bosch and leaders of the Revolutionary Social Christian Party (PRSC) agreed on the Pact of Rio Piedras, a plan to cooperate in overthrowing Reid and restoring the 1963 Constitution. In a more secret move, Bosch also reached a similar but more tenuous agreement with the ex-Trujillo servant and conservative, Joaquin Balaguer.[51] Both agreements involved utilization of disparate military factions in the projected overthrow of Reid Cabral. Many of the conservative senior officers were riding high on corruption involving import rackets. The younger and lower-echelon officers were easily approachable by the various anti-Reid factions who also feared cancellation or manipulation of the promised elections. These clandestine accords, combined with deteriorating economic and social conditions in the country, especially in Santo Domingo (unemployment was as high as 40 percent), precipitated the coup in April, 1965. It is quite possible that in the early hours of the uprising as many as three or more separate military factions were vying for power: one faction supporting Bosch, another Balaguer, and one right-wing faction supporting

---

[50] For a discussion of the Reid Cabral regime and its relations with labor, see Franco, pp. 170–177 and Bodenheimer, *Viet Report* (September–October, 1967).

[51] This secret Balaguer-Bosch understanding has been confirmed in several personal interviews. See also Dan Kurzman, "Dominican Constitutionalism," *The New Leader* (July 18, 1966), p. 10.

Wessin y Wessin. And it was at this point, when the military split and broke into internecine combat, that the Dominican crisis made international headlines.

DOMINATION THROUGH INTERVENTION
AND OCCUPATION

Within three days the constitutionalist forces routed Wessin y Wessin's troops while the other military factions wavered. Obviously the crucial question was whom the United States would back. There is no doubt that the PRD leadership was counting on rather automatic U.S. support for the return of the legally elected Bosch government. It seems they were convinced of U.S. democratic intentions.[52] At the point when the constitutionalists were in control of Santo Domingo—April 27—the United States could have prevented bloodshed and chaos, furthered the development of social reform, and destroyed the anti-reformist military forces by supporting exiled Juan Bosch. It was simply a matter of permitting Bosch to reenter the country to take command of the constitutionalist forces. On several occasions Johnson confidant Abe Fortas and ex-Ambassador Martin visited Bosch in San Juan, Puerto Rico, making it clear that Washington would *not* support his return to Santo Domingo. The FBI and CIA kept him under constant surveillance and thwarted his various overt and covert attempts to return.[53]

[52] During an interview in exile in San Juan, Puerto Rico (August, 1965), Juan Bosch described his reappraisal of U.S. democratic intentions to Kal Wagenheim, then editor of the *San Juan Review* and *New York Times* stringer in Puerto Rico. A quote from that interview appeared in *The New Leader* (February 28, 1966), p. 10:
I believe that in the Dominican Republic Latin America has been given a lesson: the lesson is that it is not possible to establish a democracy with the help of the United States, and neither is it possible to establish a democracy against the United States.
It seems that the constitutionalist military leaders were also convinced their rebellion would *not* arouse the San Isidro right-wing forces led by General Wessin y Wessin to armed opposition. That is, they expected a relatively peaceful palace coup. See Franco, p. 195.

[53] This information has been confirmed in several personal interviews. See also: Juan Bosch, "A Tale of Two Nations," *The New Leader* (June 21, 1965), pp. 3–7, and Juan Bosch: "An Anti-Communist Manifesto," *New York Review of Books*, Vol. IX, No. 7 (October 26, 1967), a review

Public statements notwithstanding, the Johnson Administration decided on April 24 that it would send in the Marines if the rebels gained the upper hand.[54] A massive buildup of troops and equipment was set in motion. When the United States made it apparent, through Ambassador William Tapley Bennett, Jr., that it was going to back the Wessin forces and that the rebels would have to fight or surrender, the PRD civilian leadership passed to the rebel military commanders, who by this time had armed and organized a sizable proportion of the civilian population within Santo Domingo.

On April 28, when it became clear that Wessin's forces had been routed, the Marines landed, ostensibly to evacuate Americans, but in reality to bolster the military and lay the groundwork for U.S. occupation. This whole process was portrayed as a response to a rump military junta set up by U.S. military attachés and led by Wessin's ally Colonel Bartolomé Benoit. The Marines quickly solidified the fractionalized military forces; wavering elements realized the rebels were doomed in the face of U.S. firepower. The so-called "neutral" landing force quickly equipped the junta units with badly needed radios, food, weapons, medical supplies, and logistic support. Surrounding Santo Domingo, they succeeded in containing and eventually splitting the rebel forces.[55]

In effect, the rebel movement's power base passed from the political leadership to the barrel of a gun. For the first time in recent Dominican history Santo Domingo was in control of

---

of Régis Debray's *Revolution in the Revolution?*, where Bosch wrote: "When I realized that the Americans would stop at nothing to prevent my return to Santo Domingo, I asked the Congress to elect Colonel Camaño constitutional president . . ."

[54] Reports on the decision to intervene are very contradictory and the real reasons have been withheld by the Johnson Administration. The Senate Foreign Relations Committee hearings on the intervention were never made public—a prerequisite agreed to by Senator Fulbright before Administration officials consented to testify. But Max Frankel was evidently "leaked" some of the hearings' highlights, which he described in "Secret U.S. Report Details Policy in Dominican Crisis," *New York Times* (November 14, 1965). Tad Szulc, *Dominican Diary* (New York, 1965) corroborates this information.

[55] For details see Szulc, *Diary;* Dan Kurzman, *Revolt of the Damned* (New York, 1966); and Theodore Draper, "The Dominican Crisis: A Case Study in American Policy," *Commentary* (December, 1965), pp. 33–68.

Dominicans completely independent of the United States. Without PRD leadership, with its links to the United States, particularly to the social democratic liberal community, violence and destruction on a massive scale were inevitable. The rebels' independence became most apparent to the American embassy staff when the constitutionalist forces twice approached the Georgia plantation Ambassador William Tapley Bennett, Jr., for the negotiation of a cease-fire. Bennett agreed to talk only if the rebels gave up their arms (i.e., surrendered). And after they refused, his response was obvious scorn and the threat of annihilation. When confronted with an independent political force the United States' response was military violence.

The effects of the rebels' independence and consequent power were tellingly demonstrated when the United States threatened to destroy the constitutionalists by a full-scale attack, including bombing, on the rebel-held sector of downtown Santo Domingo.[56] This attack was deterred, partly because the rebels threatened to set off explosives in the banks (including Chase Manhattan and First National City), the headquarters and offices of many U.S. businesses operating in the Republic, the electric plant and the telecommunications center, all of which were within the rebel-held sector. The United States backed off and thereby demonstrated some of its true interests.

The stated reasons for American military intervention are still veiled in confusion, primarily because many of the official documents have never been made public and the political figures who formulated and executed the policy are still in power. In President Johnson's first public statement on April 28, 1965, the United States intervened to ". . . give protection to hundreds of Americans who [were] still in the Dominican Republic and to escort them safely back to this country."[57] The President's statement was based on embassy and press cables which exaggerated the constitutionalist threat to American lives. Dispatches described firing squads holding terrorized American tourists at gunpoint in the Embajador Hotel. Moreover, the heads of assassinated victims were supposedly paraded through the streets of downtown Santo Domingo. In reality, from the

56 Max Frankel, New York Times (November 14, 1965).
57 "Statement by President Johnson, April 28, 1965," as reproduced in U.S. Senate, Committee on Foreign Relations, Background Information Relating to the Dominican Republic (Washington, 1965), p. 51.

outbreak of the rebellion not one American civilian was killed by accident or on purpose by the constitutionalists.[58]

By April 30, President Johnson, after reiterating the purported threat to American lives, hinted at another justification for intervention:

> . . . there are signs that people trained outside the Dominican Republic are seeking to gain control. Thus the legitimate aspirations of the Dominican people and most of their leaders for progress, democracy, and social justice are threatened and so are the principles of the inter-American system.[59]

By May 2, however, President Johnson clarified the above:

> The evidence that we have on the revolutionary movement indicates that it took a very tragic turn. Many of them trained in Cuba, seeing a chance to increase disorder and to gain a foothold, joined the revolution. They took increasing control. What began as a popular democratic revolution that was committed to democracy and social justice moved into the hands of a band of Communist conspirators. . . . Our goal, in keeping with the great principles of the inter-American system, is to help prevent another Communist state in this hemisphere.[60]

[58] In fact, the only atrocities ever documented during this period were all within the military junta's territory. Murder of civilian prisoners took place between May 22 and June 5, 1965. A report submitted to the OAS by a special team of three Latin American criminologists sent to investigate alleged brutalities reached the following conclusions, according to Drew Pearson:
> That there had been mass murders and that most of the population had been too terrorized to testify. The Commission was not able to arrive at the number killed though one prison under General Imbert's supervision, once containing 3,000, now has been reduced to 500.
> General Imbert was picked by the American Embassy to head the military junta immediately after the landing of American Marines. He has been kept in power only by the Marines and U.S. aid. . . .
Drew Pearson, "A Report of Imbert Atrocities," *Washington Post* (August 13, 1965). See also *Washington Post* (June 10, 1965), and the *New York Times* (June 10, 11, and 23, 1965) as well as the criminologists' report to the OAS.

[59] "Statement by President Johnson, April 30, 1965," Committee on Foreign Relations, p. 53.

[60] "Statement by President Johnson, May 2, 1965," Committee on Foreign Relations, pp. 56–57. A review of Dominican events supporting the Administration's position on Communist infiltration and control can be found in *Dominican Action—1965: Intervention or Cooperation?*,"

The charges of Communist infiltration and control have been refuted by liberal journalists who were on the scene, liberal Senators such as J. William Fulbright, noted resident researcher at Stanford University's Hoover Institute, Theodore Draper, and Juan Bosch himself.[61] While agreeing that Communist conspiracies are a real danger to democratic revolutions, they proceed to question the strategic influence of the small and fractionalized Dominican Communist parties. Given such criteria one could delegitimize any revolution threatening U.S. interests by uncovering a handful of Communists. Undoubtedly Communists are present in every Third World conflict today; but, from a radical perspective, there is no reason to assume Communists cannot also be bona fide nationalists. The supposition that a Communist Party member will place the interests of an international Communist conspiracy above those of a nationalist revolution cannot be substantiated from a historical or practical point of view. It should be noted that the international Communist conspiracy within the rebel movement never appealed for Cuban, Soviet, Chinese, or any other Communist aid, even while under severe duress.

What, then, were the real motives and circumstances of the U.S. intervention? American liberals and social democrats, including Tad Szulc, Dan Kurzman, J. William Fulbright, and Theodore Draper all agree that the troops intervened to bolster the flagging junta forces. But they fail to offer any comprehensive explanation of why the United States *opposed* a return to a democratic order under the constitutionalists. In their opinion, faulty information about the rebel forces was supplied and

The Center for Strategic Studies, Georgetown University (Washington, 1966). This pamphlet was partially authored by Eleanor Lansing Dulles, ex-State Department official (1942–62) and sister of the late Secretary of State John Foster Dulles and former CIA director Allen Dulles.

61 Tad Szulc, Diary; Dan Kurzman, Revolt; Senator J. W. Fulbright, "The Dominican Republic," Speech before the U.S. Senate, September 16, 1965, and The Arrogance of Power (New York, 1966), Chapter 4; the following works by Theodore Draper: "The Dominican Crisis; A Case Study in American Policy," Commentary (December, 1965), 33–68; "The Roots of the Dominican Crisis," The New Leader (May 24, 1965); "A Case of Defamation: U.S. Intelligence versus Juan Bosch," The New Republic, two parts (February 19 and 26, 1966); and Juan Bosch, "A Tale of Two Nations," The New Leader (June 21, 1965), pp. 3–7, and "Communism and Democracy in the Dominican Republic," War/Peace Report (July, 1965), pp. 3–5.

evaluated by incompetent policy makers who were overly pre-occupied with Cuba and anti-Communism. After meticulously refuting the Administration's "cover stories" Draper awkwardly concludes: "We still do not know what was behind the anti-Bosch campaign."[62] The key to this perplexing question lies in an analysis of why the United States *supported* the right-wing junta forces. Johnson and his advisers knew from past experience they could control the military and thus guarantee U.S. domination; however, the constitutionalists, with their independent, armed civilian cadres, presented a more formidable obstacle to manipulation.

The liberals offered no comprehensive explanation for U.S. intervention because they were hopelessly confused about the priorities and objectives of U.S. policy. They assumed the primary goal was to promote democracy and social welfare, and the intervention, with its support of the right-wing military, became a paradox. But if one assumes the most important U.S. foreign policy objective is maintaining control and domination over Dominican development, the intervention and occupation becomes quite logical. Johnson and his advisers knew from past experience they could penetrate, manipulate, and control the military, thus guaranteeing U.S. domination and its consequent benefits; the constitutionalists, however, lacked a formal structure to penetrate and were willing to employ illegal and violent means which frustrate manipulation. Given the objective of domination, President Johnson had little choice about which side to support.

The forces determining U.S. priorities and objectives in the Dominican Republic were rooted in powerful American economic interests and domestic political considerations. The U.S. corporations with a direct and indirect stake in the outcome of Dominican events had ready access to U.S. Administration officials, and when the April, 1965, rebellion broke out they most likely expressed their deep concern. A considerable number of individuals with financial, legal, and social connections to the East Coast sugar complex were well stationed throughout the upper echelons of the U.S. Government. For example, prominent New Dealer and Johnson confidant Abe Fortas was a twenty-year director of the Sucrest Corporation, the third largest East Coast cane refiner. State Department expert and ad-

62 Theodore Draper, "A Case of Defamation: The U.S. Intelligence vs. Juan Bosch," *The New Republic* (February 26, 1966), p. 18.

viser to several presidents on Latin America (including Kennedy and Johnson) Adolf A. Berle, Jr., was postwar Board Chairman of Sucrest as well as a large stockholder. OAS Ambassador and special envoy to the Dominican Republic Ellsworth Bunker was past Chairman, President, and thirty-eight-year director of the second largest East Coast cane refiner, the National Sugar Refining Co.; roving Ambassador W. Averell Harriman (sent to Latin America by Johnson to explain the Dominican intervention) is a limited partner in the New York banking house of Brown Brothers, Harriman, which owns approximately 5 percent of National Sugar's stock. Molasses magnate J. M. Kaplan is a heavy contributor and influential adviser to many Democratic Party candidates and the ADA. State Department consultant and ex-U.S. Ambassador to the Dominican Republic (1957–1960) and Panama (1960–63) Joseph S. Farland has been a director of South Puerto Rico Sugar Co. since 1964. Former Deputy Secretary of Defense Roswell Gilpatric is the managing executive partner of Cravath, Swaine and Moore, the Wall Street legal counsel for National Sugar. Wall Street lawyer Max Rabb, in the firm of Stroock, Stroock and Lavan (legal counsel for Sucrest), was a member of the National Committee for Johnson and Humphrey.[63]

63 Ex-FDR Under Secretary of the Interior Abe Fortas was described by Washington reporter Ben H. Bagdikian as "the most intimate and omnipresent of the President's friends and adivisors." See Ben H. Bagdikian, "The 'Inner Circle' Around Johnson," *The New York Times Magazine* (February 28, 1965) and Charles B. Seib and Alan L. Otten, "Abe, Help!—LBJ," *Esquire* (June, 1965).

William D. Rogers, Deputy Assistant Administrator of USAID and Deputy U.S. Coordinator of the Alliance for Progress from 1963 to 1965, is a member of Arnold and Porter, prominent law firm and lobbyist which Fortas was formerly associated with. The law firm is described in the *Esquire* article as "a high-powered operation of about 40 lawyers, most of them former government officials or teachers . . . [The] business is almost completely oriented to the Federal Government cases involving taxes, anti-trust situations, savings and loan regulation cases, proceedings before the Securities and Exchange Commission, and the like."

Fortas was also a board member and general counsel of the Greatamerica Corporation, a holding company with 80 percent of Braniff Airlines: Greatamerica is controlled by Dallas businessmen Troy V. Post and Clint W. Murchison, Jr.

Adolf Berle, Jr., was honored by the Sucrest stockholders on the occasion of his retirement as Chairman of the Board in 1964 for "the firm hand of his leadership and the uniquely personal quality of his service, to and on behalf of the corporation . . ." Mr. Berle is also a partner in the

The whole East Coast sugar industry, which is dominated by National Sugar, Sucrest, and the largest U.S. refiner, American Sugar Co., is directly dependent on sizable Dominican sugar and molasses imports. Any disruption in supply, as happened

New York law firm of Berle and Berle, which specializes in Latin American affairs for U.S. corporations.

Ellsworth Bunker, whose father was a founder of National Sugar, was described by *New York Post* columnist Joseph P. Lash (January 27, 1957) as a "spokesman for the whole [sugar] industry vis-à-vis the government." Before entering the diplomatic corps in 1950, Bunker had extensive business connections centered around the East Coast cane sugar complex. His directorships included American Hawaiian Steamship, Central Aguirre Associates, General Baking Co., Guantanamo Sugar Co., and Potrero Sugar Co. He was Chairman of the U.S. Cane Sugar Manufacturers Association and during World War II served as Chairman of the Cane Sugar Refiners War Committee. He is a long-time trustee of the Atlantic Mutual Insurance Company, which uses as its legal counsel Senator George Smathers' Miami law firm, Smathers and Thompson, and whose board includes J. Peter Grace, President and director of W. R. Grace and Co. and director of the First National City Bank of New York. Bunker and his close friend molasses magnate J. M. Kaplan are both honorary directors of the New School for Social Research of New York. The Honorable Ellsworth Bunker's son John B. Bunker, is past President of Great Western Sugar Company and currently President of the second largest U.S. sugar beet refiner, Holly Sugar Company, a subsidiary of Houston Oil Field Material Company (HOMCO). Bunker's brother, Arthur H. Bunker, is a past partner and long-time director of Lehman Brothers, a large New York investment house. Director of a Lehman Brothers subsidiary, Edwin L. Weisl is a close Johnson adviser and New York County Democratic Committeeman.

W. Averell Harriman's brother, E. Roland Harriman, heads Brown Brothers, Harriman, and sits with Ellsworth Bunker on the Board of Directors of Atlantic Mutual Life Insurance Company. Another Brown Brothers partner, Knight Woolley, is a board member of Bunker's National Sugar Refining Co.

Roswell Gilpatric's law firm, Cravath, Swaine and Moore, includes among its other clients such giants as Time, Inc., and the General Dynamics Corporation.

Max Rabb was also former Secretary to Dwight D. Eisenhower's Cabinet (1953–1958).

Thomas Mann, Assistant Secretary of State for Inter-American Affairs, also prominent in the decision to intervene, "worked closely with the CIA" in the 1954 Guatemala coup and the Bay of Pigs invasion. See Alex Campbell, "The Mann to Watch," *The New Republic* (June 5, 1965), pp. 13–15. He was described by *Business Week* as a "conservative friend of business," who as ambassador to Mexico had been "excessively concerned with leftist influence."

after the Cuban Revolution, would threaten price stability and earnings in this narrow margin of profit industry. The ability of these as well as many other corporations to either place people directly in the government or have access to important government officials was and is a major factor shaping the priorities and objectives of American foreign policy vis-à-vis the Dominican Republic. Even without direct economic interests it would be difficult, if not impossible, for these gentlemen to resist or escape the assumptions and inclinations inculcated by their economic and social milieu.

The domestic political considerations operating in favor of intervention were even more subtle than the economic forces at work. Any foreign country (especially in the Third World) which attempts to become truly independent by freeing itself of American economic, military, and political manipulation and control is easily branded in the U.S. public media as Communist. The financial and military interests affected by such a move have direct access to the mass media and other organizations shaping public opinion. This could be used as leverage against those political officials responsible for protecting their interests. No domestic political figure can afford to risk the charge of being soft on "communism" which, for all practical purposes, means losing control over actual or potential (1) investments and trade opportunities returning high profits, (2) markets for goods and services, (3) sources of cheap labor, (4) sources of cheap or strategic raw materials, (5) militarily strategic bases, and (6) influence and votes in international regional organizations. Particularly after the Cuban Revolution any U.S. President would be vulnerable, and therefore sensitive to, a situation like that confronting President Johnson in April, 1965. The decision which had to be made was painfully clear. Rather than risk failure by backing a nationalist government promoting democracy and social reform, Johnson intervened militarily to insure U.S. control and head off any domestic political threat from U.S. financial and military interests. In short, domestic political interests again took priority over Dominican democracy and independence.

With the U.S. occupation, domination and control in the Dominican Republic became, for all practical purposes, absolute. Military operations involving over 30,000 U.S. troops were coordinated out of the office of General Bruce Palmer and not by the Brazilian Inter-American Peace Force Commander-in-Chief.[64] The Assistant Secretary of State for Economic Affairs, Anthony M. Solomon, went to the Republic to coordinate the work of more than sixty U.S. officials "acting for all practical purposes as the civilian government in the Dominican Republic."[65] The U.S. Special Forces' "Operation Green Chopper" flew units throughout the country to inquire about the political views of the citizens at large, to distribute food, and to promise public works.[66]

Once Santo Domingo was militarily secure, the Johnson Administration moved to reestablish control through economic, political, and social manipulation. Rejecting an original plan of establishing a provisional government with the former Bosch minister of agriculture, Silvestre Antonio Guzmán, as head (the "Bundy formula"), the Johnson Administration finally settled on a plan similar to one described by Tad Szulc of the *New York Times:*

> In Washington highly authoritative officials told me that the Administration favored a plan for Dominican elections within six to nine months. The authorship of this idea was ascribed to Assistant Secretary [of State for Inter-American Affairs, Jack Hood] Vaughn, with the explanation that the State Department was hoping for a victory at the polls by Joaquin Balaguer . . .[67]

The State Department had been in touch with Balaguer, in exile in New York, through Washington lobbyist I. Irving Davidson. Davidson represented at one time or another Ecuadorean sugar interests, Israel military interests, the Somoza and Duvalier dictatorships, and served as intermediary for Texas oil magnate Clint Murchison in an illegal Haitian meat packing deal involving Bobby Baker.[68]

[64] Szulc, *Diary*, p. 284.

[65] *Ibid.*, p. 267.

[66] *Ibid.*, pp. 314–5.

[67] *Ibid.*, p. 313. Jack Hood Vaughn in a speech to a group of businessmen said: "Government and business must work together—that is the true Alliance—that is the combination that the framers of the Charter of Punta del Este had in mind . . ."
Address before the 15th Annual Convention of the Chamber of Commerce of the United States, June 16, 1965.

[68] Upon his return to Santo Domingo Balaguer stated he was there only to visit his dying mother.
Sorting out Davidson's relationships is a complicated task; see *I. F.*

To further extend its political control, the United States forced out the military junta headed by Imbert, cutting off U.S. funds which were supplying the government payroll. By September, 1965, U.S. negotiatiors were able to put together a provisional government headed by Hector García Godoy, formerly Bosch's foreign minister and subsequently vice-president of Balaguer's Partido Reformista. The U.S. objective for this administration was to maintain stability and hold elections which would further legitimate a U.S.-backed government. In effect, Washington was creating a pro-U.S. political atmosphere and party within the country. Aiding mightily in this task was an OAS mission headed by Ellsworth Bunker, and U.S. gifts and low-interest loans amounting to over $100 million.[69]

Bosch returned from exile in September, 1965, and under strong domestic and foreign pressure, agreed to run in the upcoming elections. Well-known social democratic and liberal Bosch sympathizers Norman Thomas and Victor Reuther argued that only through elections and the subsequent establishment of a stable democratic government would the occupation troops leave the island. Obviously, no meaningful election could be held without the participation of the PRD and their candidate Juan Bosch. Thomas, Reuther, civil rights leader Bayard Rustin, lawyer and New York Reform Democrat Allard Lowenstein, Sacha Volman, and others organized the Committee on Free Elections in the Dominican Republic. They told Bosch they would send a team of "independent unofficial observers" (eventually seventy) to oversee the elections, and

Stone's Weekly (June 21, 1965); Szulc, *Diary*, p. 170; Bernard Collier, New York *Herald Tribune* (June 11, 1965).

From private interviews we have learned that Davidson also acted as an agent for Trujillo in August, 1956, when Trujillo was trying to interest Indonesian military interests in buying several thousand of his locally manufactured "San Cristobal" carbines.

[69] On February 18, 1966, the *Christian Science Monitor* reported the U.S. had "pumped more than 100 million dollars since last September in gifts and low interest loans" into the Dominican economy. "The bulk of the money—$77 million—went to pay government salaries and other budget items." According to the *New York Times* (January 23, 1967), between July 1, 1965 and June 30, 1966, the Dominican Republic received the highest per capita economic aid from the United States of any Latin American country—$32.10 compared to $13.40 for Chile, the closest competitor.

through their presence, help moderate possible fraud and coercion. Unbeknownst to Bosch and all but one or two of the
committee observers, Allard Lowenstein held several private
talks with U.S. officials in Santo Domingo and on the eve of the
elections made a secret agreement with Ambassador Ellsworth
Bunker. If Bosch won, Bunker would publicly state U.S. support for his election. And if Balaguer was the victor, Lowenstein promised to use his considerable influence to encourage a
public statement of support.[70]

Though nearly blind and over eighty years old, Thomas made
a three-day visit to the Republic at election time to lend his
prestige as head of the committee. Upon his return to New York
immediately after the election, Thomas, accompanied by Lowenstein, made a press statement that was interpreted as a
personal endorsement of the election's freedom and fairness. In
the eyes of many liberals who had opposed Johnson's intervention policy, the committee's presence and Thomas' statement
legitimized the elections. However, the Dominicans who cooperated with the committee (most of whom were Bosch sympathizers) felt betrayed by the premature statement. The committee and most Americans avoided the key question: How can
you hold a free election in a country occupied by foreign troops
who invaded to prevent one of the two main candidates from
assuming the presidency? Even more convinced than in 1962
that he would be overthrown if elected, Bosch first refused to
run. After being persuaded otherwise, however, he conducted a
campaign aimed at educating the electorate about problems
facing any Dominican government. An atmosphere of fear
pervaded the country and he never left his heavily guarded
Santo Domingo residence to campaign among the peasantry and
pro-urban strongholds.

The candidate favored by the United States, the oligarchy,
most of the armed forces, the Church, and the U.S.-backed
Dominican Labor Confederation, CONATRAL, was Joaquin
Balaguer. The ex-Trujillo servant won handily amidst charges
of fraud, coercion, and political pressure tactics.[71] The much
needed peasant backing organized in 1962 for the PRD by CIA-
financed Sacha Volman was missing. Apparently, Volman had
agreed, in accordance with U.S. State Department wishes, to

[70] From personal experience, interviews, and observations.
[71] Norman Gall, *The New Leader* (June 20, 1966).

remain outside the country during the campaign.[72] It was
obvious to most Dominicans that the United States was backing
Balaguer and that a Bosch victory was unacceptable. Never
close to U.S. social democrats and ADA liberals—the Kennedy
operatives for controlling the PRD—Johnson literally constructed a new pro-American power base (Balaguer's party and
government) that was largely dependent on, and subservient to,
United States interests.

DOMINATION THROUGH STABILIZATION AND INFILTRATION:
BALAGUER'S FIRST YEAR

Balaguer's election victory in June, 1966, vindicated U.S.
intervention and occupation in the eyes of the Johnson Administration and its supporters. A new Constitution was drawn up
and most of the U.S. objections to the 1963 document were
excluded. Financial and technical resources were quickly
brought to the assistance of the new regime. Supplementing
generous loans and grants were nearly five hundred Americans
serving in official capacities, creating a virtual parallel government.[73] An outfit known as the International Development
Foundation, financed and staffed by the Central Intelligence
Agency, replaced Volman's operations in the training of anti-
Communist peasant leaders. The U.S. sugar quota was substantially raised to bolster revenues. On top of $3 million in military
assistance, the Pentagon sent sixty bilingual advisers to train a
3,400-man "elite" army brigade in riot control and counter-

[72] From a personal conversation with Sacha Volman, May 7, 1966.

[73] Ninety-three percent (93%) of the supporting assistance (i.e. primarily budgetary support) given by AID for fiscal year 1967 was
scheduled to go to five countries listed in the following order: Vietnam,
Korea, Jordan, Dominican Republic, and Laos. U.S. Department of
State, Agency for International Development, *Proposed Economic Assistance Plans for FY 1967* (Government Printing Office), p. 10.
The 500 official Americans serving as of January, 1967, included
almost 100 from the State Department, 160 from the Agency for International Development, 150 Peace Corpsmen, and 60 military advisers.
An undetermined number of CIA agents and unofficial Americans were
also present. Susan Bodenheimer, "The Hidden Invaders: Our Civilian
Takeover in the Dominican Republic," *Liberation* (February, 1967),
p. 14.

insurgency. In addition, AID was spending $800,000 on "public safety" (police training). The military received upward of 40 percent of the national budget; approximately 40 percent of the labor force was unemployed.[74]

Satisfied that the situation had been stabilized, United States business flocked to the Republic to make new investments in housing construction, land and tourist development, and agribusiness.[75] Strikes were virtually outlawed for one year, the government austerity program (geared to alleviating the foreign debt) frozen, and in some cases it forced reduction of wages. And a program for selling the state-owned properties was instituted. Meanwhile, left political parties were thoroughly infiltrated while the return of many feared ex-Trujillistas into positions of authority brought about a rise in political assassinations and terrorism.[76] Periodically the Dominican press carried reports of sporadic guerrilla warfare in the countryside.

CONCLUSION

The U.S. intervention and occupation had several far-reaching consequences. Large segments of Dominican society, especially the urban youth, were further alienated from the tradi-

[74] Bodenheimer, Liberation, pp. 14–15.
[75] Housing: Rockefeller's IBEC (International Basic Economy Corporation) and George A. Fuller Company Pan-Americana.

Land development and tourism: Hilton Hotels, Holiday Inn, and the American-Dominican Investment Company (of Boston) have all invested in hotels, or hotel sites. South Puerto Rico Sugar, recently bought by Gulf and Western Industries (whose head, Charles Blundorn, is a close friend and business associate of Edwin L. Weisl, Johnson adviser and political supporter), plans to turn much of its virgin beachfront land into a Caribbean vacation paradise. South Puerto Rico Sugar owns over 275,000 acres in the Republic, constituting 78.9 percent of the total cultivated land in San Pedro de Macoris province and 59.7 percent in El Seibo.

Agribusiness: Central Aguirre bought up a former United Fruit Company 30,000-acre plantation to develop vegetable production for Puerto Rican and U.S. markets. Aside from sugar, South Puerto Rico Sugar's land supports approximately 30,000 head of cattle; much of its land is undeveloped and suitable for cultivation (now being planned).

[76] For some documentation on the return of Trujillistas see Norman Gall, "The Struggle in Santo Domingo," The New Leader (January 2, 1967).

tional political leadership with its links to the United States. Anti-Americanism became even more deep seated. As one Dominican author observed, the intervention "fully revealed those who were culpable for our underdevelopment."[77] As a result of the struggle, during the late spring and summer of 1965 a whole new power base was created and two opposing camps were strengthened, reinforced, and polarized to the extent that few observers feel there will be a peaceful reconciliation. The people were armed with as many as 20,000 firearms which they still possess; they saw how their commando units could hold off and even defeat the regular army; the right-wing military elements acquired new equipment and supplies while solidifying their ties to the U.S. Armed Forces.

The more international effects of the intervention were a further weakening of the Organization of American States and the United Nations. Professor W. Friedman of the Columbia University Law School described how the United States did not even pretend to be guided by international law: "It [U.S. intervention] departs from the principle that international law does not permit interference on the ground of an objectionable political ideology."[78] The "joint" military action in the Dominican Republic was the first such "cooperative" venture in the history of the hemisphere and set the precedent for the creation of a permanent Inter-American Peace Force.

In the United States the intervention led more liberals to conclude that Vietnam was not simply a mistake, but rather part of a new approach to foreign relations. The official policy of nonintervention in the internal affairs of Latin American nations which had been proclaimed with varying degrees of credibility since December, 1933, was officially reversed. A less noted though significant effect was the weakening of the Peace Corps' political independence. Frank Mankiewicz, then director of the Corps' Latin American operations (and later Senator Robert Kennedy's press secretary) made a special trip to Santo Domingo to oppose the threatened en masse resignation of a sizable number of volunteers as a protest against U.S. policy.[79]

[77] Franco, p. 264.

[78] Letter to the Editor, *New York Times* (May 9, 1965).

[79] Szulc refers in passing to Mankiewicz's trip in May, 1965, to the Dominican Republic. Szulc, *Diary*, p. 224. Other information on this topic was obtained from interviews with several Peace Corps volunteers who were directly involved.

Juan Bosch once again left the Dominican Republic after the 1966 election, declaring that "there is no democratic exit from the present situation." It became clear that the constant priority of United States foreign policy was the maintenance of control and domination for the unequal benefit of U.S. interests. The mechanisms for achieving this objective varied from brutal suppression to subtle manipulation, with a conscious preference for the latter. Military occupation gives way to U.S.-trained and -financed "national" organizations whose dependency is invisible only to North Americans. Democracy, social progress, and independence are subservient to the primary objective and readily disposable if they jeopardize U.S. authority. What is conspicuously absent from most left-liberal and social democratic interpretations is an analysis of political and economic forces *within* American society. Interests, associations, and structures, rather than intentions and rhetoric, largely determine the motivational forces that shape foreign policy.[80] While the Kennedy and Johnson administrations employed different mechanisms of domination—political vs. military—their objectives remained the same. Kennedy had strong enough links to the PRD through ADA liberals and social democrats to take a chance with democracy and muted nationalism; he hedged his bets by stepping up military assistance. But Johnson lacked

[80] Feeling that business and financial information was most lacking in standard interpretations, we concentrated a great deal of effort on recognized business sources, special libraries, and trade journals. For analysis on corporations we found especially helpful *Moody's Industrials*. Senate and Congressional hearings as well as executive department data were utilized (e.g. Securities and Exchange Commission listings of corporation stockholders). Tracing the interests and associations of individuals presents a difficult area of research. Some basic reference sources include: various *Who's Who; Current Biography; Poor's Register of Directors and Executives; Martindale-Hubbell Law Directory;* U.S. Department of State *Biographical Register;* and telephone directories at home and abroad.

Data collected from these sources provide knowledge and leads on the potential interrelationships involved in decision-making and the exercise of power. The preliminary background knowledge gained from the above enabled us to frame questions and understand answers in interviews with individuals directly or indirectly related to crucial events. Among these individuals were corporation executives, sugar brokers, journalists, and government functionaries. A summer 1967 visit to the Dominican Republic by one of the authors provided an opportunity to conduct interviews and collect statistical data on economic, social, and military conditions.

Kennedy's connections and when revolutionary nationalist forces took up arms the ability of the United States to maintain effective control, short of occupation, was undermined.

The fate of peaceful democratic modernization in Peru, Brazil, Ecuador, or the Dominican Republic, pivots on the political, corporate, and military structures of American society. This is what the Cuban revolutionaries profoundly understood and the American people, including liberals from the Church, university, and the professions, have never confronted. Those who define Latin American problems primarily in terms of conditions external to the United States and offer assistance based on this assumption will only perpetuate U.S. domination. Without fundamental change in American society, violent confrontation is inevitable.

Foreign Exploitation of

Oil and National Development*

SALVADOR DE LA PLAZA

CONTENDING that the economic activities connected with the extraction, processing, and distribution of oil have been grouped, for methodological convenience, under the general classification Oil Economy, some writers have maintained that these activities are governed by laws of their own and therefore constitute an independent economic category, separate from the general production and distribution of products in the country, whereas history has shown that societies are governed as a whole and by a single set of laws. Those laws, moreover, were not invented by man, but simply discovered and interpreted. From our study of them we know that the pronounced contrasts between economic, social, and political structures of some countries and those structures of other countries and between different stages of historical development in the same country are determined by the forms of ownership of the means of production, the relationships inherent in these forms of ownership, and the degree of development of each nation's productive forces.

Hence, in order to interpret how the existence of petroleum in our subsoil and its exploitation by international trusts have conditioned the economic, social, and political process through which this country has lived for the past fifty years, and in order to arrive at precise solutions to the great variety of problems

*Lecture given at the Engineers' Center of Falcón State in Coro, Venezuela, February 25, 1966, and published in *Revista Cultura Universitaria*, No. 91, Caracas, 1966.

confronting Venezuela, we shall have to start with a discussion of the causes which have obstructed, retarded, and distorted the development of the Venezuelan economy in general. This discourse, therefore, will be an attempt to uncover these causes and present, as concisely as possible, a little-known aspect of the oil problem.

One hundred and thirty-five years have elapsed since Venezuela became a sovereign republic and yet, despite the fabulous wealth that has been extracted from its subsoil—between 1917 and 1964, more than 124 billion bolivars in oil alone—it continues to be an undeveloped country, a country whose independent economic development has been impeded by the survival of an outdated agrarian structure and the interference of foreign capital, whose evolution as a nation has been retarded and whose social relationships and democratic policies have not been allowed to become stabilized. This is a reality which causes profound concern to most Venezuelans who realize what will happen when the country's petroleum deposits are exhausted.

It is also a reality which has several precedents. When Venezuela won independence from the Spanish Crown, the country inherited an economic structure based on extensive landholdings and on the cultivation, by slave labor and for export, of vast coffee and cacao plantations. With the proceeds from the sale of those crops in foreign markets, the big landholders and slaveholders—who consequently also wielded political and economic power—purchased goods for their own immediate needs. Since no capital was accumulated in the country for the stimulation of manufacturing activities, rudimentary trades and crafts languished in the cities.

Although it is true that slavery was officially abolished by the middle of the nineteenth century and that even before then "free" labor relations, such as sharecropping, partnership, peonage for wages, had replaced slave labor, it is also true that during this same period foreign companies—vanguard of the European imperialist system, already in the full spate of its irresistible development—began to penetrate into the country. Because these foreign interests dominated the import and export trade and gained control of coffee, cacao, and cattle production by means of one-sided financing methods of landowners and ranchers, they were in a position to draw off the wealth created

by the labor of peasants, wage earners, and artisans, and export
it to their countries of origin, thereby preventing even more
surely any accumulation of domestic capital. A minister of
development testified to this extortion and the resulting impoverishment of the country in his 1868 report:

> Everybody knows that Venezuelans in general lack liquid capital.
> In agriculture, for example, the major crops wholly depend on
> foreign companies, from which they receive at high interest the
> funds needed for the clearing of the fields, the harvesting of the
> crop and the daily sustenance of the farmers and their families.
> As a result, the farmer is frequently subject to the creditor's
> control, not only with regard to profits and the price of the
> money, but also in relation to the very value of the crop itself.
> And if the creditor makes any profit on it abroad, it can be
> assumed that he will not surrender it to the producer. There are
> hardly any landowners in a position to throw off this yoke and
> ship elsewhere the produce of their own farms. A similar situation
> prevails with regard to other products. And here we have another
> of the causes of the discontent among so many farmers. . . .[1]

Thus, dependent on foreign capital and hampered by the
persistence of large landholdings, Venezuela remained divided
into regions which were cut off from one another and which
supplied their own requirements, while their peasant populations grew ever poorer as a result of the intensive exploitation to
which they were subjected by the owners of the great plantations and ranches.

But since the exploration for oil began in 1912, that backward agrarian structure started to break up at its foundations—
the production relations which held it up. Absentee landowners
could no longer count on the necessary abundance of servile
labor, for both the oil explorations and the attendant services
which sprang up in those areas attracted large numbers of
peasants. Similarly, the country folk flocked into the cities,
because the state—having at its disposal the increased income
from oil revenues—expanded its own organization and devoted
ever-growing sums to public works projects and to the expansion of existing services and the creation of new ones. The
plaintive lamentations of the absentee landowners give evidence
of this process: "Oil and public works are the cause of our

[1] Ramón Veloz, *Economy and Finances of Venezuela from 1830 to
1944*, Caracas, p. 150.

having had to abandon the coffee and cacao plantations, the ranches and the activities of the countryside; they are the cause of the collapse of agricultural production. . . ." Though prompted by resentment, their remarks embodied, without their realizing it, what was actually happening to absentee land-lordism as a system, inasmuch as the serfs of the soil, from whose exploitation they had wrung the juicy profits which were the basis of their economic and political power, had begun their exodus to places where they expected to find better remunera-tion for their labor and freedom from the tyranny and the abuses imposed upon them by their traditional exploiters.

Up to 1917, Venezuela's trade balance had shown a surplus, although we cannot say, for lack of data on balance of pay-ments, precisely how much of that capital returned to this country. In 1854, for example, exports totaled 35.7 million bolivars and imports 29,462 million bolivars, providing a sur-plus of 6,238 million bolivars. In 1908, fifty-four years later, exports had only increased to 83,145 million bolivars and imports to 49,180 million bolivars, while the surplus rose to 33,965 million bolivars—figures revealing the meager economic development which had taken place. In 1917, the last year in which a surplus was produced, it had dropped to 16,173 million bolivars. With the development of the oil industry, and because its exploitation had from the beginning been controlled by international trusts, the same phenomenon was to persist, vary-ing only in degree and in the personalities involved. The fabu-lous wealth wrung from Venezuelan labor and the irreplaceable natural resources extracted from the country's soil, instead of accumulating and breeding new wealth within the country as a foundation for its economic, social, and political development, escaped abroad, to contribute, through its productive employ-ment there, toward the enrichment and ever more rapid devel-opment of the industrialized countries of the world.

Although the exploitation of oil distorted the outdated agrar-ian structure in several respects, it did not destroy it, nor did it stimulate a progressive transformation of the economy. From 1917 on, due to more aggressive methods of penetration on the part of foreign capital and the use made of oil revenues by the state, the nation's supply of manufactured articles and food products was increasingly to depend on foreign sources, and the national economy was to be ever more profoundly diverted from its proper course. Since the exploitation of its oil resources

was controlled by international trusts, two violently contradictory and antagonistic economies had begun to coexist
within the nation: the highly technical economy of the oil
industry, closely linked with the economies of the countries
where the trusts originated and aimed at obtaining the greatest
possible profits for those countries, and the purely national
economy based on a backward agrarian structure. The natural
development of the latter economy was more obstructed by this
situation, as a result of the failure to take adequate measures to
get rid of the outdated agrarian system and to encourage an
autonomous development which would have taken full advantage of what the country earned from the exploitation of its oil
resources. That income—the foreign exchange brought into
Venezuela by the oil trusts for payment of wages and taxes and
for expenses—did not remain and accumulate, but, instead,
leaked out again as soon as it entered: it was used to pay for
imported products for immediate consumption. There was still a
favorable trade balance in 1917, but nine years later, in 1926,
although exports, excluding oil, had risen but slightly (to 152
million bolivars, or $28 million), imports had increased four-
fold, to 432 million bolivars, or $81 million. The surplus in the
trade balance had been replaced by a deficit of 281 million
bolivars—a deficit which was to grow by leaps and bounds in
subsequent years, and which, because of the nature of the
imports, was irrefutable proof of the stagnation that had overtaken agricultural production; of the lag in industrial development; of the country's dangerous dependence on foreign capital;
and the antinational way, which we do not hesitate to describe
as criminal, in which successive governments used the proceeds
from the exploitation of oil.

The figures supplied by the Central Bank of Venezuela in its
annual reports are eloquent. They reveal that exports, excluding
oil and iron, rose from $28 million in 1926 to $45 million in
1955, becoming stabilized up to the present time at between
$40 million and $50 million. In contrast, imports rose from $81
million in 1926 to $638 million in 1953, almost an eightfold
increase over that twenty-seven-year period. Four years later, in
1957, they amounted to $1,278 million. In 1959 they rose to
$1,330 million, and in subsequent years hovered around $900
million. Consequently, the trade balance deficit jumped from
$53 million in 1926 to $699 million in 1953, to $1,346 million

in 1957, and to $2,117 million in 1959, and was stabilized at
around $1,400 million. The figures for all these years include
the balances of services and capital, which were $147 million
and $69 million respectively in 1953, $421 million and $409
million in 1959, and jointly around $500 million in subsequent
years.

In 1964 exports totaled $59 million and imports $1,101
million, or 4,957 million bolivars. However, since the bolivar
was devalued in January of that year from 3.09 to 4.40 (rate of
exchange for purchase of the oil dollar), and from 3.35 to 4.50
(rate for sale of controlled foreign currency for payment of
imports, travel expenses, etc.), we find that in that year, for the
same quantity of merchandise bought abroad with dollars,
Venezuelan consumers had to pay a surcharge of 1,269 million
bolivars—the difference between 4,957 million and the 3,688
million they would have paid at the exchange rate of 3.35.
These additional millions paid by the consumer represented a
26 percent increase in the cost of living. This was an enormous
sacrifice imposed upon the population by the devaluation of the
bolivar, and it has continued to increase, for in 1965, according
to data from the United States Department of Commerce,
Venezuela imported merchandise from all sources to the value
of $1,300 million, or 5,850 million bolivars, at the rate of
exchange of 4.50. At the former exchange rate of 3.35, that
same volume of imports would have cost 4,017 million bolivars.
So Venezuelans paid 1,832 million bolivars extra.

How were the growing deficits in the trade balances covered
in the balance of payments? The international trusts which
control the extraction, handling, and refining of oil in our
country export 92 percent of the crude oil and oil products and
sell it abroad for dollars, returning to this country, as we have
seen, only enough for the payment of wages and taxes, for
expenses, and to purchase the oil royalty from the state. It is
precisely these dollars which have been covering the deficit in
the trade balance. They are put into circulation in the internal
market through government expenditures, in the case of those
received by the state in taxes and from sale of the royalty;
through the purchases made by the companies' workers, and,
finally, through the sundry expenditures of the companies themselves, all of these operations being covered by the sale of oil
(and now also iron) dollars made by the Central Bank of

Venezuela to the commercial banks. Since 1941, under a decree issued by the government, the oil companies have been compelled to sell to the Central Bank, at the exchange rate of 3.09 bolivars, all the foreign currency they bring into the country. It is this foreign exchange, thus controlled, that the Central Bank sells to the commercial banks.

With the end of the Second World War, world consumption of crude oil and oil products increased enormously and rapidly and the trusts stepped up oil production in this country to keep pace with the rising demand. Output (in cubic meters) rose from 41 million in 1944 to 105 million in 1952 and to 185 million in 1963. As a result, the influx of oil dollars also increased, though not in due proportion to the increase in production and the amendments introduced in 1946 and 1958 into the income tax law. From the 205 million bolivars received by the Treasury in 1944 from taxes and from sale of the royalty, these revenues jumped in 1952 to 1,475 million bolivars, and in 1958 to 2,608 million bolivars. In 1959, as a result of raising the scale of the complementary tax on income from 26 to 45 percent, 3,226 million bolivars was collected. These revenues dropped in 1960 to 3,002 million bolivars, despite the fact that output had increased by 5 million cubic meters. In subsequent years this income was stabilized around 3,200 million bolivars. Increases in the years 1956 and 1957 were due to extraordinary revenues resulting from the misnamed "sales of concessions" which were carried out by Pérez Jiménez during those years and which amounted to a total of 2,118 million bolivars, or $785 million. It should be noted that this extraordinary revenue was the result of the international trusts having undertaken to pay as an additional exploitation tax, in order to obtain new concessions covering 821,089 hectares, 2,579 bolivars per hectare instead of the 8 bolivars fixed by law. But it must be recognized that when Pérez Jiménez and his successors allowed the international trusts to enter those 2,118 million bolivars in their books as capital investment instead of sums paid in taxes—and consequently subject to amortization—those millions of bolivars acquired the status of a long-term loan without fixed expiration date, which the nation has been paying in annual installments equivalent to what it fails to receive in income taxes as a result of the reduction in taxable income that is implied by the amortization. All of this means that the unspeakable tyrant and the enlightened democrats who succeeded him in the government conspired to make the international trust a present of concessions covering 821,089 hectares, largely from national reserves including the richest deposits in the country.

Indeed, because the oil companies are mere subsidiaries of huge trusts which form an integral part of the economies of their countries of origin, our country receives only a part of the total value of the oil exported—47.8 percent in 1946 and 57.8 percent in 1963—while the rest stays abroad, increasing the wealth of foreign lands. Those dollars which are held back comprise profits, dividends, and amortizations of capital initially invested—capital which, according to a statement made by the Central Bank of Venezuela in its 1956 report, had been completely amortized by 1954. This is tantamount to saying that the billions of dollars that the trusts have since retained abroad are nothing but extraordinary superprofits; subsequent investments are merely part of the excessive profits which are amortized once more.

It should also be kept in mind that the increasing migration of the peasant population to the oil fields and the cities since 1912—a migration prompted by the demand for labor on the part of the oil companies and the state—transformed the country's population, changing its characteristics. The proportions of the rural and urban populations were inverted, the latter increasing from 34.7 percent in 1938 to 39.4 percent in 1941, 53.8 percent in 1950 and 67.5 percent in 1961, the year of the last census. In order to provide for this growing urban population, given the stagnation of agricultural production and the rudimentary development of industry, recourse could only be had to importing all types of products, including vast quantities of foodstuffs. Consequently, those who engaged in the import business, because of their growing numbers and the ease with which they grew rich, tended to form a group within the ruling classes which, in order to further increase its huge profits, was to ally itself with the foreign interests and bring pressure to bear within government circles for progressive expansion of the policy of using public revenues for "current government expenditures" rather than government investment. Also backing this policy were the industrialists, businessmen, bankers, professional men and high-level bureaucrats, who hoped to use their influence to obtain handsome profits from public works projects, attractive commissions, and the elaboration of plans and projects in which extravagant imagination has always disguised the most voracious appetite for profit.

The struggles among these groups for the control of appropriation of oil revenues conditioned the social and political activities of the majority of Venezuelans from the third decade of this century until now, with the resultant strangulation of agricultural and industrial development. The constant increase in current government expenditures—in 1958, in salaries alone, by more than 1,000 million bolivars—does not, therefore, stem from a desire to satisfy the pressing needs of the Venezuelan people, as government officials and political leaders have asserted, but from the obvious though camouflaged intention of contributing toward the further enrichment of segments of the ruling class and recruiting supporters for the various political parties they have organized and established, while encouraging, at the same time, the deep and easy penetration of foreign capital. Not only are these palpable facts which nobody can deny, but there is no other way to explain the tenacious opposition of these sections of the ruling class to productive reinvestment of the government's oil revenues. From 1944 to 1963 the state had collected 38,251 million bolivars in taxes and from the sale of oil royalties to the companies. If these billions had been reinvested in machinery and equipment, in the installation of factories, in carrying out an agrarian reform with the consequent development of agricultural and livestock production, and in the direct exploitation by the state of irreplaceable natural resources, Venezuela would not be confronted today with the problems resulting from her position as an underdeveloped country: the growing unemployment among the masses, the increase in delinquency, the general poverty in which the great majority of the people are trapped because the number who work becomes progressively smaller in proportion to the growing population, while the number who do not work, but must be fed, constantly increases.

Other industries are also being exploited. The petrochemical complex has been broken up by contract arrangements and the creation of "mixed associations" with international trusts, such as the agreement signed with Union Carbide, the biggest United States petrochemical trust, in which the minister of mines and hydrocarbons and the director of the Venezuelan Petrochemical Institute handed over to that cartel control of the production and distribution of ethylene and polyethylene, the basic products of the petrochemical industry. Thus has the nation been deprived of directly exploiting its wealth of natural gas, which is essential to ensure its independent economic development.

In order to camouflage the fact that they were distributing the oil revenues among themselves and in order to justify their alliance with foreign capital, the circles among the ruling classes to which we have already referred and of which most government figures are mere administrative agents, have formulated a pseudodoctrine, which they are now putting into practice. According to this pseudodoctrine: "The State should not reinvest the revenues from the exploitation of oil in the installation, administration and control of companies of fundamental importance for industrial and agricultural production, because that implies State invasion of the sacred territory reserved by the Constitution for 'free enterprise' and 'private initiative.' " As a corollary they add: "Since Venezuela lacks capital—public and private—in sufficient amounts to stimulate economic development, it should employ every kind of encouragement and incentive to persuade foreign capital to perform that function." This pseudotheory, or doctrine, as they call it, is repeatedly expounded in the great volume of resolutions and statements issued by both the associations representing the interests to which I have referred and the government agencies concerned.

Yet if any underdeveloped country has had more than sufficient capital at its disposal to undertake its own independent economic development, that country has been Venezuela. Thanks to the Liberator's decree of October, 1829, the subsoil of our country, unlike that of most other countries in the world, is the property of the nation, instead of belonging to the owner of the soil in accordance with traditional Roman law. As a result, and despite the appetites, betrayals, and questionable compromises of the ruling classes, the legislation on hydrocarbons required that the concessionaire exploiting oil deposits must deliver to the state part of the petroleum it extracts—the royalty—besides paying the general and specific taxes imposed (or which may be imposed) as a condition for exclusive exploitation rights, for a specified period, of the oil deposit located in the concession area. In spite of these provisions, there are still people who do not accept this ruling. For example, an officer of the Creole Oil Corporation, Dr. Rodríguez Eraso, publicly maintained during a round-table discussion at the Collegium of Engineers of Venezuela that the oil companies were the owners of the oil they exploited and that the royalty was therefore a "production cost," a kind of tax, similar to the one the parent corporations of the oil companies pay in their countries of origin.

Two countries with different views on the ownership of the subsoil must also, of necessity, have different legislation regulating the disposal, exploitation, and administration of their irreplaceable natural resources. In the United States the owner of the soil is also the owner of the subsoil. Consequently, legislation on mines and hydrocarbons in that country must be restricted to measures of conservation, regulation and control of methods of exploitation, the fixing of production ceilings in the national interest, etc.—all measures involving, in practice, "direct intervention of the state" in the exercise by private persons of their "sacred" right of private ownership of the soil and subsoil. In Venezuela, the nation, as owner of the subsoil, has the inherent right to use the natural resources for the national, or collective interest. The nation may exploit its irreplaceable natural resources directly, through the state, or it may grant or withhold concessions to private interests to exploit those resources, reserving for itself part of what is extracted (the royalty). It also has the right, which is more properly an obligation, to oversee the conservation and efficient exploitation of those resources. Under no circumstances is "state interference" with private property rights implied, even when a concession is granted, because the concession involves no transfer of property rights. In any case, those rights are inalienable under the provisions of the national constitution. Nevertheless, in the eyes of the oil trusts and their Venezuelan accomplices, the United States is the only country with "free enterprise," where the state does not intervene in or interfere with the "private activity of its citizens," and Venezuela is the country whose government is the prototype of "interventionism," to the point where, as the banker Pérez Dupuy puts it, referring to the Corporación Venezolana del Petroleo, the Venezuelan government "has even planned to exploit the country's oil directly, when that function corresponds, by natural right, to private enterprise," which means, in plain language, that these people consider that the oil should be exploited by foreign private capital. It is clear that they want the foreign trusts to be given carte blanche to act in this country as if they were the absolute masters of its soil and subsoil.

In the United States, as in Britain, the state can only directly exploit the subsoil of land which is not in the possession of private persons. In Venezuela, since the subsoil is the property of the nation, mineral deposits can be exploited only by private citizens who have been granted concessions by the state—whether or not they own the land. It is in the exercise of its right of ownership of the subsoil that the state, when granting oil concessions, reserves the right to a part of the oil extracted, known as the royalty. Consequently, of the wealth which the concessionaire has wrested from the bowels of the earth, that part to which the state has a right—and which it may elect to receive in kind or sell back to the concessionaire—is neither a tax nor a rental. Nor is it the national Treasury's share in the profits obtained by the concessionaire from the handling of the remainder of the oil extracted as a result of the concession. Whether the government sells the royalty oil back to the concessionaire or receives it in kind and sells it on the open market, that oil, when exchanged for money, furnishes capital which enters the Treasury as a national asset, and, from its very nature, cannot be equated with the other revenues accruing from taxes and contributions paid by the citizens for the upkeep of the state and the maintenance of the public services it is called upon to provide.

The Hydrocarbons Law of 1943, which is still in effect, standardized the royalty for all existing and future concessionaires at a rate of 16⅔ barrels of oil for every hundred barrels extracted. In the event that the government elects to sell the royalty oil back to the concessionaire, the same law lays down precise rules to determine, at the well, the commercial value of the oil, and also authorizes the government to enter into agreements to that end with the concessionaires. In the agreements which are still in force, certain American crude oils similar to those produced in Venezuela were chosen as a standard for determining commercial value, since prices of these crude oils were quoted daily on the market. However, the international trusts arbitrarily cut the prices of oil from Venezuela and the countries of the Middle East in February and April, 1959, and since those cuts did not affect the prices of oil produced in the United States, the concessionaires, under these agreements, have been forced to continue paying the state for the oil they deliver to it as a royalty and then buy back from it—and at prices higher than those fixed by the trusts for Venezuelan crude oils. That price difference has provided the nation, since 1959, with an annual income of more than 300 million bolivars. In other words, it proposed that the concessionaires—the international trusts—should be allowed to buy back the product of the oil royalty at the prices those same trusts have fixed for Venezuelan oil. Such a monstrous antipatriotic proposal clearly reveals that supreme organization of the ruling classes—the cynical and shameless spokesman of the foreign interests that are despoiling our country and warping its economy.

From just the sale of the oil royalty back to the companies, the national Treasury received between 1944 and 1963 the fantastic sum of 21,574 million bolivars, which amounts to 56 percent of the total revenues the state obtained during that period from the exploitation of its oil resources. In 1944 the proceeds from the sale of the royalty oil totaled 155 million bolivars. As production increased, it rose in proportion, reaching 904 million bolivars in 1954 and 1,715 million bolivars in 1963, also a result of the agreements we have already referred to. These figures show that Venezuela has had at its disposal sufficient capital for a gradual reinvestment program which, in the course of the twenty years which have elapsed, would have generated a harmonious, sustained, and independent development of its agricultural and industrial production, and would have guaranteed the solution, within the limitations of the incipient capitalist system, of the nation's problems of supply, of full employment of the masses of the working class, and of a less unequal distribution of the national income.

Since 1945, the year in which Yankee imperialism established the International Monetary Fund, the oil trusts have been applying pressure on the IMF to force Venezuela to replace its system of exchange differentials with a single rate of exchange for the purchase and sale of the dollars entering the country. This they finally achieved with the decrees issued by Betancourt on January 18, 1964, and the corresponding devaluation of the bolivar from 3.09 to 4.40. To better appreciate and measure the catastrophic consequences of those decrees, let us look briefly into the recent past.

As we have already seen, once the oil has been extracted, refined, and exported, the international trusts dispose of it as best serves their own interests. During World War II they sold oil to the Germans, and now they are supplying it to Rhodesia, despite the fact that Venezuela has expressed in the United Nations its support of the economic boycott of that country. Insofar as our monetary system is concerned, given the volume of oil production and the oil companies' need to bring dollars into the country to cover their expenses in bolivars, they have always sought to obtain higher profit margins by manipulating the money changing. The lower the exchange rate for the purchase of oil dollars, the fewer of these dollars would they have to use to obtain the bolivars necessary to cover their expenses. The importance of these maneuvers was not fully appreciated during the early years of oil exploitation, but by the thirties it became so obvious that even the government of Juan Vicente Gómez moved in 1934 to regulate exchange rates and stabilize the currency.

In 1941, by a decree of July 23 on the "control of imports and exports," or "new system of exchange," the government forced the oil companies to sell to the Central Bank of Venezuela, at the exchange rate of 3.09, all the dollars they imported. And the government established, for the protection of agricultural production, then predominant, a system of differential exchange rates: one rate of exchange for oil dollars (3.09); another and higher one for those earned by the exportation of coffee, cacao, and cattle; and still another for the sale of the dollars thus controlled to private persons (for payment of imports, expenses abroad, travel, etc.).

Clearly, what prompted Medina Angarita's government to implement, as an instrument of economic policy, the control of foreign exchange, and set up the system of differential exchange rates, was the nationalistic concept of state action against which those who plotted and carried out the coup d'état of October 18, 1945, rebelled. The roots of this nationalistic concept go back to 1937. At that time, after examining how the exploitation of oil by foreign trusts affects our economy, Professor Vandellos concluded that "there are two economies in Venezuela: the general economy and the oil economy, which maintain a certain independence of one another but are linked by the umbilical cord of the wages of the workers employed in the oil fields and the royalties and taxes paid to the government by the oil companies." To ensure simultaneously the development of domestic production and the maximum foreign exchange from oil, this situation called for the regulation of foreign exchange by the state, in order to coordinate and harmonize, within the framework of the monetary system, the different sections of our economy: a) to obtain for the nation the maximum amount in foreign currency by fixing a rate of exchange between the bolivar and the dollar very close to the gold parity of both currencies (3.06); thus the oil companies would have to bring into the country greater amounts in dollars in order to obtain the bolivars required to meet their expenses; and b) to ensure remunerative incomes in bolivars for domestic producers by fixing other rates of exchange for the purchase of foreign currency resulting from the exportation of other products. For the sale of this controlled foreign exchange to private parties, still another rate of exchange was to be established, one which would reimburse the state for the subsidy it gave farmers and cattlemen and afford a measure of protection for domestic production, but without creating any special source of revenue. The rate of exchange for these sales was fixed at 3.35.

Both the control of foreign exchange and the system of preferential exchange rates were prompted by a situation which still persists because our oil was, and still is, extracted, exported, and sold, both at home and abroad, by foreign trusts which form an integral part of the economies of their countries of origin and by the corresponding need to protect the national interest. In 1939 the Chilean professor Max, then economic adviser to the government, stated:

> In my opinion, monetary policy should be different for the two sections of Venezuela's economy (the national economy properly so called and the oil economy). Since the rate of exchange in effect for the oil economy is not applicable to the national economy without payment of subsidies to producers and exporters, a special rate of exchange should be established for that sector. This difference in exchange rates does not constitute anything at all out of the ordinary, but is imposed by the logic of the situation.

That sovereign policy of fixing a rate of exchange close to the gold parity of the bolivar and the dollar and differential rates of exchange was maintained until January, 1964, despite the pressures of the oil companies during that twenty-three-year period to force its elimination. The companies argued that it was "a policy of discrimination against them" and that "its continued application is imprudent in view of the growing competition which Venezuelan oil has to face in the world market." However, this policy was not applied consistently by successive governments to the foreign currency from exportation of other products, inasmuch as the respective rate of exchange for its purchase by tradesmen, industrialists, cattlemen, and farmers other than those engaged in the planting of coffee and cacao crops, was never fixed, and this despite the fact that, in 1962, to obtain funds to cover growing budget deficits, the government established another rate for sale of foreign exchange (4.70, later stabilized at 4.50), a monetary manipulation which served to create another indirect tax (affecting the poorer sections of the population), from which the national Treasury obtained in 1963 more than 1,200 million bolivars.

With the decrees of January, 1964, the powers of the state—for both the legislature and the judiciary supported the executive—abandoned the policy of seeking to obtain for the nation the highest possible dollar income from the exploitation of its oil. And, by so doing, they started the nation down the headlong slope of currency devaluations, with all the catastrophic consequences which other sister nations such as Brazil, Argentina, and Chile have suffered and continue to suffer. Because the bolivar has been shorn of its gold parity with the dollar, the currency of international trade, Venezuela has been forced to purchase abroad with the same amount in bolivars as before the devaluation, a smaller quantity of merchandise—a circumstance which will, due to the higher costs involved, obstruct and delay Venezuela's independent economic development. Accumulation of domestic capital will be even slower. The flow of dollars into the economy by way of wages, salaries, and other expenditures of the oil companies in this country will shrink, and the nation will receive fewer dollars for the same volume of oil or iron extracted and exported. This situation will increase still further the wealth of the trusts' countries of origin to the detriment of our own, which will become progressively impoverished because these resources are irreplaceable.

Moreover, the contradictions and antagonisms between the two economies, observed in 1937 and 1939 by Professors Vandellos and Max respectively, have not only continued to exist, but have been accentuated as production of crude oil, crude oil derivatives, and iron has increased and as industrial production has been added to the economy of agriculture and animal husbandry. This situation has also been exacerbated by the growing economic power of the foreign trusts, whose threat to Venezuela's sovereignty and independence was demonstrated, among other things, by the economic recession which has gripped the country since 1959 and which was deliberately brought about by the oil companies with their reprisals (dismissal of 25 percent of their personnel, reduction of oil exploration to a minimum, bank scares, reduction of oil prices, etc.) against this country for the decree of December 19, 1958, by which the government junta sought to increase the nation's share in the exploitation of its oil by raising the complementary income tax rate from 26 percent to 45 percent.

The oil trusts reacted swiftly. They did not delay very long in putting their threats into practice, for in February, and again in April, 1959, they reduced the prices of Venezuelan and Middle Eastern oil, a maneuver which prevented the oil taxes from increasing in due proportion to the increase in production and the raising of the complementary income tax rate. For in 1958, with production of 1,014 billion barrels in 1957, income taxes of 1,052 billion bolivars were collected on the basis of the 26 percent rate, while in 1963, with production of 1,185 billion barrels and on the basis of the 45 percent rate, income tax revenue was only 1,758 million bolivars—a sum lower than would have been collected from the trusts if the 1957 prices had been maintained together with the 26 percent ceiling on the complementary income tax.

Shell also protested against the decree, making among other threats the following: "We interpret this swift and drastic action [the decree], which has also been made retroactive, as a *violation* of the principle of *equal shares* for the nation and the oil companies, an association which has worked to the benefit of both parties. . . ."

Both Shell and Creole expressed great indignation because they believed the government junta had violated an agreement, or "secret pact," not to modify taxes without the prior consent of the trusts. And such an understanding did indeed exist, dating from the middle of 1948, when the amendment to the income tax law which introduced the so-called "additional 50–50 tax" was worked out and later sanctioned by the Congress.

Venezuela has never enjoyed a half share in the profits of the oil companies, even after the promulgation of the decree of December, 1958. The so-called "50–50" was a *myth* created by mutual agreement between the government and the companies in order to hide the vast profits the latter were earning—which amounted to as much as 34 percent of the capital invested. This false and mendacious "50–50" share was obtained by including the royalty in the total of taxes which was to serve as a basis for calculating the additional tax.

The decree of December, 1958, raising the complementary tax rate to 45 percent, put an end to that myth, uncovered the lie of the "50–50," and assured the nation of a greater share in the exploitation of its oil. If that decree had not been issued, instead of 1,758 million bolivars being collected in 1963, for example, no more than some 1,000 million would have been realized from the income tax, in view of the impact of the price cuts arbitrarily agreed upon by the companies in 1959. As an excuse, some government spokesmen insist on attributing these cuts to the "pressures" the "consuming countries" brought to bear on the price levels in the world market.

Not even the present minister of mines and hydrocarbons has ventured to cast doubt on the fact that the oil economy operates independently and from outside the country, apart from the Venezuelan national economy. In an attempt to justify the decrees of January 18, 1964, and explain why the Treasury would obtain higher revenues in bolivars with devaluation of the bolivar from 3.09 to 4.40, Dr. Pérez Guerrero stated:

> Insofar as concerns the yield in bolivars, the greater amount received (by the Treasury) is due especially to the increase in the companies' gross receipts when the higher rate of exchange is applied to their *sales of petroleum abroad.* With regard to the yield in dollars, the increase is due to the reduction in *certain operating costs* which *are paid in bolivars,* for which reason a smaller amount in dollars is required (by the companies) to cover the corresponding payments. This gives rise to a larger taxable income. . . .

In other words, the increase in revenues for the Treasury in bolivars will not be the result of higher prices for oil sold by the company, but will be due to manipulation of exchange inside the country; and the "higher taxable income" will have its origin in the smaller amount in dollars which the companies will bring into the country to cover the payment of "certain costs" in bolivars, principally wages and salaries. Consequently, it follows that the "greater taxable income" and the corresponding increase in the companies' profits will ultimately be wrung from the sweat of the oil workers, on whose backs—and those of the consumers in general—will fall the weight of the increase in the cost of living which the devaluation of the bolivar will bring in its wake. All of this shows that the bolivar was devalued in order to benefit the foreign trusts, as the minister of mines and hydrocarbons himself freely admitted:

> However, insofar as concerns the development of the [oil] industry, and exploration in particular, the oil companies *will obtain an appreciable advantage* with the application of this measure [the devaluation to 4.40]. Every new investment they make in Venezuela will call for a *smaller number of dollars* from them, in proportion to the number devoted to the purchase of goods and services [and, we add, of labor]. We realize that the factors which stimulate oil activities are many, but certainly a *reduction in investment costs* [which is to say, a more intensive exploitation of Venezuela and the Venezuelan workers, according to our interpretation] is one of them, and, under certain circumstances, it can even *be decisive.* . . .

He concludes his exposition with a prediction which reveals the antinational point of view of those who urge investment of foreign private capital as a determining factor in economic development: "The dollar income from oil will tend to increase to the extent that oil investment increases as we anticipate. . . ."

Will these new investments increase the nation's share in each unit of oil that is extracted from the subsoil? No, by no means, since the capital invested will be amortized, with payment of the respective interests, and reexported to its country of origin, the amortization installments implying a certain reduction of the income subject to the income tax and, therefore, a real siphoning off of the national wealth. This is the typical technique of extortion and exploitation of underdeveloped countries which the international trusts employ to accumulate wealth at their expense and keep them subjugated and dependent.

When the bolivar was devalued and deprived of its gold parity with the dollar to reduce the *cost of investment,* the government created *appreciable advantages* not only for the oil trusts, but for all foreign investors, thereby encouraging and facilitating the colonialization of our country which we are now witnessing—the immediate future consequences of which are not yet fully realized by the Venezuelan people. The oil companies, in order to cover the same volume of expenditures in this country, had to bring in fewer dollars—an amount almost one-sixth less than was required before the devaluation—and therefore the nation received, as a general share in the exploitation of its oil, almost a sixth part less than it did before.

If Venezuela is to progress, the very real situation I have just described makes it unavoidable that prompt action be taken to overcome and eliminate this state of dependency. Among other practical steps which should immediately be taken, we must again insist that the revenues from oil be directly reinvested, under state control, in the building up of an indigenous and independent economy—a basic and integral agrarian reform and the installation of heavy industry. Any measure or scheme which involves prolonging or consolidating the state of dependency which foreign capital has imposed upon the nation should be energetically rejected. Examples of such plans are the so-called "service contracts" or "mixed companies," in which foreign capitalists are associated with the government through the participation in such entities as the Corporación Venezolana del Petroleo, the Corporación de Guayana, the Instituto de Petroquímica. By this action, the government merely renounces, in favor of foreign trusts, the direct exploitation by the state of Venezuela's irreplaceable natural resources and their better use on behalf of the nation. On January 17, 1966, before a conference of American journalists held in the Macuto Sheraton, the minister of mines and hydrocarbons left no doubt about this, when he stated: "All the service contracts will be signed through the Corporación Venezolana del Petroleo. They will not have the same forty-year term as the concessions, but, it is estimated, between fifteen and twenty years. Great prospects for oil development *are opened up for the country and for private industry* by means of this system which is being studied. . . ." (*El Nacional,* January 18, 1966.)

Meanwhile, in the same edition, the newspaper reported: ". . . the government of the United States informed that of Venezuela that the increase in its sugar quota is conditional upon improvement in coming years of Venezuelan purchases of manufactured products and machinery in the United States. . . ." This means that Venezuela must renounce, even more than it has already renounced, any attempt to expand and diversify its foreign markets by purchasing in other countries products of better or equal quality at prices lower than those set by the American exporters—another link in the chain of dependency and colonialization of our country. Before long, Dr. Colmenares Peraza and his associates in the Distribuidora de Azúcar, who are particularly interested in getting the United States to increase the quota for them, will begin an intense propaganda campaign, in order to demonstrate with doctored figures and wily arguments that Venezuela would find it very bad business to barter coffee, cacao, "surpluses" of rice, or other products for agricultural or industrial machinery produced in Italy, Poland, or any other European country.

Venezuela finds herself still in a situation of underdevelopment, shaken from one end of her territory to the other by the most violent contrasts, with the majority of her population producing nothing and living in wretched poverty, with a growing rate of unemployment and crime among both young people and adults. Yet we have shown that there is sufficient national capital to promote the economic development of the country. It would be no exaggeration to describe as fabulous the income the Treasury has enjoyed during the last twenty years from taxes and sale of the oil royalty. The obsession of sectors of the dominating classes—and also of corrupt sectors of the dominated classes—to appropriate to themselves and distribute among themselves this fabulous income, through proliferation of bureaucracy and increases in the "current public expenditure," has led to the misappropriation and squandering of those resources. They have been spent on imported goods and extravagant building projects, consequently prolonging the backward agrarian structure and accentuating our foreign dependency—the two factors that have been such obstacles to the independent economic development of our country and have delayed our integration into a nation.

Meanwhile new palliatives are being applied, usually with a view to vote-getting. This is not an arbitrary or a defeatist supposition. It is founded on the reality that the country is living on promises which the president will not be able to fulfill, because there is a limit to public indebtedness. For quite some time, the president has sought to camouflage the growing deficit in the national budget: he has contracted foreign loans to carry out public works on the national, state, and community level in order to balance the budget by removing these works from the expenditures column in the ledgers. But those loans will have to be amortized. So, besides being artificial, that balancing of the budget is placing on the shoulders of the next generations the burden of an enormous debt which will thwart still more the social and political development of Venezuela.

All Venezuelans have an equal right to enjoy a life of economic and spiritual well-being. Above all they have the imperative obligation—a frequently forgotten and belittled one —of watching out for and fighting for, today and always, the collective national security, to assure a worthy and secure future for the next generations. If the country continues to stumble along this path Venezuela's status will be little more than a Commonwealth territory of the United States.

Mass Immigration and

Modernization in Argentina

GINO GERMANI

INTRODUCTION

CONTEMPORARY Argentina cannot be understood without a thorough analysis of the role of immigration in its development. In the first place, immigration was a powerful factor in the total process of modernization. In the second place, the intensity and volume of immigration caused a substantial realignment of the population: economically, socially, and politically. In no other country did the proportion of adult foreigners reach the level that it did in Argentina, where for more than sixty years foreigners represented around 70 percent of the adult population in the capital city (which contained one-fifth to one-third of the total population of the country), and almost 50 percent in the provinces which were heavily populated and economically important.

Immigration resulted from a conscious effort by the elites to replace the old social structure inherited from colonial society with a structure inspired by the most advanced Western countries. This plan was based on three assumptions: (1) massive immigration; (2) universal and compulsory education; (3) import of capital, development of modern forms of agriculture and a livestock-breeding industry, and heavy investment in social-overhead capital, especially railways.

The principal aims of immigration were not only to populate an immense territory that had a low population density, but also to modify the *composition* of the population. Underlying this

314

aim are other aspects of the plan: education, and the expansion and modernization of the economy. To understand these aims it is necessary to remember the point of departure for the elites which conceived and carried out national organization. Only then can we understand the essential role that immigration played in the transformation of the country, although there were consequences which were unforeseen and undesired.

The revolution that initiated the successful movement for national independence was led by an elite inspired by the eighteenth-century Enlightenment. It was composed of creoles belonging to the upper urban class, especially from Buenos Aires. It was numerically very small, and its Western and modern (1800 style) outlook contrasted sharply with the traditional nature of the vast majority of the population, urban and rural (but mostly rural). The failure of the Independence elite to establish a modern state was basically the result of this contrast. The years of anarchy and autocracy did not fail to teach the modernizing elite a lesson. They saw that a modern national state could be established only on the basis of a transformed social structure and a change in its human composition. This attitude was reinforced by ideas about the role of racial factors and the national character. The intention of many was to modify the "national character" of the Argentine people in a way that would suit the political ideal of national organization to which these elites aspired. It was necessary to "Europeanize" the Argentine population, to produce a "regeneration of the races," to use Sarmiento's expression. Insurmountable limits in the psycho-social characteristics of the existing population made it all the more necessary to physically bring Europe to America (according to the well-known formulation by Alberdi).

A CENTURY OF FOREIGN IMMIGRATION

One of the first changes introduced by the new regime which replaced colonial rule in 1810 was to open the country to foreigners, thus eliminating the strict isolation enforced by the Spaniards in their colony. The governments of the following two decades stressed the need to attract immigrants. This was especially true of Rivadavia, who took concrete steps to create a stream of European immigration into the country. But these

316 # THE NATIONALIST PIVOT

attempts were doomed to failure for the same basic reasons which destroyed the dream of establishing a modern national state soon after formal independence had been reached. Only a limited number of immigrants arrived in Argentina during the first two decades of independence, and in the next thirty years the Rosas dictatorship practically reestablished the old colonial barrier against foreigners. In the second half of the century, after the downfall of the autocracy, immigration increased. The promotion of immigration became a formal function of the state, according to the 1853 Constitution. For nearly seventy years thereafter, European immigrants arrived in Argentina in a continuous stream, broken only occasionally by domestic events like the economic crisis of 1890 or by international upheavals like the First World War.

Of the nearly sixty million Europeans who emigrated overseas, Argentina received some 11 percent, a proportion much smaller than that of the United States, but still considerably larger than that of any other immigration country.[1] But what really makes Argentina a special case is that the six and a half million foreigners who arrived* between 1856 and 1930 found a very small local population, estimated at 1,200,000 in 1856. This meant that for many decades the proportion of the foreign born was higher than that of the natives within many important sectors of the population.

During the first decade after 1853 immigration did not exceed a few thousand per year. But as soon as some of the more pressing internal problems were solved, the inflow of foreigners increased to an annual average of nearly 180,000 in the decade preceding the First World War. After the war, large-scale immigration resumed, deterred only by the great depression of 1930. From 1947 to 1952 there was another large inflow of European immigration, after which it practically disappeared.

Thus, three major periods can be distinguished in overseas immigration. The first stage ended in 1930, the second stage

[1] The other countries which received the largest share of intercontinental immigration were Canada (8.7 percent), Brazil (7.4 percent), Australia (5.0 percent), New Zealand (1.0 percent), and South Africa (1.3 percent). The United States, Argentina, and the above-mentioned countries account for some 90 percent of the total immigration of the period. See Julius Isaac, *Economics of Migration*. New York: Oxford University Press, 1947, p. 62.

* This figure refers to arrivals. For net immigration see Table I.

extends through the thirties and most of the forties, and the last
stage corresponds to the period of post-World War II. It must
be noted that after the end of the first stage another stream of
foreign immigration was added: immigration from the neighboring countries, especially Bolivia, Paraguay, and Chile. This
process became more important as the demand for industrial
labor increased. But in many ways this stream resembles the
mass internal migrations, which also occurred in response to
industrial development.[2]

In Argentina, as in other immigration countries, not all the
immigrants remained. A certain number of them returned to
their native lands or emigrated to other countries. Unfortunately, available immigration statistics do not distinguish between permanent and transitory arrivals or departures. The
figures for net overseas immigration included in Table I result
from the difference between total departures and total arrivals
for European passengers traveling second and third class.

TABLE I

NET OVERSEAS IMMIGRATION IN ARGENTINA.
1857–1965.

Years	Net immigration (in thousands)
1857–1860	11
1861–1870	77
1871–1880	85
1881–1890	638
1891–1900	320
1901–1910	1,120
1911–1920	269
1921–1930	878
1931–1940	73
1941–1950	386
1951–1960	316
1961–1965	206

Sources: Alessandro Bunge, "Ochenta y cinco,"
Revista de economía Argentina, 1944; and information provided by the Dirección Nacional
de Estadísticas y Censos.

[2] Gino Germani, "Inquiry into the Social Effects of Urbanization in a
Working-class Sector of Greater Buenos Aires," in Philip Hauser (ed.),
Urbanization in Latin America. Paris: UNESCO, 1961.

It must be noted that the idea of permanent immigration is difficult to define. It is well known that most of the overseas emigrants to South America, especially in the period under discussion, did not intend to become permanent citizens of the new country. Their chief motivation was to save enough money to return to their native villages and buy land.[3] This motive, which affected the assimilation of the immigrants, made difficult the interpretation of migration statistics. In any case, it must be noted that the "return" movement included, in addition to seasonal immigrants and temporary visitors to native lands, a number of permanent returns. These last were probably of two kinds: those returning because of their inability to adjust to social, economic, and personal conditions; and those returning because they had earned the money they desired. After the First

TABLE II

NUMBER OF FOREIGN PASSENGERS DEPARTED FOR EVERY 100
ADMITTED (SECOND AND THIRD CLASS).

Years	Departed passengers
1857–1913	40
1914–1920	151
1921–1930	38
1931–1940	67
1941–1946	79
1947–1950	14
1951–1958	56

Sources: Alessandro Bunge, "Ochenta y cinco," *Revista de economía Argentina,* 1944; and information provided by the Dirección Nacional de Estadísticas y Censos.

World War seasonal immigration disappeared, and the high rate of departures since 1951 corresponds to the last cycle of overseas immigrants, whose assimilation became increasingly difficult.

Almost half of the incoming immigrants were Italian, and a third were Spanish. A fifth of the total were Polish, followed numerically by Russians, French, and Germans. Italian immigration maintained its predominance throughout almost the

[3] José Luis Romero, *Las ideas políticas en Argentina.* Mexico: Fondo de Cultura Económica, 1956, p. 176; and Domingo F. Sarmiento, *Condición del extranjero en América.* Buenos Aires: A. B. Sarmiento, 1900, *Obras completas,* Volume V, pp. xxxvi, 73, and *passim.*

whole period. In the decade following the First World War there was a notable Polish immigration which continued during the period of low immigration, becoming then the largest national group up to 1940. Russian immigration was high between the end of the nineteenth century and the beginning of the twentieth, and again in the decade following the First World War. In this same period there are major immigrations from Germany and other Eastern European countries. This inflow included a large proportion of Jews.

TABLE III

NET IMMIGRATION BY PRINCIPAL NATIONALITIES. 1857–1958.

Years	Italian	Spanish	Polish	Others	Total
1857–1860	17	21	—	—	100
1861–1870	65	21	—	14	100
1871–1880	44	29	—	27	100
1881–1890	57	21	—	22	100
1891–1900	62	18	—	20	100
1901–1910	45	45	—	10	100
1911–1920	12	68	—	20	100
1921–1930	42	26	13	19	100
1931–1940	33	—	58	9	100
1941–1950	66	29	4	1	100
1951–1958	58	34	—	8	100
1957–1958	46	33	4	17	100

Sources: Alessandro Bunge, "Ochenta y cinco," *Revista de economía Argentina,* 1944; and information provided by the Dirección Nacional de Estadísticas y Censos.

THE DEMOGRAPHIC IMPACT OF IMMIGRATION

In 1869, Argentina had a population of a little more than 1,700,000; in 1960 it had become more than 20,000,000, thus growing almost twelve times in ninety years. Immigration decisively contributed to this extraordinary expansion. The proportion of foreigners to the total population does not accurately indicate the immigrants' contribution to national growth. For example, the proportion of immigrants in the labor force was especially large.

A number of demographers and other social scientists have in the past challenged the commonsense notion that immigration

320 | ▌ THE NATIONALIST PIVOT

always involves an increase in the receiving population.[4] Malthus maintained that immigration would produce no lasting effect, since the available or potential resources would put an absolute limit on population increase. By different routes other authors have reached the same conclusions as Malthus, and in the United States a "substitution theory" was widely discussed.[5] It is recognized now that the effects of immigration are quite complex. Most of these hypotheses cannot survive the test of facts, even though they continued to circulate as ideological arguments against immigration. In any case, nobody has contested the essential role of immigration in a sparsely populated country like Argentina.

An estimate formulated by Mortara suggests the contribution of immigrants and their children to the Argentine population. Table IV indicates that the joint contribution of immigrants and their descendants to the national population exceeds the natural increase of native population. In this sense Argentina represents

TABLE IV

COMPONENTS OF POPULATION GROWTH IN FOUR AMERICAN
COUNTRIES. 1841–1940.

Countries	Native natural increase	Percent	Immigration	Percent	Immigrants' natural increase	Percent
All America	163.0	70.9	36.0	15.6	31.0	13.5
Brazil	28.6	81.0	3.3	9.4	3.4	9.6
Argentina	5.2	41.9	3.6	29.0	3.6	29.0
Canada	8.0	78.4	1.0	9.8	1.2	11.8
United States	67.7	59.1	25.0	21.8	21.8	19.0

Summarized from Giorgio Mortara, "Pesquisas sobre populaçoes Americanas," *Estudos Brasileiros de demografia*, Monografía No. 3, July, 1947.

an extreme case, even in comparison with the United States. With regard to the other Latin American states, it is clear that immigration made a crucial contribution to population growth. During the period 1869–1959, Argentine population grew more than ten times, while the population of another immigrant

[4] Julius Isaac, *op. cit.*, Chapter VI.

[5] Joseph J. Spengler, "Effects Produced in Receiving Countries by Pre-1939 Immigration," in Brinley Thomas (ed.), *Economics of International Migration*. London: Macmillan, 1958, p. 22 ff.

country like Brazil increased six times, and Chile, where immigration was practically nonexistent, needed 110 years for its population to grow less than four times. Mortara has estimated that without immigration the population of Argentina in 1940 would have been 6,100,000 instead of over 13,000,000.[6]

The demographic impact of immigration was increased by the geographic concentration of the foreigners. About 90 percent of them settled in the Buenos Aires metropolitan area and in the central provinces of the country, a region which includes no more than one-third of the national territory. This concentration was further intensified because most immigrants went to the cities. The urban counties contained a large majority of the foreign population. After 1914 this tendency was reinforced, and in the last Census 68 percent of the immigrants lived in the big cities.

TABLE V

GEOGRAPHIC DISTRIBUTION OF THE FOREIGN BORN. 1869–1960.

Years	Buenos Aires metropolitan area* Percent	Provinces of Córdoba, Buenos Aires, Entre Ríos, Mendoza, Santa Fé, La Pampa Percent	Rest of country Percent	Total
1869	52	38	10	100
1895	39	52	9	100
1914	42	48	10	100
1947	51	35	14	100
1960	57	27	16	100

Source: Argentine National Census.
* Includes population in the rural sector of the area.

Finally, the proportion of foreigners in certain key sectors of the population was increased by the age and sex composition of European immigration. Over 71 percent of the immigrants were male, and about 65 percent were adults between twenty and sixty years of age. This proportion did not change significantly

[6] Giorgio Mortara, "Pesquisas sobre populaçoes Americanas," *Estudos Brasileiros de demografia,* Monografía No. 3. Rio de Janeiro: Fundação Getulio Vargas, 1947.

throughout the period of mass immigration.[7] This demographic concentration greatly affected the age and sex composition of the Argentine population. The most important economic and

TABLE VI

DISTRIBUTION OF THE FOREIGN-BORN POPULATION BY URBAN AND RURAL COUNTIES.*

Counties including cities of population specified in 1947 Census.	1869 Percent	1895 Percent	1914 Percent	1947 Percent	1960 Percent
Buenos Aires metropolitan area	52	39	42	51	57
100,000 and more	5	10	12	12	11
50,000–99,000	3	3	3	3	2
2,000–9,999	34	42	39	30	25
Less than 2,000	6	6	4	4	5
TOTAL	100	100	100	100	100

Source: Argentine National Census.
* The counties were classified on the basis of the size of the major cities they included according to the 1947 Census. Each category of counties also includes a proportion of "rural" population (living in centers of less than 2,000 inhabitants). Such proportion was very small (in 1947) in the first two categories, but it was increasingly larger in the other categories.

social consequences were the great expansion of the labor force and an extremely high proportion of foreigners among adult males. The demographic effects of immigration on sex and age composition began to wear off after 1930, but in the last Census (1960) they were still visible. In 1960 most of the immigrants were concentrated in the older age groups. Two-thirds of the foreigners were more than forty years old, and nearly one-third were over sixty.

IMPACT ON THE ECONOMIC AND SOCIAL STRUCTURE

The role of immigration in the rapid economic growth of Argentina can hardly be overemphasized. However, it is very difficult to separate this role from its general context. Immigra-

7 Walter F. Willcox (ed.), *International Migrations.* Vol. 1. New York: National Bureau of Economic Research, 1929, p. 540.

TABLE VII

SEX RATIO AND AGE COMPOSITION IN ARGENTINA. 1869–1960.

	Sex ratio			Percent 14–64 years old		
Census	Total population	Native born	Foreign born	Total population	Native population	Foreign population
1869	106	94	251	56.5	—	—
1895	112	90	173	57.9	48.6	85.0
1914	116	98	171	61.4	50.3	87.4
1947	105	100	138	65.2	61.9	83.7
1960	101	99	110	63.0*	61.3*	75.0*

Source: Argentine Census.
* Estimates on the basis of a sample of the 1960 Census.

tion provided the labor needed to occupy the unexploited land and to develop the agricultural production which transformed Argentina from an importing country in 1870 to one of the principal world exporters. At the same time immigration supplied the manpower to build a railroad system, public works, and housing, and to expand the commercial activities and the service sectors. Finally, it was the immigrant population which provided most of the labor and entrepreneurship in the beginnings of industrial development. But relative political stability and heavy capital investment were needed in order for this role to be carried out.

No less important was the contribution of foreign immigration to modification of the social structure. The system of stratification and many traditional social values were sharply affected by the overwhelming mass of foreign population. The old creole stock was replaced by a new type which has not yet been clearly defined.

Immigrant participation in economic areas varied a great deal. Such participation was not only a function of their original skills but also of the kind of socioeconomic structure they found in the country and the conditions under which economic expansion occurred.

Most immigrants came from the poorer strata of their native lands. About 41 percent were peasants, 23 percent were unskilled workers, and about 36 percent had various manual and non-manual skills. Up to 1890, more than 70 percent of the immigrants were peasants, but this percentage decreased sharply in following years. It is known that even those who were originally peasants did not remain in the rural areas. A considerable proportion went to the cities and worked in secondary or tertiary activities.

TABLE VIII

FARM AND NONFARM OCCUPATIONS OF THE
IMMIGRANTS. 1857–1954.

Years	Farm Percent	Nonfarm Percent	Total Percent
1857–1870	76	24	100
1871–1890	73	27	100
1891–1910	48	52	100
1911–1924	30	70	100
1925–1939	39	61	100
1940–1945	20	80	100
1946–1954	41	59	100

Sources: Alessandro Bunge, "Ochenta y cinco," *Revista de economía Argentina*, 1944; and information provided by the Dirección Nacional de Estadísticas y Censos.

The populating of the countryside through rural immigration was limited by the traditional distribution of land ownership and by the methods of the successive governments in subdividing and allocating the remaining public lands. Two facts must be recorded: throughout the history of the country, property tended to be concentrated among a relatively small number of families, with the consequent predominance of latifundium. These procedures caused serious difficulties in the realization of one of the declared aims of massive immigration: the settlement of European population in the deserted or semideserted rural areas of the country. This settlement was successful to a certain extent, but it was undoubtedly much smaller than what might have occurred if there had not been a predominance of latifundium.

In the second place, the traditional system of land distribution did not ensure peasant ownership of the land. For the whole massive immigration period, the so-called "colonization" was carried out through the intervention of commercial companies or individuals who took over the subdivision of the land and the organization of the "colonies," making these operations lucrative through what amounted to selfish speculation.

TABLE IX
FOREIGN-BORN PER EVERY 100 PERSONS IN PRIMARY, SECONDARY, AND TERTIARY ACTIVITIES. 1895–1947.

Activities	1895	1914	1947
Primary	30	37	18
Secondary	46	53	26
Tertiary	42	30	22
Total occupied population	38	47	22

Source: Argentine Census.

In many cases, the owners of vastly extensive properties in the more favored areas preferred to exploit their lands by means of renting or similar devices, rather than transferring their property.[8] We should also bear in mind that land exploitation often favored the permanence of large units; this applies not only to cattle breeding but also to extensive farming. Finally, insofar as agricultural and cattle-breeding activities developed, the land became increasingly valuable, thus making it less accessible to immigrants, who continued to arrive in great numbers. Very few immigrants acquired property after 1900.

[8] The diffusion of the system had many causes, but the interests of the big landowners, coupled with the nearly complete lack of official support for a real colonization, are the basic factors. Other complementary causes have also been mentioned. At the beginning the rent was generally low and some immigrants, even if they had the required capital, were therefore more inclined to rent. Given the high market demand, the immigrant was induced to produce as much as possible and preferred to rent large areas of land rather than buy smaller ones. This must be related to the immigrants' basic aim to get rich and return to the homeland. At the same time, the landowner found it much more convenient to rent than to sell, since the price of the land was rapidly increasing. Also, many landowners preferred cattle breeding to agriculture, and the renting system allowed them to convert from one to the other while at the same time improving the condition of the land and benefiting from its increasing value. One of the most negative aspects of the renting system was the duration of the contracts, mostly less than three years. This caused a kind of "nomad agriculture," and a very high instability of the peasant, with all its economic and social consequences. On this problem see Manuel Bejarano, "La Política Colonizadora en la Provincia de Buenos Aires," Instituto de Sociología y Centro de Historia Social, Universidad de Buenos Aires, 1962, especially paragraph two. Also see Mark Jefferson, *The Peopling of Argentine Pampas.* New York: American Geographic Society, 1926, pp. 114–15 and 141 ff. The classic book on the high concentration of land ownership is Jacinto Oddone's *La burguesía terrateniente Argentina.* Buenos Aires (no publisher indicated): 1930.

This meant that only a minority of the European peasants could settle in the country on the stable basis of land ownership. A considerable number were able to secure land only by renting, and the majority finally settled in the cities, returned to their own lands, or emigrated to other countries. Moreover, the limitations and conditions under which the immigrant appropriation of land occurred caused a great deal of instability for the peasant and his family. This was particularly true of the renters, for whom this situation meant almost always the last stage of their social ascent, since they never became owners of the land they worked on, and moreover were frequently displaced from one area to another in search of better conditions.[9]

In summary, we can say that, while the tremendous increase in agricultural production was mainly the result of European immigration, such participation rarely developed into ownership. Frequently it was subjected to the conditions established by the titleholders of the land, who either rented it to immigrants or hired them as laborers or managers. In the cattle-breeding sector the immigrants' participation was even lower. The development of this sector began earlier. Because of its nature and traditions, its expansion and modernization was undertaken by the big Argentine landowners. Also, labor was provided

TABLE X

PROPORTION OF FOREIGNERS IN SOME OCCUPATIONAL CATEGORIES IN THE PRIMARY SECTOR. 1914.

Occupational categories	Foreigners per every 100 persons in each category
Landed property owners in general*	10
Owners of cattle-breeding operations	22
Renters of cattle-breeding operations	34
Administrators, directors, managers of cattle-breeding operations (including owners and renters)	44
Administrators, directors, managers of agricultural operations (including owners and renters)	57

Source: Third National Census.
* Excluding the city of Buenos Aires.

[9] Gastón Gori, *El pan nuestro*. Buenos Aires: Raigal, 1958, p. 84.

by the native-born population, traditionally related to this kind of occupation. The rural creole workers, who did not adapt to agricultural work, either migrated to the cities or gathered in the *estancias* (cattle ranches), devoted to stock breeding.

These circumstances explain the varying participation of foreigners in the different economic activities. The figures given in Table X, although fragmentary, give a clear illustration of the foreigners' participation in the different levels of ownership and control of the primary sectors. Only 10 percent of the landowners and no more than 22 percent of the owners of stockbreeding operations were immigrants. The proportion of the foreign-born approximates the national average in the labor force only in the Census category, which lumps together administrators, managers, and renters. In the agricultural enterprises foreigners reach higher proportions than in the national average (but still below the proportion among the owners of commerce or industry).

TABLE XI

PROPORTION OF FOREIGNERS IN SOME OCCUPATIONAL
CATEGORIES IN THE SECONDARY AND TERTIARY SECTORS.
1895–1914.

Occupational and economic category	1895	1914
Owners of industry*	81	66
Owners in commerce†	74	74
Personnel in commerce (workers and white collars)*	57	53
Personnel in industry (workers and white collars)*	60	50
Liberal professions	53	45
Public administration†	30	18
Persons in artisan and domestic activities†	18	27
Business administration†	63	51
Domestic service workers†	25	38

Sources: * Second and Third National Census: special census.
† Second and Third National Census: population census.

The result of the agrarian policy which conditioned foreign immigration was not so much to populate the extensive semideserted rural areas as to create an abundant urban labor force and on a lesser scale a rural one, since a minority of the landless immigrants remained in the countryside as salaried peons. The growth of the cities, the emergence of industry, and the resulting transformation of the social structure were consequences of this process, and in turn originated new social conditions affecting the ruling elites. All these circumstances contributed to shaping the geographic and economic distribution of foreigners.

Immigrant participation in certain sectors was preponderant. As we have seen, in the secondary and tertiary sectors foreign participation in the cities was always higher than within the total labor force. The rates included in Table XI indicate the varying proportions of immigrants in some activities. According to the 1895 Census, the conduct of about 80 percent of industry and trade was in the hands of foreigners. Among salaried personnel the proportion was lower, but always higher than in the national average. The native born predominated in artisan activities, other domestic industries, the public bureaucracy, and domestic services.

The data presented in Table XI are too incomplete to offer a basis for systematic observation. Nevertheless, the figures are useful at least to illustrate the orientation of immigration and its distribution in the different strata of the occupational structure. Apparently, in the process of Argentine society's transformation, foreigners were preferentially placed in the emerging strata. Entrepreneurs, workers, and managers in strategic areas of industry and commerce were at the root of modernization. They predominated especially in the middle class and the new urban industrial proletariat, both categories belonging to the new economic structure which was replacing traditional society. It was precisely in the older economic activities that the native born continued to predominate, as well as in activities directly related to government operations.

From the economic point of view the recent industrial activities were only of secondary importance. A larger proportion of industry was directly linked with agriculture and stock breeding. This sector, some 40 percent of the total industrial production, included the industries devoted to perishable goods and the meat-packing plants, which must be considered the only "large scale" industries of that time. The remaining industry was devoted mostly to the production of inexpensive and low-quality consumer goods for the lower strata, while the market for the elite and the upper middle class was mostly supplied by imports.

Many of the industrial enterprises were small,[10] and did not
represent a key sector in the national economy of the time, even
if they supplied two-thirds of the total consumption of the
internal market.[11] Nonetheless, the growing number of local
industrial enterprises eventually played an essential role in
the transformation of Argentine society. The rapid growth of the
population and the general economic expansion stimulated the
internal market. This resulted in a great increase in the number
of industrial and business enterprises and a growth of public
services. This expansion not only absorbed immigrant labor but
stimulated a crucial change in the social structure: urbanization
and the rise of a large middle class. By 1895 the urban population had increased to 37 percent, and by 1914 the majority of
the inhabitants lived in urban centers. As noted earlier, this
increase was mostly due to the immigrants, whose proportion
was about 50 percent of the population of all ages in the
Buenos Aires metropolitan area and more than one-third in the
other large cities.

At the same time, the structure of stratification had been
drastically modified. The two-strata system of the mid-nine-
teenth century was replaced by a much more complex structure, in which the middle layers increased from less than 11
percent of the population in 1869, to 25 percent in 1895, and to
more than 30 percent in 1914. Within this emerging middle
class the proportion of foreign born was larger than in the total
labor force. This was especially true of industry, commerce, and
services.

While these estimates are imprecise, they illustrate the importance of foreign immigration in the modernization of the
stratification system.

This process, on the other hand, did not involve only the rise
of a substantial middle class. It also stimulated the transformation of the lower class by causing the emergence of a modern

[10] In 1913 only one-half of the industrial enterprises could be considered
"factory industries"; these enterprises concentrated some 60 percent of
the capital, 80 percent of the production, and approximately 65 percent
of the workers. The average number of workers per plant was 8.4; in
1947 it had risen to 14.7. See Adolfo Dorfman, *Evolución industrial
Argentina*. Buenos Aires: Losada, 1942, pp. 16–17. See also Gino
Germani, *Estructura social de la Argentina*. Buenos Aires: Raigal, 1955,
p. 130.
[11] Adolfo Dorfman, *op. cit.*, pp. 21–22.

TABLE XII

PERCENTAGE OF FOREIGN BORN IN DIFFERENT OCCUPATIONAL
STRATA. 1895–1914.

Occupational strata	(a) 1895	(a) 1914	(b) 1960
Middle strata in secondary and tertiary sectors	59	51	16
Middle strata in primary sector	43	45	16
Lower strata in secondary and tertiary sector	39	48	15
Lower strata in primary sector	25	35	15

(a) Computed from an unpublished reclassification of the 1895 and 1914 Argentine Census prepared for the Institute of Sociology of the University of Buenos Aires by Ruth Sautú and Susana Torrado.

(b) Estimates on the basis of a sample of the 1960 Census.

urban proletariat, predominantly foreign. This process did not affect the occupational structure alone. When we speak of *middle classes* and *urban proletariat,* we are also referring to attitudes, ideologies, aspirations, and self-identifications. The reality of this transition is clearly expressed in the political events of the period corresponding to the appearance of middle-class political parties, and the typical "protest" movements of the rising urban proletariat. But, as we will indicate later on, the overwhelmingly foreign origin of both the modern middle class and the modern urban workers was itself a basic factor in the political development of the country.

Between 1870 and 1910 a great part of the transition from a predominantly traditional structure to a more advanced pattern was completed, at least in the Buenos Aires metropolitan area and in the provinces of the Littoral region (which included two-thirds of the national population). However, those geographical areas and social groups less affected by foreign immigration tended to maintain archaic traits. The persistence of these internal contradictions had a lasting effect on the subsequent economic and social development of the country. It is true that the landowning elite was not an entirely closed class, even at that time; its origins were fairly recent, and a number of "new" families were able to reach the upper social level. However, regardless of the degree of fluidity within this group, the important fact is that the elite became increasingly concerned with maintaining the economic and social structure favorable to its interests. This meant strictly limiting the process of modernization which the elite itself had initiated. While its attempt to completely control the process was doomed to failure, it managed to maintain a key economic position and continued to orient the economy to the exporting of primary products. For another thing, the existence of a large proportion of the population within the less developed regions, and still mostly traditional, involved the problem of its future mobilization and integration into the modern pattern. Both problems were to acquire a dramatic expression after 1930.

The rapid rate of the transition after 1930, especially the expansion of the middle class, made social mobility an important factor in shaping the historical process. A large majority of immigrants belonged to the lower strata of their societies. Table XIII does not give a precise measure of the social composition of the immigrants, but at least it suggests the kind of people who were arriving by the thousands in those years. Only very few immigrants had middle-class backgrounds. As a result, the

TABLE XIII

SOCIO-OCCUPATIONAL STRATA OF IMMIGRANTS, ACCORDING TO
THEIR OCCUPATION DECLARED AT THE MOMENT OF
ADMITTANCE TO THE COUNTRY. 1857–1925.

Socio-occupational categories	1857– 1870	1871– 1899	1900– 1920	1921– 1924	Total: 1857– 1924
Employees in business, industry, services, agriculture; free professionals, technicians; White collar and kindred occupations	4.4	5.4	8.6	13.4	7.2
Skilled and unskilled workers, day laborers and kindred occupations	95.6	94.6	91.4	86.6	92.1

Source: *Resumen estadístico del movimiento migratorio,* Ministerio de Agricultura. Buenos Aires, Argentina, 1925.

new Argentine middle class, so heavily recruited from among the immigrants, was mostly of lower-class origin. Between 1895 and 1914 no less than two-thirds of the middle classes were of popular-class origin; that is, they were formed by individuals who either had begun their occupational careers as manual workers, or were sons of manual-worker fathers.[12] Social mobility became a normal pattern in Argentine society (or at least in the central areas), and this trait was accompanied by corresponding attitude changes and ideological expressions. Social mobility must be considered an important factor not only in explaining the process of absorption of the foreign immigrants, but also in explaining essential aspects of the Argentine political and social history in the twentieth century.

The Assimilation of the Foreign Population and Its Impact on the Culture

The problem that Argentina had to confront between 1870 and 1930 is probably without precedent in other immigration countries. Even the United States, which received the largest share of the great international migrations, was never in a similar situation; the proportion of foreigners in its total population and in the annual migratory stream, although much higher in *absolute* terms, was *relatively* much lower than in Argentina. Moreover, the size of the native-born population was large enough to ensure the possibility of real assimilation; also, the stability of the existing social structure was much stronger, which made it better equipped to resist the migratory impact. In the United States the maximum proportion of foreign-born population was 14.7 percent in 1910, and after 1920 it decreased steadily to the present 5.4 percent. In Argentina immigrants were more than one-fourth of the total population in the last decade of the nineteenth century. This proportion grew to nearly 30 percent just before the First World War, and it stayed as high as 23 percent until 1930. In 1960 it was still nearly 13 percent; that is, a proportion quite similar to the highest ever reached in the United States. But even these figures fail to suggest the immigrants' impact on Argentine society. As we have seen, the demographic concentration for certain ages and for the male sex, coupled with the regional and urban concentration, increased the proportion of foreigners in the more strategic areas of the country and in most of the important sectors of the

[12] Gino Germani, "La movilidad social en la Argentina," Appendix to Spanish translation of Reinhard Bendix and Seymour M. Lipset, *La movilidad social en la sociedad industrial*. Buenos Aires: Eudeba, 1964.

TABLE XIV
TOTAL POPULATION AND PERCENTAGE OF FOREIGN BORN IN
ARGENTINA AND THE UNITED STATES. 1810–1960.

	Total population (millions)		Percent foreign born in total population	
Years	United States	Argentina	United States	Argentina
1810	7.2	.4	11.1	*
1850	23.2	1.3	9.5	*
1870	39.8	1.7†	14.1	12.1†
1890	62.9	*	14.6	*
1895	—	4.0	—	*
1900	76.0	*	13.6	*
1910	92.0	*	14.7	*
1914	—	7.9	—	29.9
1920	105.7	8.8	13.2	24.0
1930	122.8	11.7	11.6	23.5
1950	150.7	17.0	6.8	15.8
1960	150.7	20.0	5.4	12.8

Sources: Brinley Thomas (ed.), *Economics of International Migration.*
London: Macmillan, 1958, p. 136, Francisco De Aparicio y Horacio
Difrieri (eds.), *La Argentina, suma de geografía.* Buenos Aires: Peuser,
1961, p. 94; and *Boletines de la dirección nacional de estadísticas y censos*
(various years).
* No data available.
† 1869 Census.

TABLE XV
FOREIGN BORN OVER TWENTY YEARS OLD (BOTH SEXES) FOR
EVERY 100 PERSONS OF THE SAME AGE AND SEX. 1869–1947.

Years	Buenos Aires City	Central area. Provinces of Buenos Aires, Córdoba, Entre Ríos, Mendoza, La Pampa	Peripheral area. All other states and territories
1869	67	*	*
1895	74	44	11
1914	72	51	20
1947	37	23	16

Source: Argentine Census.
* No data.

population. Immigrants comprised from two-thirds to three-quarters of the total adult population in Buenos Aires City for more than the sixty years after 1869. In the remaining provinces of the central area, this proportion remained close to 50 percent. If we consider only the adult males, we see that for many decades there were in Buenos Aires more than four foreigners for every native-born Argentine, and in the central area the immigrants were considerably more numerous than the natives. We do not have specific rates for the inter-censal years, but we can guess that this proportion must have continued during the early thirties, especially before the mass internal migrations from the peripheral regions began to accelerate the Argentinization of the population.

TABLE XVI

ARGENTINE AND FOREIGN MALES TWENTY YEARS AND OVER. 1869–1947 (THOUSANDS).

Years	Buenos Aires City		Central provinces of Buenos Aires, Córdoba, Entre Ríos, Mendoza, La Pampa	
	Argentine	Foreign	Argentine	Foreign
	males	males	males	males
1869	12	48	*	*
1895	42	174	287	309
1914	119	404	557	752
1947	614	433	2,115	747

Source: Argentine Census.
* No data.

We insist on the sheer size of the proportion because it introduces a factor rarely considered in studies on the assimilation of foreign immigrants. Usually one speaks of assimilation as a concept presupposing a native population with the capacity to assimilate the incoming groups. But how well will the host society be able to maintain its identity if the incoming population is larger than the existing one, and if the absolute size of the latter is very small in the first place? We suggest that, other things being equal, these two quantitative aspects definitely limit the absorption capacity of the receiving society. There are other, equally important conditions which affect the process:

the power structure of the receiving society; the immigrants'
position within the structure; their location in the stratification
systems of both the native and receiving societies, the differences between immigrant and native cultures, and their relative
prestige; the degree of segregation of the immigrant population
in relation to the receiving society and to its different sectors
and strata; the degree of cultural homogeneity of the immigrants; their solidarity; their attitudes; their level of education;
the strength of their original national identifications; the degree
of acceptance they find in the new country; and especially the
degree of social mobility they experience in the receiving country. Only in the case of a heterogeneous and subordinated
immigrant population, characterized by a much lower cultural
level than that of the host society and placed under conditions
of severe segregation, could a smaller native population limit
the impact of immigration on the existing culture and social
structure. An illustration of this extreme case could be a large
slave population of immigrant origin placed in a society composed of a smaller number of free individuals. But even in this
example the receiving society would eventually change in response to the immigrants' impact. In Argentina conditions were
not this extreme. The immigrants were neither nationally nor
culturally homogeneous, but there was at least one extremely
large national group. The degree of their identification with
their country of origin varied, but it was probably fairly low
because many immigrants came from backward and traditional
cultures. However, they did not regard the receiving country as
a superior culture to be imitated. Although many were illiterate,
they introduced new skills and new attitudes toward economic
activities. Also, the fact of having emigrated involved a rupture
with their traditional past. They had been released from that
past and were now "mobilized," even if their basic motivation
was not to settle permanently in the new country but to get rich,
return to the native village, and buy land. In fact, their attempts
to fulfill their purposes set them on the path which led them to
abandon their traditional mores. And this change was irreversible: unconsciously and unwillingly, the immigrants were the
bearers of modernization.[13] On the other hand, they soon
gained a better social and economic position than the native
born of the lower strata. At the same time, however, they
remained practically excluded from positions of economic

[13] Domingo F. Sarmiento, *op. cit.*, pp. 229–30, 64 ff., and *passim*.

power, which as we have seen remained firmly in the hands of the elite.

After the deluge of immigration there was still an Argentina: the country did not lose its identity. But the old and new elements had been fused and transformed. A new country emerged, and is still emerging, since the historical process set in motion by the mass nineteenth-century immigration cannot be considered complete.

In Argentina the immigration process implied the virtual disappearance (in the areas of immigrant settlement) of the existing native social types and the partial destruction of the social structure which corresponded to them. In their place emerged a new type, still not well defined, and a new structure.

Among the rural population, which made up its large majority, the typical native had adapted to the occupations and social conditions of the countryside during the colonial epoch. Many of his psychological features were those that characterize the Spaniards. The image of the *gaucho,* who later became a national myth, may illustrate the prevailing values of rural society prior to the impact of immigration. The *gaucho* was a kind of *peón* on horseback. He worked at intervals, never having a permanent occupation or home. His personal life was characterized by freedom. He could move freely in the immense open spaces of the pampas, which at that time had no limits fixed by wire fences. His work depended only on his ability, on his talent as a horseman, and on his courage. These were the values which identified him to himself and to others. There were no habits of regularity, frugality, foresight, or rational calculation in his behavior. On the contrary, these were considered negative characteristics, opposed to the manly ideal. He had no aspiration for social ascent, no special desire to acquire land. Because the *gaucho* sometimes worked as a *peón* in the *estancia,* he has quite often been confused with the ordinary peasant, which he was not. However, there is little doubt that most of his traits were shared by the rural inhabitants who formed a majority of the population. Their relation to the masters of the *estancias* was wholly particularistic, and did not correspond at all to the relationship between a salaried worker and his employer. Insofar as the master displayed some of the traits valued by the *gaucho,* especially personal courage, physical strength, and ability, the latter felt a personal adherence to him, based on sentiments of fidelity, loyalty, and admiration.

GINO GERMANI ▯ 337

The material aspects of the culture were a function of the
necessities of a life based on livestock, technically and socially
at a primitive level. Agriculture and sedentary work in general
was considered inferior; work itself was despised. In the rural
areas, and probably in the lower strata in the towns and urban
centers as well, the population lacked national identification;
their loyalty was mainly local, and it was usually personified in
the *caudillo* (political-military strong man). This, of course,
was the social basis of the dissolution of the "unitarian state"
which occurred soon after Independence.[14]

Thus Argentina in the middle of the nineteenth century,
before the beginning of mass overseas immigration, was permeated by traditional values and behavior patterns. Its more
modern sectors were found in the urban elites; that is, in a small
proportion of its inhabitants sharply contrasting with the rural
masses and also with the lower urban strata. The overseas
immigrants were the bearers of different attitudes toward agriculture, saving, economic life, and mobility aspirations. Partly
because of a different cultural heritage and partly as an effect of
displacement, they became a powerful impulse toward modernization. Certainly, even if the majority of the foreigners had little
or no education, a considerable number of professionals, technicians, and skilled workers did arrive, and they were able to
provide most of the specialized personnel for the many new
activities required by modernization in all fields. But even the
uneducated peasants became innovators. In the Argentine pampas, for example, they showed a much greater flexibility and
creativity than did the local population.[15]

Under the impact of immigration the old cultural patterns
practically dissolved. Objects of previously great material value
and symbolic meaning, like the horse, lost all importance.
Similarly, many aspects of the traditional culture, such as
clothes, tools, vehicles, food, housing, furniture, forms of lei-
sure, were totally replaced or profoundly transformed. These
changes were mainly due to material necessity, not merely to a

[14] The literature on the *gaucho* is very extensive; for evaluation and
synthesis, see Ezequiel Martínez Estrada, *Muerte y transfiguración de
Martin Fierro*. Mexico: Fondo de Cultura Económica, 1948, Vol. I,
pp. 237–92; see also, for contrasts with the immigrants, Gastón Gori, *op.
cit.*, and Gastón Gori, *La pampa sin gaucho*. Buenos Aires: Raigal,
1952.
[15] Domingo F. Sarmiento, *op. cit.*, pp. 64 ff.

wish to emulate. Each immigrant group imprinted its characteristics on the different aspects of the material and nonmaterial
culture, and in this way innovation, implicit or explicit, was
stamped with the cultural forms imported from Europe.

According to Gori, the immigrant did not easily shed his
European culture. On the contrary,

> . . . he tried to reaffirm it, especially the Swiss and German,
> through family training and the schooling of his children. He
> had staked his sights more on the consulate of his country as an
> agent of legality than in the formal representatives of Argentine
> authority, whom he mistrusted, even while being forced to accept.

According to Gori and others, the immigrant generally
spoke his mother tongue, read newspapers in his native tongue,
and maintained organizations to encourage ties with the fatherland. Whenever he could, he chose a wife of his own nationality. Sometimes, in the beginning, the immigrant agricultural
colonies chose their own authorities, and quite often geographic
isolation made such colonies akin to foreign fortresses in the
middle of the nation.[16]

In the cities the isolation and segregation which prevailed in
the rural colonies was absent, although there was, particularly
in Buenos Aires, some ecological segregation by nationality.
The term *colony* was applied to a native group residing in an
urban center; this term also referred to settlements of immigrants of any origin throughout the country. They developed
separate communities with advanced organizational structure
which included newspapers, schools, hospitals, and all kinds of
voluntary associations connected with their country of origin.

In some cases the actions of foreign governments through
these associations went farther than the attitudes of the emigrants would have justified. In the case of the Italians and the
Spanish the degree of national identification with their country
of origin was quite low. Patriotism among the Italians often
came *after* emigration, perhaps as an effect of nostalgia, as
Sarmiento noted.[17] Moreover, the strongest expressions of
national identification with the country of origin came not from
the inarticulate masses but from the elites of each national

[16] Gastón Gori, *La pampa sin gaucho.*
[17] Domingo F. Sarmiento, *op. cit.,* p. 76. Sarmiento calls this attitude
"retrospective patriotism."

sector. If, as we suggest, the national identification of the largest immigrant sectors was weak, this must be counted as an important factor in the survival of an Argentine national identity.

The prevalence of these voluntary associations is remarkable if we consider the low cultural and economic level of the majority. At first the organizations provided many services which Argentina was unable to offer. Later on, however, education, sanitary facilities, mass communication media, and other services were provided by public and private Argentine institutions, and the need for the foreign national associations was less obvious. Some contemporaries have observed that their underlying purpose was to keep alive the language and traditions of the fatherland.

The associations had other latent functions. For instance, they provided the traditional immigrants with a means of integration into the Argentine society. These functions may account for the fact that the enthusiasm for associations was much higher among the immigrants than among the native born. This fact cannot be explained simply as a consequence of the emigration and of their special situation in a foreign land. Under similar conditions half a cntury later, the degrcc of formal and informal participation of Argentine internal migrants was extremely low; in fact, one obstacle to their assimilation was precisely their disorganization upon their arrival in the city.[18]

The remarkable propensity to cooperate and to create voluntary associations among the foreign immigrants was also due to other factors. In the first place, the associations expressed values and attitudes widely different from the anarchic and at the same time "submissive-authoritarian" character predominant among the natives, especially in the rural areas. In the second place, foreign immigration included an important working-class elite, which often had not left their native lands for economic reasons alone. This elite provided leadership both to the voluntary associations and to the protest movements arising within the new industrial proletariat.

The tremendous challenge to Argentina created by the avalanche of foreigners is reflected in the writings of the decades around the end of the nineteenth and the beginning of the twentieth century. Sarmiento described Argentina as a "republic

18 Gino Germani, "Inquiry into the Social Effects of Urbanization."

TABLE XVII

VOLUNTARY ASSOCIATIONS BY NATIONALITY OF THE MAJORITY
OF THEIR MEMBERSHIP: NUMBER OF AFFILIATES FOR EVERY
1,000 NATIVE BORN AND FOR EVERY 1,000
FOREIGN BORN. 1914.

Types of Associations	No. of members for every 1,000 Argentines and for every 1,000 foreign born living in the area		No. of Associations	
	Buenos Aires City	Rest of the country	Buenos Aires City	Rest of the country
Argentine Associations	104	21	19	153
Foreign Associations:				
—one nationality:	145	151	97	752
—multi- national: (includes workers' centers)	197	14	98	83

Source: Third National Census.

of foreigners," served by a small number of nationals performing unprofitable and burdensome tasks such as keeping order, defending the territory, administering justice, and preserving the rights and special privileges of the immigrants themselves.[19] Even the Italians, who later revealed themselves as the most amenable to assimilation, appeared as a powerful threat to national independence and identity. This was a consequence of their high proportion and concentration, their powerful organizations, and the attitudes of the Italian government, which regarded the Italian immigrants and their descendants as Italian citizens, in keeping with the principle of *Jus Sanguinis*. The problem of foreign schools, the deliberate attempt to create alien national communities, the absence of an Argentine tradition among the immigrants, and their complete political alienation continued to be serious concerns of the Argentine elite for a long time.

[19] Domingo F. Sarmiento, *op. cit.*, p. 101.

The problem was aggravated by certain basic contradictions in the policy followed by the elite in fostering immigration. These contradictions resulted from the difference between the declared and manifest aims of constructing a modern nation, and the limits within which many members of the dominant group wished to restrict the process of modernization. These problems were especially apparent in the political participation of the immigrants.

One of the proclaimed aims of immigration was to provide a stable basis for the functioning of democracy. But it soon became evident that those who were expected to become the new citizens remained totally outside the political life of the country. Indeed, despite the legal facilities for obtaining naturalization (which only required two years' residence and a relatively simple procedure), almost none of the immigrants sought it. There were several reasons for this. The Constitution accorded foreigners the same rights as those of the native born, except the right to vote and to run for election. Under certain conditions, the foreigner, even without naturalization, could participate in local elections for city administration. In any case, not only economic activities but also all jobs in the civil service of the federal and provincial governments or other public bodies were open to the foreign born without any requirements for citizenship. Consequently, there was no economic incentive for naturalization. Also, many immigrants were reluctant to lose their foreign national identification, for it gave them *additional* rights, since they were protected also by their respective native governments. In most cases, the immigrant looked down on the native born as an inferior. Often he simply expected to return to his fatherland as soon as possible after getting rich. This situation caused many heated discussions between Argentines and foreigners, whose point of view was expressed by the booming foreign press. Some foreign sectors requested that naturalization be automatic but not compulsory. That is, foreigners would receive full citizenship rights, without renouncing their previous nationality and without being compelled to accept Argentine citizenship.[20] For certain nationalities and for the more highly educated, the failure to naturalize was certainly an expression of loyalty to the country of origin. But the reasons for the majority of the immigrants, especially Italian and Spanish, were probably different. Their lack of

20 Domingo F. Sarmiento, *op. cit.,* pp. 301 ff., 328 ff., and *passim.*

interest in political participation was an expression of the low political culture of the lower-class foreigners who came from countries whose voting was quite restricted and where politics was an activity monopolized by the middle and higher classes.

TABLE XVIII

NATURALIZED FOREIGNERS FOR EVERY 100 FOREIGNERS RESIDING IN BUENOS AIRES AND IN THE REST OF THE COUNTRY. 1895–1947.

Regions	1895	1914	1947
Buenos Aires City	0.2	2.3	9.5
Rest of the Country	0.1	0.9	7.2

Source: Second, Third, and Fourth National Census.

The political elite wanted a genuine functioning of the democracy anticipated in the Constitution, and immigration was stimulated with this in mind. But they found themselves faced with the paradox of a country in which 60 to 80 percent of the adult male population in the most important areas had no right to vote and was governed by the remaining minority, constituting 20 to 40 percent. But even these were not the true proportions. Only a minority of the native born effectively participated in politics, and elections took place amid the general indifference of Argentines and foreigners alike, at least among the popular classes. And the governing elite, whatever its explicit purposes may have been, for a long time resisted the relinquishing of power through elections based on effective universal suffrage. They yielded only when the urban middle and popular classes became endowed with sufficient size and solidity to impose their influence.

When the foreigners created movements that suggested active political participation, the elite became indignant and fearful. It is true that these organizations could not be considered real channels of integration into the national life, since they were found in the context of the so-called Political Centers for Foreigners[21] and not in national political parties. But other attempts by the immigrants at political participation which were not linked to their nationalities were also opposed. This happened in the case of the workers' movements, which were

[21] Gastón Gori, La pampa sin gaucho.

especially vigorous in Buenos Aires from the end of the nineteenth century on, and which lacked specific national identification. On the contrary, although the majority of the members were foreigners, they did not possess any unified national character; they were international and cosmopolitan in ideology and composition. These "cosmopolitan" societies and "workers' circles" had a real function in the assimilation of immigrants; they channeled the immigrants' activities into the political life of the country. This participation was not determined by national origin, but by location in a given sector or stratum of Argentine society. However, the immigrants' ideologies still could not be readily accepted by the liberal elite. In this sense it was historically impossible for the elites to recognize the latent integrating function of workers' organizations. In fact, the ruling group not only did not welcome the immigrants but repressed them through severe laws and systematic police persecution. The elite wanted to populate the desert, but they were not ready to introduce the necessary reforms in the agrarian structure. They wanted to integrate the immigrants into the body politic but did not want to share power with them.

In fact, political participation by the immigrants is only one aspect of this more general problem. We have given some indications of the many problems and internal tensions caused by immigration. What remains to be understood is how, after some sixty years, a relatively integrated and unified nation finally emerged. Systematic research on this subject is not available. Suggestions can be made, but we must recognize that they are speculative.

Perhaps it will be convenient to clarify first the meaning of *assimilation* as the term is used here. We will base our analysis on a preliminary distinction between *individual adjustment, participation, acculturation,* and *identification.*[22]

(a) The notion of *adjustment* refers to the manner in which the immigrant performs his roles in the various spheres of activity in which he participates. What is important here is his ability to perform the roles without excessive or unbearable psychological stress.

[22] Some parts of the following typology have been summarized from Gino Germani, "The Assimilation of Immigrants in Urban Settings." In Philip Hauser (ed.), *Handbook of Urban Studies.* Paris: UNESCO, forthcoming. The typology follows the theoretical suggestions of S. N. Eisenstadt in his *Absorption of Immigrants.* London: Routledge and Kegan Paul, 1954, Chapter 1.

(b) The concept of *participation* treats assimilation from the standpoint of the receiving society. Here we distinguish between three different dimensions. (i) *Extent* of participation: What roles is the immigrant performing within the social institutions and sectors of the host society? how much is he still connected with his fatherland? what roles is he playing in the social institutions and sectors of the host society, but socially segregated from it? (ii) Another important aspect of participation is the *efficiency* with which the roles are performed. In this case we define *efficiency* from the point of view of the receiving institutions and groups. (iii) Finally, we must take into account the *reception* given by the country to the immigrants. It is important to emphasize that participation may be granted in certain spheres of activities but not in others; indeed, this is usually the case.

(c) By *acculturation* we mean the immigrants' absorption of the cultural patterns of the host society. Such absorption may consist of relatively superficial learning or it may penetrate deeply into the personality. Acculturation is never a one-way process. It affects not only the immigrants but the receiving culture as well.

(d) Finally, an important aspect of assimilation is the degree of *identification* of the foreign born and their descendants with the new country. To what extent do they lose their previous identification, and acquire a new one? how deep is the new identification, and how does it affect their attitudes and behavior?

These four aspects of assimilation are not necessarily all present in the same group or in the same individual. It is true that in certain spheres of activity adjustment, participation, and acculturation will usually be associated, but this does not necessarily include national identification. Given the heterogeneity of the immigrants and the different conditions under which they settled, there should be a variety of situations, according to the different national origins and the educational and socioeconomic status of the individuals involved.

In terms of *individual adjustment* there are reasons to believe that massive immigration involved a high cost. The high proportion of "returnees" indicates this. Among the causes were the relative inaccessibility of land ownership and the hardships of life in the rural areas. But in the cities too the adjustment must have been relatively painful. The documents of the period under consideration abound in descriptions of the sufferings, restrictions, and poverty of the immigrants. On the other hand, many acquired a degree of economic and social well-being beyond what they could have expected at home. We know very little about the degree of family organization. It is estimated by some that family organization among the native rural population was not high. If this is true, then immigration helped to establish a pattern of more regular and organized family life among the lower strata.[23]

The *participation* of immigrants varied according to the various spheres of activity. In the economic sphere it was always high. Since immigrant participation in the nation's economic life involved upward social mobility, this must have been a powerful means of integration. Thirty years after the end of mass immigration, in the Buenos Aires area, second-generation immigrants were mostly in the middle and higher strata, and together with the foreign born constituted more than three-fourths of the individuals located at these levels.[24] Among the entrepreneurial elite this proportion was even higher: almost 90 percent at about the same date.[25]

Intermarriage was another essential means of participation and integration into the life of the country. During the period from 1890 to 1910, about 40 percent of the immigrants married outside their national group, many marrying Argentine women.[26]

The participation of foreigners in the intellectual life of the country was another means of integration. Although, of course, it was not a means of mass participation, it gave the immigrants

[23] In 1942 this difference was still observed. Cf. the remarks by Carl C. Taylor, *Rural Life in Argentina*. Baton Rouge: Louisiana State University Press, 1948, Chapter 13.

[24] The average socioeconomic status of the native Argentines whose parents were both natives was lower than that of second-generation immigrants. The average relative position of the foreigner was lower than that of the native, but slightly higher than that of the native internal migrants. Here the emigration to the city was another important factor in determining the socioeconomic status. Cf. Gino Germani, Blanca Ferrari, and Malvina Segre, "Características sociales de la población de Buenos Aires," Instituto de Sociología, Universidad de Buenos Aires, 1965 (unpublished manuscript).

[25] José Luis de Imaz, *Los que mandan*. Buenos Aires: Eudeba, 1964, pp. 136–138 (Tables 72 and 73).

[26] Franco Savorgnan, "Homogamia en los inmigrantes en Buenos Aires," *Boletín del Instituto Étnico Nacional*, 1957.

an important role among the intellectual elite, and it contributed very much to the national patterns of intellectual and artistic expression. The consequences of this fact are still controversial. Nationalists of the right as well as the neonationalists of the left feel that the typical cosmopolitanism of the Argentine intelligentsia is one of the major obstacles to the rise of an "authentic" national consciousness. Often the blame has been placed on the

TABLE XIX

ARGENTINE AND FOREIGN-BORN HEADS OF FAMILY BY
SOCIOECONOMIC STATUS.
BUENOS AIRES METROPOLITAN AREA, 1961.

Socioeconomic status	Native-born Argentine family heads			Foreign-born family heads	Total population heads of family
	Both parents Argentine born	One parent foreign born	Both parents foreign born		
Lower (unskilled and skilled manual)	45.6	30.0	33.3	48.2	41.5
Middle (lower middle and upper middle)	49.0	65.6	60.8	49.8	55.4
Upper (lower upper and upper upper)	5.4	4.4	5.9	2.0	4.1
TOTAL	100.0	100.0	100.0	100.0	100.0
	519	262	534	736	2,051

Source: "Stratification and Mobility in Buenos Aires" (Buenos Aires Institute of Sociology unpublished data). Survey based on a random area sample. Socioeconomic status is computed on the average of four indicators: occupation, income, education, and standard of living.

"oligarchy" and its intellectual establishment.[27] But whatever the evolution of the process, its existence cannot be denied.

As we have seen, the direct political participation of the foreigner was low and frequently inconsistent because of the ambivalent attitudes of the ruling elite. But this was true only of

[27] Especially by the ideologues of the "national left." Cf. Juan José Hernández Arregui, *Imperialismo y cultura.* Buenos Aires: Amerindia, 1957 and *La formación de la conciencia nacional.* Buenos Aires: 1960.

those actually born abroad, not of their children. After 1916 the proportion of second-generation immigrants began to rise among the active politicians. In 1889 their proportion among legislators (deputies and senators) was only 38 percent, but it had risen to 55 percent by 1916.[28] The degree of participation of second-generation immigrants reflected the political history of the country. Participation rose with the access to power of the middle class and decreased again when the "oligarchy" returned to power through the military revolution of 1930. After 1945 participation increased again.[29] It is worth noting that the last two constitutional presidents were second-generation Italian immigrants. If we consider the other two sectors of the leading elite—the military and the Church—we will see that the participation of immigrants' descendants is very high. In the last twenty-five years 77 percent of the generals and admirals in the army, navy, and air force and 77 percent of the bishops were of immigrant origin, mostly sons of foreigners.[30]

One aspect which alarmed the native elite was the immigrants' tendency to segregate themselves in colonies and communities often supported by their respective national governments. At least up to the First World War, Argentina appeared to many observers to be composed of juxtaposed segments, each of which claimed the loyalty of its members. Even in the economic sphere, which was a major field of interaction, the tendency to segregate by nationality appeared to a certain extent. But as time elapsed it became apparent that, below the seemingly chaotic surface of heterogeneous fragments, a sort of unity was being formed. In the first place, for the majority of immigrants ethnic segregation was really limited to certain special sectors of their life. More pervasive segregation occurred only among the higher strata. Moreover, segregation in one area did not affect the adequate fulfillment of universalistic roles within the society as a whole.[31] In fact these segregated

[28] Darío Cantón and Mabel Arruñada, "Orígenes sociales de los legisladores," Instituto de Sociología, Universidad de Buenos Aires, 1960, unpublished paper.

[29] José L. de Imaz, op. cit., p. 9.

[30] Ibid., p. 60 and p. 175. In the armed forces the high officers of Italian origin accounted for one-fourth of the total, 35 percent were of Spanish origin, while the remaining 16 percent were of French or Anglo-Saxon (including German) descent. Among the bishops, the Italian influence was higher: one-half were sons of Italian peasants.

[31] Cf. S. N. Eisenstadt, op. cit., Chapter 1.

structures functioned as intermediaries between the national society and the immigrants. Thus, even while preserving the cultural traditions of their members' homelands, they nonetheless facilitated social integration. In any case a certain degree of survival of native cultural traditions was perfectly compatible with a high degree of integrated participation in other spheres, especially in a society comparatively free from antagonistic ethnic tensions.[32]

[32] In Argentina there is some anti-Semitism. However, its degree and diffusion are not higher than in other Western countries, such as the United States or France. Some episodes which have received international attention are an expression of the complex political situation, but not of a widespread or intense racial prejudice. In a survey it was found that about 22 percent of the family heads in a random sample of the Buenos Aires metropolitan area gave anti-Jewish answers (when asked specifically about Jews). For similar questions, the verbal attitudes reported in studies in West Germany, France, and the United States indicated a similar or smaller proportion of prejudiced answers. Cf. Gino Germani, "Antisemitismo ideológico y antisemitismo tradicional," *Comentarios*, 1962, No. 34. In any case, it is well known that the prejudice against Italians or the Spanish is much lower. In the same survey the anti-Italian answers were 4.4 percent and the anti-Spanish 3.5 percent. These reactions were obtained from respondents of all national origins and all social classes. The attitudes of native Argentinians classified by socioeconomic status (see Table A) showed the usual correlation between low education (and socioeconomic level) and prejudice.

TABLE A

Attitudes toward Immigrants by Native-born Family Heads. Percentage of Respondents who would "exclude" the different national or ethnic groups. Buenos Aires metropolitan area, 1961.

National and ethnic groups "excluded"	Low socioeconomic status	Middle socioeconomic status	High socioeconomic status
Italians	12	3	1
Spanish	9	2	0
Jews	34	22	14
North Americans	24	13	5
English	18	10	3
Polish	17	10	7
Rumanians	15	8	7

The hostility against Italians and Spanish was the lowest and very small at all socioeconomic levels. The anti-North American and anti-English attitudes indicated more of an ideological orientation than an ethnic prejudice. There was strong evidence that negative reactions regarding the Jews and other lower-class Eastern Europeans were more frequently

Another integrative force was the fact that the immigrants' descendants frequently entered the same voluntary associations as their parents. In this way, such organizations gradually lost their specifically ethnic character. For example, the use of the language of origin in many foreign associations decreased steadily until it almost disappeared, to be replaced by Spanish. It is obvious that the end of immigration in 1930 was a factor in this process.

The participation of immigrants in these organizations varied according to nationality and socioeconomic level. The participation of Italian and Spanish immigrants of the popular classes was less frequent and briefer. Although the large voluntary associations were primarily composed of persons from the lower strata, the proportion of members was probably smaller than for the higher strata. Separate social stratification systems were probably maintained only at the higher class levels. But this segregation was certainly much more limited among the lower strata, and continued to decrease in time.

In addition to the progressive Argentinization of the foreign voluntary associations and the lower formal participation among the working class, there were other factors which favored integration into the national society. In the lower strata the ecological segregation of ethnic groups steadily diminished. In the Buenos Aires area, for example, there was a gradual reduction of the "ghetto" areas occupied by given nationalities. It is important to add that these zones did not have some of the characteristics common to cities in the United States. In some cases in the big cities, for example, certain types of slum, like the *conventillo*,* had a real integrative function for the different nationalities. Obviously the disappearance or drastic reduction of ecological segregation was in many cases due to the replacement of the immigrants by their children.

The process of assimilation should be considered as part of the emergence of new cultural forms and a new human type.

---

an expression of "traditionalism" than of ideological anti-Semitism. Cf. Gino Germani, "Antisemitismo ideológico y antisemitismo tradicional," *Comentarios,* 1962, No. 34; and Francis Korn, "Algunos aspectos de la asimilación de inmigrantes en Buenos Aires," Instituto de Sociología, Universidad de Buenos Aires (unpublished paper based on the same survey).

* A one- or two-floor building with a central courtyard around which the rooms are located. Usually one family lives in each room.

This synthesis is the outcome of the interaction of the native and foreign cultures.

This observation brings us to the problem of *acculturation*. Even though we lack scientific studies concerning this process, there is an abundant literature, mostly impressionistic essays, attempting to characterize the society born of massive immigration.[33] The result of mass immigration was not the assimilation of the immigrants into the existing Argentine culture. The outcome was a synthesis that created a new cultural type, which is still not well defined. In this emerging culture it is possible to recognize the contributions of the different national groups, particularly the Italian and the Spanish. But all of them are substantially modified and submerged in a context which gives them a new meaning. Particularly visible in most of the largest cities is the Italian influence in language, gestures, food, and many customs. The Spanish influence, no less strong, is perhaps less visible because it is more easily confused with creole elements. Some popular products of this fusion, like the tango, have great emotional and symbolic importance as expressions of the new Argentine society.

The bearers of this new cultural type are the children of the immigrants and their descendants. They are almost completely acculturated. Italian, Yiddish, Polish, and other Eastern European languages are seldom spoken by second-generation immigrants. Also, they would never refer to themelves as belonging to a particular national stock. For example, an Italian immigrant's son would mention when asked that his father was Italian, but nobody would differentiate people on the basis of their ancestry. Instead, Italian language and customs have been adapted to new cultural patterns. The Italians' sons do not speak Italian, but everybody regardless of their national origin understands Italian and would be able to learn to speak it quite easily. This is not only because of its similarity to Spanish (in Spain, Italian is not so easy) but because Italian is so familiar in many ways. Words, idioms, the typical pronunciation of Spanish in Buenos Aires and the central area, as well as manners, inflections, facial expressions, and gestures, all bear the mark of many generations of Italians.

The immigrants' upward social mobility facilitated the accul-

33 Among Argentine writers the most important are Ezequiel Martínez Estrada, Jorge Luis Borges, José Luis Romero, Carlos Alberto Erro, Eduardo Mallea, and Raúl Scalabrini Ortíz.

turation of their children. Often the second generation was assimilated into a different social class, values, style of living, and expectations that greatly diverged from those of the previous generation. This is of course a well-known phenomenon in a country of heavy immigration, but the huge proportion of immigrants in Argentina accentuated its consequences.

THE ARGENTINIZATION OF ARGENTINA AND THE SURVIVING FOREIGN POPULATION

Let us now examine to what extent the process of assimilation was facilitated by the interruption of mass overseas immigration thirty-five years ago. We may also consider the role of the mass internal migrations in this process.

The Census of 1947 is the only one to give some information on the national origin of the parents. By that time more than one-half of the population was born of native Argentine par-

TABLE XX

NATIONAL OR FOREIGN ORIGIN OF THE POPULATION. 1947–1960.

National origin	Whole country— 1947* (all ages) Percent	Buenos Aires City—1947* (all ages) Percent	Buenos Aires metropolitan area—1961†	
			Heads of family Percent	Population aged 18 and over Percent
Argentine born from Argentine parents:	53.3	30.9	25.2	33.1
Argentine born from foreign parents (one or both)	31.1	41.1	39.3	39.3
Foreign-born:	15.6	28.0	35.5	27.6
	100.0	100.0	100.0	100.0

Sources: * 1947 Census and † "Stratification and Mobility in Buenos Aires."

ents. The rest were sons of immigrants or immigrants themselves. The proportion of the foreign element was higher in
Buenos Aires. By 1961 only one-quarter of the heads of family
were third-generation Argentines on both parents' sides, this
proportion increasing to one-third among the adults. One-half
of the families living in Buenos Aires included at least one
member born abroad.

Thus, the composition of the population is still rather heterogeneous, even taking into account no more than the birthplace
of the present population and of their parents, and disregarding
the origin of grandparents. Only a process of rapid synthesis
and a large cultural distance between the first- and second-
generation immigrants can explain the degree of homogeneity
apparently achieved. The impact of time on the foreign population was another factor in facilitating the homogenization. Not
only the immigrant group is becoming older, but it is composed
of a higher proportion of persons with longer residence in the
country.

TABLE XXI

FOREIGN-BORN POPULATION BY AGE GROUPS. 1947.

Age Groups	Buenos Aires metropolitan area	Rest of country
Up to 39 years old	26.2	25.3
40–59 years old	51.8	50.1
Over 60 years old	21.2	24.5
Age unknown	0.8	0.1
	100.0	100.0

Source: Fourth Argentine Census.

Some information on the degree of assimilation and identification of the surviving immigrant population may be found in
recent surveys. In Table XXIII only the two major immigrant
groups were included.

Some differences may be noted between Italians and the
Spanish, especially between lower and higher socioeconomic
strata, the former being more easily assimilated than the latter.
On the whole, however, these two immigrant groups seem
largely assimilated. Even if they have not lost all emotional ties
with their fatherlands, they show an increasing identification
with their new country. Practically nobody in these two groups

GINO GERMANI ▮ 353

TABLE XXII
PERCENTAGE OF FOREIGN-BORN POPULATION BY NUMBER OF YEARS
OF RESIDENCE IN THE COUNTRY. 1947–1961.

Years of residence	Entire country	Buenos Aires City. 1947*	Buenos Aires metropolitan area 1961†
Up to 9	7.9	6.9	13.9
10–19	16.5	20.7	17.5
20–29	25.5	26.7	12.1
Over 30	45.2	41.5	56.5
Unknown	4.9	4.2	—

Source: * Fourth National Census (unpublished data).
† "Stratification and Mobility in Buenos Aires."

TABLE XXIII
SOME INDICATORS OF ACCULTURATION, PARTICIPATION, AND
IDENTIFICATION IN ITALIAN AND SPANISH POPULATION AGED
18 YEARS AND OVER. BUENOS AIRES
METROPOLITAN AREA, 1961.

Indicators	Socioeconomic status:† high	medium	low
Feel closer to Argentina than to home country:			
Italian immigrants	48.6	48.7	46.8
Spanish immigrants	28.9	46.4	51.3
Not affiliated to any foreign association:			
Italian immigrants	88.9	95.7	95.3
Spanish immigrants	75.0	86.3	89.5
Do not wish to return permanently to native land:			
Italian immigrants	94.4	91.7	93.2
Spanish immigrants	83.5	92.7	94.5
Closest friends are Argentinians, or Argentinians and foreigners in same proportion:			
Italian immigrants	100.0	89.5	86.1
Spanish immigrants	78.6	91.7	88.2
No communication with persons in home country:			
Italian immigrants	34.3	46.1	47.6
Spanish immigrants	13.8	40.1	51.0

354   ▌ THE NATIONALIST PIVOT

TABLE XXIII (Cont.)

Indicators	Socioeconomic status:†		
	high	medium	low
Never experienced discrimination:			
Italian immigrants	94.3	92.2	94.9
Spanish immigrants	96.6	96.0	93.9
Never or seldom read in native language:			
Italian immigrants	80.0	71.9	88.9
No preference for films, theatre, etc. in own language:			
Italian immigrants	21.4	54.1	49.7
Speak only Spanish or Spanish and own language in the same proportion when at home:			
Italian immigrants	92.9	67.6	39.2
Number of respondents:			
Italian immigrants	20	274	335
Spanish immigrants	33	228	257

Source: Data summarized from Francis Korn, "Algunos aspectos de la asimilación de inmigrantes en Buenos Aires." Instituto de Sociología, Universidad de Buenos Aires. Unpublished paper based on the "Stratification and Mobility in Buenos Aires" survey.

† Composite index of occupation, education, income, and consumption level.

wishes to return to his ancestral land. With the exception of the upper class, one-half of them feel closer to Argentina than to their fatherlands. Only a minority of the Spanish and Italians participate in foreign associations or have predominantly foreign friends. Among the Italians, the use of their native language seems confined to their homes.

Argentina has been rather successful in achieving a high degree of cultural homogeneity and national identification, as well as in capturing the loyalty of immigrants. However, many Argentine writers have challenged this suggestion. Such doubts have been expressed not only when the country was submerged in the flood of foreign immigration, but also in recent years. One prominent Argentine historian has described the present society as a "hybrid mass, formed by creole and foreign elements coexisting without predominance by either."[34] In other

[34] José Luis Romero, Argentina: imágenes y perspectivas. Buenos Aires: Raigal, 1956, p. 62.

Argentinians we find a nostalgia for the homogeneous creole society. This attitude is typical not only of right-wing nationals but also of liberal intellectuals like Erro, Borges, or Mallea.

The political instability since 1930, the economic stagnation of the last fifteen years, and especially the fragmentation of many groups and institutions have been imputed to the lack of real community feeling. However, Argentina was stable and economically prosperous when the degree of cultural homogeneity was much lower and the threat to national identity far more serious. The present troubles have other causes, even if they are in part an expression of the painful process of national integration. In fact, one of the consequences of the great internal migrations was precisely to halt the segregation of the old creole population and to facilitate its fusion with the descendants of immigrant stock.

Perhaps doubts and fears could simply be dispelled or confirmed by empirical evidence alone, even if such evidence were actually available. The contrasting interpretations may be caused by divergent expectations of the degree and kind of cultural homogeneity and national consciousness that can be achieved in Argentina. If one takes into account the risks involved in the incorporation of such a mass of foreigners in so short a time, then the present situation can be viewed with optimism. But if this same situation is measured by the yardstick of a country with a longer historical tradition of homogeneous culture, then of course there is less cause for optimism. The problem is primarily one of time, and this is a limit which even the most efficient assimilation cannot possibly overcome

Puerto Rico: An American

Showcase for Latin America

MANUEL MALDONADO-DENIS

IN JANUARY, 1965, Sixto Alvelo, twenty-three-year-old Puerto Rican worker, reported to the U.S. Army Recruiting Station at Fort Brooke, San Juan, Puerto Rico. When his turn came the recruiting officer requested that he step forward, thus formally entering within military jurisdiction. Alvelo flatly refused. In a written statement prepared beforehand he read to the Army officer the reasons for his refusal: he could not conscientiously serve in the armed forces of a nation not his own, since he considered that he had only one country: Puerto Rico. Consequently, he would not take the oath to the American flag required of all recruits, and if forced to enter the U.S. Army he would do so under protest. (Later Alvelo would categorically state that he would under no circumstances serve in the U.S. Army.)

Before this incident, Puerto Rican youths belonging to the Nationalist Party had already been sentenced to five years of imprisonment for their refusal to serve in the American Armed Forces. Alvelo became a symbol of resistance to the military draft and to American domination of Puerto Rico.

Very soon other recruits followed his example. At first the U.S. Attorney decided to prosecute them and the whole apparatus of the federal authorities here was put into action. Visits by the F.B.I. and by U.S. Army Intelligence to their homes and those of their neighbors were combined with continued harassments and attempts to intimidate. (In the case of Alvelo, the long hand of the F.B.I. reached to his employers. He is at present unemployed and unable to find a job because of the continuous harassment and intimidatory tactics employed by the F.B.I.)

A committee for the defense of Sixto Alvelo was created for the purpose of explaining his case to the Puerto Rican public and for raising funds for his defense. The Movement for Independence (M.P.I.), an organization to which Alvelo belongs, launched a massive campaign against the draft and its application to Puerto Rico. As a result of mounting pressures and public sympathy for Alvelo and the other Puerto Rican youngsters the U.S. Attorney in San Juan decided to drop the prosecution. As of this moment nearly a thousand young Puerto Ricans have refused to serve in the American Army, and the number increases every day. A growing awareness of the basic injustice involved in serving in the armed forces of a nation that imposes a "blood tax" upon the Puerto Rican youth without allowing us representation in Congress, the example of the antidraft movement in the United States, and heightened consciousness about the atrocities being committed daily by American troops in Vietnam have contributed to this trend.

The crux in the draft cases as well as in other areas where federal legislation applies to Puerto Rico lies in the "plenary" powers of Congress to pass all laws that are "not locally inapplicable." The powers of the Puerto Rican government under Commonwealth status are akin to those of a local government. But the larger powers that truly determine the destiny of Puerto Rico—for example, the application of the Selective Service Act to our island—are vested in Congress, a body in which we have a kind of errand boy who can neither speak nor vote and who is called "Resident Commissioner of Puerto Rico in Washington." Of the powers of the U.S. Congress with respect to Puerto Rico—putting strictly local matters aside—it can be said as Blackstone did of the British Parliament, that it can do everything except turn a man into a woman or a woman into a man.

In Puerto Rico, the draft must be seen within the context of a broader military build-up. According to the conservative estimates of Admiral R. S. Craighill, Chief of the Tenth Naval District, there are approximately 14,000 Puerto Ricans serving in the U.S. Armed Forces and 1,000 of them are in Vietnam. During the Korean War more than 1,000 Puerto Ricans were killed and countless maimed or made human wrecks. Since

1917, when U.S. citizenship was imposed upon the Puerto
Rican people by Congress, notwithstanding the opposition of
the ruling party in Puerto Rico and of the Puerto Rican House
of Delegates (at that moment the only truly representative body
of the Puerto Rican people), the policy of the home country
toward its colony was clear: here was a human quarry, in a
densely populated region, which could be counted upon to serve
as cannon fodder in American wars.

In an action unique in the annals of colonialism, an act was
passed by the U.S. Congress in 1917 that made compulsory
military service one of the many "privileges" that went hand in
hand with the great boon of American citizenship. Thus Puerto
Ricans have had to fight in whatever war the United States
deems necessary for the preservation of "the free world."
Alvelo and others have now courageously challenged this abu-
sive practice.

When President Eisenhower spoke in his farewell address
about "the military-industrial complex" he had the United
States and its "territories" in mind. Puerto Rico is a small island
(3,435 square miles), densely overpopulated (its population,
estimated at 2,668,000, faces an increase that is 50 percent
higher than the U.S. and the U.S.S.R.) and with scarce natural
resources, compared with other countries in the Caribbean. Yet
it has sustained the brunt of the military-industrial complex by
becoming a tax-free haven for American investors and a
splendid military base that promises to offset the "loss" of Cuba
in the Caribbean.

Thus the American Armed Forces are the greatest landholders in Puerto Rico. It is estimated that they own around
100,000 acres of Puerto Rican territory. In terms of cultivable
land this amounts to about 13 percent of the total area of the
island. Among the thirteen military bases that the United States
operates in Puerto Rico is Roosevelt Roads Naval Base, a vast
military complex that includes guided missiles as well as an
enormous area for maneuvers of all kinds. Admiral Craighill
was quoted in a local newspaper as saying that "all the ships
and planes of the Navy that are going to Vietnam receive
previous training in Puerto Rico." The small offshore island of
Vieques—formerly a thriving municipality—is on the verge of
disappearing, since its inhabitants have been left with only
5,000 acres out of a total area of 31,000 (the other 26,000

acres are completely controlled by the Tenth Naval District). It is no secret that the Pentagon would like to swallow the rest of Vieques.

Meanwhile, in the western part of Puerto Rico an immense S.A.C. base called Ramey Field operates. B-52's take off on an around-the-clock basis, carrying their nuclear bombs over Puerto Rican territory. (The Oakland *Tribune* reported recently that a nuclear device had fallen on the coast of Puerto Rico. This was, of course, denied by the Pentagon. Given the "credibility gap" the chances are that only the fact that Puerto Rico is American territory saved the Pentagon from another "Palomares" incident when a nuclear arm was lost off the coast of Spain.) Ramey Field is one of the most important S.A.C. bases in the Atlantic and a springboard for American control of its Mediterranean—the Caribbean.

We have, therefore, two military installations in the midst of our small island. With great fanfare an announcement was made about a treaty to "denuclearize" Latin America, but as far as the United States is concerned this does not include Puerto Rico. A recent AP dispatch from the UN signed by William Oatis speaks for itself: "The projected treaty to keep nuclear weapons out of Latin America would not bar U.S. nuclear bases from Puerto Rico unless the U.S. should change its position." The article then quotes a statement by William C. Foster of the U.S. Arms Control and Disarmament Agency made on December 10, 1965: "We do not wish to have included in the proposed nuclear free zone the Virgin Islands, since that is U.S. territory or the Commonwealth of Puerto Rico, because of its international relationships with the U.S. In the case of both these areas the U.S. must deal with disarmament problems affecting other nuclear powers." On the basis of this statement we can clearly see that the United States would "denuclearize" Puerto Rice only if other nuclear powers were willing to do the same. Since there are no other nuclear powers in Latin America except the United States this means that the situation will remain the same. It is evident from Mr. Foster's statement that the Puerto Rican people are not to be consulted on so vital a matter and that the basic decisions are to be made, as usual, by the imperialist power.

American control of Puerto Rican territory extends not merely to areas considered "vital" to "national defense," but also applies to such historic monuments as El Morro fortress, acquired by the United States as a result of the Spanish-American War. The "Commonwealth" government, in its own very pusillanimous way, has been trying in recent years to recover from the United States those lands not considered "vital" for national defense. It had almost been agreed that with the closing of some military installations ordered by Secretary McNamara, about 15,000 acres would revert to the people of Puerto Rico. However, the tug of war between Congress, the Pentagon, and the National Park Service has culuminated in a public rebuke to the Commonwealth claims by Representative Wayne Aspinall, Chairman of the House Committee on Interior and Insular Affairs. In typical imperialist fashion Mr. Aspinall has stated that there is "not a chance" that we will get back what belongs to us: "There is no possibility, none whatsoever," the Congressman has said, that the Federal government "will ever give the land up."

The Pentagon incidentally does not pay a cent for the use of Puerto Rican territory in its aggressive policies. After all, this country "belongs" to them. Why should they pay?

The other side of the military build-up in Puerto Rico is its American-dominated economy. The lavish praise showered upon our little island by Madison Avenue ads and by American politicians reflects, to be sure, the image of what they would like to see in Latin America: a completely "open" country subject to American domination where the profits are high, no taxes have to be paid on investments, the "natives" are under control, and complete obsequiousness of those in power. In typical barnstorming fashion Vice-President Humphrey added his voice to the chorus in a $100-a-plate dinner by praising the Puerto Rican "revolution," the same one that is "making Puerto Rico's experience the model for the peaceful and democratic future of the hemisphere." The United States, he reminded us, spent $350 million in Puerto Rico during 1965, undoubtedly contri- buting to the success of this "peaceful revolution." And then he repeated, for the nth time the greatest compliment that can be paid our "success story": we are the "showcase" of the Caribbean.

Let us take a look at the showcase. One of the things the Vice-President pointed out was that the per capita income in Puerto Rico had risen from $270 to $830 a year as a result of a "revolution." Further that Puerto Rico has one of the highest economic growth rates—comparable to Japan. Besides, prosperity is everywhere evident: San Juan is thriving and full of luxury hotels and apartment houses, stores are open, sales are high, and the people are happy and satisfied. What else can they want?

There is another side to the picture. Tourism has made San Juan the recipient of all the tastelessness, the vulgarity, and the corruption of prerevolutionary Havana. In a recent year 723,-500 tourists spent more than $139.6 million in Puerto Rico. And yet the monster threatens to devour its children. Because of the tempo of Americanization many tourists now see nothing exotic about San Juan, just a Miami Beach with a Spanish accent. "Old San Juan by night" is fast becoming a decadent, corrupt city, where catering to the tourist requires subordinating aesthetic considerations to the dollar. This is a high price to pay for "progress": a tropical extension of the American mainland where the tourists can flock—a land they can call their own.

Near the luxury hotels and the plush apartment houses are the slums of San Juan with their dire poverty. The "prosperity" ushered in by "Operation Bootstrap" has not filtered down to the masses. A recent study by Dr. José Vázquez Calzada of the Center of Demographic Studies at the University of Puerto Rico noted that personal income has increased, although not rapidly enough, but that its distribution has become even more inequitable. He goes on to quote: In 1940 per capita income in Mississippi—which is the lowest of any state—was 80 percent higher than in Puerto Rico, and in 1960 it was 81 percent higher. If families earning less than $3,000 are defined as poor for the island as they are for the mainland, then 60 percent of Puerto Rican families "do not have enough income to satisfy their basic needs adequately." The poor distribution of income is shown by another set of figures quoted by Dr. Vázquez: 20 percent of the richest families received 51.1 percent of total personal income in 1963, while 20 percent of the poorest families received only 5 percent of total personal income. The extent of poverty in Puerto Rico is also illustrated by the number of people who must resort to federal food surpluses in order to survive. In a population of approximately 2.5 million, 910,502 received surplus food during 1966 according to figures released by the U.S. Department of Agriculture. Add to this the estimate made by Dr. Hubert C. Barton, a Commonwealth government economist, that the rate of unemployment in Puerto

Rico may be as high as 30 percent of the available labor force
and a clearer picture of the Puerto Rico not shown in the ads
appears. Poverty, unemployment, and dependence upon food
"gifts" from the metropolis are still the lot of the majority of
Puerto Ricans.

In the greenhouse industrialism fostered by Operation Bootstrap the colonial character of an economy that "consumes
what it does not produce and produces what it does not
consume" becomes painfully evident. As a market for American
goods Puerto Rico ranks with giants like Brazil and Venezuela.
In a consumer-oriented economy almost totally dependent upon
imports from the metropolis, it is no wonder that there is a
$228 million deficit in our balance of payments, according to
the colonial Secretary of Commerce. The same trend toward a
completely dependent economy can be seen in the fact that from
1950 to 1960 the government debt with Wall Street bankers
went up from 14 percent to 41 percent of total net income.

That the Puerto Rican economy is less and less Puerto Rican
is attested by the fact that nearly 80 percent of the firms established in Puerto Rico under Operation Bootstrap are controlled
by American capital. Tax exemption up to seventeen years on
profits, an abundant labor force, low wages, and a government
willing to provide the overhead capital has made Puerto Rico an
investor's paradise in the Caribbean. This has been the genius of
men like Luis Muñoz Marín and Teodoro Moscoso, who have
genially devised a way to hand out a country's patrimony without batting an eye in the process. The profits made on these
ventures are fabulous, since the right "climate" exists in the
island. Contributing to this climate is an abundant labor force, a
reserve army of laborers that can be freely tapped by the
prospective investor. In its December 27, 1966, edition the
Wall Street Journal elatedly tells us: "The appalling rate of
unemployment [in Puerto Rico]—variously estimated at between 12 percent and 30 percent—is helping attract industry at
a record clip from the continental U.S. where the labor pinch is
currently severe." But the availability of labor is not the only
reason why companies are flocking to Puerto Rico. The article
adds: "For one thing, local income and property taxes, as well
as license fees, are often suspended for up to 17 years, depending on a company's product and the extent to which it aids
industrialization of the area. In addition, the Puerto Rican
government doles out generous subsidies for everything from

transportation to training." There is every reason for Wall Street to exult about Operation Bootstrap. For even if the boastful name Commonwealth accompanies Puerto Rico in its showcase functions, Section 931 of the Internal Revenue Code of the United States uses a much less complimentary term to refer to those areas that are exempt from paying federal taxes. This legislation provides that United States corporations which are operating in a "possession" of the United States and which meet certain prerequisites shall be exempt from paying federal taxes. Under this section Puerto Rico is regarded as a possession and is thus tax exempt. A possession, I hasten to add, in more than a purely legal sense. For the United States "possesses" the island militarily, economically, and politically, and it has been trying for more than sixty years to possess her completely by destroying Puerto Rican culture and personality. That it has not completely succeeded in this attempt is a tribute to the resistance by Puerto Rican nationalists.

Foremost among the apologists of Commonwealth status as a showcase for Latin America is Luis Muñoz Marín, ex-Governor of Puerto Rico and, as a prominent member of the democratic left, the darling of the American Liberal Establishment. As a leader of the generation that came to power under the banner "bread, land, and freedom" in 1940, Muñoz Marín has evolved from a defender of socialism and Puerto Rican independence to the foremost ideologist of colonial rule in the Caribbean. His party, the Popular Democratic Party (PPD), has followed a policy of concession after concession to the United States to such an extent that American control over the Puerto Rican economy is much more pervasive today than it was three decades ago. Furthermore independence has been associated with fearsome consequences through propaganda and education, as well as through a rewriting of history that portrays the struggle for independence as something that runs "contrary" to our traditions.

The policy of Muñoz Marín and his generation—with a benevolent nod from Washington—has in the last decade greatly contributed to an increase in the strength of the Statehood Republican Party (SRP). The PPD's constant reiteration of "permanent" and "irrevocable" union with the United States separates them from the advocates of statehood only in their evaluation of the economic consequences of the respective political formulas. Essentially the two parties have come to resemble—in terms of real alternatives—the two-party system in the United States.

Growing popular discontent with Commonwealth status in the early sixties led to an exchange of letters between President Kennedy and Governor Muñoz in 1962 and as a result a U.S.-P.R. Status Commission (STACOM) was formed. Weighted heavily on the American side (seven of the thirteen members were Americans) as well as on the Commonwealth and statehood sides (the independence advocate resigned, alleging partiality on the part of the other members of the Commission), STACOM spent two years and half a million dollars and came out with a report that left us essentially where we were in 1962 when the Muñoz-Kennedy letters were exchanged. Their only concrete proposal was for a plebiscite between statehood, independence, and Commonwealth (for which they reserved their most elaborate adjectives).

As a result of the possible reopening of the case of Puerto Rico under Resolution 1514 (XV) of the UN, which states that colonial powers must take all steps to give independence to all territories that have not yet achieved it, pressures have apparently been put upon the PPD to carry out a plebiscite in July, 1967. (The plebiscite must be considered—for UN purposes—a purely "domestic" affair, in accordance with the statements Ambassador Goldberg made recently to that effect.) The real meaning of this plebiscite lies in its giving a kind of ratification to the actual colonial ("Commonwealth") status. Furthermore, the results of this plebiscite do not bind Congress, so that, as the San Juan *Star,* a Cowles publication, said in an editorial:

> Nobody has said that the results would be a mandate to Congress or a directive to Congress to grant the status chosen by the people at the polls. And Congress has not said that it will grant what the people choose. What has been said is that it would represent a public opinion poll of qualified electors on the question of political status.

It is with this mock plebiscite that the United States and its obedient servants in Puerto Rico seek to hoodwink world public opinion so they will not have to comply with those UN resolutions that require all colonial powers to devolve upon the subject peoples all the powers that it has taken away from them. A plebiscite that would amount to a true act of self-determination would have to comply with this prerequisite before the people are duly consulted on the subject. (The State Department announced recently that it will adopt a policy of "non-intervention" with respect to the plebiscite. Given the continued "intervention" in our affairs since 1898 by the United States, the assertion must be somebody's idea of a joke.)

If one were to believe Muñoz Marín, the democratic left, and the Voice of America, Puerto Rico seems to be the only country on earth that does not want independence. And yet it is not the Puerto Rican people but the leaders in power that have chosen colonialism and created a colonialist mentality in the people.

If Puerto Rico is to survive as a nation and as a people, the only way to achieve that goal is through independence. True, Washington has said that it will grant us independence if we so desire. But here, as elsewhere, there is a credibility gap between what Washington says and what it does.

Puerto Rico would seem to be Henry Cabot Lodge's dream about a "pacified" country. It is the opposite of "unpacified" Vietnam. And yet in both cases the United States has shown that it lacks what Jefferson called "a decent respect for the opinions of mankind." For even though it speaks about the possibility of granting independence to our island, it belies it by ordering its secret police to haunt, harass, and persecute independence supporters; by the military occupation of our territory; by the creation of thermonuclear bases in our midst; by condoning the prolonged imprisonment of political prisoners (some of whom are serving sentences totaling up to 432 years as a result of the 1950 Nationalist uprising).

Vietnam seems to represent the reverse of Puerto Rico because it is fighting for its independence and to keep the United States out. As a result there is napalm, phosphorus, germ warfare, and saturation bombing.

So far, American imperial policy of *divide et impera* has been successful in Puerto Rico. So there is no need for napalm . . . For as long as Puerto Ricans do the job of fighting those Puerto Ricans who fight for independence, the imperialist power can stay on the sidelines. But if one day the Puerto Rican people unite to demand their independence, then I am certain that the iron fist beneath the velvet glove will show. Puerto Ricans will then see with their own eyes the true face of the American empire and they will fight as people are the world over to recover what is rightfully theirs.

Control and Coöptation in

Mexican Politics

BO ANDERSON and
JAMES D. COCKCROFT

I. INTRODUCTION

THIS PAPER represents an attempt to describe and account for
some basic features of the Mexican political system. The analysis is structural rather than historical. That is, we have not tried
to narrate how the Mexican system came into being, but have
rather attempted to set forth a somewhat abstract formulation,
which we believe can account for certain broad tendencies in
Mexican politics in the sense that many concrete policies and
changes in policies and political events are more or less direct
manifestations of the principles our formulation contains. The
formulation consists of (1) a description of what we believe is
the basic and enduring *goal-structure* of the Mexican political
system, and (2) a set of structural principles which seem to
determine, broadly speaking, how the elements in the goal-
structure are implemented, and what the relations between
different groups in the system will be like. Hence, we believe
that some basic tendencies of the Mexican polity can be made
meaningful by our formulation. However, we do not attempt to
analyze the question why in Mexico there gradually developed a
polity having these properties; nor do we try to answer the
somewhat more fundamental and general question about what
the conditions are for a political system to develop these
properties. (We do believe that these questions are important,
however; if we knew the answer we would know more about the

problem of how to combine basic democracy with rapid economic growth, starting from a state of rather extreme underdevelopment, than we now know.)

We do not claim to have isolated all the major principles which determine the structure of Mexican politics. We also regard our present formulation as a first tentative statement, although we believe it to be essentially correct.

Also our formulation is intended to apply only to *modern* Mexican *national* politics. Economically and culturally Mexico is a very heterogeneous society. In many local areas grass-roots politics is structured by "traditional factors" like kinship (including ritual kinship or the *compadrazgo*); and sometimes indigenous or Indian political forms of organization have survived in some modified form. (Sieverts, 1960; Friedrich, 1965.) This is more common in some states of the Mexican Union than in others. Politics in some southern states, Guerrero is often mentioned as a prime example, is very much traditional. In some of the economically more developed states, like Sonora and Baja California, politics seem less traditional. There are a host of important general questions that could be raised about the way that such traditional subsystems operate within the context of the national polity and economy. One could ask, for instance, how the power position of local bosses (*caciques*) is changed by the welfare and development policies that are carried out by the federal government or the regional commissions, modeled on the TVA (for instance, the Papaloapan Commission, Poleman, 1964). Such a study of political subsystems will not be undertaken in this paper, however.

We will attempt to illustrate our model with descriptions of concrete cases drawn from contemporary Mexican politics. The information about these comes from accounts in books and newspapers and also from interviews we have conducted in Mexico at various times during the period 1963–64. These cases are only assumed to be illustrative of the mode of analysis used in this paper.

2. THE GOAL-STRUCTURE OF THE MEXICAN POLITY

An adequate understanding of the structure of a political system presupposes an analysis of its *goal-structure*. Therefore

in this section we shall attempt to characterize the major goals
of the Mexican polity and the relations that hold between these
goals. The term "goals" refers to aims that are consciously
being promoted by those in the polity that make major decisions. There is, in fact, a great deal of consensus in Mexico
about what the goals are, and how they relate to one another,
although groups and individuals differ a great deal with respect
to the weights and priorities to be given to the different goals.
The following picture of the goal-structure of Mexican politics
has been pieced together from official speeches and statements, newspaper editorials, and interviews with politically
active persons.

The following major goals are present in the Mexican polity:
political stability, economic growth, public welfare, and Mexicanization. Let us now first characterize what we mean by these
terms.

Political stability refers to a state where (1) the basic
political institutions are seen as legitimate by the bulk of the
population, (2) the incumbent decision-makers are granted the
right to make binding decisions, even by those who do not
always agree with their decisions, (3) the succession of office-
holders proceeds according to rules specified in advance that are
accepted by most people as binding. After the overthrow of the
regime of Porfirio Díaz in 1911, Mexico went through more
than a decade of frequent insurrections, civil wars, and general
fragmentation of the political system. Beginning in the twenties,
however, the system has gradually gained a considerable degree
of stability. A rather dramatic and much-publicized example of
change toward stability arose right after the 1964 elections,
when González Torres, the unsuccessful candidate of the main
rightist opposition party (PAN, Partido de Acción Nacional),
publicly acknowledged that the candidate of the ruling party
(PRI, Partido Revolucionario Institucional), had won a clear
majority of the popular vote. Prior to this, PAN typically
used to attribute PRI victories in elections to large-scale fraud.

Economic growth, in the sense of industrialization and modernization of agriculture, was promoted by the Díaz regime and
was encouraged by the revolutionary regimes in the 1920s,
following the economic chaos of the civil wars. A very determined effort to make Mexico a modern industrial country has
been under way since the end of the Second World War. (For
descriptions of different aspects of the Mexican Economic

Modernization program see Vernon, 1963, 1964; and Flores, 1961).

Public Welfare. The revolutionary program heavily stressed the need for raising the material and cultural level of the Mexican masses. In the agrarian sector, a massive land reform program has been carried out in order to help the peasants obtain ownership to their land, and to enable landless laborers to acquire some land of their own. (Whetten, 1948; Flores, 1961). For the urban workers low-cost housing, subsidized staple foods, and a federally determined minimum wage level (it varies from state to state) are among the welfare policies. The middle class, especially that sector which consists of government employees, also has available low-cost housing, cheap vacation plans, and other benefits.

Mexicanization refers to the policy of securing control over the major economic companies and activities in the country for either private Mexican citizens or public agencies. Before the revolution, and for a substantial time after the revolution, foreign companies controlled many aspects of the Mexican economy. Since the 1930s the Mexican government has by expropriation or purchase obtained control over many enterprises that used to be foreign owned. The most famous case is, of course, the expropriation of the oil companies in 1938, which led to a bitter conflict with the United States. (See Cronin, 1960, Chaps. 7–10.) There are also many other less well-known cases, like the nationalization of the electric power industry (see Vernon, 1964) and landholdings. (See Cronin, 1960, Chap. 6; Flores, 1961, Chap. 17.) Nationalism is certainly a driving force behind these measures. More important, however, is the belief that if national economic planning for growth is to be successful (and the Mexican government is committed to a policy of rather centralized economic planning), it is necessary that Mexican authorities be able to make all major economic decisions about investments, allocation of resources, and so on. Mexico has encouraged foreign capital to invest in Mexico, but demands that the majority of the shares be under Mexican control.

Let us now turn to the question of how these goals are related to one another. For the purpose of this analysis we shall concentrate on *short-term* relationships. We are going to use the goal-structure to analyze political decision-making, and in Mexico, as in most other systems, political and economic planning seems to be conceived over periods of five to ten years. A president is elected for six years; he cannot constitutionally be reelected, and policies often change somewhat when a new administration comes in, so it is often not worth it to plan ahead in detail for longer periods than a presidential period.

Our conception of how the major goals of the Mexican polity are related to one another (goal-structure) is depicted in the points listed below. (The term "investment" here refers to investments made into infrastructure and industrial enterprise, and does not cover investments into "human capital" through welfare policies.)

THE GOAL-STRUCTURE OF THE MEXICAN POLITY
Arrows represent postulated causal relations.

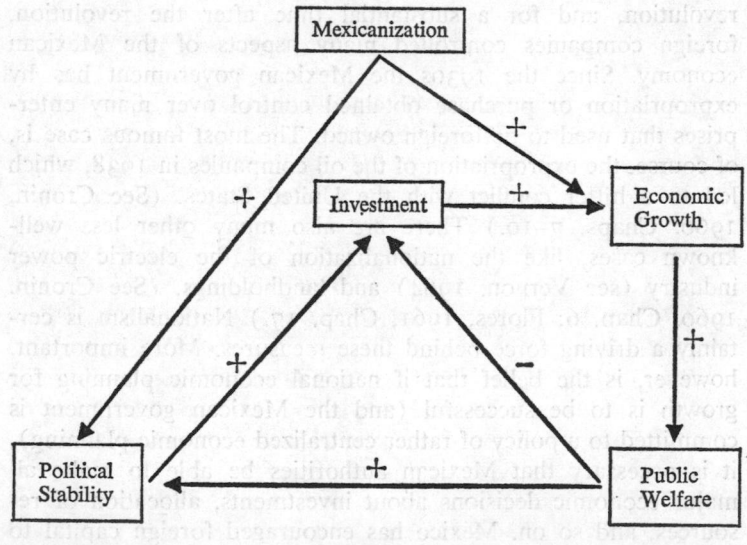

(1) Political stability clearly facilitates investments and other means toward economic growth. Stability and order make economic planning feasible, both for private entrepreneurs and public agencies. An unstable regime would have difficulty attracting foreign and domestic capital. Loss of work

hours due to political strikes, damage done to equipment, buildings, and other facilities during disorders would also impede the growth of the economy.

(2) Economic growth is clearly a prerequisite for the maintenance and extension of welfare services and policies. If a country wishes to industrialize and at the same time undertakes to construct a welfare state, then the economic growth rate has to be substantial if both sets of goals are to be met. It has been remarked that serious political problems are created in countries that attempt to build extensive welfare services before they have reached a high enough level of wealth. (Dore, 1964.) Even in countries with a certain amount of wealth and a steady growth rate, welfare policies may slow down industrialization and economic growth. Wage increases and benefits for the workers may mean less capital available for critical investments. Land-reform measures might sometimes lead to fragmentation of landholdings into economically unviable units.

(3) Following a line of thought that goes back to Durkheim (1933), we also assume that industrialization contributes to political stability by creating "organic solidarity," that is, interdependence due to division of labor among the various parts of the country. Localism, the traditional individual's sense that he owes his primary allegiance to "La Patria Chica" rather than to the nation, may be expected to diminish in importance as a result of this. The mobility of the labor force that industrialism tends to create should work in the same direction.

(4) Welfare policies contribute to political stability. In Mexico no regime that did not try to improve the lot of the poor masses, maintain a minimum wage level, give land to at least some of the landless, provide cheap housing and subsidized staple foods, and organize public works and other welfare facilities would get much popular support.

(5) Mexicanization has, we believe, contributed a great deal to political stability in Mexico. Apart from satisfying nationalistic sentiments, Mexicanization has provided ambitious and competent Mexicans with access to important economic command posts, whether as private owners or public officials. (To a similar end, Mexico requires foreign companies that operate in Mexico to train Mexicans for managerial positions in the companies.) The opportunities thus given to aggressive, competent individuals to acquire power, wealth, and prestige within the system prevents them from joining restless strata that might be a

372   ■ THE NATIONALIST PIVOT

threat to the regime. (Emerson, 1960; Zelditch and Anderson, 1965.)

(6) It also seems clear that the Mexicanization program has contributed a great deal to economic development in Mexico. Through control over the petroleum industry, for instance, the Mexican government has gotten a whole industry of synthetic fibers and other chemical products well under way. (Bermúdez, 1963, 21f.)

This analysis has shown, we believe, that the relationships between the goals are rather complicated. All goals cannot be maximized simultaneously. Compromises are made necessary, especially between the goals of industrialization and public welfare. Both these goals affect that of political stability, which in turn is seen as a main responsibility and concern of the power-holding political groups. And in Mexican history political stability has never been something to be taken for granted. In Mexico, therefore, the political elements will have to take the major share of the responsibility for how compromises between economic growth and public welfare are achieved. The state, represented by the federal government and the top organs of the ruling party, exercises a great deal of influence over business, as well as over labor unions and agrarian organizations, to this end. (The business community has considerable political influence, but how this is exerted falls outside of the scope of this paper.)

Well-organized interest groups exist in Mexico which attempt to promote one or the other of the goals in ⌐.[1] Interest groups differ from one another in the priority ordering they want to see given to the goals in ⌐. The agrarian organizations demand a rapid completion of the land reform at the expense of those landholders who still own or control more land than the *Código Agrario* allows. The middle class, including many governmental officials, seems to regard land-reform measures, and especially economic aid to marginal farmers, as welfare measures that should be given low priority in order that capital not be diverted from more profitable enterprises. The labor organizations demand wage increases and other benefits for the urban working classes. (Business groups demand government regulation. For a description of several of these organizations, see Scott, 1964; Brandenburg, 1964; and Kling, 1961.)

[1] The symbol refers to the goal-structure of the Mexican polity as illustrated in Figure I. It is used throughout this article.

2.1. The national political leadership in Mexico is strongly committed to the goal-structure ⌐ and is cognizant of the interrelations between the various goals.

Mexican presidential administrations have differed with respect to the emphasis given to the different goals, but we think it is fair to say that every regime from around 1920 on has pursued the goals in ⌐, and been fairly well aware of their interrelations. In fact, certain changes over time in the political climate in Mexico can be interpreted as reflections of changes in priorities given to the elements in ⌐. The Cárdenas administration (1934–40) was very much concerned with agrarian reform (to a large extent a welfare issue) and Mexicanization. (The oil industry was nationalized in 1938.) This regime, governing during the world-wide depression, could hardly have stressed economic growth and industrialization. In contrast, the Alemán regime (1946–52) stressed industrialization. The heavy emphasis on industrialization necessitated, or was seen to necessitate, holding back wage increases and other welfare measures. This took the form of repressive measures against militant labor union and agrarian agitation, and accounts for the bad name of Miguel Alemán in left-wing circles in Mexico.

3. THE OLIGARCHIC PATTERN

The Mexican national leadership seems, by choice or necessity, to be committed to tolerating a substantial amount of political pluralism. It is taken for granted, and indeed sometimes encouraged, that occupational groups attempt to promote their interests and demands through organizations. Political parties other than the ruling PRI are also tolerated, although not allowed to challenge effectively the PRI monopoly on power.

3.1. The political leadership in Mexico is committed to a substantial amount of pluralism, but is determined to preserve for the foreseeable future the de facto power monopoly of the PRI.

Our next two principles deal with conflict between interest groups.

3.2. The top decision-makers in Mexican national politics act so as to minimize the overt conflicts between interest groups giving different priorities to the elements in Γ.

3.3. If conflict arises between interest groups involving priority ordering of goals in Γ, the top leadership of the PRI and the government reserves for itself the right to make final and binding decisions.

Several writers about Mexican politics have emphasized that interest groups play an important role in the political system. The ruling party, the PRI, consists of three segments: the agrarian (peasants and agricultural laborers) sector (CNC, Confederación Nacional Campesina), the labor sector (CTM, Confederación de Trabajadores Mexicanos), and the middle-class sector (CNOP, Confederación Nacional de Organizaciones Populares). The only major interest groups that are excluded from the party are certain business groups. (For further organizational details, see Scott, 1964.) In the party policy-making and in executive bodies at the local, state, and national levels, there will always be representatives from each one of the three sectors. The various interest groups therefore have a voice in the nominations for public offices like federal and state deputies, senators, state governors, and president of the republic. (He who gets the PRI nomination, then, can be virtually sure of getting elected.) There is no doubt that in the prenomination struggle the various interest groups try to promote candidates sympathetic to their causes. It seems to be clear, however, that the top leadership of the party maintains rather tight control over who gets the actual nominations. Nominations are made at party conventions, but before the name of an aspirant is put before the convention, he will have to be approved by the national committee (Comité Ejecutivo Nacional), the top group of the PRI. Thus, the national committee has effective veto power.

We interviewed a representative of the national committee of the PRI who had been sent to a northern state to supervise the selection of candidates for the 1964 elections. He told us that there had been six aspirants for the two Senate posts from the state. The national committee allowed only two names to be placed before the convention which then had the option of accepting or rejecting these two men. During the discussion he maintained that this procedure should not be called imposition of candidates by the national committee; the committee passes on candidates that have been made available on the local scene. He also emphasized that Mexico, because of its turbulent history, needs a party that maintains "social peace" by seeing to it that equilibrium is maintained between the various special interest groups. He also said that, in his opinion, the middle-class sector of the party, the CNOP, can be said to represent the "national interest" more than the more specialized agarian and labor sectors. The CNOP represents a "more varied collection of interests" than the other sectors, according to him.

We interviewed the representative from the national committee in the presence of high PRI officials on the state level (including the president of the state committee). Everybody was very deferential toward the national committeeman. The latter did not hesitate to interrupt the others and was addressed by the honorific title "Don." (Anderson and Cockroft, *Field Notes,* Summer, 1964).

The national committee consists of seven members and is one of the most powerful political bodies in Mexico, second only to the office of the president of the republic or the secretary of the interior (Gobernación).

While we agree with Robert Scott and others that interest groups are very important in Mexican politics, we believe that they play an essentially secondary role, and that the real power lies in an inner circle of the ruling party. (It is hard to say how large this group is or how it is structured.) The interest groups *articulate* demands and needs, but the decisions on how to combine and harmonize these demands on the national level in the light of long-term goals are made by the ruling circle. The leaders are, however, at the same time, very much concerned with getting to know the points of view of various interest groups. The decisions of the top leadership are carried out by a bureaucracy staffed by various kinds of professionals. They often seem to have a "middle-class" orientation, but they hardly act in their professional roles as representatives of any interest groups. The *técnicos,* strongly committed to *dirigismo,* seem concerned with efficiency and economic modernization, often viewed in a long-term perspective. That the bureaucrats and politicians consult with representatives of the interest groups is obvious, but consultation is not necessarily acquiescing to pressures and demands, but can be purely for purposes of information and coöptation (see section 4). Leaders of interest groups on the local and national level are very busy trying to influence

administrative decisions and seek redress for grievances and
local problems, like shortage of water for irrigation, maltreat-
ment of peasants by local officials and so on (compare La-
Palombara, 1960). Thus, several of the peasant leaders we
interviewed make regular trips to Mexico City on behalf of the
members of their organizations. This holds both for leaders of
the official CNC and those representing dissident groups. It is
obvious that some detailed empirical studies of political and
bureaucratic practice need to be done before we can say anything beyond these generalities about the role of the interest
groups in the formulation of long-term policies on the one hand
and administrative implementation on the other.

There have been some very recent developments that suggest
that the oligarchic control over nominations may change. The
regime has lately been experimenting (in Baja California) with
a nomination procedure based on direct primaries. In these
internal elections the members of PRI, by direct and secret
ballot (see for instance *El Día,* April 14, 1965, and *Política,*
April 15, 1965, 24) selected candidates for various offices.
These elections were reported to have proceeded quietly. The
leader of PAN in Baja California declared that the chosen
PRI candidate for governor was "an honorable man" and he
expected that the coming constitutional elections could be
"clean"[2] (*El Día,* April 14, 1965). This experiment with direct
internal election was explicitly set up in order to select candidates with popular support. It was conceded that the old
system, still practiced in the other states, often led to the selection of candidates with little support among the population.
(See for instance *Excelsior,* April 7, 1965.)

4. THE COÖPTATION PATTERN

The ruling party in Mexico was built up during the 1920s and
1930s to provide a political instrument for the modernization
and nationalization of the polity. It was from the very beginning
ideologically and socially very heterogeneous. Apart from an
adherence to the principles of the revolution, as set forth in the
constitution and various other documents, membership required

[2] A PAN leader in Baja California later bitterly alleged that the elections held in the state in August, 1965, were fraudulent.

no specific ideological commitments. Marxists and other social-
ists became members, as did traditional liberals and people
without any coherent political beliefs at all. The party has by
and large continued to be pragmatic and ideologically vague. At
times strongly ideologically oriented groups have split away
from the PRI. In the late 1940s, for instance, the former leader
of the labor sector, Vicente Lombardo Toledano, split away to
form his own Partido Popular Socialista (PPS), which claims
to be Marxist. (We shall have more to say about this party and
its peasant organization later, in section 5:1.) In the last five
years or so, there has been a great deal of unrest in the peasant
sector of the ruling party. An independent peasant organization
(CCI, Central Campesina Independiente), was formed by people who used to be active in CNC, the PRI peasant sector. This
group is especially strong in Baja California and is led by a
rather charismatic leader named Alfonzo Garzón. (We discuss
this movement in section 5:2). Both the PPS and the CCI are
very critical of PRI and "the ruling oligarchy." The two
organizations have organized mass demonstrations in favor of
radical agrarian policies in their strongholds (the PPS and its
peasant organization in the Yaqui and Mayo valleys in Sonora,
and the CCI in Mexicali, Baja California). Several of their
leaders have been jailed and the authorities have used rather
harsh methods to "restore order." (*Hispanic American Report,*
November, 1962.) However, and here we have to anticipate
sections 5:1. and 5:2., in spite of their bitter criticism of the
PRI, both the PPS and the CCI *give the PRI a kind of qualified
support,* especially at election times. The dissidents do not
attempt to build political parties that could aspire to become
serious rivals of the PRI. (It is true that elements of the CCI
supported the uncompromising Frente Electoral del Pueblo in
the 1964 elections, but this was an exception to the main trend
and later caused the CCI to split.) The PPS openly supported
the PRI presidential candidate, Gustavo Díaz Ordáz, in this
election, and Alfonzo Garzón seems lately also to have found
that he has something in common with the PRI. In a report of a
meeting between Garzón and the new president of the PRI
(head of the Comité Nacional), agreement was said to have
been reached about certain issues (". . . with respect to the
future of Baja California"; *Siempre,* March 31, 1965, 57).
The PPS and CCI are not the only dissident groups that have
kept or built ties with the PRI. In the 1960s left-wing groups

inside and outside the PRI formed an organization called Movimiento de Liberación Nacional (MLN). This group was very critical of the PRI, but its majority did not break with the party in 1964. Its chief sponsor, ex-president Lázaro Cárdenas, endorsed Díaz Ordáz, the PRI candidate. We were told by a man who had been a local leader of the MLN in a northern state, that the best thing for him and people like him would be to support the PRI and work inside the party for a more radical line. In return, he and others seemed to expect that the left would get some influence; that maybe some cabinet post would be given to a person sympathetic to their point of view. (Anderson and Cockroft, *Field Notes,* Summer, 1964.)

A change in the electoral system, put into effect for the first time in 1964, guarantees that some officially "approved" opposition groups get representation in the federal Chamber of Deputies. Twenty-five seats are divided among the legally registered opposition parties in proportion to their total showing in the elections. Since the total number of deputies is 200, the PRI retains a comfortable majority.

We believe that the leadership of the PRI rather systematically attempts to make dissidents give at least qualified and partial support to the party, and that the PRI is willing to give dissidents a hearing and certain concessions in return for such limited support.

This mechanism of control has been called coöptation. "The process of absorbing new elements into the leadership or policy-determining strata of an organization as a means to averting threats to its existence or stability is called coöptation." (Selznik 1949, 259.) In the Mexican case the *intent* of the PRI is certainly to avert threats to the stability of the polity and the coöpted dissident groups certainly *come to believe* that they will get a measure of influence (see section 5:1.), but the extent to which they get any real influence, that is, get some parts of their programs enacted, is hard to determine. Coöptation is an exchange process, and can thus hardly be an enduring phenomenon unless the coöpted groups, led by rather astute politicians, receive some concessions. Our data do not allow us to penetrate this process any further.

4.1 The top leadership in the ruling party in Mexico systematically attempts to coöpt dissident groups into at least partial support of the PRI. The PRI is ready to make limited policy concessions to such groups in return for limited support.

The coöptation principle reflects, we think, a very basic concern that goes back to the times right after the revolutionary wars: the need to "nationalize" politics in the country. After the wars, politics in Mexico was very fragmented. Local bosses (called *caudillos* or, on a smaller scale, *caciques*) controlled many areas of the country, maintained their own armies or bands of strongmen, and often acted independently of or in defiance of the national authorities. Ideologically most of these bosses seem to have claimed to be representatives of "the true" revolution. Some combined anarchism and what little was known of Russian Communist practices with extreme left-wing ideologies (Friedrich, 1965). The party that began to be built in the 1920s had as one of its tasks to overcome this fragmentation, to build an organization which, although ideally sensitive to local needs and demands, could be an instrument in the construction of a modern, rather centralized state and the maintenance of social peace. As we have already said, the party chose to be ideologically pragmatic and vague, in order to accommodate the various groups. Groups of different persuasion were offered rewards and concessions in return for loyalty to the party and the regime. It was also, however, made very clear that the party would not tolerate any strong centers of power that were outside of the party or not allied with the party. If coöptation failed strong-arm methods were used. Many of the local caudillos and caciques were assassinated, on orders from the regime. Gradually there emerged the pattern we have seen: the PRI attempts to coöpt dissident groups and these know that in order to have any impact at all it is wise for them to maintain friendly relations with the PRI. Repression of uncoöptable groups is nowadays most of the time less harsh, but it still exists. While the PRI and its presidential candidate won support from many of the leftists, bitterly critical of the "oligarchy," in the 1964 elections, some leftist groups formed the Frente Electoral del Pueblo (FEP). This organization was hostile to the PRI and had its own candidate for the presidency. The FEP was *not* allowed to register as a legal political party. It was also regarded as ineffectual and unrealistic by many people sympathetic to its views on issues. (A strong split developed, for instance, within another dissident group, the MLN, over whether or not to support the FEP.) Thirty members of the FEP, the CCI, and the Mexican Communist Party were arrested in April, 1965, in Mexico City and many documents were confiscated (*Política,* April 15, 1965, 5).

We thus have another principle of politics in Mexico.

4.2. If coöptation of dissident groups fails, then repression is likely to occur.

The measures taken against the FEP and the Communists presumably represent premeditated decisions by the national authorities. There is also another type of repression in Mexico which represents survivals of earlier political forms. Local political and military authorities sometimes resort to violence against dissident groups, especially, it seems, in the countryside.[3]

> In Baja California, for example, an agrarian settlement, not far from Ensenada, is ruled by a cacique, who seems to base his power on his connections with the CNC and the state government. Opponents to him within the settlement have been assassinated by his alleged "pistoleros."
>
> As we have already said, politics in the state of Guerrero has the reputation of being controlled by traditional bosses. In the late 1950s there occurred violent and bloody clashes between soldiers and demonstrators in the cities of Iguala and Chilpancingo. The governor responsible for these measures of violence was later removed by the president of the republic. (Anderson and Cockroft, *Field Notes,* 1964.)

The PRI has been more concerned with coöpting left-wing than right-wing dissidence. The reason for this is partly that the PRI regards itself as the only legitimate heir to the Mexican revolution. This revolution was made in order to accomplish large-scale social change. The conservative and clerical groups that were bitterly opposed to the revolution had no place in the revolutionary party. They had to be reckoned with, but could not be coöpted. Left-wing dissidents, however, could challenge the PRI on its own ground. The regime has tolerated a conservative opposition party, the Partido de Acción Nacional

---

[3] For accounts of politically inspired violence in different parts of Mexico, see the weekly *Política,* the section entitled "La Nación."

(PAN). The PAN voters come from different social strata. There are the big businessmen, the members of the small-town clerically oriented middle classes and also the religious peasants in some parts of the country. (See for instance Foster, 1948, for a description of peasant conservatism.) The party also attracts workers and peasants who are discontented with the ruling PRI, which is often seen as corrupt and inefficient. The PAN won some local elections, for instance in Mérida, Yucatán, in 1964, but has never been able to challenge the power of the PRI in any serious manner. It used to accuse the PRI of large-scale fraud in the counting of ballots. Recently PAN has accepted the legitimacy of the basic gains of the revolution and a Christian Democratic faction of the party is making itself noticed. In talking with PRI officials one sometimes gets the impression that PAN is regarded as a legitimate opposition party which fulfills an important role in Mexican politics (the revolution was among other things made in the name of democracy), but which is not expected to seriously challenge the role of the PRI, sometimes referred to as *"el partido oficial,"* as representative of the mainstream of Mexican politics.[4]

To summarize, then, the PRI seems to be ruled by an oligarchy which, using both the carrot and the stick, keeps dissident groups under control. The ruling group considers and arbitrates the conflicting demands of many, often rather militant, interest groups, but also has rather explicit long-term plans for how Mexico is to develop economically, politically, and socially. The oligarchy perpetuates itself. The incumbent president of the republic, for instance, has the decisive voice in determining who his successor is to be and he selects the president of the Comité Nacional of the PRI. As we have seen, the top leadership of the party maintains tight control over nominations and elections. The minority-party seats in the Chamber of Deputies and the Baja California direct-primary experiment demonstrate, however, that the oligarchy also thinks ahead

---

[4] We said earlier that in Mexico a rather modern political system on the national level coexists with remnants of a traditional system. This is well illustrated by the contrast between the Baja California direct primaries with the following incident observed by an anthropologist in the state of Oaxaca: On election day in 1964 in a Zapotec community nobody cast a vote. In spite of this some 500 votes were recorded for both the PRI and the PPS. The count was made by the two officials from the lists of residents. Nobody in the town seemed to mind. (W. H. Geoghegan, *Field Notes,* Summer, 1964.)

toward a more democratic polity, when the "political maturity" (*madurez cívica*) is greater than it is now. (It is, of course, no coincidence, that the experiment with direct primaries was undertaken in Baja California, one of the most modernized states in the country.) In fact, some public pronouncements by the PRI president suggest that the oligarchy sees democratization of Mexico as proceeding in set stages. A new stage was said to have been entered with the institution of the direct primaries and the minority-party seats.

5:1. THE PARTIDO POPULAR SOCIALISTA AND ITS PEASANT LEAGUE

The purpose of this section is to illustrate further the main argument about the structure of Mexican politics that is set forth in sections 2 to 4. The information comes from printed sources and from interviews conducted in 1964 with leaders in the Union General de Obreros y Campesinos Mexicanos, the peasant league of the PPS.

Vicente Lombardo Toledano was head of the labor sector of the PRI up until 1941. In the late forties, after having been pushed aside by the ruling Alemán group in the PRI, he founded the Marxist Partido Popular Socialista. In collaboration with Lombardo a peasant leader, Jacinto López, who had earlier been active in the CNC, founded the agrarian organization Unión General de Obreros y Campesinos Mexicanos. This organization has branches in more than a dozen states, but has its main strength in Sonora, primarily in the Yaqui and Mayo river valleys. The organization comprises both members of agricultural collectives (*ejidos;* for the meaning of the word "collective" here see, for instance, Whetten, 1948) and landless laborers who demand land [*solicitantes de tierra*].

In the Yaqui valley the Unión General claims to have some 11,000 members (700 *ejidatarios* and some 10,000 *solicitantes*), organized in 117 local groups. The organization has a democratic structure: decisions are made by an assembly of the chairmen of the locals. A secretary coordinates the activities from a small office in Ciudad Obregón, the main city of the region.

The main activity of the organization consists of putting pressure on the political authorities on the municipal, state, and national levels to obtain full compliance with the agrarian reform laws. The valley has good, irrigated land, suitable for cotton, wheat, and some corn. There are many ejidos in the Yaqui valley, but much land is also in the hands of private families. Maps of the land tenure situation show that members of some families of revolutionary fame and families related to these by marriage (Obregón, Tapia, Calles) own large, sometimes continuous holdings. In order to comply with the letter of the law, the land a kin group owns is divided up among quite a few members. This is regarded by the peasant organization as a violation of the spirit of the land-reform laws.

The Unión General demands a change in this situation. A substantial part of the privately owned land should, the organization claims, be made into ejido land, so that at least some of the many landless *solicitantes* can get titles to land of their own. The organization has sponsored mass demonstrations and land invasions in order to put pressure on the authorities.

In spite of its agrarian militancy, the Unión General maintains somewhat strained, but not unfriendly relations with the PRI. Our informant characterized the relations between the organization and the state government at that time (1964) as "cordial." It had been worse earlier when the son of Alvaro Obregón, the revolutionary leader and later president of the republic (a member of one of the great landholding families), was governor of Sonora. When Díaz Ordáz was nominated as the PRI presidential candidate, the Unión General followed the decision of Lombardo Toledano to support him. Díaz Ordáz met with Jacinto López and the Yaqui valley leader of the Unión General in Hermosillo, the capital of Sonora. At that time the peasant leaders turned over to him a detailed account of the land tenure situation in the Yaqui and Mayo valleys. (This meeting was given some national publicity, see *Siempre*, May 6, 1964.) Díaz Ordáz was very concerned with the situation (our notes from interviews with Jacinto López and Yaqui valley informant). He used language to the effect that the situation was a scandal (*"es un desmadre"*) and indicated that he would try to do something about the situation. The Unión General leaders were evidently rather impressed with Díaz Ordáz, who used to be regarded as a member of the right-wing of the

PRI. "He matured during his campaign, came to understand domestic and agrarian problems," they said. (Our *Field Notes,* 1964.)

Lombardo Toledano seems, in spite of his Marxist ideology and leadership of an opposition party, to retain some access to and influence in the inner circle of the government. The PPS got a number of the minority-party seats in the national Chamber of Deputies after the 1964 elections, and Jacinto López was seated as a representative of the party. López clearly seemed to regard this as a gain. He and his organization now have a national platform from which they can make their views heard. López and our other informants from the Union General are clearly gradualists. They believe that change can only come slowly in Mexico, as a result of pressures and organization work. The organization was, nevertheless, denounced as Communist by some PRI leaders from the middle-class sector we interviewed in Hermosillo, Sonora.

5:2. THE CCI EXPERIENCE:
DISSENT FOLLOWED BY COÖPTATION

The CCI received its initial impetus from Alfonzo Garzón of Baja California, after a left-leaning state governor there (1953–59) had named the charismatic peasant leader head of the state branch of the CNC, the PRI's peasant sector. However, when the CNC and PRI failed to adequately meet the demands of Baja California peasants, already aroused by the dumping of saline water from the U.S. Colorado River which destroyed their crops (*Hispanic American Report,* XV, 989–90), Garzón broke from the PRI to form his own peasant movement, the nucleus of the national CCI, which was officially founded about a year later (HAR, XVI, 14–16). He took an overwhelming majority of Baja California's peasants with him (our interviews).

As the salinity problem worsened, new CCI locals formed in other states, and finally, Communist-oriented members of the CCI (less so Garzón's group) openly backed the "illegal" presidential candidate of the FEP. In 1964 the PRI stepped up its pressures on Garzón and his followers to "reenter the fold." Garzón had vainly essayed the tactic of political candidacy against the PRI in 1962, when he ran for mayor of Mexicali but was refused recognition as a candidate. The failure of FEP candidate Ramón Danzós Palomino, himself a peasant leader from the north (the impoverished La Laguna area), in the 1964 presidential elections, may have further disillusioned Garzón with the efficacy of political dissent. In any case, repression of CCI demonstrations continued apace, and by 1964, Garzón seemed willing to reconsider his relationship with the PRI.

The CCI people we interviewed emphasized that their organization was working solely for the interests of the peasants. They seemed determined not to let their organization be used for any broader political purposes, and expressed rather strong resentment against the Communist Party, which they accused of being more interested in broad political questions than in the problems of the peasants. Within the CCI friction between the Communists and their sympathizers and Garzón and his group has occurred from the time the organization was founded.

The CCI, then, is clearly a dissenting group, but it is important to note that its dissent, although very vigorous, has been confined to a sharply limited set of issues. This strategy, of course, makes a reconciliation with the official party, once the issues that brought about dissent have been attended to, much easier than a line of more diffuse and less delineated dissent. In the interviews the CCI men often condemned certain groups within the PRI, but indicated that there were others that they respected. For example, speaking about a peasant leader in Mexicali who had chosen to stay in the official CNC where he led a dissident faction, they emphasized that he was "clean and honorable." The PRI on its part kept lines of communication open with the CCI, at least with its branch in Baja California, the Liga Agraria Estatal. Before the 1964 elections, one of the PRI candidates for senator from this state contacted leaders of the Liga in order to hear their points of view on current issues.

The Díaz Ordáz administration concluded an agreement with the United States which promises to end the dumping of salt water into the Colorado River. It has also been announced that large sums of money will be used by the government to rehabilitate the Mexicali valley land that had been ruined by salt water. (*El Día,* March 26, 1965.) At least some of the goals that the CCI had been agitating for have thus been achieved. In September, 1964, Garzón declared Communist members of the CCI *personae non gratae* (*Política,* October 15, 1964). Danzós, his followers from the Laguna, and all Communist members of the CCI in turn declared Garzón and his group expelled from the CCI. In effect, a second CCI was formed behind Danzós.

Garzón, meanwhile, began to cooperate more openly with the PRI. Demonstrations by Garzón's CCI became less common, although various of his followers continued to be smeared as "Communists" and jailed from time to time. Garzón and his group seemed to have made their peace with the PRI at the time of the gubernatorial election in Baja California in August, 1965. Garzón was photographed frequently with the PRI candidate, and at least according to the PAN, Garzón openly campaigned for the PRI among the peasantry (El Día, July 30, 1965). Thus, Garzón and the CCI seemed to be following the same road toward coöptation by the PRI as Jacinto López and the Unión General did in Sonora a year earlier.

The PRI still had to reckon with the uncoöptable Danzós faction of the CCI, however. As we would expect, repressive measures were used against them. When small-scale milk producers in Puebla protested a new pasteurization law which threatened to encourage large monopolies in October, 1964, they invited Danzós to address a rally. Danzós and other "Communists" were jailed. The PRI labor movement and the CTM rallied behind the state governor in a show of unity. This may have been a mistake, for among Puebla's students and workers the occasion of the milk-producers' protest and severe repression of demonstrators was a perfect pretext for expressing their own complaints about the relatively unprogressive and stagnant administration of the governor, an army general accused of nepotism. When massive demonstrations demanding the governor's resignation mounted, and a few labor unions began to cancel their affiliation with the CTM (some observers say that worker soviets were even formed in some cases), the problem assumed national proportions. The president of Mexico called in high national and local PRI officials and worked out an immediate solution. The demands of the dissidents were swiftly met. The Puebla governor stepped down behind the façade of "a leave of absence." The people who booed him turned out the next day to cheer the new governor, who was flown in from Quintana Roo where his progressive administration had been described by PPS leader Lombardo Toledano as "an example for all governors to follow." (Política, November

1, 1964, also, *Excélsior* and *El Día,* October 15 through November 1, 1964.)

The Puebla experience was one of dissent, followed by repression, followed by a kind of coöptation. When repression failed, coöpting the demands of the dissenters by naming a new governor with a more liberal program succeeded.

6. MEXICAN POLITICAL PATTERNS
AS FUNCTIONS OF THE GOAL-STRUCTURE

The two broad tendencies in Mexican politics that we have tried to demonstrate in the previous three sections, the oligarchical and the coöptation patterns, should be related to the nature of the goal-structure that we described in section 2. In an underdeveloped society with sharp latent and often manifest conflicts between interest groups, regions, and to some extent ethnic groups, and a tradition of political violence, a regime that is strongly committed to political stability, substantial economic development, and social welfare faces a task that must often seem insurmountable. If the regime, by choice or necessity, is *also* committed to a certain amount of political pluralism, then it cannot choose the way of Communist one-party states. Under conditions of economic backwardness increments in welfare policies and wages and other benefits must be carefully controlled, if there are to be resources available for economic growth. The demands and expectations of the population have to be met to some extent to ensure the necessary amount of political stability required for continuous economic growth. Dissident political groups, based on substantial or important social strata that believe that their demands have not been met adequately, will tend to develop. If the regime is unable to or does not want to suppress these, then it has to develop ways of co-existing with them, but in such a way that they do not threaten the stability of the polity. The regime will very likely tend to develop mechanisms like the control and coöptation pattern described in our analysis.

If our analysis is right, the Mexican polity provides an example of a complicated system of exchanges between interest groups and an oligarchy that provides decisive and sometimes rather ruthless leadership. It is what Shills (1962) calls a tutelary democracy. Political "interest group" theory, which has had a tendency to view politics solely as shaped by contending interest groups, and hence to ignore the role of leadership on the national level, should have much to learn from the study of this system.

In conclusion we shall mention, but not analyze here, one important cost that may be inherent in this type of political system. The absence of a real contest between opposing political parties breeds political apathy and indifference. We know that popular participation in Mexican politics is quite low compared to more advanced democracies (Almond and Verba, 1963, Chapters 3–9). We are referring to real involvement in politics, not the kind of sham participation that occurs when a busload of peasants is brought in to cheer a candidate in return for beer and food. It is quite clear that the top leadership desires active citizen participation in public affairs, but the basic structural features of the polity may make it impossible to reach this goal. The minority-party seats in the Chamber of Deputies and the experiment with direct primaries may be first steps toward making a fuller participation possible. If in the future direct primaries are adopted in all the states of the Mexican union and are used for nominating candidates for all local offices, from mayor to state governor and federal deputy and senator, then it is likely that the two features of the Mexican polity this paper has dealt with will change rather drastically.

REFERENCES

Almond, Gabriel, et al., *The Politics of Developing Areas*, Princeton: Princeton University Press, 1960.

Almond, Gabriel, and Sidney Verba, *Civic Culture*, Princeton: Princeton University Press, 1963.

Bermúdez, Antonio J., *The Mexican National Petroleum Industry*, Institute for Hispanic-American and Luzo-Brazilian Studies, Stanford University, 1963.

Brandenburg, Frank, *The Making of Modern Mexico*, Englewood Cliffs, N.J.: Prentice Hall, 1964.

Cronin, E. David, *Josephus Daniels in Mexico*, Madison: The University of Wisconsin Press, 1960.

Dore, Ronald, "Latin America and Japan Compared," in John J. Johnson (ed.), *Continuity and Change in Latin America*, Stanford, California: Stanford University Press, 1964.

Durkheim, Émile, *The Division of Labor in Society*, New York: Free Press, 1964.

Emerson, Rupert, *From Empire to Nation*, Boston: Beacon Press, 1962.

El Día, Mexico City daily.

Excélsior, Mexico City daily.

Flores, Edmundo, *Tratado de economía agrícola*, Fondo de Cultura Económica, Mexico-Buenos Aires, 1961.

Foster, George, *Empire's Children: The People of Tzintzuntzán*, Smithsonian Institution, Institute of Social Anthropology, Publication No. 6, México, 1948.

Friedrich, Paul, "A Mexican Cacicazgo," *Ethnology*, Vol. IV. No. 2 (April, 1965), pp. 190–209.

Hispanic American Report. Published by the Institute for Hispanic-American and Luzo-Brazilian Studies, Stanford University.

Kling, Merle, *A Mexican Interest Group in Action*, Englewood Cliffs, N.J.: Prentice Hall, 1961.

LaPalombara, Joseph, "The Utility and Limitations of Interest Group Theory in Non-American Field Situations," *Journal of Politics*, Vol. 22 (February, 1960), pp. 29–49.

Poleman, Thomas, *The Papaloapan Project*, Stanford: Stanford University Press, 1964.

Política, Mexico City weekly.

Scott, Robert E., *Mexican Government in Transition*, Urbana: University of Illinois Press, 1964.

Selznik, Philip, *TVA and the Grassroots*, Berkeley: University of California Press, 1949.

Shils, Edward, "The Military in the Political Development of the New States," in John J. Johnson (ed.), *The Role of the Military in Underdeveloped Countries*, Princeton: Princeton University Press, 1962.

Siempre, Mexico City weekly.

Siverts, Henning, "Political Organization in a Tzeltal Community in Chiapas, Mexico," *Alpha Kappa Delta*, Vol. III, No. 1 (Winter, 1960), pp. 14–28.

Vernon, Raymond, *The Dilemma of Mexico's Development*, Cambridge, Mass.: Harvard University Press, 1963.

—— (ed.), *Public Policy and Private Enterprise in Mexico*, Cambridge, Mass.: Harvard University Press, 1964.

Whetten, Nathan, *Rural Mexico*, Chicago: University of Chicago Press, 1948.

Zelditch, Morris, Jr., and Bo Anderson, "On the Balance of a Set of Ranks," in Joseph Berger, Morris Zelditch, Jr., and Bo Anderson, *Sociological Theories in Progress*, Boston: Houghton Mifflin, 1965.

Political Strategies of

National Development in Brazil

HÉLIO JAGUARIBE

HISTORY AND POLITICAL DEVELOPMENT

BRAZIL is the largest Latin American country in area (3,294,-
600 square miles), in population (more than 82 million inhabitants in 1965), and in absolute gross national product (the
GNP in 1965 was above U.S. $27 billion). The country, with a
territory larger than the United States without Alaska, occupies
more than half of South America, extending from 5 16′ 19″
north to 33 45′ 09″ south and from 34 45′ 54″ east to 73 59′
32″ west. This territory encompasses five major regions, presenting the main features indicated in Table I.

The Brazilian population, one of the fastest growing in the
world (3.1 percent yearly) is ethnically mixed. According to
official statistics, 62 percent are white, predominantly of Portuguese descent, 26 percent are "brown," mostly mulattoes with
some Indians and mestizos (about 300,000), 11 percent are
Negro, and 1 percent are Oriental, mostly Japanese. Scholars,
however, agree that the percentage of whites is a little smaller
and that of mulattoes correspondingly larger, because color
classifications are self-stated and lighter mulattoes tend to class-
ify themselves as whites.

The social structure of the population is more difficult to
estimate, because census data are not collected for this purpose.
According to the available statistical data, the following class
distribution of the population seems reasonably accurate: (1)

TABLE I
BRAZILIAN REGIONS

Region	Area	Percent of: Population	Percent of: National Income	Main features
North	42	4	4	Amazon basin; equatorial and tropical forest; very humid; thin layer of humus over crystalline; extractive economy (rubber, fishing); extensive cattle breeding in some parts.
Northeast	11	22	9	Fertile coastal plain; sugar cane plantation in manorial system; arid hinterlands; cattle breeding and cotton; textile industry needing modernization; SUDENE plans.
East	15	35	36	Tropical fertile alongside coast; cacao in northern part, coffee in southern part; active, diversified, emerging industry.
South	10	35	50	Temperate fertile area, coffee in northern part, cereals in southern part; active, diversified, emerging industry.
Center-West	22	4	3	Tropical inland humid area; extensive cattle breeding.

Source: Instituto Brasileiro de Geografia e Estatística-IBGE (Brazilian Institute of Geography and Statistics), Anuario Estatístico, 1963.

upper and middle class, 15 percent; (2) working class and lower white collar, 35 percent; (3) peasants, 50 percent.

Fifty-one percent of the population is illiterate, most of these being peasants. The urban population (about 45 percent of the total) is growing faster (5.4 percent) than the rural (1.6 percent). The rapid and profound changes introduced by recent industrialization have only marginally affected the countryside, which keeps its archaic and traditional character. There is a corresponding high concentration of land and large amount of very small estates, the output of which is considerably below the value of the local minimum wage. The large properties (with more than 100 hectares) represent less than 11 percent of the rural establishments but own 79.7 percent of the agricultural area. The small properties (with less than 10 hectares) represent 45 percent of the total establishments but own only 13.3 percent of the agricultural area, according to official statistics.

Stages of Brazilian Development

The course of Brazilian history is similar to that of most Latin American countries. Change has been very gradual; the old colonial and semicolonial structures were recently only affected by socioeconomic development. This disparity between a rapidly moving political plan and a slowly changing socioeconomic basic structure is in the Brazilian case particularly wide.

After Independence the country was ruled by Pedro I (1822–31) and Pedro II (1831–89), after whom there was a short-lived positivist military republic under Marshals Deodoro da Fonseca and Floriano Peixoto (1889–95). Then followed a stable but static oligarchical republic (1895–1930), a radical revolution (1930), a radical regime (1930–37), and a semifascist (1937–45) regime. A populist democracy, chaotic but reform-minded and developmental, brought the country into the fifties and early sixties. This government was overthrown by a reactionary military coup in 1964.

All these events concur with the development of the country through three stages: (1) the colonial (1500–1850); (2) the semicolonial (1850–1930); and (3) the transitional (since 1930).[1]

The colonial stage begins with the Portuguese settlement of the newly discovered land. It lasts until the middle of the nineteenth century, when the Eusebio de Queiros Act, forbidding overseas slave traffic, forced the gradual substitution of free

[1] Cf. from an economic point of view Celso Furtado, *Formação econômica do Brasil,* Fundo de Cultura, Rio de Janeiro, 1959 (there is an English translation published by Berkeley University Press); from a sociopolitical point of view, Hélio Jaguaribe, *Economic and Political Development: A Theoretical Approach and a Brazilian Case Study.* Cambridge: Harvard University Press, 1968.

labor for slaves. In those three and a half centuries the country remained basically an exporter of raw materials produced by slave labor: wood in the first decades of the sixteenth century; sugar from the late sixteenth to the twentieth century; gold and precious stones in the eighteenth century; hides and miscellaneous tropical agricultural products in the early nineteenth century. These have been Brazil's main products and exports.

All this economic activity is surprising in view of the country's small population[2] and the fact that the wealth was controlled by a handful of patrician landowners and merchants. In the middle of the seventeenth century, when the sugar industry was most active, the total annual exports were worth about 3.6 million pounds sterling, or about 27 tons of gold.[3] The export of gold, diamonds, and precious stones was also extremely high. Until 1803, Humboldt estimates the total Brazilian production of gold at 194 million pounds sterling, most of which was extracted in the eighteenth century. The extraction of diamonds in the eighteenth century is estimated at 3 million carats, worth at the time about 10 million pounds sterling.[4]

The Eusebio de Queiros Act of 1850 altered the patterns of income and encouraged the development of an internal market. While the Brazilian economy, at the semicolonial stage, was still dominated by the external demand for its major exports, domestic formation and accumulation of capital was increasing. There was a corresponding increase in the country's self-generated capacity for investment. The population grew from 8 million in 1850, to about 14 million at the fall of the Empire, and 33 million in 1930. The economic expansion, although quantitative rather than qualitative, was even larger, stimulated

[2] According to Caio Prado Júnior, *Historia econômica do Brasil* (São Paulo: Editorial Brasiliense, 3rd edition, 1953) the population of Brazil in the periods under discussion was:

Year	Free	Slave	Total
1576	—	—	57,000
1776	—	—	1,900,000
1800	2,000,000	1,000,000	3,000,000
1823	2,813,351	1,147,515	3,960,866
1850	5,520,000	2,500,000	8,020,000

[3] Roberto Simonsen, in his *Historia econômica do Brasil,* São Paulo: Cia. Edit., Nacional, 3rd ed. 1957, p. 115, estimates Brazilian production of sugar, until Independence, at 300 million pounds sterling at that time, of which 200 million was produced in the seventeenth century.

[4] *Ibid.,* pp. 284 and 289.

by the ever-increasing exportation of coffee. Coffee production and exports began growing in the second half of the nineteenth century, reached 16 million bags (of 60 kilograms each) at the turn of the century, and climbed to a peak of 30 million bags on the eve of the world depression of 1929.[5] Exports rose from an annual average of 55 million pounds sterling in 1841–50, to 291 million in 1891–1900, and to a peak of 806 million in 1921–30.[6]

The colonial stage had led to the formation of a central government which provided political unity, maintaining the inherited cultural unity of a loosely articulated, archipelagic society. The various production centers of that society, composed of patrician landowners and slave peasants, were directly connected to their European metropolitan centers: Portugal until Independence; Great Britain after that. Otherwise, there was only the empty space of unexplored land or the areas of subsistence economy, economically no less empty. With the semicolonial stage began the conversion of that archipelagic society into a national society, first by integrating into an internal market the formerly unconnected centers of production, and later by integrating into a single political structure the plantation society of the nineteenth century.

With the increasing city expansion an urban middle class developed, mostly in Rio de Janeiro and the major provincial capitals: Recife, Salvador, São Paulo, and Pôrto Alegre. The army, enlarged in the last third of the nineteenth century due to the war with Paraguay, became the most important agency of social and political promotion of the rather marginal middle class. The fact that Brazilian urbanization had preceded its industrialization had led to the formation of a large marginal

---

[5] Even before the Great Depression, Brazilian coffee production exceeded international demand, thus lowering prices. According to Celso Furtado (*op. cit.,* p. 208 ff.) the sterling price of the coffee bag declined from 4.09 in 1893 to 2.91 in 1896 and 1.48 in 1889. To correct that trend, Brazilian exporters, through the Taubate Agreement of 1906, created a system providing for the limitation of exports to the effective demand, the balance of the production being bought and stored by the government. More than 30 percent of the coffee produced was being stored in the late twenties, and its accumulated value of more than $2 billion clearly indicated that this system could not be maintained for long. The Great Depression destroyed it entirely, imposing, from September, 1922, to September, 1931, a price drop from 22.5 cents a pound to 8 cents.

[6] Cf. Caio Prado Júnior, *op. cit.*

middle class in a society which, based on a plantation export economy, had little room for the kinds of services that are usually rendered by the middle classes. That economically marginal middle class, however, was the best-educated segment of the population. It constituted the public opinion of the big cities and performed an increasingly important political role. Its absorption by a military and civil bureaucracy purposefully expanded for such a role was the solution found by the ruling oligarchy. This arrangement subsidized the marginal middle class at the expense of the public treasury while preserving its own interests and power.

This system, which has become known as "politics of clientèle"[7] and which led to a special kind of state, the "Estado Cartorial" (literally, notarial state), consists fundamentally in the exchange of superfluous jobs for votes. The "Cartorial" state includes the middle class in an ever-expanding military and civilian bureaucracy by allowing it to nominally render public services but actually providing more or less useless jobs for the political clientèle. This system preserves the status quo and maintains, within the appearance of a democratic regime, the oligarchical rule of the establishment.

The Crisis of Transition

The semicolonial structure came to an end in the 1920s through the combined effects of internal and external forces. The external forces have already been mentioned. In the long run, there was too great a discrepancy between the growth of the international demand for Brazilian coffee and the domestic increase of its production(artificially kept at a high pace by the Taubate Agreement) as well as the rate of growth necessary for continued economic expansion. Moreover, the Great Depression caused such a drastic reduction in the quantity and value of imports by the industrialized countries that no economy based on coffee exports could survive unchanged.

In addition to these circumstances, the intensive growth of an urban middle class preceding the industrialization of the country

[7] The terms "politics of clientèle" and "Estado Cartorial" were coined, together with the corresponding phenomena first analyzed, in my study "Politica de clientela e politica ideologica" (*Digesto Econômico*, São Paulo, 1951), and have later been developed in "O nacionalismo na atualidade brasileira" (ISEB, Rio de Janeiro, 1958).

far surpassed the ability of the semicolonial structure to adapt
to it. There was a double phenomenon in this direction. Culturally, the development of an educated urban middle class
eventually brought the country to the spiritual atmosphere of
post-Victorian Europe.[8] Politically, the increasing importance
of the army and civilian bureaucracies made it impossible for
the oligarchical establishment to keep these forces under their
control. Cultural modernity and military-bureaucratic strength
allowed the middle class to achieve control of the state by a
revolution in 1930, ideologically based on the principles of
secret vote and honest ballot computation.

This was the second time in Brazilian history that the emerging middle class had seized control of the state by revolution.
The first attempt was the republican revolution of 1889. Positivist republicanism in the earlier revolution and radical liberalism
in the later were the respective ideological motivations. In both
cases, the army was the most effective instrument of the rising
middle class. The republican revolution was a simple military
coup with the marginal participation of a few leaders of the
Republican Party. It attempted to establish an austere and
"scientific" petty-bourgeois government and directed all its
efforts toward a new constitutional organization. It never occurred to the republican revolutionaries that the effective bases
of the *ancien régime* were not the Emperor and the former
monarchical features of the Brazilian state, but the system of
rural property and its exploitation. The control of this system
by the patrician oligarchy guaranteed to that class the socio-
political control of the country, whatever the constitutional
form of government might be. The inevitable consequence of a
purely formal change in the organization of the state was immediately apparent in the first presidential elections held by the
new government: the landowners recovered full control of
political power, because their control of the nation's economy
remained unaltered.

[8] Typically expressive of the new spiritual atmosphere in literature,
music, and plastic arts was the Modern Art Week, celebrated in São
Paulo in February, 1922, under the intellectual leadership of Graça
Aranha and Mario de Andrade, challenging, in a way which aroused
enormous scandal and protest, the current academic style. The social
sciences and philosophy, then divided between the positivist and the
scholastic schools, would only in the next decade start feeling the effect
of modern thinking, and only after the Second World War would they be
moved by the great currents of thought of our time.

The second middle-class revolution was both broader and deeper. The army was still a decisive factor in the conquest of power. But this time it did not take the initiative of the movement. Civilians began the revolution by arming their own ranks and assaulting military barracks and arms depots in Rio Grande do Sul. The army, furthermore, did not side as a whole with the revolutionaries. The division of military sympathies between the two camps roughly followed a generational line, with the young officers supporting the revolution. This division later induced the chiefs of the army, allegedly in order to prevent a longer and bloodier civil war, to overthrow the last president of the "Old Republic," Washington Luis, and allow Getulio Vargas, the leader of the revolution, to take over the government.

The results of the radical revolution of 1930 have been more far-reaching than those achieved by the republicans in 1889. It is true that the revolution never achieved a consistent theoretical and programmatic formulation of its aims, which remained at the vague level of socio-democratic reformist generalizations or slogans. It is also true that the more radical revolutionaries, the *tenentes* and their civilian companions who wished to introduce rapid and profound, albeit not clearly formulated, changes in Brazilian society, gradually lost their influence to the more moderate and politically sensitive sectors. Nevertheless, with the revolution of 1930, Brazil changed irreversibly, because the semicolonial structures no longer satisfied the country's international and domestic needs. Even if the radical revolution failed in formulating and in carrying over an alternate model for democratic development, it still served to break down the old structures and traditions and to set in motion a process of spontaneous change which could later be accelerated and oriented more deliberately.

Like the republicans of 1889, the radicals of 1930 were unable to change the system of property and exploitation of the Brazilian countryside. This time, however, the accumulation of unsalable stocks of coffee and the drastic drop in the quantity and price of coffee exports were acting as objective factors of change. The new government, supported by the rising middle class, was not willing in the name of its own principles to return power to the rural oligarchy. The economic situation created by the coffee surplus and the Great Depression, and the new *realpolitik* of the middle class and its leader, Getulio Vargas, gave the revolution of 1930 a meaning and outcome that the

revolutionaries themselves had not been able to formulate and
to forecast.

Politically the revolution created a government which ceased
to be an executive committee of the coffee planters and exporters. The government now depended chiefly on the support
of the military and civilian bureaucracies, which were enlarged
in order to provide new jobs for the always underemployed
middle class. The necessity of maintaining this new form of
government led Getulio Vargas to the "New State" coup of
1937. Vargas and his followers were quite aware that if the
scheduled elections of 1938 were duly held, the rural oligarchy,
in spite of its economic setbacks, would surely win due to its
unbroken control over the rural majority of the electorate.
Vargas' New State, therefore, was primarily a device for the
governing circle to stay longer in power, and for the middle
class in general to keep sharing the control of the state without
controlling the means of production. It was as well an expression of the ideological change undergone by the middle class,
from the radical liberalism of the twenties to the fascist tendencies of the late thirties. Vargas' New State was much nearer
to Franco's Spanish Falangism or to Salazar's Portuguese Cor-
porativism than to the German or even the Italian models. It
also provided a protective shield to the prevailing interests of
the time. The middle class was assured its continued co-optation by the New State bureaucracy. It no longer had to barter
jobs for votes. For the landowners, the New State offered the advantage of not interfering in the agrarian economy of the country
and of accepting them as the official spokesmen for the countryside, thus keeping them in political control of their rural
strongholds. In terms of the interests of the urban bourgeoisie,
the New State repressed the socialist tendencies that were
beginning to menace the private appropriation of the means of
production. It also offered the benefit of favoring the expansion
of the internal market and protecting it with its right-wing
nationalism from foreign competition that could easily strangle
the developing national industry. For the working class, the
New State, although repressing any attempt to create an independent political organization, adopted a strongly paternalistic
posture, introducing important new social legislation and assuring the protection of the worker's rights.

While these changes were being made at the political level,
the country was being still more profoundly affected at the

economic level by the events following the revolution of 1930. The coffee crisis, caused by the combined effects of overproduction, unsalable accumulated stocks, and the drastic reduction in price and quantity of exports, acted as an objective impetus to economic change. On the one hand, the country could not continue to import the industrial goods required for its consumption.[9] On the other hand, the decrease in coffee prices, although much smaller in Brazil than in the international market,[10] made other investments more attractive than coffee. Thus, a spontaneous process of import substitution created the conditions for the country's industrialization. The industrial goods that the balance of payments precluded importing could now be profitably made at home (this acted as a powerful indirect protectionism). Beginning with textiles, a large range of light and medium industries was gradually installed during the thirties, according to the necessities of import substitution and the profit margins.[11] The Second World War accelerated import substitutions because of the external limitation on supplies due to war restrictions.

The National Front

A consequence of industrialization was the emergence of two new social groups, the industrialists and the proletariat. Before the expansion of Brazilian industry, the owners and managers of manufacturing concerns belonged to no specific social group. Some, like the pioneer Viscount of Maua, who were formerly self-made men with modest clerical or technical occupations, considered themselves members of the petty bourgeoisie. Most of the industrialists of the Old Republic did not distinguish themselves from the commercial bourgeoisie and belonged, in an indiscriminate form, to the ruling oligarchy, which had a rural basis.

[9] Cf. Celso Furtado, op. cit., p. 218.

[10] Due to the domestic policies of coffee protection, the average decline in the price of coffee from 1929 to 1932–34 was only 25 percent in Brazil, while its international price decreased 62 percent. Cf. Celso Furtado, op. cit., p. 219.

[11] Brazilian industrialization, which only in the thirties became an irreversible and self-expanding process, had already had an important upsurge in the Empire from 1845 to 1875 with the Viscount of Maua, and another less spectacular but longer phase in the Old Republic dating from the First World War.

The new industrialists, however, because of their increasing number and the specificity of the interests of their sector, soon realized that they were a special group within the bourgeoisie. The new industrial bourgeoisie was committed to economic and social development: they opposed the rural oligarchy and the traditional export-import merchant bourgeoisie, who depended on the maintenance of the old modes of production and trade and represented the semicolonial establishment based on those modes. To expand their production they needed to maximize the rate and the margin of autonomy of the domestic process of capital formation and enlarge the internal market by increasing the population's capacity to consume and by incorporating into the economy those marginal populations which barely subsisted.

The fact that the industrial bourgeoisie, as a rapidly growing social group, was the result of the process of import substitution determined its particular role in the national society. For purely objective reasons (often not understood by the individual industrialists) the industrial bourgeoisie was a natural ally of the proletariat—its counterpart in the same process. Both classes grew out of the process of socioeconomic development, and the integration and consolidation of Brazil as a nation. Both were committed to changing the semicolonial structures into modern ones. In order to do this, both needed to convert the semifeudal Brazilian society into one which was basically democratic and development-oriented.

This coincidence of interests between the industrial bourgeoisie and the proletariat marked the appearance of a new sector in the middle class, composed of various executives and technicians required by the new industry. The traditional middle class was essentially marginal; its survival depended on the Cartorial state. But the new middle class was composed mostly of younger people who had acquired the new skills needed for the technical and administrative operation of the new industry and for the distribution of its products. The new middle class also generated a new intelligentsia, no longer primarily or exclusively concerned with literary or artistic affairs but fundamentally engaged in a deliberate effort to promote the economic, social, cultural, and political development of Brazil as a nation. For the first time in its history, Brazil was subjectively felt by its citizens to be in the process of becoming an autonomous polity with a special national identity.

These new social groups, united by their common interests

and summoned by the new intelligentsia to an awakening consciousness of their new roles, were also led to adopt a new political position. It was under these circumstances that Getulio Vargas, the former leader of the radical revolution of 1930, was able to lead these new forces and to launch the country in a new and broader political direction.

The personality and political significance of Getulio Vargas have not yet been accurately appraised, partly because his lasting impact on recent events still makes him controversial. In his peculiar combination of personal opportunism and social awareness, he successively played three different roles in the course of his political life: the radical liberal, until 1937; the proto-fascist, from 1937 to 1943; and the center-left laborite, from the last two years of the New State until his tragic suicide in 1954. Most analysts have either viewed him in only one of these three roles, or they considered all his political positions merely as tactical maneuvers at the service of opportunistic power politics.

Actually, like most men of power, Getulio Vargas was both a manipulator of people and symbols in order to achieve his own political designs, and a most effective representative of the three new social aspirations of his time: radicalism, fascism, and welfare laborism. His embodiment of these aspirations enabled him to ride the great waves of political change, from 1930 to 1954. It was because the old semicolonial establishment had exhausted all its economic and socio-political possibilities that the Brazilian middle class could successfully wage the radical revolution of 1930, bringing to power the formerly defeated candidate of the opposition. It was because the radicals were neither able to change the socioeconomic structure of the country nor to accept a regression to the political status quo of pre-1930 that the Vargas movement was driven to semifascist solutions. The middle class, still affected by economic marginality, feared its own proletarianization as much as it resented the rising political importance of the working class. This led them to support the coup staged by Vargas in 1937. That same middle class lost thereby its former revolutionary impetus of the twenties and early thirties. This loss allowed Getulio Vargas, who understood the inevitability of the final defeat of the Axis in the Second World War, to change his political role for the last time. He opposed the worn-out radical liberalism of the twenties as well as the semifascist regime he was still leading.

He attempted to shift the socio-political basis of the New State from the middle class to a coalition formed by the working class and the industrial bourgeoisie. From 1943 until the downfall of the New State, while the formal government apparatus remained the same, Vargas actively tried to strengthen the working-class unions and to convert them to the support of his future regime.

This attempt was frustrated by the military coup of 1945. It is interesting to observe that this coup, in which the army once again acted as the military-political agent of the middle class, was justified as an antifascist movement for restoring democracy. Actually, however, what really scared the military, who had been the staunchest supporters of the New State while it was in effect a semifascist regime, was precisely the fact that Vargas was then successfully shifting his regime from the right to the left.

The military coup of 1945 notwithstanding, there was no change in the course of events set in motion by Vargas. PTB and PSD,[12] the two new parties organized by Vargas in 1945, brought him back to power with a massive vote in the elections of 1950, succeeding the inexpressive conservative government of Marshal Dutra (1945–50).[13] After the tragic suicide of Vargas in 1954, the PSD-PTB coalition elected Juscelino Kubitschek (1955–60), who continued the same basic policies.

The period from 1945 to 1960, Brazil's fastest phase of development, was ruled by the national front. The national front—not its actual name—was a loose coalition of social forces representing a process of national development based on the expansion of Brazilian industry. Its members were the

---

[12] PTB—Partido Trabalhista Brasileiro (Brazilian Labor Party), representing the working class, substantially based on the unions created and supported by the ministry of labor; PSD—Partido Social Democrático (Social Democratic Party), representing, without any connection with the social democracy of Germany, a wide and heterogeneous socio-political spectrum, from modern industrialists to traditional rural landowners, and basically formed by the politico-administrative machine of the New State.

[13] Marshal Eurico Gaspar Dutra, the conservative former war minister during the New State regime, despite having sided with the military coup that overthrew Vargas in 1945, was finally supported by the latter as a lesser evil against Brigadier Eduardo Gomes, candidate of the UDN—União Democrática Nacional (National Democratic Union), the anti-Vargas coalition party, and won the 1945 election because of such support.

national bourgeoisie, including the industrial bourgeoisie and its new commercial counterpart—the traders for the domestic market of national manufacturing—the technical middle class, and the proletariat. This coalition never reached a complete social and economic consciousness of its role, in spite of the serious efforts undertaken by the new intelligentsia in formulating the "ideology of national development."[14] What kept this coalition together was not an explicit agreement but its common interests and consequent opposition to the rural landowners, the commercial bourgeoisie, and the traditional middle class. At the political level, the national front failed to produce an authentic and well-established party for national development. The most that was achieved was a tactical but enduring alliance between the two parties founded by Vargas: the PSD, commanding a solid plurality in Congress; and the PTB, with a substantial popular support.

In spite of these shortcomings, the national front in the fifties brought the country to the brink of self-sustained socioeconomic development. The second Vargas government (1950–54) started the first serious effort at national planning and for the first time achieved the formulation of a general developmental policy which would combine economic growth with social democracy. This government, however, could not achieve its goals, owing to the conspiratorial opposition of the reactionary forces, appalled by the idea of liquidating the semicolonial establishment. Overthrown by another military coup in 1954, Vargas refused to sign his resignation and committed suicide. In so doing he explicitly condemned what he saw as the antinational conspiracy of reactionary forces supported by Western imperialism.

The tragic death of Vargas, however, had the merit of awakening the consciousness of the popular forces which brought about the succession against the UDN (National Democratic Union) anti-Vargas coalition of Juscelino Kubitschek. More to the center in social and international affairs, the Kubitschek government was exceptionally active in the field of economic development. Vargas' former plans were revised and reshaped in a broader and more systematic form, and together

14 On the effort of the Brazilian intelligentsia to create a bourgeoisie-middle-class-proletarian alliance for a nationalist and socially progressive development during the fifties, see Frank Bonilla, "A National Ideology for Development: Brazil," in K. H. Silvert (ed.), *Expectant Peoples: Nationalism and Development,* New York: Random House, 1963.

with many other new projects, were adopted under the name of Target Plan as the new administration's five-year plan.

Politically more moderate than Vargas, Kubitschek was able to reduce to manageable proportions the rebellious attempts of the reactionary forces[15] and so was able to achieve practically all the goals of his program. During his government the national front reached its highest level of political articulation and socioeconomic understanding. However, the conditions to which the Kubitschek government owed its success precluded the possibility of its continuation in the years to come, except at the cost of new and still more creative solutions. The fact that these new solutions were not found or adopted brought the country to the tremendous crisis of the middle sixties, which will be analyzed in the third section of this study.

DEVELOPMENT TARGETS AND THEIR ACHIEVEMENT

The spontaneous process of import substitution brought about by the crisis of 1930 caused a substantial change in the economic structure of the country, but it was halted in the late forties. Brazilian exports recovered from their depression but did not surpass the 1929 level, while the national income increased 50 percent and the structure of imports was changed by industrialization. Once the surplus of foreign exchange accumulated during the war was unwisely spent on nonpriority matters, the country had to face a serious imbalance between its import capacity and import needs. The new requirements of the industrial sector were indispensable: fuel, raw materials, spare parts, and machinery. Restricting such imports would have had the double consequence of depressing industry's employment and of reducing the supplies needed for the domestic manufacture of consumer goods.

To correct this situation the government introduced a selective, quantitative control of imports, keeping the same exchange parity but giving import priority to capital goods and to equipment needed for domestic production. The judicious use of scarce foreign exchange had a double effect. On the one hand, it

[15] Two small-scale coups were attempted against Kubitschek by some sectors of the air force, Jacare-Acanga and Aragarcas. The great majority of the armed forces remained loyal to the government and easily smashed the coups.

gave stronger stimulus to industry by subsidizing, first implicitly and later explicitly, imported raw materials and equipment for expansion. On the other hand, balance-of-payments planning led to general economic planning and to the formal introduction of the practice, and the public expectation of, government by planning. From the import substitution of consumer goods, Brazilian industry was deliberately led to the import substitution of capital goods. In the second Vargas government emphasis was given, on the one hand, to the modernization and expansion of maritime and railway transport facilities (Lafer's plan for re-equipment), together with the creation of the National Development Bank, which provided for the continued expansion of priority sectors. On the other hand, emphasis was given to Romulo Almeida's plans for the production and expansion of infrastructural goods and services: the creation of Petrobrás, a publicly owned corporation for finding, exploiting, refining, and transporting oil; a plan to nationalize coal mining; and the creation of Electrobrás, a publicly owned corporation for power generation, which only much later was approved by Congress because of opposition by the existing foreign-controlled power companies.

In the Kubitschek government, whose campaign slogan was to achieve fifty years of progress in five years of government, the Target Plan, incorporating former plans in a much larger and more systematic framework, adopted thirty-one targets divided among six general groups: energy, transport, food, basic industries, education, and the construction of Brasilia, the next capital.[16] The Target Plan was based on the assumption that the economy could achieve self-sustained growth by reaching the minimum production necessary to satisfy expected demand. The expected demand was deduced by correlating past demands (in absolute, per capita, and per unit GNP terms) with present demands and with additional demands which were to be generated by the Target Plan itself. The plan, therefore, was mainly concerned with the achievement of minimum results compatible with the limits of the economy and the existing institutional framework. To achieve these minimum results, specific projects using public and private agencies and resources were prepared for each sector under the coordination of the Development

[16] All data on the Target Plan has been collected, where no other source is mentioned, from ECLA's study, "Fifteen Years of Economic Policy in Brazil," *Economic Bulletin for Latin America*, Vol. IX, No. 2, November, 1964.

Council. The overall budget for the Target Plan presented the following forecasts:

TABLE II

FINANCIAL FORECAST OF THE TARGET PLAN (1957–61)

			Import goods and services		
Sector	Estimated cost of domestically produced goods and services	U.S.$ millions	Equivalent in billions of cruzeiros	Estimate of total investment in billions of cruzeiros	Percent of total
Energy	110.0	862.2	44.3	154.3	43.4
Transport	75.5	582.6	30.0	105.3	29.6
Food	4.8	130.9	6.7	11.5	3.2
Basic Industry	34.6	742.8	38.1	72.7	20.4
Education	12.0	—	—	12.0	3.4
TOTAL	236.9	2,318.5	119.1	355.8	100.0

Source: BNDE, VI, "Exposição sobre o programa de reaparelhamento econômico," *Economic Bulletin for Latin America,* ECLA, Vol. IX, No. 2, November, 1964.

For matching the foreseen expenditures the Target Plan estimate of mobilizable resources presented the following percentage itemization:

TABLE III

PERCENTAGE ITEMIZATION OF FINANCIAL RESOURCES FOR THE TARGET PLAN
(1957 ESTIMATES)

Origin of Resources	Percent
Federal budget appropriations	39.7
State budget appropriations	10.4
Financing by federal agencies (BNDE–National Bank of Brazil)	14.5
Resources of private enterprises and mixed-economy companies	35.4
	100.0

Source: Development Council, Target Plan, 1959 Report, p. 34; see Antonio Patriota, "The Economic Development of Brazil," *Hispanic American Report,* special issue, 1961.

Energy

More than 40 percent of the Target Plan resources were meant to increase the capacity for energy production (chiefly electric power and oil), because the energy lag was the most serious bottleneck in the Brazilian economy. The existing capacity of electric power generation was 1,883,000 kilowatts in 1950 and 3,550,000 kilowatts in 1956; this was to be increased to 5 million kilowatts by 1960 and 9 million kilowatts by 1965. The results were fairly near the forecast. By 1960 the installed capacity was increased to 4,800,000 kilowatts (96 percent of the target) and to 5,205,000 kilowatts in 1961.

The domestic production of crude oil under Petrobrás responsibility and refining (mostly by Petrobrás) were in 1955, respectively, 5,600 and 108,300 barrels daily. For supplying the domestic consumption of 180,000 barrels daily, $43.1 million worth of petrol and $73.4 million worth of fuel oil had to be spent in that year in imports. The plan's targets for 1960 were to achieve a daily production of 100,000 barrels of crude oil and 308,000 barrels of refined products. In 1960 the production of crude oil was increased to 75,500 barrels daily (75.5 percent of target) and the refining capacity enlarged to 218,000 barrels daily (71 percent of target). In 1961 the daily production of crude oil was increased to 95,400 barrels, while the refining capacity rose to 308,000 barrels daily.

Transport

The second largest area of investment in the Target Plan was transport, with a provision for a substantial increase in railway, road, and maritime facilities.

For the railway system the plan foresaw the incorporation of 440 new diesel-electric engines, 12,000 passenger carriages and goods wagons, together with the laying of 291,000 new rails and the construction of 1,624 kilometers of new tracks for interconnection. In 1960, 440 engines but only 7,052 wagons (58.8 percent of target) were incorporated into the system; 80 percent of the rails had been manufactured, and 1,195 kilometers of track had been laid.

The progress in road construction was impressive. There were 22,250 kilometers of federal highways in 1955, of which only 2,376 kilometers were paved. The highway targets of the plan foresaw the construction of 10,000 kilometers of new federal roads, with 3,800 kilometers to be improved and 3,000 kilometers to be paved. The achievement (1961) surpassed the plan: federal highways were extended to 35,419 kilometers and the paved ones to 9,591 kilometers. Moreover, with federal help, state highways were extended from 54,291 kilometers to 72,751 kilometers.

Regarding maritime transportation, the plan's targets and achievements were the following:

TABLE IV
MARITIME TRANSPORTATION
(SHIPS OVER 100 TONS)

	Situation in 1955	Target	Achievement	Percent
Coasters	600,000	200,000	179,000	89.5
Tankers	217,000	330,000	299,000	90.6
Ocean vessels	150,000	30,000	64,000	213.3

Intermediate Industries

The most important provisions concerning intermediate industries concerned steel and Portland cement.

In 1956 the national consumption of steel ingots was 1,704,-000 tons, of which 1,365,000 were domestically made, 80 percent of it by the publicly owned plant of Volta Redonda. The steel target was to increase Volta Redonda's capacity from 1.2 million to 2.3 million tons of ingots by 1960, and the total domestic production to 3.5 million tons by 1965. In 1960 the domestic production reached 2,279,000 tons of ingots (81 percent of target), while the rolling capacity had been increased from 1,074,000 tons to 1,707,000 tons. Estimates indicate that the plans now being carried out, concerning the new plants of Usiminas, Ferro e Aço, Cosipa and others, reached the target in 1965.

The production of Portland cement in 1955 was 2.7 million tons, out of a consumption of 3 million tons. The plan's target by 1960 was the production of 5 million tons. In 1960, 4.4 million tons (89 percent of target) were manufactured. Production in 1962 went beyond 5 million tons.

Capital-Goods Industries

The goals set by the plan in the area of capital-goods industry concerned the manufacture of vehicles, ships, and equipment.

In 1955, Brazilian production of vehicles was limited to 2,500 lorries made by the publicly owned FNM. The targets and achievement for the manufacture of vehicles were the following in the 1957–60 period:

TABLE V
VEHICLE PER UNITS TARGET AND ACHIEVEMENT
(THOUSANDS OF UNITS)

Vehicles	Target	Achievement
Lorries and buses	170.8	154.7
Jeeps	66.3	61.3
Utility trucks	52.6	53.2
Private cars	58.0	52.0
TOTAL	347.7	321.2 (92.3 Percent)

The Plan had also forecast the proportion of the vehicle parts to be domestically manufactured. Targets and achievements were the following:

TABLE VI
PERCENTAGE OF DOMESTICALLY MADE VEHICLE PARTS
(PERCENT OF TOTAL WEIGHT)

Vehicles	Envisaged for 1960	Attained June, 1962
Private cars	95	89.3
Lorries	90	93.0
Buses	—	86.4
Utility trucks	90	94.3
Jeeps	95	90.9

Concerning shipbuilding, the targets of the plan were the construction of two new shipyards for large vessels and the reequipping of fourteen smaller existing ones, in order to reach an annual production capacity of 160,000 tons. The projects approved and being carried out in 1960 will eventually assure an annual production of 158,000 tons (98.7 percent of target).

The other target of the plan in the area of capital-goods industries was concerned with the establishment or expansion of the metal-transforming and the heavy electrical equipment industries. The plan did not set any quantitative goal for such industries; but it provided for a substantial increase in the domestic production of equipment. According to the Development Council, the production of machinery and equipment in the period 1955–60 increased 100 percent and that of heavy electrical equipment more than 200 percent. Estimates of the three-year plan of 1962 concluded that the achievements of the Target Plan had led domestic industry to supply in 1960 two-thirds of the overall domestic demand for equipment.

The more controversial goal of the Target Plan was the construction of a new capital, Brasilia, on the semiarid and formerly unsettled highlands of the state of Goias, 1,200 kilometers from Rio de Janeiro. The decision to build a new capital at the geographic center of the country had been approved by the successive constitutions since the republican revolution, but the project never received more than lip service. While the strategic reasons which formerly influenced that decision had been superseded by contemporary weaponry, the social, economic, and political reasons were, in principle, still more relevant. Most experts, however, emphasized the necessity of postponing this project until the country (presumably in the seventies) could afford its execution without causing inflation and without slowing down the pace of economic development. But Kubitschek, fearing that future administrations might hesitate to start that project, decided to include it among the targets of his government and gave it top priority.

Without attempting any critical appraisal of the pros and cons of Brasilia, it should be pointed out that the city was built very quickly, and was inaugurated on April 21, 1960, with working facilities for 100,000 inhabitants. The road network expressly built for linking Brasilia to other cities presents the following figures:

TABLE VII

LENGTH OF ROADS TO BRASILIA

	Kilometers
Belo Horizonte-Brasilia	700
Goiana-Brasilia	200
Belém-Brasilia	2,000
Fortaleza-Brasilia	1,500
Acre-Brasilia	2,500

The cost of the construction of Brasilia, at 1961 prices, based on estimates at current prices for the period 1957–62 by the Getulio Vargas Foundation, was about 300,000 million cruzeiros.

Income Impact

The impact of the Target Plan on the national product in absolute and per capita terms has been considerable, no less than the structural differentiation caused by massive industrialization.

As the following table shows, the gross domestic product from 1955 to 1960 increased by 41.1 percent, and per capita by 16.3 percent. From 1949 to 1954 the increases were 29.5 percent for the total product and 11.6 percent for the per capita growth.

TABLE VIII

GROSS DOMESTIC PRODUCT (1949–61)

Year	Total (crs. $billions)		Per capita (crs. $1,000)	
	Current Prices	Constant Prices, 1949	Current Prices	Constant Prices, 1949
1949	215.2	215.2	4.3	4.3
1954	555.2	278.9	9.5	4.8
1955	691.7	297.8	11.5	4.9
1960	2,385.3	394.7	34.2	5.7
1961	3,522.0	425.0	49.0	5.9

Source: Fundação Getulio Vargas, *Anuario estatístico Brasileiro*, 1963.

The effects of industrialization are reflected in the sectoral differences in the growth of the real product, as shown in Table IX.

TABLE IX
INDICES OF THE REAL PRODUCT PER SECTOR

Sector	1949	1954	1955	1960
Agriculture	100	120.5	129.8	154.0
Industry	100	146.7	162.3	266.3
Commerce	100	136.7	143.5	195.7
Transport and Communication	100	147.7	152.4	219.1
Government	100	112.6	115.4	130.0
Services	100	116.1	119.7	139.0
Rent	100	119.3	123.7	148.0
GROSS DOMESTIC PRODUCT	100	129.6	138.4	183.0

Source: Fundação Getulio Vargas, *Anuario estatístico Brasileiro*, 1963.

Industrial growth from 1949 to 1954, compared to the growth of the real product, has been 113.2 percent larger; and from 1955 to 1960, 145.5 percent larger.

The regional distribution of the national income, on the other hand, although remaining extremely uneven, reflected in the last half of the decade the efforts of the plan to develop the Northeast, prepared and carried forward by Celso Furtado through SUDENE (North East Superintendency).

TABLE X
REGIONAL DISTRIBUTION OF THE NATIONAL INCOME

Regions	1950	1955	1960
North	2.2	2.0	2.2
Northeast	16.4	13.9	15.9
Center-South	79.5	81.5	79.4
Center-West	1.9	2.6	2.5

Source: Three-year plan, Table XXVI.

Accordingly, the Northeast per capita income, which in 1950 represented 48.5 percent of the national average, declined to 42.9 percent in 1955 but rose in 1960 to 50.6 percent.

Inflation

If the period 1955–60 witnessed a rapid growth of and a relevant structural change in the economy, it was also marked by an increasing acceleration of the rate of inflation. This process is better understood if one compares the rise in the cost of living with the growth of the real per capita product:

TABLE XI

INDEX OF COST OF LIVING IN RIO DE JANEIRO AND PER CAPITA
REAL PRODUCT
(1952–61)

Year	Cost of Living	Per Capita Real Product
January, 1952	100	100.0
August, 1956	222	107.4
October, 1961	867	129.8

Source: *Desenvolvimento e conjuntura*, February, 1962; see also *Economic Bulletin for Latin America*, Vol. IX, No. 2, November, 1962.

The real per capita product has grown 7.4 percent from 1952 to 1956 and 20.8 percent from 1956 to 1961. The rise in the cost of living was 22 percent from 1952 to 1956 and 290.5 percent from 1956 to 1961. This means that while the increase of the rate of growth of the real per capita product from the first to the second period was 270 percent, the increase of the rise in the cost of living was 1390 percent.

The many factors determining the increase of the rate of inflation were basically caused by the growing deficits of the union and their financing by sheer money emission.[17] In terms of percentage of the gross domestic product, the deficits of the Union presented the following figures:

[17] The most noteworthy specific factors have been: military expenditures (more than 20 percent of the federal budget); federal subsidies to consumption (transportation, wheat, newsprint); coffee retention and accumulation (more than 2 percent of gross domestic product in 1958–60); construction of Brasilia; private price increase in excess of costs; public investment in excess of available funds.

TABLE XII

RECEIPTS AND EXPENDITURES OF THE FEDERAL
GOVERNMENT AS A PERCENTAGE OF GNP

Year	Receipts	Expenditures	GNP (crs. $billions)
1955	8.0	9.2	691.7
1956	8.3	12.2	884.4
1957	8.1	11.2	1,056.5
1958	8.9	11.3	1,310.0
1959	8.8	11.1	1,788.9
1960	9.2	12.4	2,385.6
1961	9.0	12.9	3,522.0

Source: ECLA, *Economic Bulletin for Latin America*,
Vol. IX, No. 2, November, 1964, Table 29; and Fundação
Getulio Vargas, *Anuario estatístico Brasileiro*, 1963.

Once having achieved such immense proportions, the annual
time-lag between taxation and collection was itself increasing
the government's financial imbalance, because taxes for the
preceding years were paid in ever less valuable currency.

It became apparent by the end of the Kubitschek government
that the cost of its extraordinary achievements was uncon-
trollably rising prices, and that the subsequent maintenance of
the same rate of growth would be impossible without a drastic
change in the social, economic, and political structure.

THE NEW STRUCTURAL CRISIS

Toward the end of the Kubitschek government it was clear
that the Kubitschek model of development, in spite of its
achievements, had exhausted its potential. The government
itself implicitly admitted this by openly adopting a policy of
problem-postponement.

As a matter of fact, the Kubitschek government had adopted
two types of postponements: one strategic and one tactical. The
latter was the most visible because it was used at the end of his
term to transfer the accumulating unsolved problems to the next
administration. The former, however, was inherent in the
Kubitschek model of development and eventually caused its exhaustion. This strategic postponement consisted of buying a

truce from the reactionary forces by leaving untouched the foundation of their power—the regime of property and exploitation of the rural-agricultural complex—in exchange for their tolerating the execution of the Target Plan. Implicit in that bargain was the Kubitschek government's conviction that changing the urban-industrial complex would necessitate a change in the rural-agricultural system by unleashing the natural economic forces that would unify the internal market.

Actually the opposite happened. The basic duality of the Brazilian economy was represented in the semicolonial stage by the contrast between the dynamic export system and the static sector of subsistence economy. In the transitional stage, because of Kubitschek's agreement with the rural obligarchy, this duality created an increasing discontinuity between the modern urban-industrial sector and the archaic rural-agricultural sector.[18]

Seen in a broader perspective, the transitional stage of Brazilian development consists basically of three structural crises. The first, in the twenties and early thirties, was caused by the external and internal disruption of the semicolonial system; it forced the country to produce its own consumer goods by a spontaneous process of import substitution. The second crisis, in the late forties, was caused by the exhaustion of the spontaneous process of import substitution; the country was forced to plan its industrial development and go on to the more advanced level of capital goods production. The third crisis, incipient in the early fifties and clearly evident in the next decade, was caused by the failure of socioeconomic development within the existing institutional framework. This problem in its early stages had been faced by the second Vargas government, which failed to overcome the resistance of the reactionary coalition of the rural oligarchy, the commercial bourgeoisie, and the traditional middle class. The Vargas government was finally overthrown by this coalition. It was precisely to prevent a direct confrontation with such forces that President Kubitschek adopted a policy of strategic postponement. In doing so, however, he only succeeded in transferring the problem to his successors.

[18] Cf. Ignacio Rangel, *Dualidade básica da economia brasileira*, ISEB, Rio de Janeiro, 1957. For a more recent, vivid, and broad analysis of the problems caused by the unevenness of Brazilian development in the late fifties and early sixties, see Irving Louis Horowitz, *Revolution in Brazil*, New York: E. P. Dutton, 1964.

It was impossible to continue socioeconomic development within the structural distortion of existing social institutions.[19] Socially there was an increasing imbalance between the urban-industrial and the rural-agricultural systems. There was also an increasing regional imbalance, with the strengthening of the Center-South at the expense of the rest of the country. Economically the structural distortions affected intrasectoral relations between the private and public sectors, and between the high- and low-income groups. Politically, the structural distortions caused a lack of representativeness in the process of power formation and delegation; this alienated the masses and invalidated the authenticity of the political parties.

Social Distortions

A rapid analysis of these structural distortions indicates that the imbalance between the urban and the rural complexes, as well as between the Center-South and the rest of the country, consists largely of an enormous and increasing difference between the levels of any socially relevant indexes: productivity and income, education, sanitation, social mobility, institutionalization, personal freedom, and political participation.

The rural-agricultural complex remains in every respect archaic and semifeudal. The introductory data of this study have already indicated that the countryside is divided by the contrast between the latifundia (11 percent of the rural establishments own 79.8 percent of the agricultural land) and the minifundia (45 percent of the total establishments own all together only 13.3 percent of the arable land). While the peasants represent 50 percent of the population, their share of the national income is less than 15 percent.[20] They live within a subsistence economy, the value of their consumption being

---

[19] These social distortions, although presenting peculiar features in each case, are common to Latin America in general. See, mostly for its economic aspects, Albert Hirschman (ed.), *Latin American Issues,* New York, Twentieth Century Fund, 1961.

[20] These facts are based on data for 1960, when the national income was crs. $1879 billion, urban wages crs. $718 billion, and total agricultural income crs. $536 billion. The peasants' income is estimated to be 50 percent of the agricultural income, due to the prevailing custom of paying peasants half of the produced crops.

sensibly below the local minimum wage. This consumption corresponded in 1960 to an annual per capita income of $40.[21] They have the country's lowest literacy standards (almost nil) and health. Every other index tells the same kind of story.

Similarly the regional contrast between the Center-South and the rest of the country illustrates the same overconcentration of productivity, wealth, education, sanitation, etc. in the former, while the latter is a depressed area increasingly dependent on the Center-South. The North, the Northeast, and the Center-West have 29 percent of the country's population, yet this population shares only 14 percent of the national income.

The reasons for this double imbalance are also twofold. First, the imbalance is caused by the same laws of capital and technological concentration that strengthen the developed nations and highly productive sectors at the expense of the backward ones.[22] Second, it results from the unbroken political dominance of the rural oligarchy. A web of interrelated interests and values rewards and perpetuates the landowners' preference for semifeudal modes of production and organization.

Among the relevant consequences of these imbalances are the food shortage and the restriction of the domestic market. In spite of various modern farms, chiefly in the state of São Paulo, most of the food production for the domestic market still constitutes a marginal activity. Plantation owners authorize the peasants, as part of their rent, to use certain tracts of land for their own subsistence crops and for supplying the market. The amount of food produced in this way, however, is not primarily determined by the market demand or prices but by the availability of arable land granted to the peasants. This is the cause of the prolonged imbalance between the urban demand for food (rising at a 12 percent annual rate) and the rural supply (rising at a 5 percent annual rate); this difference is continually increasing.

The restrictive effect on the domestic market is likewise very significant. Fifty percent of the country, represented by peasants

[21] This is based on an estimate for the peasants' income of crs. $218 billion and an exchange rate of crs. $1900/U.S. $1 billion for a peasant population of 35 million.

[22] Cf. Aníbal Pinto, "La concentración de progreso técnico y de sus frutos en el desarrollo latinoamericano," *Trimestre Económico*, Vol. XXXII (1), March, 1965, No. 125.

living at subsistence levels, are automatically excluded from the consumption of domestic products. The fact that half of the other urban 50 percent, earning a minimum wage, is practically paid for buying food, imposes an additional restriction on the market. Only 25 percent of the Brazilians, therefore, are really consumers of the products of domestic industry. This is the reason why Brazilian industry is so easily affected by insufficient demand and is unable to benefit from the large-scale savings provided by modern technology; on the contrary, it is overcharged by fixed costs.

Economic Distortions

Economically the intrasectoral distortions which impoverish most of the population and enrich a small part of it were, at the same time, stifling the country's capacity for saving and investment, thus creating a structural inflation which in 1964 became a galloping one.

The impoverishment of the public sector had two causes: insufficient tax revenues and underpricing of the goods and services produced by the publicly owned concerns. Taxation has been too low or nonexistent on rural incomes. In the urban areas its effect has been weakened by its regressiveness and by the concentration of income, practically excluding from direct taxation the working class and the lower-middle class. Moreover, the supervision of tax collection has been careless. The underpricing policy imposed on the federally owned concerns, as a means of reducing inflation, was forcing the transport system (federal maritime companies and railways) to operate below cost, transferring to the union the ever-increasing burden of balancing their deficits.[23] Even the technically well managed steel plant of Volta Redonda was being forced by the government to sell its steel practically at cost, which resulted in its dependence on new federal resources for continuing expansion.

The results of the economic distortions can be seen in Table XIII:

[23] According to the three-year plan, 1962 (Table V), the subsidies granted by the union to the transportation system and other activities of consumption have risen from 0.1 percent of the GNP in 1947 to 0.7 percent in 1960, amounting in that year to about crs. $165 billion, equivalent to more than U.S. $868 million.

TABLE XIII

FEDERAL BUDGET IN CURRENT FIGURES AND IN PERCENTAGES OF
GROSS NATIONAL PRODUCT (1960–63)

	Receipts		Expenditures		Balance	
Year	crs. $bill.	Percent of GNP	crs. $bill.	Percent of GNP	crs. $bill.	Percent of GNP
1960	233	9.2	265	12.4	32	13.7
1961	317	9.0	420	12.9	103	32.4
1962	512	9.0	727	14.1	215	41.9
1963*	737	9.0	1,512	18.5	775	105.1

* Estimates based on provisions of the three-year plan, 1962.
Source: *Anuario estatístico Brasileiro,* 1963; and *Economic Bulletin for Latin America,* Vol. IX, No. 2, November, 1964, Table 29.

The table indicates that the budget deficits went from more than 10 percent of the GNP in 1960 to more than 100 percent in 1963. Under these conditions the rational concept of a budget had become meaningless. As far as the gross domestic product is concerned, the table indicates that the constant rise in public consumption brought the union's expenditure from 12.4 percent to 18.5 percent of the GNP, increasing its relative share to more than 49 percent. On the other hand, the receipts, practically corresponding to fiscal revenues, are always the same proportion of the gross domestic product. The difference, of course, has been balanced by printing money.

Political Distortions

Politically the lack of representativeness in the processes of power formation and delegation (political input) has hindered the development of an ideologically meaningful and programmatically consistent party system. At the bottom of this lack of representativeness is the fact that the illiterates, who are nearly all peasants, are not allowed to vote—although they constitute half of the population. In addition, the prevailing politics of clientèle has blurred the meaning of the political parties.

Organized as national entities, but actually constituting loosely organized local and regional groups, the parties act in two ways. First, they express the interests of their state bases and clientèles. Second, they reflect the political issues they had to face in their Congressional activity or under the pressure of public opinion in the big cities. While the second level implies ideological and programmatic options, the first is based purely on intraparty or local interests. The parties, as bodies of elected officials, are the expression of broad political issues. But as political agencies, they function as a means of protecting local interests. This explains their difficulty in reaching any programmatic coherence. The three major parties, in spite of their internal contradictions, gradually succeeded in acquiring a basic national image.[24] The PSD, although it had a rural basis, became associated in the Vargas, Kubitschek, and Goulart governments with the efforts of industrial development under federal sponsorship. The UDN, with the same rural basis, was known in the big cities as a liberal-conservative party which favored laissez-faire and private business positions. The PTB had always reinforced its working-class image and its left-wing ideology, although in its expansion from the big cities to the countryside it had to incorporate all the conflicting local interests and tendencies. Behind such national images, however, these parties were expressing the regional influences that were shaping their state branches. These influences were mostly determined by the relative stage of development which each region had achieved.

In such a large and diverse country as Brazil it is only a half-truth to say that the country as a whole is presently in a "transitional stage." Basically three different regional stages of development should be distinguished in the country. (1) The North, the Northeast with the exception of Recife, and the hinterland of the Center-East and the Center-West, representing about 41 percent of the electorate, are still in a traditional and archaic stage. Regardless of party labels, the kind of politics which

[24] Before the Second Institutional Act of November 27, 1965, issued by the military government, which suppressed all political parties, Brazil had 14 parties. The three major parties, commanding about 75 percent of the votes for Congress and presenting some political meaning (see footnote 12) were: PSD, Partido Social Democrático (Social Democratic Party); PTB, Partido Trabalhista Brasileiro (Brazilian Labor Party); UDN, União Democrática Nacional (National Democratic Union). For a well-selected collection of data on electoral and political affairs, see Henry Wells, Charles Daugherty, James Rowe and Ronald Schneider (eds.), *Brazil: Election Factbook*, No. 2, September, 1965, Washington, D.C., Institute for the Comparative Study of Political Systems.

actually takes place in such regions is extremely traditional, yet is expressed purely in terms of clientèle politics. (2) The subregion of Recife and the coastal zone of the Center-East, including most of the big cities, is one on the brink of rapid economic development. In such regions, clientèle politics coexist with ideological politics, and there is a marked polarization of political beliefs between left and right. The southern part of the country—primarily São Paulo—generally enjoys a better developed economy. It is more inclined to modern forms of conservatism or welfare laborism.[25]

The discrepancy between the federal roles of the parties and their regional bases had weakened their internal functions, reducing them to little more than electoral labels and machines. The voters, as a rule, did not feel a sense of participation in the parties. It is true that voting in important elections has been much more partisan. But the fact is that a useful relationship between the voters and the parties had practically ceased to exist in between elections. The voters' lack of participation in the parties was an important factor in perpetuating the control of the parties by a small and close-knit circle of professional politicians whose members changed more through retirement and co-optation than through competition based on merit.

All these influences reduced the parties' ability to effectively represent social groups and interests. Among the many consequences of this failure, two deserve special mention. One result was that important class and group interests sought expression through other means. Trade unions have been a noteworthy spokesman for the working class, commercial associations have become typical agents of the commercial bourgeoisie, while the army kept its role as a middle-class pressure group. The failure of the political parties to be adequately representative also affected the value of Congress as a chamber for national discussion and bargaining. Class and group interests, instead of being channeled to and through Congress, have sought more direct forms of expression, chiefly since the Kubitschek government. This fact has directly contributed to the increase in socio-polit-

[25] For an analysis of the three major parties in terms of class ideologies, also taking into account the influence of the stage of development of each region on the parties' local sections, see Hélio Jaguaribe, "As eleiçoes de 1962," *Tempo Brasileiro*, December, 1962, Ano 1, No. 2, Rio de Janeiro; a Spanish version was published in *Desarrollo Económico*, January–March, 1964, Vol. 3, No. 3, Buenos Aires.

ical tension and polarization which led to the denouement of
the military coup of 1964. The weakness of the parties, on the
other hand, largely explains the reason that the military easily
achieved complete control of the country in April, 1964, and in
the next year were able to dissolve the parties almost without
protest.

The other result of party inadequacy has been the formation of
super-party ideological camps and fronts. While clientèle politics was the major party activity until their final dissolution, the
rising socio-political tension and the corresponding polarization
of public opinion found expression not only in the press but also
in new Congressional and extra-Congressional political groups.
The Congressional groups at the end of the Kubitschek government were the Fronte Parlamentar Nacionalista (Nationalist
Parliamentary Front), mobilizing the left wing, and the Ação
Democrática Parlamentar (Parliamentary Democratic Action),
mobilizing the right-wing congressmen regardless of their parties. Later, during the Goulart government until the April coup,
the more active groups were the Fronte de Mobilização Popular
(Popular Mobilization Front), which gathered the radical left
under Brizola; and a coalition of right-wing groups under Carlos
Lacerda, of which the most vocal was the women's association,
Campanha da Mulher pela Democracia-CAMDE (Women's
Campaign for Democracy).

The ideological confrontation of left-wing and right-wing
blocks, expressing the radical polarization of the big cities,
powerfully contributed to the sliding of the Goulart government
from its initial (and viable) center-left position to its later (and
nonviable) radical-left posture. This confrontation also exerted
a similar effect on the army, as the most representative and
effective political agent of the middle class.

Another serious political shortcoming affected the function of
the state and the action of the government (political output).
This shortcoming is reflected in the politics of clientèle and
consists in the Cartorial state's basic inability to function usefully. The eventual result of the Cartorial state's methods was a
number of more or less parasitical functionaries, assigned to
more or less useless public jobs. Nevertheless, the Cartorial
state had to face the need for effective public services for a
rapidly industrializing country. At first Vargas' New State tried
to impose some rationality upon the incoherence of clientèle
politics. The Departamento Administrativo do Serviço Publico

—DASP (Public Service Administrative Department) was created to transform the Cartorial state into a functional state by reorganizing its agencies, training its personnel, and adopting convenient stimulus and penalty devices. It was also stipulated that new public servants would be selected mostly on the basis of public competition. But the continued growth of the Cartorial state after Vargas did not allow these reforms to take place. Vargas' second government and the Kubitschek government made a new attempt to ensure minimum efficiency in important state functions. New agencies were created, duplicating or superseding the old unserviceable ones, either as mixed societies or as executive commissions of working groups. In the execution of permanent, economic, productive activities, the preferred agency was the mixed society. In the undertaking, coordination, and supervision of plans, the preferred agency was the commission or working group. Although most of these agencies were successful, they finally proved to be insufficient. Paradoxically, Brazil became more capable of performing complex nonroutine tasks than the usual daily ones. But without the latter, the former became increasingly difficult or altogether futile. The methods of the Cartorial state precluded even minimum efficiency in a society increasingly dependent on state action.

It is interesting to note that the laissez-faire critics of Brazilian policies have used state inefficiency as their major argument in condemning state intervention in economic affairs. What has never occurred to these critics is that the underdevelopment of the state reflects the underdevelopment of the economy and of the society in general, whose correction requires the intervention of the state.

Alternative Solutions

The new structural crisis consequently affected the national integrity of the country and its social order. A nation is a society presenting a specific identity to which its members give the allegiance that binds them together in a special relationship. National development requires an endogenous growth which will preserve and strengthen the nation's self-determination and individuality.

A social order, on the other hand, means a specific social and economic structure founded on a certain pattern of relationships among the social classes and groups. The maintenance of this order requires a certain social stability which can be preserved by a useful combination of rewards and coercions.

The Brazilian structural crisis imperiled the country by increasing the conflicts between social groups and eroding their common solidarity, and by strangling the country's capacity for endogenous growth. The crisis disrupted social stability, invalidating the usefulness of rewards and coercions.

These two effects of the crisis were basically understood by many, especially after the Kubitschek government. But the remedy to these effects could not be agreed upon because the solutions required for each of them were mutually incompatible.

To preserve the nation it would be necessary to change the socioeconomic structure and adopt a more suitable pattern of relationships between classes and groups. However, these solutions would lead to sacrifices of the existing order, not to its preservation. To preserve the existing social order, it would be necessary to strengthen its stability, most conveniently by reinforcing the existing mechanisms of rewards and coercions, and by similarly reorienting the process of economic and social development. Such reorientation would require considerable foreign influence to compensate for the internal lack of dynamism inherent in the preservation of the status quo.

According to the first hypothesis, the social structures should be readjusted to allow maximum development of the country as a nation. According to the second hypothesis, the national structures should be readjusted to insure maximum stability of the existing social order.[26]

MODELS FOR NATIONAL DEVELOPMENT

Any plan for national development must first meet two types of prerequisites. One refers to the conditions under which a society can maintain itself as a nation. The other refers to the conditions under which a nation can achieve endogenous development.

[26] For a discussion on that question from the perspective of the "reform-revolution" issues and models, see Albert Hirschman, *Journeys Toward Progress,* New York, Twentieth Century Fund, 1963.

It is beyond the scope of this study to analyze in detail either of the prerequisites.[27] Historically they vary according to the level of technology in each era, as well as to the socio-political conditions prevailing in the country and neighboring countries. Within these variations, the prerequisites are fundamentally determined by the availability of the natural and human resources of the country. The Central American and Caribbean countries do not seem to satisfy even the minimum prerequisites for national development. Brazil, with the largest area, population, and gross national product, seems to be among the best qualified for development, even if some of its internal problems are particularly serious.

Regarding the conditions under which national development may be achieved,[28] it is enough to make two observations. First, models for national development must be considered empirically, irrespective of personal preferences. It would be senseless to claim that any model in itself is better or worse than any other. Each model is more or less suitable to the social, economic, cultural, and political structure of a particular country.[29]

In the second place, it should be noted that the structural conditions of an underdeveloped country at a given time determine the variety of models for national development open to it. Under present conditions there are basically three varieties available, depending on whether (1) the entrepreneurs of the national bourgeoisie, (2) the technical and managerial sectors of the middle class, or (3) the counterelite of revolutionary intellectuals are the dynamic force capable of promoting the changes required for national development. For each of these three structural situations, the three corresponding models of development are respectively, national capitalism, state capitalism, and developmental socialism.[30]

[27] For an analysis of such prerequisites, see Hélio Jaguaribe, *op. cit.*, Part I.

[28] Cf. *ibid.*, Chapters 5–7.

[29] The suitability of a model of national development to the socio-political structure of a country is determined by the degree to which the application of the model is likely to readjust the existing social forces for the greatest internal development.

[30] For a discussion on the relevance of these models to the Latin American countries, see Hélio Jaguaribe, *op. cit.*, Part I, Chapter 7.

National Capitalism

In Brazil, from 1930 onward, it became increasingly clear that national capitalism would be the most suitable model for promoting national development. More than that, an analysis of what was actually accomplished in the country, from the second Vargas government until mid-1963, shows that the national-capitalist model was continuously adopted by Brazilian governments.

Fundamentally, what is essential and common to the policies applied by Vargas, Kubitschek, Quadros and, until mid-1963, by Goulart, was an effort to undertake the endogenous socio-economic development of the country. This meant preserving the private enterprise system under the direction of the national entrepreneurs, and using the state as an agency for planning, coordinating, and supplementing such efforts.

The experience of the fifties and early sixties, however, while confirming the fitness of that model, has also made clear that some fundamental contradictions had not been solved. Rather, they had become an obstacle to its efficient application. These contradictions were the social, economic, and political distortions of structure that have already been analyzed.

This study does not claim to analyze how and why the application of the national-capitalist model to Brazil caused these distortions. What can be said, very briefly, is that the Brazilian experience has shown that the pure-and-simple application of the national-capitalist model required both a less heterogeneous society and a greater consciousness by the national bourgeoisie of its own class interest and social role.

The enormous differences separating the rural-agricultural world from the urban-industrial world, and favoring the Center-South region at the expense of the others, have proved too great for the national bourgeoisie to reconcile. In spite of the stimulus of the state, the national entrepreneurs have naturally been led to increase the development of the already more developed sector and region, thus widening the gap instead of reducing it. The insufficient class and role consciousness of the national bourgeoisie, moreover, never permitted the accumulation of enough political strength to reinforce the state.

Another factor which hindered healthy development was the increased interference of the United States in the affairs of

countries outside the Soviet bloc. As a result of this interference, there was an important change in one of the variables
determining the proper model for national development: the
external socio-political situation.

Insufficiently aware of its class interest and of its socio-political role, the Brazilian national bourgeoisie was influenced by
the United States to overemphasize its "bourgeois" features at
the expense of its "national" features. It was led into an absurd
"common cause" with the old traditional sectors against the
interference of the state in economic affairs. It was led, therefore, to forget that the state should be an agent of the national
bourgeoisie. Without the state's interference, it could neither
overcome, internally, the resistance of the traditional forces
against socioeconomic development, nor could it be protected,
externally, from the overwhelming pressures of the bourgeoisies
of the highly developed countries, particularly the United States.

National Laborism

The experience of applying the national-capitalist model to
Brazil indicated the necessity for a readjustment of that model
by incorporating some features of state capitalism.

In spite of all the difficulties presented by the national-
capitalist model, Brazilian conditions in the early sixties would
not have been better met by a switch from the national-capitalist to the state-capitalist model. Such an attempt would certainly have been politically impossible and socioeconomically
disastrous. The technical and managerial sector of the Brazilian
middle class, which constitutes the new middle class, had
neither the desire nor the ability to seize revolutionary control
of the state against a coalition of the landowners and the
bourgeoisie. On the contrary, it had become incorporated into
the "new establishment," sharing most of the values of the
bourgeoisie. It was particularly reluctant to play a more active
role in events, even if such a role would fit its now more conservative values. Therefore, rather than drag itself against the
establishment, the middle class kept its associaton with the
national bourgeoisie and preserved its feeling of belonging to
the upper and not the lower strata of society.

The kind of readjustment required by the national-capitalist
model was, in general, compatible with the mood and ten-

‖ THE NATIONALIST PIVOT

dencies of the new middle class in the early sixties. It also suited
the expectations and effective means of action of the national
bourgeoisie, not to speak of the proletariat.

Basically the readjusted model was national laborism. The
readjustment was to consist, in the first place, of reinforcing the
role of the state as the major agent of socioeconomic development, and not simply as an agent for the national entrepreneurs.
In the second place, it was to consist of drastic intervention in
the rural-agricultural world, aimed at liquidating the semifeudal
forces still entrenched. The countryside would then be open to
rational exploitation by the conversion of cooperative farms and
large state farms, depending on local conditions and the nature
of the crops. Complementary policies would have to be applied
to the reduction of regional inequalities, mostly connected with
the urban-rural imbalance.

In the third place, the national-labor model would realign the
interests of the national bourgeoisie and the proletariat by
raising the technology and the scale of industry, thereby increasing the number of jobs, the wages, and the consuming capacity
of the workers, together with the productivity and business
capacities of the entrepreneurs. Such a policy would require a
substantial enlargement of the state's capacity for investment
and a more consistent policy of preservation and consolidation
of the national growth. This would require a systematic division
of entrepreneurial responsibilities between the state and the
national entrepreneurs, according to the principle of assigning
the state to the infrastructural and large intermediate industries,
and the private sector to the industries of transformation. No
less a systematic division of sectors between national and
foreign capital would be required, as well as a policy for the
determination of ceilings of foreign ownership and control of
productive enterprises.

The Model for Social Stability

Another way of dealing with the structural distortions would
lead to the preservation of the social order, at the expense of the
national structures and the national individuality. This model
can be described in terms of three major requisites.

In the first place, this model would require, as would the
national-laborism model, a substantial reinforcement of the

state. Such reinforcement, however, would not be for permitting a greater intervention in the economic sphere, but for preserving stability.

In the second place, it would require the promotion of the tightest possible economic and political integration of the country into the Western system, under United States leadership— the Atlantic Community. This integration would consolidate the parties, generally in terms of their existing functions. This integration would also ensure maximum use of foreign assistance, which would compensate for the lack of internal dynamism caused by the preservation of the status quo. A third result of integration would be enlargement of markets, with a new emphasis on the Latin American Common Market, thereby incorporating the whole of Latin America (under expected Brazilian regional leadership) into the Atlantic Community.

In the third place, this model would reestablish, under state supervision, a free market, assuring private enterprise full control and management of the economy, along with the transference of most of its productive activities from the public to the private sector.

The most appropriate name for such a model is colonial fascism. Indeed, in the last analysis fascism is simply a model for promoting economic development without changing the existing social order. The German and Italian examples, however, were characterized by the fact that in each of these countries there was an important industrial complex, owned and managed by a dynamic bourgeoisie. In the alliance between the middle class and the bourgeoisie, the German and Italian bourgeoisies let the middle class take over the political leadership of their respective countries, in exchange for preserving their ownership and management of industry. In the Brazilian case, however, this solution would be doubly impossible. Internally there is the incompatibility between a nationally oriented development and the maintenance of the existing social order. Externally there is the dependence of the model on the West in general and the United States in particular, due to its need for foreign assistance and foreign markets. The adjustment of a fascist model to dependence on foreign metropolitan centers transforms it into colonial fascism. This is, therefore, why that designation has been given to the model which can deal with the Brazilian structural distortions in terms of the existing social order.

The Quadros Government

The Jânio Quadros government, inaugurated on January 31, 1961, and abruptly ended on August 25 of the same year by the resignation of the president, has been singled out by its unpredictability. Not so, however, for the usually alleged reason: the mercurial character of Quadros, manifested most notably in his unexpected resignation. Besides, and in spite of the oddities of his personality, what has lent Quadros' government its acknowledged unpredictability has been the rapidity with which events have moved after the Kubitschek government and the rapidity —if not always the adequacy—with which Quadros was led to react to them, often by changing his former positions.

The most unexpected of Quadros' shifts was certainly the meaning and direction he gave to his government a couple of months after his inauguration. Elected by the UDN, although in a nonpartisan campaign, he was linked by his political past to the conservative forces which had overthrown Vargas and opposed Kubitschek. The supporters of his candidacy were expecting from him a basically conservative government, under the disguise of popular gestures.

Whatever might have been Quadros' previous intentions, when confronted with the pressing problems created by the structural distortions analyzed above, he quickly understood that the traditional conservative remedies would be inoperative. He realized the necessity of establishing financial stability and pursued economic policies which he hoped would halt the inflationary spiral. In this respect he followed the conventional remedies. But he also understood the structural character of the Brazilian inflation and the fact that its effective correction—if the country was to be maintained and strengthened as a national society—could not be dissociated from the overall problem of economic and political development. Thus he oriented his government in terms of national economic development and sociopolitical change, in accordance with the model of national laborism.

The problem with Quadros was not so much the lack of a full theoretical understanding of his adopted model, but rather the fact that his new insight into the real problems of the country was not followed by a corresponding understanding of the conditions and instruments necessary for the execution of the required policies. The surprising impact of his personality, transmitting an extraordinary impression of power, increased by the relevance of the decisions he was taking, made him a victim of the power illusion he imparted. He played a Bonapartist role—which tended to be required by the circumstances—without having Bonaparte's armies. In that respect he committed a double and equally fateful mistake. The first was ignoring that the authority of the president, undermined by a restive Congress, would not be enough for changing the socioeconomic structure of the country, particularly in a direction that would antagonize the most powerful international interests. Used to handling politics above the parties and through a charismatic and nonmediated appeal to the masses, Quadros never realized the necessity for organizing the latter in support of his policies, to neutralize the well-structured resistance of domestic and international conservative interests.

Quadros' second mistake was to ignore that the loyalty of the military whom he entrusted with the command of the armed forces—already predominantly conservative—had been acquired by him when he was playing a very different role. His political meaning as president became the reverse of his former role as São Paulo's governor. For a certain time the links of tradition and personal relationship, as well as the magic of presidential authority, added to his personal charisma, kept his military chiefs and the armed forces in line. However, when the expert Carlos Lacerda, then head of the state of Guanabara, felt that he could ostensibly lead the Quadros opposition, mobilizing against him all the domestic and foreign interests vested in the preservation of the status quo, Quadros suddenly realized that he had literally no support in any relevant sector of the establishment. Since he had not foreseen any other base for his policies, he lost assurance and resigned. He preferred to anticipate a crisis he understood to be inevitable rather than wait for it. He also preferred to step down rather than be ousted, and he probably supposed that the national commotion which would follow the news of his resignation could still bring him back on the crest of a mass protest movement.[31] The fact that even for this last move he had not counted on any organized groups

---

[31] For a complete analysis of Jânio Quadros' resignation see Hélio Jaguaribe, "The Crisis in Brazilian Politics," in Irving L. Horowitz (ed.), *Revolution in Brazil: Politics and Society in a Developing Nation,* New York: E. P. Dutton & Co., 1964, pp. 138–164.

dispersed the effects of the spontaneous "Quadros-come-back" manifestations which actually took place in the big cities. And the army of Marshal Denys, too happy with that white coup to allow its results to be lost, immediately took over full control of the country, removing any possibility of Quadros' return and trying to prevent his succession by Vice-President Goulart.

The Goulart Government

By other means, and under the official command of a very different personality, the Goulart government staged two new attempts for solving the structural distortions of the country in a way intended to combine national development with socio-political change.

Goulart's first steps had been very difficult. Initially he had had to counteract the coup of Marshal Denys, aimed at preventing him from succeeding the former president. Later he had had to engage in a long and perilous struggle to overcome the parliamentarian limitations which he had tactically accepted as a compromise to overcome the veto of the military. Only in January, 1963, more than a year after being sworn in, was he given back full presidential powers, by a massive 4 to 1 plebiscite vote. From then until its end the Goulart government attempted to carry forward two different political experiments. They have become respectively known, according to the definition given by the late San Tiago Dantas, as the "positive left" and the "negative left" experiments.[32]

The positive left experiment, under Dantas' leadership and with the technical orientation of Celso Furtado (then respectively the minister of finance and the minister for planning), was the most conscious and deliberate attempt at implementing national laborism ever tried in Brazil. That attempt, however, hardly went beyond the basic formulation of its policies—in Celso Furtado's three-year plan—and the initial steps for its implementation through the measures adopted and the negotiations initiated by San Tiago Dantas.

For a complex set of reasons—ranging from personal resent-

[32] Cf. San Tiago Dantas, "A evolução da política brasileira," *Digesto Econômico*, 174, November–December, 1963, São Paulo. For a general view of Dantas' political studies, lectures, and speeches, particularly on foreign policy, see *Revista de Política Internacional*, Ano VII, No. 27, September, 1964, Rio de Janeiro.

ments to the fear of losing out to his brother-in-law, political rival deputy Leonel Brizola—less than six months after their appointment Goulart dismissed the Dantas-Furtado Cabinet.

Owing to the brevity of the experiment, it is impossible to appraise the national-laborism model either in its testing by experience or in the form by which its implementation was attempted.[33] The national-laborism model is not likely to mobilize the social forces to which it is addressed if these are not prepared, by former experience or by active organization, to realize that such a model represents, for their peculiar class and group interests, not a total but just the maximum viable satisfaction compatible with their reciprocal harmonization. It was precisely because the negative left, under Brizola's irresponsible adventurism, could address to the masses the most revolutionary promises and appeals that the viable compromise offered by the positive left was made to look irrelevant, if not as a disguise for a social treason. Correspondingly, the fallacious appeal by the right-wing conservatives to unrestricted advantages for the bourgeoisie could mislead the national entrepreneurs and make them believe that the viable compromise offered by the positive left was not worth its price.

The second experiment of the Goulart government could not be appropriately considered as representing another, albeit more radical, version of the national-laborism model.[34] First of all, because of the lack of consistency peculiar to the negative left, independent of its nature and degree of implementation. Nevertheless this second experiment was oriented toward revolutionary social change: land and income redistribution, economic nationalism, nationalization of large sectors of production, political mobilization of the urban and rural masses, control of the state by new social forces, and international neutralism and nonalignment were, among others, the proclaimed goals to be attained.

While the first experiment of the Goulart government, under Dantas' leadership, was not allowed by the president himself to

[33] For an account of Brazilian socio-political events and problems in the last thirty years, with particular emphasis on the sixties, and the study of the Dantas-Furtado experiment, see Thomas E. Skidmore, *Political Change in Brazil*, 1930–1964. New York: Oxford University Press, 1967.
[34] Cf. Thomas Skidmore, *op. cit.*; see also Otavio Ianni, Paulo Singer, Gabriel Cohn, and Francisco Weffort, *Política e revolução social no Brasil*. Rio de Janeiro, 1965.

be effectively tried, the second political experiment was never implemented due to the military coup of April 1, 1964. In the first case, sophisticated ideas were placed at the service of national development and social reform without being given effective trial. In the second, a social revolution from the top was attempted without the previous formation of revolutionary cadres or the effective participation of the masses.

The Military Government

The military coup which overthrew President Goulart in April, 1964, was originally an expression of a very broad opposition to his government. This opposition acquired a militant counterrevolutionary character at the end of 1963.[35] The unexpected ease with which the first rebel troops carried with them the rest of the armed forces, and the ease with which the armed forces took full control of the country, led the coup to a fast and increasing radicalization by the right. On the other hand, these same facts led the army, as the core of the armed forces, to concentrate all power in the military as a corporation, reducing to nominal or dependent participation the politicians who had taken part in the anti-Goulart counterrevolution—a counterrevolution aware of its meaning and unsatisfied with it, which felt the compensatory necessity of labeling itself a "revolution." Carlos Lacerda, a veteran and the ablest of the Brazilian counterrevolutionists, rapidly found himself in a marginal position, long before he decided to openly recognize and to oppose the Castelo Branco regime for its pretense of an authentic "revolutionary" message. He would, later in 1966, once again shift his position, this time to assume—in complete contradiction with all his political past—a center-left national-laborism posture, fiercely opposed to the Castelo Branco regime.

The message of the Castelo Branco regime, however, although originally reduced to the simplistic terms of a middle-class and conservative moralism and anti-Communism, was reformulated in a very elaborated form by the new minister of planning, Roberto Campos. Diametrically opposed to Celso Furtado, Campos prepared for the Castelo Branco regime a model for social stability, with strong colonial-fascist propensities. This model he succeeded in bringing into existence.

[35] Cf. Alberto Dines et al., Os idos de março e a queda em abril, Rio de Janeiro, 1964; see also Thomas Skidmore, op. cit.

The total control of the state by the military and its self-legitimation by Institutional Acts provided the most formidable reinforcement of the state ever attempted in Brazil, and equipped the government with means of coercion seldom paralleled even in the most authoritarian regimes. With socio-political stability thus assured, the Campos policies were oriented toward achieving financial stability. He had the advantage, in his attempt to control inflation, of not being encumbered by the usual difficulties. The tough military dictatorship eliminated working-class resistance to the more than proportional reductions of their real wages. The bourgeoisie, although alarmed by the recession caused by the anti-inflationary policies, was still too frightened by the last tendencies of the Goulart government and too concerned with the imminent risk of hyperinflation to accept the sacrifice of a period of bad business. The middle class, although enjoying its former influence, was the least patient. Its most influential sector, the military, was, however, given a fair pay rise and compensated by many other advantages resulting from its now direct and unchecked control of the state.[36] On the other hand, insofar as the loss of autonomy and internal development of the economy was concerned, with its gradual denationalization, there was no actual problem from the point of view of the new model, oriented toward the maximum use of foreign participation. Great strides were made, therefore, in the direction of financial stability. The rate of inflation was reduced by the end of 1965 to about 45 percent per year, half the rate of 1964, although this trend was sensibly slowed down in 1966.

The second requirement of the model, the total realignment of Brazil with the United States, was constantly proclaimed as the government's major external goal and was in all forms actively pressed forward. New facilities for foreign investment and capital movement were rapidly provided. Foreign aid, which had been practically suspended during the Goulart government, was again channeled to Brazil with larger amounts promised. The political aspects of the new Brazilian foreign

[36] The preexisting tendency in Brazil of appointing the military to manage state-owned corporations was led to a new height by the Castelo Branco regime. Another relevant technique for increasing military pay and influence was the setting up of innumerable military commissions of inquiry (*Enquerito Policial-Militar*—IPM), endowed with the widest and judicially uncontrollable powers.

policy were also made visible in a fast pace of participation in the occupation of the Dominican Republic.

A third basic feature of the model, the emphasis on private capital and free enterprise, has also been put into practice. In that respect, however, due to the resistance of the military nationalists, the selling out of state-owned concerns could not be seriously contemplated. The government was even forced to reinstate its loyalty to Petrobrás and its policy of state oil monopoly.

The rather successful implementation of the model for social stability, nevertheless, was neither capable of preventing the formation of a strong extreme-right nationalist opposition among some military sectors, nor has it been able to overcome the intrinsic contradictions of the model itself.

The right-wing nationalist opposition was an unavoidable result of the training and professional ideology of the military, reinforced by the practice of assigning them to manage most of the state-owned corporations. While nationalism could be identified with left-wing tendencies, as was the case before the military coup, the right-wing nationalists in the army could be induced to accept antinationalist policies as a necessary means to liquidate the left wingers. Once a right-wing military regime had taken over power, however, that sort of justification could no longer stand. Right-wing nationalists were making their voices heard. For tactical reasons there was a fusion of positions in the "hard line," between the ultra-rightists (who are not always nationalists) and the right-wing nationalists. They became altogether both ultra-rightists and nationalists. And they almost succeeded in striking a coup within the coup in the weeks preceding the "Second Institutional Act" of October 27, 1965.[37]

The right-wing nationalists, however, are not capable of prevailing over the colonial-fascist tendency, nor is the hard line likely to be altogether liquidated while this regime keeps its military character. The former is not possible because right-wing nationalism is not viable under present Latin American conditions. An emphasis on the preservation of the existing

---

[37] The "hard line" is ultimately composed of a non-openly defined clique of colonels, strategically situated in the army system of command, who have been ideologically influenced and led by Carlos Lacerda before he shifted to oppose the military regime and adopted, even if only for temporary tactical reasons, a center-left position.

social order needs external compensatory assistance both for economic and political reasons, and therefore cannot be nationalistic without losing support and viability, both domestically and internationally. Despite its lack of viability, however, the hard line is not likely to be eliminated by the prevailing soft line, since the very existence of the "rabid right wingers" justifies that of the nonrabid ones, as the lion is indispensable for the role of the tamer.

The model for social stability in its Castelo Branco form, acquired at the cost of national individuality, is doomed in the long run by its unsolvable internal contradictions. These are of two kinds: one affects its internal mechanism, which suffers from the results of overconcentration of income and the power it generates. The other affects the relationship of the regime with its external metropolitan center. In other words, one contradiction results from its "fascist" and the other from its "colonial" features.

The first contradiction results from the well-known impossibility, classically formulated by Marx, of maintaining a process of economic and political concentration over an extended period. The fact that Marx's predictions did not take place in Western Europe in no way affects the theoretical validity of his thesis. It simply shows that Western European societies, by the combined effect of working-class pressures, through unions and socialist parties, and the later more enlightened use, by the bourgeoisie, of the enormous increase in productivity brought about by technology, have provided the minimum redistribution of income, education, social opportunity, and power to keep these societies running and developing. In the case of a country like Brazil, a colonial-fascist model would, after a few years, so aggravate the imbalance between the growth of the population and the creation of new jobs, at all levels of occupation, that the new establishment would soon be forced to adopt a kind of apartheid policy, to prevent the starving peasants from migrating to the cities and joining the explosive marginal masses. Even such extreme policies, nevertheless, could not prevent the irrepressible political explosion of the system, combined with its economic crisis of supercapitalization and underproduction. In practice, of course, events would never be pushed to their theoretical limit and the regime would tend to be changed by the imposition of circumstances long before its viability was completely exhausted.

Concerning the external or "colonial" contradiction of the model, the crux of the matter lies in the fallacy of "complementarity" between developed and underdeveloped economies and the resulting assumption that external stimulus can compensate for the lack of internal growth. The dominant economy needs the raw materials of the dependent economy and cannot give to it, in exchange, any durable assistance or provoke any lasting dynamic effect of growth if the dependent economy, besides its export sector, does not develop a self-centered economy with a domestic market. The colonial-fascist model, however, is precisely intended to prevent the social changes which would be required for the development of an autonomous and growing economy. In so doing, it blocks the expansion of its own economy—whatever the factors available abroad might be. If the metropolitan center needed labor the colonial-fascist model could, at least, have its equilibrium prolonged by "exporting" its surplus population. Exporting such surpluses, however, would be entirely unfeasible for a country of the dimensions of Brazil, even if the metropolitan center had an unlimited tendency to import labor. This is not the case, moreover, in a country like the United States, where the cybernetic revolution is liberating more native labor than can be conveniently reoriented. A Brazilian–United States colonial-fascist relationship, therefore, would produce a declining stimulus in the Brazilian economy, while hindering the development of the country. In the long run, it would also prove less beneficial to United States economic interests than a relationship of increasingly differentiated and complex exchanges based on an independent and developed Brazilian economy.

Under such conditions, the result of a colonial-fascist relationship between the two countries would be that the dominant classes in Brazil—with the exception of the minority groups participating in the export sector—would not recover from abroad the dynamic impulse they had to suppress at home in order to prevent social change. Cumulative unemployment would increasingly push the system to its political and economic collapse.

As a conclusion it must be mentioned that the Brazilian military regime is not likely either to keep control of the country long enough to reach an impasse or to consistently maintain its original colonial-fascist orientation.

The complexity already achieved by the Brazilian urban-industrial sector is not compatible with a long-run colonial-fascist military regime. In the course of time (in a process which could hardly last more than a few years) the fears that have led the more progressive sectors of the Brazilian middle class to associate with the reactionary forces will be diluted. Change will then inevitably take place, both at the political and socioeconomic levels. The military will have to either return power to political parties and the social forces represented through them, or they will have to change in an essential form the orientation of their regime.

The first hypothesis, as things stand at this writing (late 1966), is more likely. The pressure of the urban-industrial complex, needing to reopen the country for economic growth and thus accepting the minimum social changes required, will induce or force the military to accept these minimum social changes.

The second hypothesis would drive the military to remain in power, with a substantial shift of ideology and policies. A "Nasserist" conversion, leading to reorienting the country toward socioeconomic development and national individuality, as well as to a new participation of the masses in the socio-political process, would extend for a much longer period the military's possibilities of maintaining power.

Battles and the War

in Latin America*

OTTO MARÍA CARPEAUX

INTRODUCTION

AMERICAN readers have not personally experienced the material, intellectual, and emotional situation of the Brazilian audience for whom this essay was originally written.

Since 1964, we have lived under a regime that has suspended the political rights of hundreds of citizens, without stating what they are guilty of, giving them no opportunity to defend themselves, and providing no right of appeal; that has expelled from the armed forces about one-fourth of the officer corps, also without due process of law; that summarily delivers citizens to military courts in peacetime; that considers every citizen a potential traitor and defines "nonconformity" as a crime (in the foreword of the new Law of National Security); that does not provide a legal definition of "nonconformity"; that made the judges liable to summary transferal; that extinguished all political parties; that reduced Congressional prerogatives to a bare minimum. Congress itself was purged; the President of the Republic can legislate by decree; and the President is no longer elected by the people but chosen from among the military chiefs by the expurgated Congress; there is no possibility of an opposition candidate; the state assemblies, which elect state governors, have also been purged; the labor organizations are under the strict surveillance of the political police, who must approve union elections. The people are denied the right of

* Translated by Fernando A. de Mello-Vianna.

assembly and intellectuals are prohibited from publicly expressing their opinions; the students too are relentlessly persecuted.
Opposition by the people under this regime is feeble. There is
no organized resistance against those in power who rule Brazil.

Hope is difficult to keep alive because those in power have
tanks and machine guns and we, the others, have only our free
consciences.

This essay was written to explain to Brazilian readers that the
real power in Brazil belongs not to the Brazilian military: the
true capital of Brazil is Washington. This had to be said. But
how say it?

The minister of justice in Brazil has ordered certain books
seized and closed one of the most widely read political newspapers in the country without due process of law. However,
there is still some freedom of the press in Brazil, although it is
under the permanent threat of a new and Draconian press law.
But it so happens that even the liberty that is granted (and so
easily revokable) is more apparent than real. To this the author
of this essay bears witness. He was for almost twenty years the
chief editorial writer for one of the largest morning papers of
the country, and was forced to resign his post because of
economic pressure from advertising agencies—"Brazilian"
agencies with home offices in New York City. Ever since, he
has been denied the opportunity to practice his profession as a
journalist. He can only voice his opinions infrequently, and then
only in books. This essay is from a book that attempted to
inform Brazilian readers about what was really happening.

In the beginning there was heaven and earth and the Monroe
Doctrine. And with the Monroe Doctrine began the misinterpre-
tation or perversion of history.

On December 2, 1823, the President of the United States,
James Monroe, sent a message to Congress in which he warned
the European powers against establishing their *political systems*
anywhere in the Americas; it was made clear that the United
States would find this intolerable and that they would defend the
continent against it.

The textbooks have it that President Monroe wished to
protect the lately acquired independence of the former Spanish
colonies, and Brazil, against Spain and Portugal. On the contrary, the independence of the Latin American countries was to
be protected for commercial reasons. Great Britain's Foreign
Minister, George Canning, had suggested to Washington the

THE NATIONALIST PIVOT

previous August an Anglo-American declaration. Washington
did not react until November, when Secretary of State John
Quincy Adams informed Canning that the United States would
prefer a unilateral declaration. The Doctrine had little to do
with Latin America; on the contrary, it had an entirely different
objective.

At that time Alaska belonged to Russia (it was only sold to
the United States in 1867) and the Czar wanted to secure bases
on the Pacific Coast for the Russian whalers. The Pacific Coast
of North America, what is now California, belonged to Mexico,
and it was poorly guarded. The Russians had set up a fishing
post near what is now San Francisco, and it was this the United
States was vetoing in the name of Mexico's independence and
territorial integrity. Barely twenty-five years later the United
States seized this same California from Mexico—in the name of
the Monroe Doctrine.

After 1823 the United States expanded greatly and was eager
to acquire even more land for expansion. The slaveowners and
cotton planters in the South sought new territories to plant
cotton and breed slaves; the pioneers of the Middle West turned
their attention to the Rockies, California, and the Pacific. John
Frémont, who was later a candidate for President, gained
nationwide popularity by organizing an expedition for "geographic exploration" of these Far Western Mexican territories,
but when the war broke out it was in Texas.

Several U.S. planters and slaveowners had settled in Texas,
then part of the Mexican state of Coahuila, founding ranches
and villages. On November 7, 1835, they organized a rebellion
against the Mexican Government and on March 2, 1836, proclaimed the independent Republic of Texas. When they applied
for admission to the Union, Washington hesitated because
northern businessmen and industrialists did not wish to wage war
with Mexico for the benefit of southern slaveowners. However, in
1845, Texas was admitted into the Union as the twenty-eighth
state and at the same time President Polk dispatched to the
frontier an army under the command of General Zachary
Taylor.

The Mexicans, less powerful, were defeated. It was obvious
all along that the peace treaty would provide that Texas be
turned over to the United States. Then it happened that Sutter
discovered gold in California (which had been defended against
the Russians in the name of the Monroe Doctrine) and since

the Americans were already in the process of "softening" them up, they also demanded the vast territories between Texas on the Atlantic Coast and California on the Pacific. By the Treaty of Guadalupe Hidalgo, signed February 2, 1848, Mexico surrendered to the United States the present states of Texas, California, Arizona, New Mexico, Nevada, Utah, and half of Colorado: 2,490,000 square kilometers, more than half of all Mexican territory.

The Mexican War is somewhat forgotten. When we speak of Los Angeles we think of Hollywood, and few recall its full name, which is very un-Hollywood—Santa María de los Angeles. Only in Mexico one still says: "Poor Mexico, so far from God and so close to the United States!"

At the end of the nineteenth century, of the vast American colonial empire of Charles V, Spain had kept only the islands of Cuba and Puerto Rico. For decades these colonies had fought against Spanish domination without any help from the Monroe Doctrine. Nor were the voices of two great thinkers, the Cuban José Martí and the Puerto Rican Eugenio María de Hostos, both poets and idealists, heard in the United States. When the first wave of industrialization had run its course and the consumption of sugar and tropical fruit increased rapidly in the United States, the martyrdom of the Cubans and Puerto Ricans was suddenly discovered and an irresistible movement of *idealism* swept the United States. War was declared against Spain to free the two islands and change them into republics, with their independence fully guaranteed by the Monroe Doctrine.

In 1898, on the occasion of riots in Havana, the United States consul asked Washington for military intervention "to protect the lives and property of American citizens" (we are to hear this request often; lately from the United States ambassador in the Dominican Republic). On April 19, 1898, the United States Senate approved a declaration supporting Cuba's independence. War broke out, Spain collapsed, and on January 1, 1899, the island was occupied by the Americans.

Independence for Cuba it is true, but independence *sui generis*. The so-called Platt Amendment was imposed on Cuba, which gave the United States the right to intervene militarily in *independent* Cuba as often as necessary. In 1901 the Cubans swallowed the pill of incorporating the Platt Amendment into the Cuban constitution. And in 1906, 1916, and 1920 occasions did arise for intervening. The Platt Amendment no longer exists but it has left a deadly inheritance—the United States base in Guantánamo, an alien fortress in an "independent" country.

And Puerto Rico? With this smaller island the amenities were not observed. When it was surrendered by Spain it became an American colony. Not until 1947 did the United States deign to grant the Puerto Ricans the right to elect their own governor. The constitution of this new Commonwealth of Puerto Rico had to be sanctioned by the United States. The island is today a part of the Commonwealth of the United States. This is what some other Latin American governments want for their countries.

The idealism of Martí and Hostos was betrayed. The two islands remained colonies, merely changing owners.

With the conquest of California the United States had become a great Pacific power. The conquest of Cuba and Puerto Rico strengthened its position as a great Atlantic power. But maritime trade between the two coasts had always been impractical; it was necessary to sail thousands of miles around South America. The United States was forced to maintain two separate fleets which, moreover, could not be joined. It was necessary to join the two oceans by a canal, and this could only be done through one of the isthmuses of Central America. However, Central America is not American territory. Therefore, it is necessary to annex one of the small Central American republics. The initial target was Nicaragua but the plan was eventually executed in Panama.

Once a Panamanian friend told me rather wistfully: "My country is unknown in the world. Everything about it that is known is not ours: the scandal was French and the Canal is American."

The French project to dig through the Isthmus of Panama, headed by Ferdinand de Lesseps, had ended shamefully in the greatest scandal of all time involving parliamentary corruption. However, the engineer Philippe Bunau-Varilla went to Washington where he captured the interest of Senator Mark Hanna—a name familiar to all of us. Backed by President Theodore Roosevelt, Hanna persuaded the United States Senate to abandon the Nicaraguan project and authorize the President to negotiate the Panamanian project with Colombia, since Panama was a Colombian province.

For quite a while Colombia had been under firm American

influence. President Marroquín and his ambassador to Washington, Martínez Silva, were inclined to favor the Bunau-Varilla–Hanna–Theodore Roosevelt projects. Meanwhile, in Bogotá a strong resistance appeared against the plan of ceding the Canal Zone to the United States. President Marroquín was forced to recall Martínez Silva and replace him by the less compliant Ambassador Concha. Bunau-Varilla started to act as if he were the United States Secretary of State. With Hanna's agreement he cabled President Marroquín: "The Canal will be built with or without Colombia." He also apprised influential newspapers of dissatisfaction in Panama and that the Panamanians wished to secede from Colombia. Everything had already been settled. Secretary of State John Hay collaborated in the writing of the treaty authored by Bunau-Varilla, which called for Colombia to make all desirable concessions. When Ambassador Concha went on vacation, his secretary, Herrán, who was chargé d'affaires, signed the treaty. Only Senator Hanna knew Secretary Herrán's motives, since he had failed to consult his Government.

The Hay-Herrán Treaty was signed in Washington on January 22, 1903. In Bogotá a wave of protests rose. The senate of Colombia unanimously repudiated the chargé d'affaires. But Bunau-Varilla had already brought to Washington a Panamanian delegation headed by Manuel Amador, which sought United States support for the Colombian province of Panama to become an independent republic. President Theodore Roosevelt agreed. Amador demanded $6 million to bribe Colombian generals and pay the Panamanian "revolutionaries." Instead, Bunau-Varilla had apparently sized up the situation and offered only $100,000, which Amador readily accepted. The Panamanian "revolution" broke out on November 2, 1903, and on the same day the American cruiser *Nashville,* which Hay had sent a few days earlier from San Francisco, arrived to lend its support. On November 6, the United States recognized the independence of the Republic of Panama, which in turn ratified the Hay-Herrán Treaty, surrendering to the United States sovereignty over the Canal Zone and granting it the right to intervene militarily in the internal affairs of the independent Republic of Panama—as it has done, since then, several times. And so the Republic of Panama remains "independent" until the present day.

* * *

The Panamanian incident begins a new phase in United States policy in Latin America: "show" of warships in ports of small republics, debarkation of Marines, military occupation of whole countries for years—in short, what President Theodore Roosevelt called the Big Stick policy. The same policy was enforced until 1933 by his successors, including the liberal Democrat Woodrow Wilson. The policy had been formulated before Theodore Roosevelt by Secretary of State Richard Olney who stated in 1895: "Today the United States is practically sovereign on this continent and its fiat is law upon the subjects to which it confines its interposition." The Big Stick policy is a new version of the Monroe Doctrine. The United States had said it would not permit the independence of Latin American republics to be attacked or violated. Now only the United States would have the right to attack or infringe upon the independence of Latin American republics.

What underlay this new interpretation were economic and even alimentary reasons. We have already mentioned the increase in sugar and fruit consumption in the United States. Now another and much stronger reason had been created—oil, brought about by the overwhelming success of the automobile; and the first great oil-producing countries in the New World, besides the United States, were Mexico and Venezuela.

To secure the steady production of these goods and raw materials it was necessary to maintain undisturbed order in the countries producing them. However, this goal was far from being achieved in the restless Caribbean and Central American republics. Only in Cuba and Panama had the United States secured the right to interfere *manu militaire*. But they exercised the same right in other countries nevertheless.

On the other hand, Mexico, the other major oil producer, overthrew the thirty-four-year dictatorship of General Porfirio Díaz in 1911. It was painful for the United States to lose such a faithful friend, to the advantage of President Madero and peasant leaders like Pancho Villa. There was an attempt to crush the revolution by eliminating its principal leader; the assassination of Madero was conspired within the walls of the United States Embassy in Mexico City. (This statement, which seems monstrous, is described in the scholarly *Historia diplomática de la revolución Mexicana* by Isidro Fabela.) Challenging the revolution after Madero's death, American Marines occupied Veracruz, and in 1916 a strong American Army under

the command of General Pershing invaded Mexico on a punitive expedition. Then the miracle happened: the Mexicans
resisted, and the Americans retreated and never came back.
This is a possibility that will be remembered forever.

In Nicaragua, American intervention stretched over a long
period. In 1909 this country was occupied by United States
troops. In 1911, American officials took over the customs
administration. In 1926 the Marines disembarked to prevent the
inauguration of a newly elected but troublesome president. In
1928 new presidential elections were held "under the supervision of U.S. officers," who also helped suppress the popular
Mexican-style revolt of Sandino. These interventions ceased
abruptly when dictatorial powers were assumed by President
Somoza, whose family rules Nicaragua to this day.

Haiti was occupied by United States troops from 1915 to
1934. One can imagine the treatment granted the population by
occupying forces, considering the natives were black. Later,
American travelers expressed surprise at the strong resentment
against the United States in Haiti.

The most intricate affair of the Big Stick era was the Dominican Republic. American interventions dated back as far as the
nineteenth century, and in 1905 the usual step of sending Washington officials to administer the country's customs was taken.
In 1914, President Ramón Baez was "placed under the protection of the United States." In 1915, the Marines went ashore to
"ensure the public order." Finally, on November 29, 1916,
Admiral Thomas Snowden officially took over the Government
of the Dominican Republic, remaining for eight years. It should
be pointed out that this occupation began in 1916, before
Bolshevism took hold in Russia, and before the United States
had reason to fear Communism.

The year that marked the withdrawal of American troops
from Haiti, 1934, also saw the United States giving up its right
to intervene militarily in Cuba; the Platt Amendment was
abolished. The President of the United States was now not
Theodore, but Franklin D., Roosevelt. Military intervention and
occupation in the Caribbean and Central America came to an
end. The Good Neighbor Policy was inaugurated.

Nowadays the extreme right wing denigrates Franklin D.
Roosevelt—a great man and a great idealist. However, Richard
Hofstadter has pointed out that no one gets elected President
without being a great opportunist. The Big Stick was broken in

the economic crisis of 1929. Busy restoring its own shaken economy, the United States temporarily lost its taste for meddling in other peoples' lives. They did not, of course, envisage the possibility of abandoning their hegemony in the Americas. Only this time, instead of maintaining it by force, they tried to create institutions to perpetuate it, grounding them in treaties and conventions. The result was the Inter-American System, the OAS.

The Inter-American System is an occult science. Some men know by heart the articles and paragraphs of the Bogotá, Rio de Janeiro, and Caracas conferences—a fascinating but highly theoretical study. We have always held the view that the alliance of an immensely powerful country with twenty very weak countries was not an alliance but a thinly disguised way of imposing servitude. The articles and paragraphs of the OAS Charter are respected only when they please the powerful partner; otherwise they are disregarded. In April of 1965 this thesis was extensively confirmed when the United States, under a thin pretext, invaded the Dominican Republic in violation of Articles 15 and 17 of the charter, which prohibit the intervention of an American state in the internal affairs of another American state "under any circumstances and for whatever reasons." Since then inter-American law has ceased to exist and we need not waste time with its provisions, which are now abolished by force.

Following the principle of nonintervention strictly, Roosevelt's Government best served the interests of the United States and of American corporations that had invested money in Latin American enterprises—by maintaining internal peace in all the countries. Political stability was to be assured, even at the price of recognizing dictatorships or semidictatorships that existed in Guatemala, Cuba, Venezuela, Peru, and Brazil; on the contrary, he supported them in the interests of political stability. However, this stability was not achieved for the simple reason that dictatorships breed instability.

This instability is the characteristic trait of Latin American political history during the nineteenth and first half of the twentieth century. A number of explanations have been advanced: the extreme individualism of the Iberian people, resulting in street riots and palace revolutions that can only be crushed by the dictatorship of a strong man, the caudillo; the lack of unity, partly the result of miscegenation and other racial factors. Europeans, in general, gave up the idea of any explanation and preferred to consider the history of Latin American countries as a foolish sequence of rebellions headed by brutish generals and bribed demagogues and devoid of any sense. These "explanations" are nonsense; the real reasons are quite different. They were brilliantly discussed by Merle Kling in his study of political instability in Latin America, published in the *Western Political Quarterly*.

Eighty percent of Venezuelan oil, 90 percent of Chilean copper, and in general the majority of the mining companies in Latin America are owned by foreign companies, mostly American. The land is in the hands of the native oligarchies, the estate owners; but the products—coffee, cacao, bananas, sugar—are dependent upon the American market. Until there is a strong native bourgeoisie, only a small percentage of the national income is available for allocation for well-paid administrative positions, or remuneration for generals and superior officers, or participation in export companies and banks. It is not enough to satisfy the needs of all the groups and clans and therefore there is a struggle for the political power that governs the distribution of positions. This is the reason for the political instability that at every hour threatens to burst the dams of legality, expressing itself in coups d'état and revolutions.

Merle Kling concluded that political instability is the effect of the incompatibility between a colonial economy, highly dependent upon the outside, and a legal sovereignty which is fictitious; that is, it exists on paper, and has to yield alternately to national coups d'état and American interventions.

During the Truman and Eisenhower years the policy of political stabilization of Latin America by support of oligarchies and dictatorships had, once again, pressing economic reasons— the United States had inherited Great Britain's role in Latin America. In Brazil, for example, in 1939, 55 percent of foreign capital was in the hands of the British and 28 percent in the Americans'; by 1949 the figures had reversed, American investments representing 54 percent and British 29 percent. Someone had had to fill the vacuum left by the weakened British; and it was worth the while.

Usually American industry works by selling as much as

possible and accepting a lower margin of profit in order to increase sales. After 1945 there was the possibility of reaping profits of from between 33 and 42 percent of capital invested in Europe, which the European countries repaid with Marshall Plan money. In Latin America profits can reach from 90 to 150 percent. In 1960 a delegation of American businessmen was in Brazil to investigate the possibility of recovering within a year or two, in the form of profits, the total expenses incurred in establishing an industry. This is discussed by Hellmut Kalbitzer, economist and deputy from West Germany, in his book *The Third World and the Great Powers* (Frankfurt, 1962); in it, he quotes from an American source (*Newsweek*) the following figures: in 1961 the $500 million invested in Latin America yielded a profit of $770 million.

We have another witness, the best of all. President John F. Kennedy, in *The Strategy of Peace,* states: "In 1960, we [the United States] invested abroad $1,700 million and obtained from these investments a profit of $2,300 million"; and he continues: "But when we examine the share of these investments located in the underdeveloped countries, that is, in the countries that need most capital formation, we can observe that we invested $200 million in them and we took out $1,300 million." In the words of President Kennedy, the investment of foreign capital in Latin America means the decapitalization of Latin America. It should be further remarked that a major part of that foreign capital is invested in areas that are not useful to the economy of the "aided" country. In Brazil a large and prosperous American concern gets all its profits from renting linen and bedding for luxury hotels and restaurants. More or less on the same level are the massive sales of articles like Coca-Cola or certain electrical appliances, which only serve to weaken the already small purchasing power of the Latin American consumer and limit his ability to make more needed expenditures. This publicity success is sometimes seized upon by certain Latin American economists who interpret it as proof of *unnecessary expense and misdirected consumption* (an ironic conspicuous consumption) and demand salary and wage cuts.

Since these investments are highly profitable, they have to be insured against revolt and riot, or take-over and confiscation, high taxes and other harassments by the authorities. After the Big Stick policy and the failure of the Good Neighbor Policy the only solution was to hand over the Big Stick to Latin American governments that represent the landed oligarchies and the higher echelons of the import-export trade. These groups, economically dependent on the United States, have the same interests as the American investors. The Big Stick of the American Marines was exchanged after 1945 for the Big Stick of the Latin American generals. The Dominican Republic had thirty-two years of peace and stability under Trujillo's dictatorship. Nicaragua enjoys peace, stability, and the dictatorship of the Somoza family.

In Venezuela, the first country in which the new policy was put into effect, it was not necessary to carry a Big Stick since General Juan Vicente Gómez exercised a ruthless and merciless dictatorship from 1908 in alliance with the growing oil interests. Only the death of Gómez in 1935 interrupted this political idyll; an American observer was incredulous of the people's manifestations of joy as they mobbed the streets of Caracas when they learned of his death and stormed the police precincts to liberate political prisoners. After this the attempt to support the constitutionally disguised dictatorship of General Medina failed; and the enthusiasm of the days of 1945, after the fall of the fascist regimes in Europe, made possible the restoration of democracy and the election of President Rómulo Gallegos. The new government curtailed the military, promised agrarian reform, and demanded higher royalties from the oil companies; in other words, they simultaneously attacked the interests of the military, the landholders, and the Americans. The attacked interests soon reformed their *Unholy Alliance* to oppose it. In 1948, President Gallegos was deposed by a military coup headed by Colonel Chalbaud, who was in turn assassinated and replaced by General Pérez Jiménez. The United States gave its full support to these officers—at first discreetly, and later openly. During the coup of 1948 in Caracas the U.S. military attaché remained in the ministry of war until the final outcome was known, whereupon he congratulated the winners. In 1953, President Eisenhower on the advice of Secretary of State John Foster Dulles conferred upon dictator-President General Pérez Jiménez the Legion of Merit; in the letter that accompanied the decoration, Eisenhower stated that the dictatorship of Pérez Jiménez should be a model for all Latin American countries. Herbert Matthews, a *New York Times* reporter, called this

letter the "most deadly proof of political incompetence" and
"highly detrimental to the prestige of the United States in Latin
America." Matthews was impatient; he should have reserved his
superlatives for other actions by Washington, the first of which
took place the following year in Guatemala.

In 1944 in Guatemala the dictatorship of General Ubico was
deposed and Dr. Juan José Arévalo was elected President of the
Republic. He was an educator who had studied in Argentina, a
moderate progressive whose cautious reform policies soon worried the United Fruit Company, which dominates agriculture
and the railroad system in the country. Arévalo's successor,
Colonel Jacobo Arbenz, even committed the crime of taking the
promised agrarian reform seriously. In 1954, Foster Dulles
started a moralistic press campaign against Arbenz, using religion as a weapon. In a school in Rio the nuns displayed a map
of Central America made in the United States in which a picture
of the devil was drawn over Guatemala. However, following the
new rules of letting others carry the stick, the Guatemalan coup
was executed by natives. Colonel Castillo Armas fled to Honduras where, with direct American aid, he organized an expedi-
tionary force. Shortly afterward he invaded, deposed Arbenz,
and assumed the dictatorship that was recognized by Washington. Unexpectedly the affair created a sensation, and to soften
the repercussions, Foster Dulles had the United Fruit Company
prosecuted for anti-trust violations, which was interpreted in the
American press as a sign of impartiality. The prosecution did
not mention United Fruit's monopoly in Guatemala, only its
affairs within the United States; and the judgment is still
pending.

Next, there was Cuba, whose dictator, Batista, was supported
by the United States. Until the end an American military
mission followed Batista's troops faithfully and actively. After
their defeat the United States expected the victors to be hostile
to it. But this hostility was not immediate, nor were the Communists immediately influential in Castro's government. The
ensuing conflict was caused by United States propaganda as well
as that of the sugar companies, the tourist business, and the
Havana night-club owners. The last act of the tragedy was the
Bay of Pigs, the attempted invasion of the island by Cuban
exiles organized by the CIA in May, 1961. It marked the end of

* * *

the traditional alliance that Merle Kling referred to; the new one would be called Alliance for Progress.

Cuba inspired urgent worry that the whole continent could catch fire. The hitherto dominant groups would be lost and a military invasion of all or the majority of the Latin American countries was clearly impossible. A new approach was indicated by John F. Kennedy, even before he assumed the Presidency, in *The Strategy of Peace* where he outlined the following program of action:

Until then the United States had given $24,800 million in aid to Europe, $19,500 million to Asia, but only $2,800 million to Latin America. However, even this $2,800 million had not benefited Latin American populations on the whole but the dominating oligarchies, and under the pretext of military aid, the executive branches of these oligarchies. Opposing this policy, Kennedy proposed that the United States defend the interests of the middle class (small industrialists and businessmen) and the labor force against the great economic powers. The social reforms that these groups had obtained in the United States during the New Deal had still to be achieved in Latin America before the doors of the continent would be opened to Communism, as had happened in Cuba. In his book Kennedy had already warned that if we did not implement the necessary social reforms, including the agrarian and fiscal reforms, and if the great masses of Latin America did not begin to participate in the growing world prosperity, our revolution and our dream would fail.

The revolution and the dream were formulated as the Alliance for Progress—an attempt to achieve political stability for Latin America without carrying a Big Stick, without coups, and without (even against) the oligarchies.

The Alliance for Progress demanded reforms in the shape of sacrifices from Latin American oligarchies, who obviously had no intention of giving up. There was an amazing development: the United States, while Kennedy was President, gave up the attempt to impose its will. The fact is that the middle classes that are the backbone of the Democratic party in the United States either did not exist in Latin America, were ineffectual, chose to follow fascist demagogues, or sided with the oligarchies. In view of this, Kennedy's aides began to despair. Only

THE NATIONALIST PIVOT

this can explain the fact that progressive democrats like Adolf
Berle, Adlai Stevenson, Averell Harriman, and Lincoln Gordon
began to behave like antidemocrats and were antiprogressive in
relation to Latin America, aligning themselves with the enemies
of social reform.

The first Latin American director of the Alliance for Progress
accurately defined the resistance of the oligarchies:

> Minorities extremely wealthy and powerful that exercise an over-
> whelming influence over the destiny of millions of human beings,
> refuse to sacrifice a small amount of their comfort and revenues,
> practically tax exempt. These minorities actively oppose the
> reforms proposed by the Alliance for Progress, especially the
> progressive income tax, agrarian reform, and other projects
> designed to create an educated middle class capable of partici-
> pating in political life.

This way the Democratic party was caught in the trap of the
reactionary classes; and the Alliance for Progress was changed,
first into an Alliance without Progress, and then to Alliance
against Progress.

The sum of $430 million, a negligible amount in view of the
needs of the continent, was spent. And how spent? Building
schools, hospitals, roads, and dredging harbors. All very nice,
but they do not change in the least the social structure of the
regions benefiting from them; on the contrary, they help relieve
the ruling classes of some of their social responsibilities. In
addition, the funds were sometimes disposed of for ulterior
political motives, favoring reactionary administrations and excluding those suspected of having progressive ideas. Finally,
Kennedy's Government reverted to the tactic of tolerating dictatorships and granting diplomatic recognition to de facto governments.

Financial help on a larger scale was only possible through the
International Monetary Fund, whose policy of austerity and
fighting inflation solely through monetary policies tends to
maintain the existing international division of labor; this results
in permanent depreciation of prices of exportable raw materials
which ruins underdeveloped countries by lowering the already
low standard of living. Unconditional financial aid is given only
for military purposes: nothing less than $500 million during the
last ten years. This amount looks small when compared with the
military expenditures of the Great Powers. But it is a lot for

Latin American armies, small in number, and lacking modern weapons, incapable of defending their countries in the event of serious foreign threat, and serving only (the expression recurs even in debates in the U.S. Senate) as forces for internal security—that is, to crush opposition movements.

The new American foreign policy in Latin America (and Asia) was bitterly criticized by Supreme Court Justice William O. Douglas: "We established fascist governments in these countries. Our businessmen bribed the Administrations to obtain favorable contracts. The CIA pours in money at election time." And we might add that when election results are unfavorable to American interests, they are annulled by coups. Since 1961 there have been coups d'état in Ecuador, the Dominican Republic, Argentina, Guatemala (to prevent the reelection of Arévalo), San Salvador, Honduras, and Bolivia with the active participation of American ambassadors in these countries.

Finally Le Monde noted in its edition of March 25, 1965, that Undersecretary of State Thomas C. Mann had announced a new U.S. policy in reference to military coups: the United States would not automatically recognize de facto governments. Only six days later the political regime of the largest of Latin American countries, Brazil, was changed and the new government was automatically recognized by the United States.

Since then there has been no holding back. The words of John F. Kennedy, in The Strategy of Peace, should be repeated:

> If we persist in believing that all Latin American agitation is Communist inspired—that every anti-American voice is the voice of Moscow, and that most citizens of Latin America share our dedication to an anti-Communist crusade to save what we call free enterprise for the Free World—then (the time may come when we will learn to our dismay that *our* enemies are not necessarily *their* enemies and that our concepts of progress are not yet meaningful in their own terms).

Well, the United States is no longer convinced of this. It is only as a pretext that they continue to affirm it. Since it is clear that Latin America is not ready to follow the U.S. in a crusade against Communism or in defense of free enterprise, it must be forced.

456   ▓ The Nationalist Pivot

This is the case at present. The policy reverses the facts and the language to describe it. The implantation of dictatorships is called *defense of democracy,* and the violation of inter-American law is presented as the reestablishment of the juridical norms of American coexistence. This was the case with the Dominican Republic.

In July, 1963, President Juan Bosch had established a new price for sugar, designed to hurt the South Porto Rico Sugar Corporation. In August the President abolished the abuse whereby Dominican army officers were receiving commissions for buying arms in the United States. This established a community of interests between the penalized military and its foreign corporate contacts. In September, when President Bosch was in Washington visiting Kennedy, he was deposed by a coup and replaced by a junta of generals and profiteers. After Kennedy's death this de facto government was recognized by the United States. But when in April, 1965, the people of the Dominican Republic took up arms to restore democracy, President Lyndon Johnson sent the Marines ashore to prevent an act of "Communist subversion." Not satisfied with this violation of the Charter of the Organization of American States, Washington decided to take the opportunity to end for good the aspirations for independence of Latin American countries, proposing in its place "interdependence"—the status of associate state that Puerto Rico has—in effect, colonies of the United States.

This is a list of the battles of Latin America—many battles, and with one or two exceptions, almost all lost. But this is not the last chapter. We will follow Great Britain's example of losing all the battles but managing to win the war.

The Alliance That Lost Its Way

EDUARDO FREI MONTALVA

JACQUES MARITAIN, the French philosopher whose thought has inspired the development of the Christian Democratic movement, maintains that history moves simultaneously in opposite directions: while the energies of society are debilitated by inaction and the passage of time, the creative forces of freedom and the spirit tend inevitably to revitalize the quality of those energies.

The evident historical importance of the Alliance for Progress, both as a human activity and as a conceptual program, makes it impossible for it to escape the workings of this general principle; thus, the generous initial concepts, the commitments and the hopes which arose after the early success of some of its programs have gone hand in hand with the renewed attacks against democracy, the loss of markets for Latin American primary commodities, the decline of foreign investment, the consolidation in power of unjust regimes and the acceptance of alternative, evolutionary processes which only retard the revolutionary changes that so many of these countries need.

The Alliance for Progress is committed to the achievement of a revolution which, as a political instrument, should be placed at the service of democratic ideas and the interests of the majority so that it will bring forth a substantial change in the political, social, and economic structures of the region. This change must be swift, and the responsibility for bringing it about belongs not just to a group of leaders or to a technocratic elite but to the whole of society. The Latin American origins of the Alliance for Progress were specially evident in the non-

457

Marxist political parties which had no links with the national oligarchies and were strongly opposed to the traditional Latin American right.

The Latin American revolution, as a force for rapid and substantial change, has been germinating for the last decade; it is now a permanent and dynamic torrent which is weakening the political and social institutions of the continent. The form taken by this drastic change will depend on the time which elapses before the forces of revolution are finally released. The greater the delay, the greater will be the accumulated pressure and the greater the violence of the eventual explosion.

The Latin American revolution has clearly defined objectives: the participation of the people in the government and the destruction of the oligarchies; the redistribution of land and the ending of the feudal or semifeudal regimes in the countryside; the securing of equal access to cultural and educational facilities and wealth, thus putting an end to inherited privilege and artificial class divisions. Finally, a main objective of the revolution is to secure economic development, coupled with a fair distribution of its products and the utilization of international capital for the benefit of the national economy.

These are precisely the same objectives as those of the Alliance. Obviously a revolution thus defined is not the only means whereby rapid change can be achieved in Latin America, but it is the one with which the Alliance has been identified from its very beginnings.

The immediate goal of those who support the Alliance should not be the achievement of perfect inter-American cooperation and solidarity; their task is rather to accelerate the liberation of the forces of freedom, justice, and solidarity among peoples who are hindered in their advance by the intellectual limitations of those unwilling to adapt to anything new, and by the material limitations retarding development. The task is to construct a dynamic image of the Alliance on the basis of facts and not to permit it to become a mere formula. The responsibility for the success of the Alliance is that of the whole hemisphere, because, as John F. Kennedy said, "Those who make peaceful revolution impossible will make violent revolution inevitable."

International cooperation is essential to secure these objectives. However important the internal effort of the developing countries may be, it will inevitably be insufficient in view of the enormous requirements of economic development and structural change. It would not be difficult under a totalitarian regime to arrange for the rapid accumulation of resources and thus advance economic development by sacrificing democracy; but neither the permanent values of the people of Latin America nor the international community as a whole would really benefit from such a solution. This is why international cooperation as established by the Alliance for Progress is absolutely necessary.

There are two basic positive aspects of the Alliance as it was originally proposed: first, it established principles for hemispheric cooperation with a clear ideological orientation expressed by its forthright support for a democratic revolution in Latin America; second, it represented a change in the hitherto prevalent concept of financial and economic assistance given by the United States. In the future, this assistance would cease to be given haphazardly or lent to this or that country to face emergencies, and it would no longer be designed to solve problems solely in a form determined by the donor. According to the terms of the Alliance, donor and recipient nations cooperate. Foreign aid is only part of a program of common achievement previously agreed on by countries which subscribed to the Charter of Punta del Este. Such arrangements for multilateral mutual cooperation were certainly new in the history of economic relations within the hemisphere. If we concentrate on these two basic characteristics and ascertain whether they have led to the achievement of concrete results during the last few years, we shall have a clear understanding of the evolution of the Alliance and the reactions it has elicited in Latin America.

II

At Chapultepec in 1945 the countries of Latin America laid great emphasis on the economic problems which industrial development and the instability of their external markets would engender in the postwar era. They suggested to the United States the advisability of making formal arrangements for concerted action in the economic field. At that time the prevalent doctrine was based on the acceptance of the notion that the free market is a final arbiter in all questions regarding international prices and movements of capital. An agreement on such matters was therefore considered superfluous.

In 1948 at the Bogotá conference this attitude was maintained by the representatives of the Washington government. The United States was too concerned with the reconstruction of Europe and aid to Asia to pay attention to her southern neighbors, who, according to Secretary of the Treasury George H. Humphrey, had only to open their frontiers and grant facilities to investors from the United States for their troubles to be at an end.

In the years immediately following World War II, Latin America did not have to face excessively grave problems, because the foreign assets saved during the war and the bonanza created by the Korean conflict were sufficient to alleviate short-term pressures. But serious difficulties were accumulating for the future. The Economic Commission for Latin America (ECLA) repeatedly pointed out that there were structural failures which could lead the Latin American economies into a period of stagnation. The economic recession at the end of 1953 and 1954 showed clearly how disadvantageous the situation of these countries really was. It was on the basis of this position that at the Petropolis conference Latin America searched for a solution grounded on greater cooperation with the United States. On that occasion it was agreed, with the United States abstaining, to form a Commission of Experts who were given responsibility for preparing a draft proposal for the creation of an Inter-American Bank.

The notorious failure of the 1957 Economic Conference of the Organization of American States marked the beginning of a period of evident deterioration in hemispheric relations, culminating in the lamentable events which marred the visit of Vice President Nixon to Latin America in 1958. That same year, President Kubitschek of Brazil addressed a letter to President Eisenhower on the need to reformulate inter-American relations, and soon after announced his now famous *Operación Panamericana*. Two months later Secretary of State John Foster Dulles replied, advising the younger nations of Latin America to implement reforms and step up their internal effort to solve their economic problems.

In spite of the disproportion between the original conception of *Operación Panamericana* and the response of the Secretary of State, the attitude of the United States was already changing. Two years later, in the Act of Bogotá, Latin America obtained formal U.S. acceptance of the idea of the interdependence of social and economic development and also succeeded in weakening the former insistence of the United States that private capital should be the principal instrument for financing the region's economic development. At that time too the Special Fund for Social Development was created, with a contribution of $500 million from the government of the United States.

The Bogotá meeting marked a change in inter-American politics and opened the possibility of realizing Latin American aspirations as to the direction hemispheric cooperation should take. The seeds of the Alliance had been sown and on March 13, 1961, President Kennedy announced his decision to carry out the Alliance for Progress. In August of that same year the Charter of Punta del Este was signed.

Latin American public opinion received the Alliance with enthusiasm; it was regarded as the beginning of a period which would open enormous possibilities for the economic and social development of Latin America. At the same time it marked the end of an unhappy period in which, as President Kennedy said, North Americans had not always grasped the significance of the Western Hemisphere's common mission. In fact, the Alliance was essentially a Latin American conception which became reality because it was accepted by the United States and especially by President Kennedy, who understood it and injected new life into it.

In spite of its limitations the Charter of Punta del Este had an immediate and significant impact. In the first place, from a political point of view it was clearly seen that the United States supported basic change. As a result, economic and political interests became active in opposition. An unholy alliance of the extreme right and left took form to prevent the charter's implementation. The reactionaries, mindful of their vested interests, maintained that the Alliance was a utopian and unrealistic program; the Marxist groups described it as an instrument of imperialism, useless for bringing about the needed change. Though using different reasons and channels, both were in accord—neither for the first time nor for the last. The victims have been the Latin American people, because this collusion prevented the reforms necessary for instituting a rapid and authentic democratic process in the hemisphere.

Thus started a long controversy on the nature of the Alliance. Its ideas have been interpreted and reinterpreted; its objectives, principles, and achievements have been openly and covertly distorted. Moreover, governments which had accepted and wanted to put the Punta del Este program into operation were either overthrown or found themselves threatened by the reactionary forces of the continent or by the violence of the extreme left.

This has resulted in many divergent opinions being formed about the Alliance. Some regard it as a scheme to finance corrupt governments uninterested in reforming anything; others think of it as a program to make the rich richer. To the landed, industrial, and financial oligarchies, the Alliance represents a danger, because by placing an exaggerated emphasis on social revolution, it deters foreign investors. To others, emergency aid is only a way of propping up a false stability which in turn prevents the working class from truly understanding its situation and opportunities, thus retarding the real revolution. Many others, especially those representing governments, complained that the work of the Alliance was being slowed up by the requirement that planning and reform precede the granting of aid.

If we compare the speech made by Secretary of the Treasury Dillon at Punta del Este with the text of the charter itself, we will see that certain clear definitions presented in the speech were expressed much more ambiguously in the charter. On the other hand, those who attended the meeting of Punta del Este will surely remember the efforts made by some Latin American delegations to diminish the force of the *Declaración de los pueblos de América* in order to obscure the need for implementing basic structural reforms. The decisiveness and skill with which Richard Goodwin of the United States delegation acted at the time secured a final text which, though weakened in some respects, was sufficiently clear to be considered a true interpretation of the real situation in Latin America.

Other criticisms have been made, but the ones that really matter have come from those effectively committed to the ideals of the Alliance—those who have expressly given it their backing or have supported national or international policies which coincide with the objectives of the Alliance.

Has the Alliance achieved these objectives? Has it preserved democracy and helped to implement substantial changes? Unfortunately the answer is negative; the Alliance has not achieved the expected success. It cannot be said that since 1961 there has been a consolidation of democratic regimes in Latin America. On the contrary, various forces have threatened democratic governments, seeking either to overthrow them or to prevent the implementation of their programs. Nor have structural reforms taken place at the expected rate.

This does not mean that the Alliance has failed. It has brought about many beneficial changes. Under its auspices there have been advances in education, in public health services, in communal improvement, in the development of rational economic programs, and in better understanding between Latin America and the United States. But these constructive achievements could have been secured simply with the financial assistance of the United States, plus, of course, the demand that these additional resources should be used rationally by the recipient countries. The problem is that what was fundamental to the Alliance for Progress—a revolutionary approach to the need for reform—has not been achieved. Less than half of the Latin American countries have started serious programs of agrarian reform. Drastic changes in the tax system are even scarcer, while the number of genuinely democratic regimes, far from increasing, has actually declined. In other words there has been no strengthening of the political and social foundations for economic progress in Latin America. This is the reason why the ultimate objective of the Alliance—the formation of just, stable, democratic, and dynamic societies—is as distant today as it was five years ago. Several experiences indicate that economic progress alone does not suffice to ensure the building of truly free societies and peaceful international coexistence. The problem does not stem solely from the inadequate flow of internal financial resources. What has been lacking is a clear ideological direction and determination on the part of the political leaders to bring about change. These two factors are intimately related and they involve the collective political responsibility of all the members of the Alliance.

Many Latin American governments have used the Alliance as a bargaining lever to obtain increases in U.S. aid precisely so as to avoid changing their domestic situation. These governments have committed themselves to internal reforms which later they knowingly allowed either to become a dead letter, or worse, to be completely controlled or used for the benefit of those in power.

For some of those who signed the Charter of Punta del Este, the important fact was the promise of the United States to help find $20 billion for Latin America. The reforms and the structural changes were regarded only as marginal conditions, clearly less important than the increase in financial aid. That is why the meaning of the Alliance was distorted and its origins often forgotten. To avoid compulsory reforms—in other words, to avoid revolution—the Latin American right wing willingly cooperated with the Marxists in regarding the Alliance as a creation of the United States exclusively. From this position they made unfair demands on the United States, destroying the true meaning of the national effort to accomplish the tasks of the Alliance. The Alliance ceased to be mentioned or studied in Latin America except when it involved a commitment on the part of the United States, while in the United States the executive branch, Congress, the intellectuals, and even public opinion accepted it as a vital task—but a distorted task because, unfortunately, the United States also fell into the trap.

It is unnecessary to point out names or dates, but at some stage the imaginative, dynamic commitment of countries united by a common ideal was gone. The name Alliance for Progress became yet another label for all forms of aid. Uncoordinated emergency loans became "Alliance loans"; technical and financial aid freely given to dictatorships was also "Alliance aid." The Alliance in fact became just one more source of assistance instead of a concerted program of mutual cooperation. Even though the aid retained its financial value, its ideological significance was completely lost. The flow of dollars given by the United States was carefully watched, but there was no equivalent effort on the part of Latin Americans to reform and become more democratic. Hence the Alliance has not reached the people of Latin America for whom it was created.

This is one of the most serious criticisms made of the Alliance: that the people have not been able to participate in it. Could it have been otherwise? The people are grateful for the assistance received, but they have no sense of belonging to the scheme. The revolutionary awareness of the Latin American people has evolved in such a way that it can now be considered as a norm—giving direction to their principal activities. The Alliance has failed to channel this awareness, and it has not provided the needed leadership; in fact, it does not belong in this revolutionary mainstream.

The Latin American institutions which collaborate with the Alliance do not include trade unions, student federations, peasant leagues, cooperatives, etc., yet it is vital that such organizations should take part in an enterprise which is essentially popular and whose success depends fundamentally on its capacity to satisfy the demands made by the community. From a political point of view this is one of the weakest aspects of the Alliance; its task is to carry through a revolution which will bring about economic and social development, and for this it is absolutely necessary that the people as a whole be committed to it. The loyal participation of the community in this effort to build an egalitarian society is the only way in which the objective can be achieved. This is why the Alliance must incorporate all sectors of society in its work of transformation.

III

Another grave problem of the Alliance is its inability to promote the integration of Latin America. The process of integration lacks speed and direction; it is hard to avoid the conclusion that it has stagnated. This is certainly the case with the Latin American Free Trade Area. The number of approved concessions declines annually; even now there is not a single product enjoying preferential treatment in all the LAFTA countries. Although the Treaty of Montevideo has been in operation for only five years, the rate of increase of the intrazonal trade has actually started to decline.

Faced with this frustrating experience, one is inclined to look at the success of the Central American Common Market. Yet the objective of the Alliance is a *Latin American* common market, which means that integration must be successful in both groupings. Again we come up against the absence of a political decision on the part of each individual country and a lack of leadership in the Alliance as a whole. The forces of nationalism, and of those committed to the status quo, have been stronger than those representing the real interests of these countries. Noisy voices are raised to decry the more advanced schemes of integration as utopian. But what is really utopian and illusory is to pretend that the countries of Latin America will be able to develop and achieve their destiny in the world of the future if each is locked up in its own isolated compartment.

The alternatives are clear: either the Alliance achieves one of its most important objectives by giving integration the needed vital impulse, or in a few years it will become evident to all that in the 1960s a great opportunity was lost because of petty nationalism.

The United States has only recently decided to support the integration of Latin America; previously its position seemed to be rather negative. The United States has an important responsibility to discharge if the Alliance is really going to achieve one of the fundamental objectives of the charter: the strengthening of the economic integration agreements, in order to build a common market which will widen and diversify trade among the countries of Latin America. In addition to liberalizing the trade of these nations, it is necessary to arrange stabilization schemes for the prices of some primary commodities to ensure that the income they produce does not go below certain acceptable levels.

The armaments race also conspires against the strengthening of the Alliance. The annual expenditure of the Latin American countries on armaments has reached $1.5 billion. Yet the average yearly sum made available by the United States to Latin America in the period 1961–65 was $1.1 billion. The two figures clearly show that present arms purchases seriously undermine the objectives of the Alliance. A Latin American country in 1965 had, in proportion to population, approximately the same number of men under arms as the United States. India, with twice the population of Latin America and having had two armed conflicts in recent years, has fewer soldiers than Latin America.

Nobody can possibly suppose that these weapons and armies are going to deter an aggressor from outside Latin America. Equally, the assertion that to stop subversion these countries must purchase fifty-ton tanks, supersonic aircraft, and battleships defies belief. The armaments race encourages distrust and nationalism and these in turn are among the chief enemies of integration. It also diverts important resources which should be utilized to satisfy the urgent need for economic and social development. It is therefore essential that a decision be taken at the highest levels of the Alliance to establish a quantitative limitation on arms purchases.

IV

More than a year has elapsed since President Johnson showed his determined support for the Alliance by announcing an extension of the period during which it will be in force. The commitments undertaken in 1961 will not now lapse in 1970, but only when the desired objectives have been achieved. Washington's various expressions of dedication to the Alliance have certainly kept hope alive, but the substantial decisions needed to inject life into this cooperative enterprise are still waiting.

The first and most important decision involves the restoration of the original character of the Alliance as a common enterprise solidly based on the needs of its member countries. For this to be achieved, its concept as a multilateral undertaking must be revived; this in turn demands a greater delegation of technical and political responsibility to the Inter-American Committee of the Alliance for Progress and the Committee of Experts. This is not just a doctrinaire need; it has a direct practical purpose, namely, the integration of the people into the work of the Alliance. This integration will take place when the Alliance identifies itself with Latin American interests, concepts, and purposes. On the other hand, the need to bring about change, and the intimate relation between this and the securing of foreign financial aid, implies the adoption of decisions which, as a matter of principle, can only be taken by each nation independently. It is inadmissible that the mere fact of making available financial aid gives any nation the right to demand that another implement specific types of structural changes. This would constitute an intolerable infringement of national sovereignty. That is why, in this situation, it is necessary to use multilateral channels for the supply of foreign assistance. Any other system might lead to new forms of scarcely veiled paternalism.

It is also important that the Alliance should openly become identified ideologically with the more progressive groups in Latin America. The future of this continent will not be contained within well-worn political and economic channels, as was so often and unsuccessfully tried during the last few decades. The Alliance must regain its essential popular character by participating in and supporting the organizations and activities of all sorts of social groups, and by granting technical and financial aid for cooperatives and for community projects in matters of health, housing, and education. In general, it must support the work of the basic popular organizations within each community. The best way to show the real meaning and direction of the Alliance is to give a decided impulse to the really important transformations such as agrarian reform. The social and political impact of this reform is so great that if the Alliance were really to support it, it would vastly strengthen the collaboration of the progressive forces of Latin America.

The salvation of the Alliance depends on the implementation of all these measures: the support of integration, the discouragement of the armaments race, and the finding of a cooperative solution for the problems of external trade. The problem is not one of financial resources only, though at certain times these have been scant when compared with the legitimate needs of the region. It is essentially a political problem requiring the expression of the will to change, together with the acceptance of the measures needed to bring about this change. People do not support governments because they have dutifully complied with directives from this or that international organization; they support them when they offer a promising political and economic alternative to present frustrations, and the hope of moving into a better future.

The necessary measures can be secured only by overcoming age-old resistance and destroying privileges which have remained unassailed over the years. To achieve this will also return to the American continent its true revolutionary mission. This is both possible and necessary because, as Toynbee said, "If America can bring herself to go this far, she will, I believe, have worked her passage back to a point at which it will become possible for her to rejoin her own revolution." The American Revolution was a truly glorious revolution. It was glorious for two reasons. The basic issues that it raised were spiritual, not material; and, even if this may not have been the intention of some of the Founding Fathers, it was, in effect, as Jefferson perceived and Emerson proclaimed, a revolution for the whole human race, not just for the people of the Thirteen Colonies.

Part III

THE POLITICAL-ACTIVIST PIVOT

Violence, Revolution, and
Structural Change in Latin America

JOHN GERASSI

A GREAT DEAL is being written in America these days about Pax
Americana and American hegemony in the underdeveloped
world. No longer able to blot out the obvious, even calm,
rational, conscientious academicians are publicly lamenting
America's increasingly bellicose policies from Vietnam to the
Dominican Republic. Suddenly, as if awakened from a techni-
color dream, intellectuals are discovering such words as "imperialism" and "expansionism." And they are asking: Why?
Who's to blame? What can be done to stop all this?

The questions are childish, the assumptions false, the implications naïve. They reflect a liberal point of view, one that
claims that there is a qualitative difference between U.S. policies
today and yesterday. In fact, American foreign policy has
varied only in degree, not in kind. It has been cohesive,
coherent, and consistent. What has varied has been its strength
—and its critics.

The basic difference between American imperialism today
and American imperialism a century ago is that it is more
violent, more far-reaching, and more carefully planned today.
But American foreign policy, at least since 1823, has always
been assertive, always expansionist, always imperialist. Of
course, it has rarely been pushed beyond America's capabilities.
Thus, when the United States was weak, its interventions
abroad were mild. When its strength grew, so did its daring.
Today, as the most powerful nation on earth, with a technologi-

471

cal advance over other countries of mammoth proportions, the United States can be imperialistic on all continents with relative security.

The main reason why we have not had the opportunity to discuss this imperialism frankly and openly within the United States—in its journals, in academia, and on platforms—is because Americans' interpretation of history has been dominated by liberal historians whose basic view of life is characterized by their inability or unwillingness to connect events. Thus, when viewing Latin America, where American policy has always been crystal clear, American historians will admit, indeed will detail, U.S. interventions in specific countries of Central America or the Caribbean, will sometimes even posit an imperialist explanation for a whole period of American history, but will never draw overall conclusions, will never connect events, economics, and politics to arrive at a basic tradition or characteristic. To such historians, for example, there is little if any correlation between the events and policies of 1823 and those of 1845, between 1898 and 1961.

Most liberal historians will admit today that the United States has often been imperialistic in Latin America up to 1933. Yet, slaves of their own rhetoric, they will inevitably cite the rhetoric of Franklin Delano Roosevelt, the greatest liberal of them all, to insist that with the New Deal, American imperialism came to an end. They can make this statement because they are committed to the proposition that it is the American State Department which makes foreign policy—simply because it is supposed to— and also because of their own fear of being identified with Marxist ideology, a fear that leads them to refuse to interpret imperialism as economic.

Rare is the liberal historian who first asks himself just what imperialism is, or, if he does, rarer still is he who simply and succinctly admits that imperialism is a policy aimed at material gain. And this, in spite of the fact that he knows full well that there has never been a stronger or more consistent justification for intervening in the affairs of other countries than the expectation to derive material benefit therefrom. Imperialism has always operated in three specific, recognizable, and analyzable stages: (1) to control the sources of raw material for the benefit of the imperializing country; (2) to control the markets in the imperialized country for the benefit of the imperializing country's producers; and (3) to control the imperialized country's internal development and economic structure so as to guarantee continuing expansion of stages (1) and (2).

That has been our policy in Latin America. It began in recognizable manner in 1823 with President Monroe's declaration warning nonhemisphere nations to stay out of the American continent. Because of its rhetoric, America's liberal historians interpreted the Monroe Doctrine as a generous, even altruistic declaration on the part of the United States to protect its weaker neighbors to the south. To those neighbors, however, that doctrine asserted America's ambitions; it said, in effect, Europeans stay out of Latin America because it belongs to the United States. A liberal, but not an American, Salvador de Madariaga, once explained its hold on Americans:

> I only know two things about the Monroe Doctrine: one is that no American I have met knows what it is; the other is that no American I have met will consent to its being tampered with. That being so, I conclude that the Monroe Doctrine is not a doctrine but a dogma, for such are the two features by which you can tell a dogma. But when I look closer into it, I find that it is not one dogma, but two, to wit: the dogma of the infallibility of the American President and the dogma of the immaculate conception of American foreign policy.[1]

Indeed, in the year 1824, Secretary of State (later President) John Quincy Adams made the Monroe Doctrine unequivocally clear when he told Simón Bolívar, one of Latin America's great liberators, to stay out of—that is, not liberate—Cuba and Puerto Rico, which were still under the Spanish yoke. The Monroe Doctrine, said Adams, "must not be interpreted as authorization for the weak to be insolent with the strong." Two years later, the United States refused to attend the first Pan American Conference called by Bolívar in Panama for the creation of a United States of Latin America. Further, the United States used its influence and its strength to torpedo that conference because a united Latin America would offer strong competition to American ambitions, on the continent as well as beyond. The conference failed and Bolívar concluded, in 1829: "The United States appear to be destined by Providence to plague America with misery in the name of liberty."

Nor was the United States yet ready to put the Monroe

1 Salvador de Madariaga, *Latin America Between the Eagle and the Bear*, New York, Frederick A. Praeger, 1962.

Doctrine into effect against European powers, at least not if they were strong. In 1833, for example, England invaded the Falkland Islands, belonging to Argentina, and instead of invoking the Monroe Doctrine, the United States supported England. England still owns those islands today. Two years later, the United States allowed England to occupy the northern coast of Honduras, which is still British Honduras. England then invaded Guatemala, tripled its Honduras territory, and in 1839 took over the island of Roatan. Instead of reacting against England, the United States moved against Mexico. Within a few years Mexico lost half of its territory—the richest half—to the United States.

In 1854 the United States settled a minor argument with Nicaragua by sending a warship to bombard San Juan del Norte. Three years later, when one American citizen was wounded there and President Buchanan levied a fine of $20,000 which Nicaragua could not pay, the United States repeated the bombardment, following it with Marines who proceeded to burn down anything that was still standing. The next year, the United States forced Nicaragua to sign the Cass-Irisarri Treaty, which gave the United States the right of free passage anywhere on Nicaraguan soil and the right to intervene in its affairs for whatever purpose the United States saw fit. If that does not make America's material interest in Nicaragua obvious to a liberal, nothing will.

The liberal historian will insist, however, that during this period the State Department was often isolationist, indeed that it tried to enforce America's neutrality laws strictly. That is true; but that does not mean, once again, that America was not imperialistic, for policy was not—and is not—made by the State Department but by those who profit from it. This was quite clear during the filibuster era, when American privateers raised armies and headed south to conquer areas for private American firms. In 1855, for example, William Walker, a Nashville-born doctor, lawyer, and journalist, who practiced none of these professions, invaded Nicaragua, captured Granada, and had himself "elected" president of Nicaragua. He then sent a message to President Franklin Pierce asking that Nicaragua be admitted to the Union as a slave state, even though Nicaragua had long outlawed slavery. Walker was operating for private American corporations bent on exploiting Central America. The trouble was that these companies were the rivals of Cornelius Vanderbilt's Accessory Transit Company whose concessions Walker, as "President," canceled. Vanderbilt thereupon threw his weight, money, and power behind other forces and they defeated Walker at Santa Rosa. He was then handed over to the United States Navy, brought back to the United States, and tried for violating neutrality laws. This had happened to him once before, after failing to conquer Lower California and he had then been acquitted. Now, he was again acquitted, and, in fact, cheered by the sympathetic jury.

Was the jury corrupt? Was it imperialist itself? Or was it simply reflecting the teachings, the propaganda, the atmosphere of the United States?

When the first colonizers to the United States had successfully established viable societies in their new land, they launched themselves westward. Liberal historians tell us that this great pioneering spurt was truly a magnificent impulse, a golden asset in America's formation. In their expansionism to the west, the early Americans were ruthless, systematically wiping out the entire indigenous population. But they were successful, and, by and large, that expansion was completed without sacrificing too many of the basic civil rights of the white settlers. Thus, early America began to take pride in its system.

Later, as American entrepreneurs launched the industrialization of their country, they were equally successful. In the process, they exploited the new settlers, i.e., the working class and their children, but they built a strong economy. So once again they showed themselves and the world that America was a great country, so great in fact that it could not—should not—stop at its own borders. As these entrepreneurs expanded beyond America's borders, mostly via the sea, and so developed America's naval power, they were again successful. Thus once again they proved that their country was great.

It did not matter that Jeffersonian democracy, which liberal historians praise as the moral backbone of America's current power, rested on the "haves" and excluded the "have nots" (to the point of not allowing the propertyless to vote). Nor did it matter that Jacksonian democracy, which liberal historians praise even more, functioned in a ruthless totalitarian setting in which one sector of the economy attempted, and, by and large, succeeded in crushing another. The rhetoric was pure, the results formidable, and therefore the system perfect. That system became known as "the American way of life," a way of life in which the successful were the good, the unsuccessful the bad. America was founded very early on the basic premise that he who is poor deserves to be poor; he who is rich is entitled to the fruit of his power.

Since America was big enough and rich enough to allow its entrepreneurs to become tycoons while also allowing the poor to demand a fair shake—civil rights and a certain mobility—the rhetoric justifying all the murders and all the exploitations became theory. Out of the theory grew the conviction that America was the greatest country in the world precisely because it allowed self-determination. From there it was only a step to the conclusion that any country which could do the same would be equally great. The corollary, of course, was that those who did not would not be great. Finally, it became clear to all North Americans that he who is great is good. The American way of life became the personification of morality.

From America's pride in its way of life followed its right to impose that way of life on non-Americans. Americans became superior, self-righteous, and pure. The result was that a new Jesuit company was formed. It too carried the sword and the cross. America's sword was its Marines, its cross was "American democracy." Under that cross, as under the cross brandished about by the conquistadors of colonial Spain, the United States rationalized its colonialism. Naval Captain Alfred Thayer Mahan even developed a theory based on Social Darwinism to prove that history is a struggle in which the strongest and fittest survive.[2] The Protestant clergy also joined in to ennoble American imperialism.[3]

The jury that tried Walker for violating America's neutrality laws—which he had clearly violated—expressed that imperialist duty and colonialist spirit when it cheered Walker out of the court. It was simply reflecting its deep-rooted conviction that Nicaragua would be better off as a slave state in the Union than as a free country outside it. To that jury, as to the American people today, there can be only one democratic system worthy of the name—the American. There can be only one definition of

[2] Alfred Thayer Mahan, *The Influence of Seapower Upon History*, Boston, Little, Brown and Company, 1890.

[3] Kenneth M. MacKenzie, *The Robe and the Sword: The Methodist Church and the Rise of American Imperialism*, Washington, D.C., Public Affairs Press, 1961.

freedom—American free enterprise. Thus, there is no need for the State Department to proclaim an imperialist policy; the Vanderbilts or the Rockefellers or the Guggenheims, the United Fruit Company or the Hanna Mining Company or the Anaconda Company can do what they please. After all, they represent democracy; they are the embodiment of freedom. What's more, they know that when the chips are down, American might will stand behind them—or in front.

Within the last century America's colonial expansionism, based on and strengthened by the American way of life, has become consistently bolder. In 1860 the United States intervened in Honduras. In 1871 it occupied Samaná Bay in Santo Domingo. In 1881 it joined Peru in its war against Chile in exchange for the port of Chimbote (as a United States naval base), nearby coal mines, and a railroad from the mines to the port. In 1885 it again torpedoed the Central American Federation because it feared such an organization might jeopardize an Atlantic-Pacific canal owned by the United States.

Meanwhile, in 1884, official United States Government commercial missions were launched throughout Latin America for one purpose only, and as one such mission reported, that purpose was successfully carried out: "Our countrymen easily lead in nearly every major town. In every republic will be found businessmen with wide circles of influence. Moreover, resident merchants offer the best means to introduce and increase the use of our goods." (Nothing, of course, has changed in this respect. Notice, for example, a report in *Newsweek* magazine of April 19, 1965: "American diplomats can be expected to intensify their help to United States businessmen overseas. Directives now awaiting Dean Rusk's signature will remind United States embassies that their efficiency will be rated not only by diplomatic and political prowess but by how well they foster American commercial interests abroad. Moreover, prominent businessmen will be recruited as inspectors of the foreign service.")

In 1895, President Cleveland intervened in Venezuela. In 1897, and again in 1898, the United States stopped further federation attempts in Central America. In 1898, after fabricating a phony war with Spain, the United States annexed Puerto Rico, the Philippines, and Guam, and set up Cuba as a "republic" controlled by the United States through the Platt

478   ⬛ THE POLITICAL-ACTIVIST PIVOT

Amendment (1901). This amendment gave the United States
the right to intervene in matters of "life, property, individual
liberty, and Cuban independence." That is, in everything.

The near-absence of significant public outcry in the United States
against this policy of open imperialism in both the Caribbean and
Pacific shows once again that the people of the United States
were convinced that it was her destiny to expand, and that her
superiority demanded it.[4]

After 1900, even liberal historians lament America's foreign
policy. Theodore Roosevelt, who is nevertheless admired as one
of America's greatest presidents, intervened by force of arms in
almost every Caribbean and Central American country. Naturally, the real beneficiaries were always American businessmen.
It is worth repeating an often-quoted statement in this respect:

I helped make Mexico, and especially Tampico, safe for American oil interests. I helped make Haiti and Cuba a decent place for
the National City Bank boys to collect revenue in. I helped pacify
Nicaragua for the international banking house of Brown Brothers. I brought light to the Dominican Republic for American
sugar interests. I helped make Honduras "right" for American
fruit companies. . . .[5]

That harsh but accurate indictment was supplied by a much-
decorated United States patriot, Major General Smedley D.
Butler of the United States Marine Corps.

Against such interventions, some local patriots fought back.
In Haiti, where United States Marines landed in 1915 and
stayed until 1934, 2,000 rebels (called *cacos*) had to be killed
before the United States pacified the island. And there were
other rebellions everywhere. In Nicaragua, one such rebel had
to be tricked to be eliminated. Augusto César Sandino fought
American Marines from 1926 until 1934 without being defeated, though the Marines razed various towns in Nicaragua,
and, by accident, some in Honduras to boot. In 1934 he was

[4] Brady Tyson, *The Roots and Causes of U.S. Policy Towards Latin
America,* unpublished manuscript, 1966.

[5] Maj. Gen. S. D. Butler in *Common Sense,* November 19, 1933, quoted
in C. Wright Mills, *Listen Yankee,* New York, McGraw-Hill Book Company, Inc., 1960.

offered "negotiations," was foolish enough to believe them,
came to the American embassy to confer with Ambassador
Arthur Bliss Lane, and he was assassinated. (Such incidents are
so common in American foreign policy that no intelligent rebel
who has popular support can ever again trust negotiation offers
by the United States, unless the setting and the terms of these
negotiations can be controlled by him. It seems as if Ho Chi
Minh *is* just that intelligent.)

On March 4, 1933, the United States officially changed its
policy. Beginning with his inauguration address, Franklin D.
Roosevelt told the world that American imperialism was at an
end and that from now on the United States would be a good
neighbor. He voted in favor of a nonintervention pledge at the
1933 Montevideo Inter-American Conference, promised Latin
American countries tariff reductions and exchange trade agreements, and a year later abrogated the Platt Amendment. His top
diplomat, Sumner Welles, even said in 1935, "It is my belief
that American capital invested abroad, in fact as well as in
theory, be subordinated to the authority of the people of the
country where it is located."

But, in fact, only the form of America's interventionism
changed. FDR was the most intelligent imperialist the United
States has had in modern times. As a liberal, he knew the value
of rhetoric; as a capitalist, he knew that whoever dominates the
economy dominates the politics. As long as American interventionism for economic gain had to be defended by American
Marines, rebellions and revolutions would be inevitable. When a
country is occupied by American Marines, the enemy is always
clearly identifiable. He wears the Marine uniform. But if there
are no Marines, if the oppressors are the local militia, police, or
military forces, if these forces' loyalty to American commercial
interests can be guaranteed by their economic ties to American
commercial interests, it will be difficult, even impossible, for
local patriots to finger the enemy. That FDR understood. Thus,
he launched a brilliant series of policies meant to tie Latin
American countries to the United States.

In 1938, FDR set up the Interdepartmental Committee of
Cooperation with American Republics, which was, in effect, the
precursor of today's technical aid program of the Organization
of American States (OAS). (The OAS itself had grown out of
the Pan American Union which had been set up by Secretary of

State James G. Blaine as "an ideal economic complement to the United States."[6]

FDR's Interdepartmental Committee assured Latin America's dependency on the United States for technical progress. During the war, the United States Department of Agriculture sent Latin America soil conservation research teams who helped increase Latin America's dependency on one-crop economies. In 1940, FDR said that the United States Government and United States private business should invest heavily in Latin America in order to "develop sources of raw materials needed in the United States." On September 26, 1940, he raised the ceiling on loans made by the Export-Import Bank, which is an arm of the American Treasury, from $100 million to $700 million, and by Pearl Harbor Day most Latin American countries had received "development loans" from which they have yet to disengage themselves. Latin America's economic dependency was further secured during the war through the United States lend-lease program, which poured $262,762,000 worth of United States equipment into eighteen Latin American nations (the two excluded were Panama, which was virtually an American property, and Argentina, which was rebellious).

Roosevelt's policies were so successful that his successors, liberals all whether Republican or Democrat, continued and strengthened them. By 1950 the United States controlled 70 percent of Latin America's sources of raw materials and 50 percent of its gross national product. Theoretically at least, there was no more need for military intervention.

Latin American reformers did not realize to what extent the economic strangle hold by the United States insured pro-American-business governments. They kept thinking that if they could only present their case to their people they could alter the pattern of life and indeed the structure itself. Because the United States advocated, in rhetoric at least, free speech and free institutions, the reformers hoped that it would help them come to power. What they failed to realize was that in any underdeveloped country the vast majority of the population is either illiterate, and therefore cannot vote, or else lives in address-less slums and therefore still cannot vote. What's more, there is no surplus of funds available from the poor. Thus, to

6 John L. Mecham, *A Survey of United States—Latin American Relations,* Boston, Houghton Mifflin Company, 1965.

create a party and be materially strong enough to wage a
campaign with radio and newspaper announcements for the
sake of the poor is impossible. The poor cannot finance such a
campaign. That is why the United States often tried to convince
its puppets to allow freedom of the press and freedom of elections; after all, the rich will always be the only ones capable of
owning newspapers and financing elections.

Now and then, of course, through some fluke, a reformist
president has been elected in Latin America. If he then tried to
carry out his reforms, he was always overthrown. This is what
happened in Guatemala where Juan José Arévalo and then
Jacobo Arbenz were elected on reformist platforms. Before
Arévalo's inauguration in 1945, Guatemala was one of the most
backward countries in Latin America. The rights of labor,
whether in factories or in fields, including United Fruit Company plantations, had never been recognized; unions, civil liberties, freedom of speech and press had been outlawed. Foreign
interests had been sacred and monopolistic, and their tax concessions beyond all considerations of fairness. Counting each
foreign corporation as a person, 98 percent of Guatemala's
cultivated land was owned by exactly 142 people (out of a
population of 3 million). Only 10 percent of the population
attended school.

Arévalo and Arbenz tried to change these conditions. As long
as they pressed for educational reforms, no one grumbled too
much. Free speech and press were established, then unions were
recognized and legalized, and finally, on June 17, 1952, Arbenz
proclaimed Decree 900, a land reform which called for the
expropriation and redistribution of uncultivated lands above a
basic average. But Decree 900 specifically exempted all inten-
sively cultivated lands, which amounted to only 5 percent of
over 1,000-hectare farms then under cultivation. The decree
ordered all absentee-owned property to be redistributed but
offered compensation in twenty-year bonds at 3 percent interest,
assessed according to declared tax value.

America's agronomists applauded Decree 900. In *Latin
American Issues,* published by the Twentieth Century Fund,
one can read on page 179: "For all the furor it produced,
Decree 900, which had its roots in the constitution of 1945, is a
remarkably mild and fairly sound piece of legislation." But,
since much of Guatemalan plantation land, including 400,000

acres not under cultivation, belonged to the United Fruit Company, the United States became concerned, and when Arbenz gave out that fallow land to 180,000 peasants, the United States condemned his regime as Communist. The United States convened the OAS in Caracas to make that condemnation official and found a right-wing colonel named Carlos Castillo Armas, a graduate of the U.S. Command and General Staff School at Fort Leavenworth, Kansas, to do its dirty work. It fed him arms and dollars to set up a rebel force in Honduras and Nicaragua and helped him overthrow Arbenz. No matter how good a neighbor the United States wanted to appear, it was perfectly willing to dump such neighborliness and resort to old-fashioned military intervention when the commercial interests of its corporations were threatened.

Since then, of course, the United States has intervened again repeatedly, most visibly in the Dominican Republic in 1965. Today, there can no longer be more than two positions in Latin America. As a result of the Dominican intervention, in which 23,000 American troops were used to put down a nationalist rebellion of 4,000 armed men, the United States has made it clear that it will never allow any Latin government to break America's rigid economic control.

And what is that control? Today, 85 percent of the sources of raw material are controlled by the United States. One American company (United Fruit) controls over 50 percent of the foreign earnings (therefore of the whole economic structure) of six Latin American countries. In Venezuela, the Standard Oil Company of New Jersey (Rockefeller), through its subsidiary the Creole Oil Corporation, controls all the bases of the industrialization processes. Venezuela is potentially the second richest country in the world. Its $500 million-plus net annual revenue from oil could guarantee every family, counting it at 6.5 persons, an annual income of almost $3,000. Instead, 40 percent of its population lives outside the money economy; 22 percent are unemployed; and the country must use over $100 million a year of its revenue to import foodstuffs, although the country has enough land, under a proper agrarian reform, to be an exporter of food.

Chile, with enough minerals to raise a modern industrial state, flounders in inflation (21 percent in 1966) while, despite all the talk of "Revolution in Freedom," there is only freedom for at most one-fifth[7] of the population—and revolution for no one. So far, the best that Eduardo Frei has been able to do is to launch sewing classes in the slums. The right accuses him of demagogy, the left of paternalism; both are correct, while, as the *Christian Science Monitor* (September 19, 1966) says, "Many of the poor are apathetic, saying that they are just being used, as they have in the past."

The continent as a whole must use from 30 to 40 percent of its foreign earnings to pay off interest and service charges, *not the principal,* on loans to the industrialized world, mostly the United States. The Alliance for Progress claims that it is helping Latin America industrialize on a social-progress basis. Now more than six years old, it has chalked up remarkable successes:[8] right-wing coups in Argentina, Brazil, Honduras, Guatemala, Ecuador, the Dominican Republic, and El Salvador. In exchange, United States businessmen have remitted to the United States $5 billion in profits while investing less than $2 billion. And the Alliance itself, which is supposed to lend money strictly for social-progress projects, has kept 86 percent of its outlay to credits for U.S.-made goods, credits which are guaranteed by Latin American governments and are repayable in dollars.

But then, under Johnson, the Alliance no longer maintains its social pretenses. In fact, no U.S. policy does, as President Johnson himself made clear last November when he told American GI's at Camp Stanley, Korea (and as recorded and broadcast by Pacifica radio stations): "Don't forget, there are only 200 million of us in a world of three billion. They want what we've got and we're not going to give it to them."

Interventionist and imperialist policies of the United States in Latin America are now successfully in the third stage. Not only does the United States control Latin America's sources of raw material, not only does it control its markets for American manufactured goods, but it also controls the internal money

[7] Federico G. Gil, *The Political Systems of Chile,* Boston: Houghton Mifflin, 1966, p. 512. See also his "Chile: 'Revolution in Liberty,' " in *Current History,* Vol. 51, No. 303, November, 1966, pp. 291–95.

[8] Jorge Graciarena, "Desarrollo y política," in *Argentina, Sociedad de masas,* by Torcuato S. Di Tella, Gino Germani and Jorge Graciarena eds., 1965. Buenos Aires: Eudeba, pp. 249–271. Also, Henri Edmé, "Révolution en Amérique Latine?", *Les Temps Modernes,* XXI, No. 240, May, 1966, 2035.

economy altogether. Karl Marx once warned that the first revolutionary wave in an imperialized country will come about as the result of frustration on the part of the national bourgeoisie, which will have reached a development stage where it will have accumulated enough capital to want to become competitive with the imperializing corporations. This was not allowed to happen in Latin America.

As American corporations became acutely plagued by surplus goods, they realized that they would have to expand their markets in underdeveloped countries. To do so, however, they would have to help develop a national bourgeoisie which could purchase these goods. This "national" bourgeoisie, like all such classes in colonialized countries, had to be created by the service industries, yet somehow limited so that it did not become economically independent. The solution was simple. The American corporations, having set up assembly plants in São Paulo or Buenos Aires, which they called Brazilian or Argentinian corporations, actually decided to help create the subsidiary industries themselves—with local money. Take General Motors, for example. First, it brought down its cars in parts (thus eliminating import duties). Then it assembled them in São Paulo and called them Brazil-made. Next it shopped around for local entrepreneurs to launch the subsidiary industries—seat covers, spark plugs, etc. Normally, the landed oligarchy and entrepreneurs in the area would do its own investing in those subsidiary industries, and having successfully amassed large amounts of capital, would join together to create their own car industry. It was this step that had to be avoided. Thus General Motors first offered these local entrepreneurs contracts by which it helped finance the servicing industries. Then it brought the entrepreneurs' capital into huge holding corporations which, in turn, it rigidly controlled. The holding corporations became very successful, making the entrepreneurs happy, and everyone forgot about a local, competitive car industry, making GM happy.

This procedure is best employed by IBEC (International Basic Economy Corporation), Rockefeller's mammoth investing corporation in Latin America. IBEC claims to be locally owned by Latin Americans, since it does not hold a controlling interest. But the 25 to 45 percent held by Standard Oil (it varies from Colombia to Venezuela to Peru) is not offset by the thousands of individual Latin investors who, to set policy, would all have to agree among themselves and then vote in a block. When one corporation owns 45 percent while thousands of individual investors split the other 55 percent, the corporation sets policy—in the U.S. as well as abroad. Besides, IBEC is so successful that the local entrepreneurs "think American" even before IBEC does. In any case, the result of these holding corporations is that the national bourgeoisie in Latin America has been eliminated. It is an American bourgeoisie. (See the analysis in this section by Carlos Romeo, a brilliant young Chilean economist who both worked with Che Guevara as a practical planner and taught with Régis Debray at the University of Havana, where together they worked out the theoretical consequences of Latin America's reality.)

IBEC and other holding corporations use their combined local-U.S. capital to invest in all sorts of profitable ventures, from supermarkets to assembly plants. Naturally, these new corporations are set up where they can bring the largest return. IBEC is not going to build a supermarket in the Venezuelan province of Falcón where the population lives outside the money economy altogether and hence could not buy goods at the supermarket anyway. Nor would IBEC build a supermarket in Falcón, because there are no roads leading there. Thus, the creation of IBEC subsidiaries in no way helps develop the infrastructure of the country. What's more, since such holding corporations have their tentacles in every region of the economy, they control the money market as well (which is why U.S. corporations backed, indeed pushed, the formation of a Latin American Common Market at the 1967 Punta del Este Conference. Such a common market would eliminate duties on American goods assembled in Latin America and exported from one Latin American country to another). Hence no new American investment needs to be brought down, even for the 45 percent of the holding corporations. A new American investment in Latin American today is a paper investment. The new corporation is set up with local funds, which only drains the local capital reserves. And the result is an industry benefiting only those sectors which purchase American surplus goods.

Having so tied up the local economic elites, the United States rarely needs to intervene with Marines to guarantee friendly governments. The local military, bought by the American-national interests, guarantees friendly regimes—with the approval of the local press, the local legal political parties, the local cultural centers, all of which the local money controls. And the local money is now tightly linked to American interests.

Latin American reformers have finally realized all this. They now know that the only way to break that structure is to *break* it—which means a violent revolution. Hence there are no reformers in Latin America any more. They have become either pro-Americans, whatever they call themselves, who will do America's bidding, or else they are revolutionaries. (Perhaps the best example of this awakening is described in Fabricio Ojeda's "Toward Revolutionary Power." Ojeda, once a well-off student who hoped to bring about reforms through the electoral process —and got himself elected National Deputy—eventually became a revolutionary and guerrilla chief.)

American liberal historians, social scientists, and politicians insist that there is still a third way: a nonviolent revolution which will be basically pro-democracy, i.e., pro-American. They tell us that such a revolutionary process has already started and that it will inevitably lead to equality between the United States and its Latin neighbors. Liberal politicians also like to tell Americans that they should be on the side of that process, help it along, give it periodic boosts. In May, 1966, Robert Kennedy put it this way in a Senate speech: "A revolution is coming—a revolution which will be peaceful if we are wise enough; compassionate if we care enough; successful if we are fortunate enough—but a revolution which is coming whether we will it or not. We can affect its character, we cannot alter its inevitability."

What Kennedy seemed incapable of understanding, however, was that if the revolution is peaceful and compassionate, if Americans *can* affect its character, then, it will be no revolution at all. There have been plenty of such misbred revolutions already. Let's look at a couple.

In Uruguay, at the beginning of this century, a great man carried out the modern world's first social revolution, and he was very peaceful, very compassionate, and very successful. José Batlle y Ordóñez gave his people the eight-hour day, a day of rest for every five of work, mandatory severance pay, a minimum wage, unemployment compensation, old-age pensions, paid vacations. He legalized divorce, abolished capital punishment, set up a state mortgage bank. He made education free through the university, levied taxes on capital, real estate,

profits, horse racing and luxury sales (but not on income, which
would, he thought, curtail incentive). He nationalized public
utilities, insurance, alcohol, oil, cement, meat-packing, fish-
processing, the principal banks. He outlawed arbitrary arrests,
searches and seizures; separated the state from the church,
which was forbidden to own property. He made it possible for
peons to come to the city and get good jobs if they didn't like
working for the landed oligarchy. All of this he did before the
Russian Revolution—without one murder, without one phony
election.

But what happened? A thriving middle class became more
and more used to government subsidy. When the price of meat
and wool fell on the world market, the subsidies began to
evaporate. The middle class was discontent. Used to government support, it demanded more. The government was forced to
put more and more workers, mostly white-collar, on its payroll.
The whole structure became a hand-me-down because the
people had never participated in Batlle's great revolution. Nobody had fought for it. It had come on a silver platter, and now
that the platter was being chipped away, those who had most
profited from the so-called revolution became unhappy.

Today, in Uruguay, more than one-third of the working force
is employed by the government—but does not share in the
decision-making apparatus. And the government, of course, is
bankrupt. It needs help, and so it begs. And the United States,
as usual, is very generous. It is rescuing Uruguay—but Uruguay
is paying for it. It has too much of a nationalistic tradition to be
as servile as the banana republics, but on matters crucial to the
United States, Uruguay now toes the line. It either abstains or
votes *yes* whenever the U.S. wants the Organization of American States to justify or rationalize U.S. aggression. And, of
course, free enterprise is once again primary.

The oligarchy still owns the land, still lives in Europe from its
fat earnings. There are fewer poor in Uruguay than elsewhere in
Latin America, but those who *are* poor *stay* poor. The middle
class, self-centered and self-serving, takes pride in being *vivo,*
shrewd and sharp at being able to swindle the government and
one another. Uruguay is politically one of the freest countries in
the world and Montevideo is one of the most pleasant places to
live, but only if one has money, only if one has abandoned all
hope of achieving national pride—or of a truly equitable society.

In 1910, while Uruguay's peaceful revolution was still un-

488   ▓ THE POLITICAL-ACTIVIST PIVOT

folding, Mexico unleashed its own—neither peacefully nor
compassionately. For the next seven years blood was shed
throughout the land, and the Indian peasants took a very active
part in the upheaval. But Mexico's revolution was not truly a
people's war, for it was basically controlled by the bourgeoisie.
Francisco I. Madero, who led the first revolutionary wave, was
certainly honest, but he was also a wealthy landowner who
could never feel the burning thirst for change that Mexican
peasants fought for. He did understand it somewhat and perhaps for that reason was assassinated with the complicity of the
U.S. ambassador, Henry Lane Wilson.⁹ But he was incapable
of absorbing into his program the unverbalized but nonetheless
real plans that such peasant leaders as Pancho Villa and
Emiliano Zapata embodied in their violent reaction to the long
torment suffered by their people.

The bourgeoisie and the peasants, according to Gunder Frank,

. . . faced a common enemy, the feudal order and its supporting
pillars of Church, army, and foreign capital. But their goals
differed—freedom from domestic and foreign bonds and loosen-
ing of the economic structure for the bourgeoisie; land for the
peasants. Although Zapata continued to press the interests of the
peasants until his murder in 1919, the real leadership of the
Revolution was never out of the hands of the bourgeoisie, except
insofar as it was challenged by the Huerta reaction and American intervention. The elimination of feudal social relations was of
course in the interests of the emerging bourgeoisie as well as of
the peasants. Education became secularized, Church and state
more widely separated. But accession to power by the peasantry
was never really in the cards.¹⁰

Thus kept out of power, the peasants never genuinely benefited from their revolution. They did receive land periodically,
but it was rarely fertile or irrigated, and the *ejidos,* communal
lands, soon became the poorest sections of Mexico. The bour-
geois-revolutionary elite grew into Mexico's new oligarchy, and
while some of its members did have darker skins than the

⁹ Jesús Silva Herzog, *Breve historia de la revolución Mexicana,* Vol. 1.
Mexico: Fondo de Cultura Económica, 1960, pp. 285–305.
¹⁰ Andrew Gunder Frank, "Mexico: the Janus Faces of Twentieth Century Bourgeois Revolution," *Monthly Review,* Vol. 14, No. 7, November,
1962, p. 374.

old Spanish colonialists, the peasants were never integrated into the new Institutional Revolutionary Party power structure.

Today, not only do they rarely vote (in the 1958 presidential elections, for example, only 23 percent of the population voted officially, and that only after frauds upped the count), but they barely profit from the social laws instituted by the revolution. As Vincett Padgett, who is no revolutionary, has written: "To the marginal Mexican, the law and the courts are of little use. The formal institutions are not expected to provide justice. There is only acceptance and supplication. In the most unusual of circumstances there is for the marginal man the resort to violence, but the most significant point is that there exists no middle ground."[11]

In Mexico today, peasants still die of starvation. Illiteracy is about 50 percent, and 46 percent of school-age children do not attend schools at all. Most of the cotton is controlled by one U.S. outlet, Anderson-Clayton, and 55 percent of Mexican banks' capital is dominated by the United States. Yet Mexico's revolution was both anti-American and violent. What went wrong?

What went wrong is that the revolution failed to sustain its impulses. It is not enough to win militarily; a revolutionary must continue to fight long after he defeats his enemy. He must keep his people armed, as a constant check against himself and as a form of forcing the people's participation in his revolutionary government. Yet he must also be careful not to guide this popular participation into a traditional form of party or state democracy, lest the intramural conflicts devour the revolution itself, as they did in Bolivia.[12] He must make the transition from a generalized concept of anti-Americanism to a series of particular manifestations—that is, he must nationalize all the properties belonging to Americans (or Britons or Turks or whoever is the dominating imperialist power). Like all of us who can never find ourselves, psychologically, until we face death, until we sink to such an abyss that we can touch death,

[11] L. Vincett Padgett, *The Mexican Political System,* Boston: Houghton Mifflin, 1966, p. 231.
[12] John Gerassi, *The Great Fear in Latin America,* rev. ed., N.Y.: Collier-Macmillan, 1965, p. 221. Also Richard W. Patch, "United States Assistance in a Revolutionary Setting," in Robert D. Tomasek (ed.), *Latin American Politics: Studies of the Contemporary Scene,* Garden City: Doubleday & Co., 1966, pp. 310-346.

smell it, eat it, and then, and only then, rise slowly to express our true selves, so too for the revolution and the revolutionary. Both must completely destroy in order to rebuild, both must sink to chaos in order to find the bases for building the true expression of the people's will. Only then can there be a total integration of the population into the new nation.

I am not trying here to define a psychological rationalization for violent revolution. What I am maintaining is that if one wants an overhaul of society, if one wants to establish an equitable society, if one wants to install *economic* democracy, without which all the *political* democracy in heaven and Washington is meaningless, then one must be ready to go all the way. There are no shortcuts to either truth or justice.

Besides, violence already exists in the Latin American continent today, but it is a negative violence, a counterrevolutionary violence. Such violence takes the form of dying of old age at twenty-eight in Brazil's Northeast. Or it is the Bolivian woman who feeds only three of her four children because the fourth, as she told me, "is sickly and will probably have died anyway and I have not enough food for all four."

Liberals, of course, will argue that one can always approximate, compromise, defend the rule of law while working for better living conditions piece by piece. But the facts shatter such illusions. Latin America is poorer today than thirty years ago. Fewer people drink potable water now than then. One-third of the population live in slums. Half never see a doctor. Besides, every compromise measure has either failed or been corrupted. Vargas gave Brazilian workingmen a class consciousness and launched a petroleum industry; his heirs filled their own pockets but tried to push Brazil along the road to progress. They were smashed by the country's economic master, the United States. Perón, whatever his personal motivation, gave Argentinians new hopes and new slogans; his successors, pretending to despise him, bowed to U.S. pressure, kept their country under their boot and sold out its riches to American companies.[13] In Guatemala, as we saw, Arévalo and then Arbenz tried to bring about social and agrarian reforms without arming the people, without violence. The U.S. destroyed them by force, and when the right-wing semidictatorship of Ydígoras Fuentes decided to allow free

---

[13] Torcuato S. Di Tella, "Populism and Reform in Latin America," in Claudio Véliz (ed.), *Obstacles to Change in Latin America*, London: Oxford University Press, 1965, pp. 47–74.

elections in which Arévalo might make a comeback, America's great liberal rhetorician, President Kennedy, ordered Ydígoras' removal, as the Miami *Herald* reported.[14] In the Dominican Republic, a people's spontaneous revulsion for new forms of dictatorships after thirty-two years of Trujillo was met by U.S. Marines. And so on; the list is endless.

Latin America's revolutionaries know from the experience of the Dominican Republic, of Guatemala, and of Vietnam that to break the structure is to invite American retaliation. They also realize that American retaliation will be so formidable that it may well succeed, at least under normal conditions. In Peru, in 1965, Apra Rebelde went into the mountains to launch guerrilla warfare against the American puppet regime of Belaúnde. Gaining wide popular support from the disenfranchised masses, it believed that it could go from phase number one (hit-and-run tactics) to phase number two (open confrontation with the local military). It made a grievous mistake, because the United States had also learned from its experience in Vietnam. It knew that it could not allow the local military to collapse or else it would have to send half a million men, as it had in as small a country as Vietnam. The U.S. cannot afford half a million men for all the countries that rebel. Thus, as soon as Apra Rebelde gathered on the mountain peak of the Andes for that phase number two confrontation, the U.S. hit it with napalm. Apra Rebelde was effectively, if only temporarily, destroyed; its leaders, including Luis de la Puente Uceda and Guillermo Lobatón, were killed.

But the guerrillas have also learned from that mistake. Today, in Guatemala, Venezuela, Colombia, and Bolivia, strong guerrilla forces are keeping mobile and are creating such havoc that the U.S. is forced to make the same mistake it did in Vietnam: it is sending Rangers and Special Forces into combat. In Guatemala, as of January 1, 1967, twenty-eight Rangers have been killed. The United States through its partners in Venezuela and Bolivia has again used napalm, but this time with no success. In Colombia, the U.S. is using Vietnam-type weapons as well as helicopters to combat the guerrillas, but again without notable success. New guerrilla uprisings are taking place (as of May, 1967), in Brazil, Peru, and Ecuador.

But, even more important, a new attitude has developed—an

[14] December 24, 1966.

attitude that had been clearly enunciated by Che Guevara who died in Bolivia seeking to organize rebellion. That attitude recognizes that the United States cannot be militarily defeated in one isolated country at a time. The U.S. cannot, on the other hand, sustain two, three, five Vietnams simultaneously. If it tried to do so, its internal economy would crumble. Also, its necessarily increasing repressive measures at home, needed to quell rising internal dissent, would have to become so strong that the whole structure of the United States would be endangered from within.

The attitude further exclaims with unhesitating logic that imperialism never stops by itself. Like the man who has $100 and wants $200, the corporation that gets $1 million lusts for $2 million and the country that owns one continent seeks to control two. The only way to defeat it is to hit each of its imperialist tentacles simultaneously. Thus was Caesar defeated. Thus also was Alexander crushed. Thus too was the imperialism of France, of England, of Spain, of Germany eventually stopped. And thus will the United States be stopped.

Che Guevara had no illusions about what this will mean in Latin America. He wrote: "The present moment may or may not be the proper one for starting the struggle, but we cannot harbor any illusions, we have no right to do so, that freedom can be obtained without fighting. And these battles shall not be mere street fights with stones against tear-gas bombs, nor pacific general strikes; neither will they be those of a furious people destroying in two or three days the repressive superstructure of the ruling oligarchies. The struggle will be long, harsh, and its battlefronts will be the guerrilla's refuge, the cities, the homes of the fighters—where the repressive forces will go seeking easy victims among their families—among the massacred rural populations, in the villages or in cities destroyed by the bombardments of the enemy."

Nor shall it be a gentleman's war, writes Che. "We must carry the war as far as the enemy carries it: to his home, to his centers of entertainment, in a total war. It is necessary to prevent him from having a moment of peace, a quiet moment outside his barracks or even inside; we must attack him wherever he may be, make him feel like a cornered beast wherever he may move. Then his morale will begin to fall. He will become still more savage, but we shall see the signs of decadence begin to appear."

Che concludes candidly: "Our soldiers must hate; a people without hatred cannot vanquish a brutal enemy."[15]

This analysis is the inevitable and necessary conclusion of anyone who faces squarely the history of American imperialism and its effect on the imperialized people. Latin America today is poorer and more suffering than it was ten years ago, ten years before that, and so on back through the ages. American capital has not only taken away the Latin American people's hope for a better material future but their sense of dignity as well.

This analysis will shock the liberals and they will reject it. But then they are responsible for it, for American foreign policy has long been the studied creation of American liberals. That is why an honest man today must consider the liberal as the true enemy of mankind. That is why he must become a revolutionary. That is why he must agree with Che Guevara that the only hope the peoples of the world have is to crush American imperialism by defeating it on the battlefield, and the only way to do that is to coordinate their attacks and launch them wherever men are exploited, wherever men are suffering as the result of American interests. The only answer, unless structural reforms can be achieved in the United States which will put an end to the greed of American corporations, is as Che Guevara has said, the poor and the honest of the world must arise to launch simultaneous Vietnams.

In *Revolution in the Revolution?*, Régis Debray tried to give the first of many theoretical systemizations as to how this coordinated, armed struggle can be waged.[16] American readers, who generally had never heard of Debray until that pamphlet became a best seller, are quick to condemn him for his lack of analytical preliminaries. But Debray is no superficial pamphleteer; though he makes some important errors in *Revolution in the Revolution?*, he is a serious student of the Latin American scene and had published some extremely lucid essays on the political and methodological aspects of revolution (one of which is included in this section) prior to *Revolution in the Revolution?*, which was meant as a working paper anyway.

In this paper, the most important change in tactics that he suggests is the constant creation of guerrilla fronts in underdeveloped countries. These fronts, he says, must be headed by the revolu-

---

[15] *Message to the Tricontinental*, 1967, Havana: pamphlet.
[16] *Monthly Review*, July–August, 1967 (N.Y.).

tionary vanguards, commanded by the revolutionary elite itself. It is crucial, he claims, that the political and military leadership be combined into one command, indeed into one man. Leaving the military considerations aside, what this means politically is that the standard practices of the Communist parties must be abandoned. No longer can bureaucrats sit in the cities coordinating strikes, electoral campaigns, and quasi-subversive fronts. From now on, revolutionaries must wage direct war against imperialism. Not to do so, says Debray, is to betray the revolution, to betray the people.

At the beginning of August, 1967, Latin American revolutionaries and Communists met in Havana to discuss these new concepts of direct confrontation with imperialism. The meeting was called the Organization of Latin American Solidarity (OLAS), and out of it came a new International, a Marxist-Leninist-Revolutionary International, which carefully spelled out the necessity of armed struggle as the only way of defeating imperialism and establishing a socialist world. The traditional Communist parties of the Americas, and of course the observers and representatives from the socialist countries of Europe, which all uphold Russia's policy of coexistence, objected to the Cuban position. But, backed by representatives from the guerrilla fronts of Latin America, the Cuban line prevailed. As long as imperialism exists, as long as the United States dominates a single country beyond its borders, as long as U.S. companies exploit the poor and the underdeveloped, no Communist has the right to call himself a Communist unless he fights, unless his solidarity with combatants is expressed in deeds and not words. Thus, Russia itself was condemned for giving material aid to oligarchical countries, and the Moscow-lining Communist parties were chastised for their opportunistic tactics of legal struggle through the electoral process established by the imperialists and repressive governments. OLAS demanded clearcut definitions, and it defined its own position.

But the traditional Communist parties were not very happy. Though they did not walk out of the conference, they made it clear that they would not accept the OLAS hard line. This, said Fidel on August 10, at the closing session of OLAS, was nothing less than treason.[17] Those who support peaceful coexistence with imperialism, when imperialism is slaughtering

17 OLAS proceedings, Code D/64. Havana: mimeographed. (The relevant sections of that speech are included in this section.)

JOHN GERASSI ▮ 495

and exploiting so many people all over the world, are not revolutionaries, no matter what they call themselves. They belong to
a new, vast "mafia," whose ultimate goal is to serve the desires
of a new form of the bourgeoisie. Fight, Fidel said, or pass
forevermore into the enemy camp.

Message to Students*

CAMILO TORRES RESTREPO

STUDENTS are a privileged group in every underdeveloped country. The few college and university graduates are supported at a very high cost. In Colombia, especially, with the great number of private colleges and universities, the economic factor has become crucial.

In a country whose population is 60 percent illiterate, students comprise one of the few groups possessing instruments for social analysis and comparison, and for finding possible answers to Colombia's problems.

Furthermore, the university student, at those colleges where there is freedom of expression, has two privileges: he can climb the social ladder through the academic ranks, and he can at the same time be nonconformist and rebellious without jeopardizing his rise in society. These factors have made students a crucial element in the Latin American revolution. During the agitational phase of the revolution, the students' efforts have been highly effective. In the organizational phase, their work has played a secondary role. In the direct struggle, notwithstanding the honorable exceptions which have occurred in revolutionary history, their role has not been crucial.

We know that agitational efforts are important, but that their real effects are lost if they are not followed by organization and the struggle for power. One of the principal reasons for the transitory and superficial nature of the students' contribution to the revolution is the lack of commitment in their economic, familial, and personal struggles. A student's nonconformity

* From *La Gaceta*, Núm. 13 Bogotá, March–April, 1965. Translated by Morton Marks.

tends to be either emotional (because of sentimental reasons or frustration), or else purely intellectual. This explains the fact that at the end of his university career, his nonconformity disappears or is, at best, hidden away, and the rebellious student no longer exists. He becomes a bourgeois professional who buys the symbols of bourgeois prestige, and barters his conscience for a high salary. These circumstances present grave dangers for a mature and responsible reply on the part of students at this moment in Colombia's history.

The workers and peasants are experiencing the political and economic crisis in all its harshness. The student, generally isolated from them, believes that a superficial or purely speculative revolutionary attitude is sufficient. This lack of contact can make the student a traitor to his historical vocation; thus when the country demands a total commitment, the student answers with nothing but words and good intentions. When the mass movement demands a daily and constant effort, the student replies with shouts, stonings, and sporadic demonstrations. When the people demand an effective, disciplined, and responsible presence in their ranks, the student answers with vain promises or excuses. The student's revolutionary convictions must lead to real commitment taken to the ultimate consequences. Poverty and persecution should not be actively sought after, but they are the logical consequence of total struggle against the existing system. Under the present system, they are the signs that authenticate a revolutionary life. The same convictions should lead the student to participate in the economic hardships and social persecution which workers and peasants suffer. Therefore, commitment to the revolution passes from theory to practice. If it is total, it is irreversible, and the professional cannot renege without betraying his conscience, his historical vocation, and his people.

At this moment of revolutionary opportunity, I don't want to preach. I want only to encourage students to make contact with authentic sources of information to determine their responsibility and what must be their response. Personally, I believe that we are rapidly approaching the zero hour of the Colombian revolution. But only the peasants and workers can say this with authority. If they, the students, "ascended to the people," without paternalism and in the spirit of learning, they could then objectively judge the historical moment.

It would, however, be fruitless and disgraceful if Colombian

498   ▌ THE POLITICAL-ACTIVIST PIVOT

students, who have been the spark of the revolution, remained
at its margin for any reason—due to lack of information, to
superficiality, egoism, irresponsibility, or fear.

We hope that students will respond to their country's call in
this transcendental moment of its history, and that they will be
encouraged to hear and follow it with boundless generosity.

Latin America: Some Problems

of Revolutionary Strategy*

RÉGIS DEBRAY

"Dark days await Latin America. . . . Once the anti-imperialist struggle has begun, it must be continuous, and it must hit hard, where it hurts, constantly, and never take one step back; always forward, always striking back, always answering every aggressive act with stronger pressure from the popular masses. It is the way to triumph."

ERNESTO CHE GUEVARA
Cuba: Historical Exception or the First Anti-colonialist Advance? (1961)

The duty of a revolutionary is to make the revolution.
Second Declaration of Havana (1962)

THE FOLLOWING COMMENTS are an attempt to answer the question, How has the Cuban Revolution modified the bitter class struggle in Latin America, which pits the popular masses against national oligarchies in power and imperialism? How does one explain the slowness and the obvious difficulties encountered by the revolutionary process in that crucial link in the imperialist chain? To the extent that the Cuban Revolution, from its earliest days, has been an important element in the vanguard of Latin American revolution—to the extent that the

* *Casa de las Américas,* No. 31, July–August, 1965 (Havana). Translated by Morton Marks and Robert Novick.

Cuban people and their leaders, after six years of struggle, have abandoned none of their proletarian internationalism—the question is one of the most vital in the continuing, sometimes agitated debate.

We lack a historical study of the complex phenomena of reaction which follow the victory of the socialist revolution. There have been three socialist revolutions of the greatest importance in the space of fifty years, Russia, China, and Cuba; these make such a work long overdue. A concrete study of tactical and strategic guises assumed by revolutionary parties in bordering countries and the imperialist blockade that stems from it would, given the evident historical differences, permit the forging of the tools necessary to answer our question. Fascism in Europe, the imperialist wars of intervention in Southeast Asia, and the growing militarization of political regimes in Latin America, cannot evidently be considered as cyclical, mechanical returns to former states of class domination. This, least of all, when they are not analyzable by means of a unilateral category such as "the negation of a negation." The concrete differences in space and time do not prevent our making some analogy between today's Cuba and the young Soviet Union. How can we fail to be reminded, after reading the statements of 1959 and 1960, in which the Cuban leaders evoke the imminence of new revolutions on the American continent, of Lenin's speeches of 1919 and 1920, in which he expressed his certainty of the imminent uprising of the European proletariat? Lenin, unlike Trotsky, soon abandoned this illusion, just as the Cuban leaders, so it would appear, have abandoned it today. Are we not reminded, on seeing the spontaneous outburst of guerrilla activity patterned on the Cuban model (except in Venezuela and Colombia), of the imitation of the Bolshevik model by the Spartacists and by Béla Kun's Hungarian Commune, both suppressed at the beginning of 1919?

Has not imperialism in its relations with the Soviet Union and Cuba passed through the same stages? First come wars of intervention; in Cuba, the Bay of Pigs. Next, economic aggression: general blockade, the breaking of the blockade by signing limited economic agreements—with England taking the lead in both cases. Then comes incoherent and hasty reformism in the countries bordering on the "subversive focus" (the agrarian measures taken in Danubian Europe after the Hungarian Revolution had the same justification as the agrarian reform proposed by the Alliance for Progress—and the same fate). This analogy is not a comparison, but it is a specific evaluation of the present situation, which puts into focus what is radically new in Cuba's relations with imperialism.

A notable synchronization has characterized continental revolutionary attempts and failures: 1959, 1960, 1961—years of sparkling heroism, of guerrilla foci appearing spontaneously in Santo Domingo, Paraguay, Colombia, Central America. In Brazil, Julião agitates in the Northeast and Brizola repels a military coup d'état in Rio Grande do Sul. In Peru the first occupations of the land take place and the first revolutionary peasant unions are organized in Cuzco. The years 1962 and 1963 reveal defeat and division within the movement. In Colombia, Ecuador, Peru, and Paraguay, attempts at armed struggle fail. In Brazil, Julião's Peasant Leagues are split by internal divisions and the *Tiradentes* movement failed to organize politically as Julião desired. In Argentina the military frustrate the popular electoral victory of March 18, 1962, when the Peronista, Framini, is elected by an overwhelming majority as governor of Buenos Aires. In Venezuela, Betancourt comes to power, and the revolution is made more difficult. In Chile, Frei is victorious, due to the women's vote; and in Brazil we have the installation of an openly fascist dictatorship. Reaction sweeps the continent.

Today we know that none of these defeats was final. Rather, they have forced the revolutionary movement to move on to a higher level of organization. In 1964 armed struggle has taken root and been consolidated in Venezuela and Colombia on a popular base that today is unbreakable. The immense explosives factory that imperialist exploitation has unwittingly installed in Latin America can finally dispense with *imported* revolutionary models and can find its way in accord with its own history, character, and social formation.

Latin America is turning toward its historical roots, putting an end to the ideological colonialism it has had to suffer for so long. In our language, retarded by metaphor, we can say that South America has gone through, immediately after Cuba, its "1905," *which it has left behind*. Today we can reflect upon that experience. This effort encounters a serious obstacle: there exists among the Latin American nations, as this historical synchronization indicates, a latent unity of destiny. The show of solidarity with Cuba demonstrates it very well; this unity is

spontaneously experienced from Mexico to Uruguay. There is a
lot of talk today, always uttered in expert tones, of the "twenty
Latin Americas." Any traveler going from Bolivia to Argentina,
or even from Salta, in the north of Argentina, to Buenos Aires,
or from Lima to Cuzco, must feel that he has journeyed through
different worlds and several centuries. But this is a superficial
impression.

Is not underdevelopment, that colonial deformation, inequality in social and economic development within the same country, between the countryside and the capital? Or to put it
another way, is not that inequality the superimposition of two
levels of development, an intrusion of capitalist penetration into
the interior of a country with feudal monoproduction? Does not
this misery perhaps condition this wealth, and vice versa? If
underdevelopment is not a natural phenomenon, but rather the
result of history, South America then possesses historical unity.
If to free itself from the Spanish yoke it had to militarily "exist
as a group," then it must act in this way to free itself of the
Yanquis. If Bolívar refused to consider Colombia free as long
as Upper and Lower Peru were not also freed, it is equally or
more realistic for Fidel Castro to believe Cuba's liberation will
not be complete while Venezuela and Colombia are enslaved. If
one can rightly speak of *the* Latin American revolution, it is not
on Latin America's account, but rather, dialectically speaking,
on account of the common enemy, the United States. And it is
for this reason that the ideas of Bolívar acquire power again in
the strategy of the revolutionary vanguards following the Cuban
Revolution.

In contrast to these internal, national, and international
divisions, North American imperialism considers South America as a unit of production first, then as a coherent field for
political maneuvers. Imperialism carries on its exploitation
through the Alliance for Progress, the Inter-American Bank for
Development (IBD), and other specialized organizations. The
Inter-American Defense Council, the OAS, etc. assure "political-
military protection."

Let us now discuss the form of economic relations that binds
South America to North America. At bottom, the "colonial
pact" survives intact: raw materials against manufactured
goods, petroleum against gasoline, cocoa against chocolate, iron
against automobiles, etc. According to the Economic Commission for Latin America (ECLA), an agency of the UN, the

deterioration of conditions of commercial exchange led to an indirect loss of $2,660 million in 1961 for South America as a whole. This, together with the income from foreign investments sent home ($1,735 million) and with the funds exported through amortization of debts ($1,450 million), totals more than three times the theoretical amount of aid funds and annual investments promised to the continent through the Alliance for Progress—$2,000 million.

Behind the marvelous promises, what strategic plan motivated imperialism when it launched the Alliance for Progress in Punta del Este in 1961? It tried to hide the traditional colonial pact, and the military dictatorships that this entailed, behind a revolutionary front (the prototype of the latter is still Pérez Jiménez of Venezuela, decorated in his time by Eisenhower). This was done through a mere show of national industrialization, inflated overnight artificially by a massive export of predominantly private North American capital. This capital was readily attracted by cheap labor; the enormous supply of available reserves; the free trade that allows profits to be sent home; the absence of fiscal control; and finally, a very high profit rate for the United States. In this way the origin of that capital channeled investments into the branches most profitable for the monopolies—chiefly the extractive industries, whose development was further subordinated to the world-wide strategic plan for the exploitation of raw materials by the United States. For example, the very important Bolivian tungsten and antimony mines have been left in reserve, since the United States does not need them at the moment and their development would depress the world market.

This economic impulse might have offered a "national appearance" if mixed pseudo-companies of administrative councils —with Spanish initials and "national bourgeois" representatives—were established. A new class of national co-administrators would have been developed to serve as a screen for foreign exploitation. In the countryside they could have liquidated the feudal relationships of production—payment in kind for real estate rental, servitude or peonage, landed estates, fallow lands, very low productivity per acre—which are the cause of the explosive political situation among the greater part of the peasantry. They could have begun a timid capitalist development. But those advanced forms of capitalist penetration threatened to end the colonial pact by allowing processing industries to work raw materials on the spot. Then these "national bourgeoisies" could have traded with the whole world, thus ending commercial monopoly.

Aware of these dangers, the Alliance for Progress reserved the greater part of its aid funds for *unproductive* investments—roads, hospitals, schools, etc.—to avoid creating competing industries. They were confident they could cure the dangerous symptoms of "underdevelopment" by hiding its causes. It was a political maneuver under an economic guise. As its own promoters confess, that plan has been a total failure, because in order to wipe out agrarian feudalism, it would have been necessary to transform the relationships of production *as a whole*. Agrarian feudalism, as in Colombia and Brazil, is an integral part of the development of the farming-exporting, commercial, and even industrial bourgeoisie. If contradictions really exist between those two sections of the ruling class, they must be *secondary* contradictions, which would be surmountable in the face of the main danger, which is revolution. The process of inflation has provoked growing unemployment, salary reduction, and sharp economic contraction; and that inflation, instead of being compensated for by an increase in production, could be corrected only through new loans from the outside. (An increase in production might have induced overproduction, because of the absence of an internal market accessible to the peasant masses. This market could be created only through a radical transformation of the semifeudal relationships of production). These loans would necessarily be short term, thus closing the vicious circle of "underdevelopment"—going into debt to pay one's debts—because the aid funds have never reached half the sum originally promised.

Let us now outline the nature of those famous aid funds of the Alliance for Progress. Such funds are presented, without any disguise, as a specific form of exportation of capital. Fowler Hamilton, director of foreign aid, declared to a group of North American businessmen: "Every dollar that leaves our pocket must reenter the U.S. after having bought for us goods for the amount of one dollar."

(1) The Alliance for Progress, in effect, allows the conquest of new markets or the consolidation of old ones. In the majority of cases, the borrowed funds must be employed in importing manufactured goods from the United States, at prices 50 to 200 percent higher than those on the world market. In Colombia

and in the Andes, the gifts in kind (powdered milk, packaged butter) that are distributed by members of the Peace Corps (young *Yanquis,* voluntarily recruited to serve simultaneously as spies and Boy Scouts in South America) serve as a tool of blackmail and political penetration among the peasants.

(2) The export of agricultural surpluses (Decree 480) satisfies two demands:

(a) It eases the crisis of national overproduction in the United States.

(b) Although payable in local currency, transportation, distribution, and packaging are at the expense of the "aided country." This is for the greater profit of the North American freight enterprises, who can charge superelevated fees.

(3) Every country "aided" within the Alliance for Progress must assure on its part:

(a) The maintenance of an enormous apparatus of North American civil servants and technicians, with a scandalously high life style (imported food, private golf and sports clubs, servants, etc.).

(b) The infrastructural projects (highway construction, forest removal, water and electricity services) are in zones where North American companies operate and where their future capital will be invested. Those projects are evidently handed over to North American concerns, who follow their own plans and estimates and use their own technicians, equipment, etc.— an ingenious way of lowering the expenses of exploitation by letting them fall back onto the exploited.

The Alliance for Progress arranges, covers, and reinforces the process by which the decapitalized countries of South America increase and feed the accumulation of capital in the United States.

Balkanization, actually the heritage of the intracontinental wars of the nineteenth and early twentieth century, coincides with the needs of North American strategy. It operates to tie up or control commercial exchanges among the countries of South America, to reserve for itself a monopoly on buying and selling, and politically, to organize Holy Alliances at a low cost. Two months before the Chilean presidential elections of September, 1964, Bolivian anti-Chilean nationalism underwent a mysteriously spirited upsurge. It was a throwback to the Pacific war of 1879, which deprived Bolivia of access to the sea. Simultaneously (a startling coincidence), Argentina laid claim against

Chile for its territories in Patagonia (between Chiloé and Chulut). Both countries began to mobilize their military reserves until the election of the Christian Democrat Eduardo Frei brought a halt to the agitation.

Ecuador against Peru; Peru against Bolivia and Chile; Bolivia against Paraguay; Chile against Argentina. Balkanization facilitates the colonialization of the small countries in a most cynical manner. An example: Bolivia. On August 22, 1963, the government of Paz Estenssoro signed a commercial treaty with the United States which obliged it to break off all trade with Europe and neighboring countries and to import only from the United States. In exchange Bolivia would receive funds in aid from the Alliance for Progress.

The existence of separate American nations, sometimes even hostile toward one another, is an irreversible fact. The revolutionary struggle can only be a fight for *national* liberation. To assign to national revolutionary movements the prior condition of continental unity is equivalent to sending them to the Greek calends. On the occasion of the last disturbances in Panama, provoked by *Yanqui* Zonists in January, 1964, some Trotskyists tried to launch the slogan "Return Panama to Colombia." These same elements brandish old man Trotsky's slogan "the socialist U.S.A." But neither returning to the letter of past history, nor evoking a mythical future (as the U.S.A. does today) can do away with the *present,* with the fact of Balkanization, unless one is trying to betray the present struggle of every nation by imposing a nonexistent unity. The Caribbean revolutionaries who have not forgotten their old project of creating a Federation of the Antilles know very well that their beautiful dream has been lost in daily, fragmented, and insular tasks.

In this sense one can see much more clearly how difficult the theoretical and practical work of national liberation is for Latin Americans. Southeast Asia has available to it the immense base of influence and theoretical planning from People's China, the Democratic Republic of Viet-Nam, and North Korea. Africa gets the support of Algeria, Congo-Brazzaville, Ghana, and Zanzibar. Among the vanguards of those two continents there is solid friendship and common forms of action, of which the Afro-Asian conferences serve as proof. Latin America, however, remains cut off and isolated from the world-wide movement.

Cuba aside, a great part of the American revolutionary organizations are still under the ideological influence of the European workers' movements whose ideology is often alien to Latin America's real problems.

Delay and division on the part of the revolutionary parties in Latin America have dramatic results. Whether or not the parties want it, they are joined by force, *from outside*. The Cuban Revolution, in spite of itself and in spite of them, has sealed that unity. History would not be truly dialectical if the formidable lesson that a revolution is for the people who have made it were not also a lesson for the continental counterrevolution. And from the Rio Grande to the Falkland Islands, the Cuban Revolution has, to a large extent, *transformed the conditions of transformation*. Therefore, from its inception, from the very fact that the revolution exists in the imperialists' eyes, Cuba has condemned to failure every attempt at a merely mechanical repetition of Sierra Maestra. The door that Cuba has opened by surprise, under the very nose of imperialism—the socialist revolution—has been solidly barred from within by the national oligarchies, and from without by imperialism. How can its brothers manage to force the door open again? By exercising a stronger and more lasting pressure, or by each opening a new door in the least defended spot in the wall.

What is this transformation brought about by Cuba? Cuba has made the class struggle in Latin America pass quickly to a level for which neither the exploited classes nor their vanguards were prepared.

In the practical realm we all know that Cuba has liquidated geographical fatalism. That, together with Browderism, had a great influence on the Communist parties of Latin America immediately after the Second World War. Today it is possible to take power and keep it. Strictly considered, this concept, which upsets habits, provokes a shudder. Even in the most intense moments of the Colombian Civil War (1949–1957), this idea was as foreign to the Colombian Communist Party as it was to the worn-out left-wing liberals, when they had a real peasant army. Only the Brazilian Communist Party, in the same situation after the failure of the insurrection of 1936, had fixed for itself the goal of seizing power. On the occasion of the Manifesto of 1950 (which was more a sectarian and "leftist" outbreak than a strategy), the Brazilian CP tried to create two bases

for a revolutionary army among the peasants, in northern
Paraná and Goiás, of which there are still traces today in
Formosa in northern Argentina.

Since the Cuban Revolution the Chilean CP has fixed as a
goal the conquest of power by the ballot box (Twelfth Congress, March, 1962); the Argentine CP has taken up as a
standard the slogan launched by its secretary Codovilla at their
Twelfth Congress (March, 1963): "Towards the seizure of
power through mass action." At their Third Congress (1961),
the Venezuelan CP had been the first to consider seriously the
establishment of a democratic and popular power, leaving to the
course of revolutionary practice itself the responsibility of deciding what road to take. As a result of the oppression unleashed by Betancourt, the only way was armed struggle. The
same evolution, three years later, takes place in Colombia
where the Colombian CP, after the beginning of the guerrilla
war in Marquetalia, abandons its peaceful line to create a front
against repression. Thus, as the Colombian comrades predicted
a long time before, the self-defense of the masses is transformed
into a tactical guerrilla offensive. But at the very moment in
which the example of Cuba showed that the conquest of power
was not a priori unrealistic, the unilateral repercussions of the
Twentieth Congress of the Soviet CP and the general orientation
taken then by the international workers' movement, led the
Communist parties to adopt a "national democratic" line, a
"united front with the bourgeoisie." This was the peaceful road
that had been defended not long before by the Colombian CP
(Ninth Congress, 1963); the Mexican CP (Thirteenth Congress); the Bolivian CP before the schism (Second Congress,
1964, in which the peaceful road is considered "the most
probable"); the Chilean CP (Thirteenth Congress); the Argentine and the Brazilian Communist parties.

The example of the Brazilian CP is revealing. Under the
direct influence of de-Stalinization, in 1958, it makes an about-
face, very much part of its tradition. The declaration of March,
1958, calls upon Communists to form a "united democratic and
nationalist front," whose leadership would logically fall into the
hands of the national bourgeoisie. One year later, Cuba. Since
then the militants of the Brazilian CP (headed by pro-Soviet
Carlos Prestes) have turned into "docile lambs," a supple-
mentary force of the "advanced" bourgeoisie and the electoral
support of Marshall Lott (who ran against Quadros in 1960).

The bourgeoisie considers them more ferocious the more sheep-like they become. Then the CP of Brazil (pro-Chinese) is founded, taking away valuable cadres, above all in the south, from Prestes' party. A good part of the middle classes, frightened by the Cuban Revolution, leans toward Lacerda and the military. The illustrious national bourgeoisie abandons Goulart in midstream, and gives rise to the coup d'état of April 1, 1964. The Brazilian CP is left disorganized, smashed by repression and internal dissension, unable to lead the violent and popular discontent. This is but one example of the historical contretemps provoked by international centralism, which turns out to be a transposition of slogans and tactics which were elaborated for a different historical situation. In the face of this incapacity, Cuba serves as an unwitting model for fifty Latin American revolutionary organizations, all on the fringes of the Communist parties, and all resolved on direct action. All these years of revolutionary action force us to recognize that heroism is not enough. There is a lack of ideological maturity, and above all, political sense, as well as a lack of sectarianism and firmness in the preparation of the armed struggle. They are too young, and too unthinkingly modeled after Cuba. They are prisoners of that model. Those so-called Castroite organizations are in jeopardy, at least in their present form: MOEC (Peasant Student Worker Movement) in Colombia; URJE (Revolutionary Union of Ecuadorian Youth) in Ecuador; MIR (Movement of the Revolutionary Left) and FIR (Revolutionary Leftist Front) in Peru; "Vanguard Socialism" in Argentina (with its myriad subdivisions); MAC (Movement of Peasant Support) and the left wing of the Socialist Party, in Uruguay (Sendic, organizers of the union of sugar-cane cutters). Until now the revolutionary front has not been able to respond to the heightened level of the revolutionary struggle—and Cuba has stood alone.

In the theoretical field, as a consequence of its practical triumph, Cuba rehabilitates Marxism. It has been trapped in Latin America since 1930 between the two poles of APRA, and the mechanical Marxism that had no contact with national reality. Let us not forget the Popular American Revolutionary League, the Latin American Kuomintang. It was born in 1924 as a united front (at the continental level of anti-imperialist parties and groups) and transformed into a party in 1929, with sections in every country. APRA was the seedbed of a whole generation of anti-imperialist, petit-bourgeois movements: of

Betancourt and ADD, of Perón's *justicialismo* in a certain sense, and of Bolivia's Revolutionary National Movement (the last two with fascist influence).

The "Indo-Americanism" of the founder and chief of APRA, Haya de la Torre, has perpetrated under the name of Marxism the greatest historical betrayal that Latin America has seen in thirty years. For at least twenty years Haya de la Torre was the anti-imperialist guide for an entire generation of enlightened bourgeoisie, even of the proletariat itself (in any case, in Peru). "Hegel, plus Marx, plus Einstein, equals Haya de la Torre," a follower of the Master could say. "The Aprista Doctrine," wrote Haya in 1936 in *Anti-Imperialism and APRA,* "means within Marxism a new and methodical confrontation of Indo-American reality with the thesis that Marx had postulated for Europe." This confrontation led to his famous notion of historical time-space. From it he concluded that since in Europe socialism springs from the internal contradictions of capitalism, and since capitalism takes the form of imperialism in Latin America, it was necessary to encourage imperialist domination. To accelerate national liberation, this sophism sought theoretical justification in a hypocritically mechanistic materialism and in a pretended law of succession of social formations. Since it would appear one cannot skip levels (or stages), North American imperialism has a possible use. This idea led Haya, beginning in 1945, to become one of the leading and most prestigious agents for North American imperialism. In proving that Marxism as a universal theory of history has its point of entry in Latin America, Cuba wipes out, in one stroke, all the falsifications of Marxism, and with it, all its spokesmen—Haya, Betancourt, Paz Estenssoro, and others.

In creating a vacuum, Cuba has also created a new demand for an authentic Marxism, able to conceive of the national experiences of South America. Not only Cuba's independence in the Chinese-Soviet split, but the entire daily practice of its leaders, both in the Sierra Maestra and in power, indicates that Latin America be transformed into a new center of revolutionary planning that accords with its own conditions. At the same time, Cuba unwittingly reveals that in many parts of the continent this planning still remains for the future. Since the death of José Carlos Mariátegui, founder of the Peruvian CP and author of *Seven Essays of Interpretation of Peruvian Reality,* the greatest Marxist work to come out of America

before the Cuban Revolution, the majority of Marxist theoreticians and leaders have imported from Europe prefabricated
strategies and concepts. Never, until Fidel Castro and the
Venezuelan and Colombian revolutions, had Marxism found a
point of articulation with a Latin American social reality, so
atypical from a European viewpoint.

The real weight of the Cuban Revolution is perhaps most
strongly felt within the revolution itself. It serves to put an end
to Soviet, Chinese, and even *Cuban* revolutionary models; to the
sterile comfort of schemes and formulas; to the separation of
the masses; to the cult of organization for the sake of organization. In this sense Cuba has demonstrated that Marxism "no
longer served" and that it was necessary to recover the revolutionary inspiration of Marxism-Leninism: that it was necessary
once again to sink Marxism into the reality of a class action.
That need is everywhere felt, but not yet everywhere satisfied.
Thus, Latin America is trying to find its own revolutionary
path, and in light of Cuba, knows that it must create a path
based on its own experience. The *Second Declaration of Havana* did not spring from the heads of the Cuban leaders one
exultant night; nor was it shoved abusively on the Latin American masses as some kind of mysticism. It is the point at which
all the experiences and latent aspirations of the continent's
exploited masses converge.

Cuba has also raised the level of material and ideological
imperialist reaction more quickly than it has the level of the
revolutionary leadership. If imperialism has drawn more advantages from the Cuban Revolution than the revolutionary
forces have, this is not due to imperialism's higher intelligence.
Imperialism is in a better position to carry out what it learned
from the Cuban Revolution, because it controls all the material
means of organized violence, plus a nervous impulse its survival
instinct adds.

On the material level, we cannot emphasize enough the incredible reinforcement of apparatus for repression which was begun
in 1960. The other side of the gilded medal that is the Alliance
for Progress is a new and intensive military aid to Latin
American governments. At Punta del Este Mr. [Douglas]
Dillon launched optimistic plans designed to transform Latin
America into that "paradise of gilded latrines," whose failure
was immediately analyzed by Che Guevara. In July, 1961,
Kennedy submitted to Congress "a special military program, des-

tined to guarantee the internal security of Latin America against subversion." According to the *New York Times* of July 4: "The program represents a radical change in the military programs for the Western Hemisphere. Until now the principal aim had always been to equip air and naval units for a common defense of the hemisphere against an attack from the outside. Today, greater importance is conceded to the internal defense against subversion." During 1961, $21 million were earmarked for "anti-subversive equipment."

Every year the antiguerrilla school in Panama graduates an unknown number (due to military secrecy, but in the thousands) of young officials and Latin American policemen. Among the graduates are battalions of Colombian antiguerrillas, Ecuadorian parachutists, Peruvian commandos, Bolivian rangers, Argentine police (now equipped with heavy weapons), and many other military groups, formed and organized by North American military missions, which had existed in an embryonic state before the Cuban Revolution. Today all those groups are engaged in liquidating insurrection within their countries. It is chiefly in the area of information and infiltration that North American aid has intensified its efforts. The FBI and the CIA directly control the local police. In Brazil, no one except Brizola, who had the police archives burned in Rio Grande do Sul when he was governor there, thought it reprehensible that the FBI and the CIA seized the secret files of the political police in full view of the "national bourgeois regime." Argentina, with twenty million inhabitants, relies on seven political police agencies, independent and mutual rivals. In Venezuela, Sotopol, Digepol, SIFA, PTJ, etc. do the job, not to mention the agents the CIA recruits on the spot. "Twenty years ago," an Ecuadorian military information officer said proudly, "we were still relatively innocent. When students went out in the streets we shot at them, which had bad results. Today we know that of the hundred weapons for stifling revolution, firearms are the last."

Judge for yourself: the six or seven important guerrilla centers that have appeared in Latin America since 1959 have been wiped out or were destroyed at birth as a result of being denounced, frequently by infiltrators.

On the political level the triumph of the Cuban Revolution tends to radicalize, organize, and unify the various elements of the bourgeoisie into a single counterrevolutionary front faster than revolutionary organizations become radicalized and uni-

fied. Cuba's rapid transformation into a socialist country has
been used to frighten the so-called national bourgeoisie and the
educated sectors of the middle classes. The paradoxical result of
a revolution that was at first bourgeois-democratic, like the
Cuban Revolution, is that it has revealed and consolidated the
wavering class consciousness of the neighboring national bourgeoisie, above all, where they exist as a social class—in Chile,
Argentina, Uruguay, Brazil, Colombia.

This consolidation to the right leaves in many places a central
vacuum for a revolutionary vanguard. It is an emptiness all the
more surprising because Latin America is a mine of solid and
committed revolutionary groups, all ready to sacrifice themselves, but not yet able to coalesce into an organized vanguard.
This vanguard is waiting to be built, and many young militants
recognize it as an exhausting task. "Ah, if only we had a man or
a party to follow"—is the phrase repeated among thousands of
young militants, from Panama to Patagonia. Among all the
spectacles of misery and abandonment that America offers,
perhaps none is as absurd, as maddening, as this one.

Overnight Cuba stamped the language, style, and content of
revolutionary action with a resounding youthfulness. Because of
the demographic situation, this youthful tone has reverberated
throughout the continent. These young people, who have short
memories, have no intention of following anyone except those
who fight beside them. In America, especially in its political
behavior, there is a dramatic separation between generations. It
is enough to observe the age structure in the semicolonial countries of South America to realize that this separation reflects a
real division, which will deepen.

The cabal of social democratic "leaders," the so-called "generation of 1920," who grew up together in exile in the shadow
of the revolutionary sacrifices of their people, have happily
faded away. The Cuban Revolution, which they have betrayed,
has publicly unmasked them. The Haya de la Torres, the
Figueras, the Betancourts, the Muñoz Maríns, the Arévalos, the
Frondizis, the Paz Estenssoros, came to power immediately
after the Second World War, and until the last three years have
retained in their hands the entire Latin American anti-imperialist movement. Cuba has pushed them off the revolutionary
scene, where they still conjured illusions.

The frustrated feelings of these petty bourgeoisies are openly
displayed. In the 1950s it was still possible for Betancourt to

become the leader of the popular anti-imperialist resistance. After Fidel's lightning trip to Venezuela in 1959, Betancourt found his position considerably changed. Betancourt's paranoid imbalance can be seen in the rabid insults he soon hurled against "Castro-Communism" (his term became popular all over the continent). Yet the man who used it is at bottom a petty, despairing politician, condemned to an armored car and solitude, who got carried away and let his mask slip before 500,000 people in Silence Square, Caracas.

The Fidelista movement is the dividing point between two generations. It starts between the two historical moments of the revolution: the bourgeois and the socialist. The Cuban Revolution has never been forgiven for having built a bridge between those two moments. At the culmination of one era and the start of another, Cuba has fixed forever the climactic moment in which a tradition was reversed. The historical fate of the Cuban Revolution is, in effect, to have been able to join the material and moral support of those old liberal politicians (which it had to quickly get rid of) with the spirit of determination and honesty of those young men with no political past, named Fidel and Raúl Castro, Camillo Cienfuegos, Ernesto Che Guevara, Almeida, and so many others.

This represents a singular fusion of contradictions. At the most intense moment of the clandestine struggle the 26th of July movement was able to collect money in the middle of New York City, in the name of the "rights of man"; to accept material assistance from Pepe Figueres, President of Costa Rica, for the defense of democracy; to receive officially financial aid from the Venezuelan people, recently freed from Pérez Jiménez's dictatorship, and to get from Larrazábal, President of the Democratic Junta, an armed airplane. It received a protective world-wide notoriety, thanks to the capitalist publishing chains *Life* and *Paris-Match*. All of this takes nothing away from the extraordinary merits of the 26th of July, but it is necessary to remember these things in order to evaluate the *differences* in equivalent movements today. "Do you think that a [Herbert] Matthews* would come out here to interview us, or that Figueres would send us guns?" the man in charge of an independent Colombian republic a few hours from Bogotá said to me with a smile. At this moment the peasants, who needed

* Of the *New York Times*, who interviewed Fidel in the Sierra Maestra (ed.).

everything, were preparing to meet the offensive that the regular army in collaboration with the *Yanqui* military mission had been preparing for several years. Destined to be far removed from the centers of international support, to lack money and weapons, to be the victims of a systematic campaign to discredit the aims and meanings of the fight carried on by the national and international press, to face solitude and hunger—such is the bitter converse of the courageous slogan that is ineluctably imposed on these revolutionaries: "Don't rely on anything but your own forces."

After the Cuban Revolution the sacrifice in human lives and the length and complexity of the revolutionary war have increased. It is not as easy today as it was five years ago to establish a broad liberation front, when every anti-imperialist stance is accused of Castro-Communism and is outlawed. It is much less easy to forge a popular army when the regular armies have for the past five years been psychologically and militarily trained in "irregular" warfare and the police agencies are trained to infiltrate clandestine networks and are enlarging the scope of their repression. Now is the time to change language and viewpoint, in Europe and elsewhere, when we attempt to understand the difficulties that confront our comrades in that part of the world.

The comments, or their absence, of the "objective" French press on the Venezuelan revolution, show this very well. Whoever does not wish to free himself from the Cuban model is likely not to understand contemporary history. On adopting their new strategy of the "long war," what have the Venezuelan FALN done but take into account the new situation created by Cuba? More than half of the North American investments in Latin America are located in Venezuela. It is the country most infiltrated and therefore the most carefully watched by the United States. After the failure of its urban insurrectional form (which was not its proper form), the Venezuelan revolution has found its second wind, its final balance, in this long-term effort: the passage from a guerrilla army to a regular popular army in the interior of the country. This leaves to the city all its political importance, to take care of the possibilities of mass legal efforts and daring alliances. In the interior, even more than in Caracas, the mass effort is directly connected to the armed struggle. This evolution bears a close resemblance to that of the Chinese revolution, which many thought was on the verge of death after the bloody failures of Canton and Shanghai in 1927. But it was only in this way that the Communist leaders could discard the Bolshevik model and develop an authentically Chinese form. This was the model victoriously defended by Mao against Li Li-san. Born out of defeat, the retirement to the countryside, with the long march and the installation of revolutionary peasant bases, meant victory. But if an inventory of sacrifices is ever compiled, the blood spilled in Shanghai or Caracas should not be recorded on the debit side of the revolution, as if it were the result of an error in judgment.

In both cases, in order to prove theoretically that an isolated urban insurrection cannot achieve victory in a semicolonial country with a peasant majority, it has been necessary to first realize it *in practice*. If it was sufficient to prove a revolutionary theory theoretically, a few competent theoreticians would be enough to make "good" revolutions, without useless detours, by deductive means. Even if a strategy of the long war, carried out from the countryside and moving to the cities, had been tacitly accepted by the commanders of the guerrilla fronts in 1962, it had to wait for confirmation upon events elsewhere. Two years later it had to be ratified by urban leaders, at which time there appeared to be a divergence of aims between the countryside and the city. Anyone who visited the rural fronts before the elections of December, 1964, could bear witness to the orientation of Douglas in Falcón, or Urbina and Gabaldón in Lara. They called for reestablishing the guerrilla war on political rather than military terms. This meant patiently building peasant cells of support in each town; daily efforts at propaganda and making contacts; plowing new lands in the jungle; campaigns for literacy among combatants and peasants; reinforcement of the contact organization with the urban areas; supply and information networks. All of this political, organizational effort culminated in the establishment of a fixed revolutionary base, with its own school, courts, and broadcasting station (already installed in Falcón).

Out of all this underground activity the press picks out only the military aspects, which are the least essential. While the urban guerrilla war eroded into a war of attrition, in which time acted against the revolutionary forces, the rural guerrilla war silently and calmly took advantage of that same time to establish the political infrastructure for future military actions. In the euphoria of the recent popular victories, a political underestimation of Betancourt's government and of North American imperialism swept the ranks of the urban militants, who for obvious reasons still did not have a full grasp of the new post-Cuban conditions. Hence the underestimation of the repressive capacity of the government and the military power of imperialism. This explains the unexpected dismantling, more rapid than was foreseen, of the legal and illegal political organization in Caracas and the state capitals. Thus, in the country most directly colonialized by the United States, the Venezuelans have been the first to experience the "people's war" in post-Cuban conditions. They have paid dearly for their pioneer role. Now that the reformist method, having been put to the test in Peru, Brazil, and Chile, seems to have incontestably failed, we would be happy to see the revolutionaries of brother countries utilize the immense wealth of experience gathered by the Venezuelans —experience which could benefit everyone.

Recently there has been a great deal of discussion about Chile. In fact, that country is now in the reformist vanguard as a result of the Christian Democrat's election victory. Their leading political position reveals the extent to which mass movements have arisen in that country in the last few years. The policy followed by the workers' movement in Chile, after its relegalization of Ibáñez in 1958, could partially explain not a reactionary victory, but the way this policy took the continent's reformists by surprise.

One does not have to read Clausewitz to know that the basis of every tactic, revolutionary or not, consists of choosing one's battleground; and, whenever there is a bourgeois regime, of not engaging in decisive battles when they take place on the enemy's territory. In this case the territory is representative democracy, whose class nature is even more marked in Latin America than in Europe.

In this light Chile presents a special case—parliamentary tradition, minor role for the army, secondary importance of agrarian feudalism, etc. However, we must keep in mind the central importance of the Catholic Church (the women's votes for Frei over Allende were crucial); the control by the ruling class of all the propaganda media; the way the "charitable organization" Caritas could freely buy the votes of the *callampas* (working-class slums of Santiago) through the free distribution of food products offered by the Alliance for Progress. The impressive anti-Cuban campaign carried on by the

United States assured from the outset the superiority of the bourgeoisie in the electoral field. If there really were in Chile before September 4, 1964, some workers' sections skeptical about claims of a popular victory in the election, the FRAP (Popular Action Front) convinced them of the contrary.

(1) All working-class demands were tabled prior to the opening of the electoral campaign, in spite of inflation and growing unemployment, in order not to invite reaction and frighten the middle classes. The democratic parties, fully reconverted into electoral machines, gave assurances of Salvador Allende's victory to their militants, thus diverting the masses from the propositions of real power. Three months before the elections, FRAP was alarmed by the military mobilization of neighboring countries (Argentina, Bolivia, Peru) and rumors of a military coup d'état in the event of a popular victory. These rumors gained credence with the Brazilian coup d'état. FRAP considered itself obliged to secretly take formal and hasty measures to protect its leaders and prepare for an eventual move underground. These measures did not contribute to raising the level of popular consciousness and preparation.

(2) The loss of the election was explained by FRAP in terms of an alliance with "centralist" as well as frankly reactionary parties, and by the fact that concessions were made to refugees from the liberal and even conservative parties. There was even a front-page report in *Vistazo,* the Communist youth magazine, of a banquet given for Allende by the Grand Lodge of Chilean Freemasons, whose membership includes the great names of Chile's commercial bourgeoisie. Very little separated Frei's Christian Democratic program from Allende's program except that Allende was for progressive nationalization of the copper mines, and Frei for their "Chileanization." But Frei found more direct methods for reaching the masses.

(3) All offensive actions on the part of the working class were postponed "for later." This included not answering the opponent's offensives for fear of frightening the electorate. Chile is the only Latin American country where the break in diplomatic relations with Cuba had not been accompanied by mass demonstrations. Since the break was carried out shortly before the elections, FRAP was content to issue a communiqué, and Allende, their presidential candidate, to state that he would, if necessary, submit the case to the International Tribunal in The Hague. Instead of affirming their solidarity with Cuba, FRAP

kept putting distance between itself and the Cuban Revolution and other revolutionary groups, especially by failing to censure the torrents of abuse hurled by reaction against "the bloody dictatorship of Fidel Castro." Many sectors thought there was, in effect, nothing to reply to, and that Cuba was indefensible.

(4) It is one thing to make use of a bourgeois weapon such as an election in a regime of representative democracy, and quite another to use that election in a bourgeois way. It is one thing to defend the honesty of a particular election and respect for the constitution at a given moment against reaction, and another to take up in an absolute way, abstracted from any class position, the fervent defense of bourgeois law and the letter of its constitution. In the development of the Chilean electoral campaign the left and the right vied to see who could go further in their peaceful declarations and humanitarian condemnations of violence. Thus, we read in the program of the Chilean CP, approved by the Twelfth Congress in March, 1962:

> The thesis of the peaceful road is not a tactical form, but rather is a proposition tied to the platform of the Communist Party . . . [the peaceful road] completely corresponds to the interests of the march toward socialism and the eminently humanist character of Marxist-Leninist theory. The present correlation of national and international forces has increased the chances for leading the revolution without an armed struggle.

Without even taking into account the unreasonable optimism of this last thesis in Latin America five years after the Cuban Revolution, one cannot help being surprised at seeing how the "theoretical humanism" of Marxism can serve to justify abandoning all political and theoretical precision. It would clearly be unjust to explain the reactionary victory in the Chilean presidential elections, and in the last legislative elections in March, 1965, solely on the basis of the mistakes made by the revolutionary forces. In fact, it could be explained in terms of the general situation in South America after the Cuban Revolution. What does say something about those errors of direction is how this electoral result has been transformed into a *revolutionary defeat*—in Chile as well as in the rest of Latin America. Taking for granted the temporary superiority of the imperialist forces and the extreme fragility of the electoral terrain for popular contests even in a country like Chile, this particular election is unparalleled by any other "democratic movement in South America." Reaction, reducing itself to limited forms of socializing demagoguery to keep power, received an equal number of votes from men, who are less susceptible than women to conservative and clerical pressure. If reformism had not spread those illusions among the masses, if it had not tried to turn the Chilean election into a crucial "test" before the eyes of all the Latin American militants, then it would doubtlessly today be in the position of retaking the offensive on a new base.

The Chilean experience gives rise to two conclusions:

1) It is impossible for a "developed" country in America that belongs to the "Southern cone" (Chile, Argentina, Uruguay) or to Central America (Costa Rica) to escape being determined by the structure of the continent as a whole and pressed between the meshes of the imperialist network. Now Chile's workers' movement (motivated by a real superiority complex which tends to overestimate its specific nature as an "evolved" democracy) has tried to make an abstraction of the Latin American national liberation movements and of the historical moment, already described, created by the Cuban Revolution throughout the entire continent.

2) Opportunism shares a common feature with adventurism: the underestimation of North American imperialism, which does not stop short of making military coups d'état.

It is well known in Cuba and elsewhere that given the lack of preparation of the Chilean democratic organizations, Allende's electoral victory would not have brought about any fundamental change in the structure of the state apparatus, and that the Chilean ruling class and imperialism would not have been cast into oblivion by popular action. This radical underestimation of imperialism appeared with much greater clarity in the case of reformism in one part of the Brazilian revolutionary movement. Because if there ever was a historical example of the vanity of reformist efforts, it is in Brazil. As the limits of this article keep us from analyzing a matter that really calls for a separate study, we shall only point out that the Brazilian Communist Party, as its present self-criticism testifies, abandoned all class independence to take advantage of an alliance with the

"national bourgeoisie," represented by Goulart. This opportunistic line automatically provoked its opposite among a great
part of the Brazilian revolutionary forces; that is, a petit-
bourgeois radicalism that sneered at the patient efforts of the
masses, in certain sectors influenced by Francisco Julião, and to
some extent by Brizola. And if the fascist coup d'état encountered no resistance, it is also because it took the CP, which was
in the middle of a legalistic euphoria, completely by surprise,
and also because the only sectors prepared for the struggle
preferred to postpone things, *not yet* wishing to take the defensive against a corrupt and impotent regime, and not *yet* wanting
to unite the most conscious masses into a revolutionary base.

We only want to raise the question why, a short time after the
Cuban Revolution and in spite of all that it taught, at the responsible leadership level in several countries, there have been
illusions about a peaceful step toward socialism. Perhaps the
secret (not really much of a secret) should be sought in the
general framework of present reformist tendencies within Latin
America. Permit us to reproduce the statement that a "highly
qualified" representative of those tendencies was kind enough to
give us, in an Andean nation where a popular insurrection survived at that moment in a latent state:

Our aim in Latin America is to consolidate the national democratic states, such as Bolivia, Chile, Mexico, Brazil [this was at
the time of Goulart], so that these can one day serve as poles of
attraction for the less advanced neighboring states. Those national states can only be effectively strengthened, to the detriment
of North American imperialism, which tends to dominate the
competing national economies so that they are able to escape
their commercial monopoly. North American imperialism is the
natural enemy of the national bourgeoisie. Now, the only chance
for these national bourgeoisie to develop economies free from
foreign influence, is to resort to the disinterested aid, free from
political strings, of the socialist camp. It is for that reason that
the primary task of the socialist camp is to tirelessly reinforce
their economic strength. There are two reasons for this. First, it
must be able to send long-term loans and technicians to those
countries, that is, to weaken or check North American spheres of
influence. Second, the revelation of the material and cultural
progress of the socialist countries will add to the prestige of
socialism and will increasingly attract to it the national democratic states.

At this moment, then, it is necessary to wait for the national bourgeoisie to mature, since they clearly cannot appear overnight. The growth of a national bourgeoisie means the simultaneous growth of *two* contradictions: the first with imperialism, which no longer exercises its exploitation as it once did, and the second with the nascent proletariat, which it is beginning to exploit. With a strong bourgeoisie, there is a strong proletariat. It is necessary for us to count on this double contradiction. Since national industries are still too weak, there are not the necessary conditions for a revolution. The weakness of the working class and of its parties should not, however, lead us to a sectarian policy of isolation, to which, on the other hand, we would be inclined by a lack of experience or leaders. It would be necessary for us to be able to arrange the broadest alliances, without fearing that the middle class takes the lead in these. Numerous petty or middle bourgeoisie have excellent political attitudes. Today, they are the only realists. On the other hand, international conditions play an increasingly crucial role in revolutionary victories. It would be better not to be hasty, but to turn those international conditions to the advantage of socialism: the Cuban economy grows stronger; that of the socialist camp also; new socialist countries appear in other parts of the world.

Today, here in ——, to attempt revolution, to begin armed struggle against the representatives of that national bourgeoisie on the road to formation, and now in power, would only serve to delay or compromise the advent of the objective conditions. The most progressive elements in the government and the bourgeoisie would be thrown, ipso facto, into the arms of the North Americans. The defeat of the insurrection would allow the most backward elements to once again take the lead, perhaps to wipe out the beginnings of agrarian reform, and even to denationalize the mines. The U.S. would thereupon demand the closing down of the Soviet Embassy that we maintain under heavy penalties and in spite of all provocations, and the departure of the socialist commercial missions. The greatest danger in Latin America is impatience, Jacobinism; to pass on to even less favorable conditions, and to sacrifice a certain future to illusion.

The partisans of reformist strategy steadily decrease in Latin America, for the simple reason that they cannot stand up to the test of experience. Reformism supposes for Latin America the development of states of "national democracy under bourgeois leadership," not aligned to the United States, and progressively able to achieve independence from it. However, the history of the past twenty years has shown that:

(1) A "national bourgeois" party takes over a popular

revolution and seizes power, as the Institutional Revolutionary Party did in Mexico, Acción Democrática in Venezuela, the Revolutionary Nationalist Movement in Bolivia. This progressive petty bourgeoisie, without having the infrastructure of economic power preexistent to its political predominance, then transforms the state not only into an instrument of political control, but also into a source of political power. The state, culmination of the social relations of exploitation in capitalist Europe, becomes in a certain sense the instrument of its restoration. As the institutional expression of the given processes of production in a society, the state, by virtue of a short circuit characteristic of semicolonial countries, is transformed into an instrument of production of the nonexistent processes of production. The proliferation of public jobs, the only source of employment for thousands of unemployed, serves as a substitute for the development of a production apparatus. Without control of the state, this bourgeoisie, economically speaking, is nothing. Political power means everything to it, and it would do anything to preserve it. One does not get into public office if one is not a party member. In Venezuela there is not a single ministerial typist who does not pay dues to the AD before learning to type. Party dues are directly deducted from the salaries of public servants, as union dues are deducted from workers' salaries. A group of fat and cynical people make up the higher and middle range of public servants; of private secretaries; of dishonest lawyers; of businessmen; of police; of officials compromised in the resale of arms; of indebted diplomats; of labor leaders who get into the Ministry of Labor and grow fat off the state apparatus that is, in its own right, parasitic. To wear down and strangle anyone who gets close to its booty is a matter of life and death for them. Threatened by popular demands, this newrich bourgeoisie betrays the nationalist ideology that at first characterized its leadership of the masses (above all, the peasant masses, by the constantly renewed promise of a "real" agrarian reform). It changes costumes and dedicates itself to collaborate ever more shamelessly with imperialism, whose interests it handles on the spot. Giving and getting: oil, mining, and commercial concessions, in exchange for a few "royalties" and "aid" funds, which are then rapidly invested in highways and private swimming pools. From this angle the regimes of Venezuela and Bolivia (with or without Paz Estenssoro) present startling similarities. The same agrarian reforms, the scandalous ransoms of land in Venezuela and the division of uncultivated lands in eastern Bolivia into private lots, the same populist demagoguery that assures the regime a good name abroad, periodic electoral frauds, maintenance of a kind of parliament, public spectacles to demonstrate support by the workers; all of this presents a semblance of democracy. It is surrounded by "a people in arms," that is, mercenaries recruited among unemployed workers and the lumpen. (In Venezuela, the half dozen legal and extralegal police agencies, in Bolivia the MNR "militias," made up of illiterate Indians and rail workers, the only proletarian union in which governmental terror had any results.) This bourgeoisie must defend its political power against those who gave it to them, the workers and the students who, spurred by Communist and nationalist youth, headed the struggle against Pérez Jiménez for ten years—and against Gómez for twenty—and who, in Bolivia, suffered the long calvary of mining massacres and all the insurrections suppressed by "Rosca." In the end the regimes of "national democracy" give birth to a monster (except for this, there is no teratology in history). This could well be called *demobourgeois fascism,* the supreme transformation of the contradictions into which a bourgeois regime with no bourgeois class enters, a liberalism without liberals.

(2) When a bourgeois politician, or some part of the "national bourgeoisie," refuses to betray his national vocation by selling out to the United States, he then tries democratic-bourgeois reforms: a real antifeudal agrarian reform, the extension of voting rights to the illiterate, the establishment of diplomatic and commercial relations with all countries, control of the profits of the large North American companies, etc. To resist the pressures of the North American ambassador (known to Ecuadorians as "the viceroy"), the press campaigns, the institutional obstacles the parliamentary majority sets up (the harvested fruit of electoral fraud), the "President" is obliged to resort to the popular masses. He seeks the support of the workers' parties and unions, and perhaps the backing of the peasant leagues (as in Brazil). From that moment on the regime sees itself threatened by the specter of an army coup d'état. Cornered between the working and peasant classes, whose enthusiasm the regime has sparked and who press it from behind, and, on the other side, the army, mobilized by the injured oligarchy and the grimaces of the North American De-

partment of State, who block it from the front, the "President" totters, looks for a way out, a respite. He compromises, but it is too late; the entire ruling class, alerted by the precipitous rush of events, has already guessed that the mechanism set in motion will lead to his downfall. The triumph of a policy of national independence implies the adoption of socialist measures: this truth, once discovered, provokes panic. The bourgeoisie then abandon their sorcerer's apprentice, and it matters little to them that constitutional legality, which was their champion against "subversion," is trampled by the military. On any pretext (in Brazil, a measure of clemency from Goulart for the mutinous sailors), the prefectures are occupied; the provincial garrisons do not answer the president's telephone calls; some tanks advance toward the presidential palace; the streets are empty: the coup d'état is here. The "President" and a handful of advisers are left in the air. Precisely because constitutional legality has been respected throughout the process, no other kind of army opposes the regular troops. Nor are the people armed. There may be a last-ditch effort, condemned to be nothing more than a symbol, the small popular demonstrations that appear here and there, and are dispersed by rifles. Unable to pose a serious alternative to the armed representatives of *his own class* and the Department of State, the "President" takes a plane to Uruguay or Panama. In this way Arbenz fell in 1954 (with direct help from the United States Army, which equipped, trained, and organized Castillo Armas' mercenaries), Bosch in Santo Domingo in 1963, and Goulart in Brazil in 1964, as well as Arosemena in Ecuador, Arévalo and Villeda Morales in Central America, and so many others, all replaced by a military junta or regime. This tragicomedy has known no exceptions, even with the Bonapartist variations of the national bourgeoisie such as Vargas (Brazil, 1954) or Perón (Argentina, 1955). The order of the acts and the scenes remains essentially the same; just as this farce is related to us, the history of the bourgeois heroes of reformism has the earmarks of religious myth. Reformism, which is inverted dogmatism, hides in a cyclical theory of history so as to better cover its ears to the real lessons of history. Like the beautiful phoenix, if it dies one night the morning will witness its rebirth. The bourgeois heroes of progress, those unfortunates, have such a strong predilection for romance, while their tragedy ends in comedy every time.

Such is the second term of the alternative: a bourgeois (an

individual or group of individuals), though he might be courageous enough to accept literally the nationalist ideology offered
by his class, is not brave enough to break with it—even though
he may be entrusted with converting his class. In carrying
through bourgeois reform of feudal society, he is strangled by
his own class, which turns the army—the instrument of its
political domination—against him. Far from admitting its in-
consistencies, the nationalist bourgeoisie decries the distance
that separates *what it is*—bourgeois and ally of agrarian feudalism and of foreign capital, from *what it says it is*—national and
anti-imperialist. The bourgeoisie would prefer that they be
taken at their own word—to a point. In politics, as in everything else, the golden mean is bourgeois virtue.

How does an alternative arise? From the explosive situation
the Cuban Revolution created in Latin America. It has given an
example to the whole world. Like Russia before 1917, Latin
America is ready to give birth to two revolutions, the bourgeois-
democratic and the socialist, and it cannot realize one without
realizing the other. "[It] cannot contain the one by postponing
the other." Therefore, it is risky to rely on the "national
bourgeoisie," even where one has developed, to make the
bourgeois-democratic revolution, for it knows very well what
that process will unleash. To say that it is up to the proletariat
and the peasantry to fulfill the historic task of the bourgeoisie is
to say that the present alternative is not between the (peaceful)
bourgeois revolution and the (violent) socialist revolution. The
promoters of the Alliance for Progress have asserted this in
accord with the reformist point of view. But today they confess
that it is simply a struggle between revolution and counterrevolution. In this way the good Kennedy types in Washington
have put aside their doubts and have deliberately welcomed
counterrevolution. The Thomas Mann doctrine which relates to
the recognition of de facto governments illustrates this. In view
of this, imperialism has only two choices: avoid the bourgeois-
democratic revolution (military coup d'état), or when it comes
about anyhow, change it essentially (demobourgeois fascism).
If the creature is already there, cage it; if it is merely conceived,
abort it. It does not matter what the reformist Communists and
Christian Democrats in Chile think about this; there is no third
alternative. There is yet more: since Cuba has put an end to
accidents (the 1910 "democratic" Mexican and the 1932 Bolivian revolutions belong to the *belle époque* of carelessness,

before the Cuban Revolution), the abortion *manu militaire* is the rule today. One can see this in the suppressions by military coups d'état during the past two years.

Consequently, whoever persists in playing at revolution, whether liberal or socialist, from above (without an armed popular organization), within the rules of constitutional legality, plays a strange game in which there is an election which can only be lost in one of two ways. Either one can be sent to prison, to exile, or to a common grave (demobourgeois fascism). Arbenz (Guatemala, 1954), or Betancourt (Venezuela, 1959): betrayed or betrayer. When the day of the real confrontation arrives, it will only be necessary to have a few more rifles. In a supreme irony of history, the surest road in Latin America to a future that will sing of blood and tears has been baptised "the peaceful road to socialism."

The Brazilian experience of "basic reforms," attempted by Goulart's government, reunites the conditions of victory at the highest level: a powerful mass movement supported by the central power, one of the most solid Communist parties on the continent, located at the very heart of the state apparatus, and an army infiltrated from top to bottom (or so it was believed) by a strong democratic, even revolutionary, movement. Hope crystallized among those in Latin America who thought it more economical to seize control of the bourgeois state from *within*. The fall of Goulart, a beautiful example, wrecked these hopes almost everywhere. It was bad luck that Goulart tried to drag the Communist Party down with him. A few days before the coup d'état the Brazilian Communist Party's general secretary answered the questions of his worried friends. "We're in power now, let's not get alarmed." The party infiltrated the bourgeois governmental apparatus without completely dominating it, thus permitting reaction to kill two birds with one stone. Now the militants cannot hide their bitterness. Torn apart, the Brazilian Communist Party is crumbling away in the bitter struggles, reciprocal accusations, and recapitulations. The forced awakening is as sad as the dreams were beautiful.

The implacable course of real class struggle always makes its voice heard. The Colombian Communist Party, under the orientation of its general secretary, Vieira, has known how to adapt itself to historical conditions when it was necessary, and has openly attached itself to the cause of the peasants of Marquetalia. One could guess that by coordinating its activities

with those of the Venezuelan guerrillas of the Andes and of
Lara, and by extending the guerrilla war along those frontierless
plains that join both countries, as it is trying to do, the
Colombian guerrillas have accelerated in a singular way the
liberation of the two neighboring countries—Colombia and
Venezuela. Now a Bolivian unity of national struggle has been
realized, *without which American liberation would be delayed
for a long time.* In regard to those whose numbers are dwindling
and who obstinately refuse to criticize their failures (Peru,
Chile, Brazil), their very silence denounces them, revealing
their mistaken emphasis on patience. This cardinal virtue of the
revolutionaries is not respectable when it is raised in theoretical
argument against all the evidence that reasoning and reality
offer. On the contrary, anyone could easily denounce the impatience of the Castroite youth when they articulate the ways and
goals of the revolution. But has anyone ever considered this
paradox: that it has been those same patient parties who have
yielded to this blind realism, and to the policy of immediate
gains and long-range losses? Does not true revolutionary patience consist of building the fundamental revolutionary apparatus through a long struggle, choosing once and for all the
class banner (which does not exclude alliances), and organizing the exploited around this nucleus? Does it not consist
of the irreversible growth of the 26th of July movement in
Cuba, of the Venezuelan FALN, and the Colombian self-
defense militias which were transformed into a guerrilla army
before they had been a regular army? The "impatient ones"
show the most surprising tactical flexibility. They arrange the
broadest alliances without compromising their positions, and
they face the long war calmly. Castroite impatience does not say
"Let's seize power tomorrow," but rather, "No matter how long
and twisting this road may be, and precisely for that reason, we
must never lose sight of the final aim—destruction of the semicolonial state—in order to avoid useless detours."

Without a common source, this passion for efficiency and a
direct blow, aimed at the foundations of the state, its army, and
its police, would not be shared by thousands of militant revolutionaries from Guatemala to Brazil. It is not necessary to
produce statistical tables to show that the Latin American
masses are victims today of a kind of *peaceful genocide,* on
the part of imperialism and the ruling class. Without including

deaths resulting from the wars that periodically devastate the continent (300,000 killed in Colombia between 1948 and 1958), we choose two figures at random from the official tables: in the suburbs of Recife in Brazil's Northeast, of every 1,000 newborn infants, 500 die before they are two years old. The life expectancy of adults who labor in the Bolivian mines or on the fazendas of Northeast Brazil barely passes thirty. This is a cross section of America. Latin America suffers, much more than the rest of the Third World, a greater population increase (approximately 3 percent per annum), which the generally feudal processes of production now in force make really dramatic. Compared with the Western world, this growth in population would create different rates of historical development everywhere. For example, the program the Communist Party of the Soviet Union adopted at the Twenty-second Congress fixes a limit of one generation—at the most half a century, but even this seems too short—for the building of Communism. But many Brazilian Communists, in setting time limits, do not allow more than a few years for the building of a new society, however unrealistic this may seem. The Soviet Union's increase in productive capacity is helped by a population growth that is not excessive. Brazil's population rate of increase, on the other hand, is: over the next twenty years it will double its population from 60 to 120 million inhabitants. This may go some way to explain the *state of emergency* in which our American comrades live. If they fail to act quickly or if they stay where they are, they will be more easily killed off, one by one. This passion for action explains the impatience of Castroites as well as vague feelings of imminent salvation, the hungry man's mysticism which stalks the peasants of Northeast Brazil. Once one understands the fact that the levels and therefore the rates of possible change vary in different parts of the world one can begin to understand that the margin of time between formulating a strategy for taking power and the tactics that follow it up is smaller in South America than in Europe. One can also understand why slogans imported directly from Europe (for example, those referring to peaceful coexistence) encounter so much difficulty in being adapted to real Latin American situations. It is easy to admit that the inequalities in world-wide development, especially population growth, are explained by unequal revolutionary patterns and forms of action. But it is

530 ■ THE POLITICAL-ACTIVIST PIVOT

equally clear that those differences of timing within world-wide revolutionary action can seem to provoke contradictions within the revolutionary world to exactly the extent that the differences are not recognized for what they are and taken into account.

For this reason, some reformists consider the Castroite conception of revolution a dangerous adventure. To gain time, to conserve energy, guarantee the legality of the organization, send the most militant to the European socialist countries (and have them come back denationalized, without any connections with their real milieu, rejected or ignored by the militants in the interior), is correct conduct for the vanguard. Reformism regards every initiative that tends to further the armed struggle, that is, to answer with illegal weapons the undeclared war (which goes under the names of silicosis, infantile parasites, brutalization, slow death . . .) that imperialism unleashes against its victims will be "premature" and provocative. The leaders and militants of the new Castroite generation, the Cubans themselves, view the conditions for the armed struggle more generally. The development of the objective conditions are in danger of being arranged by the enemy and compromised or retarded if the Latin American revolutionaries fail to advance seriously the *long* struggle for power by "realistic" efforts and specific revolutionary actions.

Whoever sees the opposition between the two attitudes as internal and inevitable is probably looking for an escape through the backdoor of neutrality. European Marxism, it will be said, is tainted with positivism (it has an empirical basis): "It is enough to be familiar with [the objective conditions] to act correctly." And Cuban Marxism is tinged with voluntarism (it has an Idealist base): "It is not always necessary to expect that all the conditions for the revolution will be given," Che Guevara once wrote; "the insurrectional center can create them."

But this attempt to compare two things that are not comparable is unrealistic. As with every false theory, it gives rise to nothing practical and reflects nothing. It would be fitting to point out here, as we have tried to do elsewhere, that the methodological instructions grouped under the name "Castroism" constitute, in the concrete conditions of the majority of Latin American nations, "a guide for action." As such, so-called Castroism, which is Leninism, is not in any way closed. Assimilated and recreated by the Latin American masses, it is the guiding force for the first steps of continental liberation. Let us listen closely to the murmur that reaches us from the neighboring mountains of Venezuela and Colombia. Latin America is entering a long era of struggle, where difficult but certain victories await it.

Havana:
*A New International Is Born**

$$\begin{array}{c}\text{\tiny\rule{0pt}{0pt}}\end{array}$$

JOHN GERASSI

To MOST American reporters present, what was fascinating about the Organization of Latin American Solidarity (OLAS) conference, which took place in Havana during the first ten days of August, 1967, were its various sideshows. Some were disturbing, as when Stokely Carmichael, the main attraction besides Fidel himself, quipped that "America is going to fall and I only hope to live long enough to see it." Some were curious, as when leaders of Latin American Communist parties huddled in corners of the Havana Libre (ex-Hilton) Hotel's spacious, marble-floored corridors ironing out a common strategy like conspirators in an old-time Preminger movie. And some were enchanting, as when the huge triple-decked outdoor stage of the plush Tropicana night club suddenly came alive with multicolored waterfalls and luscious mulatto girls as naked as Latin Quarter chorus cuties. But what was truly dramatic during OLAS went almost unnoticed: the birth of a new International.

In launching the new, Fifth International, Fidel was risking a great deal—and he knew it. On the one hand, he could expect the United States-dominated Organization of American States (OAS) to find in it justification for an armed assault on Cuba. On the other, he could conceive that Russia's anger might be transformed into material retaliation, which would deprive Cuba of the oil it needs to keep running and the raw materials it requires to develop. Indeed, many Cubans were already talking

* *Monthly Review,* Vol. 19, No. 5, October, 1967.

of a "double blockade," and only partly in jest. But to be true to himself and to the Cuban Revolution, Fidel had to do what he did—and most Cubans, fully aware of the possible consequences, jubilantly and enthusiastically approved.

In essence, the new International was simply the systematization and continentalization of Cuba's own revolution—armed struggle through guerrilla forces which gradually gain the support of the peasant masses. As such, OLAS's task was to spell out the economic, political, cultural, and military reasons why armed struggle is necessary and to establish the machinery by which guerrillas in any one country of Latin America can count on the active support of those in any other. Thus, OLAS would officially have to reject Russia's "peaceful coexistence" policy; more, it would have to explain why such a policy necessarily leads to a betrayal of the poor and the exploited peoples of the Americas. Finally, OLAS would have to commit itself, more or less openly, to an outright interventionist position.

It is true, and perhaps Fidel was banking on it, that Russia could not afford, propagandistically, to punish Cuba for its revolutionary fervor, especially when most radicals and left-wingers already criticize Russia's lukewarm support of Vietnam. Indeed, during OLAS, one revolutionary, Comandante Francisco Prada, third in command of Venezuela's FALN (Armed Forces of National Liberation), publicly lamented the fact that Vietnam was "tragically alone."

Besides, Cubans have been silently convinced ever since the 1962 missile crisis that Russia was capable of abandoning them in a showdown with the United States. They might have harbored a false sense of security after Kennedy was reported to have made his no-invasion promise.

But Vietnam changed all that. With America's increasing aggressiveness in that hapless country the Cuban leaders realized that Kennedy's promise was not worth very much—in fact, the State Department has since denied that there was such a promise. Thus they are certain that once the United States settles the Vietnam war one way or another, it will go after Cuba. On August 10, at the close of OLAS, Fidel explicitly stated that this was his conviction. He read a *Daily News* editorial which said (in re-translation), "Let's stick a memo in Uncle Sam's hat to trample Castro under foot with all necessary force to destroy his Communist regime, as soon as we win the war in Vietnam."

Though he scoffed that "If the danger posed to this country depends on a United States victory in Vietnam, we will all die of old age," Fidel made it clear that it was in Cuba's national interest, as well as in the interest of all revolutionaries in the small countries of the underdeveloped world, to create as many Vietnams as possible.

Sometime in 1965, Che Guevara, who had long thought this to be the case, disappeared from Cuba to help organize the revolutionary movements of Latin America. To do so, he needed a fresh approach and a fresher commitment. The Communist parties of Latin America by and large accept Russia's coexistence policy. Like Russia, they claim that by playing the game of legality, entering elections, organizing the working class, etc., they will eventually be brought to power without bloodshed.

Che disagreed. He realized that the United States and its oligarchic partners in Latin America occasionally tolerated Communist legality only because it was ineffective and unproductive. Che knew that in every country of Latin America the "national bourgeoisie," which Karl Marx once expected would lead the first revolutionary assault on imperialism, was completely tied materially to American corporate interests. Furthermore, Che, who never underestimated his enemy, saw that American imperialism was not static but dynamic, that it could generate enough mobility within the cities to create a sense of progress in the urban masses strong enough to neutralize the traditional proletariat as a revolutionary force. Instead, said Che, it had to be the peasants who would make up the revolutionary force, and it is with them that the revolutionary vanguard must work. And since the peasants were neither organized nor controlled by the Communist parties, these parties could not be considered a revolutionary vanguard. The young French philosopher Régis Debray, picking up these thoughts and adding them to Che's book on *Guerrilla Warfare,* then constructed the basis for a new concept of revolution through the building up of small guerrilla bands in remote areas, where peasants are totally outside society and where advanced military technology loses its advantage. The role of the traditional Communist Party in these operations was discounted.

Naturally, Communist leaders were not very enthusiastic over these developments. At a meeting in Prague in May, 1967, they denounced the forthcoming OLAS meeting as divisionistic, and

supported the Venezuelan Communist Party which had already
been denounced by Fidel himself.

The Venezuelan case is the key to understanding the whole
new process of revolution in the Americas. Back in 1961 it was
mainly the Communists—the traditional, Moscow-line party,
with relative strength in the cities—that launched the country's
first armed struggle through the creation of the FALN. The
orders, the money, the arms, and the food came from the city as
the Party continued to lead the armed operations from its
Central Committee headquarters. For a while, as the result of
armed uprisings by leftists and Communists within the armed
forces, it looked as if the armed struggle was rapidly gaining
strength. But, as Presidents Betancourt and then Leoni came
down hard on the Party, jailing the leaders and declaring their
activities illegal, the FALN suffered greatly. It was then that the
CP decided to abandon the armed struggle and return to
legality. It ordered its field commanders to give themselves up.

Douglas Bravo, a member of the Central Committee of the
Communist Party and commander-in-chief of the FALN, refused. He was trounced out of the Party and was denounced as
an adventurer. His men were then cut off from funds and material and, it is said, were even betrayed. "The right-wing
leadership of the Communist Party behaved like a spurned
mistress—denouncing, lying, trying its best to isolate its former
lover," Comandante Ellias Manuit, one of Venezuela's chief
guerrilla fighters who was also kicked out of the CP, told me
recently. To Manuit, Bravo, Prada, and the other fighters, this
was an outright betrayal. Fidel thought so too. He said: "Maybe
some day the Venezuelan people will ask them [the Communist
leaders] about the millions of dollars they collected throughout
the world on behalf of the guerrilla movement which they
abandoned; whose members they left without shoes, clothes,
food, and even the bare necessities; and which they have
accused and attacked without scruples of any kind." And
Prada, who was chairman of the Venezuelan delegation to
OLAS, told me, "For the sake of their own legal standing, they
have abandoned every one of their principles, betrayed their
comrades, and are in effect now in partnership with the repressive forces against the people."

What it all comes down to this: If you are a revolutionary,
you must fight; if you do not fight, you are not a revolutionary.
And that was OLAS's motto, derived from the Second Declara-

tion of Havana: "The duty of every revolutionary is to make the revolution."

But it is a dangerous concept, especially for Russia which wants to avoid a confrontation with the United States at all costs. And the Cubans have no illusions about what to expect. In a crucial and brilliant speech, Raúl Castro on July 22 told a graduating class of the Superior School of the Ministry of Armed Forces: "Our country is very small and very narrow and behind us is the sea, so that we have no space to retreat. We must be ready. It is the price that we must pay to maintain our revolution and we may have to maintain it with our own resources alone." And to the rumor propagated by Humphrey in Alaska that Kosygin had come to Cuba at the suggestion of Johnson in order to tell Cuba to cool it, Raúl said that Cuba used to have two "Papas": first, Spain; then, the United States. Now: "We have no Papas! . . . Do we have [Russia's] help? Yes, we have. Is it good? Yes, it is good. Can we depend exclusively on it? No."

In Santiago on July 26, Fidel repeated the admonition to an excited but jubilant crowd of half a million people, most of them peasants who had come from all over the country. Flanked by members of the Central Committee of the Cuban Communist Party (who are all revolutionaries now) and by the guest of honor, Stokely Carmichael, Fidel Castro shouted:

> It is necessary that all Cubans, all of us, be clear about certain things. We are not going to speak of the correlation of forces between imperialism and ourselves; we are not going to speak of how many planes they can send over our heads, or how many soldiers they can send. We are not going to speak of foreign help. We must say realistically that we are thousands of miles from any country that can give us any kind of help, and in case of an invasion here, we must learn to accustom ourselves to the idea that we are going to fight alone . . . and there is one word that is absolutely forbidden in revolutionary terminology—defeat; and equally the synonym of defeat—surrender. And, in addition, there is a phrase that as a matter of profound principle will be forever abolished from the terminology of this revolution and that phrase is "Cease Fire."

Four days later, in the swank ballrooms and former casino rooms of the Havana Libre, OLAS got under way in earnest. The general sessions were public, and it was there that Stokely

Carmichael made his dramatic entry into the revolutionary process of the underdeveloped world. I had been with Stokely at the Dialectics of Liberation Congress in London earlier in the month, and I had heard him repeatedly refer to the black rebellions as the prelude to revolutionary warfare in the United States. I had also heard him there refer to the Negro ghettos as the underdeveloped, imperialized portions of the United States. But now, on the podium, flanked by Rodney Arismendi, the biggest name in Latin American Communism, by three genuine fighters from Latin America, including Comandante Prada of the Venezuelan FALN and Comandante Néstor Valle of the Guatemalan FAR (Armed Revolutionary Forces), and by Haydée Santamaría, one of the two women survivors of Fidel's 1953 assault on the Moncada barracks, facing some of the most courageous and dedicated revolutionaries of the continent, Stokely said:

We greet you as comrades because it becomes increasingly clear to us each day that we share with you a common struggle; we have a common enemy. Our enemy is white Western imperialist society; our struggle is to overthrow the system which feeds itself and expands itself through the economic and cultural exploitation of non-white, non-Western peoples. We speak with you, comrades, because we wish to make clear that we understand that our destinies are intertwined. We do not view our struggle as being contained within the boundaries of the United States, as they are defined by present-day maps. . . . When black people in Africa begin to storm Johannesburg, when Latin Americans revolt, what will be the role of the United States and that of African Americans? It seems inevitable that this nation will move to protect its financial interests in South Africa and Latin America, which means protecting white rule in these countries. Black people in the United States then have the responsibility to oppose, at least to neutralize, that effort by the United States. . . . [Together our task is] starting a new history of man.

The real work, however, was carried out in the Commission sessions from which both observers and press were banned. During these sessions, which lasted a week, the clash between the *fidelistas* and the *ortodoxos* gained momentum. In crucial Commission I, which was to decide the ideological and political definition of a permanent OLAS, Arismendi, who is Secretary-General of the Uruguayan Communist Party, and John William

Cooke, a Communist-hating ex-Peronist who was chairman of the Argentine delegation, exchanged such fiery insults that the session had to be postponed lest it degenerate into blows. At another time, when the Venezuelans referred to Communists as counterrevolutionaries, Arismendi threatened to walk out for good.

As the revolutionary hard-line prevailed more and more, the clash between the two sides became hotter and hotter. Ideologically, it was a fundamental clash, for from it may come about not only the split but also, if the revolutionaries can successfully repeat the Bolivian operation elsewhere in the Americas in the next year or two, the demise of the Communist Party structure on the continent. The traditional Communists were best represented by Manuel Cepeda, a member of the Central Committee of the Communist Party of Colombia, while the *fidelistas* were supported most vehemently by Prada and President Dorticós himself. Rodney Arismendi agilely tried to develop an intermediary position, recognizing, on the one hand, that armed struggle is the highest form of revolutionary activity but that it is not the exclusive one, and, on the other, that all Communist parties do belong to the revolutionary vanguard even if they no longer necessarily dominate it. This was quite a compromise, since traditional Communists have never before allowed their monopoly of the vanguard to be challenged. Also, Arismendi's compromise tacitly recognized that in the struggle between FALN and the Communist Party of Venezuela, FALN predominates. But the compromise failed.

Taking the following quotes out of actual speeches made by Cepeda, Prada, Arismendi, and Dorticós, the debate could have sounded thus:

Question: What is the object of OLAS?

Dorticós: The organization throughout the continent of a wide movement of solidarity . . . capable of supporting the development of revolutionary strategy in a systematic and permanent way.

Arismendi: The union of all the organizations and parties that fight in the arena of Latin American liberation along the channels of unity.

Question: Is there only one way or are there many ways to fight imperialism?

Cepeda: We are against formulating a single line. . . .

We [propose] a combination of all the methods of struggle.

Dorticós: If someone wishes to discuss whether in most conditions in this continent the only way, either today or in the near future, for the liberation of the peoples is or is not the armed struggle, it would be enough to explain to him that there is someone who does not have the slightest doubt that the armed struggle is the only way. That someone is United States imperialism.

Arismendi: It would be absurd to believe that Latin America offers a dull and uniform picture where a dry formula for liberation can be worked out for each country.

Cepeda: We do not exclude the use of all the expressions of struggle of the masses. Civic action is not an obstacle to armed struggle; they complement and support each other.

Prada: The peoples of America have already decided the road they will take. . . . The road of armed struggle is inevitable.

Cepeda: We will not waste even a tiny particle of legal action while we can.

Arismendi: In general it will be an armed revolution . . . [but] it is particularly dangerous not to see the strategic unity of the historical process.

Dorticós: And if imperialism chooses violence and armed struggle, who can deny the peoples and argue with their militant revolutionary vanguards, who are intelligent, capable, and worthy of these qualifications, the right to choose revolutionary violence, revolutionary armed struggle as the suitable, dramatically inevitable reply?

Cepeda: This violence will have many forms of expression.

Question: Though disagreeing on the kind of violence, you thus all do agree that it is ultimately inevitable and desirable?

Arismendi: No. Revolutionaries are not anxious for violence. We want a world in which it does not reign, once the causes that engender it—exploitation in all its forms, of man by man, of one class by another, of a nation by another—no longer exist. In Uruguay we have said many times before that we wish to follow the least painful road; but we know we are in Latin America, that imperialism is threatening us, and that our people's struggle will be hard and difficult, and that it is already a bloody one.

Prada: Let us not worry too much about the opinion of

others who, while claiming to represent [the peoples], are
frightened by the revolutionary thrust, hesitate to march in the
front ranks, and are reluctant to be replaced by those who
are willing to fight until final victory.

Cepeda: The tactics of the enemy are manifold. He does
not put into practice one but several lines of action. The tactics of the Latin American popular movement will also have
to be manifold.

Prada: This is the time of great definitions. The question
is to determine whether we are willing to lead the revolutionary process on to the achievement of true and complete victory or whether, on the contrary, we are willing to lead it
into stagnation and regression.

The Communist parties of the world apparently chose "regression." On July 30, 1967, for example, *Pravda* published an
article by Luis Corvalan, head of Chile's Communist Party. In it,
Corvalan told Castro to stop his meddling, denounced the
fidelista line as "adventurism," and warned that any criticism of
any Communist Party by any revolutionary was "a gift to
imperialism." Then, on August 4, *L'Humanité,* organ of the
French Communist Party, blasted Prada and the other OLAS
hard-liners as "worshippers of the Peking line." That same day,
the Ecuadorian Communist Party in its official weekly, *El
Pueblo,* explained that it had refused to attend OLAS because
the conference contradicted the 1964 decisions of Latin American Communist parties to let each country adopt its own way
of struggle.

These criticisms did not soften Havana. On the contrary,
Cuba and the hard-liners pushed through a resolution condemning the Venezuelan Communist Party leadership as "opportunistic," "reformist," and "serving the interests of imperialism."
Only El Salvador, Bolivia, and Uruguay, whose delegations
were dominated by traditional Communists, voted against
the resolution. The next day, another resolution, which was
meant to remain secret to the outside world, blasted Russia for
giving financial and technical assistance to Latin American
countries governed by oligarchies. And finally, in his August 10,
OLAS-closing, four-hour speech, Fidel brought his gripes
against Russia out into the open: "If internationalism exists, if
solidarity is not just a word, the least we can expect of any state

of the socialist camp is that it will lend no financial or technical assistance of any type to those [oligarchic] governments."

At that point all but a handful of the 5,000-odd delegates, observers, guests, and ordinary Cubans who had packed the Chaplin Theater in Havana's once fashionable Miramar section jumped to their feet and cheered. On the stage behind Fidel were the chairmen of the delegations from all twenty-seven countries, among them Cepeda, Arismendi, and Communist leaders from Chile, Bolivia, and El Salvador. They did not applaud. Nor did the observers from Eastern Europe sitting in the audience. Next to Arismendi was Raúl Castro. When he noticed that the Uruguayan Communist was standing stiffly, his arms crossed, Raúl shot his clapping hands high above his head and laughed. The audience went wild. And as the television cameras focused first on the tall, immobile, lanky Uruguayan, then on the short, rocking, beaming, Cuban *comandante,* all Cubans finally understood that the left in Latin America, indeed in the world, had come to an irreconcilable split. There now existed two clearly delineated camps—the revolutionaries and the others.

And still, Fidel was not through. These parties, he said when he resumed his speech, belong to a world-wide conspiracy against Cuba, against true revolutionaries who lay down their lives for the cause. Fidel then went on with increasing harshness, saying, in effect, that these parties who mouth the co-existence line, these parties who defend Russia's opportunism, who refuse to condemn Venezuelan Communist Party's betrayals, who sit here today not daring to applaud the true meaning of revolutionary solidarity, these parties belong to an "international mafia" whose ultimate goal is not the revolution but, on the contrary, its destruction.

The traditional Communists did not walk out. But the split is inevitable. The new revolutionary vanguards of Latin America no longer expect help from any Communist Party. They have formulated new concepts, they are seeking out new leaders, they are establishing new tactics. It is very significant that the two heroes of OLAS whose photos were plastered all over the Havana Libre were not Karl Marx and Lenin but Simón Bolívar and Che Guevara—he who in the past proclaimed a revolution of all the Americas against the domination of Spanish imperialism, and he who today leads the revolutionary struggle also of all the Latin Americans against the domination of United States imperialism. Both men saw the struggle as long, hard, and bloody. And both men thought they could win against superior odds and weaponry simply because theirs was the side of justice. Bolívar was right everywhere on the continent. Che has already been proven right in Cuba and is doing well in Bolivia.

To most sophisticated Cubans, Castroism-Guevaraism-Debrayism, or the New International, has taken a giant stride forward from the "clichés" and "catechism," as Fidel put it, of traditional Marxism-Leninism. For one thing, it both integrates and honors man by making the struggle his own and keeping him armed in the collective society it establishes. Almost every Cuban today is armed, and is thus constantly a potential counterrebel should he be dissatisfied with the regime. He participates not only in the tasks he accepts but volunteers for additional duty, especially in agriculture. It is not true that he does so reluctantly and out of social and political pressure. Many times during my six-week stay in Cuba, during which I toured the whole island, I had the opportunity to talk to such volunteers. Their spirit was high, their fervor genuine—whether they were hoeing *malangas* or planting coffee trees. They have no patience with the dullness and rigidity of bureaucrats who are constantly being weeded out of the offices. Cuba's youngsters thirst for knowledge and never fear controversy. They read Trotsky and even Schlesinger. They enjoy pop music and look at abstract art. They criticize their old press and are developing new journalistic concepts (and a new newspaper, *Juventud Rebelde* ["Rebellious Youth"], which in its first year of existence has shown amazing flexibility). They discuss their mistakes, face their problems, and criticize their mentors. They admire the United States' New Left and are more interested in the discussions that take place in New York's Free University than in Moscow's numerous academies. They are armed and want to follow Che into the battlefields of the Americas, but they know they must let the peoples of the Americas do the fighting while their own task is to continue the revolution at home. Cuba's revolutionaries do not talk very much about the Permanent Revolution—but they live it.

Waves of the Future*

FIDEL CASTRO

. . . The imperialists pretend to commit with impunity all kinds of misdeeds in the world. They daily bomb North Viet Nam with hundreds of planes: that is the imperialist system, those are the laws of imperialism. They invade the fraternal Dominican Republic with 40,000 soldiers, they openly set up a puppet government there with their occupation troops; that is the order of imperialism, those are the laws of imperialism. A state such as Israel, at the service of the imperialist aggressors, gets hold of a great part of the territory of other countries, establishes itself there at the very margin of the Suez Canal and is already claiming the right to participate in the control of that canal—so all that's lacking now is for them to ask that a pipeline be installed from the Aswan Dam to irrigate the Sinai Peninsula; they are there, and nobody knows how long they'll stay, and the longer it takes the longer they'll stay: that is the order imperialism wants to establish, those are the laws imperialism wants to impose upon the world. To send missions of murderers with poisoned bullets to kill leaders of other states, to constantly send armed infiltration groups to a country they have been harassing for eight years. That is the imperialist order! Those are the laws imperialism wants to impose upon the world! And we are a small country, but we will not accept that order! We will not accept those laws.

We are not a country of adventurers, of provocateurs, of

* Speech delivered at the closing of the first conference of the Organization of Latin American Solidarity (OLAS) at the Chaplin Theater (Havana), August 10, 1967. Official Cuban Government translation. (The word "olas" means "waves" in Spanish [ed.].)

543

irresponsible people, as some have wanted to picture us. We simply refuse to accept that order and those laws of imperialism. And if the price of this attitude should be to be sunk in the Bartlett Basin, to have the entire population of this country swept away—if that were possible—we would prefer this to accepting that order and those laws that imperialism wants to impose upon the world.

Go out on the streets in this country and ask any citizen—young or old; father, son, or mother—ask him what he prefers, which he prefers: the acceptance of that Draconian order, submission to the dictates of imperialism, or death. And you will find that there are very few who think differently, who prefer to accept that imperialist order. But do not think that all of them will be counterrevolutionaries; there will also be some who, invoking Marxism-Leninism, will say that that is what has to be done—that is, that we should accept submission to the imperialist Draconian order. There are some of these, and they are everywhere.

There are currents, there are attitudes. And we do not impose attitudes on our people. We have tried to teach and learn; we have tried to educate ourselves as consistent revolutionaries and also help the people to educate themselves as consistent revolutionaries.

No one will think the problems of this country are easily solved, that the dangers that menace this country are insignificant and small.

No one will be able to make light of the circumstances which this small country resolutely faces, without any hesitation, at the very doorstep of the most powerful imperialist country in the world—and not only the most powerful one, but the most aggressive; and not only the most powerful and aggressive, but the bloodiest, the most cynical, the most conceited of the imperialist powers of the world.

Here is a case which expresses the essence of imperialist thought. It is an article from the New York *Daily News* headed "Stokely, Stay There." We would indeed be honored if he wishes to remain here! but he is the one who doesn't want to stay here because he considers it his fundamental duty to fight. But he must know that whatever the circumstances, this country will always be his home.

The article states: "While we are busy in Viet Nam, it is

hard for us to crush Castro—although the Government could, and should, stop discouraging Cuban refugees who plan Castro's destruction." A fine discouragement!

"But let's stick a memo in Uncle Sam's hat to trample Castro under foot with all necessary force to destroy his Communist regime as soon as we win the war in Viet Nam."

If the danger posed to this country depends on a U.S. victory in Viet Nam, we will all die of old age. But see how they express themselves, with incredible irritation, with what contempt they speak of "a Negro inciter," of "the miserable island," of "trampling under foot." Because it must be said that the imperialists are annoyed by a lot of things, but most of all they are annoyed by the visit of a Negro leader—of a leader of the most exploited and most oppressed sector of the United States—by the strengthening of relations between the revolutionary movement of Latin America and the revolutionary movement inside the United States.

It is logical that the exploiters, who for centuries practiced racism against the Negro population, now consider as racists all those who struggle against racism.

They say that they have no program. Well, that shows that often a movement can begin before the program. But it is also false that a movement has no program; what is happening is that the Negro sector of the population of the United States at this moment, overwhelmed by the daily repression, has concentrated its energies on defending itself, on resisting, on struggling.

But it will not be long before they will discover something that is inevitable according to the laws of society, the law of history. And that is that this Negro sector—because it is the most exploited and repressed sector, the most brutally treated in the United States—will arise the revolutionary movement in the United States; just as from the most mistreated and most exploited, the most oppressed of the Negro sectors, will come the revolutionary vanguard within the United States. And around this revolutionary movement that does not arise from that sector because of race problems, but arises because of social problems, because of exploitation and oppression, and because that sector constitutes the most suffering, the most oppressed; and by the law of history—just as in all periods of history: as happened with the plebeians in Rome, the field serfs

of the Middle Ages, with the workers and farmers of contemporary times—in the U.S., from that oppressed sector of society
will arise the revolutionary movement.

And that is a social truth, that is a historic truth. And
don't be impatient; from that oppressed sector will arise that
revolutionary movement—vanguard of a struggle—that will one
day liberate the whole U.S. society!

That's why we must reject—as injurious and slanderous
—the attempt to present the Negro movement of the United
States as a racial problem.

And we hope they don't continue to harbor the illusion
that anyone has been misled here. The drawing together of the
revolutionaries of the United States with those of Latin America
is the most natural thing in the world, and the most spontaneous. And our people admire Stokely for the courageous
statements he has made in the OLAS Conference, because we
know that it takes courage to do this, because we know what it
means to make such statements when you are going to return to
a society that applies the most cruel and brutal procedures of
repression, that constantly practices the worst crimes against the
Negro sector of the population; and we know the hatred that his
statements will arouse among the oppressors.

And, for this reason, we believe that the revolutionary
movements all over the world must give Stokely their utmost
support, as protection against the repression of the imperialists,
in such a way that everyone will know that any crime committed against this leader will have serious repercussions
throughout the world. And our solidarity can help to protect
Stokely's life.

And, because all these inevitable facts of the process are
developing, the revolutionaries are getting together, internationalism is being practiced. We believe that the attitude of this
U.S. revolutionary leader is a great lesson, a great example of
militant internationalism, very characteristic of revolutionaries.
And we undoubtedly sympathize much more with this type of
revolutionary than with the super-theorizers, who are revolutionary in word and bourgeois in deed.

This internationalism is not just proclaimed; it is practiced! And the Negroes of the United States are offering resistance, they are offering armed resistance. They didn't go around
making theses, they don't start talking about objective conditions
first in order to seize a weapon and defend their rights. We don't

have to appeal to any philosophy—and, even less, to a revolutionary philosophy to justify inaction.

And we believe that if there is any country where the struggle is hard, where the struggle is difficult, that country is the United States. And here we have U.S. revolutionaries giving us examples and giving us lessons.

We always have to bring along some cables, some papers, some news items, especially in a meeting of this nature. We sincerely believe that we would not be fulfilling our duty if we did not express here that the OLAS Conference has been a victory of revolutionary ideas, though not a victory without struggle.

In OLAS, a latent ideological struggle has been reflected. Should we conceal it? No. What is gained by concealing it? Did OLAS intend to crush anyone, to harm anyone? No. That is not a revolutionary method, that does not agree with the conscience of revolutionaries. Let's be clear about this—*true* revolutionaries!

And we believe it is necessary that revolutionary ideas prevail. If revolutionary ideas should be defeated, the revolution in Latin America would be lost or would be indefinitely delayed. Ideas can hasten a process—or they can considerably delay it. And we believe that this triumph of revolutionary ideas among the masses—not all the masses, but a sufficiently vast part of them—is absolutely necessary. This does not mean that action must wait for the triumph of ideas—and this is one of the essential points of the matter. There are those who believe that it is necessary for ideas to triumph among the masses before initiating action, and there are others who understand that action is one of the most efficient instruments for bringing about the triumph of ideas among the masses.

Whoever stops to wait for ideas to triumph among the majority of the masses before initiating revolutionary action will never be a revolutionary. For, what is the difference between such a revolutionary and a latifundium owner, a wealthy bourgeois? Nothing!

Humanity will, of course, change; human society will, of course, continue to develop—in spite of human beings and the errors of human beings. But that is not a revolutionary attitude.

If that had been our way of thinking, we would never have initiated a revolutionary process. It was enough for the ideas to take root in a sufficient number of men for revolutionary action to be initiated, and through this action the masses started to acquire these ideas; the masses acquired that consciousness.

It is obvious that in Latin America there are already in many places a number of men who are convinced of such ideas, and have started revolutionary action. And what distinguishes the true revolutionary from the false revolutionary is precisely this: one acts to move the masses, the other waits for the masses to have a conscience already before starting to act.

And there is a series of principles that one should not expect to be accepted without an argument, but which are essential truths, accepted by the majority, but with reservations on the part of a few. This useless discussion about the means and ways of struggle, whether it should be peaceful or nonpeaceful, armed or unarmed, the essence of this discussion—which we call useless because it is like the argument between two deaf and dumb people—because it is that which distinguishes those who want to promote the revolution and those who do not want to promote it, those who want to curb it and those who want to promote it, is useless. Let no one be fooled.

Different words have been used: the road is the only one, it is not the only one, it is exclusive, it is not. And the conference has been very clear in this respect. It does not say *only* one road, although that might be said: it says a fundamental road, and the other forms of struggle must be subordinated to it, and in the long run, it is the only road. To use the word *only,* even though the sense of the word is understood and even if it were true, might lead to errors about the imminence of the struggle.

That is why we understand that the declaration [Second Declaration of Havana], by calling it the fundamental road, the road that must be taken in the long run, is the correct formulation. If we wish to express our way of thinking, and that of our party and our people, let no one harbor any illusions about seizing power by peaceful means in any country in this continent; let no one harbor any illusions. Anyone trying to tell such a thing to the masses will be completely deceiving them.

This does not mean that one has to go out and grab a rifle and start fighting tomorrow, anywhere. That is not the question. It is a question of ideological conflict between those who want to make revolution and those who do not want to make it. It is the conflict between those who want to make it and those who want to curb it. Because, essentially, anybody can realize if it is possible, or if conditions are ripe, to take up arms or not.

No one can be so sectarian, so dogmatic, as to say that one has to go out and grab a rifle tomorrow, anywhere. And we ourselves do not doubt that there are some countries in which this task is not an immediate task, but we are convinced that it will be their task in the long run.

There are some who have put forward even more radical theses than those of Cuba: that we Cubans believe that in such and such a country there are no conditions for armed struggle, but they claim that it is not so. But the funny thing is that it has been claimed in some cases by representatives who are not quite in favor of the theses for armed struggle. We will not be angered by this. We prefer them to make mistakes trying to make revolution without the right conditions than to have them make the mistake of never making revolution. I hope no one will make a mistake! But nobody who really wants to fight will ever have differences with us, and those who do not want to fight ever, will always have differences with us.

We understand very well the essence of the matter, and it is the conflict between those who want to impel the revolution and those who are deadly enemies of the ideas of the revolution. A whole series of factors have contributed to these positions.

This does not always mean that it is enough to have a correct position and that is all. No, even among those who really want to make revolution many mistakes are made; there are still many weaknesses, that is true. But logically we will never have deep contradictions with anyone—no matter their mistakes—who honestly have a revolutionary position. It is our understanding that revolutionary thought must take a new course; it is our understanding that we must leave behind old vices, sectarian positions of all kinds, and the positions of those who believe they have a monopoly on the revolution or on revolutionary theory. And poor theory, how it has had to suffer in these processes; poor theory, how it has been abused, and how it is still being abused! And all these years have taught us to meditate more, analyze better. We no longer accept any "self-evident" truths. "Self-evident" truths are a part of bourgeois philosophy. A whole series of old clichés should be abolished. Marxist literature itself, revolutionary political literature itself, should be renewed, because repeating clichés, phraseology, and verbiage that have been repeated for thirty-five years you don't win over anyone, you don't win over anyone.

There are times when political documents, called Marxist, give the impression that you go to the archives and ask for a form: form 14, form 13, form 12; they are all alike, with the same empty words, which logically is a language incapable of expressing real situations. And many times the documents are divorced from real life. And many people are told that this is Marxism . . . and in what way is this different from catechism, and in what way is it different from a litany, from a rosary?

But we consider ours a Marxist-Leninist party, we consider ours a Communist Party. And this is not a problem of words, it is a problem of facts.

We do not consider ourselves teachers, we do not consider ourselves to have drawn the guiding lines, as some people say. But we have the right to consider ours a Marxist-Leninist party, a Communist Party.

We are deeply satisfied, and it is with great joy, not nostalgia, with happiness, not sadness, that we see the ranks of the revolutionary movement increasing, the revolutionary organizations multiplying, Marxist-Leninist spirit making headway —that is, Marxist-Leninist ideas—and we felt deeply satisfied when the final resolution of this conference proclaimed that the revolutionary movement in Latin America is being guided by Marxist-Leninist ideas.

This means that conventlike narrowmindedness must be overcome. And we, in our Communist Party, will fight to overcome that narrow concept, that narrowmindedness. And we must say that as a Marxist-Leninist party we belong to OLAS; as a Marxist-Leninist party we belong not to a small group within the revolutionary movement, but to an organization which comprises all true revolutionaries, and we will not be prejudiced against any revolutionary.

That is, there is a much wider movement on this continent than the movement constituted simply by the Communist parties of Latin America, we are a part of that wide movement, and we shall judge the conduct of organizations not by what they say they are but by what they prove they are, by what they do, by their conduct.

And we feel very satisfied that our party has wholeheartedly entered into this wider movement, the movement that has just held this First Conference.

The importance of the guerrilla, the vanguard role of the guerrilla. Much could be said about the guerrilla, but it is not possible to do so in a meeting like this. But guerrilla experiences in this continent have taught us many things—among them the terrible mistake, the absurd concept that the guerrilla movement could be directed from the cities.

That is the reason for the thesis that political and military commands must be united.

This is the reason for our conviction that it is not only a stupidity but also a crime to want to direct the guerrillas from the city. And we have had the opportunity to appreciate the consequences of this absurdity many times. And it is necessary that these ideas be overcome, and this is why we consider the resolution of this conference of great importance.

The guerrilla is bound to be the nucleus of the revolutionary movement. This does not mean that the guerrilla movement can rise without any previous work; it does not mean that the guerrilla movement is something that can exist without political direction. No! We do not deny the role of the leading organizations, we do not deny the role of the political organizations. The guerrilla is organized by a political movement, by a political organization. What we believe incompatible with correct ideas of guerrilla struggle is the idea of directing the guerrilla from the cities. And in the conditions of our continent it will be very difficult to suppress the role of the guerrilla.

There are some who ask themselves if it is possible in any country of Latin America to achieve power without armed struggle. And, of course, theoretically, hypothetically, when a great part of the continent has been liberated, there is nothing surprising if under those conditions a revolution succeeds without opposition—but this would be an exception. However, this does not mean that the revolution is going to succeed in any country without a struggle. The blood of the revolutionaries of a specific country may not be shed, but their victory will only be possible thanks to the efforts, the sacrifices, and the blood of the revolutionaries of a whole continent.

It would therefore be false to say that they had a revolution there without a struggle. That will always be a lie. And I believe that it is not correct for any revolutionary to wait with arms crossed until all the other peoples struggle and create the conditions for victory for him without struggle. That will never be an attribute of revolutionaries.

To those who believe that peaceful transition is possible in some countries of this continent, we say to them that we cannot understand what kind of peaceful transition they refer to, unless it is to a peaceful transition in agreement with imperialism. Because in order to achieve victory by peaceful means, if in practice such a thing were possible, considering that the mechanisms of the bourgeoisie, the oligarchies, and imperialism control all the means for peaceful struggle . . . And then you hear a revolutionary say: They crushed us, they organized two hundred radio programs, so and so many newspapers, so and so many magazines, so and so many TV shows, so and so many of this and so and so many of the other. And one wants to ask him: What did you expect? That they would put TV, the radio, the magazines, the newspapers, the printing shops, all this at your disposal? Or are you unaware that those are precisely the instruments of the ruling class to crush the revolutions?

They complain that the bourgeoisie and the oligarchies crush them with their campaigns, as if that is a surprise to anyone. The first thing that a revolutionary has to understand is that the ruling classes have organized the state in such a way as to maintain themselves in power by all possible means. And they use not only arms, not only physical instruments, not only guns, but all possible instruments to influence, to deceive, to confuse.

And those who believe that they are going to win against the imperialists in elections are just plain naïve; and those who believe that the day will come when they will take over through elections, are supernaïve. It is necessary to have been present in a revolutionary process and to know just what the repressive apparatus is by which the ruling classes maintain the status quo, just how much one has to struggle, how difficult it is.

This does not imply the negation of forms of struggle. When someone writes a manifesto in a newspaper, attends a demonstration, holds a rally, propagates an idea, they may be using the famous so-called legal means. We must do away with that differentiation between legal or illegal means, and call them revolutionary or nonrevolutionary means.

The revolutionary, in pursuit of his ideal and revolutionary aims, uses various methods. The essence of the question is whether the masses will be led to believe that the revolutionary movement, that socialism, can take over power without a struggle, that it can take over power peacefully. And that is a lie! And those who assert anywhere in Latin America that they will take over power peacefully will be deceiving the masses.

We are talking about conditions in Latin America. We don't want to involve ourselves in any other problems, which are already large enough, of those of other revolutionary organizations in other countries, such as those of Europe. We are addressing Latin America. And of course, if they would only confine their mistakes to themselves . . . but no! they try to encourage the same mistakes of those who are already mistaken on this continent! And to such an extent that part of the so-called revolutionary press has made attacks against Cuba for our revolutionary stand in Latin America. That's a fine thing! They don't know how to be revolutionaries over there, yet they want to teach us how to be revolutionaries over here.

But we are not anxious to start arguments. We already have enough to think about. But of course, we will not overlook the direct or indirect, the overt or covert attacks of some neo-Social Democrats of Europe.

And these are clear ideas. We are absolutely convinced that in the long run there is only one solution, as expressed in the Resolution: the role of the guerrilla in Latin America.

Does this mean that if a garrison rises in rebellion because there are some revolutionaries in it we should not support the rebellion because it is not a guerrilla struggle? No! It is stupid to think, as one organization did, that the revolution would be made with the rebellion of garrisons only. It is stupid to have a rebellion in a garrison, and afterwards let it be crushed by overpowering forces, as has happened on some occasions.

New situations arise, new situations may arise; we do not deny that. For example, in Santo Domingo a typical case came up of a military uprising that started acquiring a revolutionary character.

But, of course, this doesn't mean that the revolutionary movement must be on the lookout for what may come up, for what may take place. Nobody was able to foresee, nobody was able to estimate the form, the character that the revolutionary movement acquired, especially after the imperialist intervention.

In other words, by stressing the role of the guerrilla as an immediate task in all those countries where true conditions exist, we do not discard other forms of armed revolutionary struggle.

The revolutionary movement must be in a position to take advantage of, and even support, any expression of struggle that may arise and develop or that may strengthen the positions of the revolutionaries. What I do not believe is that anyone who considers himself a revolutionary will wait for a garrison to rebel in order to make a revolution. I do not believe that there can be any revolutionary dreaming of making a revolution with the rebellion of garrisons.

The uprising of military units may constitute a factor, unforseeable factors may arise; but no really serious revolutionary movement would begin with these eventualities as a starting point.

Guerrilla warfare is the main form of struggle, but that does not exclude all other expressions of armed struggle that may arise.

And it is necessary—it was very necessary—that these ideas be clarified, because we have had very bitter experiences; not the blows or reverses of a military order, but the frustrations of a political nature, the consequence—in the long run sad and disastrous for the revolutionary movement—of wrong concepts. The most painful case was that of Venezuela.

In Venezuela the revolutionary movement was growing, and the revolutionary movement has had to pay dearly the consequences of the absurd concept of wanting to lead the guerrilla warfare from the city, of wanting to use the guerrilla movement as an instrument for political maneuvers, of wanting to use the guerrilla movement as an instrument of low politics; the consequences that may be derived from incorrect attitudes, from wrong attitudes, and, on many occasions, from immoral attitudes.

And the case of Venezuela is a very worthwhile case to take into consideration, because if we do not learn from the lessons of Venezuela, we never will learn.

Of course, the guerrilla movement in Venezuela is far from being crushed, in spite of treason. And we, gentlemen, have every right to use the word treason.

We know that there are some who do not like it; a few will even feel offended. I hope that some day they will be convinced that they have no reason to be offended, unless they carry in their hearts the seeds of treason.

The case of Venezuela is eloquent in many respects, because in Venezuela a group which was in the leadership of a party, with all these wrong concepts, almost achieved what neither imperialism nor the repressive forces of the regime could achieve.

The party, or rather, not the party but the rightist leadership of the Venezuelan Party, has come to adopt the position practically of that of an enemy of revolutionaries, an instrument of imperialism and the oligarchy. And I do not say this for the sake of talking; I am not a slanderer, I am not a defamer.

We have some unfinished business with that group of traitors. We are not encouragers of polemics; we have not been inciters of conflicts; far from that, for a long time we have silently borne the publication of a series of documents and a whole series of attacks from that rightist leadership, in the same degree as that leadership forsook the guerrilla fighters and took the road of conciliation and submission.

We were the victims of deceit. First they spoke to us about a strange thing (for many of these problems began with a series of strange things); they began to talk of democratic peace. And we would say: "What the devil does that democratic peace mean? What does that mean? It is strange, very strange." But they would say: "No, that is a revolutionary slogan to widen the front, to join forces, to face an ample front." "An ample front?" "Well, an ample theoretical front; who will oppose it?" "No, trust us."

Then, after a few months, they began to speak of tactical retreats. Tactical retreats? How strange is all that!

Because if they had told us the truth we might have disagreed, we might have doubted, anything, but never . . .

A tactical retreat: that is what they said to the militants; they said that to the people.

The tactical retreat was followed by an attempt to end the struggle, an attempt to suppress the guerrilla movement. Because anyone knows that in a guerrilla movement there is no tactical retreat; because a guerrilla that retreats is like an airplane which, cutting the engine in mid-flight, falls to the ground. Such a tactical retreat must have been conjured up by those genius inventors of high-flown revolutionary theories. Whoever has an idea of what a guerrilla is, and begins to listen to talk of retreat by the guerrillas, says: "This man is talking a lot of nonsense. A guerrilla can be totally withdrawn, but he cannot retreat."

Bit by bit they begin unmasking themselves, until one day they completely unmask themselves and say: "Let's have an election," and they become electoralists.

But even before they declared themselves in favor of elections, they committed one of the most vile deeds that a revolutionary party can commit: they began to act as informers, as public accusers of the guerrillas. They took advantage of the case of Iribarren Borges, and with that episode took the opportunity to accuse openly and publicly the guerrilla movement, practically throwing it into the jaws of the beasts of the regime. The government had the weapons and the soldiers with which to pursue the guerrillas who would not retreat; the so-called party or the rightist leadership of the party had taken control of the guerrillas' command, and armed, both morally and politically, the repressive forces that persecuted the guerrilla forces.

We must ask ourselves honestly, how could we, a revolutionary party, cover up such a conventlike and chapel-like attitude of a party that was trying to morally arm the repressive forces, that persecuted the guerrilla forces.

Then came the phraseology. They began accusations, saying that we were creating divisions. That we were guilty of creating divisions!

They were not discussing a group of charlatans. They were talking about a group of guerrillas that had been in the mountains for years, combatants who had gone into the mountains and had been completely abandoned, had been forgotten. But can a revolutionary say: "Yes, once more you are correct that they have been deceiving us, that they began speaking to us about this and about that, and then afterwards do something else?"

And, naturally, we publicly expressed our condemnation, after a series of statements had already been issued by the right-wing leadership against our party, condemning it in a treacherous manner, using the Iribarren incident to spread calumnies and to attack revolutionaries.

Logically that provoked the airy and indignant protest of that right-wing leadership, which made us the butt of a series of tirades. They did not answer a single one of our arguments, they were unable to answer even one, and they wrote a maudlin reply—to the effect that we were ignoble, that we had attacked an underground party, that we were fighting a most combative, a most heroic anti-imperialist organization. And they drafted a reply against us.

Why has it been necessary to bring that reply here? Because that document became the argument of a gang, a whole gang of detractors and slanderers of the Cuban Revolution. And that incident served as the beginning of a real international conspiracy against the Cuban Revolution, a real conspiracy against our revolution.

And we feel that it is a problem that must be clarified; at the very least the truth must be clarified.

I am going to read this answer, if you'll pardon me, even though it is a bit lengthy. Of course, it is an answer full of phrases which aren't at all kind about us, but if you'll permit me I would like to read this answer, which was made public, the so-called "answer of the Communist Party of Venezuela to Fidel Castro." And I hope it will give us a starting point to refute some things that have been said about Cuba and about the revolution.

It says: "Fidel Castro, Secretary General of the Communist Party of Cuba in power, and Prime Minister of the Socialist Government of Cuba, taking comfortable advantage of his position, has attacked the Communist Party of Venezuela, an underground Party, with hundreds of its militants in prison, with dozens of them fallen in the mountains and the streets of the country, and subject to an inexorable persecution daily, falling new victims even as Fidel Castro is speaking.

"The same man who is tolerated in all his verbal excesses, thanks to the fact that Cuba occupies the front line of the anti-imperialist struggle, should have the elementary finesse of being careful of his language when referring to the Communist Party struggling in the country most intervened in by Yankee imperialism in all of Latin America, that is fighting it under the most difficult conditions.

"With a world audience, and saying who he is, Fidel Castro has not hesitated to insult a Communist Party which is hardly able to answer due to repression.

"Therefore, Fidel Castro's action is ignoble, advantage-taking, and treacherous, and lacking the nobility and gallantry that have always characterized the Cuban Revolution.

"Fidel Castro has expressed a negative judgment concerning the murder of Iribarren Borges, even claiming a right to express an opinion on this matter.

"Nevertheless, with surprising cheek, he wants to deny the same right to the CPV. Fidel Castro evidently does not want the Communist Party of Venezuela, which acts in Venezuela, which is in Venezuela, to express an opinion, to pass judgment on a Venezuelan political event which took place on Venezuelan soil and closely affects the life of the CPV. On the other hand, he can do so from Cuba.

"According to his peculiar point of view, we are on speaking terms and play up to the government. He does so and is trying to be the voice of an intangible revolutionary oracle. This strange way of reasoning shows an irresponsible arrogance and self-sufficiency, improper in a chief of state.

"As to the fact itself, the CPV said exactly the same thing that Fidel Castro did—no more, no less. On the other hand, we assert that what does play up to reaction and imperialism are speeches such as that of Fidel Castro"—they don't even thank me—"slander like that which he has hurled against our party, his efforts to divide it, and such matters as the murder of Iribarren Borges.

"The CPV claims its right of planning its own policy without anybody's interference. Cuba has marched along a hard, revolutionary road with honor; by this she is an example and inspiration to us. But the one thing that we have never been, are not, and never will be, is agents of Cuba in Venezuela, or for any other Communist Party in the world.

"We are Venezuelan Communists, and we do not accept the tutelage of anyone, no matter how great their revolutionary merits may be.

"If there is any revolutionary group in Venezuela that submits with pleasure to the tutelage and patronage of Fidel Castro, that is its business. The CPV will never do it. If Fidel Castro does not like it, so much the worse for him. Now then: Why does Fidel Castro intervene precisely at this time against the CPV? Because the CPV has already begun to defeat in practice, and not only ideologically, the antiparty faction of Douglas Bravo; because the party and the Communist youth have attained great political and organizational successes in applying their policy; because our recent feat, the rescue of comrades Pompeyo, Guillermo, and Teodoro, has filled all the militant Communists of the country with enthusiasm and renewed energy; and because, finally, the anarchistic, adventurous policy of the antiparty group has shown the inevitability of its failure and has helped enormously in the clarification of problems under discussion.

"That is precisely why Fidel Castro has thrown all the weight of his prestige against the CPV in a desperate attempt to help the anarchistic group of adventurers, which he patronized and urged on so the CPV would go under.

"Nevertheless, our policy and the facts prove daily what the adjectives 'hesitant,' 'halting,' and 'opportunistic'—that Fidel Castro applied to the leadership of the CPV—are worth. And that is proved here in Venezuela, even in spite of the things Fidel Castro has done to us, and surely, will continue doing to us.

"But let him and the whole CPV understand this clearly: we will not even discuss the sovereignty of the CPV.

"Fidel Castro has described the leadership of the CPV as cowardly, in a new demonstration of that irritating tendency of his to believe himself to have a monopoly on bravery and courage. We Venezuelan Communists do not suffer from childish exhibitionism; we do not go around proclaiming our qualifications in this field. When Fidel Castro was a child, that great patriarch of Venezuelan Communism Gustavo Machado was already storming Curaçao and invading Venezuela, arms in hand.

"And from then on, the history of the CPV, which is a political history, was also the history of the men who confronted Gómez's terror and that of Pérez Jiménez; the men who directed the insurrection of January 23, 1958; the men who were responsible for Fidel Castro's receiving a plane loaded with arms when he was still in the Sierra Maestra; and the men who, during the last eight years, if they have hesitated in anything, it has not been in sacrificing their lives.

"This answer of ours is the best demonstration we can give Fidel Castro of what the leadership of the CPV is really like. Accustomed to believe in his power as a revolutionary High Pasha, he thought his speech would doubtlessly crush and confound us. He couldn't be more mistaken, and now Fidel Castro will see why Yankee imperialism and its agents insist so much on liquidating this Venezuelan Communist Party.

"In his speech, Fidel Castro shows that he wants to

Tʜᴇ Pᴏʟɪᴛɪᴄᴀʟ-Aᴄᴛɪᴠɪsᴛ Pɪᴠᴏᴛ

assume, once more, the role of a sort of arbiter of the revolutionary destiny of Latin America—a superrevolutionary who, if he had been in the place of all the Communists of Latin America, would have already made the revolution.

"On another occasion we referred to the characteristics of the Cuban struggle and to the place where Fidel Castro would still be if it had occurred to him to hoist the red flag in the Sierra Maestra. At the moment we only want to reject the role of revolutionary 'papa' that Fidel Castro adopts.

"We firmly reject his presumption of it being he and only he who decides what is and what is not revolutionary in Latin America. In Venezuela this question is decided by the CPV and its people, by no one else. But to this Fidel Castro—highest dispenser of revolutionary diplomas, who asks what would North Viet Nam say if Cuba were to trade with South Viet Nam—we only want to ask him if he thinks of what the Spanish people have to say about his trading with Franco and the Spanish oligarchy, or what the Negro peoples of Zimbabwe, Rhodesia, and the patriots of Aden might say about his trading with imperialist Britain. Or is it that what Fidel Castro considers as opportunism in others, in him would be washed away by the holy waters of his own self-sufficiency?

"This is unpleasant polemics and one that makes the enemy jump with joy, but which evidently cannot be deferred any longer. Fidel Castro himself forced us to the limits with his speech. Let it be, then. We will argue. And just as we claim our affiliation in Simón Bolívar and the fathers of our homeland in our anti-imperialist struggle, so we tell Fidel Castro that the descendants of Simón Bolívar and Ezequiel Zamora will never forgive anybody for the insolent and provoking language he used in his speech on March 13.

"The Venezuelan believes himself neither above nor below anybody else; but if there is one thing that will provoke his militant, faithful pride, it is an insult.

"And already Fidel Castro must have started to realize that he has stumbled against something different, that he has come up against the Venezuelan Communists.

"We realize that such acts as that of Fidel Castro will cause us difficulties but we do not despair.

"We have the calm conviction of those who know they are right, and we have the revolutionary passion to defend it.

March 15, 1967

Political Bureau of the Central Committee
of the Venezuelan Communist Party
Pompeyo Márquez
  Guillermo García Ponce
    Alonso Ojeda Olaechea
      Pedro Ortega Díaz
        Eduardo Gallegos Mancera
          Teodoro Petkoff
            German Lairet."

"Without comments" it says on the top. "Answer of the Communist Party of Venezuela to Fidel Castro." And below: "Reproduced and distributed by Second Front—Alpha 66, 109 South West 12 Avenue, Miami, Forida. 33-130."

Do not think that I have taken this letter from a spokesman of a party or from a political newspaper. Thousands of issues of this letter were sent to Cuba from the United States by the Organization "Second Front—Alpha 66." Those same persons that sent that gang with guns, and bullets with cyanide, to murder Prime Minister Fidel Castro, as they said.

And this really needs some commments. In the first place, I am not going to refer now to what I said that night, because it would take too long. It is not true that we made personal insults against anyone. We did not call anyone in that party a coward; we said that the political line was cowardly. I was not insulting, offending anyone, or saying so-and-so are cowards.

Naturally, far from answering any of the things that were stated, they drew up this document, published it, and it was one of the many that they had written, and naturally, we have complied; our party has been working on a document to answer this and all the intrigues of those gentlemen, which will be released at an opportune moment.

But naturally a series of imputations are made in this document, the same ones that have been made against the revolution, against our party, and not only by imperialism, not only by imperialism.

Among other things, these gentlemen did not hesitate in

accusing us, in accusing our party, of intervening in the internal affairs of the Venezuelan Party and of intervening in the internal affairs of Venezuela.

They accused us of having agents in Venezuela, they insinuated that the guerrilla group of combatants who refused to retreat and surrender was a group of Cuban agents. These were exactly the same as the slanderous imputations made by the U.S. State Department.

In this document Cuba was also accused of pretending to be an arbiter, of pretending to direct the Latin American revolutionary movement—exactly the same accusations that imperialism makes against us. In this document they even include lies, even mentioning arms which came from Venezuela —but these did not come when we were in the Sierra Maestra; they were 150 weapons that came when our troops advanced on Santiago de Cuba, in December, when the columns of Camilo Cienfuegos and Ernesto Guevara had already taken an important part of Santa Clara.

In fact, they accuse us, and attribute to themselves the sending of a planeload of arms . . . They almost try to say that the war was won with these arms . . . And they were not the ones who sent these arms. And they are so short of arguments, so short of arguments that they have had to resort to such lies.

Maybe some day the Venezuelan people will ask them about the millions of dollars they collected throughout the world on behalf of the guerrilla movement—which they abandoned; whose members they left without shoes, clothes, food, and even the bare necessities; and which they have accused and attacked without scruples of any kind. Some day—I repeat— maybe the Venezuelan people will ask these swindlers how much they collected throughout the world: the figures, the numbers, the data.

And what did they do? For our part, we do not ask them anything; we are not interested. When we help somebody, we truly help him, we do not ask him to render us an account of what he did with this aid.

Nevertheless, there is an argument which is an old stand-by, and it is going to have a full answer. This was a malicious argument. (Perhaps, if it were not for these painful circumstances, we would not have to discuss this problem.) This is the argument of our trade with Spain, with England, and the other capitalist countries. Of course this argument, or this problem, was not being discussed at all.

This was not what was discussed.

Why, then, did these gentlemen bring this problem into the discussion? Why did they bring this argument into the discussion? They did so in reference to our critical position of the financial and technical aid extended to the Latin American oligarchies.

In the first place, there has been a deliberate attempt to distort our views. Furthermore, these gentlemen of the rightist leadership of the Communist Party of Venezuela had a goal, and they pursued it in a very immoral manner. Once, when Leoni's administration was trying to establish diplomatic relations with the Soviet Union, we were asked what we thought of it; these gentlemen were also asked, and they responded negatively to the idea.

Why do these gentlemen resort to this argument and drag in a problem that was not being discussed with them? This is very clear; this forms part of the plot, of the conspiracy in which they and their fellows are participating with imperialism in order to create a serious conflict between the Cuban Revolution and the socialist countries. It is unquestionable that this argument is one of the lowest, most despicable, most treacherous, and most provoking things. It pretended to present a contradiction between our position and our trade with capitalist countries. Furthermore, as this argument, until recently, was not openly published—for the capitalist press published it, and the letter was published by the counterrevolutionary organizations —but this low argument was also employed sotto voce in small groups by the conspirators and detractors of the Cuban Revolution.

In the first place, they are lying when they state that Cuba is opposed to trade. In every international body, in every economic conference, in all the organizations in which Cuba has taken part as a state, we have constantly denounced the imperialist policy of blockade, and we have denounced the acts of the Government of the United States against our country as a violation of free trade and of the right of all countries to trade with one another. Cuba has inflexibly maintained that position at all times; that has been a policy pursued by our country which the facts throughout the history of the commercial relations of our country can bear out. Our position does not refer to commerce; it never referred to commerce. And that position of ours is known by the Soviet peoples; we have stated our viewpoint to them.

We refer to the problem of financial and technical help of any socialist state to the Latin American oligarchies. Let these things not be confused; do not try to confuse one thing with another; do not ever try to confuse one thing with the other. Some socialist states even offered dollar loans to Mr. Lleras Restrepo because he was in difficulties with the International Monetary Fund.

And we asked ourselves: How can this be? This is absurd! Dollar loans to an oligarchic government that is repressing the guerrillas, that is persecuting and assassinating guerrillas. And the war is carried out with money—among other things—because the oligarchies have nothing with which to wage war except money, with which they pay mercenary forces.

And such things seem absurd to us—as does everything that implies financial and technical aid to any of those countries that are repressing the revolutionary movement, countries that are accomplices in the imperialist blockade against Cuba, which we condemn. It is unfortunate that we have to go into this problem in detail, but naturally, it is the number-one argument employed by this gang.

And it is logical. Cuba is a small country against which the United States practices a cruel blockade. At Gran Tierra we explained to some of those present here how the imperialists do everything within their power to prevent our obtaining even such insignificant things as a handful of seeds of a kind of rice, cotton, or anything else; seeds of any kind of grain, of vegetables, any kind at all.

No one can imagine to what lengths the imperialists go to extend their economic blockade against our country. And all those governments are accomplices, all those governments have violated the most elemental principles of free trade, the rights of peoples to trade freely; those governments help imperialism in its attempts to starve the people of Cuba.

And if that is true, if that is the case, and if internationalism exists, if solidarity is not a word worthy of respect, the least that we can expect of any state of the socialist camp is that it will lend no financial or technical assistance of any type to those governments.

It is truly repugnant that this vile argument is used to

test the revolutionary steadfastness of this country, or to provoke conflicts with it. And truly, this nation's steadfastness, its
policy based on principle, its decision to act in a responsible
way—to prevent wherever possible polemics and conflicts. Yes!
But never believe under any circumstances, no mattter how
difficult it may be, that in the face of any problem, no matter
how great, will they be able to put our dignity and our revolutionary consciousness up against the wall! Because if that was
how we were, if that was the kind of leadership our party had,
we would have surrendered long ago in the face of the great and
mortal dangers—the dangers engendered by imperialism, by our
firm political position.

And it is equally repugnant that they try to find a
contradiction between this position and Cuba's commercial
policy with the capitalist world. The imperialists have tried to
break the blockade. And the question is not what countries we
do trade with, but with how many countries throughout the
wide world do we not trade with simply because, one by one,
and under the incessant and growing pressure of the imperialists, they break trade relations with us.

We have never broken off those relations. Imperialism
has taken care of that, in the same way that it has seen to it that
they break off diplomatic relations with Cuba, one by one. We
have never broken them off with anybody. They are weapons
imperialism has used against the Cuban Revolution, in diplomatic relations, in commercial relations.

And it is worthwhile to speak about commercial relations, for some of the mafia—and I cannot define, in any other
way, those who attack our revolution in such a slanderous and
base fashion, without any serious and powerful argument—have
spoken of our not breaking off diplomatic relations with the
state of Israel. Neither did our country break off relations with
Albania when a great number of countries from the socialist
camp did; we did not break off relations with Federal Germany,
but Federal Germany did not want to accept our establishing
relations with the German Democratic Republic. And even
though we knew that the consequences would be the breaking
off of diplomatic and commercial relations, this country had not
the slightest hesitation of being among the first to establish
diplomatic relations with the German Democratic Republic.
And this country has never hesitated in the least to put our
political principles above economic interest, for if this were not

so, we would have found a million reasons to reconcile ourselves with imperialism a long time ago, more so in these times
when it has become quite fashionable to do so.

The slightest insinuation of our following a sordid policy
of interests in our international stand is to forget what this
country has paid for its unyielding stands, its solidarity with a
great number of countries—Algeria among them—notwithstanding the fact that this gave another country, which was one
of the biggest buyers of Cuban sugar, an excuse to justify the
pressures exercised by imperialism against them and to stop
buying our sugar. And many are the facts.

And our people always saw—and we thought that
everyone understood quite clearly—that each time an imperialist pressure against anyone selling or buying from us failed, it
was a victory of our revolution in the face of the blockade. We
spoke about Europe and what it could and would not accept;
why Europe offered resistance; why Europe, in spite of its
economic and industrial development, has to resist the competition of Yankee monopolies—Yankee imperialist attempts to
take over the economy of those countries—and how, owing to a
question of interest, it was impossible to accept imperialist
pressure; and because Cuba paid, and paid promptly, and
because Cuba was a growing market, the imperialists had
utterly failed in having the whole capitalist world break off—as
they wished—commercial relations with Cuba.

What has this to do with our arguments? What has it to
do with our statements? If imperialists had succeeded, the road
of the revolution would have been much more difficult.

Do we trade with the socialist camp? Yes, a trade which
is practically all barter, the so-called clearing currency, which
has a value only in the country with which the agreement is
signed. And if any of the things that the country may need, such
as medicines of a certain kind, things essential for the life of our
people, the trade organizations in any socialist country may
have to say: "We do not have it, we must look for them in other
markets and pay in the currency of that country." And it is here
that imperialism tries to crush us. And if we have bought
medicines in capitalist countries, because we cannot get them or
any similar product in a socialist country, to save the lives of
sick people, of children, to reduce—as we have reduced—the
child mortality rate, the mortality rate in general, and attain the

position Cuba has today—for instance, in public health and in many other fields, we apparently are criminals, we apparently are people without principles, we apparently are immoral, we apparently are the opposite of what we proclaim.

We are not instigators of conflicts, we do not seek unnecessarily, gratuitously, to create conflicts of that nature. I believe that in a high degree, facing a powerful enemy, the interdependence among the movements, the parties, the revolutionary states, will grow.

We may very much want it, a country as small as ours, without having any possibility of economic autarchy, in need principally of the arms to defend ourselves from Yankee imperialists. No one can imagine us acting in an irresponsible manner and creating problems that can be avoided. But between that position and that attitude of Cuba, and the idea that this country can be intimidated with provocations of that sort, there is a profound abyss.

And actually at the bottom of this there is a conspiracy of these elements of the reactionary mafia within the revolutionary movement and Yankee imperialism, a conspiracy to create a conflict between our revolution and the states of the socialist camp. Because, in fact, what they attempt, what they demand, what they urge, is that the socialist camp also join in the imperialist blockade against Cuba.

It is more or less what they really want and they do not hide it. The same March 18, three days after the famous answer, an AP news dispatch came from Caracas—because it became fashionable to have a party spokesman quoting a spokesman of that right-wing leadership, who had frequent dealings with the AP, frequent conversations with the AP—and the AP, cheerful, informative, reported: "Fidel Castro has no ideology. 'He is a revolutionary but he is not a politician,' a leader of the underground Venezuelan Communist Party told the Associated Press today."

I do not know what interest Leoni may have in persecuting these clandestine, yielding, cringing denouncers of the Cuban Revolution, or why they talk about the great feat of the liberation of the distinguished Tom, Dick, and Harry. And really the only one who has profited from that is neither the people of Venezuela nor the revolutionary movement, but Leoni. Because he now has some bloodhounds who only need to ask Leoni to give them some rifles for them to set out and punish those criminals, bandits, trouble-making and dividing Cuban agents.

Since these "journalists," as part of their mission, often have to play the role of journalists, and occasionally like to promote certain contradictions, the journalist added: "When asked if the CPV was not siding with the enemy by trying to have the Soviet Union withdraw its backing of Castro, the spokesman answered: 'We coincide dangerously with the Venezuelan government, but remember that we support the Cuban Revolution and the Cuban Communist Party.' " Evidently I was the bad one, the intruder, the provoker, the revolutionary *Piache* (Johnny-come-lately) etc., etc. " 'Our attack is not against the Cuban Revolution, but against Castro, who has insulted us.' "

"He made it clear"—he made it clear!—"that the Communist Party of Venezuela wished that the Soviet Union would get Castro out of the way." He accuses me of trying to interfere in their internal affairs. And he says that nothing arouses his fury and his revolutionary ardor and his pride more than when someone tries to meddle with them. Not to have imperialism or Leoni meddle, but to have somebody make a criticism with all the justified reasons that I have explained here—"that the Communist Party of Venezuela wished that the Soviet Union would get Castro out of the way." And they put forth the thesis that somebody might get Castro or anybody out of the way, remove or install anybody.

Where did he get such far-fetched theories? Although, ugh, it isn't strange, because we are already fed up with far-fetched theories.

This gentleman states that the Communist Party of Venezuela would like the Soviet Union "to get Castro out of the way." Let's forget Castro. Really, these gentlemen are naïve, they are far-fetched, they are ridiculous. It is not Castro but a revolution that they have to get out of the way! Even a cold could get Castro out of the way! But no one can get a true revolution out of the way!

Am I perhaps a slanderer? In the mafia there are some who will react just as those who doubted our witnesses and questioned our evidence, and who will say: "That is a lie, a slander." But on August 1 of this year, an AP news dispatch datelined in Washington, from Ary Moleón—and these gentlemen play a role in all of this—reports: "The highest Venezuelan diplomatic official here advised today not to hastily label the meeting in Havana of the Organization of Latin American Solidarity as Communist, saying that those who attend are in effect anarcho-Castroites."

Finally they exchanged vocabulary. Pompeyo and his retinue talking about our interference in the internal affairs of Venezuela. Tejera Paris and his clique saying: "No, no, no. They aren't Communists, they are anarcho-Castroites. A purely ideological exchange, ideological trade between Tejera Paris and Pompeyo, between the State Department and the right-wing leadership of the Communist Party of Venezuela. Now they are lending each other concepts and words."

When has imperialism ever been seen treating Communism with so much finesse? When has it ever treated Communism with so much sweetness, decency, finesse, if the image they have tried to paint of Communism is of the worst, the most heartless, degenerate, depraved, cruel and savage of human beings?

And suddenly: No! Have a care! Don't name these people Communists.

Communist is a most sacred, a most respectable, most venerable, most decent, friendly, conciliatory word. Tejera Paris, the great ideologist of tropical Communism.

"Venezuelan Ambassador to the White House, Enrique Tejera Paris, said that this distinction is fundamental." Of course it's fundamental. That theory is clear "if we want to understand a situation that is more complex than applying simple titles," he continued.

What care, what exquisite delicacy, what subtlety, what distinction!

In simple Communist terms, what can we call these people? They are anarcho-Castroites. And they are bad!

"Tejera observed that the present meeting in Havana is not only to protest against the other governments of the hemisphere, but against the established Communist parties in Latin America."

And what a defense lawyer has appeared here, saying that this meeting was called to attack the parties! And since when have the imperialists worried so exquisitely about the parties? Who appointed Tejera Paris as defense counsel for the parties?

Did the diplomat remember that the Communist Party of his country has accused Castro's regime of intolerable intervention in the internal affairs of Venezuela and of appointing himself referee of the Latin American revolution?

Be careful, do not get mixed up; these are Castro anarchists; they are dangerous, they are bad; do not call these people Communists, do not forget that the Venezuelan Communist Party accused Castro of intervention in the internal affairs of Venezuela; do not forget that it accused him of trying to make himself an arbiter.

Did anything like this ever happen before? Did anyone ever talk with such refined language, exquisite courtesy, of the Communists of this continent?

I believe that what is intolerable is this, what is really painful is this. Offense, diatribes, and slander from imperialism are a thousand times preferable to the praise of imperialism. Tell me who defends you, and I will tell you who you are. Tell me who attacks you, and I will tell you who you are.

This we know, that never has any oligarchy, any imperialist, any imperialist henchman, printed one of my speeches by the thousands. Never! Not a phrase, not a line, not a word.

Leoni did not have my speech printed; he did not distribute it; if he read it, he probably pushed it away with a feeling of nausea. Alpha 66, a well-known organization of counterrevolutionaries in Miami, which, in complicity with the CIA, has organized personal attacks with potassium cyanide and silencers, had thousands of copies printed of the declaration of that leadership and distributed them all over the world.

Heirs to Bolívar? What an insult to the memory of Bolívar! They would have accused Bolívar himself of being an interventionist. What accusations would they not have made against him?

To call themselves sons of Bolívar, followers of Bolívar? To speak about hundreds of dead? What right have they to speak in the name of the dead, they who betray the dead? What right have they to invoke martyrs, they who are thinking of running for office as representative, senator, and mayor, and canvass for votes with the pictures of the fallen and betrayed heroes?

Because that declaration against Cuba was made in March. In April they issued a long document. If I were to read it—it is a long one, I am not going to read it—you would see their cliché style; this one was a hybrid product of three or four models, because it is long. It is the document in which they propose an alliance with the bourgeois parties, and it ends by saying:

"Finally, the armed movement is not at this moment capable of playing a decisive role, because of the stagnation of the guerrilla fronts and the armed struggle in general, a situation made more serious by the false political ideas and operations prevailing in the terrorist-anarchist group."

Adventurist-anarchist, terrorist-anarchist, Castro-anarchist! Some day Johnson will start talking about the terrorist-anarchists!

"In view of this national movement, the Central Committee has resolved that the party should take active part in the next electoral process, under the slogan 'Neither continuation nor Caldera—a change'; a change favoring the democratic freedoms and national sovereignty, a change toward the independent development of Venezuela.

"The electoral process is being conducted under conditions of governmental advantage and repression. The party will struggle against such a situation, to turn the elections into a battle against the reactionary clique leading the AD and the government." Amen.

That is, the dead for the campaign posters!

And in this country we know about these things, our people know about these things, and these things only produce nausea and repugnance, because we had our fill of this. No one will be able to tell our people that these are the actions of Communists—nobody; for even at the beginning of Communism, in the middle of the last century, when the Communist Manifesto was written, Marx said that the Communists should support the most militant and progressive sectors of the bourgeoisie. These so-called Communists join the politicians of the bourgeoisie to oppose the heroic guerrilla fighters.

Our people and the Venezuelan people certainly have to know that this kind of apostasy, this trade in the blood of those who have fallen, this effrontery in sending men to die, in leading them wrongly, in presenting themselves afterwards on the election posters—our people know that history does not forgive this, that history will never forgive such crime.

These gentlemen do not have to be destroyed; they have to be left alone, because they destroy themselves.

We know the environment we live in; the reactions, the temperament, the character of our peoples. And we know that the most humiliating, the most abominable, is to send men to death and later present themselves to ask for votes in the name of the betrayed dead.

And on this same road on which the mafia and imperialism coincide, here is yesterday's latest dispatch:

"The American nations are considering today a request from Venezuela to denounce the regime of the Cuban Prime Minister Fidel Castro as pernicious to the cause of peaceful coexistence for which the Soviet Union pleads.

"The question, which could explode in the rear guard of Castro's Moscow-supported regime, would be in answer to the appeal of the Conference of the Organization of Latin American Solidarity to fight for the seizure of power through armed struggle."

It says then that the Associated Press got itself a copy . . . They are the devil, they get copies from anywhere. And of that document that they say has eleven points, which they publish in this dispatch, this is point four:

"To express to the extracontinental governments that actively support the actual government of Cuba, the serious worry of the member states of the OAS, as this support tends to encourage the interventionist and aggressive activities of the Cuban regime against the countries of the Western Hemisphere, that until the mentioned activities do cease, the cause of peaceful and active coexistence of the nations of the world will be harmed.

"To this effect it is recommended to the governments of the member states of the OAS to carry out common or separate efforts toward the states which actively support the actual government of Cuba, in order to reiterate this expression of concern."

Peaceful coexistence? And this terminology in the mouth of the OAS and its clique? This terminology in the mouth of the OAS and its clique, of sending—in a few words— groups, commissions of the OAS, to visit the governments of the socialist states so that they will withdraw their aid to Cuba. It's incredible! It's incredible to be seeing and hearing these things! On what will these gentlemen base this? How can they be so shameless? How do they dare to do such a thing?

And point five: "To ask the governments which support

the Organization of Solidarity of the Peoples of Asia, Africa, and Latin America, to withdraw their support of that organization as well as of the Second Tricontinental Conference programmed to be held in Cairo in January, 1968; and reiterate the categorical repudiation of the member states of the OAS to the said organization, whose purposes—as has been shown by the resolutions of its first conference, which took place in Havana in January, 1966—are to prompt the separation of the peoples into groups divided by sectarianism and violence.

"To that effect, it recommends that the governments of the member states approach the American states and the organizations supporting the Tricontinental organization, individually or as a group, in order to insist on this proposal."

Since the governments of certain states belong and do not belong to the organizations, it follows that these gentlemen feel inspired to approach the state organizations that have been at the Tricontinental and say to them: "They are no good; repudiate those people; leave the Tricontinental."

If this doesn't smell of imperialism ordering the world around, then what does it mean, gentlemen? What is it? What have we come to? What nerve these gentlemen have! What illusions, and what shameless pretensions!

But at any rate, the machinations of such groups and imperialism are very evidently trying to isolate Cuba completely, to proclaim the total blockade of Cuba, so that not a grain of bird seed will enter this country. They coincide in their despair: they are dreaming, they are raving, they imagine atrocious, dreadful things. And this country is isolated, it is absolutely alone. Poor people! If that hypothesis were possible —and it isn't—they'd have to suffer the shock of seeing this poor, lonely country marching onward.

This small country has not accumulated enough merits in the eyes of the world, has not accumulated enough merits with regard to the revolution. And often we have imagined the conditions under which imperialism would impose a total blockade on this country, surround Cuba with its ships, and prevent everything from coming in. Would they crush the revolution? I am asking the people: Would they crush the revolution?

That is a most solid "No," coming from the heart of a revulutionary people. In short: If we were not prepared for everything—for everything—we could not call ourselves revolutionaries.

We do not deliberately search out conflict, problems, difficult situations. That will never be the attitude of the revolution. They'll never see an irresponsible, absurd attitude adopted by revolution, no! But neither will they see the revolution hesitating, the revolution giving up; they'll never see the revolution yielding one iota of its principles! For *Patria o Muerte* has many meanings. It means being revolutionaries until death, it means being a proud people until death! And the fact that we speak about *Patria o Muerte* does not mean that we have a sense of fatalism. It is the expression of determination. When we say "death," we mean that not only we would be dead, but many of our enemies would be dead, as well. Kill our people? All the soldiers of Yankee imperialism could not do it!

These facts, these attitudes, are calling us all to order; they are calling us all to reason, to clarify things. These attitudes are the result not of development, but of the deterioration of revolutionary ideas and of a revolutionary conscience.

The resolutions of OLAS do not mean that everything is done. They do not mean that the struggle is past. The Tricontinental also had resolutions, and there were those who signed the resolutions and forgot all about them afterwards.

There must be a struggle. We have to struggle. And the statement that Cuba wants to set itself up as an arbiter, a head, a leader, is more than ridiculous. No! And I am going to tell you what we really think: there is no reason why there should be leading peoples or leading men!

It is leading ideas that are needed! And revolutionary ideas will be the only and true guide of our peoples. We fight for our ideas! We defend ideas! But to defend ideas does not mean the pretension to lead anyone. It is our ideas we defend, the revolutionary ideas.

And the ideas will open the road. We know the process. At the beginning, when a few began to think about the idea of an armed struggle in our country and we began to struggle, very few believed in this possibility—very few. And for a long time we were very few. And afterwards, little by little, these ideas began to gain prestige, began to acquire conscience, and the moment came when everybody believed and the revolution won.

How difficult it was to get the idea accepted that the struggle of the people against modern professional armies was possible in order to make a revolution! And when that was finally demonstrated, after the triumph of the revolution, what happened? Everybody believed in this truth in such a way, that the counterrevolutionaries also believed that it was also a truth for them, and then followed the organization of guerrilla groups and counterrevolutionary gangs, and even the most gentle, the most peaceful of the counterrevolutionaries, the most charlatan of counterrevolutionary park-benchers, grabbed for, joined a gang, and took to the hills. Then it became necessary to show them they were mistaken, that that kind of action was a revolutionary action to be used against the oligarchies; but a counterrevolution of oligarchs, a guerrilla warfare of oligarchs and of reactionaries against a social revolution is impossible.

And how difficult it was! Until we finally showed that this was true. We have had to point out more than once that it is impossible for oligarchs to defend themselves against the people's struggle; and that it is impossible for the people to be defeated by counterrevolutionary guerrilla gangs. And the CIA knows that. Do you know who are probably the most convinced of the effectiveness of the armed revolutionary guerrilla warfare and of the incapacity of the oligarchies to oppose the armed guerrilla struggle of the people? Do you know whom? The CIA, Johnson, McNamara, Dean Rusk, Yankee imperialism. They are the most convinced.

And one would ask oneself, How is it possible that these counterrevolutionaries let themselves be deceived and dragged into the armed revolutionary struggle against the revolution if it is impossible to win? And it is, gentlemen, we are forced to admit, that these counterrevolutionaries are more consistent than many who call themselves superrevolutionaries.

They are most consistent. They wrongly believe in that and let themselves be dragged . . . Naturally, afterwards they say what they say, always—that is a rule without exception!—that they had been fooled, that they had been deceived, that they believed that the army, that the militia . . . All that. For us it is a broken record; we know that . . .

And logically, the ideas in our country have had to develop dialectically, in the struggle, in conflicts. And it will be the same in every country, and no country will be freed from this conflict of ideas. These conflicts of ideas survive even in Cuba. No, the fact that we have a revolutionary people does not mean that there are no antagonisms, no contradictions. Here we find the contradiction, the counterrevolution and imperialism, and there are also contradictions with those who share these ideas of the reactionary gentlemen of the Venezuelan Party.

And in this country we also have our micro-fraction—we can't call it a fraction, because it has no volume, it has no size, it has no possibilities, it has nothing—it is a micro-fraction that has existed. Where does that micro-fraction come from? From the old resentful sectarians. Because our revolution has its history; our revolution has its history. I said that at the beginning very few believed; afterwards many believed.

Our revolution went through that process; it passed through the process of sectarianism, and the sectarians created serious problems for us, with their ferocious opportunism, with their inexorable policy of persecution against many people; they brought corruption into the revolution. And naturally, the revolution, with its methods, its patience, made the criticism; it was generous, it was generous with that sectarianism.

And not only that. We had to be careful to prevent sectarianism from creating neosectarianism in the ranks of the revolution, and that was also prevented. But some sectarian elements held on, they swallowed their resentment, and each time they have had a chance they have expressed it. There are those who never believed in the revolution unless it was in an opportunist way, trying to profit by the efforts of the revolutionary people; trying to climb high in a shameful way. They never believed in revolution, they haven't learned in eight years, nor in ten years, and they will never learn.

Let it be clearly understood: I am not referring to old Communists, because the worst expression of sectarianism and of the activities of those sectarians has been trying to involve the concept of old Communists with their pseudorevolutionary attitudes.

We have to say that the revolution counts, and always counted with the support of the real Communists in this country.

But logically, at the time of sectarianism, many cowards who had deserted the ranks of the old party turned up again. Opportunism, sectarianism, brings all this, and isolated from the masses, tries to create forces by means of favoritism. And then followed the incomes, and more incomes, and more incomes and the privileges.

Logically, afterwards, when the revolution put a brake on sectarianism, it prevented the expressions of sectarianism of another kind, because that has always been our stand, that has always been the stand of the revolutionary leadership; it has always tried to find the best solution, has tried to always overcome those problems with the characteristic style of our revolution, without incurring excesses of any type, preferring to sin by omission rather than excess.

And here we also have our micro-fraction, integrated by old sectarian groups, which are not the same as old Communists. And I repeat, the greatest harm is that they have tried, although in vain, to install their unhealthy ideas, their resentful ideas, into the old and tried revolutionaries. They were the ones who, for example, at the time of the October Crisis thought that we should have let Yankee imperialism inspect us, search us from head to foot, let the planes fly over low, in fact everything. They have been systematically opposed to all the concepts of the revolution, to the most pure and sincere revolutionary attitudes of our people—to our concepts of socialism, of Communism, of everything.

That is, no one will be exempt. And this micro-fraction has the same attitudes of this larger group; this micro-fraction constitutes a new form of counterrevolutionary activity, in that it has the same goals as Alpha, as Faria, as Pompeyo and company; the same as McNamara, Johnson, and all those people.

Now the CIA has a new thesis. (Why does it want to prepare so many personal attacks and so many other things?) Its thesis now is that Castro has to be eliminated in order to destroy the revolution, because imperialism is losing ground. At the beginning it wanted to do away with everything revolutionary; now, the more it loses ground, the more frightened it gets. Now its thesis is to moderate the line of the revolution, to change its course so that Cuba will take a more moderate position—and in this, Alpha, Johnson, Faria, the micro-fractionists, and similar political groups coincide. And they are harboring illusions.

Really, I'm not interested in buying an insurance policy; I don't give a damn! Let them believe what they want; I don't want to be indebted to our enemies for their ceasing to consider me a true enemy; I don't want to be indebted to them for their not doing whatever they want to. They have their rights, they are in their rights. I do not intend to buy any insurance policy.

But, to all of you, I think it is unnecessary to say that the line of this revolution is not the Castro line; it is the line of a people, it is the line of a leading group that has a real revolutionary history. And it is the natural line of this revolution!

The counterrevolutionaries encourage one another; their international organization has been encouraged, greatly encouraged by the idea that insurmountable antagonisms may develop, insurmountable conflicts between the Cuban Revolution and the socialist camp. Really, the only thing that we can say is that it is an honor to our revolution that our enemies think so much about it; likewise, it must be an honor for all Latin American revolutionaries that imperialism has given so much attention to the problem of OLAS. They issued threats, they postponed the OAS Conference, they said they were going to do a lot of things, they "were going to clean the place up," and that this meeting could not take place. And the OLAS Conference has been held—a true representation of a genuine revolutionary movement, whose ideas are solid because they are based on reality. OLAS is the interpreter of tomorrow's history, interpreter of the future, because OLAS is a wave of the future, symbol of the revolutionary waves sweeping a continent of 250 million. This continent is pregnant with revolution. Sooner or later, it will be born. Its birth may be more or less complicated, but it is inevitable.

We do not have the slightest doubt. There will be victories, there will be reverses, there will be advances, there will be retreats: but the arrival of a new era, the victory of the peoples in the face of injustice, in the face of exploitation, in the face of oligarchy, in the face of imperialism, whatever the mistakes that man makes, whatever the mistaken ideas that may be obstacles on the road, they are unavoidable.

We have spoken to you with complete and absolute frankness; we know that the true revolutionaries will always be in solidarity with Cuba; we know that no true revolutionary, that no true Communist on this continent, nor among our people, will ever let himself be induced to take those positions which would lead him to an alliance with imperialism, which would make him go hand in hand with the imperialist masters against the Cuban Revolution and against the Latin American revolution.

We do not condemn anyone a priori, we do not close the doors to anyone, we do not attack anyone en masse, in a block; we express our ideas, we defend our ideas, we debate these ideas. And we have absolute confidence in the revolutionaries, in the true revolutionaries, in the true Communists.

Those will not fail the revolution, the same as our revolution will never fail the revolutionary movement of Latin America.

We don't know what awaits us, what vicissitudes, what dangers, what struggles. But we are prepared, and every day we try to prepare ourselves better, and every day we will be better and better prepared.

But one thing we can say: we are calm, we feel safe, this little island will always be a revolutionary wall of granite, and against it all conspiracies, all intrigues, and all aggressions will be smashed. And high upon this wall there will fly forever a banner with the legend *Patria o Muerte! Venceremos!*

Revolutionary Practice
and Theory in Latin America*

CARLOS ROMEO

TECHNICAL-ECONOMIC STRATIFICATION
OF LATIN AMERICAN SOCIETIES

CHARACTERISTICALLY, in highly developed capitalist societies technological levels of various sections of the economy are not sharply differentiated. In the past twenty years, even agriculture, the economy's Cinderella, has caught up with and sometimes actually surpassed industry in the amount of capital invested per worker.

In Latin American societies a marked technological stratification is clearly evident. In the forefront are the foreign installations that exploit natural resources and whose technology is in no way inferior to similar plants in the mother country. They belong, technologically speaking, to the economy of the country where the invested capital originated.

Economically, they are the offshoots of an alien economy; although physically located in the dependent countries, these foreign installations are an integral part of the economy from which they stem. The workers employed in these installations are natives of the dependent country but they belong to the exploited working class of the investor country. As members of the investor country's exploited class they occupy the lowest rung, since their wages are set by the labor market of the dependent country.

* Written in Havana in 1967.

Their average wage level is higher than the rates paid for similar jobs in the native economy. And they enjoy certain material advantages in accommodations, services, and supplies, compared to workers employed by native capitalists in the same industries and the same region.

From an economic standpoint these workers have been denationalized and now constitute a marginal social stratum that belongs to the foreign economy, and they are involved in a socioeconomic relationship which is also foreign.[1] The economic relations which these highly technified foreign enclaves maintain with the native economy are "foreign trade" relations, not only when the foreign company itself is involved but also when the workers make purchases in the "native economy."

Sharp technological contrasts can also be found within the "native economy" proper. In the first place, there is industry. It is characteristic of Latin American countries that their industries are monopolistic. Whether a single company dominates the market for its products or a cartel fixes the prices, the monopolistic structure of industry is a general rule in Latin America.

This structure makes it possible for the major industrial concerns to earn enormous profits and pay wages and salaries considerably higher than the national average. Also, copying the techniques of the big American companies, they offer all manner of material advantages and assistance to their workers and employees. They build towns for the use of their personnel, operate dispensaries with free medical and dental services, and subsidize popular dining rooms, amusement parks, sports fields, etc. The company ties its workers to it and also separates them from their natively employed fellow workers by the differential in living standards and job security.

The term "labor aristocracy" can fairly be used to describe these privileged groups among the working class in Latin America. Below this elite, the workers and employees in domestic but nonmonopolistic industries—small factories, workshops, the establishments of prosperous tradesmen, the construction industry in general, as well as retail establishments and small agencies of all kinds, etc.—are at economic levels which, from a technological standpoint, place them considerably above

---

[1] Obviously this analysis cannot be applied to foreign enterprises using *technologies similar* to those of native concerns of the same type. (Such was the case of the American and domestic sugar mills in prerevolutionary Cuba, and, in general, it is the case of plantation economies.)

the levels of agriculture and the native mining companies. They form the bulk of the urban population and therefore determine the low wage and salary rates in Latin American countries, but their living standards are ever so much higher than those of the peons on the big estates, agricultural laborers, peasants, share-croppers, squatters, and aboriginal Indians.

Therefore, the economico-technical stratum to which the workers of the nonmonopolistic industries belong is by no means the lowest in the community; there are still several strata beneath them in the interior of the country. The former group, along with the white-collar "aristocrats," enjoy to some extent the advantages of the civilization which is concentrated in the great cities. In a certain sector of agriculture, modern or rela-tively modern methods are used; this includes the sector run by the agrarian capitalists and includes the vast plantations.

Where this technological level prevails, the wage scales and life are superior to those of the peasants, sharecroppers, and squatters, and above those of the peons and tenants of the big Latin American estates. This is the result of agricultural ma-chinery, systems of irrigation and drainage, fumigation, chemi-cal fertilizers, modern dairy farms. It is possible to speak of an economico-technical stratum arising out of capitalistic produc-tion relationships, which, in turn, creates a corresponding stratum of agricultural workers distinguished both by their standard of living and their technical skills and, consequently, by their introduction to the advantages of civilization.

Below this group we find the peons on the big estates, peasants, sharecroppers, and squatters (a source of seasonal labor essential to the plantations and the harvest in general), and the Indian communities. Here we reach the very fringes of society: rudimentary methods of labor, primitive techniques, the lowest evaluation of human labor. This is the outside edge: physically, because of their geographical location, and economi-cally, because of the social role they play. Under these condi-tions, men accept what they are offered without any possibility of breaking out of the trap. Their only escape is to the outskirts of the great cities, where they can hope to find relatives willing to support them until they can find work.

In Latin American countries society resembles a series of concentric circles, representing economico-technical strata, de-pendent upon one another and differentiated by their economic and technical levels—the highest in the center and the lowest on the outer edges.

In Latin American countries there is no effective counterbalance to the domination of mercantile methods in the interchange of the products of labor. From the center, the highest strata of the national economy (and from the still higher stratum of the highly developed foreign economy), products flow toward the lower strata and the periphery of the economy. Prices include replacement costs, the monopolistic earnings of the huge capital investment modern technology requires, and the relatively high wages and other benefits the workers of big companies enjoy (to say nothing of the remunerations the wholesale and retail distribution networks receive). These prices make possible a high standard of living not only for the bourgeoisie, but also for the manual and white-collar workers who belong to the privileged economico-technical strata.

Similarly, since tax collections are adjusted to these patterns, these prices also cover the public financing and upkeep of the nation's assets (maintenance and improvement of cities, highways, railroads, sewage systems, etc.), which most benefits the higher economico-technical strata of the community. Those who pay for all this, who purchase those products, reinforce the inequitable state of affairs inherent in such a society and vote for its continued functioning. But on the economic plane there is no alternative. The dilemma is categorical: buy what is needed, or refrain from buying and go without. Products also move from the lowest strata of the national economy toward the center (and toward the even higher stratum of the highly developed foreign economy). Prices of these goods include the profits on the capital invested, the rentals of the landowners, the income from absentee plantation owners, as well as the low wages of the workers who produce the goods and the wretchedly deprived lives they lead.

Goods produced by peasants, squatters, sharecroppers, and Indians fetch low prices, which implicitly sanctions the deplorable living conditions and the underestimation of their labor. When they sell those products, when they find a buyer, their abject poverty and peripheral situation within society are once more sanctioned and confirmed. Those who buy these products take advantage of their "cheapness." The living standards of the upper economico-technological strata are dependent upon the

584 ■ THE POLITICAL-ACTIVIST PIVOT

conditions of the lower strata. *In capitalist social development, in order for the higher strata to exist, the lower social strata must be maintained.*

The polarization of wealth is therefore a *sine qua non.* This phenomenon is not new. A century ago, Marx explained how the concentration of wealth in the capitalists' hands necessarily implies the concentration of poverty among the workers. For him this polarization was a corollary of class exploitation: a society in which mutually antagonistic social classes with a marked economico-technical stratification coexist. Various social relationships to the means of production exist, some involving exploitation (capitalists, absentee landlords, investors) and others in which no exploitation is involved (peasants, the Indian communities—that is, individual or collective producers who own their own land and means of production). Since capitalistic systems of operation dominate, there is a transfer of values among the various social strata.

The unequal mercantile interchange, characteristic of capitalism, is both fully operative and of basic importance in the underdeveloped economies of Latin America. It constitutes an exploitative relationship between producers with unequal technical-economic status who exchange their products on an equal basis—which infers mutual recognition of their inequality.[2]

The underlying significance of this unequal interchange is that minimal but highly paid labor, incorporated into the value of the product, is exchanged for a great deal of very poorly paid labor. Where capitalist relationships are dominant, this unequal interchange governs, like a natural law, the redistribution of the economic surplus among the social classes.

The socioeconomic status quo finds ideological justification for the unequal evaluation of human labor and the polarization of wealth. Thus, a worker employed by an American company earns more and lives better because his labor is said to be "worth" more. In contrast, a peasant or sharecropper earns a pittance for arduous work and lives under subhuman conditions, cut off from twentieth-century civilization because his labor is "worth" very little.

The ruling class base their "scientific" interpretations on this

[2] In this connection, see "Unequal Interchange" by M. A. Emmanuel, and "International Interchange and Regional Development" by Charles Bettelheim, in "Problems of Planning," No. 2, of the Sorbonne's *Centre d'Etude de Planification Socialiste.*

ideology, which is accepted even by the oppressed classes. These interpretations try to explain the differentiation in workers' living standards in terms of labor productivity. For greater productivity, greater remuneration, and consequently, a higher standard of living.

The conditions under which the highly developed and underdeveloped countries exchange their products—in the nineteenth century, manufactured products for raw materials, and today, raw materials and manufactured products of high technological level for raw materials and manufactured products of low technological level—have not changed, and the differences in technological development have become accentuated.

Since the highly developed countries have advanced more rapidly than the backward lands, it is not amiss to speak of the "development of underdevelopment"; for in absolute terms, the underdeveloped countries have achieved only modest improvements in their living standards.

The same inequalities are also operative in the international sphere. The highly developed foreign economy exploits the national economy in the same way the national industry exploits the national agriculture. Not only do the populations—capitalists and workers alike—of the highly developed countries profit from the "cheapness" of the backward economies' products (the cheapness of the human sweat of the Third World), but city dwellers—both capitalists and workers—of underdeveloped countries benefit from the cheapness of their own agricultural and mining products.

Consequently, another process of exploitation of the lower economic strata by the upper strata is superimposed upon the exploitation of labor by the owners of capital and land. While it is true that workers in highly developed countries are exploited by the owners of capital and parasitic social groups, the degree of exploitation is mitigated by the workers' participation in the exploitation of the economies of the Third World. And the same is true of upper stratum workers in an underdeveloped economy in relation to the lower strata.

Do these facts not call for a restatement of proletarian internationalism? Was it not Lenin himself who explained the breakup of the Second International as a result of the development of a "labor aristocracy" in the rich capitalist countries?[3]

---

[3] V. I. Lenin, "Imperialism, the Highest Stage of Capitalism," *Selected Works*.

The tendency Lenin denounced fifty years ago has developed into a polarization of the world working class. The experience of the national liberation movements reveals the indifference of the working class in the rich capitalist countries to the fate of their proletarian and peasant "brothers" of the Third World, except when they must serve as cannon fodder in the struggle.

To define revolutionary strategy in Latin America today by invoking slogans which are the product of other historical conditions is, at the very least, an absurdity.

REVOLUTIONARY POTENTIAL OF THE EXPLOITED CLASSES IN LATIN AMERICA

In Latin America the structure of the social classes is doubly complicated. On a horizontal plane it would be possible to line up the exploiting classes and the exploited classes, taking into account the diversity of relationships that coexist and the peculiar structure they assume under the domination of capitalist property relations. However, this arrangement would reflect no clear class political identification. It is also necessary to arrange them on a vertical plane, in order to see how the social relationships involved in the productive process intersect.

Under this dual arrangement, the position of each class, as defined by its respective social relationship to the means of production, is modified, and so are the options open to it and its political attitude. For example, the workers of the American companies are proletarians, and from the point of view of their relationship to the means of production, which defines their position in society, they are exploited by foreign capital. Nevertheless, because they belong to the highest stratum within the national territory, they are also coparticipants in the exploitation of the lower strata. Because they belong to the working class (that is, they are exploited by capital) they are economically linked with the rest of the workers and are also politically tied. But their immediate interests tend to take precedence over their long-term interests. Thus, they are prepared to take part in general-strike movements, provided they have an interest in the demands put forward, for they do not always act in solidarity with the other workers. Since their economic problem is peculiar to them, this is perfectly understandable.

Political action, especially if its aim is revolutionary, is something else again. The workers employed by American companies have much to lose and little to gain, at least on a material level. Would their present privileged position be compatible with a socialist regime in which the will and the interests of the majority must prevail? It is unlikely that they could maintain their advantages in such a situation. Would they risk their comparatively high standard of living to improve the lot of the oppressed and exploited classes, with whom they have very little in common? Considerable revolutionary impetus would be required to bring them into the revolutionary struggle. Clearly, the revolution will not begin with them.

Let us look now at what is happening in the Middle East. Through their oil the Arab countries can make their power felt in the imperialist world. Yet most Arab governments, if not actually opposed to an oil embargo of Great Britain and the United States, are at least reluctant to back it. Such an embargo would provide an opportunity for the Arab working class to act in support of Syria and the United Arab Republic, occupying or destroying the refineries, wells, and pipe lines of the foreign companies. Until now, apart from some isolated actions in Lebanon and the operations in Aden of FLOSY (Front for the Liberation of Occupied South Yemen), against the oil companies, such measures have been conspicuous by their absence. The Venezuelan oil workers have remained silent. And as for the Americans! . . .

What shall we say of the Chilean copper workers' attitude to the struggle in Vietnam? Or, the workers of all Latin American countries who provide raw materials used against the Vietnamese? To look for proletarian internationalism, or even proletarian nationalism, among these labor aristocracies is futile. Dockworkers in Venezuela and other Latin American countries for example, reacted against Cuba as a result of the Venezuelan government's denunciation of Cuban intervention in the revolutionary struggle which is in progress in that country. At the instigation of the Venezuelan workers, the other longshoremen have agreed to refuse to load or unload ships of countries trading with Cuba! It might be asked, On which side are these "proletarians"?

And does this incident not epitomize the situation today in Latin America—for workers of the electricity companies, the telephone companies (all American), the big textile companies, and the domestic metalworks? Does it not reveal the attitude of the labor unions, especially the great labor federations, to the revolutionary struggle being waged in Latin America?

To ignore the privileged position of part of the working class within the national complex leads to gross errors in the political, and above all, revolutionary, identification of the working class in Latin America. Exploitation alone does not determine class political orientation. It is also essential to keep well in mind its relative position within the specific socioeconomic environment of Latin America. Once the dogmatic veil of class unity *à outrance* has been raised, it can be seen that the workers are a much less powerful force than their total numbers would indicate, and are much more difficult to integrate into an overall revolutionary strategy.

But other classes which by "orthodox" standards are not so revolutionary have adopted a potentially more revolutionary attitude than has a part of the working class, if not the working class as a whole. These other classes realize that they are united by a common predicament which touches the very roots of the system; they also realize that revolution is their only hope of escape from the infrahuman conditions inherent both in their position within the social structure peculiar to Latin America and in their role in a socioeconomic drama also peculiar to this continent.

Do these characteristics not compensate for a quantitative disadvantage in relation to the workers in the cities?

Not even the new vanguards of the continent are immune to the old concepts and formulae. An example of the urgent need of "liberating the present from the past" is the bitter statistical battle the leaders of the Venezuelan Frente de Liberación Nacional (FALN) are waging against the ex-leader of the Movement of the Revolutionary Left (MIR), Alberto Rangel, and the right-wing leadership of the Venezuelan Communist Party, on the proposition to integrate the country people within the Venezuelan nation.

In the final analysis the issue is the size of the social base of the guerrilla movement in Venezuela and the possibility of organizing a popular army based on the country people.

In this controversy special attention is devoted to the size of the peasant population; since it is relatively small in Venezuela (around 32 percent), the political argument centered around the value of the various government agencies' demographic censuses. (See Mario Menéndez's report on the Venezuelan FALN in *Sucesos para todos,* Mexico, December 24, 1966.)

However, the basic contribution the peasantry can offer in a revolutionary situation does not depend on the absolute or relative numbers of this class, but on its role within the system —its submerged and marginal position in relation to the other classes and the class interests inherent in that position. These are precisely the conditions affected by the guerrilla struggle, with the result that a new situation modifying the traditional orientation of this class has arisen. If the guerrilla struggle really creates a new and decisive situation for the peasantry, it is of secondary importance whether that class constitutes 70 or 20 percent of the population. The guerrilla struggle will have set them in motion and thereby will have begun developing a people's army.

Since these people need a radical change in the social system in order to improve their condition, they place themselves in the front line of revolutionary struggle. Those who seek a social basis for the revolution must of necessity call upon them, whatever their numbers. The revolutionary position is determined by the overall situation and not by numerical superiority or trade-union organization.

Thus, the politico-strategic concept that in underdeveloped countries the revolution must be consolidated in the countryside and then advance upon the cities is not solely determined by the relative size of the peasantry, in proportion to the working class. That interpretation seemed pretty obvious in the case of China, for example, when the theoretical dogma and mechanical application of working class insurrectional experience were abandoned. Nevertheless, it is still necessary to make decisions on the basis of concrete revolutionary conditions, and to have the courage to reject theory which has crystallized into dogma. That is what Mao Tse-tung did when he challenged the "orthodoxy" of the Third International.

It is true that when the term *campesinado* (country people) is used in its widest sense, it includes several different social classes and lacks the real basis the workers have for their class organization: the necessary conditions for the political work of revolutionary parties are absent. The social reality of the underdeveloped countries of Latin America *calls for an instrument of political action adapted to these conditions.*

Such an instrument of political action must operate among

the social class whose organization and "politicization" is sought. The purpose is to incorporate this social class into the political struggle with the clear objective of taking power and destroying the prevailing social system. There is no attempt at political organization with a view to electoral campaigns or unionization, i.e., forms of struggle which respect the rules of the bourgeois game. When the objective is revolution, the instrument of political action must be suited to the conditions of political struggle imposed by the ruling class.

In Latin America the first consideration means transferring the field of operations to the countryside, and the second calls for adaptation to the violence unleashed by the state apparatus and even by the landowners themselves. Then the proper political instrument emerges: the guerrilla bands. This is not a whim of petit-bourgeois romanticism. It is what Marx would have called a manifestation of society itself creating the means to solve historical problems as they arise:

. . . humanity always strives only for those objectives it can attain, for, when we focus the situation correctly, we always see that these objectives emerge only when it is already possible to achieve them, or, at least, when the material conditions for their realization are already developing. (Karl Marx, *Preface, Critique of Political Economy, Selected Works.*)

The conditions under which the revolutionary political struggle must be carried on in Latin America require that the political instrument be, at the same time, a military instrument —what might be called a politico-military movement. By means of this new instrument the revolutionary vanguard is able to awaken political consciousness in the classes whose real situation places them in the vanguard of the struggle for revolutionary change, and *thus gain sufficient momentum to bring into the struggle the other social classes* which are interested in a socialist revolution, either for ideological reasons or because of their real economic situation. That is why the guerrillas are called the "little motor" that sets in motion the "big engine." The guerrilla struggle must therefore be the *dominant form* of struggle in Latin American revolutionary strategy. And this becomes even more imperative as the fight against the repressive forces of the government, supported by imperialism, is stepped up in tempo and intensity toward a final confrontation between the organized violence of the masses and the organized violence of reaction.[4] Consequently, guerrilla warfare emerges as the proper political instrument—arising out of the characteristics of Latin American society itself and the political conditions imposed by the governing classes in that society.

The guerrillas' presence tends to alter the situation in which peasants, sharecroppers, squatters, peons, and Indians live. These people are condemned to an existence which follows the same unchanging routine from year to year, from decade to decade, from generation to generation, until it assumes in their minds the proportions of an immutable natural order. Nevertheless, that ideology includes moral and ethical values, such as self-respect, pride, honesty, justice, and rectitude, which, although adjusted to the prevailing material and intellectual conditions of life, enter into sharp contradiction with their impoverished and humiliating lot.

It is on this ideological plane, generated in a spontaneous process, that a link is established between the guerrillas, political militants in the vanguard of the struggle, and the peasants, sharecroppers, peons, Indians, etc.

First, communication must be established in order to promulgate the idea of revolution, and later, to make it seem desirable and possible. But the peasant's limited intellectual horizon does not call for a thorough exposition of that possibility, but for a palpable and irrefutable demonstration. Thus, the guerrillas must necessarily show the method or means of victory—and that is nothing less than the demonstration of violence—to ensure, above all, their own survival. If they manage to survive and defeat the reactionary armed forces they will have proved that their idea was brilliant and well expressed, as well as feasible.

The peasant is right to demand guarantees and he should receive them. He is being asked first to join the guerrilla band and later the people's army, decisions which are of vital importance in his life.

It is a question of making a clean break with a familiar routine and embarking upon another, radically different way of life, if not on the basic material plane, then in outlook and

---

[4] The development of the guerrilla struggle and its transformation into a conventional war of position between the people's army and the government army has been analyzed by Che Guevara in his *Guerrilla Warfare*, New York: Monthly Review Press, 1960.

reaction. It is a break which presupposes the conscious choice
of a path from which "there is no turning back," for by deciding
to become an active agent in the destruction of the existing
social order, he condemns himself irremediably in the eyes of
the ruling classes and their instruments of repression: the army
and the police.

Now that the idea of the imminent revolution has been
dissipated by the revolutionary experience of the past few years,
the outlook is for a protracted struggle, whose duration nobody
can predict. Under these circumstances it is no exaggeration
to say that the decision to join in the guerrilla struggle is
tantamount to consciously accepting the "death" of the social
being one has been until that moment, in order to be born again
as a totally different individual. Consequently, it should not
surprise us that the young people show more resolution in supporting the guerrilla struggle in Latin America.

To assume that resignation and conformity must prevail over
the revolutionary decision is to condemn from the outset any
revolutionary strategy based on the guerrilla struggle. Such an
assumption begins by denying that the military instrument
needed to seize power can become a reality. That is why
possibilities offered by bourgeois reformism are put forward, to
change the peasants' alternative from violence or resignation to
violence or hope.

Because there is much ignorance of revolutionary psychology
and sociology, the case must rest on the facts. Until now revolutionary attitudes have been sufficiently widespread to create and
maintain guerrilla forces—mostly made up of the country
people—for years in Venezuela, Colombia, and Guatemala.
One can say, with Fidel Castro, that one has faith in mankind,
because there are moments in history when ideology overrides
and leaves behind all other social influences. In Latin America
there is a small country of seven million people that decided to
defy the most powerful empire in the world and confronted it
under the threat of atomic bombs. This kind of attitude inspires
faith in the common man.

Illiteracy does not make the decision to *join the guerrillas* any
less crucial for the peasant or Indian than it is for the intellectual. While the dilemma may not present itself in the same way,
or in the same terms, it is essentially the same. The former have
over the latter only the advantage of being able to adapt themselves more rapidly to the material conditions of the struggle.

To fail to understand this is to fall, from the outset, into a grave error of judgment regarding the peasant as a human being.

Forced into action by the very society he seeks to destroy, the guerrilla becomes an instrument of "politics through force of arms," and is at an extraordinary disadvantage in any comparison of military forces. That is why the military phase has such dramatic importance and why the finest policy can easily end up as nothing but a lovely dream if it fails to operate correctly on the military level. For this reason the two most outstanding works on revolutionary strategy and tactics which have appeared in Latin America in the past few years—Che Guevara's *Guerrilla Warfare* and Régis Debray's *Revolution in the Revolution?*—place such emphasis on military questions, although both are essentially political works.

Consequently, the need for combat and for continuity in the struggle stressed by the new Latin American revolutionaries is no mere expression of "petit-bourgeois desperation" or a "militarist deviationism," to employ stereotyped phrases which no longer mean very much. The new revolutionaries stubbornly insist on the need to demonstrate to the masses again and again the method or lever which can make victory possible. Their purpose is the constant reenactment of the "way out"—the means of escape from the social dilemma in which the exploited masses are trapped both in the countryside and in the city.

If there is anything which is fatal to the guerrilla struggle as the active expression of a revolutionary movement, it is its political *nonexistence* in the public arena; its absence from the national, or at least the regional, panorama during the preliminary phase. It must not be forgotten that the primary objective of the revolutionary vanguard is to organize the masses and launch them as a solid bloc toward a final confrontation with the military apparatus of the government. But this task calls for contact with the masses, who must be imbued with ideological conviction if they are to be ready and willing to take the revolutionary step at the proper time. This process begins slowly— individual by individual at the beginning—but it progressively gains momentum and finally leads to active participation en masse at the crucial moment.

Although the unfavorable balance of military and political forces at the outset of the new phase of the revolutionary struggle may force the vanguard to select the most favorable politico-military terrain (usually the countryside, or even the

mountains, where society has a peasant social base), this does
not mean that it should refrain from national political action in
order to concentrate *exclusively* on the peasantry. The theory of
the guerrilla "pocket" cannot be reduced to a simple mechanical
determinist process. If the guerrillas isolate themselves at the
beginning, both geographically and politically, by concentrating
on action which unfolds outside the traditional political arena
where political force becomes *visible,* they do so simply *because
they have no alternative but to do so.*

But if there is an opportunity or possibility of making a debut
on the national or international political stage, it would be an
unpardonable error to neglect it. All the guerrilla efforts are
ultimately directed to playing the leading role on that stage, and
emerging as the most important political force in the nation on
the basis of their military power and their support by the
majority of the population.

To struggle under the most favorable conditions and in the
most effective manner does not exclude a priori any type of
struggle, but poses the problem of choosing the most suitable
methods for each occasion. This coordination consists of the
development of methods of struggle in which first the guerrillas
and later the people's army can *dominate* the situation. To
emerge in and gradually dominate the national political arena is
therefore the expression on that ultimately decisive plane of the
combat effectiveness of the new politico-military vanguard.

The Cuban experience illustrates this strategy. From July 26,
1953, to December 2, 1956 (the *Granma* landing), Fidel
Castro waged an intense political struggle, which resulted in the
creation and popularization of the eminently political 26th of
July Movement. When Castro returned to Cuba from Mexico
aboard the yacht *Granma,* that movement was sufficiently
powerful to attempt an insurrection in Santiago de Cuba under
the command of Frank País, an outstanding revolutionary
leader. That País remained in the lowlands shows the importance Castro attached to an active presence in the national
political arena. Nevertheless, the guerrilla struggle dominated
over all other methods, and was in turn directed toward the
formation of a people's army which would make it possible to
destroy Batista's armed forces, a necessary precondition for the
forces headed by Fidel Castro to seize power.

But the 26th of July Movement was also active in the
clandestine armed struggle in the cities. By acts of sabotage and

propaganda coups it kept constantly in the minds of the city populations throughout the country the presence of a revolutionary struggle, the heart of which was in the Sierra Maestra, 1,000 kilometers from Havana, isolated from the masses of the people. Thanks to the 26th of July Movement, contact was established; first by clandestine propaganda and later through a radio station in the mountains. In this way the Cuban guerrilla movement was able to steal the spotlight on the national political stage, arousing the expectations of the masses. It is not accidental that the Latin American governments whose countries harbor guerrilla bands appear to have adopted a policy of politically isolating those forces or of giving the impression that the guerrillas' forces are insignificant.

Although it is imperative for the guerrillas to dominate the national political scene, it does not justify conditioning the development of the armed struggle to that objective. To fear political isolation is to fall into the trap of political opportunism, and it implies betrayal of the main objective of the revolutionary struggle. That objective is the destruction of the government military apparatus supported by the military missions and even the Armed Forces of American imperialism.

THE NATIONAL BOURGEOISIE

Just as the myth of the antifeudal revolution survives in Latin America, so another myth persists: that the contradictions with imperialist capital will eventually make the national bourgeoisie take an anti-imperialist stand.

The protests of Third World bourgeois governments over the deterioration in the terms of exchange of their exports or the reestablishment of diplomatic and commercial relations with the socialist countries are seen by some as clear signs of a progressively more anti-imperialist attitude on the part of the national bourgeoisies. This is a fallacy. Then there are others whose personal observations of well-known developments have long since dispelled such delusions, but who still hope for a miracle from the "contradiction" between imperialism and the national bourgeoisie and continue to talk about vague and mysterious "patriotic forces" anxious to put an end to colonialism.

There is still much talk about the alliance between imperialism and the "most reactionary forces" in Latin America (meaning the landowning oligarchy), which the national bourgeoisie as a force, because it discerns its differences with both, opposes. In this way, one searches desperately for political justification to consider the national bourgeoisie as a circumstantially and temporarily progressive element in the "democratic and anti-imperialist" struggle.

All this vividly recalls the alliance against the imperialist invader—a policy which was put into practice by the Chinese Communists during the anti-Japanese war of liberation. Unfortunately, the concrete historical context differs very substantially from present conditions in Latin America.

The main role of the national bourgeoisie in the social structure of Latin America stems from its position in the productive process. In this sense it stands at the apex of the social pyramid and constitutes the highest national economico-technical link in the chain of exploitation which stretches from top to bottom of Latin American societies.

The national bourgeoisie is seated on top of a volcano and knows it. In this continent the Cuban Revolution has served to alert it to its fate should it fail to maintain control over the body politic. The landowning oligarchy is also well aware of the situation, and that is one reason why the alliance between these two classes has been reinforced.

But the post-Cuban political situation in this continent is not all that has tended to cement international solidarity between the hemisphere's national bourgeoisies and the United States. There are also underlying causes in the very structure of the Latin American societies themselves. Like it or not, the Latin American economies are molded by fully developed capitalism, and concretely in this case by American capitalism.

Unable to produce their own means of production, or at least unable to manufacture goods of like quality and with the same efficiency, the Latin American economies depend on the central hub of world capitalism for their supply. To that end they must obtain the elusive convertible foreign currency they need by exporting their products and taxing the concessions granted to foreign capital. In both respects they are captives of the United States. The dollars they receive are Yankee dollars and it is to that country that they must go for the purchases they require. Any attempt to divert those purchases to other countries results in a restriction of the market granted them in the United States.

They are organically linked to the American economy and this dependency is their lifeline.

Moreover, the foreign investments constitute an extension of the American economy into the territories of Latin American countries. To visit an American copper mine in Chile it is necessary to apply to the company offices for a permit to enter an area which is not merely private, but foreign property. Thus, the two economies are solidly linked and the national economy is a mere appendage of the American economy.

Nobody likes to play second fiddle in his own house but the national bourgeoisie has no choice but to accept and endure this situation. However aggressive the bourgeoisie may be within their own country, and even in the Latin American sphere, they are perfectly well aware that the best deals—those of greatest scope and magnitude—are closed to it, or at most its participation is limited to a minority share, intended as a sop to nationalist sentiment. We find that the trade names of American companies producing for Latin American markets reflect the name of the Latin American country or contain the word "national," and that there are a small number of prominent nationals in the list of stockholders.

It would be hard to find a clearer example of this situation than the famous "Chileanization" of the copper industry by the "revolutionary" Frei government. That regime, which has even been cited by socialist political experts as an example of anti-imperialism, managed not only to perpetuate Yankee domination of the Chilean copper industry, but also to make the national resources available to the American companies for the expansion of their operations.

Desperately anxious to expand its investments, but blocked by the chronic dollar shortage which made it impossible to import the necessary plant and installations, the Chilean national bourgeoisie devised a plan. So that foreign exploitation of the nation's copper might generate a larger flow of foreign exchange into the country's economy, without having to increase the American companies' taxes, the Frei government offered them sufficient guarantees to persuade them to expand production 100 percent. In addition, from its own funds and international loans guaranteed by the Chilean state, it supplied them with more than 70 percent of the necessary investment capital.

The national bourgeoisie not only renounced any possibility

of investing those dollars for itself, in order to expand its investments and venture into the international market, it also handed over control of those funds to the Yankee companies in exchange for being made a "partner," through the state, in some of the copper enterprises. Such behavior on the part of a national bourgeoisie reputed to be one of the strongest and most aggressive on the continent leaves little room for doubt about its subordinate role in the economic sphere.

Even to suppose that the national bourgeoisie could constitute a political force in any confrontation with imperialism is to misunderstand completely the Latin American reality. Such a confrontation, on a revolutionary plane, implies the nationalization of American property and the severing of the umbilical cord of dependence on that country. The Cuban experience leaves no room for doubt about the American reaction to such a situation. And the experience of Santo Domingo leaves even less doubt that reaction will occur long before anything of the sort can happen.

The national bourgeoisie is the natural guardian and main beneficiary of the existing social structure. If capitalistic production relationships were to disappear, the social structure would completely collapse, bringing down with it the production relations of absentee landlordism and the social and political foundations that sustain foreign productive relations, that is, American investments. So there is ample reason for landowners and capitalists, in their struggle for survival as classes, to join forces in a solid political alliance, to which American imperialism is prepared to give its full support, even when it does not take the problem of preservation of the social structure into its own hands.[5]

How could such a "theory" explain the readiness of the

[5] The leadership of the Venezuelan Communist Party, through one of its members, invoked the relatively small total of American investments in the country, concentrated mainly in the sugar industry, to explain the "facility" with which the revolution triumphed in Cuba. However, the revolutionary struggle against Yankee imperialism in Venezuela will necessarily be much longer and more difficult because it will encounter far greater resistance, because 60 percent of all American investment in Latin America is in Venezuela, concentrated in the production of oil.

Aside from the naïve "fetishism" according to which oil production is of greater "value" to capital than sugar production, it would seem, according to this Politburo member, that the resistance of American imperialism to any revolutionary development depends on the magnitude of its investments in that country.

United States to intervene in Santo Domingo (initially with 40,000 men)? How can it explain Vietnam? It is known that Yankee investments in the southern part of that country (as of 1966) did not exceed $300 million. Nevertheless, the American Government was spending some $25 billion a year on that war.* It would be strange economic arithmetic indeed that could reconcile the Venezuelan Communist Party's theory with these facts!

Everything tends to show that imperialism reaches its decisions on intervention in a particular country without regard to the magnitude of its economic interests at stake there, or, and this is the same thing, *as if all its interests were concentrated there*. (See open letter from Teodoro Petkoff to Mario Menéndez in *Política,* February 14, 1967, Mexico.)

Let us not forget that we are dealing with American imperialism, a historical instrument of world-wide scope, whose interests span the entire globe and hold captive in that network not only the countries of Latin America, but the entire Third World. Every link in the chain is vitally important to the whole, quite apart from additional reasons which may further intensify interest in a particular country.

Not only are the peoples held captive in the network of American imperialism, but so are their respective ruling classes. This is at the root of the remarkable international solidarity to be found among the forces of the world counterrevolution, especially in Latin America. The activities of the OAS (so aptly known as the "Colonial Office") on the political level, and the formation of inter-American and Central-American armed forces on the military level, clearly reveal the strength of the bond between these different interests.

Unfortunately for us, the counterrevolution is firmly united at the international level, in contrast to the division among left-wing forces.

The alternative which confronts the national bourgeoisie in every Latin American country today is whether to continue to play a secondary role at the apex of the Latin American social pyramid or be liquidated as a class. If it chooses the former, it must rely on the military and financial support of American imperialism. Again the Cuban experience is instructive. Without Yankee intervention until it was too late, the national bourgeoisie—which was undoubtedly very weak, in any case—was

* $75 billion by mid-1968 (ed.).

ejected from its positions, with no possibility of effectively resisting the impetus of the revolution.

This would not be repeated now in Argentina, Brazil, or Chile, where the Cuban lesson has been carefully weighed by the governing classes, and where they have had more than seven years to prepare. But who would trust in the power of these classes against the onslaught of the revolution? Without Yankee support they are nothing. For the national bourgeoisie in Latin America, as well as the landowning oligarchy, the bourgeois-democratic machinery is no longer reliable.

That system can function to the extent that the popular forces resign themselves to waging a political battle under the conditions imposed by the ruling classes. As Régis Debray has written in *Revolution in the Revolution?*: "Oligarchical dictatorships face the alternative of beginning to destroy them *en bloc* or of accepting them *en bloc*: there is no middle way."

Debray's assertion, more than any other, has stung those who say they accept the necessity of armed struggle in the present Latin American situation—but not in their own country; for it is always easier to agree to the general, rather than the particular. They will say that tactical theory is demonstrated in practice, and that in certain politically "advanced" countries the existence of a powerful left-wing movement, organized under the banner of Marxist parties with full legal status, clearly contradicts this assertion. Such, for example, would be the case of Chile.

But what are the terms of this class equilibrium? Respect for the bourgeois legal and constitutional forms, that is, for the rules of the game imposed by the other side. Those left-wing forces are well aware that the moment they significantly breach the rules of coexistence that equilibrium will break down. The brute force at the command of the bourgeoisie will be implacably used to prevent disruption of the established order. In the countryside, any action by the political organizations not confined to the trade-union and economic spheres will face violence from the absentee landlords as well as the rural constabularies.

The idea that it is possible to combat reactionary violence with revolutionary nonviolence is reminiscent of the situation in India before it received its independence. It is clear, however, exactly to whom the English handed independence in that country, and what has happened since.

In Latin America a class policy to mobilize the masses

behind a revolutionary transformation calls for controlled violence to answer the violence which will be unleashed by the classes in power as soon as they feel threatened.

To suppose that it is possible to escape this historical dilemma is to accept the coexistence of classes within the bourgeois framework. "The end of an epoch, the epoch of relative class equilibrium," writes Régis Debray in *Revolution in the Revolution?*. "The beginning of another, that of total class warfare, excluding compromise solutions and sharing power."

The end of an epoch, indeed: the epoch of left-wing reformism!

ECONOMIC AND SOCIAL DYNAMICS
OF BOURGEOIS REFORMISM

It has been argued that the policy of reformist economic development endows Latin American societies with a dynamic that brings about substantial change in the class structure. In this way, it is contended, the social base for guerrilla struggle—the peasantry—gradually tends to decrease because of the slight but noticeable reformist efforts. This line of argument, which expresses very well the neocolonial strategy of North American imperialism for Latin America, calls for a reply.

The behavior of the most outstanding structural characteristics of Latin American societies needs to be examined in relation to prospects for neocolonial economic development.

The following questions must be answered:

(1) What forces will bring about a change in certain production relationships among the population?
(2) What changes will result from a change in the relative importance of the different classes within the social structure?
(3) What structural changes can be provoked by this social dynamic within the neocolonial framework: appearance of new production relationships and disappearance of old ones? This brings us directly to the historical perspective that can be assigned to neocolonial reformism.

The answer to each question provides the elements necessary to answer the following one.

Let us concentrate on the two principal forms that explain the social dynamic: demographic and economic development for increasing productivity.

The first question involves situating both the projected population increase and size of the present population in the various production relationships that exist. At the present 3 percent annual rate of growth the population of Latin America will have doubled at the end of the next twenty-five years and will triple within forty years. How can this growth be absorbed within the neocolonial framework?

It is easy to become alarmed at the reformist threat. It is much more difficult—it is impossible—to show that imperialism and the national bourgeoisie are capable of coping with this human avalanche, or of solving the critical economic situation on the Latin American continent today. It requires material resources that can be accumulated and transformed into capital. Reformism will not be carried out through feudal-type relations of production. As soon as the population problem is solved, still more capital will be needed to make the present population "conform" to the neocolonial status and forget the revolution.

According to the United Nations' Economic Council for Latin America (ECLA) between 1950 and 1966 the real per capita income of Latin America has grown at the cumulative rate of 1.5 percent annually. At this rate of growth, a half century would be needed to double it. In Latin America the average life span is fifty years and many Latin Americans—for example, the miners and the Indians of the Andes—have an even shorter life span.

It might be thought that considerable progress has been made in these last seventeen years. For example, with the creation of the Alliance for Progress in 1961, conditions might very possibly have improved for neocolonialism in Latin America. It cannot be denied that at that meeting the United States promised $20,000 million over a ten-year period, and if we take reformism seriously we must agree that they take their commitments seriously. Nevertheless, after the famous Punta del Este Conference the rate of economic growth declined to a pitiful 1.0 percent annually. That is what the first five years of the Alliance for Progress accomplished.

But the teachings of the past are not valid now! According to the left-wing spokesmen of neocolonial reformism a new era has opened in the history of imperialism in Latin America—the era of Latin American economic integration. Impressed by the brilliant successes of the European Economic Community (the Common Market) and the European Association of Free Trade, they try to apply mechanically these experiences to Latin America.

What is the idea? Why do they make this comparison? For the neocolonialists American economic integration means the Latin American states, with their respective internal investments of Yankee capital, form one regional market isolated by tariff barriers from the rest of the world. The shark together with the sardines, but now in a fishbowl.

The experiences of European regional integrations indicate there would be development for all—of course, more for the North American capitalists than for those of Latin America. And there would also be exploitation of this region by the United States. Anyway, Latin America would see an upsurge in economic growth, and with it a general rise in the standard of living.

The development of the capitalist relationships would increase still further the sphere of influence of the developed zones of the continent and would precipitate large-scale peasant migration to the cities. Eventually not only the exploited masses but also the principal contradictions of the region would be concentrated there.

Relegating to Latin America low technological level production activities and keeping for themselves high technological level production activities, the United States would exploit our continent by building factories obsolete by North American standards and develop industries appropriate to underdevelopment. The unequal exchange would succeed in further strengthening the United States' higher standard of living. In this way our countries would become literally the outlying districts of the North American economy.

But all this is an old story. The future which threatens us is our past and our present. If anybody believes that the United States needs Latin American economic integration to better exploit Latin America, he does not know North American imperialism.

In the first place the idea of Latin American economic integration was born ten years ago in Latin America (in Chile, to be precise) as a bourgeois solution to limited national markets, and thus revealed that the Chileans do not have the slightest intention of carrying out the classic "bourgeois revolution" against the feudal land estate oligarchy which still dominates Latin American agriculture. Furthermore, the idea was only an illusory attempt to compete with the United States for the Latin American market—a naïve idea given the strength of Yankee capitalism. While they unite and integrate, the North American capitalists take over, as they have always taken over, the most lucrative investment opportunities when it is not to their advantage to continue exporting from the metropolises.

In what way could neocolonial development change the relative importance of classes in Latin American societies?

Let us concede at the outset that neocolonialism spurs migration from the rural areas to the cities—a supposition that implies that it should first be capable of absorbing at least a part of the big cities' marginal population.

Quantitatively, the weight of the industrial workers and the marginal population of the cities would increase, and the relative importance of the peasants, sharecroppers, squatters, Indian communities, and agricultural laborers would diminish.

How would the Latin American social structure be changed thereby? The gap between the upper and lower strata would be even greater. Wealth would be polarized even more between the cities and the interior of the country. Except for relative change in the importance of classes, the social context and its class problems would remain intact. In the political sense the upper strata of the workers would become more reformist and the lower strata potentially more revolutionary. If the structure is maintained, reformist development would succeed in making the social contradictions more acute instead of relieving them.

Nevertheless, to concede that it is possible to increase rural migration to the cities is to concede that reformism will be capable of solving the continent's agricultural problem—either by increasing agricultural productivity, or that failing, by importing food.

To increase agricultural productivity means that modern technology must be widely introduced, so the benefits will offset migration to the city and keep food available. If modern technology is used effectively, the advantage enjoyed by the agricultures of developed countries would progressively lessen.

It is not merely a matter of raising the technological level of Latin American agriculture but of making technological production profitable for agricultural capitalists and big landholders of the continent when compared with imported food (subsidized by the large economic powers) and when compared with other investment opportunities in the country.

To achieve development of agriculture has been the policy of many more-or-less reformist governments of Latin America during the postwar period. The results can be seen. According to the United Nations' Food and Agriculture Organization (FAO) between 1952–53 and 1964–65 production per capita has not risen in Latin America; rather, it has even dropped slightly. Compared to the prewar level, it is 8 percent lower. And every year the balance-of-payments noose draws tighter and tighter as capitalist accumulation strangles the continent.

Thus ECLA reports that between 1950 and 1963 the population of Latin America increased 4 percent while the net capacity to import rose only 34 percent. On the other hand, between 1948 and 1965 the imports of animal-husbandry products increased 70 percent.

To suppose, therefore, that increased rural migration to the cities will result from reformism is to ignore completely the economic and agricultural problems that confront the countries of the continent.

Those who are alarmed by reformism must focus on the most backward social relations of production: the feudal relationship between the owners of the vast estates and the peasants. They wield the "threat" of the reformist agrarian reform.

Since the Cuban Revolution the agrarian-reform question has become fashionable in Latin America. There is hardly a sellout government or bourgeois party in all Latin America that does not demagogically brandish the subject of land reform. But in the past eight years there has not been a single meaningful land reform in the whole continent.

Perhaps Chile provides the best example of class alliance between the oligarchies. Frei, with his proposed land reform, set out to create 100,000 new landowners in the course of his regime. Several years have passed since he sent his proposed law to Congress. When the debate was over, the project was not the same. Now there are to be only 40,000 landowners and the terms of the land reform have changed; included are terms the landholding oligarchy laid down before it would lend its "aid." The farce of representative bourgeois democracy was outdone only by the farce of "differences" between landowners and industrial capitalists.

After this attempt—the most serious and profound—it is not worthwhile to continue speaking of bourgeois land reform in Latin America, except to repeat that land is only one of the problems faced by the peasants and agricultural laborers. Even if a solution could be arrived at, isolated, it does not solve their situation within Latin American society.

Let us stop speaking of land reform, because it has become a fetish. The peasants' problem is not land reform, but rather a change of the social regime in its entirety.

Everything indicates that neocolonial reformism will be carried out within the structural framework typical of Latin American societies and that this reformism does not attempt or demand a reshaping of the structures—at least not in the lifetime of most of those who live in Latin America today. As Gunder Frank says, if anything is developed, it will be a matter of "developing the underdevelopment."

Message to the Tricontinental*

CHE GUEVARA

Now is the time
of the furnaces, and only
light should be seen.

José Martí

TWENTY-ONE years have already elapsed since the end of the last world conflagration; numerous publications in every possible language celebrate this event, symbolized by the defeat of Japan. There is a climate of apparent optimism in many areas of the different camps into which the world is divided.

Twenty-one years without a world war, in these times of maximum confrontations, of violent clashes and sudden changes, appears to be a very long time. However, without analyzing the practical results of this peace (poverty, degradation, increasing exploitation of enormous sectors of humanity) for which all of us have stated that we are willing to fight, we would do well to inquire if this peace is real.

It is not the purpose of these notes to detail the different conflicts of a local character that have been occurring since the surrender of Japan, neither do we intend to recount the numerous and increasing instances of civilian strife which have taken place during these years of apparent peace. It will be enough just to name, as an example against undue optimism, the wars of Korea and Viet Nam.

In the first of these, after years of savage warfare, the northern part of the country was submerged in the most terrible

* Pamphlet, written in some unknown guerrilla camp in Latin America, published in Havana in 1967. Official Cuban translation.

devastation known in the annals of modern warfare: riddled with bombs; without factories, schools, or hospitals; with absolutely no shelter for housing ten million inhabitants.

Under the discredited flag of the United Nations, dozens of countries under the military leadership of the United States participated in this war, with the massive intervention of U.S. soldiers and the use, as cannon fodder, of the drafted South Korean population. On the other side, the army and the people of Korea and the volunteers from the People's Republic of China were furnished with supplies and technical aid by the Soviet military apparatus. The United States tested all sorts of weapons of destruction, excluding the thermonuclear type, but including, on a limited scale, bacteriological and chemical warfare.

In Viet Nam, the patriotic forces of that country have carried on an almost uninterrupted war against three imperialist powers: Japan, whose might suffered an almost vertical collapse after the bombs of Hiroshima and Nagasaki; France, which recovered from that defeated country its Indo-China colonies and ignored the promises it had made in harder times; and the United States, in this last phase of the struggle.

There have been limited confrontations in every continent, although in Our America, for a long time, there were only incipient liberation struggles and military coups d'état until the Cuban Revolution sounded the alert, signaling the importance of this region. This action attracted the wrath of the imperialists and Cuba was finally obliged to defend its coasts, first in Playa Girón, and again during the October Crisis.

This last incident could have unleashed a war of incalculable proportions if a U.S.-Soviet clash had occurred over the Cuban question. But, evidently, the focal point of all contradictions is at present the territory of the peninsula of Indo-China and the adjacent areas. Laos and Viet Nam are torn by civil wars which have ceased being such by the entry into the conflict of U.S. imperialism with all its might, thus transforming the whole zone into a dangerous powder keg, ready at any moment to explode. In Viet Nam the confrontation has assumed extremely acute characteristics. It is not our intention, either, to chronicle this war. We shall simply remember and point out some milestones.

In 1954, after the annihilating defeat of Dien Bien Phu, an agreement was signed at Geneva dividing the country into two separate zones; elections were to be held within a term of eighteen months to determine who should govern Viet Nam and how the country should be reunified. The United States did not sign this document and started maneuvering to substitute the emperor, Bao Dai, who was a French puppet, for a man more amenable to its purposes. This happened to be Ngo Dinh Diem, whose tragic end—an orange squeezed dry by imperialism—is well known by all.

During the months following the agreement, optimism reigned supreme in the camp of the popular forces. The last redoubts of the anti-French resistance were dismantled in the South of the country—and they awaited the fulfillment of the Geneva Agreements. But the patriots soon realized there would be no elections—unless the United States felt itself capable of imposing its will in the polls, which was practically impossible, even resorting to all its fraudulent methods. Once again fighting broke out in the South and gradually acquired full intensity. At present the U.S. invading army has increased to nearly half a million troops, while the puppet forces decrease in number and, above all, have totally lost their will to fight.

Almost two years ago the United States started systematically bombing the Democratic Republic of Viet Nam, in yet another attempt to overcome the resistance of the South and impose, from a position of strength, a meeting at the conference table. At first, the bombardments were more or less isolated occurrences and were represented as reprisals for alleged provocations from the North. Later on, as they increased in intensity and regularity, they became one gigantic attack carried out by the Air Force of the United States, day after day, for the purpose of destroying all vestiges of civilization in the Northern zone of the country. This is an episode of the infamously notorious "escalation."

The material aspirations of the Yankee world have been fulfilled to a great extent, despite the unflinching defense of the Vietnamese antiaircraft artillery, of the numerous planes shot down (over 1,700) and of the socialist countries' aid in war supplies.

This is the sad reality: Viet Nam—a nation representing the aspirations, the hopes of a whole world of forgotten peoples—is tragically alone. This nation must endure the furious attacks of U.S. technology, with practically no possibility of reprisals in the South and only some of defense in the North—but always alone.

The solidarity of all progressive forces of the world with the people of Viet Nam today is similar to the bitter irony of the plebeians urging on the gladiators in the Roman arena. It is not a matter of wishing success to the victim of aggression, but of sharing his fate; one must accompany him to his death or to victory.

When we analyze the lonely situation of the Vietnamese people, we are overcome by anguish at this illogical fix in which humanity finds itself.

U.S. imperialism is guilty of aggression—its crimes are enormous and cover the whole world. We already know all that, gentlemen! But this guilt also applies to those who, when the time came for a definition, hesitated to make Viet Nam an inviolable part of the socialist world, running, of course, the risks of a war on a global scale—but also forcing a decision upon imperialism. The guilt also applies to those who maintain a war of abuse and maneuvering—started quite some time ago by the representatives of the two greatest powers of the socialist camp.

We must ask ourselves, seeking an honest answer: Is Viet Nam isolated, or is it not? Is it not maintaining a dangerous equilibrium between the two quarreling powers?

And what great people these are! What stoicism and courage! And what a lesson for the world is contained in this struggle! Not for a long time shall we be able to know if President Johnson ever seriously thought of bringing about some of the reforms needed by his people—to iron out the barbed class contradictions that grow each day with explosive power. The truth is that the improvements announced under the pompous title of the "Great Society" have been poured down the drain of Viet Nam.

The largest of all imperialist powers feels in its own guts the bleeding inflicted by a poor and underdeveloped country; its fabulous economy feels the strain of the war effort. Murder is ceasing to be the most convenient business for its monopolies. Defensive weapons, and never in adequate number, is all these extraordinary Vietnamese soldiers have—besides love for their homeland, their society, and unsurpassed courage. But imperialism is bogging down in Viet Nam, is unable to find a way out, and desperately seeks one that will overcome with dignity this dangerous situation in which it now finds itself. Furthermore, the Four Points put forward by the North and the Five Points of the South now corner imperialism, making the confrontation even more decisive.

Everything indicates that peace, this unstable peace which bears the name for the sole reason that no world-wide conflagration has taken place, is again in danger of being destroyed by some irrevocable and unacceptable step taken by the United States.

What role shall we, the exploited people of the world, play? The peoples of the three continents focus their attention on Viet Nam and learn their lesson. Since imperialists blackmail humanity by threatening it with war, the wise reaction is not to fear war. The general tactics of the people should be to launch a constant and a firm attack on all fronts where the confrontation is taking place.

In those places where the meager peace we have has been violated, what is our duty? To liberate ourselves at any price.

The world panorama is of great complexity. The struggle for liberation has not yet been undertaken by some countries of ancient Europe, sufficiently developed to realize the contradictions of capitalism, but weak to such a degree that they are unable either to follow imperialism or to start on their own road. Their contradictions will reach an explosive stage during the forthcoming years—but their problems, and consequently their solutions, are different from those of our dependent and economically underdeveloped countries.

The fundamental field of imperialist exploitation comprises the three underdeveloped continents: America, Asia, and Africa. Every country also has its own characteristics, but each continent, as a whole, also presents a certain unity. Our America is integrated by a group of more or less homogeneous countries, and in most parts of its territory U.S. monopoly capital maintains an absolute supremacy. Puppet governments, or, in the best of cases, weak and fearful local rulers, are incapable of contradicting orders from their Yankee master. The United States has nearly reached the climax of its political and economic domination; it could hardly advance much; any change in the situation could bring about a setback. Its policy is to maintain that which has already been conquered. The line of action, at the present time, is limited to the brutal use of force with the purpose of thwarting the liberation movements, no matter what type they might happen to be.

The slogan "We will not allow another Cuba" hides the

possibility of perpetrating aggressions without fear of reprisal, such as the one carried out against the Dominican Republic, or before that, the massacre in Panama—and the clear warning stating that Yankee troops are ready to intervene anywhere in America where the established order may be altered, thus endangering their interests. This policy enjoys an almost absolute impunity: the OAS is a suitable mask, in spite of its unpopularity; the inefficiency of the UN is ridiculous as well as tragic; the armies of all American countries are ready to intervene in order to smash their peoples. The International of Crime and Treason has in fact been organized. On the other hand, the national bourgeoisies have lost all their capacity to oppose imperialism—if they ever had it—and they have become the last card in the pack. There are no other alternatives: either a socialist revolution or a make-believe revolution.

Asia is a continent with different characteristics. The struggle for liberation waged against a series of European colonial powers resulted in the establishment of more or less progressive governments, whose evolution has brought about, in some cases, the reaffirmation of the primary objectives of national liberation, and in others, a setback toward the adoption of pro-imperialist positions.

From the economic point of view, the United States had very little to lose and much to gain in Asia. The changes benefited its interests; the struggle for the overthrow of other neocolonial powers and the penetration of new spheres of action in the economic field are carried out sometimes directly, occasionally through Japan.

But there are special political conditions in Asia, particularly in Indo-China, which create certain characteristics of capital importance and play a decisive role in the entire U.S. military strategy.

The imperialists encircle China through South Korea, Japan, Taiwan, South Viet Nam, and Thailand, at least.

This dual situation—a strategic interest as important as the military encirclement of the People's Republic of China and the penetration of these great markets, which they do not dominate yet—turns Asia into one of the most explosive points of the world today, in spite of its apparent stability outside of the Vietnamese war zone.

The Middle East, though geographically a part of this continent, has its own contradictions and is actively in ferment; it is impossible to foretell how far the cold war between Israel (backed by the imperialists) and the progressive countries of that zone will go. This is just another of the volcanoes threatening eruption in the world today.

Africa offers an almost virgin territory to the neocolonial invasion. There have been changes which, to some extent, forced neocolonial powers to give up their former absolute prerogatives. But when these changes are carried out without interruption, colonialism continues in the form of neocolonialism, with similar effects as far as the economic situation is concerned.

The United States had no colonies in this region but is now struggling to penetrate its partners' fiefs. It can be said that, following the strategic plans of U.S. imperialism, Africa constitutes its long-range reservoir; its present investments, though, are only important in the Union of South Africa and its penetration is beginning to be felt in the Congo, Nigeria, and other countries where a sharp rivalry with other imperialist powers is beginning to take place (nonviolent up to the present time).

So far it does not have great interests to defend there except its assumed right to intervene in every spot of the world where its monopolies detect the possibility of huge profits or the existence of large reserves of raw materials.

All this past history justifies our concern over the possibilities of liberating the peoples within a moderate or a short period of time.

If we stop to analyze Africa we observe that in the Portuguese colonies of Guinea, Mozambique, and Angola the struggle is waged with relative intensity, with particular success in the first and with variable success in the other two. We still witness in the Congo the dispute between Lumumba's successors and the old accomplices of Tshombe, a dispute which at the present time seems to favor the latter, those who have "pacified" a large area of the country for their own benefit—though the war is still latent.

In Rhodesia we have a different problem: British imperialism used every means within its reach to place power in the hands of the white minority, now in control. The conflict, from the British point of view, is absolutely unofficial; this Western power, with its habitual diplomatic cleverness—also called hypocrisy in plain language—presents a façade of displeasure before the measures adopted by the government of Ian Smith.

Its crafty attitude is supported and followed by some Commonwealth countries, but is attacked by a large group of countries
belonging to Black Africa, even by some that are still docile
economic vassals of British imperialism. Should the efforts of
Rhodesia's black patriots to organize armed rebellion crystallize
and should this movement be effectively supported by neighboring African nations, the situation in that country could become
extremely explosive. But for the moment all these problems are
being discussed in such innocuous organizations as the UN, the
Commonwealth, and the OAU. Nevertheless, the social and
political evolution of Africa does not lead us to expect a continental revolution. The liberation struggle against the Portuguese
should end victoriously, but Portugal means nothing in the
imperialist field. The confrontations of revolutionary importance are those which place at bay all the imperialist apparatus,
though this does not mean that we should stop fighting for the
liberation of the three Portuguese colonies and for the deepen-
ing of their revolutions.

When the black masses of South Africa or Rhodesia start
their authentic revolutionary struggle, a new era will dawn in
Africa. Or when the impoverished masses of a nation rise up to
rescue their right to a decent life from the hands of the ruling
oligarchies. Up to now, army putsches have followed one
another; one group of officers succeeds another, or replaces
rulers who no longer serve their caste interests and those of the
powers who covertly manage them—but there are no great
popular upheavals. In the Congo these characteristics appeared
briefly, generated by the memory of Lumumba, but they have
been losing strength in the last few months.

In Asia, as we have seen, the situation is explosive. The
points of friction are not only Viet Nam and Laos, where actual
fighting is going on, but also Cambodia—where a direct U.S.
aggression may start at any time—Thailand, Malaya, and, of
course, Indonesia, where we cannot assume that the last word
has been said, despite the annihilation of the Communist Party
of that country carried out by the reactionaries when they took
power. And also, naturally, there is the Middle East.

In Latin America armed struggle is under way in Guatemala,
Colombia, Venezuela, and Bolivia, and the first uprisings are
appearing in Brazil. Other foci of resistance appear and are
later extinguished. But almost every country of this continent is
ripe for a type of struggle that, in order to achieve victory,

cannot be content with anything less than establishing a government of a socialist nature. On this continent, for all practical purposes, only one tongue is spoken (with the exception of Brazil, but those who speak Spanish can easily make themselves understood, owing to the great similarity of Spanish and Portuguese). There is also such a great similarity among the classes of the different countries that an identification exists among them, as an "international American" type, much more complete than that of other continents. Language, customs, religion, a common foreign master—unite them. The degree and forms of exploitation are similar for both the exploiters and the exploited in many of the countries of Our America. And rebellion is ripening swiftly.

We may ask ourselves: how will this rebellion come to fruition? What type will it be? We have maintained for quite some time now that, owing to the similarity of national characteristics, the struggle in Our America will achieve, in due course, continental proportions. It will be the scene of many great battles fought for the liberation of humanity. Within the overall struggle on a continental scale, the battles which are now taking place are only episodes—but they have already furnished their martyrs, who will figure in the history of Our America as having given their necessary quota of blood in this last stage of the fight for the total freedom of Man. These names will include Major Turcios Lima, the priest Camillo Torres, Major Fabricio Ojeda, Majors Lobatón and Luis de la Puente Uceda, all outstanding figures in the revolutionary movements of Guatemala, Colombia, Venezuela, and Peru.

But the active mobilization of the people creates new leaders. César Montes and Yon Sosa raise the flag of battle in Guatemala; Fabio Vázquez and Marulanda in Colombia; Douglas Bravo in the western half of the country and Américo Martín in El Bachiller direct their respective fronts in Venezuela. New uprisings will take place in these and other countries of Our America, as has already happened in Bolivia; they will continue to grow in the midst of all the hardships inherent to this dangerous profession of the modern revolutionary. Many will perish, victims of their errors; others will fall in the hard battle ahead; new fighters and new leaders will appear in the heat of the revolutionary struggle. The people will produce their fighters and leaders in the selective process of the war itself—and Yankee agents of repression will increase. Today there are military "advisers" in all the countries where armed struggle exists, and the Peruvian army, trained and advised by the Yankees, apparently carried out a successful action against the revolutionaries in that country. But if the foci of war grow with sufficient political and military wisdom, they will become practically invincible, obliging the Yankees to send reinforcements. In Peru itself many new figures, practically unknown, are now tenaciously and firmly reorganizing the guerrilla movement. Little by little, the obsolete weapons which are sufficient for the repression of small armed bands will be exchanged for modern armaments and the U.S. military "advisers" will be replaced by U.S. soldiers until, at a given moment, they will be forced to send increasingly greater numbers of regular troops to ensure the relative stability of a government whose national puppet army is disintegrating before the attacks of the guerrillas. It is the road of Viet Nam; it is the road that should be followed by the peoples of the world; it is the road that will be followed in Our America, with the special characteristic that the armed groups may create something like coordinating councils to frustrate the repressive efforts of Yankee imperialism and contribute to the revolutionary cause.

America, a forgotten continent in the world's more recent liberation struggles, which is now beginning to make itself heard through the Tricontinental in the voice of the vanguard of its peoples, the Cuban Revolution, has before it a task of much greater relevance: to create a second or a third Viet Nam, or the second and third Viet Nam of the world.

We must bear in mind that imperialism is a world system, the last stage of capitalism—and it must be defeated in a great world confrontation. The end of this struggle must be the destruction of imperialism. Our part, the responsibility of the exploited and underdeveloped of the world, is to eliminate the foundations of imperialism: our oppressed nations, from which they extract capital, raw materials, cheap technicians, and common labor, and to which they export new capital (instrument of domination), arms, and every kind of article, submerging us in absolute dependence.

The fundamental element of this strategic end is, then, the real liberation of all peoples, a liberation that will be brought about in most cases through armed struggle and will, in Our America, almost certainly have the characteristic of becoming a socialist revolution. In envisaging the destruction of imperialism, it is necessary to identify its head, which is no other than the United States of America.

We must carry out a general task which has as its tactical purpose drawing the enemy out of his natural environment, forcing him to fight in places where his living habits clash with the existing reality. We must not underrate our adversary; the U.S. soldier has technical capacity and is backed by weapons and resources of such magnitude as to render him formidable. He lacks the essential ideological motivation which his bitterest enemies of today—the Vietnamese soldiers—have in the highest degree. We will only be able to triumph over such an army by undermining its morale—and that is accomplished by causing it repeated defeats and repeated punishment.

But this brief scheme for victory implies immense sacrifice by the people, sacrifice that should be demanded beginning today, in plain words, and which perhaps may be less painful than what they would have to endure if we constantly avoided battle in an attempt to have others pull our chestnuts out of the fire.

It is probable, of course, that the last country to liberate itself will accomplish this without armed struggle and that people may be spared the sufferings of a long and cruel war against the imperialists. But perhaps it will be impossible to avoid this struggle or its effects in a global conflagration and the last country's suffering may be the same, or even greater. We cannot foresee the future, but we should never give in to the defeatist temptation of being leaders of a nation that yearns for freedom but abhors the struggle it entails and awaits its freedom as a crumb of victory.

It is absolutely just to avoid all useless sacrifice. For that reason, it is necessary to study carefully the real possibilities that dependent America may have of liberating itself through peaceful means. For us, the answer to this question is quite clear: the present moment may or may not be the proper one for starting the struggle, but we cannot harbor any illusions, and we have no right to do so, that freedom can be obtained without fighting. And the battles will not be mere street fights with stones against tear-gas bombs, nor pacific general strikes; neither will they be those of a furious people destroying in two or three days the repressive superstructure of the ruling oligarchies. The struggle will be long, harsh, and its battlefronts will be the guerrilla's refuge, the cities, the homes of the fighters —where the repressive forces will go seeking easy victims among their families—among the massacred rural population, in the villages or cities destroyed by the bombardments of the enemy.

They themselves impel us to this struggle: there is no alternative other than to prepare it and decide to undertake it. The beginnings will not be easy; they will be extremely difficult. All of the oligarchies' power of repression, all of their capacity for brutality and demagoguery will be placed at the service of their cause. Our mission, in the first hour, will be to survive; later, we will follow the perennial example of the guerrilla, carrying out armed propaganda in the Vietnamese sense (that is, the propaganda of bullets, of battles won or lost—but fought—against the enemy). The great lesson of the invincibility of the guerrillas will take root in the dispossessed masses. The galvanizing of national spirit, preparation for harder tasks, for resisting even more violent repressions. Hatred as an element of struggle; relentless hatred of the enemy that impels us over and beyond the natural limitations of man and transforms us into effective, violent, selective, and cold killing machines. Our soldiers must be thus; a people without hatred cannot vanquish a brutal enemy. We must carry the war as far as the enemy carries it: to his home, to his centers of entertainment, in a total war. It is necessary to prevent him from having a moment of peace, a quiet moment outside his barracks or even inside; we must attack him wherever he may be, make him feel like a cornered beast wherever he may move. Then his morale will begin to fall. He will become still more savage, but we shall see the signs of decadence begin to appear.

And let us develop a true proletarian internationalism, with international proletarian armies; let the flag under which we fight be the sacred cause of redeeming humanity, so that to die under the flag of Viet Nam, of Venezuela, of Guatemala, of Laos, of Guinea, of Colombia, of Bolivia, of Brazil—to name only a few scenes of today's armed struggle—be equally glorious and desirable for an American, an Asian, an African, or even a European. Each drop of blood spilled in a country under whose flag one has not been born is an experience for those who survive to apply later in the liberation struggle of their own countries. And each nation liberated is a step toward victory in the battle for the liberation of one's own country.

The time has come to settle our discrepancies and place everything we have at the service of the struggle.

We all know that great controversies agitate the world now fighting for freedom; no one can hide it. We also know that these controversies have reached such intensity and such bitterness that the possibility of dialogue and reconciliation seems extremely difficult, if not impossible. It is useless to search for means and ways to propitiate a dialogue which the hostile parties avoid. But the enemy is there; it strikes every day, and threatens us with new blows and these blows will unite us, today, tomorrow, or the day after. Whoever understands this first, and prepares for this necessary union, will earn the people's gratitude.

Because of the virulence and the intransigence with which each cause is defended, we, the dispossessed, cannot take sides with one or the other form of manifestation of these discrepancies, even if we at times coincide with the contentions of one party or the other, or in greater measure with those of one part than with those of the other. In time of war, the expression of current differences constitutes a weakness; but as things stand at this moment, it is an illusion to hope to settle these differences by means of words. Time will erase them or give them their true explanation.

In our struggling world, all discrepancies regarding tactics and methods of action for the attainment of limited objectives should be analyzed with the respect that the opinions of others deserve. Regarding our great strategic objective, the total destruction of imperialism via armed struggle, we should be uncompromising.

Our aspirations to victory may be summed up thus: total destruction of imperialism by eliminating its firmest bulwark— imperialist domination by the United States of America. To carry out, as a tactical measure, the gradual liberation of the peoples, one by one or in groups; forcing the enemy into a difficult fight far from its own territory; liquidation of all of its sustaining bases, that is, its dependent territories. This means a long war. And, we repeat once more, a cruel war. Let no one fool himself at the outset and let no one hesitate to begin for fear of the consequences it may bring to his people. It is almost our sole hope for victory. We cannot elude the call of this hour. Viet Nam is pointing it out with its endless lesson of heroism, its tragic and everyday lesson of struggle and death for the attainment of final victory.

There, the imperialist soldiers encounter the discomforts of those who, accustomed to the vaunted U.S. standard of living, must face a hostile land, the insecurity of those who are unable to move without being aware of walking on enemy territory, death to those who advance beyond their fortified encampments, the permanent hostility of an entire population. All this provokes internal repercussions in the United States and encourages the resurgence of a factor which was attenuated in the full vigor of imperialism: class struggle even within its own territory.

What a luminous, near future would be visible to us if two, three, or many Viet Nams flourished throughout the world with their share of death and their immense tragedies, their everyday heroism and their repeated blows against imperialism obliging it to disperse its forces under the attack and the increasing hatred of all the peoples of the earth! And if we were all capable of uniting to make our blows more solid and more infallible so that the effectiveness of every kind of support given to the struggling peoples were increased—how great and how near that future would be!

If we—those of us who on a small point of the world map, fulfill our duty and place at the disposal of this struggle whatever little we are able to give; our lives, our sacrifice—must some day breathe our last breath in any land not our own yet already ours, sprinkled with our blood, let it be known that we have measured the scope of our actions and that we consider ourselves no more than elements in the great army of the proletariat, but that we are proud to have learned from the Cuban Revolution, and from its maximum leader, the great lesson emanating from Cuba's attitude in this part of the world: "What do the dangers or the sacrifices of a man or of a nation matter, when the destiny of humanity is at stake?"

Our every action is a battle cry against imperialism, and a call for the peoples' unity against the great enemy of mankind: the United States of America. Wherever death may surprise us, it will be welcome, provided that this, our battle cry, reaches some receptive ear, that another hand be extended to take up our weapons and that other men come forward to intone our funeral dirge with the staccato of machine guns and new cries of battle and victory.

Toward Revolutionary Power*

✕✕✕
✕✕✕✕✕✕✕✕✕
✕✕✕✕✕✕✕✕

FABRICIO OJEDA

INTRODUCTION

RECENTLY I spoke to a close friend of mine. We discussed at length the current Venezuelan political scene. His opinions made me decide to write this book. The arguments he expressed —and I have always considered him to be a revolutionary within his own social class, the national bourgeoisie—revealed the great need for better understanding of the broad revolutionary problems that affect our country. We are a dependent nation, exploited by imperialism and its agents, and the life of the republic is controlled by oligarchs.

I noticed how his whole thought led him, along with reformist politicians, to feelings of fatalism, impotence, and resignation. In his mind (captive of the steady campaign of reactionary propaganda, which as Goebbels used to say, can turn lies into truths) there is room only for those ideas and strategies which fall within the framework of traditional politics. For my friend, as well as for all those who think like him, Venezuela and Latin America can change their present situations only in a slow and gradual way, without a head-on collision with oppressive forces. He believes that a struggle should develop, which, through the evolution of the present state, could progressively transform social, economic, and political institutions.

His arguments for this thesis are based upon the tremendous power of imperialism and the oligarchy, whose enormous force

* Written early in 1966 (Ojeda was murdered in jail June 21, 1966, by Venezuela's Armed Forces Intelligence Service), published in Havana in August, 1967, as a small book, *Hacia el poder revolucionario*. Translated by Morton Marks.

621

would be used against any revolutionary insurgency, or against any government which attempted to alter the present colonial situation.

These fatalistic ideas are present not only in my friend's thought. They populate the political thought of whole groups, in important sectors of the colonized, neocolonial and dependent world. In Venezuela, this also includes a large part of the working class who are under the influence of déclassé leaders in the service of reaction. Such a situation is not unique, and neither is that of my friend or of the traditional partisan cliques. The influence of reactionary ideas on the minds of the ruling groups is the logical product of the control that imperialism and the ruling bourgeoisie exercise on all the communications media, which they hold as a consequence of their control of political power.

We have already said that in the colonized, neocolonial, and dependent world, nothing escapes the control of imperialism. It grasps the basic tools for molding mind and consciousness. It owns the press, radio, television, and movies. It has in its service waiters, political leaders, governors, parliaments, historians, sociologists, et al., who, through all their activities, twist events, distort realities, and build an artificial world which, with the help of the state's coercive apparatus, fills the eyes and ears of an entire nation.

This is what is happening today and what has happened in the past. The present colonial regime prevents the free circulation of revolutionary literature and of new ideas in much the same way that the Spanish colonial regime forbade the reading of the French encyclopedists. The closing of bookstores such as Magrija and El Siglo was not done as a whim. Neither was the purge of leftist newspaper writers and workers at *El Nacional,* or the discrimination against scriptwriters and actors in the television and radio companies. It is all part of a policy—a well-studied, planned strategy applied by the ruling classes, the owners of the media, and the powerful interests who, through publishing contracts, finance the newspapers, magazines, reviews, etc.

Venezuela's neocolonial situation creates a state of affairs which many find incomprehensible if they refuse to accept what we really are: a dependent country. On the contrary, they rack their brains without ever clearly understanding the causes of our political crises, our economic development, our social system. As long as we view our country through a cracked lens, there will be a distorted image and unreal view whereby events appear as partial, circumstantial, and capricious. This is the case with the great majority of politicians, historians, and sociologists. It was the case with Laureano Villenilla Lanz, the old man with his pessimistic theory of the "necessary gendarme." And it is happening to many who are presently formulating their fatalistic theories concerning the revolutionary transformation of the country, the chance for its liberation, and the erasure of the causes of oppression and misery.

For a long time I shared these ideas. I honestly believed that our country and others in similar situations in the Western Hemisphere under the domain of the United States would remain in a situation of dependency. I also believed that, because we were of the same family—the international family —the older brother would not refuse aid to the younger. The older brother would not refuse a generous act, and would instead take the other brothers by the arm and lead them to a higher level, toward a state of full development which would enable them to have an independent existence. This mental image of mine, which required great personal effort to correct, was molded chiefly by those people for whom, in the desperation of my intellectual and political unease, I felt the greatest admiration. When I was seventeen I joined the URD* in Boronó, my hometown, where I had always lived. My joining the party followed an eloquent speech by Jóvito Villalba, whom I met that day and for whom I felt deep admiration for his struggles in 1928 and 1936. In 1948, after working for a year as a schoolteacher for the Creole Petroleum Corporation and simultaneously continuing my studies, I got to know Caracas, and turned the dream of every provincial into a reality. I lived for a long time in Caracas in the Urredista National House.

In his desire to aid my political career, Jóvito adopted an almost paternal attitude toward me. He recommended many books. The first was Harold Laski's *Introduction to Politics*. He

* Unión Republicana Democrática (URD), a liberal-left party that first opposed, then cooperated, and finally split with Rómulo Betancourt's ruling Acción Democrática (AD). "Urredismo" was Venezuela's last serious attempt at bringing about meaningful reforms through the electoral process. It failed (ed.).

spoke with me almost constantly, as did many of the prominent figures of Urredismo, such as Hernández Solís, Alfredo Tarre Murzi, Raúl Díaz Legórburu, Juan Manuel Domínquez Chacín, Humberto Bártoli, et al. Little by little they gave me greater responsibilities in public life. My thinking revolved around their advice and the books they put in my hands. For me the world was Jóvito's world. I imitated his gestures and even his tone of voice. I repeated as my own, in my first speeches, many of the expressions and phrases that he had made famous.

I had gone to Caracas to continue my studies. I planned to enroll in the National Pedagogic Institute, but politics completely absorbed me. I became enmeshed in its complex theories, with Jóvito firmly leading me by the arm. His opinions were like a dogma that I bewilderedly accepted. I listened to him discuss geopolitics and America's destiny to be united into one great nation. With him, I learned to examine our politics, but from his point of view. There are things to be done, he would always say, but not to be discussed. And those things that were in the political sphere could be done only after gaining power. But if they were discussed beforehand, they could never be carried, because they would be stopped by the powers of reaction.

The URD, he told me, apropos of a speech I had given in Cumaná, would come to power if we did not frighten the bourgeoisie and Americans with radical statements. What you are saying, he added, we will save for when we're in the government. Let's not talk about it now, because if we discuss it, we'll never be able to carry it out.

I timidly accepted the master's admonition, and only recently have I fully understood what it meant. It is the same argument that today is supported by large sectors of the country. There are many people under the same influence I was when I was reading only what the Urredista leaders recommended, when I did not try to find the truth nor break their intellectual bonds.

The personal story I have related is not an isolated case. It is the reason why the majority of speechmakers imitate Rómulo Betancourt, or they copy Caldera, and it is the reason why large sections of the population develop their own fatalistic and reformist political notions. Just as my own thought was influenced by the advice and lessons of the Urredista leaders, so too the minds of a great portion of humanity were influenced by the ideologies of imperialism and their agents.

THE SANCTIONED REVOLUTION OR
THE PRO-IMPERIALIST REFORM

Reactionary ideologists are unceasing in their efforts to fit thought into rigid patterns, within which state violence, with all its coercive agencies, plays a crucial role. They create an artificial world of freedom. Progressive ideas move unimpeded through proper channels. But only in this way, that is, through the proper channels, can one be a revolutionary, and that means revolutionary in a reactionary way. This type of revolutionary accepts the established rules, the imposed limits. Once those channels overflow and everyone is freed of feelings of submission and fatalism, state violence goes into action to defend "freedom."

This is a problem not limited only to Venezuela, nor even to Latin America, as when the Monroe Doctrine was in force. It is a problem for the whole colonized and dependent world. The progress and development of a nation is incompatible with colonial domination. In order to progress and develop, it is necessary to be freed from the economic and political domination that imperialism exercises, as well as from the oligarchic groups that have long controlled the instruments of political power.

In Venezuela, power has traditionally been in the hands of a strong and well-organized oligarchy. They are descendants of the creole nobility that rebelled first against the monopolistic control of the Companía Guipuzcoana and against the colonial laws of Spain. The obstacles created by Spanish domination to the expansion of the Venezuelan economy, by the need for the creole families to increase their profits, to join the international market, developed a power-oriented mentality in the leading socioeconomic groups. That is, the consciousness of winning and preserving power at any cost, the awareness of the uses of power on the part of the most powerful economic sector in our country, has been a constant force throughout our national history. Since independence was won from Spain, a process in which the creole nobility played a crucial role, the social composition of the Venezuelan government has been unvaried. Sociologists, historians, and politicians have developed the thesis of military-civilian struggle, in the sense that the two represent different sectors. This is in reality a constant struggle between the rising social classes and the reactionary classes, between the developing and the already consolidated economic groups.

This is what is happening today between the new social classes and the oligarchic sectors of the bourgeoisie; between the economic groups who see in nationalist politics an opportunity for expansion and the groups who see in this the disappearance of their privilege; between the national sectors, conscious of the need for independence as a factor in progress, and the imperialists, who are aware that national independence means the end of the exploitive practices.

In the independent and developed capitalist countries the formation of contradictions is different and establishes a different correlation of forces. The principal part of the struggle is between the proletariat and the bourgeoisie, or really, between socialism and capitalism, where the working class is directed toward the conquest of political power and the establishment of a proletarian dictatorship in a transitional stage on the road to Communism. Class alliances are formulated in relation to this objective. It is the union of workers, peasants, and certain sectors of the petty bourgeoisie against bourgeois capitalist society. This is not the case in the colonial, neocolonial, and dependent countries. There, the main struggle is of a different nature: it is that of a revolution of national liberation, which greatly widens the area of alliances, the type of state, and the social make-up of the revolutionary government.

In a nation having a neocolonial structure important sectors of the bourgeoisie (industrialists and farm producers) and of the petty bourgeoisie are exploited by imperialism and blocked in their development by the powerful interests of the importing bourgeoisie, by the financial oligarchy, and by the large landowners. The former group plays an important historical and revolutionary role. The winning of national independence and the liquidation of the landed interests accomplishes the greater portion of the struggle for an anti-imperialist and antifeudal revolution. This struggle differs in its objectives from a socialist revolution: the government will not be a dictatorship of the proletariat, but rather a New Democracy.

The aims that are pursued by the revolution in every historical stage, the social make-up of the revolutionary government, and the general situation created by the process itself are the consequences of objective factors. These same objective factors are crucial in the development and strengthening of the consciousness of power. This consciousness of the people and of their adversaries results from national and class interests. The area of conflict is progressively delimited and the correlation of forces favoring the revolution increases. As consciousness of power penetrates the most backward classes, and as they begin to be aware of its potency, the revolutionary arena grows huge and the conditions of power achieve their full magnitude.

Few would dispute the need for a revolutionary transformation of the present Venezuelan situation. My good friend of the agrarian bourgeoisie would not, nor would the groups controlling the political parties. Neither would leading spokesmen for the industrial bourgeoisie, much less the nonreformist leaders of the working class. There is a sort of general consensus among the majority of our people and their political, professional, cultural, and union organizations concerning the urgency of national liberation. The government itself (Betancourt's and Leoni's)— for demagogic reasons—has never stopped talking about its anti-imperialist and antifeudal leanings. The need to satisfy this necessity is so evident in our country that nobody opposes it. It is here that the ideological terrorism of imperialism and its servant classes enters into play. The right of a country to make its own revolution and free itself is undeniable, and the course that the "revolutionary movement" must take is clear.

For a long time we have been reading documents from Venezuelan industry and the political parties. In these, there is established as an urgent need of the country the necessity for a radical transformation of the present political and economic structures, in order to move national development to a higher level. There are concrete suggestions for the radical modification of the present system of landholding and eradication of the landed estate, for enlargement of the consumer market, for the elimination of unemployment and for the introduction of industrial planning as the primary way of utilizing industrialization as one of the fundamental tools for gaining national economic independence.

When such concepts are translated into the language of politics and are placed within the reality of Venezuela (a country highly infiltrated by monopoly capital), we can see how there is an open revolutionary situation.

The imperialists and those classes who in our country serve

them as agents are not blind to reality. Their ideologists constantly study the changes that are operating. Their political behavior is oriented toward intervention in any form necessary to prevent radical changes in the present situation. They know very well that "the sun cannot be hidden with one's finger"; that in the face of concrete and objective facts in Venezuela and Latin America, it is impossible to hide the need for revolutionary transformation.

President Kennedy, in numerous speeches, recognized this need and appealed to progressive "revolutionaries" in Latin America to put the revolution in motion and to develop higher standards of living. To do this, they could depend on the "generous help" of the North American people and Government who "view with horror the state of misery in which the greater part of the people of this continent live."

It did not take long for events to catch up with the words of the Yanqui president. The course of the "revolution" opened up almost immediately: the revolution of the Alliance for Progress, "which the free peoples have been successfully practicing for four years" and about which a North American columnist recently said: "The Revolution of the Alliance is in favor of peace and freedom, of forging nations independent and free of all imperialist domination."[1]

This kind of revolution or any other which counts on the prior consent of imperialism and the classes it controls can be realized without utilizing any form of struggle other than the traditional democratic forms. It operates in a gradual manner without disturbing the status quo, without clashing head-on with oppressive forces, and without challenging their sovereignty.

When one sees the problem this way, one cannot deny that my friend and those who think like him are right. . . .

THE TRUE REVOLUTION,
VIOLENCE AND GEOPOLITICAL FATALISM

An alternative to passive acceptance of the "sanctioned revolution" (which is only a revolution in the faulty theories of the imperialists) implies a substantial change in the attitude of individuals and groups.

[1] "Revolución de la Alianza," *El Nacional*, January 15, 1966, p. A–7.

The most important thing is to understand exactly the causes of the country's problems. Then one must know the range of conflicting interests and the behavior of each social class toward the whole country. A complete analysis of the situation, combined with the detailed examination of the relationships of national and international forces, determines the characteristics and possibilities of a true revolution. This applies with no other limitations than those imposed by objective realities, and with no more restrictions than those that accompany a difficult task in the face of a relatively more powerful enemy.

In Venezuela and other countries, the extent to which the need for revolution becomes apparent to the different national sectors, and the extent to which the people and their revolutionary vanguard throw themselves into the real struggle is the extent to which the imperialists and other reactionary classes rush to maintain their terrorist control. This is done with threats and shows of force against groups and classes who do not dare to risk what they have gained, or to endanger their interests in a struggle which, viewed superficially, would appear to be simply an adventure.

The recent statements by President Johnson at the beginning of the Dominican Crisis, announcing that the United States Government would not allow the appearance of "another Cuba" on the continent; the House of Representatives' resolution to support any military intervention on the part of their country in Latin America; the widening of the war in Vietnam; the proposal to create an Inter-American military force—all these constitute important statements of a political line. Such a line, besides being the only means for preserving imperialistic control, is aimed at collective terror, and makes clear to the people the immense risks, sacrifices, and difficulties that true revolutionary struggles must confront.

Just as there would be no letup in the use of their military might, the imperialists never let up in their attempt to create an artificially easy atmosphere. This presents the wavering groups and classes with a less risky and insecure path, designed to satisfy the imperialistic interests.

On the occasion of the last anniversary of the Alliance for Progress, after the military intervention in Santo Domingo crushed a democratic movement, President Johnson said: "The social democratic revolution is the alternative—the only alternative—to bloodshed, destruction and tyranny. For the past is past. And those who struggle to save it unwittingly join the ranks of their own destroyers."

But who is it that opposes social democratic revolution in the Dominican Republic, Venezuela, Peru, Guatemala, Brazil, the whole world? Who but the same North American troops increase "bloodshed, destruction and tyranny" in Vietnam? Who but the North American Government struggles to preserve the past and to bloody our country and the whole American continent?

The words of President Johnson and of Mr. Kennedy, those of the representative to the OAS apropos of the Tricontinental Conference, like those of all imperialists and their servants, contradict the facts (the military occupation of Santo Domingo, the House Resolution, etc.) and have a clear and precise nature. They are like those used by some blustering father who, with a rod in his hand, says to his misbehaving son, "If you don't behave, I'll beat you!"

The combination of words and deeds as the single expression of policy of the imperialists, their ideologists and lackeys, have always given them good results. Through them imperialists have been able to gain control of important sectors of the neo-colonized people, for whom national liberation is the road to economic and social liberation. This opens up immense perspectives for development in which the classes that are totally exploited by imperialism and the oligarchy find a favorable opportunity for the increase of productive labor.

In Venezuela, as we have said, few would dispute the need for a revolutionary transformation to put an end to the present state of underdevelopment, backwardness, and misery. The old and close friend to whom I constantly refer is conscious of that need, as are many, even within the working class, who think the same way. A problem arises when ways are considered for achieving this revolutionary transformation. It is then that doubts and discordant opinions appear. On one side are those who believe (with my friend) that there are still ways to gain national liberation through the vote or through the peaceful struggle of the masses. On the other side are those who believe (as I do) that such a conquest is possible only through popular insurrection, which would result from the proper combination of all forms of struggle, with a correct notion of the People's War.

There are, then, two camps into which the progressive classes and sectors of the country are divided, in the same way that the entire Venezuelan society is divided in two. At our present historical stage, in which the liberating revolution is the national alternative, this division will become more clearly defined as the consciousness of the people grows. The progressive classes and sectors, to which my friend belongs, are now reformist and opt for the "sanctioned revolution." They lack any clear consciousness of power, which means essentially the conquest of political power as an instrument of struggle between the rising, temporarily in transition, and the backward conservative classes, whose control is also transitory.

Many of those who today are in the revolutionary vanguard, myself included, did at one time take a position similar to the progressive bourgeoisie. We had no idea of power on January 23, 1958, nor in July nor in September of that year. For me, representative democracy was the same as it is today for my friend. Luckily, I freed myself from reformism in order to become a real revolutionary. I achieved a consciousness, and above all, a clear notion of power. This same process has been carried out by many others—some sooner, some later—as the result of objective realities which the imperialists' intensive propaganda campaign has not been able to hide.

To abandon the reformist camp and take up revolution means deciding to struggle fearlessly, to be certain of victory and to challenge, as did David, gigantic reactionary power, as all true revolutionaries of history have done, including the bourgeois revolutionaries.

The psychology of power played an important role in the conversion, since gaining power is the aim of every political movement. Yesterday's revolutionary classes, which are today's reactionaries, are what they were and what they have become precisely as a result of their psychology of power. It developed to win a war (in Venezuela against Spanish colonialism), and it was maintained to try to preserve power, also through war. The revolutionaries triumphed yesterday because they were new forces brewing within society. They had at their side the invincible support of the people (mulattoes, plainsmen, and mountaineers) and they represented the road to independence. But they will be defeated, inevitably conquered, "because they are divorced from the people; it doesn't matter how strong they appear at the moment, for they are condemned to failure."

The exercise of political power is the definitive factor within society. Politics are practiced only through power, whether revolutionary or reactionary, the two halves into which power is divided. In every historical period there are revolutionaries and reactionaries; a large sector in the middle, without a consciousness of its own, wavers from one side to the other. Their consciousness develops late, as a product of harsh struggle and class interests. But at the beginning of the whole revolutionary process, the middle sector, under the direct influence of the classes in power (the reactionary classes) plays into their hands, even as it tries to escape the oppression. Nevertheless, they slowly acquire consciousness and awareness of power. This has important consequences for the entire revolutionary movement.

This is what happens to imperialism in the general field of politics as its sustaining base grows steadily smaller. Since the Second World War the diminishing process has been accelerated, and the power of the socialist world has grown tremendously. Revolutions against imperialism have sprung up in vast areas of Asia, Africa, and Latin America. Two-thirds of humanity has been liberated and now lives outside reactionary control. This makes possible today, more than before, the revolutionary advance and victory of subjugated people, like those of Venezuela, even when they are geographically very close to the Northern Colossus; Cuba, only ninety miles away, is already freed.

The liberation of the colonized and dependent countries is strengthened by these facts. Imperialism no longer has, in spite of its strength, the same power it had twenty years ago. Its foundations have undergone steady erosion, and it faces a changed world. Such a phenomenon in political and military affairs contributes to the tempering or the frustrating (as the case may be) of the fury of the police. The world situation grows increasingly more favorable to the peoples' progress. Alongside everyone's consciousness and determination to shake off the chains of colonialism and oppression, the moral and material support of all the peace-loving countries turns the revolution into an invincible enterprise. The colonized, neo-colonial, and oppressed people, in exercising their sovereignty, are not alone. Their struggle is not an isolated cause waged at their own expense, with their own means and resources. There exists a world-wide reactionary camp in which the oppressors join hands, support one another, and arrange all their forces around the preservation of their control. There is also a world-wide revolutionary camp where the people make militant solidarity effective. This circumstance, that of the new realities in the world, eloquently explains the reason for the defeat of the imperialists in Vietnam, where 200,000 regulars of North American Armed Forces have not been able to weaken the victorious thrust of the guerrilla movement, now a People's War. It explains why the 40,000 troops landed in Santo Domingo in the face of universal criticism could not restore the *gorillas* Wessin y Wessin and Imbert Barrera into office. It explains why the imperialist blockade of Cuba, one of our era's strongest sanctions, has not been able to produce the effects predicted by the Pentagon and the State Department.

No people in the process of liberation can fight an isolated struggle; no two forces or two belligerent armies, like a rabbit and a tiger, fight before the impassive gaze of the rest. To think so would be a grave error that would lead to opportunism and resignation. Today's revolutionary struggle (as we must see it) is a struggle on the part of all the progressive forces in the world. We are in a situation having great popular appeal, and in which the objective conditions of each country constitute the principal factor. Already in Latin America, as in the early 1800s, there are several countries which have begun their struggle against neocolonialism. These include three of the Bolivarian countries (Venezuela, Colombia, and Peru), and others such as Santo Domingo, Guatemala, and Paraguay. They have taken the true path to the liberating revolution, at whose center is the principal instrument of power: the armed forces of liberation. The chances for imperialism to triumph are even further reduced to the extent that the struggle grows and liberation movements in Africa and Asia continue to develop. The domestic problems confronting the North American Government are also multiplied as a consequence of the spread of the war in Vietnam (i.e. higher taxes and higher draft calls). The entire North American Army would be insufficient to function as an occupational force in the far-flung areas shaken by revolution.

Venezuela is an important factor in the world-wide revolutionary camp. Its struggle for liberation complements that of other peoples in similar conditions. Whether we like it or not, one is necessarily the continuation of the other. Although every country, including Venezuela, must act according to its own realities, and must realize the kind of revolution its own history allows, the integration of these revolutionary movements is possible. It is not the fault of the Venezuelan revolutionaries that their struggle against the imperialists is in its first stage. Their struggle is identical to that being waged in Vietnam, in Angola, in the Congo, or to that which freed Cuba and Algeria. The fault in this case belongs to the imperialists, who have respected neither frontiers nor continents in extending their exploitation.

Venezuela struggles today against the North American yoke, as it did yesterday against Spanish colonialism; as the North Americans did against English domination, and the Brazilians did against the Portuguese Empire.

There are still people who adhere to theories of geographical fatalism and view the world as it was at the time of the Monroe Doctrine, whose slogan of "America for the Americans" reflected a situation far different from today's situation. Then our continent had to protect itself against European imperialist expansion. It was a world of great distance, with only rudimentary means of communication. These conditions have been completely changed by the presence of the common enemy in our own continent; by the scientific and technological progress which has practically wiped out distances; by man's remote-controlled intercontinental weapons; by strengthening the field of the liberated socialist countries with a population that exceeds two-thirds of humanity. The factors above place such people in an uncertain world, with their backs turned to reality, with their mistaken political notions that serve as a prop for colonial domination and its resultant underdevelopment, exploitation, and misery.

The geopolitical theses have been overtaken by the dynamics of history. The North American imperialists erased all continental frontiers. President Johnson recently said (as if any doubt remained) that the military forces of the United States will be present in any part of the world, in any country, where "freedom is endangered by Communist aggression." This aggressive conduct on the part of Yanqui imperialism openly reveals the breakdown of schemes for intercontinental cooperation. For the North American Government behaves toward Venezuela or Santo Domingo, geographically located in

America, as if they were located in Indo-China (an area that until recently was synonymous with unfathomable distance).

The analysis of the world-wide political grouping and of the international relationship of forces is made necessary by the study of our problems as a neocolonial country, and of the possibilities for its liberation. Progressive Venezuelans, whose interests coincide with those of the nation, are restrained in their development by the unfair competition of North American capital and goods; and in view of the political control that the creole oligarchy exercises, they cannot underestimate any aspects of the present world situation, nor view it in a simplistic or superficial way.

It is necessary to dig deeply into present political affairs and to look toward the future to understand the promising outlook presented to our people in their struggle for freedom. In light of facts, of historical realities, no one can doubt that the road to revolutionary action, whatever the circumstantial difficulties may be, is the only way, the surest way, for structural change in our country.

To develop a firm concept of power on the part of the popular, patriotic, and progressive classes, the first step is to be free of geographic fatalism and the thesis of the invincibility of imperialism and the forces of reaction. The second step is to be convinced, once and for all, that without seizing political power, no change in the national crisis can be effected. The implementation of an agrarian reform that would liquidate the present system of landholdings (as is the wish of the peasants and important sectors affiliated with *Federagro**) is not possible. This is shown by six years of a progressive law of agrarian reform. It is impossible without radically transforming the nation's economic and political system; it is impossible without changing the social make-up of the government, where, until today, the landed interests have predominated and maintained the concentration of landownership in a few hands.

The men who have passed through the Ministry of Agriculture and Livestock (a functional tool of agrarian reform) in the past decade have invariably been representatives of the classes opposed to a full and real agrarian reform. But even if they did belong to the progressive classes, they would not have been able to do things differently, because agrarian policy is not indepen-

* The Federation of Agronomists (ed.).

dent from the national economic complex. It forms part of a whole, a system, an indestructible unit that is entirely responsive to political control by the reactionary classes.

This same thing occurs in the industrial development of the country. No change can be operative in this important sector of the national economy if it is not a result of a modification of our whole system of dependency. The nationalistic statements that many of the member organizations have been issuing since the founding of Pro-Venezuela will remain pretty much in a vacuum. One cannot pretend that Venezuelan industry is anything more than a simple processor of imports. Such a pretense would hinder the real study of the causes that keep its industry relegated to such a position. In Venezuela, imperialism has one of its most important markets in Latin America. The bourgeoisie that are involved with this market and draw juicy profits from it will never, by themselves, support changes that would even remotely suggest the disappearance of such privileges.

The present Minister of Development, who changed his profession from worker and linotypist to lawyer, is of a socially different origin than the oligarchs. He is founder and director of one of the self-styled parties of the left, and secretary general of Pro-Venezuela, a registered association for independent industrial development. Until his arrival in this position, he had been nothing more than a member of a quisling government, controlled by the most reactionary sectors, and linked to the interests of Venezuelan and foreign capital.

An industrial policy is also an integral part of the economic complex under the control of the colonial system. The Minister of Development has had to submit, at the risk of losing his position, to the leading groups in the class structure of the government.

None of the problems that affect our country and the popular and progressive classes (concentration of landownership in a few hands; low level of industrial development; unemployment; technical and scientific backwardness; undernourishment; underdeveloped consumers' market; lack of housing, schools, health centers, and hospitals; low salaries; foreign exploitation of the chief sources of wealth; control of sovereignty, etc.) can be resolved without changing the whole national structure, or without removing its basis, which amounts to the same thing. We are not talking about marginal or superficial changes in government that could be achieved through the traditional forms of political struggle, "without doing violence to the present state of affairs," or "without a head-on clash with the oppressive forces" or an evolutionary process that "progressively transforms the system of political institutions. . . ."

Aside from the study of political theory, experience itself shows that at every historical stage our country has nothing to look for in the change from one clique to another, or from one party or group of parties to others. What we are trying to achieve is a fundamental revolutionary change in the social make-up of the government, a change in the structure of the country, and then build—independent of imperialism and oligarchy. The magnitude and causes of the national problem call for the seizing of power by an alliance of the popular, democratic, and progressive classes, with sufficient military and political power to face the forces of reaction.

It has been shown that most parts of the country would accept it; that Venezuela is living through a full and growing crisis whose seriousness calls for great efforts to end it. Neither the Alliance for Progress nor circumstantial reforms have been able to conjure away the tremendous ills. Nevertheless, many sectors, conscious of the need for revolution, have still not left the reformist camp, the camp of illusions, contributing by their attitude to the prolonging of the oppressive situation. They still believe, ingenuously (and this is the result of a poorly defined concept of power) that other means exist to solve the national problems, without the need to expose their lives, their freedom, or their private interests.

It is no longer possible to continue living in a world of illusion. The revolution must be made at any price. The process of pauperization, reabsorption of small enterprises by monopoly capital, will inevitably continue with their corresponding unemployment, backwardness, and misery. The national bourgeoisie (agrarian and industrial), the petty bourgeoisie (students, professions, small businessmen, and employees) together with the peasant and working classes, whose vanguard advances along the road of armed insurrection by means of the People's War, must come together. They must move with a single will, becoming the liberation front. They are the decisive force for victory.

The popular, democratic, and progressive classes of Venezuela, victims of imperialism's exploitation and oligarchic oppression, have come to the crossroads: either they resign themselves to prolonged existence in an increasingly restrained area, due to progressive impoverishment of the country; or else they could open the way through revolutionary struggle to winning a better life, free from exploitation and oppression, in a country whose great riches would open immense perspectives of development and progress.

At the present historical juncture, two conflicting policies are polarized into reaction and revolution. One is in a dizzying descent, supported by dying forces with no other rationale than their own pretension of power. The other is in permanent flux, led by new forces at the height of their development and strength, which, like an overflowing torrent, open their channels and wipe out all that tries to stop them.

Our country and our people live at the moment of a revolutionary crisis, where the old political schemes suffer the jarring impact of the struggle between the worn-out that requires constant tinkering, and the new that grows with unusual vigor. This struggle between life and death dislocates everything. The proliferation of political parties that for some is the expression of stability is nothing more than the product of this same revolutionary crisis, where each sector is involved in the search for its own truth and tries to break with the moribund past. Each one proposes to find the truth. Some align themselves without having found it, and are still vacillating. They are fundamentally ignorant of the crisis and they do not understand the true causes that feed it. Others, who become fully aware and develop a concept of power, understand what this means as a class tool. They decide to struggle and take the road of revolutionary politics.

Venezuela's progress is doubtlessly tied to its national liberation, and this cannot be won except through revolutionary action of determined and total struggle against the common oppressor. As a consequence, the progressive classes must necessarily take this road of struggle. To do this, it is indispensable to know that "when the need for change exists, as in Venezuela, the struggle becomes irresistible, and whether we like it or not, is sooner or later produced." Only if one is conscious that this is how it will happen, and that the enemy, no matter how powerful at first, will be conquered—then the necessary step will have been taken and the imperialists and reactionaries can be scorned.

We have already said that in Venezuela, as in the rest of the world, two policies exist: one revolutionary and the other reactionary. The first means, in our case, anti-imperialistic and antifeudal liberation, social progress and economic development; the other, colonialism, oppression, backwardness, tyranny, misery.

Two forces also exist: the patriotic and progressive revolutionaries, and the conservative and neocolonial reactionaries. And in the middle, a crowded area that wavers between one side and the other, and includes both revolutionaries and reactionaries.

My friend and I—both with revolutionary ideas—were together in the middle ground. I, in spite of my youth, was slightly more reactionary than he. His advice and the books he gave me were certainly very different from what Jóvito Villalba had given me. And they opened up the correct path to politics. Today, the roles are inverted, and my friend remains, without having changed his revolutionary ideas, in the same place where I left him five years ago. He understands the need for our liberation. Until now he has been a fervent partisan of the social ownership of land, of independent industrial development, of full democracy and sovereignty. In stating Venezuela's problems and in outlining strategic objectives, there is little difference between us. Nor is there much difference between those of us who drive for change by means of the People's War and those who remain under the influence of reformist ideology and under the terror of national and international reaction.

The reformist thesis is that imperialism and the oligarchy maintain an immense force that will be used against any insurgency or against any government that attempts to modify the present situation. This has already happened, both on our continent and elsewhere. It happened in Cuba, and failed. It happened in Santo Domingo, but did not fully achieve its objective. It happened in Brazil, and the imperialists imposed their role.

Imperialism has not rested for a moment in its aggressive conduct against Cuba. From the moment when the revolutionary government took its first step toward reclaiming its riches exploited by the North American monopolies, and began a full agrarian reform to break up the landed estates, counter-revolutionary reaction was manifested. The internal military conspiracy (Díaz Lanz, Urrutia, and Hubert Matos), prepared, armed, and financed by the State Department and the CIA in the United States and Nicaragua, effected sabotage (burning of *El Encanto,* explosion of the steamship *La Coubre,* etc.); assassination of revolutionary workers (Conrado Benítez, Ascunce Domenech, and others); the invasion of the Bay of Pigs. The expulsion of Cuba from the OAS and the multilateral breaking of diplomatic and commercial relations by the United States with Latin American countries, and the general blockade, are the concrete expression of a steady repression. Such a chain of events has been produced in two different stages of the Cuban revolutionary regime; first, with the democratic-bourgeois government, at the fall of the tyrant, Fulgencio Batista, on January 1, 1959; and second, with the socialist regime, proclaimed during the mercenary invasion in April of 1961.

The transition from the democratic-bourgeois government to the socialist regime was the direct result of popular radicalization in the face of imperialist aggression and the product of the revolutionary firmness of the new leaders, headed by Fidel Castro. But in their aggressive and confusing attitude, the reactionary forces have never made any distinction. And when it is said that the United States Government will not allow the appearance of a "new Cuba" on the continent, this refers not only to the presence of socialism but to the triumph of any national liberation movement under the revolutionary democratic-bourgeois regime. Nor is Communism the only thing the reactionary democratic-bourgeois regime opposes, as they try to demonstrate, but they also oppose the people's liberation and an end to exploitation and colonialism.

The imperialists would not be bothered, said Raúl Castro, on May 1, 1959, if we hoisted the Red flag with the hammer and sickle on the flagstaff of the national capitol, or if we realized agrarian reform or set into motion a policy that affected the large North American interests in our country. The reactionaries would not care, even if the people seemed very attached to these symbolic gestures. But what stands out, in every case, are the interests which they guarantee through political and economic control of the weaker peoples. The Cuban government has been characterized precisely by deeds, by direct action against neocolonialism and imperialist oppression. Thus the enraged attitude of the United States toward the revolution. Nevertheless, since the facts and not the formalities are what galvanize the popular will, Cuba has resisted defeat and its people advance toward the building of a new society.

There have been seven years of ferocious and open struggle by imperialism against the small Cuban nation, with no truce. All the power of reaction has been aimed at that people without being able to bring it down. The failures of the reactionary forces clearly indicate that it is not possible to defeat a people who have made the decision to fight.

In our present world, where the grouping of revolutionary forces is greater than that of counterrevolution, no people who move toward liberation can be defeated, irrespective of geographical location or other circumstances.

Vo Nguyen Giap, in his book *Viet-Nam: Liberation of a People* says: "The war of liberation of the Vietnamese people has helped to bring out this historical truth: at the international juncture of today, a weak people that rises up and determinedly fights for its liberation, is able to conquer its enemies whoever they may be, and to win the final victory . . ."

The lesson we must learn is that the imperialists have failed in Cuba, because the people of the island, the majority of whom were in favor of the revolution and its liberation policy, had resolved to perish rather than return to the previous state of exploitation and misery. Furthermore, they have not been alone, left to their fate, in the daily fight against immense reactionary power. Cuba has always had the support of the socialist world and of peace-loving people. And the great contradictions within the world-wide capitalist system have worked to Cuba's advantage.

Proof that the imperialists and other reactionaries use their anti-Communist fight as a pretext, a smoke screen, behind which they hide their real purposes, is seen in the case of Santo Domingo, where the fight for the return to constitutional democracy is completely different from that waged by the Cuban people in defense of their socialist government. In the Dominican Republic, the United States Government has once again been exposed. Many governments, in violation of the principles of free determination, could be explained with respect to Communist Cuba. These governments had to adopt different attitudes in the face of open North American military intervention on the other Caribbean island. It was this behavior that helped strengthen the firm stance of the Dominican people, who, with weapons in hand, stopped the return of military gorilla rule.

The constitutionalist leader Colonel Francisco Caamaño

Deño recently said that North American Marines and the airborne battalions did not go to Santo Domingo to save lives. It was their aim to restore to power Wessin y Wessin's military clique, or more recently, Imbert Barrera; to impede constitutional restoration and block the return of Juan Bosch to the presidency of the Republic, an office to which he had been democratically elected. There was no sign of a Communist-inspired revolutionary insurgency, or even of a strong movement for national liberation. The immediate aim of the country was the return to constitutional normalcy, to democratic legality, interrupted in 1963 by the barracks revolt headed by Imbert Barrera and Wessin y Wessin.

Juan Bosch is a reformist politician and not a revolutionary. His government was trying to turn representative democracy into a reality, to realize certain reforms, very tenuous at best, in the area of economic and social development, and to maintain the standing of public freedom. The Constitution of 1962 supports the free play of political ideas. It also opened the door to certain modifications in the landholding system and the economic development of the country. The application of these reforms on the part of the legitimate government was more than enough for the militarist gorillas. Under the pretext of a Communist threat, and aided by the weakness of the constitutional president, the militarists threw him out of office and reestablished a dictatorship. The most reactionary Dominican military clique, with the direct support of the oligarchy and imperialists, finally put an end to the first attempt at democracy after thirty years of total power in the hands of Trujillo. The maneuvers of the antipopular and neocolonialist forces during the electoral process were broken against the majority will of the Dominican people, expressed in their vote for Juan Bosch (as a demonstration of popular sovereignty). These forces will not take long to impose, with violence, and with the blessing and support of the United States, their reactionary policies.

The popular and democratic forces did not sit on their hands in the face of this usurpation. In April, 1965, a civilian-military alliance deposed the junta headed by Donald Reid Cabral. He had assembled the Congress, dissolved in 1963, which in accordance with the new constitution, named the provisional president of the Republic. Meanwhile this caused the return of the titleholder, Juan Bosch. The reactionary sectors of the armed forces, under the direction of General Wessin y Wessin, aligned themselves with the deposed junta, and dug in at the old San Ysidro Air Base. From there, they tried to crush the popular movement. The people were armed by the constitutional regime, thus eliminating the possibility of victory for the reactionary forces. When the constitutional triumph was assured with massive support, the North American Government invaded the island. The subterfuge the United States used was that it was necessary to evacuate and protect American residents of the island and to protect their possessions. Having taken up position in Dominican territory, the U.S. troops began to play a role alongside the military reactionaries. First, they propped up the strongholds of Wessin y Wessin. When they realized that the civilian-military alliance would not be terrorized or yield one inch, they went through the motions of a formal charge. They gave their patronage to the support of a new junta, headed by Imbert Barrera, without the presence of Wessin y Wessin. The popular resistance kept up with great fervor and heroism, aided to a large extent by world-wide condemnation of North American military aggression.

The imperialist forces, who had for a long time occupied Dominican territory, had to retreat and give in to negotiations, without having fully achieved their objectives. North American military power, quickly deployed, could not avoid the partial defeat of Dominican reaction that at last had to accept a transitional government. This excluded from power the most noted *gorillas,* provided for the incorporation of constitutional officials into the army, a general amnesty, the return of those exiled during the rule of Reid Cabral, and the free activity of all the political parties, including those of the extreme left.

The Dominican Crisis, which has still not been completely resolved, served to end the masquerade of the United States Government; to show, once again, that a people committed to struggle, with political right on their side, cannot be defeated. If one tried to make the North American military invasion of Santo Domingo look like a victory, all they could hope to claim would be a Pyrrhic victory: the losses were greater than the gains.

All the Latin American peoples, all the progressive institutions of the world, move as one against the interventionist policies of the United States and in support of the people whose land was occupied by U.S. Marines. Johnson's Government, even within the United States, suffered one of its hardest moral defeats of recent time. The Dominican people, on the other hand, received lively demonstrations of support and endorsement that made their position stronger and inspired them on the revolutionary road against military occupation, toward independence.

Here again, one sees that "in the face of a powerful and aggressive enemy, victory is assured only with the union of an entire nation in the middle of a solid and wide national front, based on the alliance of workers and peasants . . ."

In Brazil, as in the Dominican Republic in 1963, reactionary forces were imposed. There had also been a regime of a truly progressive nature, with universal suffrage. João Goulart, who succeeded President Jânio Quadros (forced to resign by reactionary coercion) was brought down by the military *gorillas,* with the support of the United States. The pretext for moving against this constitutional government was the same used to defeat Juan Bosch: Communist infiltration.

Quadros and Goulart, the same as Juan Bosch and other traditional politicians on our continent (similar to certain members of Venezuela's generation of 1928, such as Jóvito Villalba), insisting on their inclusion in "Western culture," operate as reformers. According to their thesis, the progress of peoples "can be achieved through evolution [which] progressively transforms the system of political institutions."

The development of this theory in Latin America is a direct result of geographic fatalism. Its practice has been constrained by its own creators (the imperialists), as happened recently in Brazil. The dangers that are attributed to revolutionary change do not disappear in the face of the "immense power of reaction" nor do they disappear before the timid and wavering nature of reform. And this never pulls the popular masses and progressive forces together to form a front, at a given moment, against the reactionary forces. The latter, equally and irrevocably, are opposed to any demonstration of revolutionary or reformist change which could endanger their interests and make their class privileges vulnerable.

The Brazilian military reaction, serving imperialism, the large landowners, and the powerful middle-class bourgeoisie, did not encounter the least resistance in the face of the successful coup. Quadros' policy, like Goulart's, if it lacked revolutionary content, did introduce certain reforms. In the international sphere, it established relations with the socialist countries, and internally it adopted several measures beneficial to the industrial and agrarian bourgeoisie. The nationalization of certain North American interests, and the promulgation, under Goulart's government, of certain agrarian measures, were enough for the oligarchic-imperialist alliance to consummate its use of force.

In the governments resembling those overthrown in Brazil, or previously in Cuba (Carlos Prío Socarrás), in Peru (Bustamante and Rivera and Manuel Prado), in Argentina (Juan Domingo Perón and Arturo Frondizi), in Venezuela (Isaías Medina Angarita and Rómulo Gallegos), in Chile (Carlos Ibáñez), in Ecuador (Velazco Ibarra and Carlos Arosemena), etc., etc., reaction constitutes the determining force, holding in its hands the principal instruments of power, among them, the armed forces. The popular and progressive sectors, whose only recourse in this case are the norms of democratic formalism and the illusory majesty of the constitution, revolve around the rule of that which is not bound by law.

The reactionary forces, who know what power is for, permit freedom only when it does not affect their interests and privileges. In Brazil and other Latin American countries, the governments that tried to go beyond their real capacity, stepped beyond what is allowed by reaction. Such governments, without a popular policy defined to avoid a clash with the interests of the ruling classes, never succeed in waking the consciousness of the people, or in placing at their sides the progressive sectors, whose support is necessary in defeating "coupism."

Nonrevolutionary politicians think that everything stems from the majority vote needed to win the government. They think that if a democratic representative government is formed, and if it aims at the total enforcement of the law, no one would dare challenge the law. They have not yet understood—and this comes out in all their statements—that in order to exercise real power, force is required; force that is able to confront and successfully defeat the reactionary classes affected by constitutional change. This is precisely the difference between imperialism and the other reactionary forces in the case of Cuba, Santo Domingo, and Brazil. In the first case, real power had passed into the hands of the people. In the second place, the people had decided to win at any price, and in Brazil, where the democratic government had only a formal nature, military "gorillism" found it easy to impose its will.

In the largest nation in Latin America, which has the greatest

air, sea, and land army and 70 million inhabitants, all imperialism had to do was move a few marshals and generals to end
the governments of Quadros and Goulart. In Cuba, on the
contrary, imperialism called upon all its resources, except direct
military aggression (and this was because of popular support
for the revolution and the international grouping of force that
impeded it), without the slightest change in the rising tide of
revolution. And in Santo Domingo, where the landing of the
Marines was carried out, the heroic resistance of the people
frustrated imperialist efforts.

This appears paradoxical, but for those who finally understand that the people's forces are not related solely to numbers
of inhabitants, but also to the level of their morale, consciousness, and power psychology, what is happening in Brazil, Cuba,
and Santo Domingo is the specific revelation of the need for
placing political power in the hands of the people.

Index

About the Editors

Josué de Castro, born in Recife, Brazil, is a physician and an expert in nutrition. He has taught at the University of Brazil and was chairman of the United Nations Food and Agriculture Organization. He has served Brazil as legislator and diplomat. However, since the military coup in 1964, Dr. de Castro has lived outside his country. He is, at present, the President of the Centre International pour le Développement in Paris. Josué de Castro is the author of the classic *Geography of Hunger,* which was published in the United States in 1952 and has been translated into eight languages, and *Death in the Northeast,* as well as other books and numerous articles.

John Gerassi, a former Latin American editor of *Time, Newsweek,* and *Ramparts,* and correspondent for the *New York Times,* and a former professor of International Relations at San Francisco State College (from where he was fired for joining a student demonstration against purported adminis-

tration racism), is the author of *The Great Fear in Latin America; North Vietnam: A Documentary;* and the editor of *Venceremos! The Speeches and Writings of Che Guevara.*

Irving Louis Horowitz is Professor of Sociology at Washington University (St. Louis), and Director of Studies in Comparative International Development. Professor Horowitz is Senior Editor of *Trans-action,* the largest social science magazine in the United States, author of *The Rise and Fall of Project Camelot: Studies in the Relationship Between Social Science and Practical Politics; Three Worlds of Development: The Theory and Practice of International Stratification; Revolution in Brazil: Politics and Society in a Development Nation;* and *Radicalism and the Revolt Against Reason.* He has served in various teaching and research posts in Latin America, including the University of Buenos Aires, and the National University of Mexico.

About the Contributors

Bo Anderson is Professor of Sociology at Michigan State University, and before that he taught at Stanford University. He is co-author of *Sociological Theories in Progress*.

Otto María Carpeaux is a naturalized Brazilian citizen who writes for *Correio da Manhã* and is Director of the Library of the National Faculty of Philosophy in Brazil.

Fidel Castro, leader of the Cuban Revolution, is Prime Minister of Cuba.

James D. Cockcroft is Professor of History at Antioch College, and before that he taught at the University of Texas in Austin. He has written many articles on Latin America for professional and political magazines, and received his graduate training at Stanford University.

Régis Debray is a French Marxist who studied with the Communist philosopher Louis Althusser and taught at Havana University before he became a cause célèbre in Bolivia.

Celso Furtado is presently Visiting Professor of Economics at the Sorbonne. Prior to that, he was at the Economic Growth Center at Yale University. He is the former chief of the Development Division of the United Nations Economic Commission for Latin America, and head of the Development Program for Northeast Brazil (SUDENE) under the Goulart administration.

He is the author of *Development and Underdevelopment; The Economic Growth of Brazil;* and *Diagnosis of the Brazilian Crisis*.

Eduardo Frei Montalva is President of the Republic of Chile and leader of that country's Christian Democratic Party. He is considered by many as the hemisphere's leading liberal reform politician.

Gino Germani is Professor of Sociology in the Department of Social Relations at Harvard University. He was formerly Chairman of the Department of Sociology at the University of Buenos Aires. He is the author of *Politics and Society in an Era of Transition;* and *Social Structure of Argentina* (both originally published in Spanish).

Fred Goff, born and raised in Colombia, is a staff member of the North American Congress on Latin America (NACLA) and a student organizer for the University Christian Movement.

Pablo González-Casanova, educated in history in Mexico and in sociology and political science in Paris, was for several years Director of the School of Political and Social Science of the National University of Mexico, and is currently Director of the University's Institute of Social Research. He is the author of many books, including *Democracy in Mexico;* and *North American Ideology of Foreign Exchange*.

Che Guevara was killed by government forces in the Bolivian

jungle on October 8, 1967, while leading a guerrilla expedition. He had been a leader of the Cuban Revolution. The diaries he kept during his Bolivian expedition were released by the Cuban government.

Hélio Jaguaribe is Associate Director of the Brazilian Institute for Studies on Development, and past head of the Political Science Department of the Superior Institute of Brazilian Studies. He taught at Harvard and Stanford between 1964 and 1967 and is the author of *Economic and Political Development: A Theoretical Approach and a Brazilian Case Study.*

John J. Johnson is Professor of History at Stanford University, and Director of its special program in Latin American studies. He is the author of several well-known works on Latin America, including *Political Change in Latin America;* and *The Military and Society in Latin America.*

Merle Kling is Dean of the School of Arts and Sciences, and Professor of Political Science at Washington University in St. Louis. He is the author of *A Mexican Interest Group in Action;* "Towards a Theory of Power and Political Instability in Latin America," in *Political Change in Underdeveloped Countries,* and other books and essays on Latin America and Communist affairs.

Michael Locker is a staff member of the North American Congress on Latin America (NACLA), and a former organizer for Students for a Democratic Society. He was on the staff of the Radical Education Program. He currently teaches at Brooklyn College of the City University of New York.

Manuel Maldonado-Denis is a professor at the University of Puerto Rico at Rio Piedras. He is the editor of *Revista de Ciencias Sociales* and author of numerous articles in political sociology.

Emilio Maspero is Secretary General of the Latin American Confederation of Christian Trade Unionists (CLASC), located in Santiago, Chile.

Fabricio Ojeda, a Venezuelan student leader, then National Deputy, resigned to join the guerrillas. He was a column commander and President of the National Liberation Front when he was captured alive and then murdered in jail by Venezuela's Armed Forces Intelligence Service (SIFA).

Salvador de la Plaza, a Venezuelan economist, was the principal of the Agrarian Reform Law in his country, which Romulo Betancourt enacted when he was President, but which de la Plaza claims was not carried out. He is the author of *The Structure of National Integration* (in Spanish), and is a regular contributor to *El Nacional* (Caracas).

Raúl Prebisch is probably the foremost economist of Argentina, and has been for many years the guiding force in the United Nations Commission for Latin America, serving as Secretary General of the 1964 United Nations Conference on Trade and Development. He is the author of *An Introduction to Keynes;* and *Towards a Dynamic Development Policy for Latin America.*

Carlos Romeo, a Chilean economist, worked with Che Guevara in the Ministry of Industries and taught with Régis Debray in the

Faculty of Philosophy at Havana University.

Paul N. Rosenstein-Rodan served as a member of the expert committee of the Organization of American States. He is a Professor of Economics at Massachusetts Institute of Technology.

John Saxe-Fernández is a sociologist from Costa Rica, currently teaching at Hofstra College in New York. He is working on the role of the Latin American military in the evolution of United States foreign policy. His writings have appeared in social science journals of both Mexico and Brazil.

Rodolfo Stavenhagen, trained in anthropology in Mexico and sociology at the University of Paris, is currently engaged in a long-term study of the social and economic structure of contemporary rural society, under auspices of the Center for Agrarian Research; he is also on the faculty of the National University of Mexico.

Camilo Torres Restrepo was a Colombian Roman Catholic priest and sociologist from an oligarchical background. He died in 1966 fighting with the guerrilla forces of the ELN, the Army of National Liberation.